ISBN 978-1-332-01915-1
PIBN 10269737

JOURNAL

OF THE

TWENTY-SIXTH ANNUAL COUNCIL

OF THE

Protestant

EPISCOPAL CHURCH,

IN THE

DIOCESE OF WEST VIRGINIA,

HELD IN

ST. MATTHEWS CHURCH, WHEELING,

MAY 20, 21, 22 AND 23, 1903.

CHARLESTON:
THE TRIBUNE PRINTING COMPANY,
1903.

Diocese of West Virginia.

Officers, Committees, Etc., for 1903.

Bishop,

RT. REV. GEO. W. PETERKIN, D. D., LL. D., Parkersburg.

Bishop Coadjutor,

RT. REV. W. L. GRAVATT, D. D., Charles Town.

Secretary of the Council,

REV. ROBERT DOUGLAS ROLLER, D. D., Charleston.

Treasurer of Council,

L. E. SANDS, Wheeling.

Standing Committee, P. O., (Charles Town, W. Va.),

Rev. G. A. Gibbons, President.
Rev. J. S. Douglas.
Rev. A. J. Willis.
Mr. J. Gassman.
Mr. Isaac H. Strider.
Judge Frank Beckwith.

Missionary Committee,

The Bishop of the Diocese, (*ex-officio*) President.
The Bishop Coadjutor, (")
Rev. J. Brittingham.
Rev. J. F. Woods.
Rev. S. S. Moore, D. D.
Mr. B. M. Ambler.
Mr. Simms Powell.
Mr. L. E. Sands, Treasurer.

Diocesan Committee on Foreign and Domestic Missions,

Rev. D. W. Howard.
Rev. G. A. Gibbons.
Rev. J. S. Gibson.
Gen'l W. P. Craighill.
Mr. C. C. Coe.
Dr. G. A. Aschman.

Trustee of the Episcopal and Contingent Fund (Special.),

Robert M. Browne, Wheeling.

Trustees of Kenyon College.

Rt. Rev. Geo. W. Peterkin, D. D., LL. D.
Rt. Rev. W. L. Gravatt, D. D.
Mr. Jos. D. DuBois.

Trustees of Permanent (Episcopal) Fund,

Mr. Robert M. Browne. Mr. B. M. Ambler. Mr. H. H. Moss.
Central Banking and Security Co., Parkersburg, Treasurer.

Registrar of the Diocese,

Mr. B. M. Ambler, Parkersburg.

Standing Committee on Constitution and Canons,

Rev. Jno S. Gibson.
Rev. D. W. Howard.
Rev. J. S. Douglas.
Mr. W. S. Laidley.
Mr. Joseph Trapnell.

Committee on Education,

Rev. G. W. Easter.
Rev. J. Howard Gibbons.
Rev. A. M. Lewis.
Mr. W. G. Hubbard.
Mr. C. L. Thompson.

Committee on Sunday Schools.

Rev. W. P. Chrisman.
Rt. Rev. C. C. Penick, D. D.
Mr. Lawrence E. Sands.
Dr. G. A. Aschman.

Examining Chaplains,

Rev. S. S. Moore, D. D.
Rev. J. S. Gibson.

Trustees of the Virginia Theological Seminary,

Rt. Rev. G. W. Peterkin, D. D. LL. D.
Rt. Rev. W. L. Gravatt, D. D.
Rev. S. S. Moore, D. D.
Mr. Joseph Trapnell.

Chancellor of the Diocese,

Hon. J. P. Rogers, Wheeling.

Woman's Auxiliary,

Mrs. G. A. Aschman, Wheeling, President.
Valley Convocation, Miss M. G. McSherry, Vice-President.
Kanawha Convocation, Mrs. Ely Ensign, Vice-President.
North Western Convocation, Miss Gertrude Lamb, Vice-President.

Delegates to Missionary Council,

Rev. J. S. Gibson.
Rev. J. S. Douglas.
*Rev. S. S. Moore, D. D.
Gen'l B. D. Spillman.
Mr. J. T. Waters.
*Mr. H. W. Potts.

*Elected by the Council.

Clergy of the Diocese of West Virginia.

May 20th, 1903.

Rt. Rev. Geo. W. Peterkin, D. D. LL. D., Bishop....*Parkersburg, W. Va.*
Rt. Rev. W. L. Gravatt, Bishop Coadjutor..........*Charles Town, W. Va.*
Rev. Geo. A. Gibbons, Rector of Emmanuel, Moorefield, and in charge of Missions in Hampshire Co..........*Romney, W. Va.*
Rev. Jno. F. Woods, Rector of St. Johns, Willow Island, and in charge of Cresaps and Wirt Co. Missions ....*Wheeling, W. Va.*
Rev. Robert Douglas Roller, D. D., Rector of St. John's Charleston ....*Charleston, W. Va.*
Rev. Jacob Brittingham, Rector of St. Luke's, Wheeling ....*Wheeling, W. Va.*
Rev. C. C. Pearson, in charge of St. Mark's, Berkeley Springs ....*Berkeley Springs, W. Va.*
***Rev. Chas. M. Campbell,* in charge of Boone Co. Missions ....*Racine, W. Va.*
Rev. S. Scollay Moore, D. D., Rector of Trinity Church, Parkersburg ....*Parkersburg, W. Va.*
***Rev. Andrew J. Willis,* Rector of Grace Church, Middleway; St. Bartholomews Leetown, and of the Church of the Holy Spirit, Summit Point..........*Middleway, W. Va.*
**Rev. W. H. Neilson*..........*Plainfield, N. J.*
Rev. Geo. W. Easter, Rector of All Saints Union, and in charge of the Church of the Messiah, Alderson........*Union, W. Va.*
Rev. Jno. S. Gibson, Rector of Trinity Church, Huntington, and in charge of Grace Church, Kenova....*Huntington, W. Va.*
Rev. B. M. Spurr, General Missionary, and Supt. Reynold's Mem. Hospital ....*Moundsville, W. Va.*
**Rev. Norman F. Marshall,* in charge of Holy Trinity, Bramwell, and of Grace Church, Eckman..........*Bramwell, W. Va.*
Rev. Andrew G. Grinnan, Rector of St. Paul's, Weston ....*Weston, W. Va.*
Rev. Thos. W. Cooke, Rector of Christ Church, Clarksburg ....*Clarksburg, W. Va.*
**Rev. Gerald Card* ....*Canada.*

Rev. Chas. E. Shaw, Rector of St. Ann's, New Martinsville ....*New Martinsville, W. Va.*

Rt. Rev. C. C. Penick, D. D., Rector of Christ Church, Fairmont ....*Fairmont W. Va.*

Rev. David W. Howard, Rector of St. Matthew's, Wheeling ....*Wheeling, W. Va.*

Rev. Jno. S. Douglas, Rector of Trinity Church, Martinsburg ....*Martinsburg, W. Va.*

Rev. Jno. Tilton Marley, Rector of Trinity Chuch, Morgantown, and Warden of the Episcopal Hall......*Morgantown, W. Va.*

Rev. Jas. L. Fish, in charge of Grace, Elkins, and St. Barnabas, Davis.... ....*Elkins, W. Va.*

Rev. Thos. J. Olliver Curran, in charge of St. Andrew's, Wheeling........ ....*Wheeling, W. Va.*

Rev. J. Howard Gibbons, Rector of Christ Church, Point Pleasant, and of Bruce Chapel........................*Point Pleasant.*

Rev. Jacob A. Hiatt, (Deacon) in charge of Grace, Ravenswood, and St. John's, Ripley ....*Ravenswood, W. Va.*

***Rev. Guy H. Crook*, Rector of St. James, Lewisburg, Church of the Incarnation, Ronceverte, and in charge of St. Thomas, White Sulphur, Grace, Clover Lick, and St. Peter's' Glen Jean.......................*Ranceverte, W. Va.*

Rev. Arthur M. Lewis, in charge of St. David's Powellton, Calvary, Montgomery, and Church of the Redeemer, Ansted........ ....*Powellton, W. Va.*

Rev. Everett Heath Brosius, in charge of Christ Church, Bluefield, and of the Church of the Heavenly Rest, Princeton................................*Bluefield, W. Va.*

Rev. Jno. S. Alfriend, Rector of Zion Church, Charles Town...... ....*Charles Town, W. Va.*

Rev. Wilson Page Christman, Rector of Trinity Church, Moundsville....... ....*Moundsville, W. Va.*

**Rev. Paca Kennedy* (Deacon).......................*Oxford, England.*

Rev. Thos. C. Darst, (Deacon) in charge of St. Andrew's, Mannington, and assisting Bishop Penick, Fairmont....... ....*Mannington, W. Va.*

Rév. Robt. N. Meade, Deacon, in charge of Grace, Eckman,, and Welch Mission..........................*Bramwell, W. Va.*

Rev. Jas. D. Miller, Rector of Mt. Zion, Hedgesville, and in charge of St. John's, Harper's Ferry....*Harper's Ferry, W. Va.*

Rev. Paris B. Stauffer, in charge of Ascension, Hinton, and Raleigh Co. Mission.............................*Hinton, W. Va.*

Rev. Geo. C. Shaw, Deacon, in charge of Grace, St. Mary's, Messiah, Waverly, and Christ Church, Williamstown.................... ... ...*St. Mary's W. Va.*

**Rev. C. E. A. Marshall*, Rector of Trinity Church, Shepherdstown...... ....*Shepherdstown, W. Va.*

**Rev. Creetus A. Dowell*, Deacon, in charge of St. Paul's, Sistersville ....*Sistersville, W. Va.*

**Rev. Jno. Warnock*, Rector of St. Mark's, St. Albans, and in charge of St. Luke's and St. Matthews, Charleston........ ....*Charleston, W. Va.*

**Rev. Edward D. Irvine*, Rector of Christ Church, Wellsburg, and of St. John's Brooke Co.............*Wellsburg, W. Va.*

**Rev. Edward B. Snead*, (1903) Buckhannon, Sutton.......*Buckhannon.*

**Not present. *Not entitled to seats.

JOURNAL

Of the Twenty-sixth Annual Council of the Protestant Episcopal Church in the Diocese of West Virginia.

ST. MATTHEWS CHURCH, WHEELING, W. VA., May 20, 1903.

The Twenty-sixth Annual Council of the Diocese of West Virginia met this day at 10 a. m.

The Rev. S. S. Moore, D. D., read morning prayer.

The Rev. Charles E. Shaw read the ante communion.

The preacher was the Rev. R. D. Roller, D. D., from the text St. Mark xvi. 20.

The Rt. Rev. W. L. Gravatt was celebrant at the Holy Communion, Bishop Peterkin assisting.

After the service, the Rt. Rev. G. W. Peterkin, D. D., LL. D., called the Council to order.

A call of the roll showed a quorum of both orders to be present.

The Bishop appointed the Rev. J. T. Marley and Mr. V. A. Weaver a committee on credentials of lay delegates.

On motion the Council adjourned until 2:30 o'clock.

2:30 P. M.

The Bishop called the Council to order.

The Bishop read the statistical part of his address, reserving the rest until the morrow.

The Committee on Credentials submitted the following report which was received by the Council:

The Committee on the Certificates of Lay Delegates beg leave to respectfully report, that the certificates of the following delegates are in due form.

J. T. MARLEY,
V. A. WEAVER.

PARISHES.

	Parish.	P. O.	Church.	Delegates.
1.	All Saints 1871.	Union	All Saints	1. J. M. Rowan.
				2. Jos. D. Logan.
				3. A. S. Johnston.
2.	Bangor	St. Albans	St. Marks	
3.	Bethel	Clarksburg	Christ	
4.	Christ	Fairmont	Christ	
5.	Christ	Wellsburg	Christ	*1. George A. Baxter.
				2. Joseph Fauset.
				*3. E. A. Piper.
6.	Emmanuel	Moorefield	Emmanuel	1. C. James Lobb.
				2. Wm H. Shearer.
				3. Dr. Lisle Gamble.
7.	Greenbrier	Lewisburg	St. James	
8.	Kanawha 1788.	Charleston	St. Johns.	1. W. S. Laidley.
				2. J. Lynn Richardson.
				*3. W. G. Hubbard.
				*1. Alfred Phillips.
				2. J. T. Waters.
				3. Lewis Summers, Jr.
9.	Norbourne 1769.	Martinsburg	Trinity	*1. J. Gassman.
				2. W. B. Colston.
				*3. H. A. Alexander.
10.	Norbourne 1769.	Hedgesville	Mt. Zion	1. Lee Lingamfelter.
				*2. R. B. Kilmer.
11.	Nelson 1888.	Middleway		1. Wm. Gilbert.
				*2. W. C. Frazier.
		Lee Town		1. Chas. E. Jones.
				2. Geo. T. Shirley.
		Summit		1. James Grantham.
				2. J. W. Strider.
12.	Pt. Pleasant	Pt. Pleasant	Christ	1. P. C. Eastham.
				2. H. E. Spilman.
				3. Lewis S. Pomeroy.
				*4. J. W. Heslup.
13.	Ravenswood	Ravenswood	Grace	*1. G. B. Crow.
				*2. W. T. Greer.
				3. F. H. Green.
14.	St. Andrews	Charles Town	Zion	*1. R. Henderson.
				*2. Scott Kenedy.
				*3. George R. Wendling
15.	St. Andrews	Shepherdstown	Trinity	1. H. W. Potts.
				*2. John O. Aglionby.
16.	St. Johns	Willow Island	St. Johns.	
17.	St. Lukes 1852.	Wheeling	St. Lukes.	*1. Jas. P. Rogers.
				*2. L. E. Sands.
				*3. Wylie Irwin.
				1. A. A. Taylor,
				2. E. B. Bowie,
				3. W. A. Wilson.

18. St. Matthews	Wheeling	St. Matthews	*1. Dr. G. A. Aschman.
			*2. Jos. C. Brady.
			*3. J. D. DuBois.
19. St. Pauls	Weston,	St. Pauls	1. Er Ralston.
			2. A. H. Kunst.
			3. E. G. Davisson.
			1. D. M. Bailey.
			2. E. M. Vandervort.
			3. R. Harrison.
20. Trinity 1846.	Parkersburg	Trinity	*1. B. M. Ambler.
			2. H. H. Moss.
			*3. Simms Powell.
			*1. W. G. Peterkin.
			2. C. C. Martin.
			*3. F. Fowler.
21. Trinity.	Moundsville	Trinity	*1. A. J. Martin.
			*2. Friend Cox.
			*3. V. A. Weaver.
22. Trinity.	Morgantown	Trinity	*1. Capt. W. C. Marshall.
23. Trinity	Huntington	Trinity	*1. C. L. Thompson.
			2. Edmund Sehon.
			3. F. R. Van Antwerp.
			1. Jno. W. Ensign.
			2. C. D. Emmons.
			3. F. D. Fuller.
24. Wetzel 1851.	New Martinsv'le	St. Annes	*1. S. R. Martin.
			2. S. B. Hall.
			*3. Edgar H. Bostock.
25. St. Johns	Cross Creek	St. Johns	
26. Tyler	Sistersville		1. A. Bruce Hunt.
			2. Geo. B. VanAmen.
			3. Geo. F. Durham.

MISSIONS.

Mission.	P. O.	Church.	Delegate.
Taylor Co	Grafton	St. Matthias	
Hampshire	Romney	St. Stephens	W. W. Baird.
			G. W. Parsons.
Hampshire	Okonoko	Epiphany	Henry M. Russell.
			Ned Russell,
Upshur	Buckhannon	Transfiguration	
Elk River	Sutton	St. Johns.	
Morgan Co.	Berkeley Spr'gs.	St. Marks	F. R. Reed.
Harpers Ferry	Harpers Ferry	St. Johns	
New River	Hinton	Ascension	
Cresaps	Cresaps	Grace	
Coal Valley	Montgomery	Calvary	W. R. Johnson.
Advent	Ansted	Redeemer	R. C. Taylor.
Princeton	Princeton	Heavenly Rest	
Wayne Co.	Kenova	Grace	Charles C. Coe.
Bluefield	Bluefield	Christ	*R. A. Anderson.
Bramwell	Bramwell	Holy Trinity	John D. Hewitt.
Ripon	Ripon	St. Johns	
Powelton	Powelton	St. Davids	D. Swain.
Elm Grove	Elm Grove	St. Pauls.	
Wheeling	Wheeling	St. Andrews	

St. Lukes	Charleston	St. Lukes	
St. Matthews	Charleston	St. Matthews	
Madison	Clover Lick	Grace	
Norbourne	Bunker Hill	Christ	Joseph Morgan.
Spruce Run	Lorentz	Sprnce.	
St. Thomas	White Sulphur	St. Thomas.,	
Davis	Tucker	Christ	
Christ Memorial	Williamstown	Christ	*J. W. Snodgrass.
Grace	Eckman	Grace	
Elkins	Elkins	St. Barnabas	
St. Marys	St. Marys	Grace	*R. H. Browse.
St. Andrews	Mannington		*F. A. Armstrong.

Those marked * were present.

Bishop Gravatt read his address as follows:

BISHOP GRAVATT'S ADDRESS.

June 4th-8th: Annual Diocesan Council, Trinity Church, Parkersburg. I preached the closing sermon of the Council Sunday evening, June 8th.

JUNE.

15th, Sunday: P. M. officiated at St. Philips, Charles Town.

17th, Tuesday: Attended a meeting of the Board of Trustees of the Virginia Theological Seminary.

19th, Thursday: At Lincoln for the Bishop of Virginia, preached and confirmed 1.

20th, Friday: At Theological Seminary Va., ordained to the priesthood Rev. A. M. Lewis and for the Bishop of Virginia I ordained to the priesthood Rev. Page Dame, Rev. Elliott, Meredith and Rev. M. S. Eagle.

20th, Friday: P. M. at Glen Collin for the Bishop of Virginia, confirmed 4.

29th, Sunday: In Zion Church, Charles Town, nativity of St. John Baptist, I preached the annual sermon for the Masons.

JULY.

6th, Sunday: Read service and preached in the Hotel at Black Mountain, N. C.

9th, Wednesday: Celebrated the Holy Communion at Black Mountain.

20th, Sunday: St. Mark's Church, Berkeley Springs. A. M. preached. P. M. officiated at Evening Service.

23rd, Wednesday: Officiated at a funeral in Middleway.

27th, Sunday: Officiated morning and evening in Emmanuel Church, Moorefield.

AUGUST.

1st: Preached in the School House, Paw Paw.

3rd, Sunday: A. M. preached in Epiphany Church, Okonoko, and celebrated the Holy Communion. Preached in the same Church at evening service.

4th, Monday: Preached in Zion's Church, Hampshire Co.

5th, Tuesday: Preached in St. Stephen's Church, Romney.

10th, Sunday: Preached at the Old Sweet Springs.

12th, Tuesday: Preached in the Presbyterian Church, Hillsboro.

13th, Wednesday: Preached in the Methodist Church, Huntersville.

14th, Thursday: Preached in the Presbyterian Church, Marlinton.

17th, Sunday: Preached in St. Thomas' Church, White Sulphur, A. M. P. M. evening prayer.

21st, Thursday: Preached in the Church of the Redeemer, at Ansted.

22nd, Friday: Preached at Caperton.

23rd, Saturday: Visited Nuttallburg.

24th, Sunday: A. M. Preached in the School House at Beauty. I baptized an infant.

24th, Sunday: P. M. Preached in the Presbyterian Church at Dubree.

31st, Sunday: A. M. Preached in Ascension Church, Hinton.

31st, Sunday: P. M. Preached in Messiah Church, Alderson.

SEPTEMBER.

7th, Sunday: A. M. St. James, Lewisburg, preached and confirmed 4. P. M. Incarnation, Ronceverte, I preached.

14th, Sunday: A. M. Preached in Zion Church, Charles Town.

15th to 18th: Attended the Fall meeting of the Eastern Convocation in Charles Town.

17th: Made an address to the clergy.

18th: Made an address to Convocation.

21st, Sunday: A. M. Preached in Trinity Church, Moundsville and confirmed 4.

21st, Sunday: P. M. Preached in St. Andrew's, Wheeling, and confirmed 10.

22nd, Monday: Met the Vestry in Moundsville.

23rd, Tuesday: Visited Fairmont and confirmed in private one sick person.

OCTOBER.

12th: 11 A. M. Visited Grace Church, Middleway, preached and administered the Holy Communion. 3:30 P. M. Preached in the Church of the Holy Spirit, Summit Point.

15th, Wednesday: Administered the Holy Communion to a sick person in Charles Town in the absence of the Rector.

21st, 22nd and 23rd: Attended Missionary Council in Philadelphia.

24th, Friday: Attended a meeting of the House of Bishops in Philadelphia.

29th, Wednesday: Assisted in marriage service in Trinity Church, Parkersburg.

30th, Thursday: Officiated at a marriage in Zion Church, Charles Town.

NOVEMBER.

2nd: Visited St. Philip's Church, Charles Town and preached.

11th: Attended a meeting of the Board of Turstees at the Va. Theological Seminary. .

13th, Thursday: Visited St. Andrew's on tne Mountain and made an address.

14th, Friday: Officiated in Zion Church, Charles Town.

15th, Saturday: Officiated at a funeral ın Zion Church, Charles Town.

16th, Sunday: Took part in the service in Zion Church, Charles Town, A. M. 3 P. M. Preached in St. Andrew's on the Mountain. 8 P. M. Preached in St. Philip's, Charles Town.

19th, Wednesday: Officiated at a marriage in Zion Church, Charles Town, A. M. P. M. Officiated at service in Zion Church for the Rector, who was absent holding a mission in Moorefield.

21st, Friday: Officiated at a funeral in Elmwood Cemetery, Charles Town.

21st, Friday: Officiated in Zion Church, Charles Town, in absence of the Rector.

23rd, Sunday: Officiated in Zion Church, Charles Town.

30th, Sunday: A. M. Addressed the Sunday School in Bruce Chapel. 11 A. M. Preached and confirmed 2. 8 P. M. Preached in Christ Church, Point Pleasant and confirmed 4.

DECEMBER.

1st: Visited the Church in Spillman, preached and confirmed 4.

2nd, Tuesday: Visited Grace Church, Ravenswood, and preached.

3rd, Wednesday: Attended a meeting of the congregation in Trinity Hall, Parkersburg.

4th, Thursday. A. M. Visited St. Paul's Church, Sistersville. P. M. Visited New Martinsville and met the congregation at the Rectory.

5th, Friday: Visited Clarksburg.

7th, Sunday: Preached in St. Paul's Church, Weston, 11 A. M. 2 P. M. Preached in the Chapel of the Hospital for the Insane. 8 P. M. Visited the Church of the Transfiguration, Buckhannon, and preached.

8th, Monday: Was unable to keep appointment at Spruce Run, the roads being impassible.

14th, Sunday: Failed to reach Lewisburg in time for appointment, due to a wreck on the C. & O. 8 P. M. Preached in the Church of the Incarnation, Ronceverte, and administered the Holy Communion.

15th, Monday: Visited Eackles' School House and preached.

16th, Tuesday: Preached in the Church of the Incarnation, Ronceverte.

21st, Sunday: A. M. Preached in St. Peter's, Glen Jean. P. M. Preached at Beury.

25. Christmas Day: Officiated in Trinity Church, Martinsburg.

28th, Sunday: A. M. Assisted in the service at the opening of Emmanuel Church, Staunton, Va. P. M. Preached in Emmanuel Church.

JANUARY, 1903.

4th, Sunday: A. M. Officiated in Trinity Church, Shepherdstown, preached and administered the Holy Communion. P. M. Officiated in Trinity Church, Martinsburg.

9th, Friday: Preached in School House, Centralia.

11th, Sunday. Preached and consecrated St. John's Church, Sutton, A. M. P. M. Officiated at evening service.

12th, Monday: Visited Parkersburg.

13th and 14th: Attended the winter meeting of the Northwestern Convocation in St. Matthew's Church, Wheeling.

13th: P. M. Confirmed 1 person in St. Matthew's Church, Wheeling.

14th: P. M. Visited Reynold's Memorial Hospital at Glendale, made an address and delivered diplomas to graduates. Afterwards I inspected the building, examined all the books, and found everything in the most perfect order.

15th, Thursday: Visited Pennsboro, baptized 5 adults, preached in the Methodist Church and confirmed 4.

16th, Friday: Preached in the Presbyterian Church at Mannington, and confirmed 10.

17th, Saturday: P. M. Met the Seabury Club in St. Matthews Church, Wheeling.

18th, Sunday: A. M. Preached in St. Luke's Church, Wheeling. 3 P. M. Visited the Sunday School of St. Paul's Church, Sistersville, and made an address. 8 P. M. Officiated at evening service in the same church. After service met with the Vestry.

25th, Sunday. Visited Trinity Church, Morgantown, preached at morning service. 7:30 P. M. Preached in same church and confirmed 2.

31st, Saturday: Visited Parkersburg to confer with Bishop Peterkin.

FEBRUARY.

1st, Sunday: A. M. Preached in St. Matthew's, Charleston, and administered Holy Communion. P. M. Preached in St. Luke's Church, Charleston.

2nd, Monday: Preached in St. David's Church, Powellton, and confirmed 4.

3rd, 4th and 5th: Attended Kanawha Convocation, St. Jonn's Church, Charleston.

Wednesday, A. M.: Celebrated Holy Communion and in the evening made an address.

6th, Friday: A. M. Visiteu St. Mark's Church, St. Albans, preached and after the service met the congregation. P. M. Preached in Calvary Church, Montgomery, and confirmed 2.

8th, Sunday: A. M. Preached in Ascension Church, Hinton. 3 P. M. Preached in Presbyterian Church at Fort Spring. 7:30 P. M. Preached in St. James' Church, Lewisburg.

15th, Sunday: A. M. Preached in Christ Church, Clarksburg, and confirmed 7. 3:30 P. M. Preached at North View Mission. 5 P. M. Confirmed 1 sick person in private. 7:30 P. M. Preached again in Christ Church.

16th, Monday: Visited Parkersburg and confirmed in private 1 sick person.

22nd, Sunday: Visited St. Matthias' Church, Grafton.

27th, Friday: Officiated at a Lenten service for the Rector of Zion Church, Charles Town.

MARCH.

1st, Sunday: Preached in Zion Church, Charles Town, and celebrated Holy Communion.

4th, Wednesday: Preached in Holy Trinity Church, Richmond.

8th, Sunday. A. M. Visited Trinity Church, Moundsville, and confirmed 2. P. M. Visited St. Paul's Church, Sistersville, made an address to the Sunday School and preached at evening service.

10th, Tuesday: Made an address at the Lenten service at Trinity Church, Moundsville. P. M. Was unable to keep appointment at Belington because no place could be found to hold service. I went to Elkins instead and met the congregation at a reception.

11th, Wednesday: Preached in Grace Church, Elkins, and confirmed 2.

12th, Thursday. Visited St. Barnabas Church, Davis, preached and confirmed 6.

15th, Sunday. A. M. Preached in Christ Church, Fairmont, and confirmed 4. Afternoon confirmed 1 sick person in private.

16th, Monday: Visited Trinity Church, Morgantown, and confirmed 2 sick persons in private. Preached in the Church at night and confirmed 3.

17th, Tuesday: In Christ Church, Clarksburg, I ordained to the diaconate the Rev, C. A. Dowell, Dr. S. S. Moore, of Parkersburg, preaching the sermon. After morning prayer, confirmed 1 candidate from Morgantown, presented by Rev. J. T. Marley.

22nd, Sunday. I preached and consecrated the new church at Spillman. A. M. P. M. Preached in Christ Church, Point Pleasant.

23rd, Monday: Preached in St. John's Church, Ripley, and confirmed 7.

25th, Wednesday: Preached at Mt. Carbon and confirmed 2.

26th, Thursday: Preached in the Church of the Redeemer, Ansted.

28th, Saturday: Visited Thurmond.

29th, Sunday: Preached in All Saints Church, Union, A. M., and administered Holy Communion. P. M. Preached in same church and confirmed 4.

30th, Monday: Visited Hinton.

31st, Tuesday: Preached in the Baptist Church, Beckley, and confirmed 1.

APRIL.

5th, Sunday: Palm Sunday. Preached in St. Luke's Church, Wheeling, A. M., and confirmed 16. 3:30 P. M. Preached in St. Paul's Church, Elm Grove, and confirmed 2. 7:30 P. M. Preached in St. Matthew's Church, Wheeling, and confirmed 31.

6th, Monday: Visited St. John's Church, Brooke Co., and after service had a conference with the congregation about fixing the church and maintaining the services.

7th, Tuesday: 9 A. M. Made an address at the Lenten service in Christ Church, Wellsburg. P. M. Preached in Christ Church and confirmed 2.

8th, Wednesday: Preached in St. Luke's Church, Wheeling.

9th, Thursday: A. M. Made an address at the Lenten service in St. Luke's Church, Wheeling. P. M. Visited Grace Church, St. Mary's preached and confirmed 2 and celebrated the Holy Communion.

10th, Friday: Good Friday: Visited the Church of the Advent, Waverly, preached and confirmed 1. P. M. Visited Christ Church, Williamstown, preached and confirmed 2.

12th, Sunday. Easter Day. Visited St. Ann's Church, New Martinsville, preached and celebrated Holy Communion.

12th, Sunday: Easter P. M. St. Paul's, Sistersville, made an address to Sunday School, at the evening service preached and confirmed 1.

19th, Sunday: Preached in Zion Church, Charles Town, and confirmed 9. P. M. Visited St. Philip's, Charles Town, and made an address.

25th, Sunday: Visited Trinity Church, Martinsburg. Preached and confirmed 11 and 1 sick person in private. P. M. Visited Mt. Zion Church, Hedgesville, and preached.

MAY.

2nd: Visited Bramwell and after service met with the congregation to advise them about their work for the future.

3rd, Sunday: Preached in Holy Trinity, Bramwell, and celebrated the Holy Communion. P. M. Preached in Christ Church, Bluefield, and confirmed 2.

5th, 6th and 7th: Attended the Eastern Convocation in St. Bartholomew's Church, Lee Town.

6th: Celebrated Holy Communion.

7th: P. M. Made an address closing the Convocation.

8th, Friday: Visited St. John's Church, Harper's Ferry, confirmed 2.

17th: 3:30 P. M. Preached in St. Andrew's on the Mountain and confirmed 3. 7:30 P. M. Preached in Zion Church, Charles Town.

SUMMARY.

Baptisms	6
Confirmations	192
Marriages	3
Burials	3
Visits	113
Sermons	118
Addresses	52
Ordinations	5
Consecrations	2
Lay Readers Licenses	5

Money received—

From Woman's Auxiliary, Zion Church, Charles Town	$100
From St. Andrew's Guild, Charles Town	30
From Friend in Fairmont	50
From Friend in Maryland	25
From Friend in Charles Town	10
	$215

Amounts paid out—

Six grants for Mission work	$180
One grant for Theological Student	25
	$205
Balance in hand	10

Bishop Peterkin announced the following committees:

STATE OF THE CHURCH.

Rev. John S. Gibson, Mr. Geo. R. Wendling,
Rev. G. A. Gibbons, Dr. G. A. Aschman,

PAROCHIAL REPORTS.

Rev. R. D. Roller, D. D., Mr. W. G. Hubbard,
Rev. R. N. Meade, Mr. H. A. Alexander,
Rev. Jas. L. Fish, Friend Cox,

ADMISSION OF NEW PARISHES.

Rev. S. S. Moore, D. D., Mr. W. C. Frazier,
Rev. A. G. Grinnan, Capt. W. C. Marshall,

FINANCE.

Mr. L. E. Sands, Mr. G. B. Crow,
Mr. V. A. Weaver, Mr. A. J. Martin,
Mr. J. C. Bradley, Mr. R. Henderson,

EPISCOPAL AND PERMANENT FUND.

Rev. C. C. Pearson, Mr. Geo. A. Baxter,
Rev. John S. Alfriend, Mr. Simms Powell.

UNFINISHED BUSINESS.

Rev. Dr. Roller, Mr. Alfred Phillips,

Bluefield Mission filed an application to be admitted into union with the Council as a Parish. Referred to Committee on New Parishes.

The Rev. G. A. Gibbons explained that the charge of $59 against him in the account of the Trustee of the Episcopal Fund, was for printing expenses in connection with the Standing Committee, and not personal.

On motion of Bishop Gravatt the Secretary sent the following telegram to the Council of Virginia:

"Loving greeting to the Council of Virginia from the Council of West Virginia, now in session."

On motion of the Rev. David W. Howard the printed programme of services and hours for meeting of the Council was adopted. The programme is as follows:

SAINT MATTHEWS CHURCH, WHEELING, W. VA.

Twenty-sixth Annual Council and Twenty-fifth Anniversary of the Consecration of

THE RT. REV. GEO. W. PETERKIN, D. D., LL. D.
Ascension Day, 1903.

WEDNESDAY, MAY 20TH.

Morning Prayer, Sermon and Holy Communion, 10:00 A. M. Preacher, Rev. Robert D. Rollèr, D. D. Council called to order, 11:30. Luncheon served in Sunday School room, 12:30 P. M. Session of the Council, 2:00. Annual meeting of Woman's Auxiliary, 2:00. Special Missionary Service and Sermon, 8:00. Preacher, The Rt. Rev. Dr. Penick. Service of St. Aidan's Mission for Deaf Mutes, 8:00. Conducted by Rev. A. W. Mann.

ASCENSION DAY.

Celebration of the Holy Communion, 7:30 A. M. Morning Prayer and Historical Sermon, 10:00. Preacher, Rev. John S. Gibson. Luncheon served in Sunday School Room, 12:30 P. M. Session of the Council, 2:30, Special Festival Service in commemoration of Bishop Peterkin's Consecration, 8:00. Preacher, The Rt. Rev. Thomas U. Dudley, D. D., LL. D.

FRIDAY, MAY 22ND.

Morning Prayer, Litany and Address, 10:00 A. M. Speaker, Bishop Van Buren, of Porto Rico. Session of the Council, 11:00. Luncheon served in Sunday School room, 12:30 P. M. Session of the Council, 2:30. Reception to Bishops, Clergy, lay delegates and parishioners, 8:00. To be held in Sunday School room.

SUNDAY AFTER ASCENSION DAY.

Celebration of the Holy Communion, 8:00 A. M. Morning Prayer and Sermon, 10:30. Evening prayer and Bishop's charge to Clergy and Laity, 7:30. The Bishop requests all who can possibly do so to remain until the closing of the Council, on Sunday Evening, May 24th.

The Committee on Constitution and Canons was elected as follows:

Rev. John S. Gibson,
Rev. D. W. Howard,
Rev. J. S. Douglas.
Mr. W. S. Laidley,
Mr. Joseph Trapnell.

On motion the Council adjourned.

THURSDAY, 2:30 P. M.

The Council was called to order by the Bishop. Prayers were said by the Rev. G. A. Gibbons.

The minutes of the previous day were read and approved.

The Secretary read the following telegram from the Diocese of Virginia:

Winchester, Va., May 20th, 1903.

Sec'y of the Protestant Episcopal Church,
Wheeling, W. Va.

The one hundred and eighth council of Diocese of Virginia sends greetings to the Council of the Diocese of West Virginia, with hearty congratulations to Bishop Peterkin on the twenty-fifth anniversary of his consecration with thanks to the Great Head of the Church for the work which has been done in his Diocese during that time.

EVERARD MEAD, *Sec'y.*

Mr. B. M. Ambler read the following letter which was ordered printed in the Journal:

7 KAWAJUCHI CHO, Osaka, Japan,
April 8, 1903.

B. M. AMBLER, ESQ.,
Parkersburg, W. Va.

MY DEAR BROTHER:

Having learned through you that a memorial of the consecration of Bishop Peterkin, as the first Bishop of West Virginia, is to be held at St. Matthew's Church, Wheeling, on Ascension Day of this year, I feel that at such a time the ends of the earth, as it were, ought to come together to do him honor.

In the absorbing demands of a work, which has been steadily growing in his Diocese, Bishop Peterkin might have pleaded his inability to take an active interest in the spread of the Gospel in heathen lands. It is well known, however, that there have been few meetings of the Board of Managers for Foreign and Domestic Missions which Bishop Peterkin has not attended, when it has been possible for him to do so, and that he has visited both Brazil and Porto Rico on two occasions on behalf of the church. I might mention many deep personal obligations to Bishop Peterkin, bestowed upon me while I was at work within his diocese, but I want to send this letter as an humble representative of the Japan Mission.

It is the hope of this Missionary Community, I am sure, that God may long spare the life of one who has done so much to spread His Kingdom in the hearts of men. The Empire of Japan has not yet come to acknowledge our Lord Jesus Christ, but when she does, she will have good reason to feel deep gratitude to those who, like Bishop Peterkin, have shown unflagging zeal in the cause of missions.

Hoping then, that you will at that meeting add the greetings of the missions of the Church in Japan, I am

Very affectionately yours,
JOHN C. AMBLER,
Missionary to Japan.

Mr. Geo. R. Wendling offered the following preamble and resolution which was adopted:

It is the sense of this Council that the admirable Historical Sermon delivered on Ascension day 1903, in St. Matthew's Church, at Wheeling, W. Va., by the Rev. John S. Gibson, is worthy of preservation in permanent form, and of wide circulation.

The Secretary of the Council is therefore instructed to request of the Rev. John S. Gibson a copy of the sermon and cause it to be printed in the Journal of this Council. The Secretary is also instructed to have 3,000 copies of the sermon printed and bound for distribution in the Diocese and among its friends. and to send a copy to each member of the House of Bishops.

The Report of the Trustee of the Episcopal Fund was received and referred to the Finance Committee. (See Appendix A.)

The Trustees of the Permanent Fund submitted their report. (See Appendix A.)

On motion the Rev. R. R. Swope, D. D., the Rev. N. S. Thomas and other visiting clergy were invited to seats on the floor of the Council.

The Bishop then read his annual address as follows:

BISHOP PETERKIN'S ADDRESS.

JUNE.

The Twenty-fifth Annual Council met in Trinity Church, Parkersburg, on Wednesday, June 4th, and continued in session over Sunday the 8th. We had our accustomed services and sessions, and, according to our wont, gave to Missions, both at Home and Abroad, a prominent place on our programme.

Tuesday, 10th: Attended a meeting of the Board of the Sheltering Arms Hospital, in Charleston.

Thursday, 11th: Officiated at a wedding in Williamstown.

Sunday, 15th: In Parkersburg. Baptized an infant in private, in the absence of the Rector, and officiated morning and evening in Trinity church, also visited St. Stephen's.

Tuesday, 17th, Friday, 20th: These days were occupied at the Seminary and High School, in attendance on the Commencement exercises, and the meetings of the Board of Trustees of the Seminary and of the Education Society. On Friday, 20th, in the Seminary Chapel, I admitted to the order of Deacons, Thos. C. Darst, Paca Kennedy and Robert N. Meade of the Diocese of West Virginia. I also ordained 11 candidates for the Bishop of Virginia, 2 for the Bishop of Southern Virginia and 1 for the Bishop of East Carolina.

Sunday, 22: In the absence of the Rector, I preached in St. Matthew's church, Wheeling.

Tuesday, 24th: In St. Stephen's Church, Lynn, Mass., I presided at the consecration of Rev. Dr. Jas. H. Van Buren, as Bishop of Porto Rico; I also preached the sermon.

Sunday, 29th: A. M. St. Matthew's Church, Wheeling. P. M. St. Luke's Church, Wheeling.

Sunday, 6th: A. M. St. John's, Willow Island. P. M. Church of the Messiah, Waverly.

Friday, 11th: Preached in a Hall at Belington and baptized a child.

Sunday, 13th: A. M. and P. M. St. Barnabas', Davis. In the morning consecrated the church. In the evening confirmed 2.

Monday, 14th: Preached in a school house, Harding.

Tuesday, 15th: Preached in Grace Church, Elkins, and ordained Rev. Jas. L. Fish to the Priesthood; Rev. Dr. Moore presented the candidate, and with Rev. Geo. A. Gibbons united in the laying on of hands.

Thursday, 17th. On Valley Mountain, I delivered an address on the occasion of the unveiling of a monument put up to mark the resting place of soldiers, at whose funerals I officiated forty-two years before, during the war between the States.

Sunday, 20th: A. M. Preached in Grace Church, Clover Lick, and baptized a child. P. M. Read the service in a room of the hotel near Clover Lick depot, the Rev. Mr. Gibbons preaching.

Saturday, 26th: Grace Church, Ravenswood.

Sunday, 27th: A. M. Consecrated the new Grace Church, Ravenswood, and P. M., preached and confirmed 6. The new church which is built upon the Rectory lot, takes the place of the old building destroyed by fire Sunday, October 7th, 1900, and is in every way a great improvement over the old.

AUGUST.

Sunday, 3rd: Preached in St. James', Richmond, Va.

Wednesday, 6th: In the same church officiated at a funeral.

Sunday, 10th: Preached in the hall of the Hotel at Brookside, Preston County.

Sunday, 17th: In company with Rev. Mr. Irvine, who had come to look over the field, I visited the Chapel of the Good Shepherd, Parkersburg, Grace, Tavennersville and Christ Memorial, Williamstown.

Sunday, 24th: A. M. St. John's, Ripley. P. M. Grace, Ravenswood.

Sunday, 31: Preached A. M. in Trinity Church, Towson, Md., and P. M. in the Chapel of the Holy Comforter, Lutherville.

SEPTEMBER.

Sunday 7th: A. M. and P. M St. Matthias, Grafton.

Sunday, 14th: A. M. Trinity, Shepherdstown. P. M. St. John's, Harper's Ferry.

Tuesday, 16th: Meeting of the Board of Managers of our Missions in New York.

Wednesday, 17: Meeting of Kanawha Convocation in Christ Church, Bluefield. P. M. Preached.

Thursday, 18th: In attendance on meetings of Convocation. P. M. Made an address.

Friday, 19th: Church of the Heavenly Rest, Princeton, and confirmed 1.

Sunday, 21st: A. M. Christ Church, Bluefield, and confirmed 2. P. M. Holy Trinity, Bramwell, and confirmed 1.

Monday, 22nd: Preached in the Baptist Church, Elkhorn.

Tuesday, 23rd: Visited Elkridge, and P. M. preached at Algoma.

Wednesday, 24th: Visited Vivian and Landgraf, and P. M. preached in Grace Church, Eckman.

Thursday, 25th: Preached in Methodist Church, Welch.

Friday, 26th: Preached in the Baptist Church, Williamson.

Sunday, 28: Preached A. M. and P. M. in Trinity Church, Huntington, and in the afternoon in Grace Chapel, Kenova.

OCTOBER.

Wednesday, 1st: Preached in Grace Church, St. Mary's, and ordained Mr. George C. Shaw to the Diaconate, also attended meetings of the N. W. Convocation.

Friday, 3rd: Preached in Presbyterian Church, Smithfield, Wetzel Co.

Sunday, 5th: A. M. St. Ann's Church, New Martinsville. P. M. St. Paul's Church, Sistersville, and confirmed 5.

Friday, 10th: Christ Church, near Racine, Boone Co.

Sunday, 12th: Preached morning and afternoon in a school house on Bull Creek, and in the evening in the Post Office, at the mouth of Robinson.

Sunday, 19th: A. M. St. Paul's, Ogontz, Pa. P. M. Calvary, Germantown. P. P. M. Ogontz School.

These services were in connection with the Missionary Council, which remained in session until the afternoon of Thursday, 23rd. On this day Thursday, 23rd, and on Friday, 24th, I was in attendance on a meeting of the House of Bishops.

Sunday, 26th: Preached in St. Augustine, Atlantic City.

NOVEMBER.

Saturday 1: Attended a meeting of the Guild and Vestry of Nelson Parish in Middleway.

Sunday, 2nd: Preached in the three churches of Nelson Parish, at Summit Point, Lee Town and Middleway.

Sunday, 9th: Preached A. M. and P. M. in Memorial Church, Baltimore, Md.

Monday, 10th: Addressed the Mother's Mission of Memorial Church, Baltimore.

Wednesday, 12th: At the Virginia Seminary, I attended a meeting of the Board of Trustees.

Thursday, 13th: St. John's Church, Ripon, confirmed 1.

Friday, 14th: A. M. Christ Church, Blue Ridge, confirmed 3.

Sunday, 16: Zion Church, Charles Town. P. M. St. Andrew's on the Mountain. P. P. M. St. Philip's, Charles Town.

Wednesday, 19th: Christ Church, Wellsburg.

Thursday, 20th: Visited Reynolds Memorial Hospital.

Sunday, 23rd: A. M. and P. M. Trinity Church, Morgantown.

Sunday, 30th: A. M. and P. M. St. Stephen's Church, Romney.

DECEMBER.

Monday, 1st: Went to New York, where during the week, I attended the Advent Missionary meeting, and by appointment, spoke three times. On Tuesday, 2nd, in St. Andrew's Church, Harlem, and on Sunday, 7th, in St. James Church, Fordham, and in the Church of the Incarnation, Brooklyn.

Tuesday, 9th: Attended the regular monthly meeting of the Board of Managers of our missions.

I reached home on the evening of Wednesday, 10th, and on the next day Thursday, 11th, because I seemed to have developed a bad cold, I had the Chaplains to come to my house to conduct an examination appointed for that day.

On Friday, 12th, the Doctor forbade my keeping appointments which I had at Fairmont and Mannington. At this time I hoped I would be sufficiently recovered to enable me to go to Clarksburg for Sunday, 21st, but my expectation was disappointed, and I found myself at last compelled to give up all prospect of immediate work and to take to my bed. I had no idea at the time that I was entering upon a long illness which would disable me for months. But, so it was. I found myself completely prostrated by an attack of acute Bronchitis, and after two months had passed, and I began to rally from the attack, the Doctor ordered me south. I am thankful to say that the treatment and advice I received was justified in the result. After two months absence, I reached home on Saturday, April 25th, 1903, by the blessing of God well again and ready to enter anew upon my much loved work.

I cannot forbear to take this opportunity to express my high appreciation of the affectionate solicitude manifested on my behalf all over the Diocese, and at the same time to congratulate you that you had already made such provision for the contingency, that the abundant and most acceptable labors of Bishop Gravatt fully supplied my lack of service. This has been to me but one to be added to the many and constant causes of thankfulness I have for his faithful and loving co-operation in all our work. His labors must continually grow greater as mine become less; but after my complete recovery from my recent sickness, I am encouraged to hope that we may long labor together, and be mutually helpful in bearing the care of all the Churches.

APRIL.

Sunday, 5, 1903: I was able to-day for the first time for four months to officiate in public. I preached in St. Timothy's Church. Wilson, N. C.

Tuesday, 7th: I made an address in the same church.

Sunday, 12: Easter Day. I preached in Emmanuel Church, Henrico Co., Va.

Sunday, 19th: I preached in St. James' Church, Richmond.

Sunday, 26: Resuming my regular visitations, I preached in Trinity Church, Parkersburg, and confirmed 14.

Tuesday, 28: I preached in St. Paul's Church, Weston, and confirmed 6.

Wednesday, 29: I preached in St. Paul's Chapel, Middle Run, about four miles from Weston, and confirmed 8. This is the 66th New Church building I have been permitted to preach in since I came to take charge of the work in West Virginia, twenty-five years ago, and there is one other, the Chapel at Spilman, recently consecrated by Bishop Gravatt, which I have not yet visited. Fourteen years ago, in company with the Rev. Dr. Lacy, I visited the neighborhood of Middle Run, and preached. Under the wise and energetic labors of Mr. Grinnan this work has developed until now a comfortable and sightly Chapel has been erected, at a cost of about $900, and the outlook for a congregation is very promising. The people deserve great credit in that they have put their own shoulder to the wheel, and with but little outside help, have completed and paid for their Chapel. Thus is our Church to grow in this Diocese when chapels like this shall spring up around the existing centres of influence. Ought not every strong congregation thus to be strengthening their stakes and lengthening their cords.

MAY.

Sunday, 3: A. M. and P. M. St. John's, Charleston, confirming at the morning service 8 persons.

Monday, 4: At Paint Creek attended the annual meeting of the Board of Directors and Board of Managers of the Sheltering Arms Hospital.

Wednesday, 6: Preached in St. Andrew's, Wheeling, and confirmed 14. There is abundant evidence of God's blessing upon this growing work.

Sunday, 10: A. M. Trinity, Shepardstown. Good Shepard, Duffield.

Tuesday, 12: Meeting of Missionary Board in New York.

Sunday, 17: A. M. Trinity Church, Huntington. Consecrated the Church. With the Rector, Rev. Jno. S. Gibson, were present and assisting in the services Rev. A. M. Lewis of Powellton, W. Va., and Rev. Mr. Hampton, of Ironton, O. This church building had been in use since 1886, but owing to the shifting membership of a new town and city and the heavy strain upon the congregation incident to still further equipping the Parish by building a suitable rectory, and passing from a mission station into an independent Parish, involving, of course, the raising of a much larger local revenue, the Church was never able before to free itself from debt. The whole Church property is admirable located and suitable for its purposes. The congregation is greatly to be congratulated on the happy result of many years of hard labor and patient waiting.

P. P. M. Trinity, Huntington. Confirmed 6. Grace Church, Kenova, and confirmed 1.

CHANGES IN THE DIOCESE.

Letters Dimissory.

Letters dismissory have been given to Rev. W. H. Burkhart to the Diocese of New Jersey, Rev. John R. Joyner to the Diocese of Maryland, Rev. H. B. Thomas to the Missionary Jurisdiction of Porto Rico, Rev. Lewis R. Levering to the Diocese of Newark, Rev. Walter B. Stehl to the Diocese of Easton.

Letters have been received in behalf of the Rev. Jas. D. Miller, from the Diocese of Nebraska; Rev. Paris B. Stauffer, from the Diocese of Pittsburgh; Rev. Jno. Warnock, from the Diocese of New Jersey; Rev. Edward D. Irvine, from the Diocese of Springfield.

The Clergy List has also been increased by the ordination of the

Rev. Geo. C. Shaw.

Rev. Creetus A. Dowell.

Rev. Thos. C. Darst.

Rev. Paca Kennedy.

Rev. Robert N. Meade.

The *Rev. Creetus A. Dowell* has taken charge of St. Paul's, Sisterville, vice, *Rev. Mr. Burkhardt*, removed to New Jersey.

The *Rev. Mr. Warnock* has become Rector of St. Mark's, St. Albans, vice, *Rev. Mr. Joyner*, removed to Maryland, and has also taken charge of St. Luke's, and St. Matthew's Missions, Charleston, vice, *Rev. Mr. Card*, temporarily removed to Canada.

The *Rev. Edward D. Irvine* has become Rector of Christ Church, Wellsburg, and of St. John's, Brooke Co., vice, *Rev. H. B. Thomas*, removed to Porto Rico.

The *Rev. J. A. Hiatt* has relinquished the charge of the Chapel of the Good Shepherd, Parkersburg, and Grace Chapel, Tavennersville, and taken charge of the Grace Church, Ravenswood, and of St. John's, Ripley.

The *Rev. C. E. A. Marshall* has taken charge of Trinity Church, Shepherdstown, vice, *Rev. Mr. Stehl*, removed to the Diocese of Easton.

The *Rev. Jas. D. Miller* has become Rector of Mt. Zion, Hedgsville, and taken charge of St. John's, Harper's Ferry, vice, *Rev. Mr. Shaw*, removed to New Martinsville.

The *Rev. Paris B. Stauffer* has taken charge of the Ascension Church, Hinton, and of the Mission at Raleigh, vice, *Rev. Mr. Meade*, removed to Virginia.

The *Rev. Robert N. Meade* has become assistant to Rev. N. F. Marshall at Bramwell and adjacent points.

The *Rev. Thomas C. Darst* has taken charge of St. Andrew's Mission, Mannington, and is also assisting Bishop Penick in Fairmont.

The *Rev. Paca Kennedy*, having received the Scholarship recently founded by the Alumni of the Alexandria Seminary, is pursuing his studies in Oxford, England.

The Missions at Buckhannon, Lorentz and Sutton, with several dependencies, have been thrown into one combination, and the charge accepted by the Rev. Edward B. Snead, of Richmond, Va.

The St. Matthias, Grafton, made vacant by the removal of *Rev. Mr. Levering* to Newark, has been put into combination with Cairo and Pennsboro, and we hope soon to secure some one to take charge.

The *Rev. Edward D. Irvine* has become Rector of Christ Church, Wellsburg, and of St. John's, Brooke Co., vice, *Rev. Mr. Thomas*, transferred to Porto Rico.

CANDIDATES FOR ORDERS.

Postulants.

Richard Trapnell. Edmund P. Dandridge.

For Deacons and Priest's Orders.

Howard Meyers.
T. Getz Hill.
Percy N. McDonald.
F. Van R. Moore.

For Priest's Orders.

Jacob A. Hiatt.
Creetus A. Dowell.
Thos. C. Darst.
Geo. C. Shaw.
Robert N. Meade.
Paca Kennedy.

Churches consecrated	3
Ordained to Priesthood	1
Ordained to Diaconate	4
Sermons and addresses	107
Meetings on other occasions	40
Confirmed on 16 occasions	79

MISSIONS.

Mission.	P. O.	Church.
Tayler Co	Grafton	St Matthias
Hampshire	Romney	St. Stephen
Hampshire	Okonoko	Epiphany
Upshur	Buckhannon	Transfiguration
Elk River	Sutton	St. Johns
Morgan Co	Berkeley Springs	St. Marks
Harpers Ferry	Harpers Ferry	St. Johns
New River	Hinton	Ascension
Cresaps	Cresaps	Grace
Coal Valley	Montgomery	Calvary
Advent	Ansted	Redeemer
Princeton	Princeton	Heavenly Rest
Wayne Co	Kenova	Grace
Bluefield	Bluefield	Christ
Bramwell	Bramwell	Holy Trinity
Ripon	Ripon	St. Johns
Powellton	Powellton	St. Davids
Elm Grove	Elm Grove	St. Pauls
Wheeling	Wheeling	St. Andrews
St. Lukes	Charleston	St. Lukes
St. Matthews	Charleston	St. Matthews
Madison	Clover Lick	Grace
Norbourne	Bunker Hill	Christ
Spruce Run	Lorentz	Spruce
St. Thomas	White Sulphur	St Thomas
Davis	Tucker	Christ
Christ Memorial	Williamstown	Christ
Grace	Eckman	Grace
Elkins	Elkins	St. Barnabas
St. Marys	St. Marys	Grace
Parkersburg	Parkersburg	Chapel of Good Shepherd
Parkersburg	Tavenersville	Grace

THE BISHOP'S SPECIAL FUND.

During the year contributions have been received as follows:

Boone Co. Christ Church	$ 1 00	
Charleston, St. John's	5 00	
Charles Town Zion	125 00	
Eastern Convocation	25 00	
Fairmont	98 04	
Fort Spring	1 00	
Glendale	15 00	
Huntington	15 00	
New Martinsville	20 00	
Parkersburg Trinity	190 00	
Parkersburg, Good Shepherd	200 00	
Romney	42 00	
Shepherdstown	100 00	
Union	2 00	
Wellsburg	5 00	
White Sulphur	50 62	
Wheeling, St. Matthew's	226 00	
Wheeling, St. Luke's	150 00	
Williamstown	10 00	
From without Diocese	97 00	
	$ 1,377 66	
Disbursements.		
20 grants to churches and rectories		430 16
6 grants for books, printing, etc		164 00
20 grants to ministers		631 68
2 grants to hospital		122 00
Balance		29 82
		$ 1,377 66

ADDRESS

It is with peculiar pleasure, my Brethren and Friends, that I welcome you to this Council Meeting in St. Matthews' Church, Wheeling—where twenty-five years ago I had committed to me the charge of the Diocese of West Virginia. All that relates to what we may call our anniversary exercises, has received, and will receive, such attention during our sessions, that I shall content myself at this time with a bare allusion to it. By God's good hand upon us we have come so far on the way, and in view of all our experience, in undertaking and carrying on what, by high authority had been pronounced impossible, we may well thank God and take courage. There are only two of the clergy, beside myself, present here today who were then connected with the Diocese, and many of the laymen, then prominent, have passed away. But what if the workmen change, the work still goes on. Let us be faithful wherever God has placed us, and where He keeps us, working while it is called today, because the night cometh when no man can work.

BISHOP WHITTLE.

During the exercises of our last commencement week at the Seminary, it pleased God to take to his rest Bishop Whittle, the fifth Bishop of the undivided Diocese of Virginia. For ten years i. e. from May 1868 to May, 1878, he had the churches of West Virginia under his care, first as assistant to Bishop Johns, and then as Bishop of Virginia. His first charge was in West Virginia, in Kanawha County, and he was always deeply interested in the welfare of the people, and in the growth of the Church. During all these years since my consecration he had only once visited the Diocese, and that was on the occasion of the consecration of Bishop Gravatt, Nov. 10, 1899, and he seemed then to show some of his old time vigor. He had, however, been in poor health for years, and it was only after a long and painful illness, at the last, that he passed away from earth to Paradise.

Bishop Whittle was a man of very marked personality. He had deep convictions and always the courage of those convictions. Frank and absolutely truthful in what he did and said, he seemed at times, to those who did not know him well, to be somewhat harsh and unyielding; but those of us who were admitted into the circle of his friendship knew what a tender heart was all the time beating in his manly bosom. Life was a more serious thing with him than with most persons, and he could not but be at times depressed at worldliness and error in the Church. Knowing nothing in his own experience save a pure intent, and seeing what he did see very clearly, he could not but chafe at every word or deed that was less than absolutely truthful and direct. Strictly evangelical in his views, he always seemed to feel a profound responsibility for the maintenance of the Church which was no less the Church of his love than of his heritage—in the spirit of the great Reformers, and its continued working along the lines marked out by them, and accepted by our forefathers. In an Episcopate of thirty-four years he never spared himself, but was instant in season and out of season. His administration was exact and painstaking, and his preaching clear and strong, and always characterized by that intense earnestness which in sacred things is eloquence. While diffident and retiring in disposition, he was approachable and genial, though uncompromising to all he conceived to be error in life or doctrine. He keenly felt his enforced retirement from active service for some years before his death, and his nearest friends could not but feel that it was far better for him to depart and be with Christ than to continue the so painful struggle for life.

In these days of so much mental and moral timidity, when many are ready to follow the trend of the multitude in one way or the other and even good men are often swayed by public opinion somewhat to relax their hold upon, even if they do not compromise the truth, and wink at what they should disallow and oppose, it is positively refreshing to think of the stalwart frame and stout heart of the late Bishop of Virginia—not only a brave but an absolutely intrepid man. Certainly you could say of him as he sleeps in expectation of the great awakening, as was said of the Scotch Reformer, John Knox: "Here lies one who never feared the face of man."

GENERAL CLERGY RELIEF FUND.

This Fund appeals to us very strongly, and ought to receive far more support than it does. If the object be properly presented, and an offering be taken up in every congregation during the year, as the General Convention suggests, we could make a very considerable addition to the General Fund, and so render the Society more able to help us and others.

I have never been able myself to see my way clear to advocate the merging of our Diocesan Fund into the General Clergy Relief Fund. There is under present conditions a flexibility of administration which makes our fund more largely and directly useful than it could otherwise be. Still we must recognize that our condition is different from that of many other Dioceses, e g. as the agent has recently stated in a circular letter, "The statistics of clerical changes prove that only a small percentage of clergymen remain in one diocese all their lives, therefore, the Diocesan relief fund they have built up in their early ministry is frequently the very fund to which they cannot appeal in later years when they need it, through no fault of their own the great body of the clergy are ineligible to local funds by reason of removals or canonical requirements." Now while this is very forcible where it does apply, still it does not apply to us because our fund, such as it is, is applicable to the whole body of canonically resident clergymen, and is not in any wise subject to the limitations and conditions that so often prevail elsewhere.

The one beneficiary, a lady, we have on the General Clergy Relief Fund list is there under peculiar circumstances; her husband having served in what is now West Virginia when it was part and parcel of the Diocese of Virginia, and never having had connection with our Diocese. I consented after some hesitation to endorse the application because the late Bishop of Virginia disclaimed all responsibility in the matter, and it did not seem right that this good woman, the widow of a faithful man, should for lack of some endorsement fail of even the very small stipend to which she was entitled.

All this by way of explanation of our relation to the General Fund.

and now it seems to me that with our own fund provided for by the offerings made on Christmas Day, and with perhaps $5,000 accumulated, that we might well heed the suggestions of the General Convention and give to this object not only one regular offering during the year, but also a portion from the communion alms. Though a small and weak diocese, we are perhaps better able than a good many others to care for our own. We have a solemn obligation to the whole Church and I trust shall the more realize the responsibility and rise to something like a proper measure of our duty.

REPORTS.

We have been for some time working on a blank form for our Parochial Reports, and have at last settled upon one that promises with a few unimportant modification, to be generally acceptable. Most of the clergy have adhered to the form as published by the Council, but some have departed from it in such wise as to make the tabulation of their reports with the others almost a matter of impossibility. Would it not be best in every case to adhere closely to the authorized form, and to express, by note, such statements and explanations as the form does not provide for. I find that in some of the reports there is included under the general head of money, raised by the congregation, certain sums that have been contributed from the outside, or raised in some other way than directly by the congregation. To speak of nothing more, if it be remembered that such figures furnish the chief basis on which the apportionment for General Missions is assigned, it will at once be perceived that it may be a very serious matter. As far as I can tell after a hasty examination the printing of our reports exactly as received would add to our apportionment for the next year the sum of at least $400. The whole difficulty could be avoided if the clergy would include in their financial summary only such sums as may fairly be said to be raised, that is, paid or contributed by the congregation. Provision is made for the proper mention of money that comes in from other sources.

THE SHELTERING ARMS HOSPITAL.

The annual meeting of the Board of the Sheltering Arms Hospital, which was held this year on Monday, May 4th, was distinctly encouraging, in spite of the anxieties caused us by labor troubles among the miners; the income of the Hospital was $7,936.48, which was within five dollars of the expenses; part of which expenses consisted in necessary repairs. During the year, 272 patients were cared for; of this number 162 were white (100 males and 62 females), and 110 were colored (82 males and 28 females). All but 50 of our patients were from the mines, nine-tenths of them free; the total number of nursing days was 7,000.

We have received more than usual from the churches during the past year, in the way of money and of supplies. The training school for nurses has been put into operation, and we have had five pupils in attendance.

Important improvements are in contemplation for the coming year. in the shape of a laundry building, which shall also have lodging rooms, that may be used for nurses or for patients. The amount of work done by the Hospital has steadily increased each year, and we believe it is more than ever worthy the confidence and support of the public.

THE REYNOLDS MEMORIAL HOSPITAL.

The number of patients for the past year was 499, of which 270 were charity cases. The total expenses of the Hospital were $11,309.71, of which amount $4,456 was raised by the personal application of the Superintendent. The additions and improvements made during the past year amounted to $39,000, all paid for. The Hospital is valued at $102,000. In January last there were four graduates of the training school, to whom Bishop Gravatt delivered diplomas, as I was detained by sickness. The presence of a hundred guests showed the general interest. Regular Sunday evening services are now maintained in the improved chapel at the Hospital.

THE EPISCOPAL HALL.

The Episcopal Hall at Morgantown has been working steadily and successfully during the past year. With the larger and more cordial support of our Church people throughout the Diocese it would still more fully meet what demands might properly be made upon it. There have been difficulties connected with its management which it would be useless to detail at this time and place, but it has always had, in spite of these difficulties, a fair measure of success. I am in close touch with the Warden, Rev. Mr. Marley, and the Proctor, Capt. Wm. C. Marshall, and they continue to enjoy my entire confidence and esteem. During the past year fifteen boys have been cared for, and we have good prospects of more for the next session of the University. In some respects the past year has been the most satisfactory in the history of the Hall. If we can move steadily along the line of our chosen plan oi work, we shall be content, even if the rate of development be somewhat below the sanguine expectations of friends. We have now on our clergy list the name of one who was trained there, and at the Seminary next year the Hall will be represented by four out of our five students. Some of these days perhaps some one will see the possibilities of such an institution, and so equip and endow it that we shall be a still greater power for the Church and for God in the community and in the State.

DIOCESAN MISSIONS.

In regard to our Diocesan Missions, you will have the report of the committee before you, and will learn from that something of the work in detail, but on this theme there is always something more to be said. It is the very backbone of our work, and we cannot nurture it too carefully. I must confess I would like to see a greater and more manifest enthusiasm about this work all over the Diocese. It is a serious question in my mind whether it ever can be properly supported and pushed unless individuals here and there, with their direct personal support, supplement the offerings usually made in our churches. If our people, or at least those who have the greater financial ability, could sometimes, in private, be reminded of the supreme importance of this work, and the part which it must play in the development of the Diocese, they would oftener make special contributions of larger sums than they are accustomed to contribute through the offertory. And yet during the twenty-five years past, only once has any thing considerable been done in this line, when a good woman undertook herself to pay, and did pay, the missionary stipends of two of our clergy during the past year. If five more persons could have been found to give as this good woman did $500.00, and ten to give $250.00, and ten to give $100.00, and twenty to give $50.00, leaving smaller sums to swell the offertory, we might be relieved of the great pressure upon us, and so lengthen our cords and strengthen our stakes that our Zion might rejoice, throughout its coasts, even to the utmost bounds. One exception must be made to the remarks just made, in that various women of the Church have together during the past year raised and paid into our treasury the sum of $350 for special missionary work in the Diocese.

The one thing that has chiefly troubled me during all these years of my service in West Virginia, and that still troubles me, is the thought of the poor support our missionary clergy, especially, receive. It is by no means sufficient for such comfortable and decent living as would ensure and promote the highest measure of efficiency in their work. How some of them manage to get along is more than I can tell. We owe them a great debt, and I trust we shall learn more fully to pay it. That I am speaking the words of truth and soberness will appear when I say, that to enable us to fix the salaries of our twenty-eight or thirty missionaries at a minimum of $800.00 and a Rectory, would require an addition of upwards of $4,000.00 to our annual Missionary Fund,—further comment is unnecessary.

My attention has been seriously turned during the last few months to the advisability of employing Deaconesses or Bible readers to aid us in this work, especially in the mining sections of the State. The population in these sections is, at the best, hard to get at and influence. It is often so scattered up and down the valleys and over the hills, that it is difficult to get the people to a central place of worship, and when to this you add the further difficulties that arise from the meetings the men often have on Sundays, and the constant strain of the household work and the care of the children on the women, the promise of great advantage from public services is much smaller than the casuel observer would think. If in the various communities where we now have missions, and in others where opportunity offers, we could establish Deasonesses, or Bible readers, as far as possible two together, we might hope to reach especially the women and children in their homes, and give them more of a training in what they ought to know and believe than they are likely otherwise to get. Such methods may not have the promise of organized congregations rapidly formed, but it will certainly lay foundations on which we, or those who come after us, may build, and if persistently and faithfully followed it must result in sowing the good seed in many places where it will bear much fruit.

In carrying out such a plan I do not consider it by any means necessary that, in every instance, we should have formally trained woman. We must have in our congregation many women who already would be able, with very little preparation, to carry on such work. It would be well if the clergy would be on the lookout for such. West Virginia has made large contributions to the ranks of trained nurses during the past few years, why not to the ranks of Deasonesses, or Bible women, to take up that work which calls aloud for them.

It will be interesting and encouraging to know that during the last six months one Deaconess and two Bible women or helpers have been secured for the work in West Virginia.

GENERAL MISSIONS.

But we all know that our interest must not stop with our home work. We are in many ways pledged to a wider outlook over a greatly extended field. Just at this time the Church is engaged in what might be called an experiment, i. e. through her Board of Managers she has inaugurated what is called the Apportionment Plan, in the distinct effort to make us all the more realize our personal responsibilities, and to bring into line those congregations, be they large or small, which have, for some cause or other, been holding back from year to year.

I think that at the least, such a plan, so presented and urged, deserves a fair trial. If that fair trial be given, we shall be able to modify and amend as may be found necessary, until we make it more generally available and efficient. Our loyalty to Christ must prompt us to follow the lead of the Church in this matter, while we pray for light and guidance upon our onward way.

I think that we, the Bishops and Clergy, are often at fault just here. What we need to further the work of missions in all its departments, is a more decided leadership. I have often said that in time past, and I desire to say it again. But I am afraid there are some called leaders who do not lead at all. Leadership in such matters cannot be realized by mild intimations as to the duty of our congregations; there must not only be personal enthusiasm, but the exercise—judicious, I grant you—but the real exercise of authority. When our people are sceptical about missions, or impatient of reminders of duty, nothing is done by those who touch the subject only with gloved hands, or perhaps not at all. Certainly in no decisive, compelling way. Yes, my Brethren, the importance of leadership deserves to be emphasized as it has not been. As some one says, let us put to usury that talent which sets another to work. The leader must use definiteness and persistence, he must uplift ideals, and to be the leader is the great responsibility of the pastor. Yes! he is not only the instructor but the leader of his congregation, he must not only care for their souls, but direct their activities. Too often I fear this is not done. You know the temptation, how hard it is wisely, and firmly, and kindly to resist it. How much easier to swim with the current, and yield all too easily to the desire of the people for what they call parochial advance, a desire that shows itself in the way of fine buildings—or at least in buildings distinctly beyond the means of the congregation, and whose erection cripples them for active and aggressive work, it may be for years; or that shows itself in decorations, or elaborate music, which, after all you can say about them, are really of secondary importance. So it is that time and energy are consumed, and as we have only a very limited amount of them, the greater interests of the Church sadly suffer. I say again that for the more vigorous and successful prosecution of our missionary work at home and abroad, we need a more decided leadership on the part of the clergy. Shall we not the more study to command and inspire our people with a high enthusiasm for the work that God calls them to do in extending His kingdom in the world.

THE PROPOSED CHANGE IN THE NAME OF THE CHURCH.

We are all aware of the particular phase which this question has assumed, at this time. The last General Convention, acting through a standing committee, has brought the matter before each Diocese in convention assembled, asking them to say whether they think a change necessary or expedient at this time and, if so, inviting them to designate the name they would prefer. This brings the whole question before us, whether we will or not, and necessitates an expression of opinion on our part.

In these conditions you find the reason for my special allusion to the subject today, and I think it right that I should not only formally bring the matter to your attention, but give a few words of explanation.

Some of you may remember that in our Council of 1887 we discussed this question pretty freely, having not only an expression of opinion by the

Bishop, but a full report of a committee, of which the present Bishop of Virginia was chairman. I am free to say that my own opinions have undergone very little, if any, change since that time. Of course we have all been compelled to think about the proposed change in the name of the Church a good deal during these years, because the subject has been brought forward time and again, and so we have had time and opportunity to make up our minds about it. The question has been discussed from almost every conceivable standpoint, and whatever our own opinions may be we are bound to give to every argument all proper consideration.

There has been so much writing on the subject since the last General Convention, and there is likely to be so much more before the next, that I hardly deem it necessary to enter upon any extended discussion of the matter. Still I venture to present certain considerations which reflect my own views on the subject, and which, as I have kept in touch with the clergy and the laity of the Diocese, I am led to believe, reflect their views also.

In trying to approach the subject with an open mind, I have, of course, read a great many newspaper articles pro and con, and also some pamphlets, and I shall no doubt be constantly using their arguments and even their words. I am glad to adopt them so far as I can, if we can thus get this whole matter intelligently before us, so that we can act with judgment and discretion.

It is very important to note just how this matter has come before the Church by the action of the committee. Not only are the Dioceses asked to say whether they consider a change of name expedient at this time, but they are asked, at the same time, to designate the name they prefer. The result has been such as to show sonsiderable confusion of mind existing in regard to the whole matter. Whatever our views as to the origin and fitness of our present name, it is a serious question whether practically any change can be considered desirable. unless with something like unanimity, some more suitable name can be suggested. Now there are no end of suggestions, but it is safe to say that each one commends itself to only a limited number of people. The truth is that it is entirely possible that there may be some who consider that our present designation is, on the whole, inadequate, and, if you choose, to some extent misleading,—at least to those who do not keep in mind the events of our past—and yet they would not venture to propse that the name, at this time, be changed; much less to suggest a substitute.

However, some do avow their preference, as a recent writer in one of our Church papers, boldly says. "Let us be straightforward and outspoken, and declare ourselves to be Catholic, and members of the One Holy Catholic and Apostolic Church. And let us not think, for a single moment, that such a declaration of the truth will lessen the number of those who turn to the American Church to find therein the rest they seek. Much more probable is it that when we boldly hang our Catholic banner on the walls, thousands will turn to us both from the Roman Communion, and from our Protestant Brethren who would not seek us if we continued to exist under the cloud of Protestant Episcopal." Of course doctors will differ, but I am disposed to say that one who could write these words has a very different outlook over the Church and over the country from that which I have and I believe from that which you have. The vision is, in my judgment, an irridescent dream.

We do, in the creeds, declare our belief in the Holy Catholic Church: but to use the word in this general sense, is a very differnt thing from so using it as, even remotely, to intimate that that we had a sole right to the use of the word Catholic.

It has been forcibly said that a name is applied to a thing to designate what it is. Now the word Catholic means universal, and when applied to the Church properly indicates the whole of the Christian body, embracing all its parts. It would follow from this that to call the Protestant Episcopal Church the Catholic Church must have one or the other of two meanings.

It must either mean that the Protestant Episcopal Church regards all the other religious bodies which claim to belong to the Church of Christ as parts of itself, or it must mean that none of them belong to it, and that the body now called the Protestant Episcopal Church, is alone the Church of Christ. As it is well known that the Protestant Episcopal Church does not make either of these contentions, it is plain that the title "Catholic Church of America" is misleading and inappropriate.

And now in regard to dropping the word Protestant from our title. We must not forget what was so clearly set forth in the late Council of Pennsylvania, both in the address of the Bishop and to the report of that committee on that address, viz: That while the word Protestant was first used in 1529 when a minority of the Diet of Spiers protested against false doctrine and wrong practice, yet that there was another element of protest that was equally prominent in the first use of this word, viz.: an appeal to a rightly constituted general council of the whole Catholic Church. In so far it therefore expressed the ground of unity on which all the Catholic reformers of the 16th century could stand consistently together in their resistance to the usurpations and corruptions of the Papacy; and that same appeal to truly Catholic authority is the very ground on which the Church of England planted herself as a Catholic Church in the commotions of those times, and which she has consistently maintained to this day.

With some I believe the proposed change is advocated without the full consideration of such facts as these, mainly because they desire to have what will appear to them to be a more technically accurate and more fully descriptive name. Perhaps this appears to some minds a short and easy way to eliminate the danger of the abuse of individualism by cutting off the name which represents and symbolizes it, as if we had any guarantee that it would in effect prove any remedy at all, forgetful too that it may be the peculiar mission of this Church of ours to demonstrate the fact, and why not partly by her very name, that evangelical liberty and apostolic order are not, when rightly understood, mutually exclusive, but rather mutually inclusive principles.

And then, I fear, that some would like to drop the word "Protestant" from our title, because they dislike that which it properly implies.

This question was first seriously brought up at the General Convention in Chicago in 1886, and although many may have voted for a change of name, who were loyal to the great Protestant principles of our Church, yet I think I am fairly and charitably stating a simple fact when I say, that the heart of the movement was then, and always has been, the spirit that objects to the name of Protestant, not mainly because in the opinion of many, it does not sufficiently affirm the historical continuity of the church, but because it all too plainly implies and affirms certain well known doctrinal principles, which at the time of the Reformation were brought to the front and emphasized as against the superstitious beliefs and customs of the middle ages. You may put the points at issue with more or less distinctness, in various ways, but I am content to adopt as my own the statement that the central idea of Protestanism is that the primary relation of the soul is to God Himself, and that the soul receives spiritual life and strength direct from Him by the immediate influence of the Holy Spirit, entering the soul by every avenue which faith offers for the reception of that influence, including of course the means of grace found in the Christian Church, and that this, because the primary relation of the soul is to God Himself, that the great work of the Christian ministry is to proclaim Christ the Eternal Word, who declares God to man, and to try to bring men to Christ, that they may know God and trust and love and obey Him, and receive pardon and peace and holiness from Him.

And on the other hand that the central idea of what for lack of a better name we call anti-Protestantism is substantially this that the primary relationship of the soul is to the church, and that the ministers of the church convey spiritual life and strength to the soul through the agency of the material element used in the sacraments, and through the spiritual efficacy of words officially uttered, and that therefore the great work of the Christian minister is to proclaim the Church, and to manipulate sacramental material and to ariticulate ecclesiastical formulas. I believe that this statement with but little modification in one way or another, will fairly present the issue involved in the Reformation controversies.

Whatever you may say about the word Protestant as having in any wise outlived and survived its original application, it is in itself a good word as meaning witnessing for the truth and against error, and, as I reminded you a moment ago, appealing to the Catholic consent of antiquity for its warrant, and having all this in mind, it is not too much now to say that perhaps there never was a time when we could so ill afford to lose or impair the meaning of this word as a characteristic of our Church. One of our Bishops has recently expressed the opinion that if we are to have a growing power in this country today, if we are to be of service in the new countries to which we have been sent, Mexico and Cuba and Brazil and Porto Rico and the Philippines, which stand out before the world as Christian countries with but little religion, and if we are to stem the tide which is running through some portions of our own land, muddy with its spring of mediaeval terms and modes of worship, we must hold fast to the name and spirit of the Church as defining and distinguishing our function and office, contending for the faith once for all delivered to the saints, and against the errors and extravagances of certain men, crept in unawares; and creeping on, too, a laughing stock to Roman and a stumbling block to Protestant Christians, in the movement toward united Christendom.

While recognizing the broad and comprehensive principles on which the Reformation of the Anglican Church was conducted would we not be wise to adopt the advice of the late Bishop Alonzo Potter in being willing to leave to churches more superstitious and as we believe less pure, usages which, though they may have the sanction of antiquity, are inconsistent with that simplicity which we have been taught to love; or which having been made directly subservient to gross errors, or having become inseparably associated with such errors in the minds of a large portion of the Christian world, were on that account wisely laid aside by the early Reformers.

May we not sum up the matter in the fewest possible words when we put this question as to the two principle names proposed. "Shall it be American Catholic? But that is imitating Rome in her restriction of the universal by the particular adjective. Shall it be the American Church? But that is an assumption of an untruth, or, at least, a very previous statement of a yet unfulfilled hope."

So, my Dear Brethren, I have put this question imperfectly before you. Shall we not all indulge the hope that this great Church of ours shall not in any wise compromise her position by making any such change in her name as would lessen the force of her appeal to those Protestant churches about us whose hold on the essentials of catholicity we may think if you choose to be somewhat defective—in the delusive hope of thereby strengthening our own position, or weakening that of any other communion.

A recent newspaper article has pertinently said that sensible men would not spend time in trying to get the name changed, unless the change meant something. The result of the success of this present movement would be not simply to continue the Protestant Episcopal Church as it is, only under a new name, but to make the new name, at least in the popular mind, stand for something which it is claimed the present name does not stand for. It is not too much to say that a new name means a new Church in some of its relations, conceptions, or ideals, and this may abundantly appear in the result, for if the name be changed at the instance of those whose conceptions and ideals of the Church are to say the least, very different, perhaps I might say almost radically different from ours, then they will quite naturally claim to be the true exponents of the Catholicity of the Church, which changed its name at their request, in order to give emphasis or expression to certain ideals which they represent. We can hardly think that such a result would be desirable "at this time."

I am happy in believing that these annual Councils mean a great deal to our people, both clergy and laity. I am sure we do a good thing in resisting the modern method of rush and hurry, which would have us transact all business in a few hours, and separate again with no refreshment of spirit, but simply wearied in body and mind. And when you consider that the members of our Council must average four or five hundred miles of travel in attending its sessions, it seems vastly important that we should adhere to our unwritten law and remain together there a few days—at least the most of us—in order that we may be somewhat filled with each others company, and take sweet counsel together about all our work. It seems important to notice this from time to time, and especially because since the Council of 1900, no less than 22 out of 44 names on our list are the names of men who have come to us in this time, and cannot be expected to know the customs and traditions of the Diocese.

I think I am as anxious as any one can be to maintain services regularly at all our Churches and missions, yes! and even at the stations, and in the outlying regions, but I am fully convinced that by prolonging our stay here together that the people are great gainers even if they do forego a few services. Our Council is meant to be a school for the clergy. It is our retreat, our protracted meeting, and if we use it aright we shall not only gather new ideas from our Brethren to whom we are not so superior as some may be disposed to think, but we shall in some mysterious—may I not say providential way—be enlightened, and strengthened and refreshed. We shall catch the spirit of the whole body, have new heart and life to put into our work; have our ideals enlarged, and our enthusiasms increased and stimulated.

I like to think of our clergy everywhere taking pleasure in their work, and anxious to find out in every way how they can make themselves more efficient in winning souls to Christ, but it is a great pity we have to be so much to ourselves; and just because in a widely scattered Diocese like ours clerical fellowship is so difficult, we ought gladly to meet in Convocations and Councils that we may each one help the other by counsel and by sympathy.

I am full of hope for the future, and there is everywhere about us that which will justify such hope. The Diocese is, on the whole well equipped for its work—there is very little debt upon any of the churches; your general funds are supported with more system and liberality than ever before; your church buildings are more numerous; your clergy list is larger than ever in the history of the Diocese; your Bishops are strong to go in and out among you; the Church we love so well is daily growing in influence all over the State; and not only so but best of all we maintain among ourselves and toward all who love the Lord Jesus Christ peace, charity and good will.

Shall we not more earnestly pray that the good Lord will honor us by giving us a greater devotion to His service, and making us in every way instrumental among these people where our lot is cast, in turning many from darkness to light, in developing in them that righteousness which exalteth a nation and causing them to shun that sin which is a reproach to any people. God bless you dear Brethren and friends and make you to abound more and more in the work of the Lord.

The Rev. G. A. Gibbons moved to refer that part of the Bishop's address relating to change of the name of the Church, to a special committee. Adopted.

The Secretary presented a communication from the Committee of the General Convention relating to change of name, which was also referred to the special committee.

The Bishop appointed that committee as follows:

Rt. Rev. W. L. Gravatt,	Dr. G. A. Aschman,
Rev. G. W. Easter,	Simms Powell,
Rev. G. A. Gibbons.	

The Rev. Dr. Moore, from the Committee on Admission of New Parishes, reported upon the subjoined application from Bluefield Mission. The report of the committee, together with appended resolution, was adopted.

At the congregational meeting of Christ Church, on Easter Monday night, April 13, 1903, it was decided to form a Parish from the Mission of Christ Church, Bluefield, W. Va., which has been in existence about 13 years.

A Vestry composed of 9 male members of the congregation was elected. The names are as follows:

Messrs. Geo. H. Wade, Treas.; Geo. H. Hill and R. C. Turner, Wardens; R. A. Lacy, Registrar; T. H. Becker, A. W. Howard, W. H. B. Loving; E. H. Smith, and F. R. Wadleigh.

The proposed Cure shall contain the territory within the district known as Beaver Pond District, Mercer Co., W. Va.

This District includes the corporation of the City of Bluefield, and the villages Ada, 4 miles distant on the East; Brush Fork, 2 miles distant on the West; Bethel, 4 miles distant on the South-east, and Belchers, 4 miles distant on the North.

The name of the proposed Cure shall be Bluefield Parish, and the name of the Parish Church shall be Christ Church.

The appointments for services, at present shall include the Parish Church, Bluefield; The Church of the Heavenly Rest, Princeton; and Athens; all in Mercer Co., W. Va.

The Parish lines will not include Princeton and Athens, but the Rector of the Parish Church will give the necessary ministrations and will have in charge the work at these places.

The apportionment for the Rector's salary at present will be as follows: Christ Church, Bluefield, $500.00 annually; the Church of the Heavenly Rest, Princeton, $25.00 annually; the congregation at Athens, $25.00 annually, and the Missionary stipends $250.00 annually. The missonary appropriation is for mission work done outside the Parish bounds.

The present membership of the proposed Parish is 91, a net gain of 19 since the last report, more than three of whom are males. The congregation owns a church property and a Rectory, both free of debt.

The total contributions from the congregation during the Parochial year just past amounted to $1,230.00 and the total of all money raised was $1,666.00.

The congregation of Christ Church, Bluefield, has during the incumbency of the present minister, which dates from Dec. 1st, 1901; and to his knowledge since its organization, acceded to the doctrines, discipline and worship of the Protestant Epeiscopal Church in the United States and to the Constitution and Canons of the Diocese of West Virginia, employing the Book of Common Prayer as the standard of worship and faith, and meeting all Diocesan and general assessments and apporitionments.

We have taken this action only after consulting with the Bishop of the Diocese.

We have given him due notice of the organization of a Parish, and have to the best of our knowledge and ability fulfilled the requirements of Canon X "Of the Formation of New Parishes."

We ask to be received as a Parish into union with the Council of the Diocese of West Virginia.

E. H. BROSIUS, *Minister.*
T. H. BECKER.
W. H. B. LOVING,
G. H. WADE, *Treas.*,
GEO. H. HILL, *Warden*,
R. CLIF. TURNER, *Warden.*
F. R. WADLEIGH,
E. H. SMITH.
R. A. LACY, *Registrar.*

I hereby certify that I have received notice of the organization of Bluefield Parish, Mercer Co., W. Va., one month before the meeting of this Council of the Diocese of W. Va., May 20th, 1903.

And I herein express my approval of the formation of this new Parish.

May 21st, 1903. St. Matthew's Church, Wheeling, W. Va.

GEO. W. PETERKIN,
Bishop of West Virginia.

The Committee on New Parishes, to which has been referred an application from the Mission at Bluefield, Mercer Co., W. Va., to be received into union with the Council of this Diocese, as a Parish, to be known as "Bluefield Parish," respectfully reports that it has carefully considered said application and finds that the papers are all in due form and that the requirements of the Canon have been fully met.

Your Committee, therefore, reports the following resolution:

Resolved. That "Bluefield Parish" is hereby received into union with the Council of this Diocese.

S. SCOLLAY MOORE, *Chairman.*

The Rev. G. W. Easter submited this report on Religious and Theological Education:

The Committee on Religious and Theological Education beg leave to report that it has received from the Treasurer of the Diocese and transmitted to the Treasurer of the Education Society of Va., the sum of $200. The total income of the fund for Religious and Theo. Education for the past fiscal year, according to the Treasurer's report, was $206.33, which added to the balance on hand June 1, 1902, made $348.03 available for its purposes, and after deducting the $200 above reported as paid to the Treasurer of the Education Society of Va., there is left in the hands of the Treasurer of the Diocese $148.03. It appears from the Treasurer's report that of 80 odd parishes, missions and preaching points in the Diocese mentioned in the Treasurer's report, only 22 made the collection required by the Canon for this fund. The committee rspectfully call the attention of the Clergy and Laity of the Diocese to this Canon and urge compliance with its requirements.

GEO. W. EASTER, *Chairman,*
J. HOWARD GIBBONS,
ARTHUR M. LEWIS.

May 21, 1903.

On motion of the Rev. J. F. Woods, the Council went into election of the Standing Committee of the Diocese. The ballot resulted as follows:

Rev. G. A. Gibbons,
Rev. A. J. Willis,
Rev. J. S. Douglas,
Mr. J. Gassman,
I. H. Strider,
Frank Beckwith.

Bishop Penick submitted the following report of Sunday School Committee.

REPORT FOR THE SUNDAY SCHOOL COMMITTEE.

Owing to the removal from the Diocese of Rev. W. H. Burkhardt, Chairman and "man of all work" of this Committee and with him all information necessary to produce an intelligent and full report of the work of this Committee, I, the remaining and ignorant clerical member of the same can only report the accompanying statement of its finances, transmitted to me by the former chairman, showing a balance of $8.00 to the credit of the Committee, which balance has also been sent me by the absent Chairman and is herewith reported and held subject to the Councils order.

Respectfully submitted,

C. C. PENICK.

May 21st, 1903.

The Committee on Credentials reported that Mr. J. W. Heslip, Christ Church, Pt. Pleasant, and R. A. Anderson, Christ Church, Bluefield, were duly certified as delegates, and they took their seats.

On motion, the Rev. D. W. Howard and the Rev. J. S. Douglas were added to the Committee on Assessments, vice Rev. N. F. Marshall and Rev. W. H. Burkhardt, removed from the Diocese.

The committee is now constituted as follows:

Rev. S. S. Moore, D. D.	Mr. L. E. Sands.
Rev. Jno. S. Gibson.	W. S. Laidley.
Rev. D. W. Howard.	Richd. Henderson.
Rev. J. S. Douglas.	J. Gassman.
Rev. A. J. Grinnan.	Simms Powell.
Rev. G. W. Easter.	R. M. Browne.
Rev. A. J. Willis.	W. T. Nuzum.

The Rev. John S. Douglas offered the following resolution:

Resolved, That the Committee on Constitution and Canons be requested to report a substitute for the present blank form of certificate of the election of lay delegate to the annual council of the Diocese.

The Rev. G. A. Gibbons presented this report of the Standing Committee of the Diocese.

STANDING COMMITTEE REPORT.

(*From June 8th*, 1902, *to May 22nd*, 1903.)

July 8th, 1902. A Committee was appointed and reported resolutions, which were unanimously adopted, regarding the resignation of Mr. B. C. Washington as a member of your Standing Committee.

The Committee approved a bill for $46.06 expenses incurred by gentlemen sent to Moundsville by the Bishop, on special and important business, and recommended by the Bishop to be paid.

Consent was given to the Consecration of the Rev. Charles Taylor Olmsted, S. T. D., as Bishop Coadjutor of the Diocese of Central New York.

For good and sufficient reasons the Committee adopted a resolution to the effect that all regular meetings of the Committee should be held first Tuesday of every other month beginning with September, at 10 o'clock A. M., in Martinsburg, as the most central place.

September 17th, 1902. Mr. T. Getz Hill was recommended to the Bishop as a candidate for Holy Orders.

November 3rd, 1902. The Committee having been called by the Bishop to consult about a paper he had prepared concerning the Rev. B. M. Spurr, the Committee unanimously concurred in the contents of said paper. At the same meeting the Standing Committee gave consent to the Consecration of the Rev. C. M. Beckwith, D. D., to be Bishop of the Diocese of Alabama. Mr. Percy N. McDonald was recommended to the Bishop as a Candidate for Holy Orders.

March 3rd, 1903. The Standing Committee of the Diocese of West Virginia, duly convened in the city of Martinsburg, this third day of March, 1903, records and spreads upon its minutes with unfeigned sorrow the death of its faithful and efficient secretary, David Howell, which occurred at his home in Charles Town, Jan. 31, 1903.

Although Mr. Howell had been on this committee less than one year, he had endeared himself to every member by his ready and accurate performance of the duties devolving upon him as secretary of the same.

His voice and counsel will be greatly missed in our meetings and the influence he exerted for good will be felt and appreciated for years to come.

To his bereaved family this committee extends heartfelt sympathy and a copy of this record.

Consent was given to the Consecration of the Rev. Sheldon Munson Griswold, D. D., to be Bishop of the Missionary District of Salina.

Mr. Creetus Atwell Dowell, a candidate for Holy Orders, was recommended to the Bishop to be ordained Deacon.

Judge Frank Beckwith was elected unanimously to fill the vacancy on the Committee caused by the lamented death of Mr. Howell, and the Judge was then elected Secretary of the Committee.

May 5th, 1903. The Rev. Thomas C. Darst (Deacon) was recommended to the Bishop for Ordination to the Priesthood.

For good and sufficient reasons, and by unanimous vote of the Committee, it was recommended that the time of Candidacy of Mr. Francis

Van R. Moore be shortened three months, and Mr. Moore was then recommended to the Bishop to be ordained Deacon.

G. A. GIBBONS, *President.*
JOHN S. DOUGLAS.
J. GASSMAN.

The Rev. John S. Gibson, for the committee appointed last year (see page 21, Journal, 1902), to consider proposed alterations in the Constitution of the Church, reported the committee could find no feature in the proposed alterations, injurious or objectionable.

The Rev. Dr. Roller nominated the Rev. S. S. Moore, D. D., and Mr. H. W. Potts as delegates to the next Missionary Council, and they were elected.

The Rev. J. S. Alfriend and Judge Frank Beckwith were elected alternates.

The Finance Committee submitted their report as follows. The appended resolution was adopted:

MEETING OF THE FINANCE COMMITTEE.

Thursday, May 21, 1903, at 2 o'clock, P. M.

All members present.

The reports of the Diocesan Treasurer and R. M. Browne, Trustee of Episcopal and Contingent Funds were presented and audited.

The following resolution was adopted:

Resolved, That this Committee recommend to Council that the Treasurer of the Contingent Fund be authorized to pay out of the funds coming into his hands $300 to cover rent on residence now occupied by Bishop Gravatt at Charles Town.

LAWRENCE E. SANDS, *Chairman.*
V. A. WEAVER. *Secretary.*
G. B. CROW,
A. J. MARTIN,
J. C. BRADY,
RICHARD HENDERSON.

Mr. Geo. R. Wendling offered this resolution, which was adopted:

This Council thanks the Trustees of the Permanent Fund for the fidelity and integrity with which they have discharged their duty and request them to make such corrections in their report as they may wish to make, and bring their reports down to June 1, 1903, and place it in the hands of the Secretary for publication in the Journal.

On motion the Council adjourned.

FRIDAY, May 22d, 11 A. M.

The Council was called to order by the Bishop.

The minutes of yesterday were read and approved.

The Rev. J. S. Gibson, from Committee on Constitution and Canons, reported a new form of certificate of lay delegates. Under the rules it went over until to-morrow.

The Rev. S. S. Moore, Commissioner of the Church Building Fund, submitted this report.

DIOCESE OF WESTERN VIRGINIA.

Total amount contributed since 1881 to 1903 for the Church Building Fund	$649 83
Contributed the past year—	
Martinsburg (Trinity Church)	4 00
Parkersburg (Good Shepherd Church)	2 00
Point Pleasant (Christ Church)	50
Union (All Saints' Church)	76
Sistersville (St. Paul's Church)	2 40
Huntington (Trinity Church)	3 00
Shepherdstown (Trinity Church)	7 53
	$20 19

Loans have been made as follows:

Charleston, Huntington, Bramwell and Weston (all paid with interest)	$7,000 00
Hinton (not yet fully paid)	1,250 00

Gifts have been made as follows:

Kenova, Charleston, Bramwell, Boone Co., Spilman and Weston, amounting to	$ 1,000 00
The Permanent Fund amounts to at present	375,593 78

The Diocesan Missionary Committee submitted this report, which was received and referred to the Committee on the State of the Church:

REPORT OF THE EXECUTIVE COMMITTEE OF THE DIOCESAN MISSIONARY SOCIETY.

Your Committee submits this annual report of its work and begs leave again, as often before, to press its importance upon the attention of members of the Council and through them upon the Diocese at large.

We have had upon the list of our beneficiaries during the past year 27 names of missionaries. These men have ministered to many different points, which would count up nearly 100 in all. Their faithful ministrations have been in this year, as in all her history, one of the main sources of the Church's life and vigor in this Diocese. Four of them have now left the Diocese for other fields of usefulness and their places are only partially supplied. There has been paid to them during the year the sum of $3,050.01 to which sundry items of expense, amounting to $105, must be added, making a total of $3,155.01 expended. The report of the Treasurer shows these expenditures in detail and it is unnecessary to recapitulate them here.

Receipts for the year have been $3,330, leaving a balance in the hands of the Terasurer upon the year's transactions of $175. This with the balance in hand at the beginning of the year, makes up now the sum of $1,878.18 in the treasury, an apparently large balance, but needed at this time to enable your Committee to meet the stipends due on July 1st, for the income of the Society between this time and that will probably be small.

It is cause for congratulation that at a time, when special efforts were being made to enlarge our Permanent Fund, the aggregate contributions for this work for the year should have actually increased, as compared with last year. But a careful inspection of the Treasurer's report discloses the fact that this increase is not due to larger gifts through the ordinary parochial channels, in which there has been some diminution, and that it is due to the special efforts of the women of the Diocese, who have added nearly $375 to the contributions. But for their aid, our expenses would have exceeded our receipts. While the margin continues so small, your Committee deos not feel justified in increasing missionary stipends, which are in many cases pitifully small. In some instances these have been supplemented by gifts from the Bishop's special fund to an amount aggregating as we are informed $447.50. Properly this would be a charge against the funds of this Society, and it may be said to represent, in part at least, the needed addition to our present receipts to enable us to do the work already undertaken in the manner in which it is now being done. But there are open doors of opportunity all about us for larger and more efficient work. Will the Church in a spirit of enlarged liberality, growing with the passing years, place in our hands the means to enable us to enter some of these?

The Committee on Parochial Reports submitted the following report:

The Committee on Parochial Reports respectfully submit the following:

Baptisms, Infants	199
Baptisms, Adults	72
Total	271

Confirmations	242
Marriages	183
Burials	199
Communicants	4,378
Baptized persons connected with Parish	7,316
Families and parts	3,737
Total No. Teachers and Scholars in Sunday Schools	3,062

FINANCIAL REPORT.

Total Current Expenses	$ 44,756 69

CONTRIBUTIONS.

Total Parochial	$ 31,198 30
Total Diocesan	26,252 70
Total Extra Diocesan	5,348 99
Grand Total All Monies Raised	112,184 55

In connection herewith your Committee present the following resolutions:

Resolved, That the form of Parochial Reports be amended by inserting after "expenses current Parochial" the words—cash on hand.

Resolved, That the Secretary be instructed to have printed several hundred sheets properly ruled and headed, for tabulating the Parochial Reports.

Resolved, That the attention of Rectors and Vestrys be called to the subject of Insurance on Church Property.

R. N. MEADE.
JAMES L. FISH.
W. G. HUBBARD.
H. L. ALEXANDER.
FRIEND COX.

(The above report embraces only Parishes reporting to the Council. For a more accurate view of the condition of the Diocese see tabulated statement in Appendix E.—SECY.)

The Rev. G. A. Gibbons moved to recommit to the committee.

Pending the discussion, the Council adjourned.

2.30 P. M.

The Council was called to order by the Bishop.

Dr. G. A. Aschman moved, as a substitute for Mr. Gibbons' motion, that the report of the Committee on Parochial Reports, be adopted, with the proviso that the Secretary be authorized to make such correction of statistics as are necessary to perfect the report and publish them in the Appendix. This motion was lost.

The motion of the Rev. G. A. Gibbons to recommit was then put to the vote and lost.

Mr. B. M. Ambler moved that the report of the committee be received and the committee discharged. Carried.

Mr. George R. Wendling offered the following resolution, which was adopted by an unanimous rising vote:

The Council, with gratitude and thanksgiving, congratulates the Diocese and our Bishop upon his recovery from his recent illness. We desire, however, in our solicitude, to convey to our beloved Bishop the assurance that the Council would be glad to see him take such a temporary rest from his official cares and duties as will enable him to tully regain his physical strength and thereby prolong a life so precious to us all. The Clergy and the Laity pledge themselves to the diligent performance of any additional duties which may be laid upon them by reason of any vacation which the Bishop may desire to take.

The Rev. D. W. Howard presented from Mrs. Reyman an invitation to the Council to visit Altenheim to-morrow afternoon. The invitation was accepted with thanks.

The Rev. J. S. Alfriend, for the Committee on Episcopal and Permanent Fund, presented the following report:

The Committee on Episcopal and Permanent Fund beg leave to report that they have examined the report of the Trustees submitted to this Council, and find the amount to the credit of this fund on May 18, 1903, to be $26,610.51, of which $15,700 is well and safely invested in interest bearing securities, $2,712.00 is in pleges, notes and certificates, and $8,198.51 in cash; all of which is deposited with "The Central Banking and Security Company" of Parkersburg, the authorized Treasurer of said fund.

Your Committee finds that according to the statement of Mr. Gordon, the former Treasurer of this fund, the total amount thereof on June 1, 1901, was $21,876.33 and that total contributions since received, in money, notes and pledges, including this Ascension Day offering, is $14,402.26, making a grand total at this date, May 22, 1903, of $36,278.59. Of the sum of $14,402.26, above given as the amount contributed since June 1, 1901, $13,150.77 was laid on the plate at the offering taken in this church on last evening, in money and pledges; it is proper to state, however, that a portion of this had been previously reported to the Trustees, and is in-

cluded in their statement of May 18, 1903, and the figures here given are simply to show the result of the effort made to increase this fund since the action taken at Cnarleston two years ago, with that end in view, and to show the amount given throughout the Diocese, and brought here as a thank-offering on this occasion of the 25th anniversary of the consecration of our beloved Bishop. It shou.u be understood, therefore, that these figures are subject to such revision as tne facts may require.

We believe that this fund has been hanuleu with intelligent care and safeguarded by proper business methods. We further think that the Trustees deserve the thanks and appreciation of this Council.

In consideration of the pressing demands of the work in the parishes and diocese and the church at large, we think, that the sum total of the offering as it now stands, affords reason and hope for encouragement.

We further recommend that steps be taken at once for continued prosecution of the Permanent Fund.

Your Committee begs to report regarding the Episcopal and Contingent Fund, that the report of Mr. R. M. Browne, Trustee, which has been presented to this Council, shows the amount assessed against the various parishes and mission stations to be $3,565.00 for the year ending May 31, 1903, and the total amount paid in on said assessments to be $2,829.58, leaving a deficit of $735.22.

The concise and intelligent report of Mr. Brown is commended to each member of the Council as worthy of their careful perusal.

Owing the effort being made in behalf of the Permanent Fund, and the large amount being raised therefor, we fear the brethren may relax their efforts on behalf of this *Contingent Fund;* the Committee therefore *urges* renewed and continued effort to meet their assessments in full.

Respectfully submitted,

C. C. PEARSON, *Ch.*,
JNO. S. ALFRIEND,
GEO. A. BAXTER,
SIMMS POWELL.

The Rev. Dr. Moore presented the report of the Assessment Committee.

On motion it was recommitted to the committee.

The committee to which was referred all matters relating to the change of name of the Church, made the following report:

The Committee to whom was referred that part of the Bishop's address which treats of the proposal to change the name of the Protestant Episcopal Church in the United States of America, beg to report as follows:

We find the word Protestant was accepted as the natural designation of our Church in the first General Convention of our Church in Philadelphia in September, 1785. It is asserted that those who organized our Church as a part of the one great Church of Christ made a mistake and gave it a name that sacrifices our position.

It is perfectly clear that our Church claims Christ through His Apostles as her founder. That she asserts that her ministry has come from the Apostles themselves.

Those who would change the name of the Church declare that the word Protestant in the title puts it in the category of those who ignore or misinterpret Church history. If this be true, it is fatal objection to a name, for it means we are calling ourselves something we are not—which is not true.

The principal *objection* made to the *name* as it stands lies in the word Protestant—this is declared to be a mere *negative*—equivalent to Anti-Roman Catholic, and its use is said to cut us off from our Catholic heritage. Nothing could be farther from the truth. True, the word in common use has been abused, but the word Catholic has been still more abused. As the word Protestant was first used it included a protest against the abuses and false teaching of the Church of Rome and an appeal to the highest of our authorities—a General Council. Now that appeal to true Catholic authority is the very ground on which the Church of England planted herself as a Catholic Church. The very ground upon which we as her daughter stand. So considered it is more than a mere negative, since it includes a positive assertion of loyal Catholicity. The essence of the protest and the appeal remain unchanged. The word Protestant is one of which we should be proud. It does not stand for a mere negative. It stands for a positive principle, to surrender which would be to surrender our claim to a true Catholicity. It stands for freedom from ecclesiastical control of opinion and for the right of private judgment.

If the word Protestant is retained Episcopal must be retained with it, as indicating one form of Church government.

If we should change our name to what should we change it? The four names most prominently urged are the Episcopal Church, The Church in the United States, The Catholic Church in the United States, and the American Catholic Church. None of these is free from grave objections. The first, the Episcopal, is bad because it abandons our claim to true Catholicity. The second, the Church in the United States, is an intolerable assumption, because it unchurches all other Christians, Protestants and Roman Catholics alike; the third, the Catholic Church in the United States, and the fourth, the American Catholic Church, are objectionable because they introduce a word that has been even more abused than Protestant, and in the opinion of large numbers of our own commuicants would be understood as a step toward union with Rome and would put us a step further from the other Protestant Churches to whom we are much nearer than we are to Rome, and the American Catholic to call our national communion by that name, is to assert that she is American, and at the same time universal, which is a contradiction in terms. The very fact that those who want a change cannot agree among themselves on any one name, is a strong argument against making *any* change. Let them agree upon a name then it would be time to urge the adoption of that name.

What would be gained by such a change of name?

One thing certainly would, and it is a thing to be avoided, namely: vast litigation. The titles to Church property all over the country would certainly be disputed in the courts. This would not be the case if it were a unanimous consent, but when so much diversity of opinion exists, when so much party strife would be engendered, this result would certainly follow.

It is asserted that large numbers of people who are outside of our Church—foreigners, would flock into it. They forget that the position of our Church would be exactly the same after a change of name as it is now. If we are not actually a part of the Holy Catholic Church in which we profess our belief whenever we say the creed, we shall not become so by merely changing our name. If we have anything in common with Protestantism we shall not lose it by dropping the word Protestant from the name of the Church.

The Church of Christ in the world today has a tremendous work before her. The world in large part, is still to be brought to Christ. The home and family need protection more than they have for hundreds of years. With all that to change now would be to waste our time and energy sowing seed of discord and discussion over a mere question of names.

The committee recommends the adoption of the following:

Resolved, That in the opinion of the Diocese of West Virginia any change of name of the Protestant Episcopal Church in the United States of America at this time would be inexpedient.

Signed.

W. L. GRAVATT,
G. A. GIBBONS,
GEO. W. EASTER,
SIMMS POWELL,
G. A. ASCHMAN.

The Rev. J. S. Gibson moved to amend by striking out of the appended resolution, the words "at this time."

The ayes and noes were called for, and the motion was carried by 23 to 20.

The resolution as thus amended was adopted by a unanimous vote taken by orders, to-wit: Clergy, 24; laity, 23.

On motion, the Council adjourned until 9.30 A. M. to-morrow.

SATURDAY, 9.30 A. M.

The Council was called to order by the Bishop.

Prayers were said by the Rev. J. F. Woods.

The minutes of the preceding day were read and approved.

The Secretary was instructed to communicate to the Committee of the General Convention the action of the Council in regard to the change of name of the Church.

The Rt. Rev. C. C. Penick, D. D., offered the following, which which was adopted:

Resolved, That this Council recognizes with deep gratitude the splendid hospitality shown it by friends here, ana that we assure them we will carry with us delightful memories of this memorable Council.

Resolved, That the Treasurer of the Diocese pay to the sexton of the Church the customary compensation usually allowed for his services.

The Rev. A. M. Lewis offered the following, which was adopted:

Resolved, That the Secretary of the Council and the Rev. Dr. Moore, after consultation with the Bishop, be a committee to republish the form of Parochial Report according to the action already taken by this council together with such rearrangement of headings and columns for figures as may seem to them best calculated to facilitate its use.

The Committee on Constitution and Canons, to whom was referred the amendments presented yesterday, made the following report, which was adopted:

The Committee on Constitution and Canons to whom was referred the matter of arranging a new form of certifying the election of lay delegates and alternates to tne annual Council, respectfully report.

Resolved, That Canon iii, Title A, be amended as follows: Strike out Sec. 3, and insert in lieu thereof the following:

CERTIFICATE.

This is to certify that at a meeting of the vestry of .... Parish (or of the qualified electors of .... Church, or at a meeting of the Committee of .... Mission Station) of the County of ...., in the State of West Virginia, held on the .... day of ...., 19.., the following were elected to represent the same in the Council of the Diocese of West Virginia, to be held on the .... day of ...., 19..:

Delegates;

....

....

....

Alternates;

....

....

....

We further certify that said delegates and alternates are communicants, in good standing, and residents of the Parish (or Church or Mission Station) they represent.

Given under my hand this .... day of ...., 19..

.........................., Rector or Minister in Charge.

.........................., Registrar.

.........................., Warden or Missions Committee.

The Committee on Assessments made their report, which was adopted. (See Appendix D.)

The Rev. D. W. Howard offered this preamble and resolution:

That in consideration of the report of the special committee to the last Council pertaining to the merging of the Diocesan and the General Funds of the Clergy Relief Fund; and of the resolution made at the last Council, to refer the matter to the Council of 1903:

Resolved, That the matter of the merging of our Diocesan Fund into the General Clergy Relief Fund be considered by this session of Council, with a view to adopting the original resolution, as well as the special committee's recommendation made at the last Council.

The Rev. Dr. Moore moved to refer the resolution and that part of the Bishop's address, relating to the subject of clergy relief, to a special committee, to report to the next Council, which was adopted, and the Bishop appointed the

Rev. S. S. Moore, D. D.	Judge J. P. Rogers.
Rev. D. W. Howard.	Mr. G. Bruce Hall.

The following Committee on Sunday Schools was elected:

Rev. W. P. Chrisman.	Mr. L. E. Sands.
Rt. Rev. C. C. Penick.	Dr. G. A. Aschman.

Mr. Simms Powell offered the following, which was adopted:

Resolved, That the special offering to the Permanent Fund required by the Canon be made each year on the Sunday before Ascension Day, and further, that a special committee be appointed to keep before the people the time, place and importance of this offering.

On motion of the Rev. J. S. Gibson, the following Diocesan Missionary Committee was elected:

The Bishop (ex-officio), President.

The Bishop, Coadjutor.

Rev. J. Brittingham.	Mr. B. M. Ambler.
Rev. J. F. Woods.	Mr. Simms Powell.
Rev. S. S. Moore, D. D.	Mr. L. E. Sands, Treas.

Mr. B. M. Ambler offered the following, which was unanimously adopted:

Resolved, That the members of the Council record grateful acknowledgments, to the railroad and transportation lines for favors granted; to the press for aid in promoting the success in this session, and to the citizens generally of this community, who have manifested a kindly interest in our proceedings, and have contributed to the pleasure of our stay among them.

Resolved II, That we would gladly extend thanks personally and individually to those of our own household. We appreciate all that they have done for us, as we have been continuously impressed with the thoughtfulness and ungrudging care bestowed upon the arrangements for our comfort and entertainment. We have enjoyed the privilege of closer social contact, even more than bounteous hospitalities lavished on every hand. We have not failed to note that this Twenty-fifth Anniversary of our good Bishop's Consecration, has been made the occasion of other reunions, bringing into view the beautiful relations and the attractive forces, which elevate and sweeten life, and of which St. Matthews is now a center; and we are moved to express a feeling somewhat akin to family pride, when we look about this chief city of our State, and find how high and honorable a part our own brethren take in the noble charities and good works, that mark and largely measure the position of a people in the scale of truest worth and righteousness.

The Rev. John S. Gibson, from the Committee on the State of the Church, submitted this report:

The Committee on the State of the Church respectfully reports:

Your committee has for its purposes the ascertaining of the progress of the Church in the several directions of the spiritual, moral and material. It is sometimes difficult to measure these things, as the short period of twelve months is under review, but we meet this year under circumstances most auspicious for the work of such committee, and because at this time there is being celebrated the twenty-fifth anniversary of the consecration of the first Bishop of West Virginia, we are enabled to take a wider view in order to determine the state of the Church.

The Diocese began her independent life in 1877 as "a little one among the thousands of Judah," there being to greet and work witn the Bishop consecrated in 1878 but 14 clergy and some 1,277 communicants. In the twenty-five years over which we look these have grown in number until to-day there are, canoncially connected with the Diocese, 46 clergy, and some 4,600 communicants, and the increase in value of Church property has been some $650,000.

Beginning with no endowment funds, except that the mother Diocese, Virginia, gave $5,000 in lieu of all claims for sharing the common property, except the estates and endowments of the Theological Seminary and Episcopal High School at Alexandria, we have now vested funds aggregating $66,000, and three institutions working for the relief and uplifting of our fellows. The 24 Churches and Chapels of the beginning have grown to number 81 and there are 36 rectories instead of the 11 of twenty-five years ago. Despite the fact of an imperfectly reported work the Parochial Reports Committee made yesterday shows that the tendency is onward. The total money raised in the last conciliar year being more than ever before, over $112,000, and, as the Bishop said in his address, the contributions to every fund being larger than ever before. So the work which began to grow as it was undertaken continues to expand, and there is manifest the good hand of our God upon us.

The Diocese in this advance has been tortunate in having the leadership of a Bishop whose heart has loved her and whose energies of thought and action have been bent for her upbuilding and your committee take this occasion to express, on behalf of the Church, to the Bishop of the Diocese its gratitude for the twenty-five years of faithful and loving service he has so freely rendered, and to pray God, Our Father, for a continuance of his guidance and blessing.

JNO. S. GIBSON,
GEO. A. GIBBONS,
GEO. R. WENDLING,
G. A. ASCHMAN.

The Diocesan Committee on Foreign and Domestic Missions was elected as follows:

Rev. D. W. Howard.	Gen. W. P. Craighill.
Rev. G. A. Gibbons.	Mr. C. C. Coe.
Rev. J. S. Gibson.	Dr. G. A. Aschman.

On motion of the Rev. Dr. Moore the following Committee on Education was elected:

Rev. G. W. Easter.
Rev. J. Howard Gibbons.
Rev. A. M. Lewis.
Mr. W. G. Hubbard.
Mr. C. L. Thompson.

Mr. J. D. DuBois was elected Trustee of Kenyon. The Trustees now are:

Rt. Rev. G. W. Peterkin, D. D., LL. D.
Rt. Rev. W. L. Gravatt, D. D.
Mr. Jos. D. DuBois.

The Rev. J. S. Douglas cordially invited the Council to meet in Trinity Church, Martinsburg, next year, which invitation was accepted by the Council.

The Rev. Dr. Moore offered this resolution which was adopted:

Resolved, That the Committee on Constitution and Canons be instructed to recodify and suggest alterations and improvements in the Constitution and Canons of this Diocese and to make report to the next session of this Council.

Mr. B. M. Ambler offered this resolution which was adopted:

Resolved, That a memorial volume of 3,000 copies be prepared, embodying the historical sermon and such other matter relating to the twenty-fifth anniversary, as may be deemed advisable by a committee of three to be appointed by the Bishop.

The Bishop appointed this Committee: The Rev. D. W. Howard, Dr. G. A. Aschman, J. C. Brady.

The Rev. J. Brittingham moved to rescind the order, passed on Thursday, to publish 3,000 copies of the historical sermon in pamphlet form; carried.

Six hundred copies of the Journal were ordered printed.

The Committee on Unfinished Business reported nothing further claiming attention of the Council.

On motion, after reading the minutes, and suitable devotions, the Council adjourned *sine die*.

ROBT. DOUGLAS ROLLER, *Secretary*.

GEO. W. PETERKIN, *Prest.*

APPENDIX A.

HISTORICAL SERMON.

HISTORICAL SERMON

FOR THE

TWENTY-FIFTH ANNIVERSARY

OF

BISHOP PETERKIN'S CONSECRATION.

St. Matthew's Church, Wheeling, W. Va.,

Ascension Day, 1903.

PREACHED BY

REV. JNO. S. GIBSON,

Rector of Trinity Church, Huntington,

MAY 21st, 1903.

HISTORICAL SERMON.

St. Mark, 16:15: 19-20.

"And He said unto them, Go ye into all the world, and preach the gospel to the whole creation. So then the Lord Jesus, after he had spoken unto them, was received up into heaven, and sat down at the right hand of God. And they went forth, and preached everywhere, the Lord working with them." (Rev. Ver.)

In the great forty days between the "Mighty Resurrection" and "glorious Ascension our Lord opened the understandings of His apostles concerning the nature and methods of His Kingdom of truth, and on the mountain in Galilee gave them the great commission: "Go ye into all the world and preach the gospel to the whole creation," thus announcing "in the simplest and least ostentatious way the most original, the broadest, the sublimest enterprise that ever human beings have been called upon to accomplish." Even, that men of every clime, condition and generation should come to the knowledge of God their Father as revealed through the incarnate Son in His office of prophet, priest and king. and witnessed to by the Spirit sent forth in all hearts crying Abba, Father, by a line of human witnesses beginning with those who had "seen and handled the Words of Life," "beheld His glory as of the only begotten of the Father" from the day when at Jordan there came the voice from heaven saying "This is my beloved son," until that day, when from Olivet, He went up from them into heaven to take His power and reign.

When these witnesses received the inward power of the Holy Ghost from the gift-giving conqueror Christ, their proclamation began, and from that hour to this the going forth and the preaching have never ceased. From this hour to that extends a wondrous line of apostles, who have blessed the generations with light and love. Their witness has been heard and a great flock has been gathered throughout the world, and as it has been gathered it has been shepherded. Like the Master. the true Shepherd, these His under-shepherds have given their lives for the sheep. The dominant thought of their serving has been "to keep those whom thou has given me that none be lost," either by the drawing away from faith by doctrines erroneous, strange, and contrary to God's word, or by ungodliness or worldly lusts. Their hearts and hands have been sanctified to show themselves gentle and merciful for Christ's sake to poor and needy people, and to all strangers destitute of help."

This line of living witnesses stretching back to the very day on which our Lord ascended up on high came at length to have its members serving in the new found Western land, and after many days our own flock of Christ upon the heights of the mountains and in the deeps of the valleys of West Virginia was, by the providence of God, given into the hands of one of them for shepherding. It was a blessed day, and we turn back to it today as a man in his full career turns back to the hour when, though self-distrusting, he started forth, with his parents' blessing, to do a man's work in the world. Into these walls there came on that Ascension Day, 1878, with look of profoundest reverence and most lofty purpose, a company of Bishops with commission to consecrate another into this line of living witnesses. They were the Diocesans, or their assistants, of each Diocese then touching the territory of West Virginia, excepting Maryland. There was the silver-haired Bishop Bebell, of Ohio, true in faith and pure in life; the Bishop of Pittsburg, Jnó. Barrett Kerfoot, who from his scholastic work and spirit came to the arduous and lack-of-ease work of a Bishop in the Church of God; the sham-hating, truth-loving, impetuous-for-his-ideas-of-truth, Francis M. Whittle, of Virginia; the young Bishop of the young Diocese of Southern Ohio, Thomas A. Jaggar, a striking figure and a scholarly Bishop, who all too soon succumbed to the inevitable strain; and then the Assistant Bishop of Kentucky, whose praise is in the Churches, and whose gracious presence here today forbids aught else to be voiced save our gratitude that he was one of those, perhaps the chiefest, who, under God, led us to the choice of him whom we would this day honor.

Standing before these Bishops in the Church of God was a tall lythe young presbyter of 37 years. He had learned in a pious rectory the "way of life," and "the beauty of holiness;" he had grown, as a participant in the four years' struggle of a valiant and noble people to maintain their ideas of truth and justice, into the qualities which go to the making of a soldier "without fear and without reproach;" he had learned in his home and in his alma mater, the Virginia Seminary, that evangelical interpretation of the gospel, which while it holds the Catholic faith and order entire, yet refuses to shadow the glory and power of Jesus Christ, the one mediator between God and man, by any undue exaltation or elaboration of ceremonial or ministry.

The solemn vows are taken *ex animo* (from the soul); the commission given, as upon the head of the kneeling Bishop elect there press the hands of his consecrators, and the voice of the consecrator says, "Receive the Holy Ghost for the office and work of a Bishop in the Church of God, now committed unto thee by the imposition of our hands; in the name of the Father, and of the Son, and of the Holy Ghost, Amen.

The solemn admonition sounds in these walls; enters into his soul: "Be to the flock of Christ a Shepherd, not a wolf; feed them, devour them not. Hold up the weak, heal the sick, bind up the broken, bring again the outcasts, *seek* the lost. Be *so* merciful, that you be not too remiss; so minister discipline, that you forget not mercy; that when the Chief Shepherd shall appear, you may receive the never-fading Crown of Glory."

It is done. The Protestant Episcopal Church in the United States has received thus, the one hundred and twentieth in the line of living witnesses, and the Church in West Virginia the completion of her organization in the giving of jurisdiction and authority to the Rt. Rev. George William Peterkin, Doctor in Divinity, the first Bishop of West Virginia. And the West Virginia Church was satisfied and expectant as he began from that hour to lead, as her apostle, in the development of her life.

Twenty-five years have passed and the representatives of the West Virginia Church are again assembled on Ascension Day within the walls of St. Matthew's Church, and the central figure in the assemblage is the *First* Bishop of West Virginia.

Of those present on the day of consecration in 1878, officially or otherwise, but few are remaining on earth. All the consecrators excepting the Bishops of Kentucky and Southern Ohio have fallen asleep—resting well after years of manly toil.

Our Nestors, Rev. Jno. F. Woods and Rev. George A. Gibbons are the two presbyters remaining of the number who gave their votes for him and their welcome to him—the others are either in other fields, or gone to rest in Paradise. Of the laity then attending likewise the number has become few.

But the church then satisfied and expectant comes today in fullness of power and gladness of heart to worship God and do honor to His servant.

She looks upon him who was then the novice-bishop and sees that he wears the aspect of a veteran; she rejoices to have had the cares and toils of his manly life hers for all these years; still satisfied and yet expectant, she assures him of her deep, true love, for his person and his office, and bids him lead on, as the directing Lord shall guide, and prays God's good providence that it may be many years before the lengthening shadows merge into the glowing light for him.

A general in the midst of conflict has his thoughts otherwhere than upon himself. How goes the battle? How *fare* the men? Is the cause *safe?* A Bishop in the Church of God on such a day as this, apart from the necessary introspection which may be short, sets his thought upon the flock committed to his charge, and the other sheep not of this fold whom he must bring, and so the West Virginia Church having taken occasion of this anniversary to congratulate herself upon his years of loving service rendered her, and to assure him of her appreciation and love must turn with some sense of his thought-direction to consider the Church, the Kingdom, during these years. How has gone the struggle to upbuild—to lead—to increase—to establish the house of God in the tops of the mountains and to give the valleys light?

The history of the Church in West Virginia territory runs back to the Colonial period, although the Church in the Colonies of Virginia and contiguous Maryland, had reached beyond the respectable age of a hundred years before Governor Spottswood and the Knights of the Golden Horse-Shoe had in 1716 made their daring journey of exploration beyond the Blue Ridge and touched, perhaps, the Valley of the Shenandoah. Soon after this the Valley began to be settled from Tidewater Virginia and from immigration from Pennsylvania. There were churches established near the present site of Charles Town; in what is now Shepherdstown; at Mill Creek; and congregations gathered in Martinsburg and in Hampshire County. The history is meagre and the traditions scant and uncertain. Who built St. George's in the fields near Charles Town? The walls of vine covered stone and the beauty of site attest the taste and spirit of the worshippers. It was on the route of the army of Gen. Braddock, and within its walls no doubt many sons of the Church with him and Col. Geo. Washington heard the word. It was erected some where between 1727-1760, presumably a little after 1740, but the names of builders, worshippers and ministers are all forgotten.

The Welshman, Morgan of Morgan, who about 1740 conducted services and was instrumental in building the Church at what is now Bunker Hill is an example of faith and works to the laymen now comprising the body of the Church. Thurston at Shepherdstown in 1768, Sturges at Martinsburg in 1771, Ogilvie, Manning and Kenner ordained in England 1771-72 for service in Hampshire, the oldest County, 1754, in the State, are the names of ministers whose memory has perished from among the sons of men. They interest us much as the teachers on the outposts of the Western line then reached by the Episcopal Church in Virginia, but their names recall no memories and suggest no deeds save those of patient witnessing for God and His Christ to the first settlers in West Virginia.

In the army of Lord Dunmore threading its way through the wilderness of New River and the Great Kanawha, and establishing by the victory at Point Pleasant over the Indian allied nations the Ohio as the boundary between barbarism and civilization, there were no do- many sons of the Church, and its training in the path of duty and Gods service no doubt inspired many a heart to deeds of heroism on that hard fought day.

Then came the struggle for American liberty extending over eight years before the end was gained and America took her place among the nations. At its close the Church, even where it had been strong, found its altars deserted and its people almost shepherdless. The half-hearted among her people when there came contumely and reproach deserted to the ranks of growing sectarianism, and even her own children were consenting to the shameless despoliation of her rightful property, the saving of which by the adjudication of the courts in her favor was prevented by the death of Virginia's great jurist, Edmund Pendleton. With the strong lowland Church suffered the just-born Missions in the adjacent uplands, and though their light never went out it flickered almost to dying. The first step of progress noted after the Revolution is the building at Martinsburg by Philip Pendleton and others of its first Church. And Hedgesville, where Wm. Pendleton and Raleigh Colston were pillars, seems to have been the Western outpost moving along the Potomac from tide water. Beyond lay tne mysterious mountains. But the battles of Point Pleasant and the Revolution had made possible the journeying and settlement of immigrants, and New Kentucky lay just beyond the Virginia border, attracting by its romance and the story of its wealth; so it was not long before Western Virginia became a known land. The Valley of the Kanawha began to fill, and it was as early as 1797 that the Hudsons came to Coalsmouth with the love of tne Church in their hearts. Then come movements from up the Ohio *down* its fertile valleys, and among the first to make his home in what is now Brooke County was Rev. Joseph Doddridge, M. D.; the pioneer in the region of Wheeling and the "Pan Handle;" untiring, vigilant, able, alone, almost unremunerated; with glorious opportunity for the Church of their fathers among many of the immigrants, yet when no helpers came giving his sad note of hope deferred.

Another stream of influence and direction of progress was due to the missionary spirit shown by the Clerical Association of the Valley, whose members assembled every three months for prayer, consultation and missionary contributing for the support of missionaries to the Western part of Virginia. It sent forth into the region beyond the Alleghanies Revs. Charles Page and Wm. Lee, whose plantings have today grown into the Churches at Clarksburg, Morgantown, Parkersburg, Point Pleasant and Charleston. As population increased it was seen that the harvest was plenteous, but the laborers were few, and so very many sons of the Church were soon lost to her. And when work was begun its progress was slow. Some thought because of the distance of the Bishops and the infrequency of their presence, and began to stir for an organization more after the primitive model of smaller sections for supervision. Dr. Doddridge moved for it, including in his proposed new jurisdiction parts of Western Virginia, Pennsylvania and Eastern Ohio. Rev. Benjamin Allen in the Eastern Pan Handle did the same thing, being the first, so it is said, to move for a division of the Diocese in 1815. A truer cause may be that given by the Rev. C. W. Andrews, D. D., as to the slow growth of the Church at Shepherdstown; the lack of a settled ministry, due to the unwillingness of the people to sustain it; it being, he says, considered that a subscription of $10 per annum, and that by people of large means, was a bountiful giving to sustain the gospel. But whether it was for these or other causes it is a fact that after the pioneers had blazed the way the Church did not grow, either in numbers or influence, as her history and traditions and her claims upon many of the immigrants as being her own sons and daughters entitled her to, or as it was the hope of her devout leaders that she would. From 1783 to 1877, a period of 94 years, she increased from some half dozen points to have some twenty-four organizations and about twenty other points where services, more or less frequent, were held. Yet she had had the Episcopal supervision, and personal presence and service of every one of the great Bishops of Virginia, excepting Bishop Madison, than whom the Church has never had a more manly or godly and well-learned and efficient line of successors to those first commissioned to preach everywhere.

As we rehearse the names of the pastors of this little flock upon the hills and in the pleasant Valleys of what is now the "Mountain State," it will be realized that the Church was served by a goodly company of priests, and that any slowness to progress must be accounted for in some other way than to lay it to the charge either of godlessness or inefficiency in the ministry; and perhaps if war and non-support had not forced a practical itineracy upon the West Virginia Church prior to 1877, and it could have had a permanent ministry exercising both the gifts of preaching and shepherding, the progress might have been much greater, despite the facts of the Church being planted in new places just out of the woods, as it were, and among a population either largely alien or else alienated from the Church. In the Eastern section there ministered such men as Benj. Allen, preacher, missionary, author, poet, tractarian (not in technical or theologian parlance) the leader of the evangelical revival after 1812. C. W. Andrews, D. D., doughty champion of the Church's system, as evangelically applied, almost the assistant Bishop of Virginia; C. E. Ambler, W. D. Hanson, the uncle of our own Bishop; Theodore Carson, Isaac Gibson, James Chisholm, the faithful pastor who fled not when pestilence entered his flock, and so perished to live ever in the heart of the Virginia Church. D. F. Sprigg, D. D., the pungent paragraphist who for many years taught all the Church wholesome things through his paper the Southern Churchman, R. T. Davis, B. B. Smith, 1st Bishop of Ky, and at 90 years of age exercising the office of Presiding Bishop. Dudley Tyng, Julius Grammar, Wm. H. Meade, almost Bishop of W. Va.: James Grammar, D. D., Alexander Jones, Wm. Thos. Leavell, of true faith and staunsh devotion, living to project his influence upon the spiritual life of the Diocese of West Virginia, which came to being largely because of his earnest labors in that behalf. These and others of like spirit.

In the Northwestern section: Doddridge the planter, the seer,

John Armstrong at Wheeling, during whose ministry Bishop White confirmed a class in Wheeling; Wm. Armstrong, Edmund T. Perkins, D. D., devoted, earnest, beloved; Addison, in troublous times of civil strife; Geo. C. Currie, the eloquent Scot; James A. Latane, godly, but led into erroneous following of Geo. David Cummins in 1873; J. G. Armstrong; Jno. F. Woods, here today as one of us; David H. Greer, D. D., today a dominant spirit in the American Church; H. E. Hayden, Joshua Cowpland, R. A. Castleman, Edmund Christian, James J. Page, Saml. D. Tomkins, W. D. Hyland, Rich. T. Brown, Thomas Smith, Francis Nash, and others like these.

In the Kanawha Valley: James Craik, D. D., founder of Christ Church, Louisville, President of House of Deputies for years; Francis M. Whittle, D. D., Bishop of Virginia; F. D. Goodwin, R. A. Cobbs, who became Secretary of the Diocese of West Virginia; Thos. Hugo Lacy, E. V. Jones, C. R. Page, C. H. Page, and others. Truly Virginia could be proud of the men she sent into her Western section, if she did in Convention again and again deplore that she sent too few, and that her children in that section were too often left as sheep without shepherd.

At length 137 years after the beginning of her life in Western Virginia and fourteen years after the territory in Western Virginia had become the Commonwealth of West Virginia the Church in West Virginia was allowed, by the conservatism of the Councils and Bishops of Virginia, and against the timidity and actual protest of some of its clergy and people, to become of age and to begin its independent life. It was in 1877 that the dream of Doddridge and of Allen from 1800 to 1816, became the vision of Wm. Thos. Leavell; that the strivings of the clergy and laity of Western Virginia as they met to obtain concerted action in 1851, 1865, 1872-3, 1875, 1876 became the deed accomplished. For 62 years the workers in this scattered field sought in vain to obtain the right to have their work done at closer range, and to have it receive the direction of a Bishop to whom its importance and its promise should give inspiration and power to apply to it the full strength of a manhood consecrated to the work of a Bishop in the Church of God. The organization was fully completed when on Ascension Day, 1878, its first Bishop was consecrated. Then began another stage in the life of the Church in West Virginia, and promise was soon given that there would be a fulfillment of the hopes of those who had seen in independent organization a vast increment of vitality and strength. There was first the necessary forming of acquaintances with the field, its needs and its promise, and this was done by the personal contact of the new Bishop with every section. Then came under his leadership, and with the co-operation of a faithful clergy and laity, a gradual development of the work, and as there was preaching everywhere there was evidence of the Lord working with them. The progress which has been made in the twenty-five years seems to your preacher to have had as its basis certain well-defined principles.

First: That a Bishop's office, whatever else canonical regulation may lay upon him, is to be that of Chief Missionary, and that he is to find satisfaction in his work, not as a ruler over the Church, but as an Apostle of it, planting with his labor, nourishing with his prayers. It was under this conception, as applied in practice, that the newly organized Church began at once to revive its established work, and to spread into central West Virginia and along the Kanawha, New and other rivers.

Second: That the Protestant Episcopal Church is not an alien in this Commonwealth seeking domicile and fruitage, but that this is her heritage, and that she has message to and responsibility for all the people, and must do them good. If they dwell amid the manifold temptations of urban life, that she must there show her utmost skill; if among the fields and woods of cultivated sections, that she must witness for the God who gave their heritage; if among the narrow valleys and in dark mines, that she must speak of peace, purity, love and mercy; if upon the mountain tops, that she must exalt their hearts to Him who reigns above them.

Third: That the Church most needed by the people of West Virginia to conserve spiritual life, preserve morality, and comfort souls and bodies of men is the Protestant Episcopal Church. Not some modern adaptation of this Church to the modes of thought and administration of Modern Romanism, but the Church of Andrews of England and Andrews of Virginia. The Protestant Episcopal Church, with its noble litergy whose rubrics are laws: with its ministers, who are neither mumblers of superstition in a language unknown, nor priests offering sacrifice, but men of God, taught of God, standing to teach and lead and encourage their brethren. The Episcopal Church, in its simplicity and its beauty, old yet instinct with manly vigor; the home of the lowly and humble in heart, whether those hearts beat beneath velvet or fustian. The Church Primitive, Protestant, Catholic. The Church of Jesus Christ.

Fourth: That self-help is the great factor in developing strength, and that while the General Church has had responsibility for the planting or non-planting of the Church in West Virginia in the past, that it is now her own chief concern, and that the Church in West Virginia must bend her energies to be self-propagating; and that every candle lighted in the woods and mines must see that others catch light from it, until the beacon of the Divine burns on every hilltop.

Fifth: That the Bishop has special and near relation as head pastor to every other pastor of the flock: even the relation of perfectly frank friendship, brotherhood and sympathy. The Episcopate in West Virginia has never yet, and please God it never will, expressed its relation to the presbyterate and diaconate as regarding itself and the laity as the permanent elements in the Church life, and *so* careless and indifferent to the struggles of the co-workers, who are here regarded as the "backbone" of the work. There has therefore grown up between the clergy and Bishop of this Diocese a love and mutual confidence which may well be the envy of larger folds, and from this has flowed a worthier service and a hastening progress.

These principles, and others, as illustrated and applied by the Bishop have resulted in a great growth and strengthening of the Church in West Virginia. This growth may appear more clearly if there are given in comparative statistics the figures of the two periods, 1878, the date of the Consecration, and May, 1903, twenty-five years after. In 1878 14 clergy working in 24 parishes and missions and preaching at perhaps 20 other points. In 1903, 42 clergy officiating in 81 Churches and chapels and ministering at 100 other points. In '78 about 1300 communicants; in 1903, about 4600 communicants. In '78, 11 Rectories, in 1903, 36 Rectories. In '78 no institutions for education under Church influences, or for ministering to the broken, bruised, and fever stricken bodies of men. In 1903, a thoroughly equipped and constantly growing hospital, the Sheltering Arms, which beginning a little over a dozen years ago has done wonderful good to hundreds of men and women in the coal fields of the Kanawha and New River, and come to require between $5,000 and $6,000 to operate.

A Hall at the State University worth $25,000, intended, in the absence of ability to conduct an institution under Church auspices, to give some oversight to the youth attending upon the State University. This is really the private property of the Bishop. A hospital at Glendale, which, while at present private property, is supported largely by contributions of churchmen, and ministers in the Church's name to all sorts and conditions, and relieves many cases of distress without money compensation. A Bishop's house worth $20,000 as a home for the beloved Diocesan.

In 1878 no vested funds or endowments except $5,000 received in lieu of all claims from the mother diocese. In 1903, over $5,000 accumulated in the Disabled Clergy and Widow's and Orphan's Fund.

$23,000 endowment for the Sheltering Arms Hospital.

Over $35,000 for Permanent Fund for the support of the Episcopate.

In 1877, contributing to work of missions in the Diocese about $500 per annum. In 1903, paying an assessment of $3,000 for missions in West Virginia. In 1877, contributing some $800 to the Contingent Fund, and in 1903, paying an assessment for same of $3,500.

West Virginia was not a name in the Church's Kalendars in 1876, but in 1893 she had become a household word in Rio Grande do Sul, for her Bishop had come across the thousands of miles of sea to give her people shepherding.

West Virginia unknown in 1876 in 1901 had her name known throughout the Isle of the Sea, Porto Rico, as her Bishop did apostolic work there.

West Virginia needing evangelization, so much in 1876 sent forth to bring light into the Dragon's Stronghold, 'Ngankin, in 1902, one of the manly sons of one of her knightliest churchmen and so the West Virginia Church will soon be thankfully thought of by many of the redeemed sons of China.

West Virginia in 1876 not a name in America's great Church in twenty-four years was named among five dioceses leading in contributions.

This advance and upbuilding represents the giving of a life. It has not come by accident or easy unfolding; but, as the great material development of West Virginia is the result of the giving of brain and brawn by the toilers, *so* this has come by God's blessing upon the manly toil of a manly man and his helpers. As Virginia traces the resuscitation of her almost perished Church in the early part of the nineteenth century to her Wm. Meade, so West Virginia ascribes her progress during the first twenty-five years of the Episcopate of her first Bishop to the character of the Bishop himself. As has been recently and well said: "What had been officially reported in 1876 as impossible, he undertook in 1878 under discouragements that seemed appalling. He infused new life where activity had almost died out. His enthusiasm was felt in every organization or gathering within his jurisdiction. His personal manliness appealed to the admiration of widening circles." For twenty-five years now he has been Bishop, and the Church in West Virginia here assembled in solemn council must claim her right to give God thanks for his servant our Bishop; and to express to the Bishop her deep sense of gratitude for his faithful, wise, sympathetic, untiring shepherding of the flock.

For twenty years the Bishop bore alone the "care of all the churches" when in 1899, the Diocese, having realized the overtaxing of his strength, through multiplication of work, gave him a coadjutor. There was chosen for that office—and wisely—a man from the ranks of our own clergy; one who familiar with the field, its promise and its difficulty, would not, as one looking on from without and despising the day of small things, cry "Nolo Episcopari," but would gladly become true yoke-fellows with such a worker in such a work. Wm. Loyall Gravatt was chosen and consecrated in 1899, a man of the same intense devotion to those truths of our religion called Protestant; of the same Catholic spirit; of the same fidelity to the Protestant Episcopal Church; of the same tenderness and sympathy; and side by side these two lead on under God to the realization of the vision of the preacher of yesterday.

Are there no clouds? you ask me. Yea, but the skies of West Virginia are very beautiful. Are there no difficulties? Yea, but our journeyings in the West Virginia hills have taught us that however deep and narrow the valley may be, there soon comes again the hill top and from it vision of beauty. Are there no failures and no slowness? Aye, both; but if the potter's kiln fails today, there comes tomorrow, and the Lord reigns.

This much of the past! Now we turn to the future, what of that? We hope, but prophesy not. We give ourselves and the Church of our love and His to the Lord's guidance. He gave the spark of life in the far off colonial day; He nourished it and fanned it into flame in the days of struggle, of weakness, of growing strength; He brought the Church to the day of her majority and "set her feet in a large room," and said: "Go ye, preach, baptize;" as the preachers went he worked with them and brought forth this that ye have this day seen and heard. Surely, then brethren we can labor on and at eventide sleep with our fathers with full confidence that the Lord Ascended will continue His guiding, and that as the West Virginia Church goes forth and preaches everywhere He will work with her with signs following. And so we commend this Church, bishops, priests, deacons and people all, to God, the Father, the Son and the Holy Ghost.

Unto whom we ascribe:

APPENDIX B.

I. Report of the Treasurer of the Diocese.

II. Report of the Trustees of the Episcopal and Contingent Funds.

III. Report of the Trustees of the Permanent Fund.

TREASURER'S REPORT.

Amount of Assessment Diocesan Missions.	NAME.	Paid for Diocesan Missions.	Religious and Theo. Education.	Widows and Orphans and Disabled Clergy.
$ 20	Ansted	20 00		8 00
6	Alderson			
25	Berkeley Springs	18 00		
30	Bluefield	22 75		9 48
30	Bramwell			
10	Buckhannon			
5	Bunker Hill	1 16		
12	Bruce Chapel	6 00		
200	Charleston, St. John's	200 00		41 95
8	" St. Luke's	8 00		
8	" St. Matthew's	8 00		
125	Clarksburg	6 50		
[illegible]	Cresap's	5 00		
300	Charles Town, Zion	300 00	88 14	64 17
10	" St. Phillip's	10 00		
8	" The Mountain			
8	Davis	8 00		
10	Elkins	10 00		
5	Elm Grove	7 58		
75	Fairmont	25 41		
5	Fort Spring			
15	Grafton	10 79		
20	Harper's Ferry	88 00	8 48	7 18
25	Hedgesville	25 00		
75	Huntington	79 15	5 00	89 87
80	Hinton	17 41		2 15
8	Kenova and Ceredo	7 00	2 60	8 95
2	Keyser			
30	Lee Town	40 85		12 00
7	Lewisburg			
3	Liverpool			
75	Martinsburg	107 20		16 10
15	Middleway	18 46		1 52
15	Montgomery	9 80		
.....	Mt. Carbon	6 30		
20	Moorefield	28 81	1 27	69
25	Morgantown	51 22		
40	Moundsville	77 00	4 55	16 85
20	McDowell Missions	16 06		
10	Nuttallburg			
40	New Martinsville	35 00	9 59	6 69
10	Okonoko	10 00	2 00	
350	Parkersburg, Trinity	350 01	19 77	49 70
20	" Memorial	149 05	32 00	25 00
8	" St. Stephen's			
50	Pt. Pleasant	6 30	1 20	
20	Powellton	18 88		2 25
6	Princeton			
10	Ravenswood			
15	Ripley			
10	Ripon	16 29		
16	Romney	16 00		
8	Ronceverte	25 00		
10	St. Albans	9 93	3 20	
15	St. Marys	16 00	40	85
75	Shepherdstown	68 94	9 97	20 00
40	Sistersville	66 02	11 36	10 90
19	Summit Point	15 00		4 35
10	Sutton	10 00		
4	Spruce Chapel			
10	Spillman	10 00		

TREASURER'S REPORT—Continued.

Amount of Assessment Diocesan Missions.	NAME.	Paid for Diocesan Missions.	Religious and Theo. Education	Widows and Orphans and Disabled Clergy.
5	Smithfield			
10	Tavenersville	5 00		
75	Union	73 21	14 51	18 88
10	Waverly	10 10	1 55	55
75	Wellsburg	27 42		
75	Weston	67 09		16 50
10	White Sulphur			
425	Wheeling, St Matthew's	425 00	15 00	316 75
15	" St. Andrew's	13 51		4 34
175	" St. Luke's	175 00	17 35	48 20
25	Williamstown	30 50	9 58	2 98
5	Willow Island	2 45		
5	Brooke Co.			
6	Beckley	8 18		
5	Beury	19 10	2 00	2 00
5	Du Bree	8 00		
10	Glen Jean	5 00		
Total Amount of Assessments.	Clover Lick	18 86		
	Old Sweet Springs	57 79		
	Salt Sulphur Springs	8 71		
	Paw Paw	8 77	1 86	1 68
	Long Reach	1 90		
	Mercers	6 00		
	Racine	1 87		
	Nau	07		
	Uneeda	15		
	Chester	2 45		
	Women of W. Va	350 00		
	" Mite	28 05		
	Capt. W. R. Johnson			100 00
	Interest and Earnings			306 16
	Total Income	3,330 00	206 38	1,156 70
	Balance June 1st, 1902	1,703 19	141 70	4,982 51
		5,033 19	348 08	6,139 21
	Total Payments	3,155 01	200 00	480 00
$2,958	Balance on hand May 20, 1903	1,878 18	148 08	5,659 21

PAYMENTS, DIOCESAN MISSIONS.

Rev. R. U. Brooking	$ 100 00
Rev. E. H. Brosius	200 00
Rev. G. H. Crook	100 00
Rev. C. M. Campbell	200 00
Rev. G. Card	41 67
Rev. Thomas C. Darst	116 67
Rev. G. W. Easter	100 00
Rev. C. A. Dowell	125 00
Rev. J. L. Fish	50 00

Rev. A. G. Grinnan	50 00
Rev. J. S. Gibson	50 00
Rev. J. H. Gibbons	50 00
Rev. G. A. Gibbons	250 00
Rev. J. A. Hiatt	100 00
Rev. J. R. Joyner	75 00
Rev. L. R. Levering	187 50
Rev. R. N. Meade	225 00
Rev. J. T. Marley	100 00
Rev. J. A. Miller	150 00
Rev. C. C. Pearson	100 00
Rev. Geo. C. Shaw	50 00
Rev. Chas. E. Shaw	50 00
Rev. H. B. Thomas	100 00
Rev. A. J. Willis	50 00
Rev. J. F. Woods	200 00
Rev. P. R. Stauffer	187 50
Rev. E. D. Irvine	41 67
McCalla & Co., for Boxs. Advent offering	50 00
Church News	50 00
Printing Report	5 00
	$3,155 01

PAYMENTS, RELIGIOUS AND THEOLOGICAL EDUCATION.

Rev. N. F. Marshall, account Seminary	$200 00

PAYMENTS, WIDOWS AND ORPHANS AND DISABLED CLERGY FUND.

Col. Herbert for acct. Dr. Packard and Dr. Walker	$ 80 00
Mrs. Leavell	100 00
Mrs. Lea	150 00
Mrs. Mason	150 00
Total Payment	$480 00

RECAPITULATION.

LEDGER BALANCES.

Widows, Orphans and Disabled Clergy Fund		$5,659 21
Diocesan Missions		1,878 18
Religious and Theo. Education		148 03
Total to be accounted for		$7,685 42
Balance in Nat. Ex. Bank of Wheeling	$1,525 42	
Bonds, Notes and Cash in hands of Treas	6,160 00	
		$7,685 42

Respectfully Submitted,

LAWRENCE E. SANDS, *Treas.*

May 20, 1903.

REPORT OF TRUSTEE OF EPISCOPAL AND CONTINGENT FUNDS.

Beginning June 1st, 1902, and Ending May 31st, 1903.

NAME OF PARISH.	Amount Assessed.	Amount Paid.	Amount Paid on Arrears.	Amount Received Not Assessed.
Alderson	$ 6 00	$ 4 25	$	$
Berkeley Springs	80 00	18 50		
Bluefield	80 00	40 00		
Princeton	6 00			
Bramwell	80 00			
Eckman and McDowell Missions	20 00			
Brooke Co., St. Johns	5 00			
Buckhannon	10 00	5 50		
Bunker Hill	5 00			
Charleston, St. John's	275 00	275 00		
" St. Luke's	7 00			
" St. Matthew's	7 00			
Charles Town, Zion	425 00	400 00		
" " St. Phillip's	5 00			
St. Andrew's on Mount	2 00			
Clarksburg	125 00			
Cresaps	5 00	5 00		
Davis	8 00	8 00		
Elkins Mission	10 00	10 00		
Fairmont	75 00	75 00		
Grafton	15 00	15 00		
Harper's Ferry	20 00		16 00	
Hedgesville	50 00		50 00	
Hinton	25 00	11 41		
Huntington	90 00		90 00	
Kenova	7 00	7 00		
Lewisburg	8 00			
Ronceverte	7 00			
Martinsburg	100 00	100 00		
Middleway	80 00	48 55		
Summit Point	80 00	88 25		
Lee Town	80 00	44 80		
Moorefield	20 00	20 00		
Romney	16 00	16 00		
Keyser	2 00			
Okonoko	10 00	8 00		
Morgantown	25 00			
Moundsville	60 00	60 00	50 00	
Nuttalburg	10 00			
Parkersburg, Trinity	525 00	525 00		
" Good Shepherd	5 00	18 00		
" St. Stephens	2 00			
Tavennersville	8 00	8 00		
Point Pleasent, Christ	50 00	50 00		
Bruce Chapel	12 00			
Spillman Mission	10 00	10 00		
Powellton	20 00			
Ansted	20 00	20 00		
Ravenswood, Grace	10 00			
Ripley, St. John's	15 00			
Liverpool, Whittle	2 00			
Ripon	20 00			
Shepherdstown	75 00	66 85		
Sistersville	40 00	4 66		
New Martinsville	40 00			
Smithfield, Wetzel County	5 00			
Spruce Chapel	4 00			
St. Albans	10 00	5 00		
Montgomery	15 00			
St. Marys	15 00	10 00		
Sutton	10 00	10 00	10 00	
Union	50 00	50 00	19 90	
White Sulphur	10 00			

REPORT OF TRUSTEE OF EPISCOPAL AND CONTINGENT FUNDS—Continued.

NAME OF PARISH.	Amount Assessed.	Amount Paid.	Amount Paid on Arrears.	Amount Received Not Assessed.
Fort Spring	$ 5 00	$	$	$ ....
Waverly	5 00	5 00	....	....
Wellsburg	25 00	25 00	....	....
Weston	80 00	80 00	....	....
Wheeling, St. Matthews	600 00	600 00	....	....
" St. Luke's	175 00	150 00	....	....
" Andrew's	10 00	10 00	....	....
" St. Paul's, Elm Grove	10 00	....	....	....
Williamstown	15 00	2 81	....	....
Willow Island	5 00	5 00	....	....
Beckley	6 00	....	....	....
Beury	5 00	....	....	....
Du Bree	5 00	....	....	....
Glen Jean	10 00	....	....	....
Totals	$3,565 00	$2,829 58	$235 90	$........

RECEIPTS.

Amount received on this year's assessment	$2,829 58
Amount received on arrears	235 90
Amount received on arrears, special, Dr. Moore	100 00
Amount received special from G. W. Peterkin	200 00
Amount received from B. W. Ambler, Chmn. of Permanent Fund	1,409 00
Total	$4,774 48

DISBURSEMENTS.

Paid Rt. Rev. G. W. Peterkin	$2,000 00
Paid Bishop Coadjutor W. L. Gravatt	2,500 00
Paid R. D. Roller, Secretary, Salary and Postage	104 86
Paid Tribune Company—Printing Journal	277 28
Paid Rev. Jno. S. Gibson—Examining Chaplain	29 64
Paid Rev. S. S. Moore—Examining Chaplain	10 00
Paid Rev. G. A. Gibbons—Standing Committee	11 94
Paid G. W. Peterkin, return of money advanced last year	400 00
Total	$5,333 72

RECAPITULATION.

Balance on hand, June, 1902	$ 794 81	
Receipts for year	4,774 48	
		$5,569 29
Bishops' Salaries	4,500 00	
Contingent Expenses	433 72	
Loan returned Bishop G. W. Peterkin	400 00	
Balance on hand	235 57	
		$5,569 29

THE REPORT OF THE TRUSTEES OF THE PERMANENT FUND OF THE DIOCESE OF WEST VIRGINIA, FOR THE PERIOD ENDING MAY 18th, 1903.

The Council having ordered that the session for 1903 should be held at St. Matthew's Church, in Wheeling, on the Wednesday preceding Ascension Day, May 21, 1903, the present report is less complete than might well be wished on account of the delays in getting returns from the different parts of the Diocese.

The figures here given include only funds received up to and including the 18th day of May, 1903.

By order of Council of 1902, *The Central Banking and Security Company, of Parkersburg*, West Virginia, was named as Treasurer of the Permanent Fund, and therefore the accounts given below will include transactions had by the Trustees direct, as well as those occurring after the funds and securities were turned over to the Treasurer on July 15, 1902; and we here record our acknowledgements to the Treasurer and its officers for many courtesies and patient kindnesses.

The Treasurer's statement shows in the hands of the Treasurer (listed as investments and credits)	$18,412 00
Cash	8,198 51
	$26,610 51

DETAILED STATEMENT OF CASH AND INVESTMENT ACCOUNT.

Cash on hand report of June 1st, 1902			$ 978 44
June 2,	To paid by Mr. and Mrs Louis Bennett, note	$ 200 00	
	Interest	16 20	
June 5,	Mr. W. H. Kilmer paid		5 00
June 5.	Mr. A. H. Kreaps on account of interest		40 00
June 5,	Ch., H. E. Spilman, Treas., (Anniversary)		18 25
June 7,	Daughter of the Church		95
June 10,	Mr. A. H. Kreaps, balance interest		50 00
June 14,	Through Bishop Peterkin (25th anniversary):		
	Ligon, Clover Lick	$ 30 00	
	Salt Ridge, Huntersville	2 50	
	Ripley	6 50	
	Chapel Good Shepherd	25 00	64 00
June 14,	Trinity, Parkersburg, Dr. Sharp, Treas		103 50

June 24,	All Saints Union $9.00. Ft. Springs $2.40	11 40
June 28,	All Saints Union	20 00
July 1,	All Saints Union	25
	Christ Church, Pt. Pleasant (25th anniversary)	14 75
	Bruce Chapel $4.50, Mason City $1.00 (same)	5 50
July 3,	Trinity Church, Martinsburg	43 35
July 3,	Lucius Hoge, interest	12 00
July 3,	Mrs. V. E. C. Roome, note $100 and int	118 00
		$ 1,701 59
From this deduct costs of printing last report		9 00
		$ 1,692 59
On July 15th, 1902, the Trustees deposited this money with the Security Company		$ 1,692 59

Amounts collected by the Treasurer being aggregate of all moneys and securities handled by Treasurer		$30,973 51	
Less securities on hand	$18,412 00		
And cash above	1,692 59	20,104 59	10,868 92

CONTRA.

1902.		
Sept. 3, Paid Mr. R. M. Browne, Tr., (Bishop's salaries)	$ 500 00	
Sept. 8, Loaned to Alex Laird and others on mortgage	3,000 00	
Dec. 22, Paid Mr. R. M. Browne, Tr., (Bishops' salaries)	200 00	
1903.		
Jan. 6, Refunded C. P. Flick, Treas., St. Mathews int. paid twice	138 00	
Mar. 7, Paid to R. M. Browne, Tr., (Bishops' salaries)	300 00	
May 12, Paid to R. M. Browne, Tr. (Bishops' salaries)	225 00	
Cash in hands of Treasurer as per report of Central Banking and Security Co	8,198 51	
	$ 12,561 51	$ 12,561 51

PRESENT CONDITION OF THE FUND.

Security, bonds, pledges, notes and certificates shown by accompanying report of the Treasurer		$ 18,412 00
Cash on hand		8,198 51
Total resources		$ 26,610 51
Total reported Council 1902		22,333 44
Actual net increase is		$ 4,277 07
This is to certifiy that the Central Banking and Security Co., of Parkersburg, W. Va., had on hand at close of business on the 18th day of May, 1903, bonds, notes and items of credit belonging to the Trustees of the Protestant Episcopal Church for the Diocese of West Virginia	$ 18,412 00	
And cash to the credit of B. M. Ambler, Chairman	8,198 51	$ 26,610 51

CENTRAL BANKING AND SECURITY CO.,
By W. H. Ogdin, Cashier.

Attention is again called to the request to remit all monies for the Permanent Fund to The Central Banking and Security Co., Parkersburg, W. Va.

STATEMENT OF SECURITIES AND COLLECTIONS

Delivered to Central Banking and Security Company, of Parkersburg, as Treasurer, by H. H. Moss, R. M. Browne and B. M. Ambler, Trustees of the Permanent Fund of the Protestant Episcopal Church for the Diocese of West Virginia, including receipts by the Treasurer up to and including May 18, 1903.

1902.

July 15,	Notes and securities received from Trustees	$ 20,957 00
July 15,	Cash received from Trustees	1,692 59
Aug. 1,	Coupons The Traders Co., of Clarksburg	15 00
Aug. 4,	Interest J. H. Grimm	30 00
Aug. 9,	Interest Traders Building Association	51 00
Aug. 30,	Trinity Parish, W. H. Sharp, Treas	4 00
Sep. 9,	A. G. Patton, Cr. All Saint's, Union	4 00
Sep. 9,	C. A. Miller	25 00
Sep. 9,	E. Rutledge	3 33
Oct. 3,	Zion Church, S. Howell, Treas	277 91

Oct. 3,	St. Alban's Church, Rev. John R. Joyner............	4 68
Oct. 3,	All Saints Church, Union, W. Va., Rev. G. W. Easter..	2 43
Oct. 3,	Interest Pythian Castle Association	15 00
Oct. 11,	Interest Citizens Building Association..............	60 00
Nov. 17,	Interest W. H. Wolfe, et al.........................	150 00
Dec. 5,	Alice Kreps	90 00
1903.		
Jan. 7,	St. John's Mission, Ripon, W. Va...................	31 00
Jan. 7,	Interest Church, St. Marys, W. Va..................	15 00
Jan. 14,	Interest Church, Bluefield, W. Va...................	9 10
Jan. 28,	Interest Traders Co. of Clarksburg.................	15 00
Jan. 28,	Interest Fannie P. Brady	6 00
Jan. 28,	Interest J. C. Smith	1 50
Feb. 4,	Interest St. Matthew's Church, Wheeling, W. Va....	138 00
Feb. 4,	Interest John H. Grim	30 00
Feb. 4,	Interest H. S. Sands	6 50
Feb. 4,	Interest J. D. Jeffries	3 00
Feb. 13	Interest P. C. Eastham	3 00
Feb. 13,	Interest J. C. Mitchell	98
Feb. 13,	Interest Thos. E. Jeffries	1 50
Feb. 13,	Interest Chas. H. Copp	12 50
Feb. 13,	Interest P. Fountain	6 15
Feb. 13,	Interest Mrs. S. Kitson	2 45
Feb. 13,	Interest Mrs. W. H. Hogeman	3 13
Feb. 13,	Interest Thos. L. Broun	24 00
Feb. 24,	Interest J. R. Johnson	60 00
Apr. 23,	Interest Lillie R. Burlingham	1 30
Apr. 23,	Interest Wm. A. Wilson	6 30
Apr. 23,	Interest Citizens Building Association	60 00
Apr. 23,	Interest Sam R. Nuzum	7 60
		$23,826 45
May 18,	Interest paid in settlement of note of St. Matthews Church for $2,300	5 75
Note of Alex. Laird and others, loan secured by mortgage.....		3,000 00

The following are contributions to the Special 25th Anniversary Fund:

Mch. 24,	Woman's Auxiliary, Williamstown ....$	10 00
Mch. 24,	Mrs. F. J. McClintock, Pocahontas Co	4 00
Mch. 24,	M. A. Stewart, Richmond, Va	100 00
Mch. 24,	Kate W. Lee, Huntington, W. Va	1 50
Mch. 24,	St. Paul's Parish, Weston, W. Va.................	68 36
Mch. 31,	Trinity Parish, W. H. Sharp, Treas...............	3 55

Apr. 23,	Miss Norma Stewart	100 00
Apr. 23,	Rev. C. M. Campbell, Boone Co.....................	8 33
Apr. 23,	The Misses Campbell, Berkeley Springs	5 00
Apr. 23,	"In Memoriam" from a Church Woman............	50 00
Apr. 23,	All Saints Church, Union, W. Va	21 00
Apr. 25,	W. E. Watson, Christ Church, Fairmont	250 00
Apr. 25,	M. H. Penick, Christ Church, Fairmont	100 00
Apr. 25,	S. R. Nuzum, Christ Church, Fairmont	100 00
Apr. 25,	M. L. Hutchinson, Christ Church, Fairmont........	50 00
Apr. 25,	J. O. Watson, Christ Church, Fairmont	50 00
Apr. 25,	A. B. Fleming, Christ Church, Fairmont	50 00
Apr. 25,	Jennie L. Reed, Christ Church, Fairmont	25 00
Apr. 25,	Many R. Sipe, Christ Church, Fairmont	15 00
Apr. 25,	George DeBolt, Christ Church, Fairmont...........	10 00
Apr. 25,	Edwin G. Weed, Christ Church, Fairmont	10 00
Apr. 25,	E. F. Hartley, Christ Church, Fairmont	10 00
Apr. 25,	S. N. Jackson, Christ Church, Fairmont...........	10 00
Apr. 25,	Chas. E. Mauley, Christ Church, Fairmont	10 00
Apr. 25,	Mrs. G. W. Arnett, Christ Church, Fairmont	10 00
Apr. 25,	Rose M. Sweeney, Christ Church, Fairmont........	5 00
Apr. 25,	E. H. McDonnell, Christ Church, Fairmont.........	5 00
Apr. 25.	W. T. Hartman, Christ Church, Fairmont	5 00
Apr. 25,	R. B. Lewis, Christ Church, Fairmont	5 00
Apr. 25,	C. C. Penick, Christ Church, Fairmont	156 00
Apr. 25,	Grace Church, Rev. Robert Meade..................	13 79
Apr. 25,	Elkhorn Church, Rev. Robert Meade	1 00
Apr. 25,	Middleway Church, Rev. A. J. Willis	3 70
Apr. 25,	Lee Town Church, Rev. A. J. Willis	3 45
Apr. 25,	Summit Pt. Church, Rev. A. J. Willis	4 50
May 2,	Christ Church, Williamstown	2 00
May 2,	Christ Church, Wellsburg	17 00
May 2,	Mrs. F. S. Burche	15 00
May 2,	Mrs. E. S. Christy	10 00
May 2,	Mrs. W. B. Paden	25 00
May 2,	B. D. Spilman	100 00
May 2,	Mrs. A. N. Guice, Meridian, Miss	12 00
May 5,	St. Mark's Church, T. R. Reed, Berkeley Springs....	3 00
May 6,	Frank M. Muzzy, Philadelphia	50 00
May 6,	Dr. W. H. Sharp	50 00
May 6,	Mrs. French, Beckley Mission	4 02
May 9,	Mrs. Flora Camden	25 00
May 9,	S. D. Camden	50 00
May 14,	Edward Rutledge, Treas	61 34
May 14,	Miss N. McCandlish	12 00

May 14,	Comyn Lewis	25 75
May 14,	L. . Sands, Treas., Fairmont	529 00
May 14,	L. . Sands, Treas., Elkins	26 00
May 14,	L. . Sands, Treas., Davis	20 00
May 14,	L. . Sands, Treas., Ansted	30 34
May 14,	L. E Sands, Theas., Parkersburg	8 00
May 14,	D. Swain, Emanuel Mission	3 61
May 14,	D. Swain, St. David's Mission	15 00
May 14,	L. E. Sands, Treas., Zion Church, Charles Town....	270 25
May 14,	S. W. Washington, Zion Church, Charles Town......	20 00
May 14,	The Misses Beale, Bruce Chapel, W. Va	18 00
May 14,	Rev. A. J. Willis, Lee Town, W. Va...............	6 00
May 14,	L. E. Sands, Treas., Lee Town....................	14 50
May 14,	L. E. Sands, Treas., Middleway	7 00
May 14,	J. W. Roberts, Parkersburg	25 00
May 14,	J. S. Bragonier	24 32
May 14,	Note W. H. Sharp	25 00
May 16,	Mrs. Mary E. Rathbone	25 00
May 16,	Mrs. W. H. Small	25 00
May 16,	T. B. Camden	50 00
May 16,	A. T. Henderson	3 34
May 18,	W. G. Peterkin, Treas............................	28 00
May 18,	Lucy W. Stewart, Richmond, Va	100 00
May 18,	E. Hope Stewart, Richmond, Va	150 00
May 18,	A. C. Stewart, Richmond, Va	100 00
May 18,	Trinity Church, Martinsburg	8 66
May 18,	St. Paul's Church, Weston	2 00
May 18,	Goood Shepherd Church, Ck. L. E. Sands, Treas....	3 00
May 18,	Moundsville Church, Ck. L. E. Sands, Treas.......	1 55
May 18,	Beury Church, Ck. L. E. Sands, Treas.............	2 00
May 18,	Pt. Pleasant Church, Ck. L. E. Sands, Treas..........	20
May 18,	Bruce Chapel, Ck. L. E. Sands, Treas.............	6 00
May 18,	Middleway, Rev. A. J. Willis, Check	20 00
May 18,	Lee Town, Rev. A. J. Willis, check	50
May 18,	Edward Rutledge, Church, Martinsburg............	5 00
May 18,	Trinity Parish	102 25
May 18,	Nannie B. Bradenbaugh, Parkersburg	50 00
May 18,	M. G. Ambler, Parkersburg	10 00
May 18,	C. Nelly, Parkersburg	50 00
May 18,	J. N. Camden, Parkersburg	500 00
May 18,	W. Vrooman, Parkersburg	100 00
May 18,	G. H. Gordon, Parkersburg	5 00
May 18,	H. M. Beam, Parkersburg	5 00
May 18,	W. S. Mowris, Parkersburg	10 00
		$ 30,973 51

CONTRA.

Cash on hand and disbursements	$ 12,561 51	
Securities, etc., on hand	18,412 00	30,973 51

List of securities, bonds, notes, pledges and certificates of the Protestant Episcopal Church of the Diocese of West Virginia, May 18, 1903:

Investments—

Bond No. 26, The Traders Company of Clarksburg	$ 500 00
Bond No. 8, Pythian Castle Ass'n., of Wheeling	500 00
Note, St. Mary's Church	400 00
Note, Alice H. and Adam T. Kreps, secured by deed of trust	3,000 00
Note, W. H. Wolfe, Joanna Wolf and Bettie G. Walt	5,000 00
Note, J. H. Grimm, secured by deed of trust	1,000 00
Note, Alex Laird et al, secured by deed of trust	3,000 00
Note, St. Andrew's Church	300 00
Certificate No. 276, Citizen's Building Association	2,000 00
	$ 15,700 00
Pledges to fund	60 00
Notes given by way of contribution	2,145 00
Sundry certificates with coupons attached	507 00
	$ 18,412 00

SUPPLEMENTAL REPORT

Referring to resolution of Council, requesting the Trustees to furnish to the Secretary an additional statement to be printed in the Journal for 1903, and to include items received subsequest to the date (May 18th) of the report to Council, the Trustees are not responsible for estimates, and claim accuracy only as to moneys received or covered by definite obligations.

After May 18th they received the following:

John W. Norris, $10.00, W. T. Greer $3,00	$ 13 00
John A. Davenport, $5.00, Venable Johnson, Tr., $7.92	12 92
Bunker Hill, $0.69, C. T. Hiteshew, $5.00, H. P. Moss, $10.00	15 69
Church, Morgantown	136 27
Marlinton, $7.50, Paintsville, Ky., $10.00	17 50
Jos. Bryan, Richmond, Va	100 00
	$295 38

Prior to the meeting of Council, notice seems to have been given that at the offering to be taken on Ascension Day, it was hoped that all contributions for this Anniversary Fund would be laid on the plate. Some contributions were accordingly made on that occasion, and memoranda and estimates were also made by representatives as to what had been paid through other channels.

The following statement shows tabulated result of that offering, including all memoranda:

ASCENSION DAY OFFERING 1903.

	Actual Cash and Checks.	Memorandum of Amounts Previously Paid And Placed in Plate Ascension Day 1903.	New Pledges.
Berkeley Springs, (currency $14.00, check $10.00)	$ 24.00	$	$
Bruce Chapel		22.50	
Martinsburg	12.00	110.00	
St. Paul's, Weston		70.36	
Point Pleasant	32 50	14.75	
Spilman	12.00	18.25	
Fairmont		1,405.00	
Trinity, Parkersburg		3,306.06	
Lewisburg			
Ronceverte			
White Sulphur	78.50		
Clover Lick			
Glen Jean			
Beury			
Chapel of Good Shepherd Parkersburg	250.00		
St. Luke's, Wheeling	586.74		150.00
St. Matthew's	3,543.75	2,300.00	700.00
St. Andrew's, Wheeling	67.48		
Ravenswood	40.00		
Huntington	121.00		
St. Marys	110.00	100.00	
Geo. C. Thomas, Philadelphia	500.00		
Sistersville	31.89		
Harper's Ferry	37.00	18.00	
New Martinsville	50.00		
Moundsville	150.00		
Bluefield	5.65		
Morgantown, (check promised)			136 62 (since paid)
Romney, including gifts from 5 persons out of the Diocese	446.25	52.74	
Moorefield	17.57		
Okonoko	8.25		
Paw-Paw	8.14		
All Saint's Union	37.95		
Messiah, Alderson	1.00	9.25	
St. John's, Charleston	669.88	114.80	
Bramwell	38.44	4.00	
Eckman		14.44	
Elkhorn		1.00	
Hedgesville	8.05		
Open Offering	135.99		
Ansted		38.61	
Powellton		22.10	
Montgomery		12.32	
Mt. Carbon		3.61	
	$ 7,024.08	$ 7,634.81	$ 986.62

NOTE:—The second column is an approximation, evidently, and the discrepancy between actual results and the statement may be largely accounted for by giving there $2,300 as previously paid by St. Matthew's Church on this 25th Anniversary Fund, while that sum was reported prior to 1901, as theretofore pledged.

RECAPITULATION

Cash and checks on plate, Ascension Day, 1903	$ 7,024 03
Memorandum of amounts previously paid	7,634 81
New pledges and notes given on Ascension Day, including check promised from Morgantown	986 62
Grand total	$ 15,645 49

The Trustees find the first column of the foregoing to be correct.

They have received from Ascension Day collection:

Actual cash and checks	$ 7,024 03	
And a note for	150 00	
		$ 7,174 03

They have pledges from individuals in Parkersburg, not heretofore stated in their accounts:

6 of $250	$ 1,500 00	
2 of $25	50 00	
1 of $5	5 00	
		$ 1,555 00

This will give present condition of Fund—

Amount reported as of May 18, 1903	$ 26,610 51
Sundry amounts above listed	295 38
Ascension Day collection (including note)	7,174 03
Parkersburg pledges	1,555 00
	$ 35,634 92
Total reported to Council of 1902	22,333 44
Actual increase	$ 13,301 48

June 5, 1903.

B. M. AMBLER,
Chairman of Trustees.

APPENDIX C.

Parochial Reports for the Year Ending April 30th, 1903, Arranged According to Alphabetical Clergy List.

PAROCHIAL REPORTS

FOR THE YEAR ENDING APRIL 30th, 1902.

PAROCHIAL REPORT.

Rev. JOHN S. ALFRIEND, address Charles Town. Zion Church, Charles Town, Jefferson county. Present minister took charge March 1st, 1902.

Church Officers **— Church Wardens, B. C. Washington, Frank Beckwith; other Vestrymen, S. W. Washington, Geo. Elster, Wm. Packett, Joseph Trapnell, C. Green, Rich'd Henderson, Scott Kennedy, Rich'd Alexander, Jno. W. Russel, Thornton Perry; Registrar, S. W. Washington, address Charles Town; Treasurer, S. W. Washington, address Charles Town; Sunday School Secretary and Treasurer, Rich'd Alexander; Lay Reader, Joseph Trapnell.**

Official Acts**—Baptisms, infants 3, adults 6, total 9; presented for confirmation since last report 9, marriages 12, burials 14, catechisings 43, public services, Sundays, 113, other days 110, total 223; Holy Communion, public, 28, private 1, total 29.**

Communicants**—Number last reported 401, received by letter 2, admitted by confirmation 9, total gain 11; died 9, transferred 6, not otherwise accounted for 71, total loss 86; net loss 75; present number total 326.**

Congregations**—Confirmed persons connected with Parish 350, baptized persons connected with Parish 550, families 160, sittings in Church 600, free sittings 100, sittings in Chapel 150, sittings in Sunday School room 150.**

Rector's Salary**—As pledged from this congregation $1,250.00.**

Organizations**—Sunday Schools, officers and teachers, male 5; female, 11; total, 16; pupils, male, 34, female, 66, total, 100; advent offering, $37.00, lenten offering, $40.00, other offerings, $23.00, total Sunday School offerings, $100.00; Industrial Schools, officers and teachers 2, scholars 10, total 12; Brotherhood ot St. Andrew, members 27; Woman Auxiliary, members 70; Babies Branch Auxiliary, 19; St. Andrew's Guild, 40; Mexican Guild, 14; Chancel Chapter, 6; Children of the King, 20; Library Association, 20.**

Property**—Church, brick, insurance $9,000, value $13,000; rectory, brick,**

insurance $2,475; value $5,000; parish house, brick, insurance $1,600; value $3,000; other property, frame, insurance $2,000; value $3,000; total insurance, $15,075; total value, $23,000; indebtedness, on other property, $575; total indebtedness, $575.

FINANCIAL REPORT.

Receipts—Current Expenses—Pledges and subscriptions, $126.00; pew rent, $1,878.25; collections in Church, $186.04; total receipts for current expenses, $2,190.29. *For all purposes other than current expenses* (*i. e. Contributions*)—Cash on hand, per last report, $398.11; collections in church, $1,921.80; Sunday School, $98.57; Woman's Auxiliary, $229.79; other sources, $696.68; total receipts for contributions, $3,344.95; grand total of all receipts i. e. for current expenses and contributions, $5,534.74.

Disbursements—Current expenses (*parochial*)—Salary of Rector, $1,-250.00; other salaries, $400.00; maintaining Sunday Schools, $39.20; ordinary repairs, $66.43; interest on debt, $78.25; payment on debt, $130.00; other current expenses, $190.09; cash on hand, $36.32; total for current expenses, $2,190.29. *Contributions—Parochial*—Communion alms $54.50, Parish Missions $212.14, other objects $126.64, total for Parochial contributions $403.28. *Diocesan*—Salary of Bishops $400.00, Permanent Fund $568.16, Diocesan Missions $300.00, Convocation Missions $159.70, widows and orphans, aged and disabled clergy fund $64.11, religious and theological education $63.14, Sheltering Arms Hospital $70.07, Bishop's Special Fund $100.00, other objects $331.43, total Diocesan contributions $2,056.61. *Objects without the Diocese* — Domestic missions general, $47.48; Jews, $11.80; through American Church Missionary Society, $25.00; total domestic missions, $84.28. Foreign missions general, $60.23; for Mexico, $60.00; through American Church Missionary Society, $159.50; Brazil, $63.00; total Foreign Missions, $342.73; total foreign and domestic missions, $427.01; Woman's Auxiliary, money, $154.86; boxes, value, $74.93; total without diocese, $427.01.

Financial Summary—Contributions—Parochial, $403.28; Diocesan, $2,-056.61; extra diocesan, $427.01; total contributions, $2,886.90. *Expenses*—current parochial, $2,190.29; cash on hand, $467.55; grand total of all money raised by the congregation, $5,077.19; cash on hand, $467.55; total $5,534.74.

Remarks—St. Philips and St. Andrews Chapels and Harewood Mission—for each of which separate reports are sent—are all under my care. And decided progress can be reported. The new rector, Rev. M. F. Duty, will take charge of St. Philip's Colored Church May 31st. A Deaconess has been secured for St. Andrew's June 1st, and Deaconess House to be built at once. The net loss of 75 communicants reported is owing to a careful revision of the old Parish register and opening of a new one.—JNO. S. ALFRIEND, *Rector*.

PAROCHIAL REPORT.

Rev. JNO. S. ALFRIEND, address, Charles Town. St. Andrew's Church, Blue Ridge Mission, Jefferson county; date of organization, 1891; present minister took charge March 1, 1902.

Church Officers—Superintendent of Sunday School, John Howell.

Official Acts—Baptisms, infants 8; presented for confirmation since last report 3, marriages 1, burials 3, public services, Sundays 24, other days 10, total 34; Holy Communion, public, 2 private 1 total 3.

Communicants Number last reported 25, admitted by confirmation 3, total gain 3; net gain 3; present number total 28.

Congregations—Confirmed persons connected with Parish 28, baptized persons connected with parish 45, families 40, number sittings in chapel 150, number sittings in Sunday School room 150.

Organizations—Sunday Schools, officers and teachers, male 2, female 5, total 7; pupils, male 30, female 40, total 70; total Sunday School offerings, $250.

Property—Chapel, frame, value $600.00; insurance included in Zion Church property.

FINANCIAL REPORT.

Receipts—Current Expenses—Collections in Church, $5.00; total receipts for current expenses, $5.00. *For all purposes other than current expenses (i. e. Contributions)*—Collections in Church $10.00, grand total of all receipts i. e. for current expenses and contributions $15.00.

Disbursements—Current Expenses (Parochial)—Other current expenses $5.00, total for current expenses $5.00. *Diocesan*—Sheltering Arms Hospital $10.00, total Diocesan contributions $10.00.

Financial Summary—Contributions—Diocesan $10.00, total contributions $10.00. *Expenses*—Current Parochial $5.00, grand total of all money raised by the congregation $15.00.

Remarks—This work is among the mountain people and is vigorously pushed by the workers from Zion Church. We expect to have a Deaconess to locate here and are about to put up a house for her home. The rector goes over there two Sundays in the month and has had a most successful mission during the year, conducted by the Rev. T. S. Douglass, of Martinsburg.—JNO. S. ALFRIEND, *Rector*.

PAROCHIAL REPORT.

Rev. JNO. S. ALFRIEND, address Charles Town. Harewood Mission, Jefferson county. Present minister took charge March 1st, 1902.

Church Officers — Superintendent of Sunday School, Frank Beckwith.

Official Acts—Public services, Sundays, 12; total, 12.

Organizations—Sunday Schools, officers and teachers, male 2, female 3, total 5; pupils, male 25, female 15, total 40; total Sunday School offerings $2.50.

Property—Use public school house.

FINANCIAL REPORT.

Receipts—For all purposes other than current expenses, (i. e. Contributions)—Collection in Church $5.11, other sources $6.00, grand total of all receipts i. e. for current expenses and contributions $11.11.

Disbursements—Contributions—Parochial—Other objects, $11.11. *Diocesan*—Sheltering Arms Hospital $5.11.

Financial Summary—Contributions—Diocesan $5.11, total contributions $5.11, grand total of all money raised by the congregation $5.11, cash on hand, $6.00.

Remarks—This is a mission point where we conduct service one Sunday afternoon in the month in public school building. The Sunday School is carried on as there is none in the neighborhood. The few adult people and nearly all of the children belong to other denominations.—T. S. ALFRIEND.

PAROCHIAL REPORT.

Rev. JNO. S. ALFRIEND, address Charles Town. St. Philip's Col. Church, Charles Town, Jefferson county. Date of organization, 1891. Present minister took charge March 1, 1902.

Church Officers—Church wardens, John Wesley Talbot, Philip Jackson; other vestrymen, Ezekiel Morris, Lucien Warwick; Registrar, Philip Jackson, address Charles Town; treasurer, Wesley Talbot, address Charles Town; Superintendt of Sunday Schools, B. C. Washington.

Official Acts—Burial 1, Catechisings 5, public services, Sundays 25, total 25; holy communion, public 2, total 2.

Communicants—Number last reported 50, present number total, 50.

Congregations—Confirmed persons connected with parish 52, baptized persons connected with parish 79, families 25, individuals not thus included 10, number sittings in Church 250, number free sittings 250.

Organizations—Sunday Schools, officers and teachers, male 2, female 8, total 10; pupils, male 36, female 48, total 84; total Sunday School offerings $5.00.

Property—Church, frame, value $900.00; rectory, frame, value $525.00; insurance on church and rectory, $1,150; total value, $1,425.00.

FINANCIAL REPORT.

Receipts—Current Expenses—Collections in Church $18.73, other sources $313.80; total reeeipts for current expenses $332.53. *For all purposes other then current expenses, (i. e. Contributions)* — Collections in Church $20.00, other sources $8.46, total receipts for contributions $28.46; grand total of all receipts i. e. for current expenses and contributions, $360.99.

Disbursements—Current Expenses (Parochial)—Other salaries $300.00, other current expenses $18.73, other objects $13.80, total for current expenses $323.53. *Contributions—Parochial*—Other objects $8.46; total parochial contributions $8.46. *Diocesan*—Diocesan missions $10.00; total diocesan contributions $10.00. *Objects without the Diocese*—Foreign missions general, $10.00; total foreign missions $10.00; total foreign and domestic missions, $10.00.

Financial Summary—Contributions—Parochial $8.46, diocesan $10.00, extra diocesan $10.00, total contributions $28.46. *Expenses*—Current parochial $323.53; grand total of all money raised by the congregation $351.99.

Remarks—The services of this Church have been maintained for the past fiscal year by students from the Theological Seminary of Virginia, assisted by the Rector. Rev. M. F. Duty, a colored minister, will take charge June 1st, 1903.—T. S. ALFRIEND, *Rector*.

PAROCHIAL REPORT.

Rev. JACOB BRITTINGHAM, address 66 So. Penn. St. Lukes Church, Island Parish, Wheeling, Ohio County. Date of organization June 22, 1881. Present minister took charge March 3, 1889.

Church Officers—Church Wardens, Jas. P. Rogers, Lawrence E. Sands; other vestrymen, M. A. Wilson, E. B. Bowie, C. H. Copp, A. A. Taylor, Thos. Johns, Wylie Irwin, M. R. Wolff; registrar, M. A. Wilson, address Cor. Main and 12th; treasurer, Lawrence E. Sands, Wheeling; superintendent of Sunday Schools, Lawrence E. Sands; Sunday School Secretary and Treasurer, Robt. L. Boyd; lay reader, A. A. Taylor.

Official Acts—Baptisms, infants 9, adults 2, total 11; presented for confirmation since last report 18, marriages 17, burials 15, catechisings 12, public services, Sundays 100, other days 70, total 170; holy communion, public 16, private 1, total 17.

Communicants—Number last reported, 258; received by letter 10, admitted by confirmation 18, total gain 28; transferred 14, removed without letter 6, total loss 20; net gain 8, present number total 266.

Congregations—Confirmed persons connected with Parish 281, baptized

persons connected with Parish 382, families 171, individuals not thus included 31, whole number of individuals 413, number sittings in Church 400, number free sittings 400, number sittings in Parish House 200, number sittings in Sunday School room 200.

Rector's Salary—As pledged from this Congregation $1,500; total, $1,500.

Organizations—Sunday Schools, officers and teachers, male 4, female 9, total 13; pupils, male 20, female 80, total 100; advent offering $10.25; lenten offering $40; other offerings $94.55; total Sunday School offerings $144.80; Brotherhood of St. Andrew, members 5; Womans Auxiliary, members 20; King's Daughters, 42; Chancel Chapter, 18; Jr. King's Daughters, 20; Jr. Woman's Auxiliary, 7.

Property—Church, frame, insurance $6,000; value $12,000; rectory, insurance $2,000; value $5,000; Parish house, insurance $4,500; value $9,000; organ, value $2,500; total insurance $13,000; total value $28,500; indebtedness, loan, $1,000.00; total indebtedness $1,000.00.

FINANCIAL REPORT.

Receipts—Current Expenses—Cash on hand, per last report, $22.98; pledges and subscriptions, $2,469.87; collections in Church, $773.47; total receipts for current expenses, $3,266.32. *For all purposes other than current expenses, (i. e. Contributions)*—Cash on hand, per last report, $22.98; pledges and subscriptions, $2,469.87; collections in Church, $773.47; Sunday School, $144.80; Woman's Auxiliary, $175.98; other sources, Jr. Woman's Auxiliary, $22.00; Chancel Chapter, $393.60; King's Daughters, $171.15; total receipts for contributions, $4,173.85.

Disbursements—Current expenses (Parochial)—Salary of Rector $1,500, salary of assistant $500, other salaries $220.50, ordinary repairs $170.49, interest on debt $75.28, payment on debt $300.00, other current expenses $300.05, total for current expenses $3,266.32. *Contributions — Parochial —* Communion alms $29.51, extraordinary repairs and improvements $488.60, charity $22.00, day nursery $51.15, total parochial contributions $591.26. *Diocesan*—Salary of Bishops $150, permanent fund $736.74, diocesan missions $175.00, convocation missions, Chester $25, widows and orphans, aged and disabled clergy fund $48.20, religious and theological education $17.35, Sheltering Arms Hospital $31.61, Bishop's special fund $150.00, St. Mary's W. Va. $15.00, total diocesan contributions $1,348.90. *Objects without the Diocese*—Domestic missions general $59.31, Jews $8.15, total domestic missions $67.46; foreign missions general $93.92, for China $45.00, Brizil, W. Aux. Ins. 5, total foreign missions $143.92; total foreign and domestic missions, $211.38; Woman's Auxiliary, money, $22.00; Woman's Auxiliary boxes, value, $108.98, total without diocese, $337.36.

Financial Summary—Contributions—Parochial $591.26, diocesan $1,-348.90; extra diocesan $337.36, total contributions $2,277.52. *Expenses*, current parochial $326.65, grand total of all money raised by the congregation, $5,543.84.

PAROCHIAL REPORT.

Rev. ROBT. U. BROOKING, address Wickliffe, Va., St. John's Church, St. Johns Mission, Rippon, Jefferson county. Present minister took charge June 1, 1903.

Church Officers—Church Wardens, Dr. Howard Osburn, Mr. Corbin La Rue; other vestrymen, Robt. Wire, John Kanode, Lafayette Sommers, John B. Page; registrar, Robt. Wire, address Rippon, W. Va.; treasurer, Dr. Howard Osburn, address Rippon, W. Va.; superintendent of Sunday Schools, Dr. Howard Osburn; Sunday School Secretary and Treasurer, Mrs. E. H. Kanode.

Official Acts—Baptisms, infants 1, total 1; presented for confirmation since last report 1, catechisings 13, public services, Sundays 69, other days 7, total 76; holy communion, public 14, total 14.

Communicants—Number last reported 28, admitted by confirmation 1, total gain 1; transferred 1, total loss 1; present number total 28.

Congregations—Confirmed persons connected with Parish 29, baptized persons connected with parish 65, families 24, individuals not thus included 1, whole number of individuals 110, number free sittings 180.

Rector's salary—As pledged from this congregation $150, from diocesan missions $100, as pledged from other congregations $400, from convocation missions $50, total $700.00.

Organizations—Officers and teachers, male 1, female 4, total 5; pupils, male 11, female 13, total 24; advent offering $549, lenten offerings $6.59, other offerings $10.90, total Sunday School offerings $22.98; Brotherhood of St. Andrew, members 3, Woman's Auxiliary, members 20, other organizations, Ladies' Aid 14; location of schools mentioned above, St. John's Rippon.

Property—Church, insurance $2,000.00; value, $3,000.00; total insurance, $2,000.00; total value $3,000.

FINANCIAL REPORT.

Receipts—Current Expenses—Pledges and subscriptions $150.00; collections in Church $34.95; for maintenance of Sunday School $15.00, money raised by Ladies' Aid $69.00, total receipts for current expenses $268.95. *For all purposes other than current expenses, (i. e. Contributions)*—Collections in Church $74.34, Sunday School $22.98, Woman's Auxiliary

$22.48, special for Chancel furniture $58.50, box sent by Aux. valued at $15.00; permanent fund $31.00; total receipts for contributions $224.30; grand total of all receipts i. e. for current expenses and contributions $493.25.

***Disbursements Current Expenses (Parochial)*— Salary of Rector $150.00, other salaries $16.50, maintaining Sunday Schools $15.00, ordinary repairs $69.00, other current expenses $18.45, total for current expenses $268.95. *Contributions—Parochial*—Communion alms $22.65, special for chancel furniture placed in memory of Rosa Nelson Neill Osburn $58.50, total parochial contributions $81.15. *Diocesan*—Salary of Bishops $20.00, permanent fund $31.00, diocesan missions $16.29, convocation missions $7.50, widows and orphans, aged and disabled clergy fund $2.16, Sheltering Arms Hospital $4.67, total diocesan contributions $81.62. *Objects without the Diocese*—Domestic missions general $8.54, deaf and dumb $2.00, Jews $1.95, total domestic missions $12.49; foreign missions general $8.54, Brazil $3.02, total foreign missions $11.56, total foreign and domestic missions $24.05; Woman's Auxiliary, money $22.48, Woman's Auxiliary Boxes, value $15.00, total without diocese $37.48.**

***Financial Summary—Contributions*—Parochial $81.15, diocesan $81.62, extra diocesan $61.53, total contributions $224.30. *Expenses*—Current parochial $258.95, grand total of all money raised by the congregation $493.25.**

***Remarks*—I have accepted a call to Harrisonburg, Va., and have handed my resignation to take effect June 1st, 1903. Respectfully, ROBT. U. BROOKING.**

PAROCHIAL REPORT.

Rev. ROBT. U. BROOKING. Address Wickliffe, Va. Christ Chapel, Blue Ridge Mission, Jefferson county. Present Minister took charge June 1st, 1900.

Church Officers—Church Warden, Marion Pomeroy.

Official Acts—Presented for confirmation, since last report 3, burials 1. public services, Sundays 10, other days 1, total 11; holy communion, public 1, total 1.

Communicants—Number last reported 3, admitted by confirmation 3, total gain 3; net gain (or loss) 3, present number total 6.

Congregations—Confirmed persons connected with Parish 7, baptized persons connected with Parish 20, families 5, individuals not thus included 2, while number of individuals 40, number free sittings 125.

Organizations—Sunday Schools, officers and teachers, male 1, female 3. total 4; pupils, male 22, female 24, total 46.

Property—Church, insurance $500.00; value, $800.00.

FINANCIAL REPORT.

Receipts—Current Expenses—Collections in Church $3.00.

Disbursements—Current Expenses (Parochial)—Insurance $1.00, Sunday School $2.00, total for current expenses $3.00.

Financial Summary—Expenses, current parochial $3.00, grand total of all money raised by the congregation $3.00.

Remarks—The Sunday School ran during the summer. At Christmas the people of St. Johns Church, Rippon and Wickliffe, Va., gave contributions of toys and money to have a Christmas tree for the mountain children. The choirs of the said churches furnished the music. This was the first Christmas celebration ever held in Christ Chapel and was much appreciated by both children and adults.

PAROCHIAL REPORT.

Rev. E. H. BROSIUS. Address Bluefield, W. Va. Christ Church, Mission, Bluefield, Mercer county. Present minister took charge December 1, 1901.

Church Officers—Church wardens, Geo. H. Hill, R. C. Turner; other vestrymen, Geo. H. Wade, T. H. Becker, A. de W. Howard, R. A. Lacy, W. H. B. Loving, F. R. Wadleigh, E. H. Smith; registrar, R. A. Lacy, Bluefield; treasurer, Geo. H. Wade, Bluefield; superintendent of Sunday Schools, R. C. Turner, Bluefield; Sunday School secretary and treasurer, Henry Becker.

Official Acts—Baptisms, infants 4, adults 1, total 5; presented for confirmation since last report 4, burials 4, public services, Sundays 46, other days 19, total 65, holy communion, public 14, total 14.

Communicants—Number last reported 72, admitted by confirmation 4, added otherwise 30, total gain 34; died 1, removed without letter 10, lapsed 2, not otherwise accounted for 2; total loss 15; net gain 19; present number total 91.

Congregations—Confirmed persons connected with Parish 91, baptized persons connected with Parish 140, families 45, individuals not thus included 12, whole number of individuals 170, number sittings in Church 200.

Rector's Salary—As pledged from this congregation $300.00, from diocesan missions $150.00, from general board $100.00, as pledged from other congregations $250.00, total $800.00.

Organizations—Sunday Schools, officers and teachers, male 2, female 3, total 5; pupils, male 17, female 20, total 37; advent offering $2.75, lenten offering $8.06, other offerings $3.86, total Sunday School offerings $14.67.

Other organizations, Ladies' Guild, Chancel Chapter, Social Guild, Charity Chapter.

Property—Church, wood; insurance, $1,500; value, $2,000; rectory, wood; insurance, $800.00; value, $1,500; total insurance, $2,300; total value, $3,500; indebtedness, organ $435.54; total indebtedness $435.54.

FINANCIAL REPORT.

Receipts—Current Expenses—Cash on hand, per last report $18.05, pledges and subscriptions $683.11, collections in Church $37.32, offerings for general missions $60.00, total receipts for current expenses $748.48. *For all purposes other than current expenses, (i. e. Contributions)*—Money borrowed $435.54; Easter offering $56.05; Sunday School $14.67; special offering for organ $50.00, Com. Alms and organiaztion $361.25, total receipts for contributions $917.51; grand total of all receipts i. e. for current expenses and contributions $1,665.99.

Disbursements—Current expenses (Parochial)— Salary of Rector $300.00, other salaries $64.20, insurance $35.10, ordinary repairs $11.88, payment on debt $209.10, other current expenses $52.53, other objects $9.24, total for current expenses $682.05. *Contributions Parochial*—Communion alms $16.20, extraordinary repairs and improvements $267.97, organizations $12.61, organ $480.00, total parochial contributions $776.78. *Diocesan*—Salary of Bishops $30.00, diocesan missions $30.00, widows and orphans, aged and disabled clergy fund $2.65, Sunday School Advent offering $2.75, for Welch $5.00, total diocesan contributions $70.40. *Objects without the Diocese*—Total foreign and domestic missions $68.06; total without diocese $68.06.

Financial Summary—Total contributions $1,230.45. *Expenses*—Current parochial $1,458.83; grand total of all money raised by the congregation $1,665.99.

PAROCHIAL REPORT.

Rev. E. H. BROSIUS. Address Bluefield. Heavenly Rest, Mission, Princeton, Mercer county. Present minister took charge December 1, 1901.

Church Officers—Registrar, H. B. Barbor, address Princeton; treasurer, H. B. Barbor.

Official Acts—Baptisms, infants 2, total 2; presented for confirmation since last report 1, marriages 1, public services, Sundays 9, other days 2, total 11; holy communion, public 4, total 4.

Communicants—Number last reported 21, admitted by confirmation 1, total gain 1; transferred 1, removed without letter 3, total loss 4; net loss 3; present number total 18.

Congregations—Confirmed persons connected with Parish 18, baptized persons connected with Parish 20, families 10, number sittings in Church 150.

Rector's Salary—As pledged from this congregation $50, from diocesan missions $150, from general board $100.00, as pledged from other congregations $500, total $800.00.

Property—Church, wood. Indebtedness, due the Minister $30.00, due on diocesan assessment for missions $6.00, due on diocesan assessment for Bishop's fund $6.00, total indebtedness $42.

FINANCIAL REPORT.

Receipts—Current Expenses—Pledges and subscriptions $39.42, collections in Church $10.93, total receipts for current expenses $50.35; grand total of all receipts i. e. for current expenses and contributions $50.35.

Disbursements—Current expenses (Parochial)—Salary of Rector $20.00, other objects $4.75, total for current expenses $24.75.

Financial Summary Grand total of all money raised by the congregation $50.35.

PAROCHIAL REPORT.

Rev. C. M. CAMPBELL. Address Racine. Christ's Church. Short Creek, Boone county. Present minister took charge April 1, 1902.

Official Acts—Marriages 2, burials 2, public services, Sundays 12, other days 2, total 14; holy communion, public 3, total 3.

Communicants—Number last reported 7, lapsed 5, total loss 5; net loss 5; present number total 2.

Congregations—Confirmed persons connected with Parish 7, baptized persons connected with Parish 10, families 4, individuals not thus included 10, whole number of individuals 20.

Rector's salary—From diocesan missions $200.00, total $200.00.

Organizations—Sunday Schools, officers and teachers, female 2, total 2; pupils, male 8, female 8, total 16.

Property—Church, Log; value $400; total value $400.

FINANCIAL REPORT.

Receipts—For all purposes other than current expenses, (i. e. Contributions)—Collections in Church 87 cents; total receipts for contributions 87 cents; grand total of all receipts i. e. for current expenses and contributions, 87 cents.

Disbursements—Diocesan—Diocesan missions, 87 cents; total diocesan contributions, 87 cents.

Financial Summary—Contributions, diocesan 87 cents; total contributions 87 cents; grand total of all money raised by the congregation 87 cents.

Remarks—An admirer of the Bishop, but not connected with the Church gave $5.00 to the Permanent Fund, for the Ascension Day offering.

PAROCHIAL REPORT.

Rev. C. M. CAMPBELL. Address Racine. St. Paul's Mission, Bull Creek, Boone county. Present minister took charge April 1, 1902.

Official Acts—Baptisms, infants 1, total 1; public services, Sundays 6, other days 1, total 7; holy communion, public 2, total 2.

Communicants—Number last reported 7, removed without letter 1, not otherwise accounted for 2, total loss 3; net loss 3, present number total 4.

Congregations—Confirmed persons connected with Parish 6, baptised persons connected with Parish 10, families 4, whole number of individuals 10.

FINANCIAL REPORT.

Receipts—For all purposes other than current expenses, (i. e. Contributions)—Other sources, 57 cents; total receipts for contributions, 57 cents; grand total of all receipts i. e. for current expenses and contributions, 57 cents.

Disbursements—Diocesan—Permanent fund 50 cents, diocesan missions 7 cents, total diocesan contributions 57 cents.

Financial Summary—Contributions—Diocesan 57 cents, total contributions 57 cents; grand total of all money raised by the congregation, 57 cents.

Remarks—The services are held in a school house on Bull Creek. There is no Sunday School, for the lack of someone to conduct it.

PAROCHIAL REPORT.

Rev. C. M. CAMPBELL. Address Racine. Emmanuel Mission, Mouth of Robinson, Boone county. Present minister took charge April 1, 1902.

Official Acts—Burials 1, public services, Sundays 6, total 6; holy communion, public 3, total 3.

Communicants—Number last reported 4, added otherwise 1, total gain 1; died 1, total loss 1; present number total 4.

Congregations—Confirmed persons connected with Parish 4, baptized

persons connected with Parish 7, families 2, individuals not thus included 8, whole number of individuals 15.

FINANCIAL REPORT.

Receipts—For all purposes other than current expenses, (i. e. Contributions)—Collections in Church 15 cents, other sources $1.33, total receipts for contributions $1.48; grand total of all receipts i. e. for current expenses and contributions $1.48.

Disbursements—Diocesan—Permanent fund 83 cents, diocesan missions 15 cents, total diocesan contributions 98 cents. *Objects without the Diocese*—Domestic missions general 25 cents, total domestic missions 25 cents; foreign missions general 25 cents, total foreign missions 25 cents; total foreign and domestic missions, 50 cents; total without diocese 50 cents.

Financial Summary—Contributions—Diocesan 98 cents, extra diocesan 50 cents; total contributions $1.48; grand total of all money raised by the congregation $1.48.

Remarks—As we have no building, the services are held in an old log cabin. It is expected that the Sunday School will be reopened in the near future.

PAROCHIAL REPORT.

Rev. WILSON PAGE CHRISMAN. Address Moundsville, W. Va., Trinity Church, Trinity Parish, Moundsville, Marshall county. Date of organization 1848 Present minister took charge June 1st, 1902.

Church Officers—Church wardens, V. A. Weaver, C. R. Oldham; other vestrymen, Friend Cox, A. J. Martin, C. L. Walton, C. A. Weaver, J. T. Gallaher, M. P. Hendrickson, A. R. Laing; registrar, J. T. Gallaher, address Moundsville, W. Va.; treasurer, C. L. Walton, address Moundsville, W. Va.; superintendent of Sunday School, Friend Cox, address Moundsville, W. Va.; Sunday School secretary and treasurer, Frank H. Weaver.

Official Acts—Baptisms, infants 6, adults 2, total 8; presented for confirmation since last report 6, marriages 5, burials 2; public services, Sundays 105, other days 112, total 217; holy communion, public 24, total 24.

Communicants—Number last reported 50, received by letter 7, admitted by confirmation 6, added otherwise 4, total gain 17; died 1, transferred 8, removed without letter 1, lapsed 2, total loss 12; net gain 5, present number total 55.

Congregations—Confirmed persons connected with Parish 72, baptized

persons connected with Parish 139, families 47, individuals not thus included 29, whole number of individuals 153, number of scattered communicants in your section not connected with any Parish 11, number sittings in Church 200; number free sittings 200; number sittings in Chapel 25 number sittings in Sunday School room 225.

Rector's Salary—As pledged from this congregation, $1,250.00; total $1,250.00.

Organizations—Sunday Schools, officers and teachers, male 4, female 5, total 9; pupils, male 42, female 64, total 106; advent offering $20.00, lenten offering $31.25, other offerings $44.80; total Sunday School offerings $96.05; other organizations, Trinity Guild $171.45. Location of Schools mentioned above, Moundsville, W. Va.

Property—Church, frame, insurance $4,000.00, value $8,000.00; rectory, frame, insurance $2,000.00, value $5,000.00; Parish house, brick, insurance $5,000.00, value $20.000.00; total insurance $11,000.00; total value $33.000.00; indebtedness, on Parish house $2,600.00; total indebtedness, $2,600.00.

FINANCIAL REPORT.

Receipts—Current expenses—Pledges and subscriptions $1,145.87, collections in Church $412.50; other sources, Trinity Guild $171.45, from Sunday School $44.80, total receipts for current expenses $2,255.52. *For all purposes other than current expenses, (i. e. Contributions)*—Collections in Church $377.95, Sunday School $51.25, Parish house $5,556.46; grand total of all receipts i. e. for current expenses and contributions $8,241.18.

Disbursements—Current expenses. (Parochial)—Salary of Rector $1,145.87, insurance $93.00, maintaining Sunday Schools $69.80, ordinary repairs $781.13, interest on debt $102.91, other objects $62.81, total for current expenses $2,255.52. *Contributions — Parochial* — Communion alms $14.12, Parish missions $3.55, other objects, Sunday School $1.65, Parish house $5,556.46, total parochial contributions $5,575.78. *Diocesan* — Salary of Bishops $60.00, permanent fund $151.55, diocesan missions $40.00, convocation missions $15.86, widows and orphans, aged and disabled clergy fund $16.85, religious and theological education $4.55, Sheltering Arms Hospital $12.15, Theological Seminary $7.20, total diocesan contributions $308.16. *Objects without the Diocese*—Domestic missions general $13.39, colored people $3.55, Indians $1.90, deaf and dumb $3.60, Jews $3.32, through American Church Missionary Society $2.45, total domestic Missions $28.21; foreign missions general $13.31, for Mexico $1.85, through American Church Missionary Society $3.35, total foreign Missions $18.51; total foreign and domestic missions $46.72; American Church Building fund $2.75, general clergy relief fund $2.70, Bible and Prayer Book Society $5.00, other objects, general missions $44.55, total without diocese $101.72.

Financial Summary — Contributions — Parochial $5,525.28, diocesan $308.16, extra diocesan $101.72, total contributions $5,985.60. *Expenses*—Current parochial $2,255.52; grand total of all money raised by the congregation $8,241.18.

PAROCHIAL REPORT.

Rev. GUY H. CROOK. Address Ronceverte, W. Va. Assistant, Roger A. Walke. Incarnation Church, Greenbrier Parish, Ronceverte, Greenbrier county. Present minister took took charge June 23, 1901.

Parochial Statistics—Church wardens, A. B. C. Bray, F. H. Hauck; other vestrymen, L. N. Simms, J. W. P. Eagle, S. T. Peck; registrar, Col. L. N. Simms, Ronceverte, W. Va.; treasurer, Col. L. N. Simms, Ronceverte, superintendent of Sunday School, Mrs. F. A. Hauck; lay reader, Roger A. Walke.

Communicants—Number last reported 16, received by letter 1, added otherwise 4, total gain 5; net gain 5; present number total 21.

Congregations—Confirmed persons connected with Parish 22, baptized persons connected with Parish 38, families 14, individuals not thus included 1, whole number of individuals 39, number sittings in Church 80, number free sittings 80.

Rector's Salary—As pledged from this congregation $150.00, from diocesan missions 50, total $200.00.

Organizations—Sunday Schools, officers and teachers, female 3, total 3; pupils, male 12, female 11, total 23; lenten offering $14.00, other offerings $21.69, total Sunday School offerings $35.69; other organizations, Ladies' Aid $63.00.

Property—Church, wood, insurance $500.00, value $900.00; rectory, wood, insurance $1,500, value $2,500.00; building lots, value $500.00; total value $3,900.00; indebtedness, on rectory $2,000.00; total indebtedness, $2,000.00.

FINANCIAL REPORT.

Receipts—Current Expenses—Pledges and subscriptions $149.00, collections in Church $49.93, interest from investments $300.00, Sunday School $21.69, Ladies' Aid $48.50, total receipts for current expenses $599.12. *For all purposes other than current expenses, (i. e. Contributions)*—Pledges and Subscriptions $500.00, collections in Church $46.63, Sunday School $14.00, total receipts for contributions $560.65; grand total of all receipts i. e. for current expenses and contributions $1,159.75.

Disbursemnts—Current expenses, (Parochial)—Salary of Rector $150.00, salary of assistant $77.00, other salaries $24.00, maintaining Sunday Schools $21.69, interest on debt $90.00, other current expenses

$49.92, total for current expenses $412.61. *Contributions — Parochial* — Communion alms $2.00, extraordinary repairs and improvements $500.00, total parochial contributions $502.00. *Diocesan* — Salary of Bishops $3.00, permanent fund $9.75, diocesan missions $7.00, religious and Theological education $3.63, Sheltering Arms Hospital $5.00, Theological Seminary $2.00, Bishop's Special Fund 50 cents, total diocesan contributions $30.88. *Objects without the Diocese*—Domestic missions, general, $3.50, total domestic missions, $3.50; foreign missions general $2.00, total foreign missions $2.00; total foreign and domestic missions $5.50; general clergy relief fund $1.00, total without diocese $6.50.

Financial Summary—Contributions, Parochial $560.63, diocesan $30.88, extra diocesan $6.50, total contributions $598.01; expenses, current parochial $599.12; grand total of all money raised by the congregation $1,-197.13.

PAROCHIAL REPORT.

Rev. GUY H. CROOK, address Ronceverte; assistant, Roger A. Walke, St. James Church, Greenbrier Mission, Lewisburg, Greenbrier county. Present minister took charge June 23, 1901.

Church Officers—Church Wardens, D. C. T. Davis, J. W. Harris; other Vestrymen, H. L. Van Sickler, Kent Snyder, H. Frazier; Registrar, Kent Snyder, address Lewisburg, W. Va.; Treasurer, H. L. Van Sickler, address Lewisburg; Lay Reader, Roger A. Walke.

Official Acts—Presented for confirmation since last report 4, catechisings 7, public services, Sundays, 32, other days 9, total 41; Holy Communion, public, 4, total 4.

Communicants—Number last reported 20, admitted by confirmation 4, total gain 4; net gain 4, present number total 24.

Congregations—Confirmed persons connected with Parish 24, baptized persons connected with Parish 42, families 13, individuals not thus included 4, whole number of individuals 46, sittings in Church 200, free sittings 200.

Rector's Salary—As pledged from this congregation, $150.00; from Diocesan Missions, 50; total, $200.00.

Organizations—Other Organizations, Ladies Guild.

Property—Church, wood, insurance $1,200.00, value $2,000.00; rectory, wood, value $1,200.00; total value, $3,200.00.

FINANCIAL REPORT.

Receipts—Current Expenses—Pledges and subscriptions $151, collections in Church $30, interest from investments $96, bazaar $40, total receipts for current expenses $3.17. *For all purposes other than current expenses, (i. e. Contribution)*—Pledges and subscriptions $98, Ladies Guild $32, total receipts for contributions $132, grand total of all recipts i. e. for current expenses and contributions $449.

Disbursements—For current expenses (Parochial)—Salary of Rector $150, salary of assistant $81, other salaries $27, insurance $25, other current expenses $32, total for current expenses $315. *For Contributions—Parochial*—Extraordinary repairs and improvements $130, total Parochial contributions $130. *Diocesan*—Salary of Bishops, $4, Permanent Fund $15.50, Diocesan Missions $7, Theological Seminary $2, Bishop's Special Fund .55, total Diocesan contributions $29.05.—*Objects without the Diocese* Domestic Missions General $2.10, total Domestic Missions $2.10; Foreign Missions General $2.40, total Foreign Missions $2.40; total Foreign and Domestic Missions $4.50; total without Diocese $4.50.

Financial Summary—Contributions—Parochial $132, Diocesan $29.05, extra Diocesan $4.50, total contributions $165.55. *Expenses*—Current Parochial, $315, grand total of all money raised by the congregation $480.55.

PAROCHIAL REPORT.

Rev. GUY H. CROOK, address Ronceverte; assistant Roger A. Walke. Holy Comforter Church, Greenbrier Parish, Fort Spring, Greenbrier county. Present minister took charge June 10, 1902.

Church Officers—Church Warden, D. Y. Huddleston; Registrar, D. Y. Huddleston, address Fort Spring; Treasurer, D. Y. Huddleston, address Fort Spring.

Official Acts—Public services, Sundays 9, total 9.

Communicants—Number last reported 1, added otherwise 1, total gain 1, net gain 1, present number total 8.

Congregations—Confirmed persons connected with Parish 9, baptized persons connected with Parish 11, families 5, individuals not thus included 4, whole number of individuals 15.

Rector's Salary—As pledged from this congregation $30, total $30.

Property—Building Fund $30.

FINANCIAL REPORT.

Receipts—For current expenses—Collections in Church $13.30, personal contributions $11.00, total receipts for current expenses $24.30.

Disbursements—For current expenses (Parochial)—Salary of Rector $26.30, total for current expenses $26.30. *Diocesan*—Salary of Bishops

$3.00, Permanent Fund $4.00, Diocesan Missions $4.27, Widows and Orphans, Aged and Disabled Clergy Fund, .50, Theological Seminary $3.20, Bishop's Special Fund .20, total Diocesan contributions $15.17. *Objects without the Diocese—Domestic Missions General* $3.00, total Domestic Missions $3.00; Foreign Missions General $1.75, total Foreign Missions $1.75, total Foreign and Domestic Missions $4.75, total without Diocese $4.75.

Financial Summary—Contributions—Diocesan $15.17, extra Diocesan $4.75, total contributions $19.92. *Expenses*—Current Parochial $24.30, grand total of all money raised by the congregation $44.22.

PAROCHIAL REPORT.

Rev. GUY H. CROOK, address Ronceverte. Grace Mission, Clover Lick, Pocahontas county. Present minister took charge June 23, 1901.

Church Officers—Church Warden, Dr. Jno. Ligon; Registrar, Dr. Jno. Ligon, address Clover Lick, W. Va.; Treasurer, Dr. Jno. Ligon, address Clover Lick, W. Va.

Official Acts—Baptisms, infants 2, total 2, public services, Sundays 3, other days 4, total 7.

Communicants—Number last reported 5, removed without letter 1, total loss 1; net gain 1, present number total 4.

Congregations—Confirmed persons connected with Parish 4, baptized persons connected with Parish 10, families 3, whole number of individuals 10, number of scattered communicants in your section not connected with any Parish 9, sittings in Church 175, free sittings 175.

Property—Church, wood, value $1,000, total value $1,000.

FINANCIAL REPORT.

Recipts—For Current Expenses—Personal contributions $14.50, total receipts for current expenses $14.50.

Disbursements—For Current Expenses (Parochial)—Salary of Rector $14.50. *Diocesan*—Sheltering Arms Hospital $3.00, total Diocesan contributions $3.00.

Financial Summary—Contributions—Diocesan $3.00, total contributions $3.00. *Expenses*—Current Parochial $14.50, grand total of all money raised by the congregation $17.50.

Remarks—Contributions from this place were sent in by Dr. Ligon and I have no account of them.

PAROCHIAL REPORT.

Rev. GUY H. CROOK, address Ronceverte. Hillsboro Mission, Academy, Pocahontas county. Present minister took charge June 23, 1901.

Official Acts—Public services, Sundays, none, other days 3, total 3.

Communicants—Number last reported 2, added otherwise 1, total gain 1, net gain 1, present number total 3.

Congregations—Confirmed persons connected with Parish 3, baptized persons connected with Parish 10, families 3, individuals not thus included 1, whole number of individuals 11.

FINANCIAL REPORT.

Receipts—For Current Expenses—Personal contributions $7.50.

Disbursements—For Current Expenses (Parochial)—Salary of Rector $7.50, total for current expenses $7.50.

PAROCHIAL REPORT.

Rev. GUY H. CROOK, address Ronceverte; assistant, Roger A. Walke. Glen Jean Mission, Glen Jean, Fayette county. Present minister took charge June 23, 1901.

Church Officers—Church Wardens, W. F. Coster, C. B. Lee; Registrar, Dr. C. B. Lee, address Glen Jean, W. Va.; Treasurer, Dr. C. B. Lee, address Glen Jean, W. Va.

Official Acts—Public services, Sundays, 14, other days 5, total 19, Holy Communion, public 1, total 1.

Communicants—Number last reported 19, added otherwise 2, total gain 2, removed without letter 1, total loss 1, net gain 1, present number total 20.

Congregations—Confirmed persons connected with Parish 20, baptized persons connected with Parish 32, families 17, whole number of individuals 32, free sittings 165.

Rector's Salary—As pledged from this congregation $150.00, total $150.

Property—Church, wood, insurance $1,500, value $2,500, total value $2,500.

FINANCIAL REPORT.

Receipts—For Current Expenses—Pledges and subscriptions $151, collections in Church $13.20. *For all purposes other than current expenses (i. e. Contributions)*—Collections in Church $9.80, total receipts for contributions $9.80, grand total of all receipts i. e. for current expenses and contributions $174.00.

Disbursements—For Current Expenses (Parochial)—Salary of Rector $151.00, other salaries $5.00, other current expenses $8.20, total for current expenses $164.20. *Diocesan*—Salary of Bishops $7.00; Permanent Fund $2.00, Bishop's Special Fund .80, total Diocesan contributions $9.80.

Financial Summary—Contributions—Diocesan $9.80, total contributions $9.80. *Expenses*—Current Parochial $164.20, grand total of all money raised by the congregation $174.00.

Remarks—Strike conditions interfered greatly at this place.

PAROCHIAL REPORT.

Rev. GUY H. CROOK, address Ronceverte; assistant, Roger A. Walke. Beury Mission, Beury, Fayette county. Present minister took charge June 23, 1901.

Official Acts—Public services, Sundays 6, total 6.

Communicants—Number last reported 2, present number total 2.

Congregations—Confirmed persons connected with Parish 2, families 2.

FINANCIAL REPORT.

Receipts—Current Expenses—Collections in Church $3.00, personal contributions $50.00, total receipts for current expenses $53.00. *For all purposes other than current expenses, (i. e. Contributions)*—Collections in Church $3.75.

Disbursements—For Current expenses, (Parochial)—Salary of Rector $50.00. *Diocesan*—Permanent Fund $3.75, total diocesan contributions $3.75.

Financial Summary—Contributions—Diocesan $3.75. *Expenses* Current parochial $53.00; grand total of all money raised by the congregation $56.75.

Remarks—Strike conditions interfered so that we could scarcely work this place.

PAROCHIAL REPORT.

Rev. GUY H. CROOK, address Ronceverte; assistant Roger A. Walke. St. Thomas Church, Greenbrier Parish, White Sulphur, Greenbrier county. Present minister took charge June 10, 1902.

Church Officers—Church Wardens, R. Cary Montague; Registrar, R. Cary Montague, address White Sulphur Springs; Treasurer, R. Cary Montague, address White Sulphur Springs; Superintendent of Sunday School, R. Cary Montague; Lay Reader, R. Cary Montague.

Official Acts—Public services, Sundays, 12, other days, 19, total 22; Holy Communion, public 2, total 2.

Communicants—Number last reported 41, present number total 41.

Congregations—Confirmed persons connected with Parish 42, baptized persons connected with Parish 75, families 17, individuals not thus included 75, number free sittings 500.

Rector's Salary—As pledged from this congregation $75.00, total $75.00.

Organizations—Sunday Schools, officers and teachers, No. 1, male 1, No. 2, 2; female, No. 1, 3, No. 2, 1; total No. 1, 4; total No. 2, 3; pupils No. 1, male 13; No. 2, 17; female No. 1, 20; No. 2, 39; total No. 1, 33; total No. 2, 56.

Property—Church, wood, value $10,000.00; total value $10,000.00.

FINANCIAL REPORT.

Receipts—Current Expenses—Pledges and subscriptions $29.00, total receipts for current expenses $29.00.

Disbursements—For current expenses, (Parochial)—Salary of Rector $29.00, total for current expenses $29.00.

Financial Summary—Expenses—Current Parochial $29.00; grand total of all money raised by the congregation $29.00.

Remarks—I did not take actual charge of St. Thomas till August and am not able to give financial report as I have been confined to the mission work.

PAROCHIAL REPORT.

Rev. THOS. J. OLIVER CURRAN, address Wheeling. St. Andrew's, Wheeling, Ohio county.

Church Officers—Treasurer, Wm. A. Carroll, address 3809 Jacob St.; Superintendent of Sunday School, Wm. A. Carroll.

Official Acts—Baptisms, infants 20, adults 16, total 36; presented for confirmation since last report 24, marriages 8, burials 3, catechisings 40, public services, Sundays, 105, other days 63, total 168; Holy Communion, public 16, private 1, total 17.

Communicants—Number last reported 51, admitted by confirmation 24, restored to communion 9, added otherwise 2, total gain 35; transferred 1, removed without letter 9, total loss 10; net gain (or loss) 25; present number total 76.

Congregations—Confirmed persons connected with Parish 76, baptized

persons connected with Parish 174, families 16, individuals not thus included 15, whole number of individuals 189, number sittings in Church 100.

Rector's Salary—As pledged from this congregation, no definite; as pledged from other congregations $500.00.

Organizations—Sunday Schools, officers and teachers, male 1, female 4, total 5; pupils, male 51, female 57, total 118; advent offering $8.00, lenten offering $30, other offerings $201, total Sunday School offerings $239; Brotherhood of St. Andrew, members 8; other organizations, St. Andrews Guild: (1) Woman's Chapter 12, (2) St. Agnes Chapter 8, (3) Altar Chapter 4, total 16.

Property—Church, wood, insurance $3,500.00; value $5,000.00. Money raised from outside sources, $1,035.00; for what objects used, Salary, Improvements.

FINANCIAL REPORT.

Receipts—Current Expenses—Cash on hand, per last report $356.28, pledges and subscriptions $243.14, collections in Church $348.98, interest from investments $10.23, other sources $1,656.02, total receipts for current expenses $2,614.65. *For all purposes other than current expenses, (i. e. Contributions)*—Sunday School $239.80, total receipts for contributions $239.80; grand total of all receipts i. e. for current expenses and contributions $2,854.45.

Disbursements—For current expenses, (Parochial)—Salary of Rector $1,223.94, other salaries $104, maintaining Sunday Schools $120, ordinary repairs $48, other objects $233, total for current expenses $1,728.94. *For Contributions — Parochial* — Extraordinary repairs and improvements $336.26, other objects $135.75, total parochial contributions $472.01. *Diocesan*—Salary of Bishops $10, permanent fund $67.75, diocesan missions $15, convocation missions $5, Sheltering Arms Hospital $4.66, other objects $76, total diocesan contributions $178.41. *Objects without the Diocese*—General Missions $30,; total foreign and domestic missions $30.00.

Financial Summary—Contributions—Parochial $472.01, diocesan $178.41, extra diocesan $30.00, total contributions $680.41. *Expenses*—Current parochial $1,728.94; grand total of all money raised by the congregation $2,409.36.

PAROCHIAL REPORT.

Rev. THOMAS C. DARST, address Fairmont, W. Va. St. Andrew's Mission, Mannington, Marion county. Date of organization about 1891. Present minister took charge September 1, 1903.

Church Officers—Church Warden, Henry W. G. Bostock; other vestrymen, F. H. Armstrong, Phil. Dietz, Arnold R. Dunkle, John O. Huey, Jas. H. Bostock; Registrar, Phil. Dietz, address Mannington, W. Va.; Treasurer, John O. Huey, address Mannington, W. Va.

Official Acts—Baptisms, infants 3, total 3; presented for confirmation since last report 10, burials 1, public services, Sundays 10, other days 1, total 11.

Communicants—Number last reported 10, admitted by confirmation 10, added otherwise 1, total gain 11, net gain 11, present number total 21.

Congregations—Confirmed persons connected with Parish 21, baptized persons connected with Parish 44, families 16, individuals not thus included 6, whole number of individuals 66.

Rector's Salary—As pledged from this congregation $200.00, from diocesan missions $200.00, as pledged from other congregations $400.00, total $800.00.

Organizations—Other organizations, Ladies' Guild, 15.

Property—Church, wood, insurance $2,000, value $2,000.00; other property, Church lot, value $1,000.00; total value $3,000.00.

FINANCIAL REPORT.

Receipts—Current Expenses—Cash on hand, September 1, 1902 .55, pledges and subscriptions $92.67, collections in Church $14.76, total receipts for current expenses $107.98. *For all purposes other than current expenses, (i. e. Contributions)*—Ladies' Guild $250.00.

Disbursements—For current expenses, (Parochial)—Salary of Rector $90.00, other current expenses $7.50, total for current expenses $97.50. *Diocesan*—Permanent fund $4.00.

Financial Summary—Contributions—Parochial $357.98, diocesan $4.00, total contributions $361.98. *Expenses*—Current parochial $97.50; grand total of all money raised by the congregation $361.98.

Remarks—When the present minister took charge of St. Andrew's Mission, September 1st, 1902, Mrs. L. G. Robinson had a claim of $1,250.00 against the unfinished Church building. There was also a diocesan debt of $350.00. Since that time Mr. and Mrs. Robinson have agreed to finish the Church according to original plans and specifications and turn same over to vestry of St. Andrew's, free of all encumbrance, including diocesan debt; provided, said vestry pay to Mr. and Mrs. Robinson $1,000.00 upon satisfactory completion of Church. This has not been done as yet, therefore we are unable to give the Church's indebtedness in this report.

PAROCHIAL REPORT.

Rev. JOHN S. DOUGLAS, address Martinsburg. Trinity Church, Norborne Parish, Martinsburg, Berkeley county. Date of organization 1769. Present minister took charge October 1st, 1899.

Church Officers—Church Wardens, Capt. W. B. Colston, Mr. C. A. Miller; other vestrymen, Mr. John E. Boyd, Mr. Alexander Parks, Mr. Edw. Rutledge, Mr. A. M. Gilbert, Dr. Alonzo Andrews; Registrar, Capt. W. B. Colston, address Martinsburg, W. Va.; Treasurer, Edward Rutledge, address Martinsburg, W. Va.; Superintendent of Sunday School, Capt. W. B. Colston; Sunday School Secretary and Treasurer, Edw. Rutledge; Lay Reader, Edw. Rutledge.

Official Acts—Baptisms, infants 11, adults 5, total 16; presented for confirmation since last report 11, marriages 4, burials 10, catechisings 12, public services, Sundays 94, other days 60, total 154; Holy Communion, public 15, private 4, total 19.

Communicants—Number last reported 158, received by letter 1, admitted by confirmation 11, added otherwise 3, total gain 15; died 5, transferred 1, removed without letter 10, lapsed 5, total loss 21; net loss 6; present number total 152.

Congregations—Confirmed persons connected with Parish 180(?), baptized persons connected with Parish 280(?), families 83, individuals not thus included 10, whole number of individuals 290, number of sittings in Church 350, number free sittings 350, number of sittings in Sunday School room 150.

Rector's Salary As pledged from this congregation $800.00, total $800.00.

Organizations—Sunday Schools, officers and teachers, male 3, female 7, total 10; pupils, male 35, female 57, total 92; advent offering $17.65; lenten offering $36.02; other offerings $38.04; total Sunday School offerings $91.71; Woman's Auxiliary, members 20; other organizations, Trinity Church Guild, under which work eight different Chapters, for objects Parochial, Diocesan and General.

Property—Church, brick, insurance $5,000, value $10,000; rectory, stone, insurance $1,500, value $7,000; Parish house, new, brick, insurance $2,000, value $4,000; organ, insurance $1,800, value $1,800; total insurance $10,300; total value $22,800. Indebtedness, on Parish house $1,344.67, on organ $108.64, other debts $588.71, total indebtedness $2,042.02.

FINANCIAL REPORT.

Receipts—Current expenses—Cash on hand, per last report $166.44, pledges and subscriptions $1,264.47, collections in Church $93.13, other sources .95, total receipts for current expenses $1,524.99. *For all pur-*

poses other than current expenses, (i. e. Contributions)—Collections in Church $337.19, money borrowed $2,900, Sunday School $91.71, Woman's Auxiliary $50.30, other sources $12, Guilds $431.45, Easter offering $525.63, total receipts for Contributions $4,348.28; grand total of all receipts i. e. for current expenses and contributions $5,873.27.

Disbursements—For current expenses, (Parochial)—Salary of Rector $800, other salaries $175, insurance $32.40, ordinary repairs $31.34, other current expenses $172.09, total for current expenses $1,210.83. *For Contributions—Parochial*—Communion alms $40.38, extraordinary repairs and improvements $39.31, other objects $237.49, new Parish house $2,717.86, payment on debt $900, interest on same $14.21, maintaining Sunday School $38.04, total parochial contributions $3,987.29. *Diocesan*—Salary of Bishops $100, permanent fund $104.69, diocesan missions $107.20, convocation missions $41.36, widows and orphans, aged and disabled clergy fund $16.10, Theological Seminary $18.91, total diocesan contributions $388.26. *Objects without the Diocese*—Domestic missions general $50.83, colored people $2, Indians $3.76, deaf and dumb $7.98, Jews $1.81, through American Church Missionary Society $4.25, total domestic missions $70.63. Foreign Missions general $43.37, for Mexico $6.03, Brazil $5 77, Cuba $2.12, total foreign missions $57.29; total foreign and domestic missions $127.92. American Church Building fund $4, Woman's Auxiliary, money $50.30, general Clergy Relief fund $15.64, Bible and Prayer Book Society $3.20, other objects $7.50.

Financial Summary — Contributions — Parochial $3 987.29, diocesan $388.26, extra diocesan without diocese $208.56, total contributions $4,583.11. *Expenses*—Current parochial $1,210.83, cash on hand $79.33, grand total of all money raised by the congregation $5,873.27.

PAROCHIAL REPORT.

Rev. JOHN S. DOUGLAS, address Martinsburg. Christ Church, Bunker Hill Mission, Bunker Hill, Berkeley county. Date of organization 1769. Present minister took charge October 1st, 1899.

Church Officers—Church Wardens, Mr. Zeph S. Morgan; other vestrymen, Joseph Morgan, John K. Cunningham; Registrar, John K. Cunningham, address Rest, Virginia; Treasurer, Zeph. S. Morgan, address Gerardstown, W. Va.

Official Acts—Public services, Sundays, 16, total 16, Holy Communion, public, 1, total 1.

Communicants—Number last reported 7, added otherwise 2, removed without letter 2, present number total 7.

Congregations—Confirmed persons connected with Parish 7, baptized

persons connected with Parish 20, families 5, individuals not thus included 1, whole number of individuals 20, number sittings in Church 200, number free sittings 200.

Rector's Salary As pledged from this congregation $31.00, total $31.00.

Property—Church, brick, value $1,500. Indebtedness, due the minister $12.00.

FINANCIAL REPORT.

Receipts—Current Expenses—Cash on hand, per last report $7.93, other sources $15.07, total receipts for current expenses $23.00. *For all purposes other than current expenses, (i. e. Contributions)*—Other sources 39, other sources $82.18, total receipts for contributions $82.57; grand total of all receipts i. e. for current expenses and contributions $105.57.

Disbursements—For current expenses, (Parochial)—Salary of Rector $19.00, other salaries $3.00, other current expenses $1.00, total for current expenses $23.00. *For Contributions—Parochial*—Extraordinary repairs and improvements $63.97, other objects $13.25, total parochial contributions $77.22. *Diocesan*—Permanent fund .69, diocesan missions $1.15, Theologiacl Seminary .53, total diocesan contributions $2.37. *Objects without the Diocese*—Domestic missions general .39, total domestic missions .39; foreign missions general .41, Brazil $1.18, total foreign missions $1.59, total foreign and domestic missions $2.98.

Financial Summary—Contributions—Parochial $77.22, diocesan $2.37, extra diocesan $2.98, total contributions $82.57. *Expenses*—Current parochial $23, grand total of all money raised by the congregation $105.57.

PAROCHIAL REPORT.

Rev. C. A. DOWELL, address Sistersville, W. Va. St. Pauls Church, Sistersville, Tyler county.

Church Officers—Church Wardens, Geo. F. Durham, Geo. B. VanAmen; other vestrymen, F. D. McCoy, Ed. Roome, Geo. W. Stocking, D. E. Thoenen, A. B. Hunt; Registrar, A. B. Hunt, Sistersville, W. Va.; Treasurer, D. E. Thoenen, Sistersville' W. Va.; Superintendent of Sunday School Geo. B. VanAmen, Sistersville, W. Va.; Sunday School and Treasurer, Thos. J. McCoy.

Official Acts—Baptisms, infants 11, adults 1, total 12; presented for confirmation since last report 7, marriages 1, burials 5, public services, Sundays 86, other days 38, Holy Communion, public 14.

Communicants—Number last reported 36, received by letter 1, admitted by confirmation 7, total gain 8; died 3, transferred 8, total loss 11; net gain (or loss) 3, present number total 34.

Congregations—Confirmed persons connected with Parish 33, baptized persons connected with Parish 50, families 20, number sittings in Church 200, number free sittings 200, number sittings in Sunday School room 200.

Rector's Salary—As pledged from this congregation $900.00, total $900.00.

Organizations—Sunday Schools, officers and teachers, male 2, female 6, total 8; pupils, male 25, female 55, total 80; advent offering $11.97, lenten offering $6.64, other offerings $50.00, total Sunday School offerings $68.61; Woman's Auxiliary, members 18, Young Woman's Guild 12, Chancel Chapter 3; location of Schools mentioned above, Sistersville, W. Va.

Property Church, frame, insurance $1,200, value $3,000; rectory, frame, insurance $2,000, value $3,500, total value $6,500.00. Indebtedness, on rectory $450.00, due on diocesan assessment for Bishop's fund $15.84, total indebtedness $465.84.

FINANCIAL REPORT.

Receipts—Current Expenses—Cash on hand, per last report $54.67, pledges and subscriptions $992.00, collections in Church $401.76, money borrowed $550.00. *For all purposes other than current expenses, (i. e. Contributions)*—Pledges and subscriptions $1,010.50; Sunday School $114.00, Woman's Auxiliary $244.32.

Disbursements—For current expenses, (Parochial)—Salary of Rector $787.50, other salaries $122, maintaining Sunday Schools $71.62, interest on debt $16.50, payment on debt $100.00, other current expenses $50.00, total for current expenses $1,147.62. *For Contributions—Parochial*—Extraordinary repairs and improvements $1,010.50. *Diocesan*—Salary of Bishops $24.16, permanent fund $31.89, diocesan missions $45.94, convocation missions $2.00, widows and orphans, aged and disabled clergy fund $10.90, religious and theological education $10.66, Sheltering Arms Hospital $12.46, Theological Seminary .70, total diocesan contributions $138.71. *Objects without the diocese*—Domestic missions general $37.35, deaf and dumb $1.14, through American Church Missionary Society $1.25, total foreign and and domestic missions $39.74. American Church Building fund $2.40, Woman's Auxiliary Boxes, value $60.00, Bible and Prayer Book Society $2.55, total without diocese $64.95.

Financial Summary — Contributions — Parochial $1,010.50, diocesan $130.37, total contributions $1,140.87. *Expenses*—Current parochial $1,-147.62; grand total of all money raised by the congregation $2,734.69.

PAROCHIAL REPORT.

REV. GEO. W. EASTER, address Union, W. Va. All Saints Church, All Saints Parish, Union, Monroe county. Present minister took charge April 18, 1892.

Church Officers—Church Wardens, Jas. W. McNeer, Chas. A. Shanklin; other vestrymen, Jos. D. Logan, John W. Rowan, A. S. Johnston, E. S. McNeer; Registrar, A. S. Johnston, address Union, W. Va.; Treasurer, Chas. A. Shanklin, address Union, W. Va.; Superintendent of Sunday Schools A. S. Johnston, Union, W. Va.; Lay Reader, Jas. W. McNeer.

Official Acts—Baptisms, infants 3, total 3; presented for confirmation since last report 4, marriages 1, burials 2, catechisings weekly, public services, Sundays 88, other days 69, total 157; Holy Communion, public 17, total 17.

Communicants—Number last reported 36, admitted by confirmation 4, added otherwise 7, total gain 11, transferred 5, removed without letter 1, lapsed 1, total loss 7; net gain (or loss) 4, present number total 40.

Congregations—Confirmed persons connected with Parish 45, baptized persons connected with Parish 78, families 14, individuals not thus included 14, whole number of individuals 78, number sittings in Church 175, number free sittings 175.

Rector's Salary—As pledged from this congregation $450.00, from diocesan missions $100.00, from general board $200.00, total $750.00.

Organizations—Sunday Schools, officers and teachers, male 2, female 2, total 4, pupils, male 20, female 28, total 48; advent offering $21.64, lenten offering $25.82, other offerings Bishop's special .94, Sheltering Arms Hospital $2.35, diocesan missions $1.73, Brazil and Cuba $3.22, Mexican missions .86, general missions $2.30, total Sunday School offerings $58.86; other organizations, Parish Aid Society. Location of Schools mentioned above, Union, W. Va.

Property—Church, wood, insurance $1,350, value $2,500; rectory, wood and brick, no insurance, value $1,200; other property, value $250; total value $3,950; indebtedness, due the Minister $82.70, for repairs to rectory $26.00, total indebtedness $108.70; money raised from outside sources $26.00, for what objects used, repairs to rectory.

FINANCIAL REPORT.

Receipts Current Expenses—Cash on hand, per last report $1.72, pledges and subscriptions $471.84, collections in Church $61.97, total receipts for current expenses $535.53. *For all purposes other than current expenses, (i. e. Contributions)*—Cash on hand, per last report $3.88, pledges and subscriptions $59.50, pew rent $253.58, money borrowed $26.00, thank offerings $20.00, Sunday School $58.43, other sources $60.25, Bishop's special $2.00, total receipts for contributions $483.64; grand total of all receipts i. e. for current expenses and contributions $1,019.17.

Disbursements—For current expenses, (Parochial)—Salary of Rector $387.75, other salaries $40.00, maintaining Sunday Schools $8.36, ordinary repairs $10.80, payment on debt $42.81, other current expenses $38.33, cash on hand to balance $7.48, total for current expenses $535.53. *For Contributions—Parochial*—Extraordinary repairs and improvements $35.00, Sunday School Christmas tree $9.70, total parochial contributions $44.70. *Diocesan*—Salary of Bishops $59.51, permanent fund $56.68, diocesan missions $139.71, convocation missions $5.65, widows and orphans, aged and disabled clergy fund $18.88, religious and theological education $14.51, Sheltering Arms Hospital $7.85, Theological Seminary $6.80, Bishop's special fund $2.51, expense account .93, total diocesan contributions $313.03. *Objects without the Diocese*—Domestic missions general $36.13, colored people $3.54, Jews $2.63, through American Church Missionary Society $2.27, total domestic missions $44.57; foreign missions general $35.79, for Mexico $8.54, Brazil $4.06, Cuba $4.05, total foreign missions $52.44; total foreign and domestic missions $97.01; American Church Building Fund .76, general clergy relief fund $3.67, for sufferers in Martinique $2.71, for sufferers in Philippines $2.71, total without diocese $106.86.

Financial Summary—Contributions—Parochial $125.79, diocesan $303.45, extra diocesan $113.51, total contributions $542.75. *Expenses*—Current parochial $535.53; grand total of all money raised by the congregation $1,078.28.

Remarks—I have begun a monthly service at Mt. Prospect, Baptist or Union Church, three miles from Union on the Knobs, and hope shortly to begin another at a school house near Union.

PAROCHIAL REPORT.

Rev. GEO. W. EASTER, address Union, W. Va. Messiah Church, All Saints Parish, Alderson, Monroe county. Present minister took charge July 1, 1902.

Church Officers—Church Warden, C. W. Vandegrift; Treasurer, C. W. Vandegrift.

Official Acts—Burials 2, public services, Sundays 2, other days 2, total 4; Holy Communion, Public 1, total 1.

Communicants—Present number total 5.

Congregations—Confirmed persons connected with Parish 5, baptized persons connected with Parish 5, families 3, whole number of individuals 9, number sittings in Church 100, all free.

Property—Church, wood, value $1,300; other property $75; total value $1,375.

FINANCIAL REPORT.

Receipts—Current Expenses—Pledges and subscriptions $7.00, collections in Church $2.65, total receipts for current expenses $9.65. *For all purposes other than current expenses, (i. e. Contributions)*—Pledges and subscriptions $3.00, collections in Church $6.25; grand total of all receipts i. e. for current expenses and contributions $9.25.

Disbursements—For current expenses, (Parochial)—Salary of Rector $7.00, other current expenses $2.65, total for current expenses $9.65. *Diocesan*—Salary of Bishops $3.00, Diocesan missions $6.25, total diocesan contributions $9.25.

Financial Summary—Contributions—Parochial $9.65, diocesan $9.25, total contributions $18.90. Grand total of all money raised by the congregation $18.90.

Remarks—Deaths, removals and the lack of services for a year have brought this congregation to a very low ebb. I actually took charge in September, 1902, then in October came my vacation. During the winter months the services were necessarily suspended, because all but one of the communicants were absent. Twice when I have advertized service I have been advised not to come. It seems to me it would be better to put this congregation in charge of some one living on the railroad, who can give the people more attention with less inconvenience and expense. Every trip costs me now at least three days and $3.30, and in winter the road from here is almost impassable.

PAROCHIAL REPORT.

Rev. JAMES LOGAN FISH, address Elkins, W. Va. Grace Church, Elkins, Randolph county. Present minister took charge July 9th, 1899.

Church Officers—Church Wardens, C. H. Scott, G. Jewett; other vestrymen, S. L. Reger, G. D. Woodrow, R. H. Pembroke, J. Lingunfelter, I. P. Gassman, J. Lacy Dunlap; Registrar, J. Lacy Dunlap, address Elkins; Treasurer, I. P. Gassman, address Elkins; Superintendent of Sunday Schools, J. Lacy Dunlap, Elkins; Sunday School Secretary and Treasurer, Chas. Steffler.

Official Acts—Baptisms, infants 3, total 3; presented for confirmation since last report 2, marriages 2, burials 3, public services, Sundays, 46, other days 61, total 107; Holy Communion, public, 12, total 12.

Communcants—Number last reported 26, received by letter 4, admitted by confirmation 2, added otherwise 2, total gain 8; transferred 1, removed without letter 3, total loss 4; net gain 4, present number total 30.

Congregations—Confirmed persons connected with Parish 33, baptized persons connected with Parish 59, families 15, whole number of individuals 61, number of scattered communicants in your section not connected with any Parish 12, sittings in Church 120, free sittings 120.

Rector's Salary—As pledged from this congregation $150, from general board $200, total $350.

Organizations—Sunday Schools 1, officers and teachers, male 2, female 2, total 4; pupils male 13, female 12, total 25; Advent offering $2.00, Lenten offering $6.69, other offerings $14.39, total Sunday School offerings $23.08; other organizations, Ladies' Guild; location of schools mentioned above, Elkins, Grace Church.

Property—Church, frame, insurance $1,400, value $2,200; rectory, frame, insurance $1,000, value $2,500, total value, insurance $2,400, value $4,700; indebtedness, on church none, on rectory $1,750, other debts, interest on rectory $50, total indebtedness $1,800.

FINANCIAL REPORT.

Receipts—For Current Expenses—Pledges and subscriptions, $118.10, collections in church $63.40, other sources, Sunday School offerings, $23.08, from Ladies' Guild $150.00, interest on rectory $100.00, total receipts for current expenses $454.58. *For all purposes other than current expenses, (i. e. Contributions)*—Cash on hand toward necessary additions to rectory $140.00.

Disbursements—For Current Expenses (Parochial)—Salary of Rector $150.00, insurance $12.50, maintaining Sunday Schools $18.08, interest on debt $100.00, payment on debt $150.00, other current expenses $19.00, cash in Sunday School Treasurer's hands $5.00, total for current expenses $454.58. *Diocesan*—Salary of Bishops $10.00, permanent fund $26.00, diocesan missions $10.00, convocation missions $2.00, Sheltering Arms Hospital $2.00, convocation assessment $1.50, total diocesan contributions $51.50. *Objects without the Diocese*—Domestic missions general $10.00, total foreign and domestic missions $10.00.

Financial Summary—Contributions—Parochial $140.00, diocesan $51.50, extra Diocesan $10.00, total contributions $201.50. *Expenses*—Current parochial $454.58, grand total of all money raised by the congregation $656.08.

Remarks—There are 12 communicants in the Mingo district to whom I occasionally minister. The amount paid to missions was undesignated. The Council of Elkins calls for alterations in the rectory, such as will necessitate considerable outlay.

PAROCHIAL REPORT.

Rev. JAMES LOGAN FISH, address Elkins, W. Va. St. Barnabas Church, Davis, Tucker county. Date of organization 1894. Present minister took charge July 9th, 1899.

Church Officers—Church Wardens, St. Barnabas, A. J. McNeil, Robt. Knox; other vestrymen, F. H. Enright, Jonah M. Smith, John Van Newkirk, Dr. W. Holmes Yeakley, Harry N. Warden; Registrar, John Van Newkirk, address Davis; Treasurer, John Van Newkirk, address Davis; Superintendent of Sunday School, Robt. Knox, Davis; Sunday School Secretary and Treasurer, Miss A. E. Kellum.

Official Acts—Baptisms, infants 6, adults 3, total 9; presented for confirmation since last report 6, burials 1, catechisings 4, public services, Sundays 42, total 42; Holy Communion, public 6, total 6.

Communicants—Number last reported 18, admitted by confirmation 6, added otherwise 1, total gain 7; removed without letter 1, total loss 1; net gain 6, present number total 24.

Congregations—Confirmed persons connected with Parish 32, baptized persons connected with Parish 53, families 12, whole number of individuals 61, number of scattered communicants in your section not connected with any Parish 14, sittings in church 120, free sittings 120.

Rector's Salary—As pledged from this congregation $150, total $150.

Organizations—Sunday Schools, officers and teachers, male 1, female 1, total 2; pupils, male 4, female 11, total 15; other offerings $7.29. Location of schools mentioned above, St. Barnabas Church, Davis.

Property — Church, frame, insurance $750, value $1,450, total value $1,450; indebtedness none.

FINANCIAL REPORT.

Receipts—For Current Expenses—Cash on hand, per last report $13.09, pledges and subscriptions $185.00, collections in church $108.70, Sunday School offerings $7.29, total receipts for current expenses $314.08. *For all purposes other than current expenses, (i. e. Contributions)*—Pledges and subscriptions $105, total receipts for contributions $105, grand total of all receipts i. e. for current expenses and contributions $419.08.

Disbursements—For Current Expenses (Parochial)—Salary of Rector $150.00, insurance $13.60, maintaining Sunday Schools $7.29, other current expenses $79.99, cash on hand $63.20, total for current expenses $314.08. *For Contributions—Parochial*—Extraordinary repairs and improvements $105, total parochial contributions $105. *Diocesan* Salary of Bishops $8.00, permanent fund $20.00, diocesan missions $8.00, convocation missions $2.00, convocation assessment $1.50, total diocesan contributions $39.50. *Objects without the Diocese*—Domestic missions general $8.00, total foreign and domestic missions 8.00.

Financial Summary—Contributions—Parochial $105.00, diocesan $39.50, extra diocesan $8.00, total contributions $152.50. *Expenses*—Current parochial $314.08, grand total of all money raised by the congregation $466.58.

Remarks—The amount paid to missions was undesignated. Four baptisms took place at Douglas, where we have 3 Episcopalian families, but hold no services. We have 6 Episcopalians at Thomas, where we hold services in the Opera House. Some of the communicants included in Davis Church number do not at present live in Davis, but keep up their interest in the church, and are not reported elsewhere. For several reasons we have been holding services very irregularly at Parsons, but look forward to more regular service.

PAROCHIAL REPORT.

Rev. JAMES LOGAN FISH, address Elkins. Trinity Church, Belington, Barbour county. Present minister took charge July 9th, 1899.

Church Officers—Church Wardens, F. A. Coleman; other vestrymen, D. D. W. Brown; Treasurer, F. A. Coleman.

Official Acts—Baptisms, none; public services, Sundays and other days 14, total 14.

Communicants—Number last reported 10, added otherwise 1, total gain 1; removed without letter 3, total loss 2; present number total 8.

Congregations—Confirmed persons connected with Parish 9, baptized persons connected with Parish 16, families 5, whole number of individuals 22.

Rector's Salary—As pledged from this congregation $100.00, total $100.

Property—Organ, kneeling benches, reading desk, etc., etc., $200.

FINANCIAL REPORT.

Receipts—For Current Expenses—Pledges and subscriptions $75.00, collections in church $25.00, total receipts for current expenses $100.00.

Disbursements—For Current Expenses (Parochial)—Salary of Rector $100.00.

Financial Summary—Expenses—Current parochial $100.00.

Remarks—We have now $700 of the amount required for church building, but have not yet commenced building, as we wish to have full amount required. During the past year we have been much hindered on account of not having the use of hall; also by the removal of friends.

PAROCHIAL REPORT.

Rev. G. A. GIBBONS, address Romney, W. Va. St Stephen's Church, Romney Mission, Romney, Hampshire county. Date of organization, 1885. Present minister took charge July 1st, 1885.

Church Officers—Church Wardens, G. W. Parsons, Wm. N. Baird; other vestrymen, E. O. Wirgman; Treasurer, G. W. Parsons, address Romney, W. Va.; Superintendent of Sunday Schools, Wm. N. Baird, Romney, W. Va.; Secretary and Treasurer of Sunday School, Wm. N. Baird, Romney, W. Va.

Official Acts—Marriages 3, burials 4.

Communicants—Number last reported 25, present number total 25.

Congregations—Confirmed persons connected with Parish 25, baptized persons connected with Parish 44, families 18, individuals not thus included 8, whole number of individuals 77, free sittings 200.

Rector's Salary—As pledged from this congregation $100, from diocesan missions $250, as pledged from other congregations $192, from convocation missions $50, from American Church Missionary Society $200, total $792.

Organizations—Sunday Schools, officers and teachers, male 1, female 2, total 3; pupils, male 6, female 9, total 15; Advent offering $2.00, Lenten offering $13.08, total Sunday School offerings $15.08.

Property—Church, brick, insurance $1,200, value $1,800; chapel, wood, insurance $400, value $700; rectory, wood insurance $,1000 value $1,900; total value, insurance $2,600, value $4,400; money raised from outside sources $575; for what objects used, rectory and increase of permanent episcopal fund.

FINANCIAL REPORT.

Receipts—For Current Expenses—Pledges and subscriptions $100, other sources $157, $94.10, total receipts for current expenses $331.10. *For all purposes other than current expenses, (i. e. Contributions)*—Pledges and subscriptions $87.87, collections in church $87.00, other sources $20.00, individual gift for P. E. fund and Bishop's 25th anniversary $400, total receipts or contributions $594.87, grand total of all receipts i. e. for current expenses and contributions $965.97.

Disbursements—For Current Expenses (Parochial)—Salary of Rector $100, other salaries $23.06, insurance $6.75, ordinary repairs $11.05, interest on debt $39.00, payment on debt $250, other objects $6.88, coal and laundry $8.13, total for current expenses $444.87. *For Contributions Parochial*—Extraordinary repairs and improvements $30.00, total parochial contributions $30.00. *Diocesan*—Salary of Bishops $16.00, permanent fund $38.85, convocation missions $6, religious and theological education $2, Sheltering Arms Hospital $6.25, special individual gift for increase of P. E. fund and Bishop's 25th anniversary $400, total diocesan contributions $469.10. *Objects without the Diocese*—Through American Church Missionary Society $10, total domestic missions $10; foreign missions general $5, Brazil $5, total foreign missions $10, total foreign and domestic missions $20.00, total without diocese $20.00.

Financial Summary—Contributions—Parochial $30, diocesan $469.10; extra diocesan $20, total contributions $519.10. *Expenses*—Current parochial $444.87, grand total of all money raised by the congregation $963.97.

Remarks—We rejoice our rectory is now paid for in full. We begin the new year, therefore, with cheerful and willing hearts and minds to do whatever our hands find to do. A friend of Bishop Peterkin's has just handed me his check for $400.00 for Permanent Episcopal Fund, and Bishop's anniversary, with the statement: "I wish I could make it $4,000."

PAROCHIAL REPORT.

Rev. G. A. GIBBONS, address Romney, W. Va. Emmanuel Church, Emmanuel Parish, Moorefield, Hardy county. Date of organization, 1878. Present minister took charge July 1st, 1885.

Church Officers—Church Wardens, C. James Lobb, Thomas Lakin; other vestrymen, Wm. H. Shearer, Disle Gamble, M. D., P. W. Inskeep; Registrar, Wm. H. Shearer, address Moorefield, W. Va.; Treasurer, Wm. H. Shearer, assistant Ida V. Wood, address Moorefield, W. Va.; Superintendent of Sunday Schools, C. James Lobb, Moorefield, W. Va.; Sunday School Secretary and Treasurer, Mrs. Annie W. Shearer.

Official Acts—Burials 1, catechisings 6, public services, Sundays, 48, other days 2, total 50; Holy communion, public 7, total 7.

Communicants—Number last reported 33, removed without letter 3, present number total 30.

Congregations Confirmed persons connected with Parish 30, baptized persons connected with Parish 55, families 18, individuals not thus included 6, whole number of individuals 61, number of scattered communicants in your section not connected with any Parish 2, number sittings in Church 200, number sittings in Sunday School room 125.

Rector's Salary—As pledged from this congregation $150, from diocesan missions $250, as pledged from other congregations $142, from convocation missions $50, from American Church Missionary Society $200, total $792.

Oragnizations—Sunday Schools, officers and teachers, male 1, female 4, total 5; pupils, male 9, female 10, total 19; advent offering $2.00, lenten offering $3.30, total Sunday School offerings $5.30; location of Schools mentioned above, Moorefield, W. Va.

Property—Church, frame, insurance $1,200, value $3,000; rectory, frame, insurance $1,200, value $2,000; Sunday School room frame, insurance $750, value $1,400; total insurance $3,150; total value $6,400.

FINANCIAL REPORT.

Receipts—Current Expenses—Pledges and subscriptions $180, collections in Church $30, other sources $250, individual $170.67, total receipts for current expenses $630.67. *For all purposes other than current expenses, (i. e. Contributions)*—Pledges and subscriptions $20.00, collections in Church $66.87, total receipts for contributions $86.87, grand total of all receipts i. e. for current expenses and contributions $717.54.

Disbursements—For current expenses, (Parochial)—Salary of Rector $150, other salaries $30, other current expenses $7, total for current expenses $187. *For contributions—Parochial*—Extraordinary repairs and improvements $423.78, other objects $35.00, total parochial contributions $458.78. *Diocesan*—Salary of Bishops $20, permanent fund $14.83, diocesan missions $23.06, convocation missions .17, widows and orphans, aged and disabled clergy fund .69, religious and theological education $1.27, total diocesan contributions $60.02. *Objects without the Diocese*—Domestic missions general $4.95, Jews .25, through American Church Missionary Society $1.54, total domestic missions $6.74, foreign missions general $4.00, through American Church Missionary Society $1.00, total foreign missions $5.00; total foreign and domestic missions $11.74.

Financial Summary—Contributions—Parochial $458.78, diocesan $60.02, extra diocesan $11.74, total contributions $530.54. *Expenses*—Current parochial $187, grand total of all money raised by the congregation $717.54.

Remarks—The number of individuals, families, communicants, and Sunday School children have been considerably reduced by removals. The Church and Rectory have been newly roofed, and in every way improved and beautified. Rev. Mr. Alfriend of Charles Town, spent the better part of a week with me, preaching day and night most acceptably to all who heard him.

PAROCHIAL REPORT.

Rev. G. A. GIBBONS, address Romney, W. Va. Epiphany Church, Okonoko Mission, Okonoko, Hampshire county. Date of organization, 1886. Present minister took charge 1885.

Church Officers—Church Wardens, Mahlon H. Russell, Okonoko, W. Va.; Registrar, E. W. McGill, Woodrow, Morgan county, W. Va.; Treasurer, Henry M. Russell, Okonoko, W. Va.

Official Acts—Burials 1, public services, Sundays 24, total 24; Holy Communion, public 4, total 4.

Communicants—Number last reported 12, died 1, removed without letter 1, total loss 2; net loss 2; present number total 10.

Congregations—Confirmed persons connected with Parish 10, baptized persons connected with Parish 16, families 4, whole number of individuals 16, number sittings in Church 150.

Rector's Salary—As pledged from this congregation $42, from diocesan missions $250, as pledged from other congregations $250, from convocation missions $50, from American Church Missionary Society $200, total $792.00.

Property—Church, wood, insurance $1,000, value $1,500; total value $1,500.

FINANCIAL REPORT.

Disbursements—For current expenses, (Parochial)—Salary of Rector $42.00; total for current expenses $42.00. *Diocesan*—Salary of Bishops $8.00, permanent fund $9.25, diocesan missions $10.00, religious and theological education $2.00, Sheltering Arms Hospital $1.00, total diocesan contributions $30.25. *Objects without the diocese*—Domestic missions general $4.00, through American Church Missionary Society $3.00, total domestic missions $7.00; total foreign and domestic missions $7.00.

Financial Summary—Contributions—Diocesan $30.25, extra diocesan $7.00, total contributions $37.25. *Expenses*—Current parochial $42; grand total of all money raised by the congregation $79.25.

PAROCHIAL REPORT.

Rev. G. A. GIBBONS, address Romney, W. Va.; New Creek Mission, Keyser, Mineral county.

Church Officers Church Warden, J. W. Linthicum.

Communicants—Number last reported 7, removed without letter 1, total loss 1, net loss 1, present number total 6.

PAROCHIAL REPORT.

Rev. G. A. GIBBONS, address Romney, W. Va. Paw Paw Mission, Paw Paw, Morgan county. Present minister took charge 1893.

Official Acts—Marriages 1, burials 2, Holy Communion, public 2.

Communicants—Number last reported 7, died 1, total loss 1; present number total 6.

Congregations—Confirmed persons connected with Parish 6, baptized persons connected with Parish 14, families 4, whole number of individuals 14.

FINANCIAL REPORT.

Disbursements—For current expenses, (Parochial)—For Rector's expenses $33.00. *Diocesan*—Permanent fund $8.14, diocesan missions $8.77, convocation missions $1.00, widows and orphans, aged and disabled clergy fund $1.68, religious and theological education $1.86, total diocesan contributions $21.45. *Objects without the Diocese*—Through American Church Missionary Society $2.50, total domestic Missions $2.50, foreign missions general $2.51, total foreign missions $2.51; total foreign and domestic missions $5.01.

Financial Summary—Contributions—Diocesan $21.45, extra diocesan $5.01; total contributions $26.46. *Expenses*—Current parochial $33.00; grand total of all money raised by the congregation $59.46.

PAROCHIAL REPORT.

Rev. J. HOWARD GIBBONS, address Point Pleasant, W. Va. Christ Church, Pt. Pleasant Parish, Pt. Pleasant, Mason county. Date of organization 1851. Present minister took charge April 1, 1901.

Church Officers—Church Wardens, Hon. P. C. Eastham, Hon. J. W. English; other vestrymen, Hon. J. S. Spencer, Hon. Rankin Wiley, Col. J. P. R. B. Smith, T. S. Pomeroy, C. C. Bowyer, J. W. C. Heslop; Registrar, Hon. J. W. English, Pt. Pleasant, W. Va.; Treasurer, C. C. Bowyer, Pt. Pleasant, W. Va.; Superintendent of Sunday Schools, Hon. P. C. Eastham, Pt. Pleasant, W. Va.; Sunday School Secretary and Treasurer, Miss K. B. Stribling.

Official Acts—Baptisms, infants 2, adults 2, total 4; presented for confirmation since last report 4, marriages 5, burials 4, public services, Sundays 49, other days 53, total 102; Holy Communion public 10, total 10.

Communicants—Number last reported 56, admitted by confirmation 4, total gain 4; died 2, total loss 2; net gain 2; present number total 58.

Congregations—Confirmed persons connected with Parish 58, baptized persons connected with Parish 75, families 25, number sittings in church, free 250.

Rector's Salary—As pledged from this congregation $350, from diocesan missions $50, as pledged from other congregations $200, from American Church Missionary Society $150, total $750.

Organizations—Sunday Schools, officers and teachers, male 1, female 3, total 4; pupils, male 15, female 13, total 28; advent offering $5.80, lenten offering $8.25, other offerings $32.20, total Sunday School offerings $46.25; Woman's Auxiliary, members 16, Ladies' Guild 30, Chancel Chapter 12, Babies Branch W. A. 12.

Property—Church, brick, insurance $4,000, value $6,000; rectory, frame, insurance $1,000, value $1,200, total insurance $5,000; total value $7,200.

FINANCIAL REPORT.

Receipts—For current expenses—Pledges and subscriptions $350, collections in Church $79.62, total receipts for current expenses $429.62. *For all purposes other than current expenses, (i. e. Contributions)*—Subscriptions $100.00, collections in Church $53.65, for Bishop's Special Anniv. offering $47.25, Babies Branch W. A. $8.33, Woman's Auxiliary $27.60, other sources $421.64, Ladies' Guild ($306.81 from last year) $966.17, Chancel Chapter $29.11, total receipts for contributions $1,653.75; grand total of all receipts i. e. for current expenses and contributions $2,083.37.

Disbursements For current expenses, (Parochial)—Salary of Rector $350.00, other salaries $31.62, insurance $50.00, ordinary repairs on rectory $6.95, other current expenses $48.00, total for current expenses $486.57. *For Contributions—Parochial*—Communion alms $21.54, extraordinary repairs and improvements $803.17, other objects $558.00, total parochial contributions $1,382.71. *Diocesan*—Salary of Bishops $50.00, diocesan missions $50.00, convocation missions $2.15, religious and theological education $1.00, Sheltering Arms Hospital $9.19, offering Bishop's special anniversary $47.25, total diocesan contributions $146.41. *Objects without the Diocese*—Domestic missions general $1, colored people $1, Indians $1, deaf and dumb $1.25, Jews $1, through American Church Missionary Society $1.32, total domestic missions $6.57; foreign missions general $1, 'for China $1, for Africa $1, for Japan $1, for Hayti $1, for Mexico $1, for Philippines $1, Porto Rico $1, Brazil $1.50, Cuba $1, total foreign missions $10.50; total foreign and domestic missions $17.07; American Church Building fund .50, Woman's Auxiliary, money $27.60, general clergy relief fund .50, Bible and Prayer Book Society .50, Babies Branch W. A. $8.33, total without diocese $37.43.

Financial Summary — Contributions — Parochial $1,382.71, diocesan $159.59, extra diocesan $54.50, total contributions $1,596.80. *Expenses*—Current parochial $486.57; grand total of all money raised by the congregation $2,083.37.

PAROCHIAL REPORT.

Rev. J. HOWARD GIBBONS, address Pt. Pleasant, W. Va. Bruce Chapel, Mason county, Present minister took charge April 1, 1901.

Church Officers—Other vestrymen, J. M. H. Beall, E. L. Neale, J. Moore; Treasurer, Miss Mary Beall, Beale, W. Va.; Superintendent of Sunday School, Miss Vause Beale, Beale, W. Va.; Sunday School Secretary and Treasurer, Miss Mary Beale.

Official Acts—Presented for confirmation since last report 2, public services, Sundays 22, other days 6, total 28; Holy Communion, public 6, total 6.

Communicants—Number last reported 19, admitted by confirmation 2, total gain 2, net gain 2, present number total 21.

Congregations—Confirmed persons connected with Parish 21, baptized persons connected with Parish 56, families 15, number sittings in Church free 125.

Rector's Salary—As pledged from this congregation $150, total $150.

Organizations—Sunday Schools, officers and teachers, male 6, female 1, total 7; pupils, male 25, female 30, total 55; advent offering $3.00, lenten offering $3.50, other offerings $7.50, total Sunday School offerings $14.00; Industrial Schools, officers and teachers 5, scholars 25, total 30.

Property—Chapel, brick, insurance $1,000, value $1,500; total insurance $1,000; total value $1,500.

FINANCIAL REPORT.

Receipts—For Current Expenses—Pledges and subscriptions $1.50, total for current expenses $1.50. *For all purposes other than current expenses, (i. e. Contributions)*—Collections in Church $29.76, other sources $22.50, Spec. off. for Bp. Ann. fund $22.50, total receipts for contributions $74.76; grand total of all receipts i. e. for current expenses and contributions $224.76.

Disbursements—For current expenses, (Parochial)—Salary of Rector $150, insurance $14.00, ordinary repairs $8.50, total for current expenses $172.50. *Diocesan*—Salary of Bishops $12.00, diocesan missions $12.00, other objects $1.40, special off. Bp's Ann. fund $22.50, total diocesan contributions $47.90. *Objects without the Diocese*—Domestic missions general .33, colored people .29, Indians .25, deaf and dumb .25, through American Church Missionary Society .29, total domestic missions $1.41; foreign missions general .29, for China .25, for Africa .25, for Japan .25, for Hayti .29, for Mexico .29, for Philippines .54, Porto Rico .29, Brazil .25, Cuba .25, total foreign missions $2.95; total foreign and domestic missions $4.36.

Financial Summary—Contributions—Diocesan $47.90, extra diocesan $4.36, total contributions $52.26. *Expenses*—Current parochial $172.50; grand total of all money raised by the congregation $224.76.

Remarks—Aid is received from the D. M. S. of West Virginia and the A. C. M. S. for *all* work under my charge and is reported only under the report for Christ Church, Pt. Pleasant.

PAROCHIAL REPORT.

Rev. J. HOWARD GIBBONS, address Pt. Pleasant, W. Va. Spilman Chapel, Spilman, Mason county. Present minister took charge April 1, 1901.

Church Officers—Treasurer, H. E. Spilman, Spilman, W. Va.

Official Acts—Baptisms, infants 1, adults 2, total 3; presented for confirmation since last report 4, public services, Sundays 6, other days 7, total 13; Holy Communion, public 1, total 1.

Communicants—Number last reported 16, admitted by confirmation 4, total gain 4; transferred 1, total loss 1, net gain 3, present number total 19.

Congregations—Confirmed persons connected with Parish 19, baptized persons connected with Parish 26, families 12, number free sittings in Church 150.

Rector's Salary—As pledged from this congregation $50.00, total $50.00.

Organizations—Sunday Schools, Lenten offering $2.75.

Property—Chapel, brick, insurance $1,500, value $1,800; total insurance $1,500; total value, $1,800. Money raised from outside sources, $1,094.11; for what objects used, built a new chapel.

FINANCIAL REPORT.

Receipts—*For Current Expenses*—Pledges and subscriptions $50.00, total receipts for current expenses $50.00. *For all purposes other than current expenses, (i. e. Contributions)*—Cash on hand, per last report $9.15, collections in church $25.68, other sources $17.75, special for Bishop's Ann. offering $30.25, total receipts for contributions $82.83; grand total of all receipts i. e. for current expenses and contributions $132.83.

Disbursements—*For current expenses, (Parochial)*—Salary of Rector $50.00, total for current expenses $50.00. *For contributions*—*Parochial*—Other objects $17.75, total parochial contributions $17.75. *Diocesan*—Salary of Bishops $10.00, diocesan missions $10.00, convocation missions $2.00, religious and Theological education $1.00, other objects $6.53, Bishop's special Anniversary offering $30.25, total diocesan contributions $59.78. *Objects without the diocese*—Domestic missions general .56, colored people .56, Indians .25, deaf and dumb .25, Jews .56, total domestic missions $2.18; foreign missions general .56, for China .25, for Africa .25, for Japan .25, for Hayti .25, for Mexico .25, for Philippines .56, Porto Rico .25, Brazil .25, Cuba .25, total foreign missions $3.12; total foreign and domestic missions $5.30.

Financial Summary—Contributions—Parochial $17.75, diocesan $59.78, extra diocesan $5.30, total contributions $82.83. *Expenses*—Current parochial $50.00; grand total of all money raised by the congregation $132.83.

Remarks—Aid is received from the D. M. S. of W. Va. and the A. C. M. S. for *all* work under my charge, and is reported only under the report for Christ Church, Pt. Pleasant. The new chapel was consecrated March 22.

PAROCHIAL REPORT.

Rev. JNO. S. GIBSON, address Huntington. Trinity Church, Cabell Parish, Huntington, Cabell county. Date of organization 1872. Present minister took charge 1892.

Church Officers—Church Wardens, Cameron L. Thompson, Edmund Sehon; other vestrymen, Frank Bliss Enslow, G. A. Northcott, C. D. Emmons, F. D. Fuller, E. S. Alshire, T. L. Trimmer, H. Chambers, F. R. Van Antwerp, Jno. W. Ensign, Robt. L. Archer; Registrar, C. D. Emmons, address Huntington; Treasurer, G. A. Northcott, Huntington; Superintendent of Sunday Schools, G. A. Northcott; Sunday School Secretary and Treasurer, Herman D. Jenkins.

Official Acts—Baptisms, infants 10, adults 1, total 11; presented for confirmation since last report 6, marriages 3, burials 9, catechisings 25, public services, Sundays 125, other days 75, total 200; Holy Communion, public 25, total 25.

Communicants—Number last reported 185, received by letter 3, admitted by confirmation 6, restored to communion 1, added otherwise 8, total gain 18; died 1, transferred 3, removed without letter 8, total loss 11, net gain 7, present number total 192.

Congregations—Confirmed persons connected with Parish 205, baptized persons connected with Parish 410, families 65, individuals not thus included 70, whole number of individuals 435, number sittings in Church all free 425, number sittings in Chapel 75.

Rector's Salary—As paid from this congregation $1,000, as paid from other congregations $264, total $1,264.

Organizations—Sunday Schools, officers and teachers, male 4, female 8, total 12; pupils, male and female 75, total 75; advent offering $13.50, lenten offering $30.00, other offerings $91.50, total Sunday School offerings $135.00; Woman's Auxiliary, members 8; other organizations, Ladies' Society 35.

Property—Church, brick, insurance $18,000, value $21,000; rectory, brick, insurance $3,000 value $6,000; total value $27,000.

FINANCIAL REPORT.

Receipts—For Current Expenses—Cash on hand, per last report $784.00, all sources $5,200.00, total receipts for current expenses $5,984.00. *For all purposes other than current expenses, (i. e. Contributions)*—Collections in Church $604.71, Sunday School $135.00, Woman's Auxiliary $140.00, other sources $767.00, total receipts for contributions $1,646.71; grand total of all receipts i. e. for current expenses and contributions $6,846.71.

Disbursements—For current expenses, (Parochial)—Salary of Rector $1,000.00, other salaries $350.00, insurance $70.00, maintaining Sunday Schools $100.00, ordinary repairs $30.00, interest on debt $195.00, payment on debt $3,054.00, other current expenses $185.00, total for current expenses $5,984.00. *For contributions—Parochial*—Communion alms $68.00, extraordinary repairs and improvements $170.00, parish missions $14.00, other objects $550.00, memorials $240.00, total parochial contributions $1,-042.00. *Diocesan*—Salary of Bishops $90.00, permanent fund $100.00, diocesan missions $75.00, convocation missions $10.00, widows and orphans, aged and disabled clergy fund $26.31, religious and theological education $5.00, Sheltering Arms Hospital $125.40, Bishop's Special fund $15, bell at Ravenswood $5, Woman's Missionary $12, total diocesan contributions $463.71. *Objects without the Diocese*—Domestic missions general $48.50, through American Church Missionary Society $5.00, total domestic missions $53.50; foreign missions general $48.50, for China, special $1.05, Brazil $10.00, Cuba $7.00, total foreign missions $67.00; total foreign and domestic missions $120.50; American Church Building fund $2.85, Woman's Auxiliary, money $17.65, total without diocese $141.00.

Financial Summary—Contributions—Parochial $1,042, diocesan $463.71, extra diocesan $141.00, total contributions $1,646.71. *Expenses*—Current parochial $5,984.00; grand total of all money raised by the congregation $7,630.71; less balance at beginning of the year $784.00, $6,846.71; plus balance on hand in Ladies' Society $75.00, $6,921.71.

Remarks—Trinity Church was consecrated by Bishop Peterkin on Sunday, May 17, 1903.

PAROCHIAL REPORT.

Rev. JNO. S. GIBSON, address Huntington. Grace Church, Wayne Mission, Kenova, Wayne county. Date of organization 1890. Present minister took charge 1892.

Church Officers—Church Warden, Charles C. Coe; other vestrymen, R. Ney Williams, Frank R. Peck; Registrar, Frank R. Peck, Kenova; Treasurer, Chas. C. Coe, Kenova; Superintendent of Sunday Schools, Chas. C. Coe, Kenova.

Official Acts—Presented for confirmation since last report 1, burials 1, catechisings 10, public services, Sundays 50, other days 8, total 58; Holy Communion, public 10, total 10.

Communicants—Number last reported 11, admitted by confirmation 1, total gain 1, transferred 1, removed without letter 2, not otherwise accounted for 1, total loss 4; net loss 3, present number total 8.

Congregations—Confirmed presons connected with Parish 9, baptized persons connected with Parish 9, families 7, free sittings 150.

Rector's Salary—As pledged from this congregation, no pledge; as pledged from other congregations $12.00.

Organizations—Sunday Schools, officers and teachers, male 1, female 1, total 2; pupils, male 10, female 1, total 11; advent offering $1.95, lenten offering $1.40, total Sunday School offerings $3.35.

Property—Church, insurance $1,800, value $2,400.

FINANCIAL REPORT.

Receipts—For current expenses—Cash on hand, per last report $32.24, pledges and subscriptions $138.25, collections in Church $43.29, thank offerings $10, total receipts for current expenses $223.78. *For all purposes other than current expenses, (i. e. Contributions)*—Pledges and subscriptions $7.00, collections in Church $57.81, Sunday School $3.35, total receipts for contributions $68.16; grand total of all receipts i. e. for current expenses and contributions $291.94.

Disbursements—For Current Expenses, (Parochial)—Salary of Rector $175.00, insurance $3, other current expenses $14.20, total for current expenses $192.20. *For Contributions—Parochial*—Extraordinary repairs and improvements $31.03, total parochial contributions $31.03. *Diocesan*—Salary of Bishops $7.00, permanent fund $21, diocesan missions $7, widows and orphans, aged and disabled clergy fund $3.95 religious and theological education $2.60, Sheltering Arms Hospital $7.50, total diocesan contributions $49.05. *Objects without the diocese*—Foreign missions general $7.31, total foreign missions $7.31; total foreign and domestic missions $7.31; American Church Building fund $2.80, total without diocese $10.11.

Financial Summary—Contributions—Parochial $31.03, diocesan $49.05, extra diocesan $10.11, total contributions $90.19. *Expenses*—Current parochial $192.20, balance on hand $9.55; grand total of all money raised by the congregation $291.94.

Remarks—Population shifting. Coming of wood working industries however promises a more stable condition. The adjustment may take some time. Salary of minister as pledged was $200; losses have made payment of that sum difficult and the service is rendered for such salary as is paid. This year it was $50 more than last, but still short of the $200.

PAROCHIAL REPORT.

Rev. JNO. S. GIBSON, address Huntington, W. Va. Mingo Mission, Williamson, Mingo county.

Church Officers—Treasurer, B. Randolph Bias, Williamson, W. Va.

Official Acts—Baptisms, infants 4, total 4; burials 1, other days 12, total 12; Holy Communion, public 4, total 4.

Communicants—Present number total 6.

Congregations—Confirmed persons connected with mission 10, baptized persons connected with mission 26, families 9, individuals not thus included 2, whole number of individuals 33.

FINANCIAL REPORT.

Receipts—For current expenses—Pledges and subscriptions $84.70, collections in Church $6.00, total receipts for current expenses $90.70. *For all purposes other than current expenses (i. e. Contributions)*—Cash on hand, per last report $8.80, collections in Church .70, other sources $10.00, total receipts for contributions $18.00; grand total of all receipts i. e. for current expenses and contributions $101.40.

Disbursements—For current expenses—Parochial—Salary of minister $84.70, other current expenses, rent $6.00, total for current expenses $90.70. *For contributions—Parochial*—Total parochial contributions $10.00. *Objects without the Diocese*—Total foreign and domestic missions .70. Total without diocese .70.

Financial Summary—Contributions—Parochial $10.00, extra diocesan .70, total contributions $10.70. *Expenses* Current parochial $90.70, grand total of all money raised by the congregation $101.40.

Remarks—On May 4th, 1903, the Williamson M. and M. Co. gave a lot to be used for Church purposes.

PAROCHIAL REPORT.

Rev. ANDREW G. GRINNAN, address Weston, W. Va. St. Paul's Church, St. Paul's Parish, Weston, Lewis county. Date of organization 1848. Present minister took charge September, 1900.

Church Officers—Church Wardens, D. M. Bailey, R. H. Harrison; other vestrymen, A. H. Kunst, Er. Ralston, E. G. Davisson, M. B. Ralston, J. S. Mitchell, Louis Bennett, A. A. Warren, E. M. Vandervort; Registrar E. M. Vandervort; Treasurer, E. M. Vandervort, Weston; Superintendent of Sunday Schools, D. M. Bailey, Weston.

Official Acts—Baptisms, infants 4, total 4; presented for confirmation since last report 6, marriages 6, burials 12, catechisings 12, public services, Sundays 85, other days 57, total 142; Holy Communion, public 16, private 2, total 18.

Communicants—Number last reported 77, received by letter 2, admitted by confirmation 6, total gain 8; died 1, removed without letter 3, net gain 4; present number total 81.

Congregations—Confirmed persons connected with Parish 114, baptized persons connected with Parish 207, families 53, individuals not thus included 17, number sittings in Church 300, number free sittings 300, number sittings in Sunday School room 100.

Rector's Salary—As pledged from this congregation $800, from diocesan missions $50, total $850.

Organizations—Sunday Schools, officers and teachers, male 1, female 7, total 8; pupils, male 18, female 34, total 52; advent offering $15.62, lenten offering $20, other offerings $23.99, total Sunday School offerings $59.61; Woman's Auxiliary, members 19, Parish Guild 20, Daughters of King 11.

Property—Church, stone, insurance $5,000, value $15,000; rectory, frame, insurance $1,000 value $2,000.

FINANCIAL REPORT.

Receipts—For current expenses—Cash on hand per last report $1.42, pledges and subscriptions $653.44, collections in Church $286.66, other sources $177.40, Sunday School $23.99, total receipts for current expenses $1,142.91. *For all purposes other than current expenses, (i. e. Contributions)*—Pledges and subscriptions $172.70, collections in Church $100.86, Sunday School $35.62, Woman's Auxiliary $50.08, other sources $118.38, total receipts for contributions $477.64; grand total of all receipts i. e. for current expenses and contributions $1,620.55.

Disbursements—For current expenses, (Parochial)—Salary of Rector $800.04, maintaining Sunday Schools $17.43, ordinary repairs $36.26, other current expenses $172.69, total for current expenses $1,026.42. *For contributions—Parochial*—Communion alms 7, parish missions $28.38, cash on hand $182.12, total parochial contributions $217.50. *Diocesan*—Salary of Bishops $80, permanent fund $70.36, diocesan missions $75. convocation missions ($2.50 from W. Aux.) $12.88, widows and orphans, aged and disabled clergy fund $16.50, Sheltering Arms Hospital ($2.50 from W. Aux.) $17.80, Woman's Missionary, Woman's Aux. $10.50, box valued $26.37 from

Woman's Auxiliary, total diocesan contributions $383.04. *Objects without the Diocese*—General missions $56.79, general missions from Woman's Auxiliary $28.39, through American Church Missionary Society $3.41, total general missions $88.59; foreign missions general, Brazil, from Woman's Auxiliary $2.00, total foreign missions $2.00; total foreign and domestic missions $90.59; Woman's Auxiliary, money $3.00, total without diocese $93.59.

Financial Summary—Contributions—Parochial $217.50, diocesan $283.04, extra diocesan $93.59, total contributions $594.13. *Expenses*—Current parochial $1,026.42; grand total of all money raised by the congregation $1,-620.55.

Remarks—I held ten services at the Hospital for the Insane and officiated at eight funerals. St. Paul's Chapel, four miles from Weston, has been completed and paid for and for the first time has a report for itself.

PAROCHIAL REPORT.

Rev. ANDREW G. GRINNAN, address Weston, W. Va. St. Paul's Chapel, St. Paul's Parish, Weston, Lewis county. Date of organization 1903. Present minister took charge 1900.

Church Officers—Superintendent of Sunday Schools, Miss Hila McBride, Weston, W. Va.

Official Acts—Baptisms, adults 4, total 4; presented for confirmation 8, burials 1, public services, Sundays 18, other days 6, total 24.

Communicants—Number admitted by confirmation 8, added otherwise 1, total gain 9; net gain 9; present number total 9.

Congregations—Confirmed persons connected with Parish 9, baptized persons connected with Parish 14, families 6, number sittings in Chapel 120.

Organizations—Sunday Schools, officers and teachers, female 3, total 3; pupils, male 20, female 30, total 50; other offerings $3.25, total Sunday School offerings $3.25.

Property—Chapel, wood, insurance $750, value $1,000; other property, one-half acre of land; money received from outside sources $150; for what purpose used, from Church Building Fund Commission for erection of Chapel.

FINANCIAL REPORT.

Receipts—For all purposes other than current expenses, (i. e. Contributions)—Thank offerings $9.85, Sunday School $3.25, cash raised for building $622.44, material and labor amounting to $175, total receipts for contributions $810.54.

Disbursements—For Contributions—Parochial—Total parochial contributions $810.54.

Financial Summary—Contributions—Parochial, grand total of all money raised by the congregation $810.54.

Remarks—St. Paul's Chapel, four miles to south west of Weston was commenced in November, 1902, and completed with furniture in April, 1903. It is a pretty wooden building, ceiled in oak, and very substantial. It was paid for as follows: Cash contributions, $622.44; Church Building Fund Commission, $150.00; material and labor donated, $175.00; total $947.44.

PAROCHIAL REPORT.

Rev. JACOB A. HIATT, address Ravenswood. St. John's Church, Ravenswood Parish, Ripley, Jackson county. Present minister took charge June, 1902.

Church Officers—Church Warden, Mr. W. T. Greer; other vestrymen, Mr. G. B. Crow, Mr. Dan. P. Crow, Dr. W. W. Armstrong, Dr. Petty, Mr. C. W. Starcher, Mr. Sam. G. Starcher; Registrar, Mr. G. B. Crow, Ripley; Treasurer, Dr. W. W. Armstrong; Superintendent of Sunday School, W. T. Greer, Ripley; Sunday School Secretary and Treasurer, Mr. Warren Keenan.

Official Acts—Baptisms, adults 3, total 3; presented for confirmation since last report 7, catechisings 10, public services, Sundays 20, other days 15, total 35.

Communicants—Number last reported 29, admitted by confirmation 7, total gain 7; net gain 7; present number total 36.

Congregations—Confirmed persons connected with Parish 36, baptized persons connected with Parish 48, families 15, individuals not thus included 80, whole number of individuals 300, number of scattered communicants in your section not connected with any Parish 25, number sittings in Church 200, all free.

Rector's Salary—As pledged from this congregation $100, through Bishop Peterkin $300, total $400.

Organizations—Sunday Schools, officers and teachers, male 3, female 3, total 6; pupils, male 15, female 25, total 40; advent offering 5, lenten offering 11, total Sunday School offerings 16; other organizations, Ladies' Guild.

Property—Church, frame, insurance $1,000, value $2,000; total insurance $1,000; total value $2,000; indebtedness, due on diocesan assessment for missions $10, due on diocesan assessment for Bishop's fund $15, total indebtedness $25.

FINANCIAL REPORT.

Receipts—For Current Expenses—Pledges and subscriptions $100, collections in Church $40, total receipts for current expenses $140. *For all purposes other than current expenses, (i. e. Contributions)*—Pledges and subscriptions $75, collections in Church $40, Sunday School $15.

Disbursements—For current expenses, (Parochial)—Salary of Rector, for 11 months $91, insurance $10, maintaining Sunday Schools $15, total for current expenses $116. *For contributions—Parochial*—Communion alms $4. *Diocesan*—Permanent fund 20, diocesan missions 6, convocation missions 3, Sheltering Arms Hospital $19, total diocesan contributions $48. *Objects without the Diocese*—Foreign missions general 11, total foreign missions 11.

Financial Summary—Contributions—Parochial $120, diocesan $48, extra diocesan $11, total contributions $179. *Expenses*—Grand total of all money raised by the congregation $179.

PAROCHIAL REPORT.

Rev. JACOB A. HIATT, address Ravenswood. Grace Church, Ravenswood Parish, Ravenswood, Jackson county. Date of organization 1851. Present minister took charge June, 1902.

Church Officers—Church Warden, Mr. F. H. Green; other vestrymen, J. V. Armstrong, Chas. P. Moore, C. E. Crum; Registrar, Mr. J. V. Armstrong, Ravenswood; Treasurer, Mr. F. H. Green, Ravenswood; Superintendent of Sunday School, Mrs. Mary Green, Ravenswood; Sunday School Secretary and Treasurer, Miss Florence Hiatt.

Official Acts—Baptisms, adults 3, total 3; presented for confirmation since last report 6, catechisings 10, public services, Sundays 34, other days 20, total 54.

Communicants—Number last reported 12, received by letter 2, admitted by confirmation 6, total gain 8; net gain 8, present number total 20.

Congregations—Confirmed persons connected with Parish 20, baptized persons connected with Parish 35, families 12, individuals not thus included 25, whole number of individuals, population 1,200; number sittings in Church 200, all free.

Rector's Salary—As pledged from this congregation $75, from diocesan missions $100, from American Church Missionary Society $100, total $275.

Organizations—Sunday Schools, officers and teachers, male 1, female 5,

total 6; pupils, male 5, female 20, total 25; advent offering $2.39, lenten offering $3.25, total Sunday School offerings $5.64.

Property—Church, frame, insurance $2,200, value $3,500; rectory, frame, insurance $800, value $2,000; total insurance $3,000; total value $5,500; indebtedness, on rectory $500; total indebtedness $500.

FINANCIAL REPORT.

Receipts—For Current Expenses—Pledges and subscriptions $75. *For all purposes other than current expenses, (i. e. Contributions)*—Pledges and subscriptions $75, from the Barr legacy $120, grand total of all receipts i. e. for current expenses and contributions $195.

Disbursements—For Current Expenses (Parochial)—Salary of Rector for 11 months $66.25, insurance $10, maintaining Sunday Schools $10. other current expenses $75, total for current expenses $161.25. *For Contributions—Parochial*—Communion alms $3.00, Parish missions $1.00, other objects $10.00, total Parochial contributions $14.00. *Diocesan*—Salary of Bishops $10. permanent fund $15, diocesan missions $5, convocation missions $2, Sheltering Arms Hospital $2, total diocesan contributions $34. *Objects without the Diocese*—Foreign missions general $3.25, total foreign missions $3.25.

Financial Summary—Contributions—Parochial $175.25, diocesan $34, extra diocesan $3.25, total contributions $212.50.

Remarks—I am visiting in connection with Ravenswood, Willow Grove, giving them occasional services.

PAROCHIAL REPORT.

Rev. JACOB A. HIATT, address Ravenswood. Whittle Chapel, Ravenswood Parish, Liverpool, Jackson county. Present minister took charge June, 1902.

Church Officers Treasurer, Mr. Irvin McPhearson, address Liverpool.

Communicants—Number last reported 9, present number total 9.

Congregations—Confirmed presons connected with Parish 9, baptized persons connected with Parish 20, families 5, individuals not thus included 15, sittings in church 200, free sittings all.

Property—Church, frame, insurance $500, value $1,250, total value $1,250.

FINANCIAL REPORT.

Disbursements—For Current expenses (Parochial)—Donation amounting to $20.00 was given to minister, total for current expenses $20. *For*

Contributions—Parochial—Parish missions $2, total parochial contributions $2. *Diocesan*—Salary of Bishops $1, diocesan missions $2, total diocesan contributions $3.

Financial Summary—Contributions—Parochial $2, diocesan $3, total contributions $5. *Expenses*—Grand total of all money raised by the congregation $25.

Remarks—We have some 10 or 12 communicants at Spencer, which can and will be reached from this point. We are planning to make regular visits to Spencer this coming year.

PAROCHIAL REPORT.

Rev. JACOB A. HIATT, address Ravenswood. Church of our Saviour, Ravenswood Parish, Mason City, Mason county. Present minister took charge March.

Church Officers—Treasurer, Mrs. Lahue, address Mason City.

Official Acts—Public services, Sundays 12, total 12.

Communicants—Number last reporter 14, present number total 14.

Congregations—Confirmed persons connected with Parish 14, baptized persons connected with Parish 16, families 5, whole number of individuals 500, sittings in church 100, free sittings all.

Property—Church, brick, value $800.

FINANCIAL REPORT.

Disbursements—For Contributions Diocesan—Permanent fund $5, total diocesan contributions $5.

Remarks—I have commenced to give services to Hartford, where we have a few communicants, and expect to give monthly visits during the coming year.

PAROCHIAL REPORT.

Rev. DAVID W. HOWARD, address Wheeling, W. Va.; assistant, Rev. Thos. J. Oliver Curran. Saint Matthew's Church, Wheeling, Ohio county. Date of organization May 11th, 1819. Present minister took charge Jan'y 1, 1900.

Church Officers—Church Wardens, J. D. Du Bois, G. A. Aschman; other vestrymen, B. W. Peterson, J. C. Brady, W. S. Brady, Peebles Tatum, Hullihen Quarrier, Cyrus P. Flick, Robert Browne, Julien Hearne, Allen Brock, J. J. Holloway; Registrar, Allen Brock, address 1413 Main St.;

Treasurer, Cyrus P. Flick, address 1423 Chapline St.; Superintendent of Sunday Schools, Rev. David W. Howard; Sunday School Secretary and Treasurer, W. Schwertzfeger; lay reader, G. A. Aschman.

Official Acts—Baptisms, infants 12, adults 8, total 20; presented for confirmation since last report 32, marriages 32, burials 17, catechisings 12, public services, Sundays 101, other days 75, total 176; Holy Communion, public 43, private 7, total 50.

Communicants—Number last reported 501, received by letter 23, admitted by confirmation 32, added otherwise 5, total gain 60; died 6, transferred 11, removed without letter 7, total loss 24; net gain 36; present number total 537.

Congregations—Confirmed persons connected with Parish 562, baptized persons connected with Parish 876, families 198, individuals not thus included 117, whole number of individuals 890, sittings in church 600, free sittings 200, sittings in Sunday School room 150.

Rector's Salary—As pledged from this congregation $2,000.

Organizations—Sunday Schools, officers and teachers, male 2, female 10, total 12; pupils, male 70, female 90, total 160; Advent offering $81.00, Lenten offering $200.00; total Sunday School offerings $281.00; Parish schools, officers and teachers 1, scholars 14, total 15; Woman's Auxiliary, members 70, King's Daughters 35, Swope Guild 22, Seabury (Men's) Club 200, Chancel Chapter 11, Junior Auxiliary 30, St. Mary's Auxiliary 17, N. S. Thomas Guild 12.

Property—Church, stone, insurance $50,000, value $65,000; rectory, stone and brick, insurance $6,000, value $12,000; indebtedness on church $4,000; three memorial windows, no valuation.

FINANCIAL REPORT.

Receipts—For Current Expenses—Pledges and subscriptions $2,349.43, pew rent $3,897.71, collections in church $734.36, money borrowed $1,000.00, total receipts for current expenses $7,981.50. *For all purposes other than current expenses, (i. e. Contributions)*—Pledges and subscriptions $176.00, collections in church $760.91, Sunday School $180.00, Woman's Auxiliary and Jun. Aux. $254.00, other sources, communion alms $289.50, Swope Guild $5,000.00, Easter offering $6,500.00, total receipts for contributions $12,984.41; grand total of all receipts i. e. for current expenses and contributions $21,141.91.

Disbursements—For Current Expenses (Parochial)—Salary of Rector $2,000.00, salary of assistant $500.00, other salaries $1,905.41, insurance $470.70, ordinary repairs $568.83, interest on debt $105.22, other current expenses $1,124.58, total for current expenses $6,674.74. *For Contributions—Parochial*—Communion alms $289.50, total Parochial contributions $289.50. *Diocesan*—Salary of Bishops $784.00, permanent fund $6,500.00, diocesan missions $545.00, convocation missions $55.00, widows and orphans, aged and disabled clergy fund $316.75, religious and theological education $15.00, Sheltering Arms Hospital $122.50, Bishop's special fund $176.00, Wheeling City Hospital $5,000, total diocesan contributions $13,514.25. *Objects without the Diocese*—Domestic missions general $429.66, deaf and dumb $28.76, total domestic missions $458.42; foreign missions general $100.00, Brazil $105.00, total foreign missions $205.00; total foreign and domestic missions $663.42.

Financial Summary—Contributions Parochial $289.50, diocesan $13,-514.25, extra diocesan $663.43, total contributions $14,467.17. *Expenses*—Current parochial $6,674.74, grand total of all money raised by the congregation $21,141.91.

PAROCHIAL REPORT.

Rev. EDWARD D. IRVINE, address Wellsburg. Christ Church. Christ Church Parish, Wellsburg, Brooke county. Date of organization, 1793. Present minister took charge Jan. 15, 1903.

Church Officers—Church Wardens, G. A. Baxter; other vestrymen, A. C. Hall, Joseph Faucett, Henry Blankensop; Registrar, Mr. G. A. Baxter, address Wellsburg; Treasurer, Mr. L. H. Buchanan, address Wellsburg; Superintendent of Sunday Schools, Mr. A. C. Hall, Wellsburg; Sunday School Secretary and Treasurer, Miss Rose Wheeler.

Official Acts—Presented for confirmation since last report 1, catechisings 12, public services, Sundays 60, other days 40, total 100; Holy Communion, public 12, total 12.

Communicants—Number last reported 63, received by letter 2, admitted by confirmation 1, added otherwise 2, total gain 5; removed without letter 2, lapsed 3, not otherwise accounted for 5, total loss 10; net loss 5, present number total 58.

Congregations—Confirmed persons connected with Parish 60, families 25, whole number of individuals 125, sittings in church 165, free sittings all.

Rector's Salary—As pledged from this congregation $450.00, from diocesan missions $200, as pledged from other congregations $60, total $710.

Organizations—Sunday Schools, officers and teachers, male 2, female 3, total 5; pupils, male 15, female 25, total 40; Advent offering $6.86, Lenten offering $10.91, other offerings $42.67, total Sunday School offerings $60.34; other organizations, Parish Guild, Chancel Chapter, Choir Guild.

Property—Church, frame insurance $2,500, value $4,300; rectory, frame, insurance $1,200, value $1,700; Sunday School room in church building, frame, total value $6,000.

FINANCIAL REPORT.

Receipts—For Current Expenses—Pledges and subscriptions $435, other sources $19.43, total receipts for current expenses $452.43. *For all purposes other than current expenses, (i. e. Contributions)*—Subscriptions $156.36, collections in church $6.08, Sunday School $10.91, total receipts for contributions $173.35; grand total of all receipts i. e. for current expenses and contributions $627.78.

Disbursements—For Current Expenses (Parochial)—Salary of Rector $338.96, other salaries $36.00, insurance $12.00, maintaining Sunday Schools $35.54, ordinary repairs $20.20, other current expenses $11.73, total for current expenses $454.43. *For Contributions—Parochial*—Communion alms $6.08. *Diocesan*—Salary of Bishops $25.00, permanent fund $90.50, diocesan missions $25.00, Sheltering Arms Hospital $7.00, Advent offering from Sunday School $6.86, total diocesan contributions $154.36. *Objects without the Diocese*—Missions general by Sunday School $10.91, total missions $10.91; total foreign and domestic missions $10.91; Florida sufferers $12.00; total without Diocese $12.91.

Financial Summary—Contributions—Parochial $6.08, diocesan $154.36, extra diocesan $12.91, total contributions $173.35. *Expenses*—Current parochial $454.43; grand total of all money raised by the congregation $627.78.

Remarks—Rev. H. B. Thomas resigned Nov. 1st, 1902. This report is as complete as data at hand will allow it to be made.

PAROCHIAL REPORT.

Rev. EDWARD D. IRVINE, address Wellsburg. St. John's Church, St. John's Parish, Brooke county. Date of organization, 1793. Present minister took charge March 29th, 1903.

Church Officers—Church Wardens, John Baxter, James Williamson; other vestrymen, Norman Pool, Jas. Allison; Registrar, Sam'l Baxter, address Route III, Wellsburg; Treasurer, Jas. Williamson, address Route III, Wellsburg.

Communicants—Number last reported 22, present number total 22.

Congregations—Confirmed persons connected with Parish 22, sittings in church 300.

Rector's Salary—As pledged from this congregation $60.

Remarks—I can only report that Rev. H. B. Thomas resigned Nov. 1st, 1902, that I held my first service March 29th, 1903, and that I have held five services—one service was on the occasion of the visitation of the Bishop Coadjutor. The attendance at the Sunday services has been good.

PAROCHIAL REPORT.

Rev. ARTHUR M. LEWIS, address Powellton, W. Va. St. David's Parish, Powellton, Fayette county. Date of organization, Dec. 5th, 1886. Present minister took charge Sept. 1st, 1901.

Church Officers — Church Wardens, Thomas Price; other vestrymen, Godwin H. Powel, D. T. Evans, J. I. Absalom, D. Swain; Registrar, J. I. Absalom, address Powellton, W. Va.; Treasurer, D. Swain, address Powellton W. Va.; Superintendent of Sunday Schools, D. Swain, Powellton, W. Va.; Sunday School Secretary and Treasurer, D. Swain; lay readers, Godwin H. Powel.

Official Acts—Baptisms, infants 10, adults 2, total 12; presented for confirmation since last report 4, burials 2, public services, Sundays 42, other days 9, total 51; Holy Communion, public 6, total 6.

Communicants—Number last reported 25, admitted by confirmation 4, total gain 4; removed without letter 2, total loss 2; net gain 2; present number total 27.

Congregations—Confirmed persons connected with Parish 27, baptized persons connected with Parish 29, families 15, whole number of individuals 56, sittings in church 110, all free.

Rector's Salary—As pledged from this congregation $402.00, total $402.

Organizations Sunday Schools, officers and teachers, male 3, female 3, total 6; pupils, male 23, female 27, total 50; Advent offering $4.88, Lenten offering $7.58, other offerings $12.64, total Sunday School offerings $25.10; other organizations, Ladies' Aid Society 15. Location of schools mentioned above, Powellton, W. Va.

Property—Other property, chancel furniture, pulpit, etc., $300.00.

FINANCIAL REPORT.

Receipts—For Current Expenses—Cash on hand, per last report $182.62, pledges and subscriptions $431.30, collection in church $56.61, other sources $25.54, contingent fund $20.50, Sunday School $25.10, Ladies' Aid Society $21.95, total receipts for current expenses $763.62.

Disbursements—For Current Expenses (Parochial)—Salary of Rector $402.00, maintaining Sunday Schools $20.94, other current expenses $49.92, other objects, hymnals, etc. $13.90, Ladies' Aid Society, church work $19.-20, total for current expenses $505.96. *Diocesan*—Salary of Bishops $20.50, permanent fund $15.00, diocesan missions $20.00, convocation missions $2.00, widows and orphans, aged and disabled clergy fund $2.25, Sheltering Arms Hospital $4.00, total diocesan contributions $63.75. *Objects without the Diocese*—Domestic missions general $2.70, Jews $1.76, total domestic missions $4.46; foreign missions general $8.74, Cuba 4.00, total foreign missions $12.74; total foreign and domestic missions $17.20; general clergy relief fund $2.20, total without diocese $19.40.

Financial Summary—Contributions—Parochial $497.85, diocesan $63.75, extra diocesan $19.40, total contributions $581.00. *Expenses*—Current parochial $505.96, grand total of all money raised by the congregation, $581.00.

PAROCHIAL REPORT.

Rev. A. M. LEWIS, address Montgomery, W. Va. Calvary Episcopal Church, Montgomery Parish, Montgomery, Fayette county. Date of organization, 1878. Present minister took charge Sept. 1st, 1901.

Church Officers—Church Wardens, N. R. Cole; other vestrymen, Dr. O. J. Henderson, Hubbard Smith, W. K. Bridges, Venable Johnson; Registrar, W. K. Bridges, address Longacre, W. Va.; Treasurer, Venable Johnson, address Crescent, W. Va.; Superintendent of Sunday Schools, Mrs. O. J. Henderson, Montgomery, W. Va.

Official Acts—Presented for confirmation since last report 2, catechisings 3, public services, Sundays 25, other days 7, total 32; Holy Communion, public 3, total 3.

Communicants—Number last reported 17, received by letter 2, admitted by confirmation 2, total gain 4; removed without letter 4, total loss 4; present number total 17.

Congregations—Confirmed persons connected with Parish 17, baptized persons connected with Parish 32, families (9), individuals not thus included 5, whole number of individulas 37, sittings in church 150, free sittings 150, sittings in Sunday School room 150.

Rector's Salary—As pledged from this congregation $200.00, total $200.

Organizations—Sunday Schools, officers and teachers, female 2, total 2; pupils, male about 7, female 15, total 22; Advent offering $3.48, Lenten offering $6.12, total Sunday School offerings $9.59.

Property—Church, frame, value $1,250.00; rectory (fund) value $1,428.-75; other property, lot, value $500.00, total value $3,178.75; for what objects used general fund.

FINANCIAL REPORT.

Receipts—For Curent Expenses—Cash on hand, per last report $70.33, pledges and subscriptions $131.00, collections in church $162.01, interest from investments $78.75, other sources, Sunday School $9.59, contingent fund $15.00, Ladies' Aid Society $19.00, total receipts for current expenses $406.93.

Disbursements—For Current Expenses (Parochial)—Salary of Rector $200.00, other salaries, sexton $22.00, other current expenses $20.96, other objects $137.20, contingent fund $15.00, permanent fund $7.92, total for current expenses $403.08; balance May 1st, 1903, $3.85—$406.93. *Diocesan*—Salary of Bishops $15.00, permanent fund $7.92, diocesan missions $15, convocation missions $1.00, widows and orphans, aged and disabled clergy fund $101.00, Sheltering Arms Hospital $5.13, total diocesan contributions $145.05. *Other objects without the Diocese*—Domestic missions general $3.25, Jews $1.70, total domestic missions $4.95; foreign missions general $3.06, Cuba $3.06, total foreign misions $6.12; total foreign and domestic missions $11.07;. general clergy relief fund $4.00, total without diocese $15.07.

Financial Summary—Contributions—Diocesan $145.05, extra diocesan $15.07, total contributions $160.12. *For Expenses*—Current parochial $176.48; grand total of all money raised by the congregation $336.60.

Remarks—The financial summary, showing total raised by congregation, $336.60, also shows that the amount $45.52 was used from balance on hand at beginning of year. This is due to some outstanding uncollected amount of about $100.00, which I think can be gotten sooner or later. The church has sustained distressing loss of several of its most substantial and ready working members recently, but on the whole is in good condition, self-supporting, and increasing both in congregations and interest.

Most respectfully,

VENABLE JOHNSON, *Treasurer.*

PAROCHIAL REPORT.

• Rev. ARTHUR M. LEWIS, address Ansted, W. Va. Church of the Redeemer, Ansted, Fayette county. Date of organization, 1879. Present minister took charge 1901.

Church Officers—Church Wardens, Wm. N. Page; Committee, Wm. N. Page, R. C. Taylor, John C. R. Taylor, Wm. H. Evans, Patrick Moran, J. R. Brashears, James O. Bailey; Registrar, John C. R. Taylor, address Ansted, W. Va.; Treasurer, Wm. H. Evans, address Ansted, W. Va.; Superintendent of Sunday Schools, Wm. N. Page, Ansted, W. Va.; Sunday School Secretary and Treasurer, John C. R. Taylor.

Official Acts—Baptisms, infants 2, total 2; marriages 2, burials 1, catechisings 12, public services, Sundays 22, other days 20, total 42; Holy Communion, public 6, total 6.

Communicants—Number last reported 37, present number total 37.

Congregations—Confirmed persons connected with Parish 37, baptized persons connected with Parish 73, families 17, individuals not thus included 4, whole number of individuals 77, sittings in church 250, free sittings 250.

Rector's Salary—As pledged from this congregation $200.00, total $200.

Organizations—Sunday Schools, officers and teachers, male 2, female 4, total 6; pupils, male 22, female 40, total 62; Advent offering $6.45, Lenten offering $5.10, other offerings $31.53, total Sunday School offerings $43.08; Parish schools, officers and teachers 1, scholars 23, total 24; other organizations, Ladies' Aid Society 10. Location of schools mentioned above at the church at Ansted.

Property—*Church*, material $400.00, value $2,500.00; total material $400.00, total value $2,500; money raised from outside sources $187.50, for what objects used, Parish school.

FINANCIAL REPORT.

Receipts—*For Current Expenses*—Cash on hand, per last report $43.54, pledges and subscriptions $196.91, collections in church $95.71, other sources, B. M. Spurr $187.50, school tuition $80.50—$268.00; Ladies' Aid Society, balance on hand $34.07, expended on church work $26.32, Sunday School collections $43.08, total receipts for current expenses $673.56.

Disbursements—*For Current Expenses* (*Parochial*)—Salary of Rector $200.00, maintaining Sunday Schools $44.83, Ladies' Aid charity, etc. $26.-32, Parochial school $227.85, total for current expenses $499.00. *Diocesan*—Salary of Bishops $20.00, permanent fund $30.34, diocesan missions $20.00, convocation missions $2.00, widows and orphans, aged and disabled clergy fund $3.00, religious and theological education $5.00, Sheltering Arms Hospital $5.00, total diocesan contributions $85.34. *Objects without the Diocese*—Domestic missions general $4.00, Jews $1.75, total domestic missions $5.75; foreign missions general $2.55, Brazil $2.55, total foreign missions $5.10; total foreign and domestic missions $10.85; American Church building fund $10.85, general clergy relief fund $3.24, total without diocese $14.09.

Financial Summary—*Contributions*—Parochial $499, diocesan $85.34, extra diocesan $14.00, total contributions $598.43; grand total of all money raised by the congregation $673.56.

PAROCHIAL REPORT.

Rev. JOHN TILTON MARLEY, address 247 Willey St., Morgantown. Trinity Church, Trinity Parish, Morgantown, Monongalia county. Date of organization, 1860. Present minister took charge Nov., 1900.

Church Officers—Church Wardens, Capt. W. C. Marshall, Mr. S. B. Bown; other vestrymen, Col. J. C. Frazer, Bryan Gordon, Mr. Geo. Rogers,

Chas. Warrick, W. A. Page, L. D. Beall; Registrar, Dr. St. George T. Brooke.

Official Acts—Baptisms, infants 5, adults 1, total 6; presented for confirmation since last report 8, marriages 2, burials 2, catechisings 12, public services, Sundays 82, other days 20, total 102; Holy Communion, public 9, total 9.

Communicants—Number last reported 60, received by letter 17, admitted by confirmation 8, added otherwise 11, total gain 36; died 1, transferred 2, removed without letter 2, total loss 5; net gain 31; present number total 91.

Congregations—Confirmed persons connected with Parish 91, baptized persons connected with Parish 118, families 50, individuals not thus included 2, sittings in church 225, free sittings 225.

Rector's Salary—As pledged from this congregation $600, from diocesan missions $100, from general board $100, total $800.

Organizations—Sunday Schools, officers and teachers, male 3, female 1, total 4; pupils, male 21, female 18, total 39; Advent offering $3.00, Lenten offering $11.40, other offerings $18.00, total Sunday School offerings $32.40, other organizations Ladies' Aid.

Property—Church, wood, insurance $25.00, value $300.00.

FINANCIAL REPORT.

Receipts—For Current Expenses—Cash on hand, per last report $83.16, pledges and subscriptions $826.75, collections in church $130.67, total receipts for current expenses $1,040.58. *For all purposes other than current expenses, (i. e. Contributions)*—Pew rent $42.63, collections in church $186.27, Sunday School $32.40, Woman's Auxiliary $328.23, other sources $25.00, $6.00, total receipts for contributions $360.63; grand total of all receipts i. e. for current expenses and contributions $1,401.21.

Disbursements—For Current Expenses (Parochial)—Salary of Rector $600.00, other current expenses $430.40, total for current expenses $1,030.-40. *For Contributions Parochial*—Communion alms $42.63, other objects $321.97, total parochial contributions $364.60. *Diocesan*—Salary of Bishops $25.00, permanent fund $136.27, diocesan missions $25.93, convocation missions $10.00, widows and orphans, aged and disabled clergy fund $6.00, Sheltering Arms Hospital $18.30, total diocesan contributions $221.50. *Objects without the Diocese*—Brazil and Cuba $11.40, Woman's Auxiliary, boxes, value $10.00, total without diocese $21.40.

Financial Summary—Contributions—Parochial $364.60, diocesan $221.50, extra diocesan $21.40, total contributions $607.50. *Expenses*—Current parochial $1,030.40; grand total of all money raised by the congregation $1,637.90.

Remarks—Trinity Parish is in the best financial condition since its organization. It, last October 1st, at a Parish meeting voluntarily raised the Rector's salary to $1,000 per year for the balance of the year. Same is paid in full. This year we pay our Rector $1,000 without any outside assistance and respectfully state that we have no need this year for any aid from missionary funds. Every debt is paid and we owe no one. We thank the Diocese for what it has done for us and we will endeavor to show our appreciation by helping others who are as weak as we have been.

Respectfully submitted,

J. C. FRAZER, *Treasurer.*

PAROCHIAL REPORT.

Rev. C. E. A. MARSHALL, address Shepherdstown, Trinity Church, St. Andrew's Parish, Shepherdstown, Jefferson county. Present minister took charge February 1, 1903.

Church Officers—Church Wardens, A. S. Dandridge, H. W. Potts; other vestrymen, P. P. Marshall, F. W. Muzzey, Dr. Hopkins Gibson, Jno. O. Aglionby, Dr. D. W. Border, J. S. Bragonier; Registrar, J. S. Bragonier, address Shepherdstown; Treasurer, J. S. Bragonier, address Shepherdstown; Superintendent of Sunday School, A. S. Dandridge, Shepherdstown.

Official Acts—Baptisms, infants 1, total 1; marriages 1, burials 2, catechisings 1, public services, Sundays 32, other days about 20, total 52; Holy Communion, public 3, total 3.

Communicants—Number last reported 145, added otherwise 3, total gain 3; died 2, transferred 1, removed without letter 1, total loss 4; net loss 1; present number total 144.

Rector's Salary—As pledged from this congregation $600, total $600.

Organizations—Sunday Schools, No. 1, officers and teachers, male 3, female 6, total 9; No. 2, officers and teachers, female 3, total 3; total 12.

Property—Church, stone, insurance $3,500, value $12,300, chapel, stone, value $3,000; rectory, brick, insurance $3,250, value $6,000; chapel at Duffields, frame, insurance $500, value $1,500; total value, insurance $7,-250, value $22,800.

FINANCIAL REPORT.

Disbursements—For Current Expenses (*Parochial*)—Salary of Rector $488.00, other salaries $48.00, maintaining Sunday Schools $11.45, current expenses and other objects $134.30, total for current expenses $681.75. *Diocesan*—Salary of Bishops $66.35, permanent fund $24.82, diocesan missions $63.94, convocation missions $35.00, widows and orphans, aged and disabled clergy fund $20.00, Sheltering Arms Hospital $21.00, theological seminary $17.39, Bishop's special fund $200.00, total diocesan contributions $448.50. *Objects without the Diocese*—Domestic missions general $32.54, Indians $3.30, total domestic missions $35.84; foreign missions general $42.76, for Africa, Little Anna School $25.00, total foreign missions $67.76; total foreign and domestic missions $103.60; American Church building fund $7.53, American Bible Society $8.64, total without diocese $119.77.

Financial Summary—Contributions—Parochial $681.75, diocesan $448.50, extra diocesan $119.77; grand total of all money raised by the congregation $1,250.02.

PAROCHIAL REPORT.

Rev. ROBT. N. MEADE, address Bramwell. Holy Trinity Mission, Bramwell, Mercer county. Present minister took charge April 15, 1903.

Church Officers—Church Warden, Col. John D. Hewitt; other vestrymen, F. L. Schoen, T. M. Archer, W. D .Tyler, B. F. Keller, W. C. Brooke, A. R. Paddock; Registrar, W. D. Tyler, address Bramwell; Treasurer, W. D. Tyler, address Bramwell; Superintendent of Sunday School, W. D. Tyler, Bramwell.

Official Acts—Baptisms, infants 2, total 2; presented for confirmation since last report 2, marriages 4, burials 2, public services, Sundays 51, other days 14, total 65.

Communicants—Number last reported 30, received by letter 4, admitted by confirmation 2, added otherwise 4, total gain 10; transferred 3, total loss 3; net gain 7, present number total 37.

Congregations—Confirmed persons connected with Parish 44, baptized persons connected with Parish 74, families 17, individuals not thus included 11, whole number of individuals 74, number sittings in Church 200, all free.

Rector's Salary—As pledged from this congregation $600, total $600.

Organizations—Sunday schools, officers and teachers, male 2, female 5, total 7; pupils, male 32, female 32, total 64; lenten offering $35.06 other offerings $21.89, total Sunday School offerings $55.94; other organizations, Woman's Guild 14, Junior Charity Society 20. Location of schools mentioned above No. 1, Bramwell.

Property—Church, frame, insurance $2,600, value $5,000; rectory frame, insurance $3,000 value $4,000; total insurance $5,600; total value $9,000. Indebtedness, on other property insura nce .Pshrdlu wartmahm Indebtedness, on rectory $500, other debts $32, money borrowed $500; total indebtedness $1,032; money raised from outside sources $150, for what objects used, special repairs rectory fund and general expenses.

FINANCIAL REPORT.

Receipts—For current expenses—Rectory fund $50.44, cash on hand, per last report, general fund $3.97, pledges and subscriptions $4,466.64, rectory fund contr. and sub. $967.33, collections in church $60.24; other sources Easter offering $73.71, special repair subs. $225.00, funds without diocese $150.00, total receipts for current expenses $1,977.33. *For all purposes other than current expenses, (i. e. Contributions)*—Money borrowed $500.00, Sunday School $55.94, other sources, alms $13.97, total receipts for contributions $569.91; grand total of all receipts i. e. for current expenses and contributions $2,547.24.

Disbursements—For current expenses, (Parochial)—Salary of Rector $600.00, salary of assistant $30.00, maintaining Sunday Schools $19.20, ordinary repairs $4.86, interest on debt $85.60, cash on hand general fund $1.44, cash on hand rectory fund $128.81, total for current expenses $869.91. *For Contributions—Parochial* Communion alms $13.97, extraordinary repairs and improvements $1,663.36, total for parochial contributions $1,-677.33. *Diocesan*—Salary of Bishops $30.00, diocesan missions $30.00, widows and orphans, aged and disabled clergy fund $14.30, Bishop Peterkin memorial $38.44, total diocesan contributions $112.74. *Objects without the Diocese*—Jews $1.06, total domestic missions $1.06; foreign missions general $8.00, total foreign missions $8.00; total foreign and domestic missions $9.06. American Church building fund $2.00, total without diocese $11.06.

Financial Summary—Contributions—Parochial $877.33, diocesan $112.74, extra diocesan $11.06, total contributions $1,001.13. *Expenses*—Current parochial $1,669.91; grand total of all money raised by the congregation $2,671.04.

PAROCHIAL REPORT.

Rev. ROBT. N. MEADE, address Bramwell. Grace Mission, Eckman, McDowell county. Present minister took charge April 15, 1903.

Church Officers—Church Warden, Grace Chapel, Dr. P. H. Killey; other vestrymen, Dr. Luther Clarke, Wm. D. Ord; Superintendent of Sunday Schools, Mrs. Ord, Landgraft.

Official Acts—Presented for confirmation since last report 1, marriages 1, public services, Sundays 20, other days 2, total 22.

Communicants—Number last reported 45, received by letter 1, admitted by confirmation 1, added otherwise 1, total gain 3; transferred 22, total loss 22; net loss 19, present number total 26.

Congregations—Confirmed persons connected with Parish 27, baptized persons connected with Parish 39, families 14, individuals not thus included 6, whole number of individuals 50, number of scattered communicants in your section not connected with any Parish 1, number sittings in Chapel 125.

Organizations—Sundays Schools, officers and teachers, female 3, total 3; pupils, male 12, female 12, total 24; lenten offering $2.97.

Proptrey—Chapel, frame, insurance $800, value $1,200; total insurance $800; total value $1,200.

FINANCIAL REPORT.

Receipts—For current expenses—Pledges and subscriptions $237.59. collections in Church $55.20, total receipts for current expenses $292.79. *For all purposes other than current expenses, (i. e. Contributions)* Pledges and subscriptions $103.90, collections in church $9.53, total receipts for contributions $113.43; grand total of all receipts i. e. for current expenses and contributions $406.32.

Disbursements—For current expenses, (Parochial)—Salary of Rector $197.62, salary of assistant $63.64, insurance $16.78, other current expenses $14.75, total for current expenses $292.79. *For contributions—Parochial*—Extraordinary repairs and improvements $80, total parochial contributions $80. *Diocesan*—Permanent fund $23.90, diocesan missions $2.75, total diocesan contributions $26.65. *Objects without the Diocese*—Total foreign and domestic missions $6.78.

Financial Summary—Contributions—Parochial $80, diocesan $26.65, extra diocesan $6.78, total contributions $113.43. *Expenses*—Current parochial $292.79; grand total of all money raised by the congregation $406.32.

PAROCHIAL REPORT.

Rev. ROBT. N. MEADE. St. Antipas Mission, Welch, McDowell county. Pesent minister took charge April 15, 1903.

Church Officers—Treasurer, Jas. A. Strother, address Welch.

Official Acts—Baptisms, infants 3, total 3; presented for confirmation since last report 1, public services, Sundays 12, other days 2, total 14.

Communicants—Number last reported 10, received by letter 7, admitted by confirmation 1, total gain 8; transferred 3, not otherwise accounted for 1, total loss 3; net gain 5; present number total 15.

Congregations—Confirmed persons connected with Parish 15, baptized persons connected with Parish 28, families 10, individuals not thus included 7, whole number of individuals 43. number of scattered communicants in your section not connected with any Parish 8.

Property Other property, 2 lots, value $400; total value $400. Money raised from outside sourses $314.82, for what objects used, applied to building fund.

FINANCIAL REPORT.

Receipts—For current Expenses—Pledges and subscriptions $104, collections in Church $58.36, total receipts for current expenses $162.36. *For all purposes other than current expenses, (i. e. Contributions)*—Pledges and subscriptions, building fund $203.00, collections in Church $11.21, Woman's Guild for building fund $210.00, total receipts for contributions $424.21; grand total of all receipts i. e. for current expenses and contributions $586.37.

Disbursements—For current expenses, (Parochial)—Salary of Rector $144.36, salary of assistant $5.56, other current expenses $12.44, total for current expenses $162.36. *For contributions—Parochial*—Other objects, building fund $413.00, total parochial contributions $413.00. *Diocesan*—Permanent fund $2.00, diocesan missions $2.00. *Objects without the diocese* Total foreign and domestic missions $7.21.

Financial Summary—Contributions—Parochial, $413, diocesan $4, extra diocesan $7.21, total contributions $424.21. *Expenses*—Current parochial $162.36; grand total of all money raised by the congregation $586.57.

PAROCHIAL REPORT.

Rev. ROBT. N. MEADE. Algoma Mission, Algoma, McDowell county. Present minister took charge April 15, 1903.

Official Acts—Baptisms, infants 4, total 4; public services, Sundays 7, other days 2, total 9.

Communicants—Present number total 8.

Congregations—Confirmed persons connected with Parish 8, baptized persons connected with Parish 18, families 7, individuals not thus included 7, whole number of individuals 23.

FINANCIAL REPORT.

Receipts—For current expenses—Pledges and subscriptions $1, collections in Church $15.19, total receipts for current expenses $16.19. *For all purposes other than current expenses, (i. e. Contributions)*—Pledges and subscriptions $16, collections in Church $3.71, total receipts for contributions $19.71; grand total of all receipts i. e. for current expenses and contributions $35.90.

Disbursements—For current expenses, (Parochial)—Salary of assistant $9.19, other current expenses $7.00, total for current expenses $16.19. *Diocesan*—Permanent fund $3, diocesan missions $3. *Objects without the Diocese*—Total foreign and domestic missions $13.71.

Financial Summary—Contributions—Diocesan 6, extra diocesan $13.71, total contributions $19.71. *Expenses*—Current parochial $16.19; grand total of all money raised by the congregation $35.90.

PAROCHIAL REPORT.

Rev. ROBT. N. MEADE, address Bramwell. Maybuery, McDowell county. Present minister took charge April 15, 1903.

Official Acts—Baptisms, infants 1, total 1; presented for confirmation since last report 1, public services, Sundays none, other days 2, total 2.

Communicants—Present number total 3.

Congregations—Confirmed persons connected with Parish 3, baptized persons connected with Parish 10, families 2, individuals not thus included 1, whole number of individuals 10, number of scattered communicants in your section not connected with any Parish 2.

FINANCIAL REPORT.

Disbursements For contributions—Diocesan—Permanent fund $2, diocesan missions $2, total diocesan contributions $4.

Financial Summary—Contributions—Diocesan $4, total contributions $4; grand total of all money raised by the congregation $4.

PAROCHIAL REPORT.

Rev. ROBT. N. MEADE. Elkhorn mission, Elkhorn, McDowell county. Present minister took charge April 15, 1903.

Official Acts—Baptisms, infants 2, total 2; public services, Sundays 7, other days 2, total 9.

Communicants—Present number total 8.

Congregations—Confirmed persons connected with Parish 10, baptized persons connected with Parish 19, families 4, individuals not thus included 4, whole number of individuals 20.

FINANCIAL REPORT.

Receipts—For current expenses—Pledges and subscriptions $4, collections in church $9.60, total receipts for current expenses $13.60. *For all purposes other than current expenses, (i. e. Contributions)*—Pledges and subscriptions $9, collections in Church $4.38, total receipts for contributions $13.28; grand total of all receipts ,i. e. for current expenses and contributions $26.98.

Disbursements—For current expenses, (Parochial)—Salary of assistant $8, other current expenses $5.60, total for current expenses $13.60. *For Contributions—Diocesan*—Salary of Bishops $1, permanent fund $1.50, diocesan missions $6.50, total diocesan contributions $9.00. *Objects without the Diocese*—Total foreign and domestic missions $4.38.

Financial Summary—Contributions—Diocesan $9.00, extra diocesan $4.38, total contributions $13.38. *Expenses* — Current Parochial $13.60; grand total of all money raised by the congregation $26.98.

PAROCHIAL REPORT.

Rev. ROBT. N. MEADE. Crane Creek Mission, Mora, Mercer county. Present minister begun work here, August, 1902. Took full charge, April 15, 1902.

Official Acts—Public services, Sundays 8, other days 1, total 9.

Communicants—Present number total 8.

Congregations—Confirmed persons connected with Parish 8, baptized persons connected with Parish 17, families 11, whole number of individuals 25.

FINANCIAL REPORT.

Receipts—For current expenses—Collections in Church $14.64, total receipts for current expenses $14.64. *For all purposes other than current expenses, (i. e. Contributions)*—Collections in Church $6.35.

Disbursements—For current expenses, (Parochial)—Salary of Assistant $10.64, other current expenses $4, total for current expenses $14.64. *For Contributions—Parochial*—Other objects, building fund $6.35.

Financial Summary—Contributions—Parochial $6.35, total contributions $6.35. *Expenses*—Current Parochial $14.64; grand total of all money raised by the congregation $20.99.

Remarks—This report includes all of Rock District, Mercer county not reported at Bramwell. We hope to build a cheap frame chapel here; are of course, ready to receive help.—R. N. M.

PAROCHIAL REPORT.

Rev. J. D. MILLER, address Harper's Ferry, W. Va. St. John's Church, Harper's Ferry, Jefferson county. Date of organization 1851. Present minister took charge June 15, 1902.

Church Officers—Church Warden, Geo. H. Child; Treasurer, Geo. H. Child, Harper's Ferry; Superintendent of Sunday Schools, Barnabas Bryan, Hall Town, W. Va.; Lay Reader, Barnabas Bryan.

Official Acts—Baptisms, infants 6, adults 1, total 7; presented for confirmation since last report 2, public services, Sundays 41, other days 31, total 72; Holy Communion, public 12, total 12.

Communicants—Number last reported 33, admitted by confirmation 2, total gain 2; removed without letter 3, total loss 3; net loss 1; present number total 32.

Congregations—Confirmed persons connected with Parish 35, baptized persons connected with Parish 35, families 10, number sittings in Church 150, all free.

Rector's Salary—As pledged from this congregation $125.00, from diocesan missions $200.00, as pledged from other congregations $200.00. from convocation missions $75.00, total $600.00.

Organizations—Sunday Schools, officers and teachers, male 1, female 4, total 5; pupils, male 14, female 34, total 50; advent offering $17.00, lenten offering $17.50, other offerings $13.14, total Sunday School offerings $47.64.

Property—Church, wood, insurance $1,200.00, value $2,000.00; rectory wood, insurance $800.00, value $1,000.00; total value $3,000.00. Indebtedness on rectory $275.00, total indebtedness $275.00.

FINANCIAL REPORT.

Receipts—For current expenses—Cash on hand, per last report $90.00, pledges and subscriptions and collections $639.62, total receipts for current expenses $729.62.

Disbursements—For current expenses, (Parochial)—Salary of Rector $133.00; ordinary repairs, interest on debt, payment on debt, $320.74; other current expenses $53.28, total for current expenses $507.02. *For Contributions—Diocesan*—Salary of Bishops $16.00, permanent fund $37.00, diocesan missions $34.68, convocation missions $6.75, widows and orphans aged and disabled clergy fund $7.13, religious and theological education $3.48, Sheltering Arms Hospital $10.00, total diocesan contributions $115.04. *Objects without the diocese*—Domestic missions general $22.29, total domestic missions $22.29; foreign missions general $10.00, for Mexico .67, through American Church Missionary Society $8.80, total foreign missions $19.47; total foreign and domestic missions $41.76.

Financial Summary—Contributions—Parochial $507.02, diocesan $115.04, extra diocesan $41.76, total contributions $663.82. Grand total of all money raised by the congregation $729.62; balance on hand $65.80.

Remarks—Sunday School offerings are included in above items.

PAROCHIAL REPORT.

Rev. J. D. MILLER, address Harper's Ferry, W. Va. Mt. Zion Church, Norbourne Parish, Hedgesville, Berkeley county. Date of organization 1817. Present minister took charge June 15, 1902.

Church Officers—Church Wardens, Geo. T. Kreglow, W. H. Kilmer; other vestrymen, J. H. Miller, F. H. Robins, P. C. Myers, Morgan Shaffer, R. B. Kilmer, Jacob H. Miller; Registrar, Morgan Shaffer, address Hedgesville; Treasurer, Geo. T. Kreglow, Hedgesville; Superintendent of Sunday School, Geo. T. Kreglow, Hedgesville; Sunday School Secretary and Treasurer, Morgan Shaffer; Lay Reader, Geo. T. Kreglow.

Official Acts—Baptisms, infants 4, total 4; marriages 1, burials 2, public services, Sundays 40, other days 4, total 44; Holy Communion, public 12, private 1, total 13.

Communicants—Number last reported 70, removed without letter 5, total loss 5; net loss 5; present number total 65.

Congregations—Confirmed persons connected with Parish 65, baptized persons connected with Parish 140, families 36, individuals not thus included 450, number sittings in Church 200, all free.

Rector's Salary—As pledged from this congregation $200.00, from diocesan missions $200.00, as pledged from other congregations $125.00, from convocation missions $75.00, total $600.00.

Organizations—Sunday Schools, officers and teachers, male 4, female 5, total 9; pupils, male 20, female 30, total 50; advent offering $14.00, lenten offering $11.29, total Sunday School offerings $25.29.

Property—Church, brick, value $2,000.00; rectory, frame, insurance $250.00, value $400.00; total value $2,400.00.

FINANCIAL REPORT.

Receipts—For current expenses—Cash on hand, per last report $4.79, pledges and subscriptions $200.00, collections in Church $38.81, total receipts for current expenses $243.60. *For all purposes other than current expenses, (i. e. Contributions)*—Pledges and subscriptions $50.00, pew rent $43.09, Sunday School $26.29, Woman's Auxiliary $85.00, total receipts for contributions $204.38; grand total of all receipts i. e. for current expenses and contributions $447.98.

Disbursements—For current expenses, (Parochial)—Salary of Rector $200.00, other salaries, Sexton $20.00, maintaining Sunday Schools $5.49, ordinary repairs $2.02, other current expenses $11.33, total for current expenses $238.81. *For contributions—Parochial*—Extraordinary repairs and improvements $85.00. *Diocesan*—Salary of Bishops $50.00, diocesan missions $25.00, convocation missions $13.00, Sheltering Arms Hospital $2.52, total diocesan contributions $90.52. *Objects without the Diocese*—Jews, $1.55, total domestic missions $1.55; foreign missions general $23.56, Brazil $.3.65, total foreign missions $27.31; total foreign and domestic missions $28.86; total without diocese $28.86.

Financial Summary—Contributions—Parochial $204.38, diocesan $90.52, extra diocesan $28.86, total contributions $323.76. *Expenses*—Current parochial $243.60; grand total of all money raised by the congregation $567.36.

Remarks—Parish was without Rector from April 15, 1902, to June 15, 1902.

PAROCHIAL REPORT.

Rev. S. SCOLLAY MOORE, D. D., address Parkersburg. Trinity Church, Trinity Parish. Parkersburg, Wood county. Date of organization, 1843. Present minister took charge April 15, 1888.

Church Officers—Church Wardens, Dr. W. H. Sharp, Dr. T. B. Camden, other vestrymen B. M. Ambler, J. N. Camden, W. N. Chancellor, C. C. Martin, H. H. Moss, Simms Powell, W. J. Robb, B. D. Spilman, W. M. Trevor, W. Vrooman; Registrar, Mr. Simms Powell, Parkersburg, W. Va.; Treasurer, Dr. W. H. Sharp, Parkersburg, W. Va.; Superintendent of Sunday School, Mr. B. M. Ambler, Parkersburg, W. Va.; Sunday School Secretary, Mr. C. E. Fitzhugh; Sunday School Treasurer, Mr. M. Q. Shrewsbury.

Official Acts—Baptisms, infants 7, adults 3, total 10; presented for confirmation since last report 15, marriages 43, burials 33, public services, Sundays 120, other days 107, total 227; Holy Communion, public 41, private 3, total 44.

Communicants—Number last reported 291, received by letter 3, admitted by confirmation 15, added otherwise 3, total gain 21; died 6, removed without letter 8, total loss 14; net gain 7; present number total 298.

Congregations—Confirmed persons connected with Parish 310, baptized persons connected with Parish 500, families 190, individuals not thus included 50, whole number of individuals 600, number sittings in Church 550, number free sittings 100, number sittings in Sunday School room 200.

Rector's Salary—As pledged from this congregation $1,800, total $1,800.

Organizations—Sunday Schools, Officers and teachers, male 6, female 9, total 15; pupils, male 44, female 76, total 120; advent offering $11.98, lenten offering $20.59, other offerings $27.16, total Sunday School offerings $59.73; Brotherhood of St. Andrew, members 14; Woman's Auxiliary, members 40; Woman's Guild, members 42; King's Daughters, members 18; "Helping Hand", members 24.

Property—Church, insurance $8,000, value $30,000; rectory, insurance $3,000, value $9,000; Parish house, insurance $2,300, value $7,000; other property, insurance $3,300, value $5,000; other property, insurance $6,000, value $15,000; total insurance $22,600; total value $66,000. Indebtedness, on rectory $550, other debts $450, total indebtedness $1,000.

FINANCIAL REPORT.

Receipts—For current expenses—Pledges and subscriptions $1,027.93, pew rent $2,270.11, collections in Church $58.91, money borrowed $50, Sunday School for expenses $27.16, total receipts for current expenses $3,434.11. *For all purposes other than current expenses, (i. e. Contributions)*—Pledges and subscriptions $95.07, special contributions $190, collections in Church $1,605.36, Sunday School $32.57, Woman's Auxiliary $525.50, other sources, Woman's Guild $942.75, King's Daughters $53, "Helping Hand" $100, total receipts for contributions $3,544.25; grand total of all receipts i. e. for current expenses and contributions $6,978.36.

Disbursements—For current expenses, (Parochial)—Salary of Rector $1,800, other salaries $800, insurance $37.50, maintaining Sunday Schools $33.16, ordinary repairs $197.67, interest on debt $68.40, payment on debt,

$78, other current expenses $419.38, total for current expenses $3,434.11. *For Contributions—Parochial*—Communion alms $48.10, extraordinary repairs and improvements $955.77, parish missions $154.02, total parochial contributions $1,157.89. *Diocesan*—Salary of Bishops $600, permanent fund $196.83, diocesan missions $350, convocation missions $3.80, widows and orphans, aged and disabled clergy fund $49.76, religious and Theological education $19.27, Sheltering Arms Hospital $328.25, Sunday School work in diocese $15.63, Bishop's special fund $190, other objects, Church at St. Mary's $29.44, Church at Welch, Wo. Aux. $28, diocesan central fund, Wo. Aux. $2, Woman's Missionary, Wo. Aux. $39, King's Daughters for charity $53, total diocesan contributions $1,904.98. *Objects without the diocese* Domestic missions general $73.76, through American Church Missionary Society $60.46, total domestic missions $134.22; foreign missions general $75.83, for Africa $50, for Mexico .55, through American Church Missionary Society $25.42, total foreign missions $151.80; total foreign and domestic missions $286.02; American Church Building fund $13.86, Woman's Auxiliary, money $69.50, Woman's Auxiliary boxes, value $112, total without diocese $481.38.

Financial Summary—Contributions—Parochial $1,157.89, diocesan $1,904.98, extra diocesan $481.38, total contributions $3,544.25. *Expenses*—Current parochial $3,434.11; grand total of all money raised by the congregation $6,978.36.

Remarks—The contribution to the Sheltering Arms Hospital was made up in large part of a box sent by the Woman's Auxiliary, which was valued at $275. The work of this Society, and that of the Woman's Guild, in aid of Parochial missions and of other activities within the Parish, have been of very great value. The King's Daughters also do most helpful work, especially in caring for the communion plate and linen.

PAROCHIAL REPORT.

Rev. S. SCOLLAY MOORE, D. D., address Parkersburg, W. Va. St. Stephen's Mission, Trinity Parish, Parkersburg, Wood county. Date of organization, 1896. Present minister took charge, 1896.

Official Acts—Marriages 1, burials 1, public services, Sundays 50, total 50; Holy Communion, public 4, total 4.

Communicants—Number last reported 12, present number total 12.

Congregations—Confirmed persons connected with Parish 12, baptized persons connected with Parish 17, families 8, whole number of individuals 20, number sittings in chapel 40.

Property—Chapel, frame, insurance $600, value $900; other property, value $100; total insurance $600; total value $1,000. Indebtedness, on chapel $500; total indebtedness $500.

FINANCIAL REPORT

Receipts—For current expenses—Collections in Church $35.76, rent from investments $50, Church Society $20, total receipts for current expenses $105.76. *For all purposes other than current expenses, (i. e. Contributions)*—Collections in Church $1.89, total receipts for contributions $1.89; grand total of all receipts i. e. for current expenses and contributions $107.65.

Disbursements—For current expenses. (Parochial)—Interest on debt $21.50, payment on debt $50, other current expenses $34.26, total for current expenses $105.76. *For Contributions—Diocesan*—Diocesan missions .84, total diocesan contributions .84. *Objects without the Diocese*—Domestic missions general .50, total domestic missions .50; foreign missions general .55, total foreign missions .55; total foreign and domestic missions $1.05.

Financial Summary—Contributions—Diocesan .84, extra diocesan $1.05, total contributions $1.89. *Expenses*—Current parochial $105.76; grand total of all money raised by the congregation $107.65.

PAROCHIAL REPORT.

Rev. C. C. PIERSON address Berkeley Springs, W. Va. St. Mark's Church Mission, Berkeley, Morgan county. Date or organization 1879. Present minister took charge April 1, 1896.

Church Officers—Church Warden, Dr. J. H. Hunter; committee, F. R. Reed, Treasurer; Dr. J. Gilpin, Registrar, address Berkeley Springs, W. Va; Superintendent of Sunday School, Rector; Sunday School Secretary and Treasurer, Mrs. G. Gilpin.

Official Acts—Baptisms, infants 1, adults 1, total 2; marriages 1, burials 1, catechisings, once a month; public services, Sundays 78, other days 26, total 104; Holy Communion, public 14, private none, total 14.

Communicants—Number last reported 24, restored to communion 1, total gain 1; removed without letter 1, net gain 1; present number total 24.

Congregations—Confirmed persons connected with Parish 4, baptized persons connected with Parish 30, families 12, individuals not thus included 2, number sittings in Church 300, all free.

Rector's Salary—As pledged from this congregation $300.00, from diocesan missions $100.00, from general board $100.00, total $500.00.

Organizations—Sunday Schools 1, officers and teachers, male 1, female 2, total 3; pupils, male 10, female 8, total 18; Advent offering $3.00, Lenten offering $3.02, total Sunday School offerings $6.02; Woman's Auxiliary, members 18, other organizations, St. Marks Guild, members 20.

Property—Church 1, wood, insurance $1,500.00, value $3,000.00; rectory wood, insurance $1,500.00, value $2,500.00; total value $5,500.00. Indebtedness, due the minister $23.62, due on diocesan assessment for missions

$12.00, due on diocesan assessment for Bishop's fund $6.50, total indebtedness $42.12.

FINANCIAL REPORT.

Receipts—For current expenses—Cash on hand, per last report, Guild fund $5.85, pledges and subscriptions $187.25, collections in Church $89.13, other sources $92.25, total receipts for current expenses $328.48. *For all purposes other than current expenses, (i. e. Contributions)*—Woman's Auxiliary $30.00, other sources $160.00; grand total of all receipts i. e. for current expenses and contributions $190.00.

Disbursements—For current expenses, (Parochial)—Salary of Rector $276.38, other salaries $37.00, ordinary repairs $2.00, other current expenses $59.60, total for current expenses $328.48. *For contributions—Parochial*—Extraordinary repairs and improvements $160.00. *Diocesan*—Salary of Bishops $18.50, permanent fund $10.00, diocesan missions $13.00, convocation missions $11.00, Sheltering Arms Hospital $3.51, total diocesan contributions $56.01. *Objects without the Diocese*—Total domestic missions $16.00; foreign missions general $5.00; total foreign and domestic missions $21.00, Woman's Auxiliary, boxes, value $20.00.

Financial Summary—Contributions—Parochial $160, diocesan $56.01, extra diocesan $41, total contributions $257.01. *Expenses*—Current parochial $328.48; grand total of all money raised by the congregation $585.49.

PAROCHIAL REPORT.

Rt. Rev. C. C. PENICK, D. D., address Fairmont, W. Va.; assistant, Rev. Thos. C. Darst. Christ Church, Fairmont Parish, Fairmont, Marion county. Present minister took charge 1897.

Church Officers—Church Wardens, J. C. Smith and W. H. Sands; other vestrymen, Geo. DeBolt, Walton Miller, Paul McCoy, Sam'l Holbert, Sam'l R. Nuzum, H. Q. Turner; Registrar, Sam'l Holbert, Fairmont, W. Va.; Treasurer, Paul McCoy, Fairmont, W. Va.; Superintendent of Sunday Schools, Rev. Thos. C. Darst; Sunday School Secretary and Treasurer, Arthur Brobst.

Official Acts—Baptisms, infants 3, total 3; presented for confirmation since last report 9, marriages 9, burials 10, catechisings 46, public services, Sundays 96, other days 52, total 148; Holy Communion, public 14, private 4, total 18.

Communicants—Number last reported 122, received by letter 5, admitted by confirmation 9, added otherwise 4, total gain 18; transferred 3, removed without letter 1, total loss 4; net gain (or loss) 14; present number total 136.

Congregations—Confirmed persons connected with Parish 136, baptized persons connected with Parish 150, families 50, individuals not thus included, above 50, whole number of individuals 375, number of scattered communicants in your section not connected with any Parish 8, number sittings in Church 150, all free, number sittings in Sunday School room 100.

Rector's Salary—As pledged from this congregation $1,200.

Organizations—Sunday Schools, officers and teachers, male 2, female 5, total 7; pupils, male 24, female 30, total 54; advent offering $12.00, lenten offering $13.42, other offerings $129.95, total Sunday School offerings $155.37; Woman's Auxiliary, members 18; other organizations, Daughters of the King.

Property—Church, brick, insurance $50.00, value $3,500.00; total value $3,500.

FINANCIAL REPORT.

Receipts—For current expenses—Pledges and subscriptions $1,807.25, collections in church $324.74, other sources $218.01, total receipts for current expenses $2,350.00. *For all purposes other than current expenses, (i. e. Contributions)*—Collections in Church $418.10, Sunday School $155.00, Woman's Auxiliary $203.00, other sources $2,240.13, total receipts for contributions $3,016.23; grand total of all Receipts i. e. for current expenses and contributions $5,366.23.

Disbursements—For current expenses, (Parochial)—Salary of Rector, $1,200, salary of assistant $400, other salaries $350, insurance $50, maintaining Sunday Schools $100, ordinary repairs $50, other current expenses $50, other objects $150, total for current expenses $2,350. *For contributions—Parochial*—Communion alms $50, extraordinary repairs and improvements $250, other objects $100, total parochial contributions $400. *Diocesan*—Salary of Bishops $70.00, permanent fund $1,303, diocesan missions $70.00, convocation missions $30.00, religious and theological education $100.00, Sheltering Arms Hospital $50.00, Bishop's special fund $98.14, other objects $100.00, total diocesan contributions $1,821.14. *Objects without the Diocese*—Domestic missions general $350.00, total domestic missions $350; foreign missions general $583.52, total foreign missions $358.52; total foreign and domestic missions $933.52; Woman's auxiliary, money $53.45, Woman's Auxiliary boxes, value $150.00, total without diocese $203.45.

Financial Summary—Contributions—Parochial $2,600, diocesan $1,821.14, extra diocesan $933.52, extra $11.57, total contributions $5,366.33. Grand total of all money raised by the congregation $5,366.33.

PAROCHIAL REPORT.

Rev. ROBT. DOUGLAS ROLLER, D. D., address Charleston. St. John's Church, Kanawha Parish, Charleston, Kanawha county. Date of organization 1788. Present minister took charge 1888.

Church Officers—Church Wardens, James F. Lewis, J. Lynn Richardson; other vestrymen, W. S. Laidley, S. S. Green, J. T. Waters, D. C. Gallaher, W. G. Hubbard, Alfred Philips, C. E. Ward; Registrar, S. S. Green, address Charleston; Treasurer, Jas. F. Lewis, Charleston; Superintendent of Sunday School S. S. Green, Charleston; Sunday School Secretary and Treasurer, J. T. Waters.

Official Acts—Baptisms, infants 10, adults 3, total 13; presented for confirmation since last report 9, marriages 8, burials 12, catechisings 40, public services, Sundays 122, other days 76, total 198; Holy Communion, public 20, private 2, total 22.

Communicants—Number last reported 244, admitted by confirmation 9, restored to communion 3, added otherwise 22, total gain 34; died 2, transferred 2, removed without letter 1, not otherwise accounted for 6, total loss 11; net gain 23; present number total 267.

Congregations—Confirmed persons connected with Parish 288, baptized persons connected with Parish 525, families, or parts 175, whole number of individuals 540, number sittings in Church 500 all free; number sittings in Sunday School room 200.

Rector's Salary—As pledged from this congregation $1,300.00, total $1,-300.00.

Organizations—Sunday Schools, officers and teachers, male 2, female 12, total 14; pupils, male 60, female 54, total 114; advent offering $10.00, lenten offering $52.00, other offerings $110.00, total Sunday School offerings $172.00; other organizations, St. John's Guild, Ladies' Aid, Rector's Aid.

Property—Church, stone, insurance $18,000.00, value $48,627.12; rectory, frame, insurance $2,400, value $10,000; Parish house, brick, insurance $4,000, value $10,000; other property, lot, value $2,100; Sheltering Arms Hospital, insurance $6,000, value $10,000; total insurance $30,400; total value $80,727.12.

FINANCIAL REPORT.

Receipts—For current expenses—Cash on hand, per last report $7.35, pledges and subscriptions $2,008.14, collections in Church $509.81, Sunday School $25.50, total receipts for current expenses $2,550.80. *For all purposes other than current expenses, (i. e. Contributions)*—Pledges and subscriptions $465.00, collections in Church $327.59, thank offerings $669.63, Sunday School $146.80, Woman's Auxiliary $119.20, Ladies' Aid $2,720.62, total receipts for contributions $4,448.84; grand total of all receipts i. e. for current expenses and contributions $6,999.64.

Disbursements—For current expenses, (Parochial)—Salary of Rector $1,300.00, other salaries $445.47 and $285.27, insurance $106.20, maintaining Sunday Schools $25.50, ordinary repairs $72.25, other current expenses $316.11, total for current expenses $2,550.80. *For contributions—Parochial*—Extraordinary repairs and improvements $64.06, other objects $99.05, Parish house $2,720.62, total parochial contributions $2,883.73.

Diocesan—Salary of Bishops $275.00, permanent fund $669.63, diocesan missions $200.00, convocation missions $15.50, widows and orphans, aged and disabled clergy fund $41.95, religious and theological education $2.16, Sheltering Arms Hospital $63.05, Bishop's special fund $5.00, total diocesan contributions $1,272.29. *Objects without the Diocese*—Domestic missions general $64.99, colored people $1.01, Indians .86, deaf and dumb $9.15, Jews $9.36, total domestic missions $85.37; foreign missions general $66.00, Brazil $2.15, total foreign missions $68.15; total foreign and domestic missions $153.52; American Church Building fund $3.10, Woman's Auxiliary, money $101.09, Woman's Auxiliary boxes, value $18.11, general clergy relief fund $17.00, total without diocese $292.82.

Financial Summary—Contributions—Parochial $2,883.73, diocesan $1,-272.29, extra diocesan $292.82, total contributions $4,448.84. *Expenses*—Current parochial $2,550.80; grand total of all money raised by the congregation $6,999.64.

Remarks—The Parish House, although reported as parish property and used for parish purposes, has been bought by the Ladies' Aid Society; and at their request, the title will remain in the Society, until such time as they may be able to turn the building over to the Parish free from all debt. The ladies deserve the highest commendation for securing this property, so perfectly located and so excellently adapted to Parish uses. The Sheltering Arms Hospital is a Diocesan institution and is only reported here because located within the Parish. Kanawha Parish: Robert Douglas Roller, Rector; Coalburg and Mammoth, communicants 8, baptized persons 9; Cabin and Paint Creeks, communicants 9, baptized 15,

---

PAROCHIAL REPORT.

Rev. C. E. SHAW, address New Martinsville. St. Ann's Church, Wetzel Parish, New Martinsville, Wetzel county. Date of organization, 1851. Present minister took charge April 15, 1902.

Church Officers—Church Wardens, S. R. Martin, S. Bruce Hall; other vestrymen, Wm. McG. Hall, Leslie Williams, Jno. F. Martin, E. H. Bostoch, John Bridgeman; Registrar, E. H. Bostoch, address New Martinsville; Treasurer, S. R. Martin, address New Martinsville; Superintendent of Sunday School, Wm. McG. Hall, New Martinsville; Sunday School Secretary and Treasurer, Miss Anna Reithmiller.

Official Acts—Baptisms, infants 3, total 3; marriages 1, burials 2, public services, Sundays 104, other days 78, total 182; Holy Communion, public 16, total 16.

Communicants—Number last reported 47, received by letter 4, removed without letter 4, present number total 36.

Congregations—Confirmed persons connected with Parish 53, baptized persons connected with Parish 90, families 16, individuals not thus included 16, whole number of individuals 105, number of scattered communicants in your section not connected with any Parish 8, sittings in church 70, free sittings 70.

Rector's Salary—As pledged from this congregation $700.00, from diocesan missions $43.75, from general board $50.00, total $793.75.

Organizations—Sunday Schools, officers and teachers, male 3, female 4, total 7; pupils, male 13, female 20, total 33; Advent offering $3.07, Lenten offering $5.68, total Sunday School offerings $8.75; other organizations, Ladies' Aid Society, Sr. Ladies' Aid Society, Rector's Guild. Location of schools mentioned above, New Martinsville, W. Va.

Property—Church, wood, value $4,000.00; chapel, wood, insurance $1,000, value $2,000.00; rectory, wood insurance $,1000.00, value $4,000.00, total value $10,000.00; indeotedness, on church $1,000.00, total indebtedness $1,000.00.

FINANCIAL REPORT.

Receipts—For Current Expenses—Pledges and subscriptions $700.00, collections in church $52.52, other sources $46.67, total receipts for current expenses $799.19. *For all purposes other than current expenses, (i. e. Contributions)*—Cash on hand, per last report $500.00, pledges and subscriptions $2,500.31, collections in church $385.13, interest from investments $29.18, money borrowed $1,058.00, Sunday School $26.74, other sources $150.00, Ladies' Aid Society $216.50, Rector's Guild $108.50, total receipts for contributions $4,974.36; grand total of all receipts i. e. for current expenses and contributions $5,773.55.

Disbursements—For Current Expenses (Parochial)—Salary of Rector $700.00, maintaining Sunday Schools $15.57, other current expenses $40.85, total for current expenses $756.42. *For Contributions—Parochial*—Communion alms $20.02, extraordinary repairs and improvements $3,756.69, total parochial contributions $3,776.71. *Diocesan*—Salary of Bishops $35.00, permanent fund $50.00, diocesan missions $40.00, convocation missions $3.92, widows and orphans, aged and disabled clergy fund $6.69, religious and theological education $7.59, Sheltering Arms Hospital $5.07, theological seminary $2.00, Bishop's special fund $20.00, total diocesan contributions $180.27. *Objects without the Diocese*—Domestic missions general $12.14, Indians $3.61, deaf and dumb $2.32, Jews $1.71, total domestic missions $19.78; foreign missions general $11.14, for Mexico .98, through American Church Missionary Society $3.26, total foreign missions $15.38; total foreign and domestic missions $35.16; Bible and Prayer Book Society $2.00, total without diocese $37.16.

Financial Summary—Contributions—Parochial $3,776.71, diocesan $180.-27, extra diocesan $37.16, total contributions $3,994.14. *Expenses*—Current parochial $756.42; grand total of all money raised by the congregation $4,750.56.

PAROCHIAL REPORT.

Rev. GEO. C. SHAW, address St. Marys, W. Va. Grace Church, St. Marys Mission, St. Marys, Wood county. Present minister took charge June 16th, 1901.

Church Officers—Church Wardens, R. L. Pemberton, R. H. Brouse; other committeemen, J. C. Noland, George Kelsall; Registrar, R. L. Pemberton, address St. Marys, W. Va.; Treasurer, George Kelsall, address St. Marys, W. Va.; Superintendent of Sunday School, George Kelsall, St. Marys, W. Va.; Sunday School Secretary and Treasurer, J. C. Noland.

Official Acts—Presented for confirmation since last report 2, marriages 1, catechisings 3, public services, Sundays 52, other days 8, total 60; Holy Communion, public 2, total 2.

Communicants—Number last reported 28, admitted by confirmation 2, total gain 2; not otherwise accounted for 2, total 2; total loss 2; present number total 28.

Congregations—Confirmed persons connected with Parish 28, baptized persons connected with Parish 58, individuals not thus included 20, whole number of individuals 50, number of scattered communicants in your section not connected with any Parish 2, sittings in church 200, free sittings 200.

Rector's Salary—As pledged from this congregation $280.00, from diocesan missions $50.00, from general board $25.00, total $355.00.

Organizations—Sunday Schools, officers and teachers, male 4, female 4, total 8; pupils, male 15, female 20, total 34; other offerings $35; total Sunday School offerings $35; other organizations, Grace Guild, object parochial work. Location of schools mentioned above, St. Marys, W. Va.

Property—Church, brick, insurance $1,500.00, value $4,000.00; rectory, wood, insurance $1,200.00, value $2,200.00, total value insurance $2,700.00, value $6,200.00; indebtedness, on church $400.00, on rectory $2,000.00, total indebtedness $2,400.00.

FINANCIAL REPORT.

Receipts—For Current Expenses—Pledges and subscriptions $397.01, collections in Church $73.45, thank offerings $360.00, other sources 0250.05 total receipts for current expenses $1,080.51. *For all purposes other than current expenses, (i. e. Contributions)*—Pledges and subscriptions $100.00, collections in church $25.00, total receipts for contributions $125.00; grand total of all receipts i. e. for current expenses and contributions $1,205.51.

Disbursements—For Current Expenses (Parochial)—Salary of Rector $280.00, maintaining Sunday Schools $35.00, ordinary repairs $110.00, interest on debt $144.00, payment on debt $356.00, other current expenses $30.00, total for current expenses $955.00. *Contributions—Diocesan*—Salary of Bishops $15.00, permanent fund $100.00, diocesan missions $15.00, total diocesan contributions $130.00. *Objects without the Diocese*—Domestic missions general $3.00, total domestic missions $3.00; total without diocese $3.00.

Financial Summary—Contributions—Diocesan $130.00, extra diocesan $3.00, total contributions $133.00. *Expenses*—Current parochial $955.00; grand total of all money raised by the congregation $1,088.00.

PAROCHIAL REPORT.

Rev. GEO. C. SHAW, address St. Marys, W. Va. Christ Memorial Church, Williamstown Mission, Williamstown, Wood county. Present minister took charge June 16th, 1903.

Church Officers—Church Wardens, J. W. Snodgrass, Charles Hunter; other committeemen, H. C. Henderson, A. T. Henderson, R. Hammett; Registrar, H. C. Henderson, address Williamstown, W. Va.; Treasurer, A. T. Henderson, address Williamstown, W. Va.; Superintendent of Sunday School, H. C. Henderson, Williamstown, W. Va.; Sunday School Secretary and Treasurer, Miss Helen Henderson; lay reader, H. C. Henderson.

Official Acts—Baptisms, adults 2, total 2; presented for confirmation since last report 2, burials 2, catechisings 2, public services, Sundays 36, other days 18, total 54; Holy Communion, public 2, total 2.

Communicants—Number last reported 28, admitted by confirmation 2, total gain 2; removed without letter 1, total loss 1; net gain 1; present number total 29.

Congregations—Confirmed persons connected with Parish 29, baptized persons connected with Parish 61, families 20, individuals not thus included 20, whole number of individuals 52, sittings in church 150, free sittings 150.

Rector's Salary—As pledged from this congregation $200, total $200.

Organizations—Sunday Schools, officers and teachers, male 1, female 5, total 6; pupils, male 15, female 15, total 30; Advent offering $10.60, Lenten offering $11.25, other offerings $18.02, total Sunday School offerings $39.87; Woman's Auxiliary, members 20. Location of schools mentioned above, Williamstown, W. Va.

Property—Church, wood, insurance $1,500.00, value $2,500.00; rectory lot, value $1,000.00; total value, insurance $1,500.00, value $3,500.00.

FINANCIAL REPORT.

Receipts—For Current Expenses—Collections in church $71.86, total receipts for current expenses $71.86. *For all purposes other than current expenses, (i. e. Contributions)*—Pledges and subscriptions $193.00, Sunday School $39.87, Woman's Auxiliary $61.25, total receipts for contributions $294.12; grand total of all receipts i. e. for current expenses and contributions $365.98.

Disbursements—For Current Expenses (Parochial)—Salary of Rector $193.00, maintaining Sunday Schools $16.02, total for current expenses $219.02. *For Contributions—Parochial*—Parish missions $22.00, rectory fund $15.00, total parochial contributions $37.00. *Diocesan*—Salary of Bishops $2.31, permanent fund $16.34, diocesan missions $22.00, widows and orphans, aged and disabled clergy fund $2.98, religious and theological education $2.11, Sheltering Arms Hospital $1.83, Bishop's special fund

$10.00, total diocesan contributions $48.57. *Objects without the Diocese*—Foreign missions general $5.15, total foreign missions $5.15; Woman's Auxiliary, money $7.25; total without diocese $12.40.

Financial Summary—Contributions—Parochial $37.00, diocesan $48.57, total contributions $85.57. *Expenses*—Current parochial $219.02; grand total of all money raised by the congregation $365.86.

PAROCHIAL REPORT.

Rev. GEO. C. SHAW, address St. Marys, W. Va. Church of the Messiah, Waverly Mission, Waverly, Wood county. Present minister took charge June 19, 1901.

Church Officers—Treasurer, Mrs. Alice Corbett, address Waverly, W. Va.; Superintendent of Sunday School, Mrs. Georgia Harness, Waverly, W. Va.; Sunday School Secretary and Treasurer, Miss Tessie Meyers.

Official Acts—Baptisms, adults 2, total 2; marriages 1, burials 1, catechisings 10, public serves, Sundays 15, other days 30, total 45; Holy Communion public 2, total 2.

Communicants—Number last reported 10, admitted by confirmation 1, total gain 1, died 1, total loss 1; present number total 10.

Congregations—Confirmed persons connected with Parish 10, baptized persons connected with Parish 24, families 5, individuals not thus included 10, whole number of individuals 34, sittings in church 100, free sittings 100.

Rector's Salary—As pledged from this congregation $50.00, total $50.00.

Organizations—Sunday Schools, officers and teachers, male 2, female 4, total 6; pupils, male 25, female 35, total 60; Advent offering $4.40, other offerings $30.0; total Sunday School offerings $34.40. Location of schools mentioned above, Waverly, W. Va.

Property—Church, wood, insurance $500.00, value $1,000.00; total value, insurance $500.00, value $1,000.00; indebtedness, on church $235.00; total indebtedness $235.00.

FINANCIAL REPORT.

Receipts—For Current Expenses—Collections in church $15.00, other sources $68.00, total receipts for current expenses $83.00. *For all purposes other than current expenses, (i. e. Contributions)*—Pledges and subscriptions $50.00, collections in church $27.29, Sunday School $30.00; total receipts for contributions $107.29; grand total of all receipts i. e. for current expenses and contributions $190.29.

Disbursements For Current Expenses (Parochial)—Salary of Rector $50.00, maintaining Sunday Schools $30.00, interest on debt $16.80, payment on debt $50.00, other current expenses $20.00, total for current expenses $166.80. *For Contributions—Parochial*—Communion alms $4.00, total parochial contributions $4.00. *Diocesan*—Salary of Bishops $5.00, permanent fund $2.25, diocesan missions $11.45, convocation missions $1.65, widows and orphans, aged and disabled clergy fund $1.05, religious and theological education $1.95, Sheltering Arms Hospital .55, total diocesan contributions $23.90. *Objects without the Diocese*—Domestic missions general .40, colored people .30, Indians .25, deaf and dumb .60, through American Church Missionary Society .85, total domestic missions $2.40; foreign missions general $1.35, for Mexico .55, Brazil .60, total foreign missions $2.40; total foreign and domestic missions $4.80; Bible and Prayer Book Society .70; total without diocese $5.50.

Financial Summary—Contributions—Parochial $4.00, diocesan $23.90, total contributions $27.90. *Expenses*—Current parochial $166.80; grand total of all money raised by the congregation $194.70.

PAROCHIAL REPORT.

Rev. PARIS B. STAUFFER, address Hinton. Ascension Church, New River Mission, Hinton Summers county. Present minister took charge July 1, 1902.

Church Officers—Registrar, T. N. Read, Esq., address Hinton; Treasurer, T. N. Read, Esq.; Superintendent of Sunday School, T. N. Read, Esq.

Official Acts—Baptisms, infants 4, total 4, burials 1, public services Sundays 68, other days 46, total 114; Holy Communion, public 12, total 12.

Communicants—Added otherwise 30, removed without letter 1, present number total 30.

Congregations—Confirmed persons connected with Parish 46, baptized persons connected with Parish 79, families 38, sittings in church 100, free sittings 100, sittings in chapel 75.

Rector's Salary—As pledged from this congregation $300.00, from diocesan missions $250.00, Bishop $150.00, total $700.00.

Organizations—Sunday Schools, officers and teachers, male 2, female 1, total 3; pupils, male 7, female 30, total 37; Advent offering $6.09, Lenten offering $8.77, other offerings $1.53, $16.97; total Sunday School offerings $35.36.

Property—Church, frame, insurance $2,000.00, value $3,000.00; rectory, frame, insurance $1,500.00, value $2,000.00; Sunday School room frame; lot on which they stand, value $4,000.00; total value $9,000.00; indebtedness, on church $690.00, due on diocesan assessment for missions $15.84, due on diocesan assessment for bishop's fund $13.19, due T. N. Read for advance of minister's salary $25.00; total indebtedness $744.03.

FINANCIAL REPORT.

Receipts—For Current Expenses—Cash on hand, per last report $27.09, pledges and subscriptions $216.50, collections in church $178.81, women

$252.83, total receipts for current expenses $675.23. *For all purposes other than current expenses, (i. e. Contributions)*—Collections in church $16.81, total receipts for contributions $16.81.

Disbursements—For Current Expenses, (Parochial)—Salary of Rector $245.00, other salaries $46.00, insurance $21.00, ordinary repairs $71.20, interest on debt $41.90, payment on debt $115.00, other current expenses $39,-39, other objects $7.20, extra repairs $26.06, total for current expenses $612.75. *For Contributions—Parochial*—Communion alms $16.81, total parochial contributions $16.81. *Diocesan*—Salary of Bishops $11.41, diocesan missions $14.16, convocation missions $5.00, widows and orphans, aged and disabled clergy fund $2.15, Sheltering Arms Hospital $1.90, linens to Sheltering Arms, total diocesan contributions $34.62. *Objects without the Diocese*—Domestic missions general $5.00, Jews .75, total domestic missions $5.75.

Financial Summary—Contributions—Parochial $687.04, diocesan $34.62, extra diocesan $5.75, total contributions $727.41. *Expenses*—Current parochial $612.75; grand total of all money raised by the congregation $762.77.

PAROCHIAL REPORT.

Rev. PARIS BECKER STAUFFER, address Hinton. New River Mission, Beckley, Raleigh county. Present minister took charge July 1, 1903.

Church Officers—Treasurer, Mrs. Wirt French, address Beckley.

Official Acts—Baptisms, adults 1, total 1, presented for confirmation since last report 1, public services, Sundays 18, total 18; Holy Communion, public 1, total 18.

Communicants—Admitted by confirmation 1, added otherwise 16, total 17, present number total 17.

Congregations—Confirmed persons connected with Parish 17, baptized persons connected with Parish 20, families 18, number of scattered communicants in your section not connected with any Parish 6.

Rector's Salary—As pledged from this congregation $108, from diocesan missions, see Hinton.

FINANCIAL REPORT.

Receipts—For Current Expenses—Pledges and subscriptions $81.00, collections in church $36.00, total receipts for current expenses $117.00.

Disbursements—For Current Expenses, (Parochial)—Salary of Rector $81.00, other current expenses, $36.00, total for current expenses $177.00. *Diocesan*—Permanent fund $7.00, diocesan missions $8.18, total diocesan contributions $15.20. *Objects without the Diocese*—Total foreign and domestic missions $4.02.

Financial Summary Contributions—Parochial $117.00, diocesan $15.20, extra diocesan $4.02, total contributions $136.22; grand total of all money raised by the congregation $136.22.

PAROCHIAL REPORT.

Rev. J. F. WOODS, address 945 Main St., Wheeling. Grace Church, Cresap's Valley Mission, Cresaps, Marshall county. Date of organization, 1881. Present minister took charge 1881.

Church Officers—Missionary Committee, Mr. A. Q. Whittaker; Wardens, Mr. Quincy Cresap, Mr. R. M. Gossett, Mr. Thos. Kemp; Registrar, Mr. Quincy Cresap, address Graysville, W. Va.; Treasurer, R. M. Gossett, address Graysville, W. Va.

Official Acts—Baptisms, infants 1, total 1, marriages 1, burials 1, catechisings 3, public services, Sundays 8, total 8; Holy Communion, public 3, total 3.

Communicants—Number last reported 12, transferred 1, removed without letter 1, lapsed 1, total loss 3, present number total 9.

Congregations—Confirmed persons connected with Parish 12, baptized persons connected with Parish 18, families 7, sittings in church 75, free sittings 75.

Rector's Salary—As pledged from this congregation $30.00, from diocesan missions $200.00, from American Church Missionary Society $150.00, total $380.00.

Property—Church, wood, value $1,000.00, total value $1,000.00.

FINANCIAL REPORT.

Receipts—For Current Expenses—Total receipts for current expenses $7.50. *For all purposes other than current expenses, (i. e. Contributions)* —Collections in church $12.00, total receipts for contributions $12.00; grand total of all receipts i. e. for current expenses and contributions $19.50.

Disbursements—For Current Expenses, (Parochial)—Salary of Rector $28.00, other current expenses $7.50, total for current expenses $35.50. *For Contributions—Parochial*—Extraordinary repairs and improvements $3.75, total parochial contributions $3.75. *Diocesan*—Salary of Bishops $5.00, diocesan missions $5.00, convocation missions $2.50, widows and orphans, aged and disabled clergy fund .25, Sheltering Arms Hospital $1.00, other objects $1.25, total diocesan contributions $15.00. *Objects without the Diocese*—Through American Church Missionary Society $1.00, total domestic missions $1.00, Brazil .50, total foreign missions $1.50; total foreign and domestic missions $2.50.

Financial Summary—Contributions—Parochial $3.75, diocesan $15.00, extra diocesan $2.50, total contributions $21.25. *Expenses*—Current parochial $35.50; grand total of all money raised by the congregation $56.75.

Remarks—We are still at this mission losing members by removals, and those who have come into the neighborhood are not Episcopalians. We have contributed of our strength to other points in the Diocese, so that our loss will be their gain. The remarkable number of wet Sundays, which occurred during the past winter and the greater part of this spring, interfered very materially with the attendance at the services, and in some cases rendered the holding of services impossible.

PAROCHIAL REPORT.

Rev. J. F. WOODS, address 945 Main St., Wheeling, W. Va. St. John's Church, Willow Island, Pleasants county. Date of organization, 1853.

Church Officers—Church Wardens, F. M. Triplett, Jno. W. Norris; other vestrymen, Jno. H. Rolston; Registrar, Jno. W. Norris, address Willow Island.

Official Acts—Public services, Sundays 4, total 4; Holy Communion, public 3, total 3.

Communicants—Number last reported 11, removed without letter 1, present number total 10.

Congregations—Confirmed persons connected with Parish 10, baptized persons connected with Parish 18, families 6, whole number of individuals 40, sittings in church 100.

Property—Church, wood, value $500.00, total value $500.00; money raised from outside sources $1.00.

Rector's Salary—As pledged from this congregation $15.00, from diocesan missions $200.00, from American Church Missionary Society $150.00, total $315.00.

FINANCIAL REPORT.

Disbursements—Salary of Rector $15.00, total $15.00. *Contributions—Diocesan*—Salary of Bishops $5.00, permanent fund $10.00, diocesan missions $1.00, convocation missions $3.50, total diocesan $19.50.

Remarks—Few services have been held in St. John's church on account of its inaccessibility and the inclement weather we have had during the past year. Nothing much can be expected from this church until it is removed to a more accessible place.

PAROCHIAL REPORT.

Rev. J. F. WOODS, address 945 Main St., Wheeling, W. Va. New Cumberland Mission, New Cumberland, Hancock county. Date of organization, 1900. Present minister took charge 1900.

Church Officers—Superintendent of Sunday School, Mrs. S. G. Gaillard, New Cumberland.

Official Acts—Public services, Sundays 16, Holy Communion, public 8, total 8.

Communicants—Number last reported 4, present number total 4.

Congregations—Confirmed persons connected with Parish 5, baptized persons connected with Parish 12, families 4.

Rector's Salary—As pladged from this congregation $48.00, from diocesan missions $200.00, from American Church Missionary Society $150.00, total $398.00.

FINANCIAL REPORT.

Disbursements—Objects without the Diocese—Through American Church Missionary Society .50, total domestic missions .50, through American Church Missionary Society .50, total foreign missions .50; total foreign and domestic missions $1.00.

Financial Summary—Contributions Extra diocesan $1.00. *Expenses*—Current parochial $49.00; grand total of all money raised by the congregation $50.00.

Remarks—We have a small fund at this point toward a church building—the people that work in the mines and factories are for the most part migratory. The place for a church building, in the county, is Chester, where in time there should be a flourishing church. My congregations that assemble at the home of Mr. S. G. Gaillard are encouraging. There is one person awaiting confirmation. I give one Sunday a month to this work.

PAROCHIAL REPORT.

Rev. JOHN WARNOCK, address Charleston. St. Matthew's Mission, Charleston, Kanawha county. Date of organization, 1897. Present minister took charge May 1st, 1903.

Church Officers—Church Wardens, J. D. Lucadoe, Comyn Lewis; other vestrymen, J. Chas. Hall, Geo. Grishaber; Registrar, J. Chas. Hall, address Charleston; Treasurer, Comyn Lewis, address Charleston; Superintendent of Sunday School, Miss Peyton, Charleston.

Communicants—Number last reported 42, present number total 42.

Congregations—Confirmed persons connected with Parish 88, baptized persons connected with Parish 160, families 25, individuals not thus included 40, free sittings 200.

Rector's Salary—As pledged from this congregation $240.00, from diocesan missions $50.00, from general board $50.00.

Organizations—Sunday Schools, officers and teachers, male 1, female 3, total 4; pupils, male 10, female 20, total 30.

Property—Church, stone, insurance $500.00, value $5,000.00; chapel, St. Andrew's, log, insurance $300.00, value $650.00, total value $5,650.00.

FINANCIAL REPORT.

Receipts—For Current Expenses—Overdrawn see below, pledges and subscriptions $104.32, collections in church $9.26, thank offerings $22.50—$136.08, less amount overdrawn last report $10.35, total receipts for current expenses $125.73. *For all purposes other than current expenses, (i. e. Contributions)*—Collections in church, for foreign missions $1.00, Sunday School $11.78, cemetery sale of lots $4.50, for Bishop's salary and permanent fund $10.70, total receipts for contributions $27.98; grand total of all receipts i. e. for current expenses and contributions $153.71.

Disbursements—For Current Expenses, (Parochial)—Salary of Rector $109.59. salary of assistant $11.65, other current expenses $3.10, total for current expenses $124.34. *For Contributions Parochial*—Total parochial contributions $124.34. *Diocesan*—Salary of Bishops and permanent fund $13.75, diocesan missions $8.00, total diocesan contributions $21.75. *Objects without the Diocese*—Foreign missions general $1.00, total foreign missions $1.00; total foreign and domestic missions $22.75.

Financial Summary—Contributions—Parochial, current $124.34, diocesan $21.75, extra diocesan $1.00, total contributions $147.09; grand total of all money raised by the congregation $164.06, less total contributions paid out $147.09—$16.97, less amount overdrawn last report $10.35, total balance May 1, 1903, $6.62.

Remarks—Any missionary stipend received by Mr. Card has not been included in this report. This mission has been without a rector since August 1st, 1902, excepting services rendered by the Rev. Dr. R. D. Roller, to whom the gratitude of the missions are due. The statistics of communicants and congregations remain the same as last year, owing to the very recent appointment of the present incumbent.

PAROCHIAL REPORT.

Rev. JOHN WARNOCK, address Charleston. St. Luke's Mission, Charleston, Kanawha county. Date of organization, 1897. Present minister took charge May 1st, 1903.

Church Officers—Church Wardens, J. D. Lucadoe, Comyn Lewis; other vestrymen, J. Chas. Hall, Geo. Grishaber; Registrar, J. Chas. Hall, address Charleston; Treasurer, Comyn Lewis, address Charleston; Sunday School Secretary and Treasurer, Miss Payne.

Communicants—Number last reported 24, present number total 24.

Congregations—Confirmed persons connected with Parish, 32, baptized persons connected with Parish 56, families 8, individuals not thus included 9, sittings in church 100.

Rector's Salary—As pledged from this congregation $240.00, from diocesan missions $50.00, from general board $50.00.

Organizations—Sunday Schools, officers and teachers, male 2, female 4, total 6; pupils, male 15, female 17, total 32.

Property—Chapel, frame, value $1,200.00; rectory, frame, value, $1,400; other property, vacant lot $300.00; these are the values we have been using in all former reports, but real estate values have advanced in this neighborhood recently; total value $2,900.00; indebtedness, on other property $600.00, estimated total indebtedness $600.00.

FINANCIAL REPORT.

Receipts—For Current Expenses—Cash on hand, per last report $10.35, pledges and subscriptions $100.80 rent of rectory $75.00, collections in church $8.12, thank offerings $7.50, other sources $2.55, total receipts for current expenses $204.32. *For all purposes other than current expenses, (i. e. Contributions)*—Sunday School $12.80, other sources, for diocesan missions $8.00 Bishop's salary and permanent fund $18.00, total receipts for contributions $32.80; grand total of all receipts i. e. for current expenses and contributions $23/.12.

Disbursements—For Current Expenses, (Parochial)—Salary of Rector $99.59, ordinary repairs $107.89, other current expenses $6.15, total for current expenses $213.63. *For Contributions—Parochial* Total parochial contributions $213.63. *Diocesan*—Salary of Bishops and permanent fund $12.00, diocesan missions $8.00, total diocesan contributions $20.00.

Financial Summary—Contributions—Parochial $213.63, diocesan $20.00, total contributions $233.63; grand total of all money raised by the congregation $226.77, balance on hand last report $10.35—$237.12, total contributions paid out $233.63, balance on hand May 1st, 1903, $3.49.

Remarks—Any missionary stipend received by Mr. Card is not included in this report. We have been without a minister since August 1st, 1902, excepting services rendered by the kindness of Rev. Dr. R. D. Roller. The statistics of communicants and congregations remain the same as last year owing to the very recent appointment of the present incumbent.

PAROCHIAL REPORT.

Rev. JOHN WARNOCK, address Charleston, W. Va. St. Mark's Mission, St. Albans. Present minister took charge May 1st, 1903.

Church Officers—Church Wardens, D. J. Lewis, E. W. Chandler; other vestrymen, A. W. Howard, Thos. E. Mohler, Luke Frazier; Registrar, Thos. E. Mohler, address St. Albans, W. Va.; Treasurer, D .J. Lewis, address St. Albans, W. Va.; Superintendent of Sunday School, E. W. Chandler, St. Albans, W. Va.; Sunday School Secretary and Treasurer, T. E. Mohler.

Communicants—Number last reported 26, present number total 26.

Congregations—Confirmed persons connected with Parish 33, baptized persons connected with Parish 58, families 16, individuals not thus included 7, whole number of individuals 81, sittings in church 250, free sittings all.

Rector's Salary—As pledged from this congregation $200, from diocesan missions $120.

Organizations Sunday Schools, No. 1, officers and teachers, male 4, total 4, pupils, female 10, total 10; No. 2, officers and teachers, male 2, total 2, pupils male 10, female 5, total 15; No. 3, officers and teachers, male 1, total 1, pupils, male 8, female 8, total 17—42; Lenten offering $10.71, other offerings $37.16, total Sunday School offerings $47.87.

Property—Church, brick, value $3,000.00; rectory, wood, insurance $2,000, value $2,400; house, wood, value $250, total value $5,650.

FINANCIAL REPORT.

Receipts—For Current Expenses—Pledges and subscriptions $125, collections in church $28.59, total receipts for current expenses $153.59. *For all purposes other than current expenses, (i. e. Contributions)*—Pledges and subscriptions $15.79, grand total of all receipts i. e. for current expenses and contributions $169.38.

Disbursements—For Current Expenses, (Parochial)—Salary of Rector $125, other salaries $28.59, total for current expenses, $153.59—$79.48—$233.07. *For Contributions—Parochial*—Total parochial contributions $7.70. *Diocesan*—Salary of Bishops $5.00, total diocesan contributions $5.00—$27.80—$32.80; total without diocese $12.20.

Financial Summary—Contributions—Diocesan $5.00, total contributions $5.00. *Expenses*—Grand total of all money raised by the congregation $158.59, cash on hand $10.79—$169.38.

Remarks—The statistics are necessarily incomplete owing to the long vacancy in the rectorship. The present incumbent assumed office May 1st, 1903.

PAROCHIAL REPORT.

Rev. A. J. WILLIS, address Middleway, Grace Church, Nelson Parish, Middleway, Jefferson county. Date of organization, 1888. Present minister took charge, Nov. 1st, 1890.

Church Officers—Church Wardens, J. J. Grantham, Wm. Gilbert; other vestrymen, James Grantham, W. G. Bates; Regsitrar, Jas. Grantham, address Middleway; Treasurer, James Grantham, address Middleway; Superintendent of Sunday School, June Locke, Middleway; Sunday School Secretary and Treasurer, Mitchell Willis.

Official Acts—Marriages 3, burials 2, public services, Sundays 52, other days 15, total 67; Holy Communion, public 12, total 12.

Communicants—Number last reported 49, died 2, total loss 2, net loss 2, present number total 47.

Congregations—Confirmed persons connected with Parish 47, baptized persons connected with Parish 90, families 22, individuals not thus included 210, sittings in church 200, free sittings 200.

Rector's Salary—As pledged from this congregation $150, from diocesan missions $50, as pledged from other congregations $400, from convocation missions $100, from American Church Missionary Society $100, total $800.

Organizations—Sunday Schools, officers and teachers, male 3, female 4, total 7; pupils, male 20, female 20, total 40; Advent offering $6.04, Lenten offering $5.73, other offerings $10; total Sunday School offerings $21.77; other organizations, Rector's Aid Society 10, Parish Guild, embracing the three churches of the Parish, 30 members. Location of schools mentioned above, Middleway.

Property—Church, brick, insurance $1,000, value $2,500; rectory, frame and brick, insurance $1,500, value $2,000; lot belonging to Parish, value $350, total value $4,850.

FINANCIAL REPORT.

Receipts—For Current Expenses—Cash on hand, per last report $6.26, pledges and subscriptions $150.00, collections in church $42.67, total receipts for current expenses $199.63. *For all purposes other than current expenses, (i. e. Contributions)*—Collections in church $117.55, Sunday School $21.77, Parish Guild $15.00, total receipts for contributions $154.32; grand total of all receipts i. e. for current expenses and contributions $353.55.

Disbursements—For Current Expenses (Parochial)—Salary of Rector $150.00, other salaries $21.00, maintaining Sunday Schools $20.00, ordinary repairs $21.06, other current expenses $11.67, total for current expenses $223.73. *For Contributions—Parochial*—Used for missions, communion alms, extraordinary repairs and improvements $16.00, total parochial contributions $16.00. *Diocesan* Salary of Bishops $43.55, permanent fund $12.95, diocesan missions $18.46, convocation missions $8.00, widows and orphans, aged and disabled clergy fund $1.52, Sheltering Arms Hospital $7.18, Marshall's work $1.36, total diocesan contributions $90.02. *Objects without the Diocese*—Domestic missions general $3.00, through American Church Missionary Society $4.00, total domestic missions $7.00, foreign missions general $2.73, through American Church Missionary Society $4.47, total foreign missions $7.20; total foreign and domestic missions $14.20. Total without the Diocese $14.20.

Financial Summary—Contributions—Parochial $16.00, diocesan $90.02,

extra diocesan $14.20, total contributions $120.22. *Expenses*—Current parochial $223.73; grand total of all money raised by the congregation $342.95; cash on hand as a balance $10.00, total $353.95.

PAROCHIAL REPORT.

Rev. A. J. WILLIS, address Middleway. St. Bartholomew's Church, Nelson Parish, Leetown, Jefferson county. Date of organization, 1888. Present minister took charge Nov. 1, 1890.

Church Officers—Church Wardens, J. H. Strider, Chas. Jones; other vestrymen, Wm. Seibert, Dr. Chas. Lucas; Registrar, J. H. Strider, address Leetown; Treasurer, J. H. Strider, address Leetown; Superintendent of Sunday School, Wm. Seibert, Leetown; Sunday School Secretary and Treasurer, R. L. Strider.

Official Acts—Baptisms, infants 1, total 1; marriages 1, public services Sundays 36, other days 8, total 44; Holy Communion, public 6, total 6.

Communicants—Number last reported 38, added otherwise 2, total gain 2, net gain 2, present number total 40.

Congregations—Confirmed persons connected with Parish 43, baptized persons connected with Parish 60, families 14, individuals not thus included 100, whole number of individuals 200, number sittings in Church 200, all free.

Rector's Salary—As pledged from this congregation $175, from diocesan missions $50, as pledged from other congregations $375, from convocation missions $100, from American Church Missionary Society $100, total $800.

Organizations—Sunday Schools, officers and teachers, male 2, female 5, total 7; pupils, male 10, female 20, total 30; advent offering $16.29, Lenten offering $8.10, total Sunday School offerings $24.39; other organizations, Ladies' Aid, Parish Guild.

Property—Church, frame, insurance $1,000, value $1,800, total value $1,800.

FINANCIAL REPORT.

Receipts—For Current Expenses Pledges and subscriptions $175, collections in church $19.23, total receipts for current expenses $194.23. *For all purposes other than current expenses, (i. e. Contributions)*—Collections in church $260.51, Sunday School $24.39, Parish Guild $15.00, total receipts for contributions $299.90, grand total of all receipts i. e. for current expenses and contributions $494.13.

Disbursements—For current expenses, (Parochial)—Salary of rector $1.75, other salaries $12, other current expenses $19.93, total for current expenses $206.93. *For contributions—Parochial*—Extraordinary repairs and improvements; used for missions $15. *Diocesan*—Salary of Bishops $44.70, permanent fund $57.43, diocesan missions $40.85, convocation missions $45.17, widows and orphans, aged and disabled clergy fund $11.00, Sheltering Arms Hospital $7.94, Marshall's work $4.87, total diocesan contributions $211.96. *Objects without the Diocese*—Domestic missions general $4.75, through American Church Missionary Society $13.00, total domestic missions $17.75, foreign missions general $4.60, through American Church Missionary society $13.63, Brazil $21.93, total foreign missions $40.16, total foreign and domestic missions $57.91. Guntin Chapel $2.00, total without diocese $59.91.

Financial Summary—Contributions—Parochial $15.00, diocesan $211.96, extra diocesan $59.91, total contributions $286.87. *Expenses*—Current parochial $206.93; grand total of all money raised by the congregation $493.80; on hand .33, per receipts $494.13.

PAROCHIAL REPORT.

Rev. A. J. WILLIS, address Middleway. Church of the Holy Spirit, Nelson Parish, Summit Pt., Jefferson county. Date of organization 1888. Present minister took charge November 1, 1890.

Church Officers—Church Warden, Dr. A. P. Thomson; other vestrymen R. O. Allen, Geo. C. Whiting, N. H. Willis; Registrar, Geo. C. Whiting, address Summit Pt.; Treasurer, R. O. Allen, address Summit Pt.; Superintendent of Sunday Schools, Geo. C. Whiting; Sunday School Secretary and Treasurer, Preston Beller.

Official Acts—Baptisms, infants 3, total 3; burials 1, public services, Sundays 52, other days 8, total 60; Holy Communion, public 12, total 12.

Communicants—Number last reported 47, died 1, total loss 1, net loss 1; present number total 46.

Congregations—Confirmed persons connected with Parish 46, baptized persons connected with Parish 86, families 19, individuals not thus included 100, whole number of individuals 186, number free sittings 250.

Rector's Salary—As pledged from this congregation $225.00, from diocesan missions $50, as pledged from other congregations $325, from convocation missions $100, from American Church Missionary Society $100, total $800.

Organizations—Sunday Schools, officers and teachers, male 1, female 3, total 4; pupils, male 5, female 10, total 15; Advent offering $1.07, Lenten offering $1.74, other offerings $5.00, total Sunday School offerings $7.81. Other organizations, Ladies' Aid for Church improvements.

Property—Church, stone, insurance $2,000, value $4,000.

FINANCIAL REPORT.

Receipts—For Current Expenses—Pledges and subscriptions $225, collections in church $50, total receipts for current expenses $275. *For all purposes other than current expenses, (i. e. Contributions)*—Collections in Church $88.13, Sunday School $7.81, Parish Guild $15.00, total receipts for contributions $110.97; grand total of all receipts i. e. for current expenses and contributions $385.97.

Disbursements—For current expenses, (Parochial)—Salary of Rector $225, other salaries $25, maintaining Sunday Schools $10, ordinary repairs $1.41, other current expenses $25, total for current expenses $286.41. *For Contributions—Parochial*—Extraordinary repairs and improvements $15.00, total parochial contributions $15.00, used for missions. *Diocesan* Salary of Bishops $33.25, permanent fund $7.64, diocesan missions $15.00, convocation missions $7.66, widows and orphans, aged and disabled clergy fund $4.55, Sheltering Arms Hospital $2.50, Marshall's work $3.35, total diocesan contributions $70.75. *Objects without the Diocese*—Domestic missions general $1.41, through American Church Missionary Society $4.40, total domestic missions $5.81, foreign missions general $1.50, through American Church Missionary Society $4.50, total foreign missions $6.00, total foreign and domestic missions $11.81, total without diocese $11.81.

Financial Summary—Contributions—Parochial $15.00, diocesan $70.75, extra diocesan $11.81, total contributions $97.56. *Expenses*—Current parochial $286.40; grand total of all money raised by the congregation $383.97, balance on hand $2.00, as receipts $385.97.

PAROCHIAL REPORT.

(VACANT.) Good Shepherd Church, Mission, Parkersburg, Wood county.

Church Officers—Registrar, Mr. W. G. Peterkin, address Parkersburg; Treasurer, Mr. W. G. Peterkin, address Parkersburg; Superintendent of Sunday Schools, Mr. Simms Powell, Parkersburg; Sunday School Secretary and Treasurer, W. G. Peterkin; Lay Readers, Simms Powell and W. G. Peterkin.

Official Acts—Public services, Sundays 10, total 10.

Communicants—Number last reported 12, transferred 3, total loss 3; net loss 3; present number total 9.

Congregations—Confirmed persons connected with Parish 9, baptized persons connected with Parish 10, families 7, individuals not thus included 22, whole number of individuals 32, number sittings in Church 200, all free; number sittings in Sunday School room 150.

Organizations—Sunday Schools, officers and teachers, male 2, female 7, total 9; pupils, male 50, female 70, total 120; advent offering $20, lenten offering $20.

Property—Church, value $10,000.

FINANCIAL REPORT.

Receipts—For current expenses—Pledges and subscriptions $112.21, total receipts for current expenses $112.21. *For all purposes other than current expenses, (i. e. Contributions)*—Collections in Church $285, thank offerings $675, Sunday School $40, total receipts for contributions $1,000; grand total of all receipts i. e. for current expenses and contributions $1,112.21.

Disbursements—For Current expenses, (Parochial)—Salary of Rector two months $90, other salaries $6, other current expenses $16.21, total for current expenses $112.21. *Diocesan*—Salary of Bishops $13, permanent fund $280, diocesan missions $199, widows and orphans, aged and disabled clergy fund $20, religious and theological education $7, Sheltering Arms Hospital $20, total diocesan contributions $539. *Objects without the diocese*—Domestic missions general 144, colored people 2, Indians $1, deaf and dumb $2, Jews $1, through American Church Missionary Society $82, total domestic missions $232; foreign missions general $144, for Mexico 1, Brazil $41, Cuba $40, total foreign missions $226; total foreign and domestic missions $458; American Church Building fund $2, general clergy relief fund $1, total without diocese $461.

Financial Summary—Contributions—Diocesan $539, extra diocesan $461, total contributions $1,000. *Expenses*—Current parochial $112.21; grand total of all money raised by the congregation $1,112.21.

PAROCHIAL REPORT.

Rev. CREETUS A. DOWELL, A. B., address Clarksburg, W. Va.; now in charge of the Rev. Edward B. Snead. St. John's Mission, Sutton, Braxton county. Present minister took charge July, 1902.

Church Officers—Church Wardens, Amos Bright, J. S. Hammond; Registrar, Amos Bright, address Sutton, W. Va.; Treasurer, Amos Bright, address Sutton, W. Va.

Official Acts—Burials 1, public services, Sundays 18, other days 1.

Communicants—Number last reported 13, died 1, total loss 1; present number total 12.

Congregations—Confirmed persons connected with Parish 12, baptized persons connected ith Parish 27, families 5, individuals not thus included 6, free sittings 125.

Rector's Salary—As pledged from this congregation $100.00, from diocesan missions $150.00.

Property—Church, frame, insurance $1,000, value $1,500. Indebtedness due the minister $19.51.

FINANCIAL REPORT.

Receipts—For current expenses—Pledges and subscriptions $150, collections in Church $45, total receipts for current expenses $195.

Disbursements—For current expenses, (Parochial)—Salary of Rector $83.40, other current expenses, traveling expenses $27.28, total for current expenses $110.68. *For contributions—Parochial*—Extraordinary repairs and improvements $175, total parochial contributions $175. *Diocesan*—Diocesan missions $10, total diocesan contributions $10.

Financial Summary—Grand total of all money raised by the congregation $380.

Remarks—This report is for ten months of the year only.

PAROCHIAL REPORT.

Rev. CREETUS A. DOWELL, A. B., address Clarksburg, W. Va.; now vacant. Pennsboro Mission, Pennsboro, Ritchie county. Present minister took charge July, 1902.

Official Acts—Baptisms, adults 5, total 5; presented for confirmation since last report 4; public services, Sundays 10, other days 2, total 12.

Communicants—Number last reported 1, admitted by confirmation 4; present number total 5.

Congregations—Confirmed persons connected with Parish 5, baptized persons connected with Parish 14, families 3, whole number of individuals 19.

Rector's Salary—As pledged from this congregation $50, from diocesan missions $150, total $200.

FINANCIAL REPORT.

Receipts For current expenses—Pledges and subscriptions $60, collections in Church $13.75, total receipts for current expenses $73.75.

Disbursements—For current expenses, (Parochial)—Salary of Rector $39.80, other current expenses $13.75, other objects, traveling expenses $10.20, total for current expenses $63.75.

Financial Summary—Expenses—Current parochial $63.75; grand total of all money raised by the congregation $63.75.

Remarks — Pennsboro is a new mission station. There have been no regular services held here before my appointment. I took charge here in July and preached on the fourth Sunday evening of each month. This report is for nine months.—CREETUS A. DOWELL, *Minister in Charge.*

PAROCHIAL REPORT.

(VACANT.) Grace Mission, Newport, Wood county.

Church Officers—Treasurer, Miss Jennie Tavenner, address Newport, W. Va.; Sunday School Secretary and Treasurer, Jennie Tavenner.

Official Acts—Baptisms, infants 2, total 2; public services, Sundays 4, other days 6, total 10.

Communicants—Number last reported 10, present number total 10.

Congregations—Confirmed persons connected with Parish 11, baptized persons connected with Parish 20, families 8, individuals not thus included 20, whole number of individuals 40, number sittings in Church 100, all free.

Rector's Salary— ainfants tso6 .t4cmfwyp shrdlu mtham shrdltmahm

Organizations—Sunday Schools, officers and teachers, male 1, female 3, total 4; pupils, male 10, female 25, total 35.

Property—Church, frame, no insurance, value $1,200.00.

FINANCIAL REPORT.

Disbursements—For current expenses—Diocesan—Salary of Bishops, $3.00, diocesan missions $11.50, widows and orphans, aged and disabled clergy fund $1.00, total diocesan contributions $15.50.

Financial Summary—Contributions—Diocesan $15.50, total contributions $15.50; grand total of all money raised by the congregation $15.50.

PAROCHIAL REPORT.

228 East 9th St., Plainfield, N. J., May 18, 1903.

To the Rt. Rev. G. W. Peterkin, D. D.,

Parkersburg, W. Va.

MY DEAR BISHOP:—Since my last report I have been supplying vacant pulpits and assisting my brethren of the clergy wherever my services have been desired. During part of June, 1902, part of July and all of

August I have had charge of the services at St. Mary's Church, South Portsmouth, and at the Chapel of the Holy Cross, Middletown, R. I., and during all of January, all of February and part of March, 1903, I have had charge of St. John's Church, Far Rockaway, L. I. I have conducted fifty-one services, of which sixteen included the administration of the Holy Communion. I have assisted at twenty-one services, of which seven included the administration of the Holy Communion. I have preached forty-eight times and made nineteen addresses, conducted two funerals and assisted at one wedding. With heartfelt congratulations to the Diocese and yourself on this the Twenty-fifth Anniversary of your Consecration, and praying for a continuance of God's blessing on your work, I remain

Respectfully Yours,

WM. H. NEILSON.

REPORT OF REV. B. M. SPURR.

To the Rt. Rev. Geo. W. Peterkin, D. D.,

Parkersburg, W. Va.

MY DEAR BISHOP:—I have during the year been engaged in the management of the Reynold's Memorial Hospital, the details of which have been reported to you.

I have regularly visited the prison in Moundsville, when not otherwise engaged, and have there ministered to four men who have been executed during the year. I have also been instrumental in supplying the 950 convicts with large quantities of reading matter.

During the year I have preached fifteen times, given about seventy addresses, and celebrated the Holy Communion ten times. I now have regular Sunday evening service at the Hospital in what we call the Chapel of the Holy Comforter. At these services $15.00 has been collected which was sent to your special fund.

Respectfully Yours,

B. M. SPURR.

Reynold's Memorial Hospital,
Glendale, W. Va., May 13, 1903.

APPENDIX D.

Report of Committee on Assessments for the Year, May 1st, 1903, to April 30th, 1904.

REPORT OF COMMITTEE ON ASSESSMENTS, AT WHEELING, MAY 22, 1903.

Name of Parish.	Diocesan Miss.	Epis. & Cont. Fund.
Alderson	$ 6 00	$ 6 00
Berkeley Springs	25 00	30 00
Bluefield	30 00	30 00
Princeton	6 00	6 00
Bramwell	30 00	30 00
Eckman and McDowell Missions	20 00	20 00
Brooke County, St. John's	5 00	5 00
Buckhannon	10 00	10 00
Bunker Hill	5 00	5 00
Charleston, St. John's	200 00	275 00
Charleston, St. Luke's	8 00	7 00
Charleston, St. Matthew's	8 00	7 00
Charles Town, Zion	300 00	425 00
Charles Town, St. Phillip's	10 00	5 00
St. Andrew's on the Mountain	3 00	2 00
Clarksburg	125 00	125 00
Cresaps	5 00	5 00
Davis	8 00	8 00
Elkins Mission	10 00	10 00
Fairmont	75 00	100 00
Grafton	15 00	15 00
Harper's Ferry	20 00	20 00
Hedgesville	25 00	50 00
Hinton	30 00	20 00
Huntington	75 00	100 00
Kenova	8 00	7 00
Lewisburg	7 00	10 00
Ronceverte	8 00	8 00
Martinsburg	75 00	100 00
Middleway	15 00	30 00
Summit Point	15 00	30 00
Lee Town	30 00	30 00

Name of Parish.	*Diocesan Miss.*	*Epis. & Cont. Fund.*
Moorefield	20 00	20 00
Romney	16 00	16 00
Okonoko	10 00	10 00
Morgantown	25 00	25 00
Moundsville	40 00	60 00
Nuttallburg	5 00	10 00
Parkersburg, Trinity	350 00	525 00
Parkersburg, Good Shepherd	20 00	5 00
Parkersburg, St. Stephen	3 00	2 00
Tavennersville	10 00	3 00
Point Pleasant, Christ	50 00	50 00
Bruce Chapel	12 00	12 00
Spillman Mission	10 00	10 00
Powellton	20 00	20 00
Ansted	20 00	20 00
Ravenswood, Grace	10 00	10 00
Ripley, St. John's	15 00	15 00
Liverpool, Whittle	3 00	2 00
Ripon	10 00	20 00
Shepherdstown	75 00	75 00
Sistersville	40 00	40 00
New Martinsville	40 00	40 00
Smithfield, Wetzel County	5 00	5 00
Spruce Chapel	4 00	4 00
St. Albans	10 00	10 00
Montgomery	15 00	15 00
St. Mary's	15 00	15 00
Sutton	10 00	10 00
Union	50 00	50 00
White Sulphur	10 00	10 00
Fort Spring	5 00	5 00
Waverly	10 00	5 00
Wellsburg	25 00	25 00
Weston	75 00	80 00
Wheeling, St. Matthew's	425 00	600 00
Wheeling, St. Luke's	175 00	175 00
Wheeling, St. Andrew's	15 00	10 00
Chester	....	4 00
Williamson	....	5 00
·eeling, St. Paul's, Elm Grove	5 00	10 00
lliamstown	25 00	15 00
low Island	5 00	5 00

Name of Parish.	*Diocesan Miss.*	*Epis. & Cont. Fund.*
Beckley	6 00	6 00
Beury	5 00	5 00
Du Bree	5 00	5 00
Glen Jean	10 00	10 00
Immanuel, Mt. Carbon	5 00	5 00
Totals	$ 2,941 00	$ 3,630 00

Your committee recommends that payments on account of the assessment for the Episcopal and Contingent Fund be made to the Treasurer quarterly.

S. S. MOORE.
J. S. GIBSON.
J. S. DOUGLAS.
A. G. GRINNAN.
G. W. EASTER.

L. E. SANDS.
RICHARD HENDERSON.
J. GASSMAN.
R. M. BROWNE.
ETAOINNNNNNN

APPENDIX E.

Tabulated Statement—Vital Statistics.

Tabulated Statement—Financial Statistics.

TABULATED STATEMENT—VITAL STATISTICS.

PARISHES, MISSIONS AND STATIONS, ACCORDING TO ALPHABETICAL CLERGY LIST.		Baptisms. Infants.	Baptisms. Adults.	Confirmations.	Marriages.	Burials.	Communicants.	Baptized Persons.	Families and Parts.	No. in Sunday School.
REV. JOHN S. ALFRIEND	Zion Ch., Charles Town	3	6	9	12	14	326	550	160	116
	St. Andrew's, Blue Ridge	8		3	1	3	28	45	40	77
	Harewood									45
	St. Phillip's, Charles Town						50	79	25	94
REV. JACOB BRITTINGHAM	St. Luke's, Wheeling	9	2	18	17	15	266	382	202	113
REV. ROBERT UPSHUR BROOKING	St. John's, Ripon	1		1			28	65	25	20
	Christ, Blue Ridge			3		1	6	20	7	50
REV. EVERARD HEATH BROSIUS	Christ, Bluefield	4	1	4		4	91	140	57	42
	Heavenly Rest, Princeton	2		1	1		18	20	10	
REV. CHAS. MITCHELL CAMPBELL	Christ, Short Creek				2	2	2	10	14	18
	St. Paul's Mission, Bull Creek	1					4	10	4	
	Emmanuel Mission, Mouth of Robinson					1	4	7	10	
REV. WILSON PAGE CHRISMAN	Trinity, Moundsville	8	2	6	5	2	55	130	76	115
REV. GUY HAMILTON CROOK	Incarnation, Ronceverte						21	38	15	26
	St. James', Lewisburg			4			24	42	17	
	Holy Comforter, Fort Springs						8	11	9	
	Grace, Clover Lick	2					4	10	3	
	Hillsboro Mission, Academy						3	10	4	
	Glen Jean Mission						20	32	17	
	Beury Mission						2	2	2	
	St. Thomas', White Sulphur						41	75	62	96
REV. THOMAS J. OLIVER CURRAN	St. Andrew's, Wheeling	20	16	24	8	3	76	174	31	123
REV. THOMAS C. DABST	St. Andrew's, Mannington	3		10		1	21	44	22	
REV. JOHN SMALLWOOD DOUGLAS	Trinity, Martinsburg	11	5	11	4	10	152	280	93	102
	Christ, Bunker Hill						7	20	6	
REV. CREETUS A. DOWELL	St. Paul's Sistersville	11	1	7	1	5	34	50	20	88

TABULATED STATEMENT—VITAL STATISTICS—Continued.

PARISHES, MISSIONS AND STATIONS, ACCORDING TO ALPHABETICAL CLERGY LIST.		Baptisms. Infants.	Baptisms. Adults.	Confirmations.	Marriages.	Burials.	Communicants.	Baptized Persons.	Families and Parts.	No. in Sunday School.
Rev. A. J. Willis	St. Bartholomew's, Leetown	1	......	......	1	......	40	60	20	37
	Holy Spirit, Summit Point	8	......	......	......	1	46	36	30	19
	Good Shepherd, Parkersburg	......	..	......	......	......	9	10	7	129
Rev. Thos. W. Cooke	*Christ, Clarksburg	......	......	......	......	......	156	225	105	64
	*St. Thomas, Northview	......	......	......	......	......	34	34	10	......
	*St. Matthias, Grafton	......	......	......	......	......	80	40	21	29
	*Buffalo and Poca	......	......	......	......	......	4	4	2	......
	*Spencer	......	......	......	......	......	7	12	4	......
	*St. John's, Scary	......	......	......	......	......	8	3	2	......
	*Pennsboro Mission	......	5	4	......	......	5	14	3	......
	*Spruce Church, Atlas	......	......	......	......	......	10	15	7	......
	*Grace, Tavernersville	......	......	......	......	......	10	20	10	40
Rev. Edwin R. Weary	*Chester	......	......	......	......	......	20	25	10	......
Bishop Peterkin's Report of Scattered	Communicants	......	......	......	......	......	88	......	......	......
Totals		205	80	250	185	206	4,668	8,040	3,226	3,479

*Taken from last year's report.

NOTE:—The Bishops report 271 confirmations from council to council. The discrepancy of 21 is due to the fact that the parochial reports close April 30th.

TABULATED STATEMENT—FINANCIAL STATISTICS.

PARISHES, MISSIONS AND STATIONS ACCORDING TO ALPHABETICAL CLERGY LIST.		DISBURSEMENTS.				Grand Total.
		Current Expenses.	Contributions.			
			Parochial.	Diocesan.	Outside the Diocese.	
REV. JOHN S. ALFRIEND	Zion Church, Charles Town	$ 2,190.29	$ 403.28	$ 2,056.61	$ 427.01	$ 5,077.19
	St. Andrew's, Blue Ridge	5.00		10.00		15.00
	Harewood			5.11		5.11
	St. Phillip's, Charles Town	323.53	8.46	10.00	10.00	351.99
REV. JACOB BRITTINGHAM	St. Luke's, Wheeling	3,266.32	591.26	1,348.90	337.36	5,543.84
REV. ROBT. UPSHUR BROOKING	St. John's, Ripon	268.95	81.15	81.62	61.53	493.25
	Christ Chapel, Blue Ridge	3.00				3.00
REV. EVERETT HEATH BROSIUS	Christ Church, Buefield	682.05	776,78	70 40	68.06	1,597.29
	Heavenly Rest, Princeton	50.35				50.35
REV. CHAS. MITCHELL CAMPBELL	Short Creek, Boone Co			87		87
	St. Paul's Mission, Bull Creek			57		57
	Emmanuel, Mission, Racine			98	50	1.48
REV. WILSON PAGE CHRISMAN	Trinity, Moundsville	2,255.52	5,575.28	308.16	101.72	8,241.18
REV. GUY HAMILTON CROOK	Incarnation, Ronceverte	412.61	502.00	30.88	6.50	951.99
	St. James', Lewisburg	315.00	132.00	29.05	4.50	480.55
	Holy Comforter, Fort Spring	24.30		15.17	4.75	44.22
	Grace, Clover Lick	14.50		3.00		17.50
	Hillsboro Mission	7.50				7.50
	Glen Jean Mission	164.20		9.80		174.00
	Beury Mission	53.00		3.75		56.75
	St. Thomas', White Sulphur	29.00				29.00
REV. THOS. J. OLIVER CURRAN	St. Andrew's, Wheeling	1,728.94	472.01	178.41	30.00	2,409.36
REV. THOMAS C. DARST	St. Andrew's, Mannington	97.50		4.00		101.50
REV. JOHN S. DOUGLAS	Trinity, Martinsburg	1,210.83	4,065.62	388.26	208.56	5,873.27
	Christ, Bunker Hill	23.00	77.22	2.37	2.98	105.57

TABULATED STATEMENT—FINANCIAL STATISTICS—Continued.

PARISHES, MISSIONS AND STATIONS, ACCORDING TO ALPHABETICAL CLERGY LIST.		DISBURSEMENTS. Current Expenses.	Contributions. Parochial	Contributions. Diocesan.	Contributions. Outside the Diocese.	Grand Total.
Rev. Creetus A. Dowell	St Paul's, Sistersville	$ 1,147.62	$ 1,010.50	$ 138.71	$ 169.64	$ 2,466.47
Rev. George W. Easter	All Saints, Union	535.53	44.70	313.03	106.86	1,000.12
	Messiah, Alderson	9.65	....	9.25	....	18.90
Rev. James Logan Fish	Grace, Elkins	454.58	140.00	51.50	10.00	656.08
	St. Barnabas', Davis	314.08	105.00	39.50	8.00	466.58
	Trinity, Belington	100.00	....	....	....	100.00
Rev. George A. Gibbons	St. Stephen's, Romney	444.87	30.60	460.10	20.00	963.97
	Emmanuel, Moorefield	187.00	458.78	60.02	11.74	717.54
	Epiphany, Okonoko	42.00	....	30.25	7.00	79.25
	New Creek, Keyser					
	Paw Paw, Paw Paw	33.00	....	21.45	5.01	59.46
Rev. J. Howard Gibbons	Christ, Point Pleasant	486.57	1,882.71	159.58	54.50	2,083.87
	Bruce Chapel	172.50	....	47.90	4.36	224.76
	........Spilman	50.00	17.75	59.78	5.30	132.83
Rev. John Shackelford Gibson	Trinity, Huntington	5,984.00	1,042.00	468.71	141.00	7,630.71
	Grace, Kenova	102.20	81.03	49.05	10.11	282.39
	Mingo Mission	90.70	10.00	....	70	101.40
Rev. Andrew Glassell Grinnan	St. Paul's, Weston	1,026.42	217.50	283.04	93.59	1,620.55
	St. Paul's Chapel	....	810.54	....	....	810.54
Rev. Jacob A. Hiatt	Grace, Ravenswood	161.25	14.00	34.00	3.25	212.50
	St. John's, Ripley	116.00	4.00	48.00	11.00	179.00
	Whittle Chapel	20.00	2.00	3.00	....	25.00
	Church of Our Saviour, Mason City	....	....	5.00	....	5.00
	Grace, New Port	....	....	15.50	....	15.50
Rev. David W. Howard	St. Matthew's, Wheeling	6,674.74	289.50	13,514.25	663.42	21,141.91
Rev. Edward D. Irvine	Christ, Wellsburg	454.43	6.06	154.36	12.91	627.78

Rev. Edward D. Irvine	St. John's, Brooke Co.					
Rev. Arthur M. Lewis	St. David's, Powellton	505.96		63.75	19.40	589.11
	Calvary, Montgomery	242.96	137.20	145.05	15.07	540.28
	The Redeemer, Ansted	244.83	254.17	85.34	14.09	598.43
Rev. John Tilton Marley	Trinity, Morgantown	1,030.40	364.60	221.50	21.40	1,637.90
Rev. Chas. E. A. Marshall	Trinity Shepherdstown	681.75		488.50	119.77	1,290.02
Rev. Robert Nelson Meade	Holy Trinity, Bramwell	869.91	1,677.33	112.74	11.06	2,671.04
	Grace, Eckman	292.79	80.00	26.95	6.78	406.22
	St. Antipas, Welch	162.36	413.00	4.00	7.21	586.57
	Algoma	16.19		6.00	13.71	35.90
	Maybeury			4.00		• 4.00
	Elkhorn	13.60		9.00	4.38	26.98
	Crane Creek	14.64	6.35			20.99
Rev. James D. Miller	St. John's, Harpers Ferry	507.02		115.04	41.76	663.82
	Mt. Zion, Hedgesville	238.81	85.00	90.52	28.86	443.19
Rev. S. Scollay Moore, D. D.	Trinity, Parkersburg	3,434.11	1,157.89	1,904.98	481.38	6,978.36
	St. Stephen's, Parkersburg	105.76		84	1.05	107.65
Rev. C. C. Pearson	St. Mark's, Berkeley Springs	328.48	160.00	56.01	41.00	585.49
Rt. Rev. C. C. Penick, D. D.	Christ, Fairmont	2,350.00	400.00	1,821.14	1,136.97	5,708.11
Rev. Robt. Douglas Roller, D. D.	St. John's, Charleston	2,550.80	2,883.73	1,272.29	292.82	6,999.64
Rev. Chas. E. Shaw	St. Ann's, New Martinsville	756.42	3,776.71	180.27	37.16	4,750.56
Rev. George C. Shaw	Grace, St. Marys	955.00		130.00	3.00	1,088.00
	Christ Memorial, Williamstown	219.02	37.00	48.57	12.40	316.99
	Messiah, Waverly	166.80	4.00	23.90	5.50	200.20
Rev. Edward B. Snead	St. John's, Sutton	110.68	175.00	10.00		295.68
Rev. Paris B. Stauffer	Ascension, Hinton	612.75	16.81	34.62	5.75	669.93
	Beckley	117.00		15.18	4.02	136.20
Rev. J. F. Woods	Grace, Cresaps	35.50	3.75	15.00	2.50	56.75
	St. John's, Willow Island	15.00		19.50		34.50
	New Cumberland	49.00			1.00	50.00
Rev. John Warnock	St. Matthew's, Charleston	124.34		21.75	1.00	147.09
	St. Luke's, Charleston	213.63		20.00		233.63
	St. Mark's, St. Albans	153.59	7.70	5.00	12.20	178.49

TABULATED STATEMENT—FINANCIAL STATISTICS—Continued.

PARISHES, MISSIONS AND STATIONS, ACCORDING TO ALPHABETICAL CLERGY LIST.		DISBURSEMENTS.				Grand Total.
		Current Expenses.	Contributions.			
			Parochial.	Diocesan.	Outside the Diocese.	
REV. A. J. WILLIS	Grace, Middleway	$ 223.73	$ 16.00	$ 90.02	$ 14.20	$ 343.95
	St Bartholomew's, Lee Town	206.93	15.00	211.96	59.91	493.80
	Church of the Holy Spirit, Summit	286.41	15.00	70.75	11.81	383.97
-	Good Shepherd, Parkersburg	112.21	....	539.00	461.00	1,112.21
	Pennsboro	63.75	....	....	....	63.75
TOTALS		$49,834.66	$29,987.89	$28,350.77	$5,490.02	$113,663.34

NOTE:—There are no financial reports from Christ Church, Clarksburg, St. Thomas, North View, and St. Matthias, Grafton.

INDEX TO JOURNAL.

ADDRESS OF THE BISHOP,

Journal and Official Acts....................................22-30

Remarks as to Bishop Whittle............................31-32

General Clergy Relief Fund 32

Parochial Reports 33

Sheltering Arms Hospital 33

Reynolds Memorial Hospital 34

Episcopal Hall 34

Diocesan Missions 35

General Missions 36

Proposed Change in Name of the Church... 37

The Meaning of Our Annual Councils...... 42

ADDRESS OF THE BISHOP COADJUTOR,

Journal and Official Acts..................................12-18

APPENDICES,

Appendix A—Historical Sermon 61

Appendix B— I. Report of Treasurer of Diocese.......... 77

— II. Report of Trustee of Episcopal Fund.... 83

—III. Report of Trustees of Permanent Fund.. 86

Appendix C—Parochial Reports 95

Appendix D—Diocesan Assessments 193

Appendix E— I. Vital Statistics 201

—II. Financial Statistics 205

BISHOP, THE,

Address and Journal 22-42

BISHOP COADJUTOR, THE,

Journal and Official Acts 12-18

BLUEFIELD PARISH 43

CANDIDATES, For Holy Orders 28-29

CHANGE OF NAME 37, 43, 53-55

CLERGY,
Bishops, List Of 5-7
Changes Among 27-28

COMMITTEES,
Of the Council 19
Constitution and Canons 4
Credentials 9
Diocesan Missionary 3
Diocesan and Foreign Missions 3
Education 4
Standing Committee 3
Sunday Schools 4

COUNCIL MINUTES,
Wednesday, A. M................................ 9
Wednesday, P. M................................ 9
Thursday, P. M................................ 21
Friday, A. M................................ 49
Friday, P. M................................ 51
Saturday, A. M................................ 56

GREETINGS ON THE TWENTY-FIFTH ANNIVERSARY,
From Virginia 21
From Japan 21

LAY DELEGATES 10-12

ORGANIZED MISSIONS, Bishops List................................ 29

OFFICERS OF THE COUNCIL................................ 3

PARISHES, List Of................................10-11

REPORTS OF COMMITTEES,
Change of Name of the Church................................ 53
Constitution and Canons................................ 56
Credentials 9, 46
Diocesan Missionary 49
Education 45
Finance 48

New Parishes 43-45
Parochial Reports 50
Pemanent Fund 52
State of the Cnurch....................................... 58
Standing Committee 46
Sunday Schools 46

RESOLUTIONS AND MOTIONS,
As to Greetings to Virginia Council....................... 19
As to Hours of Meeting, Etc....................... 19
As to Historical Sermon....................... 22
As to Certificates of Delegates....................... 46
Of Thanks to Trustees of Permanent Fund....................... 48
As to Vacation for the Bishop....................... 52
Of Thanks 56
As to Form of Parochial Report....................... 56
Of Thanks 58
As to Recodifying Canons, Etc....................... 60
As to Memorial Volume....................... 60
As to General Clergy Relief Fund....................... 57

SPECIAL COMMITTEES,
As to Change of Name....................... 43
As to General Clergy Relief Fund....................... 57
As to Aniiversary Memorial Volume....................... 60

SHELTERING ARMS HOSPITAL .... [illegible]

SUMMARY OF STATISTICS (Appendix E)....................... 199

TABULATED STATEMENT (Appendix E)....................... 199

TREASURER OF THE DIOCESE....................... [illegible]

TREASURER OF PERMANENT FUND....................... [illegible]

TREASURER OF EPISCOPAL AND CONTINGENT FUND......... [illegible]

WOMAN'S AUXILIARY, OFFICERS, ETC....................... [illegible]

Resolved, That this Council call the attention of the members of this Church to the action of the House of Bishops respecting worldliness, and commends to their prayerful consideration and abstaining from all those forms of worldly amusements tending to bring reproach upon the Christain Religion; and

Resolved, That attendance upon public balls, horse racing and theatres are some of those things which in the judgment of this Council are inconsistent with the Christian Life, and improper for the members of the body of Christ.

The Parochial and Fiscal Year of the Diocese begins May 1st, and ends April 30th.

Places of Meeting Determined on by the Council.

MARTINSBURG, 1904.	CLARKSBURG, 1905.
CHARLES TOWN, 1906.	MOUNDSVILLE, 1907.
POINT PLEASANT, 1908.	WESTON, 1909.
HUNTINGTON, 1910.	SHEPHERDSTOWN, 1911.
CHARLESTON, 1912.	PARKERSBURG, 1913.

WHEELING, 1914.

ZRP

JOURNAL

OF THE

TWENTY-SEVENTH ANNUAL COUNCIL

OF THE

Protestant

EPISCOPAL CHURCH,

IN THE

DIOCESE OF WEST VIRGINIA,

HELD IN

TRINITY CHURCH, MARTINSBURG,

JUNE 1, 2, 3, AND 4, 1904.

1904:
TRIBUNE PRINTING COMPANY PRINT.
CHARLESTON, WEST VA.

Diocese of West Virginia.

Officers, Committees, Etc., for 1904.

Bishop,

RT. REV. GEO. W. PETERKIN, D. D., LL. D., Parkersburg. ....

Bishop Coadjutor,

RT. REV. W. L. GRAVATT, D. D., Charles Town.

Secretary of the Council,

REV. ROBERT DOUGLAS ROLLER, D. D., Charleston.

Treasurer of Council,

L. E. SANDS, Wheeling.

Standing Committee, P. O., (Charles Town, W. Va.)

Rev. G. A. Gibbons, President.
Rev. J. S. Douglas.
Rev. A. J. Willis
Mr. J. Gassman.
Mr. Isaac H. Strider.
Judge Frank Beckwith.

Missionary Committee,

The Bishop of the Diocese, (*ex-officio*) President.
The Bishop Coadjutor, (*ex-officio*)

Rev. J. Brittingham.
Rev. J. S. Alfriend.
Rev. S. S. Moore, D. D.
Mr. B. M. Ambler.
Mr. Simms Powell.

Mr. L. E. Sands, Treasurer.

Diocesan Committee on Foreign and Domestic Missions,

Rev. D. W. Howard.
Rev. G. A. Gibbons.
Rev. J. S. Gibson.
Gen'l W. P. Craighill.
Mr. C. C. Coe.
Dr. G. A. Aschman.

Trustee of the Episcopal and Contingest Fund (Special).

Robert M. Browne, Wheeling.

Trustees of Kenyon College.

Rt. Rev. Geo. W. Peterkin, D. D., LL. D.
Rt. Rev. W. L. Gravatt, D. D.
Mr. Jos. D. DuBois.

Trustees of Permanent (Episcopal) Fund.

Mr. Robert M. Browne. Mr. B. M. Ambler. Mr. H. H. Moss.
Central Banking and Security Co., Parkersburg, Treasurer.

Registrar of the Diocese,

Mr. B. M. Ambler, Parkersburg.

Standing Committee on Constitution and Canons,

Rev. Jno. S. Gibson.
Rev. D. W. Howard.
Rev. J. S. Douglas.
Mr. W. S. Laidley.
Mr. Joseph Trapnell.

Committee on Education,

Rev. G. W. Easter.
Rev. J. Howard Gibbons.
Rev. A. M. Lewis.
Mr. W. G. Hubbard.
Mr. C. L. Thompson.

Committee on Sunday Schools,

Rev. W. P. Chrisman.
Rev. C. E. Shaw.
Dr. G. A. Aschman.
George Rogers.

Examining Chaplains,

Rev. S. S. Moore, D. D.
Rev. J. S. Gibson.

Trustees of the Virginia Theological Seminary.

Rt. Rev. G. W. Peterkin, D. D. LL. D.
Rt. Rev. W. L. Gravatt, D. D.
Rev. S. S. Moore, D. D.
Mr. Joseph Trapnell.

Chancellor of the Diocese,

Joseph Trapnell, Charles Town.

Woman's Auxiliary,

Mrs. G. A. Aschman, Wheeling, President.
Valley Convocation, Miss M. G. McSherry, Vice-President.
Kanawha Convocation, Mrs. Ely Ensign, Vice-President.
North Western Convocation, Miss Gertrude Lamb, Vice-President.

Delegates to Missionary Council.

Rev. J. S. Gibson.
Rev. J. S. Douglas.
*Rev. S. S. Moore, D. D.
Gen'l B. D. Spillman.
Mr. J. T. Waters.
*Mr. H. W. Potts.

Deputies to General Convention.

Rev. S. Scollay Moore, D. D.
Rev. Robt. Douglas Roller, D. D.
Rev. David W. Howard.
Rev. John S. Alfriend.
Mr. Joseph Trapnell.
Mr. B. Mason Ambler.
Dr. G. A. Aschman.
Mr. C. L. Thompson.

Alternates.

Rev. J. Brittingham.
Rev. John S. Douglas.
Rev. John S. Gibson.
George A. Gibbons.
Mr. Peebles Tatum.
Judge Frank Beckwith.
Mr. Wm. S. Laidley.
Gen'l B. D. Spillman.

ted by the Council.

Clergy of the Diocese of West Virginia.

Rt. Rev. Geo. W. Peterkin, D. D. LL. D., Bishop (1878) *Parkersburg, W. Va.*
Rt. Rev. W. Loyall Gravatt, Bishop Coadjutor (1893) *Charles Town, W. Va.*
Rev. Geo. A. Gibbons, (1878) Rector of Emmanuel, Moorefield, and in charge of Missions in Hampshire County .... *Romney, W. Va.*
**Rev. Jno. F. Woods*, (1878) .... *Philadelphia, Pa.*
Rev. Robt. Douglas Roller, D. D., (1879) Rector of St. John's, Charleston .... *Charleston Kanawha Co., W. Va.*
**Rev. Jacob Brittingham*, (1881) Rector of St. Luke's, Wheeling .... *Wheeling, W. Va.*
Rev. C. C. Pearson, (1882) in charge of St. Mark's, Berkeley Springs .... *Berkeley Springs, W. Va.*
**Rev. Chas. M. Campbell*, (1886) In charge of Boone County Mission .... *Racine, W. Va.*
Rev. S. Scollay Moore, D. D., (1888) Rector of Trinity Church, Parkersburg............................ *Parkersburg, W. Va.*
Rev. Andrew J. Willis, (1890) Rector of Nelson Parish, (Grace Church, Middleway; St. Bartholomew's, Leetown, and Church of the Holy Spirit, Summit Point)..*Middleway, W. Va.*
Rev. Geo. W. Easter, (1892) Rector of All Saints Union, and in charge of Church of the Messiah, Alderson........*Union, W. Va.*
Rev. Jno. S. Gibson, (1892) Rector of Trinity Church, Huntington, and in charge of Grace Church, Kenova..*Huntington, W. Va.*
Rev. B. M. Spurr, (1894) General Missionary and Supt. Reynold's Memorial Hospital .... *Moundsville, W. Va.*
Rev. A. G. Grinnan, (1895) Rector of St. Paul's Church, Weston .... *Weston, W. Va.*
Rt. Rev. C. C. Penick, D. D., (1899) Rector of Christ Church, Fairmont .... *Fairmont, W. Va.*
Rev. Jno. S. Douglas, (1899) Rector of Trinity Church, Martinsburg, and in charge of Christ Church, Bunker Hill .... *Martinsburg, W. Va.*
Rev. Chas. E. Shaw, (1899) Rector of St. Ann's, New Martinsville.............................. *New Martinsville, W. Va.*
Rev. David W. Howard, (1899) Rector of St. Matthew's, Wheeling .... *Wheeling, W. Va.*

Rev. Jas. L. Fish, (1900) in charge of St. Barnabas, Davis.......... *Davis, W. Va.*

Rev. Thos. J. Oliver Curran, (1900) in charge of St. Andrew's, Wheeling.......... *Wheeling, W. Va.*

Rev. John Tilton Marley, (1900) Rector of Trinity, Morgantown, and Warden of the Episcopal Hall.... *Morgantown, W. Va.*

Rev. J. Howard Gibbons, (1901) Rector of Point Pleasant Parish, (Christ Church and Bruce Chapel).... *Point Pleasant, W. Va.*

**Rev. J. A. Hiatt,* (1901) in charge of Ascension, Hinton, and St. Peter's, Glen Jean.......... *Hinton, W. Va.*

**Rev. Guy H. Crook,* (1901) Rector of Greenbrier Parish, (St. James, Lewisburg; Church of the Incarnation, Ronceverte, and St. Thomas', White Sulphur) and in charge of Missions in Pocahontas County.......... *Ronceverte, W. Va.*

Rev. Arthur M. Lewis, (1901) in charge of St. David's, Powellton; Calvary, Montgomery, and Church of the Redeemer, Ansted .... *Powellton, W. Va.*

Rev. Everett Heath Brosius, (1902) Rector of Christ Church, Bluefield, and in charge of Heavenly Rest, Princeton .... *Bluefield, W. Va.*

Rev. Jno. S. Alfriend, (1902) Rector of Zion Church, Charles Town .... *Charles Town, W. Va.*

Rev. Wilson Page Chrisman, (1902) Rector of Trinity Church, Moundsville.......... *Moundsville, W. Va.*

**Rev. Paca Kennedy,* Deacon, (1902) .... *Oxford, England.*

Rev. Robt. N. Meade, (1902) in charge of Holy Trinity, Bramwell and Grace Church, Eckman.......... *Bramwell, W. Va.*

Rev. Paris B. Stauffer, (1902) Rector of Mt. Zion, Hedgesville, and in charge of St. John's, Harpers Ferry.......... *Harpers Ferry, W. Va.*

Rev. Geo. C. Shaw, (1902) in charge of St. Andrew's, Mannington .... *Mannington, W. Va.*

Rev. C. E. A. Marshall, (1903) Rector of Trinity, Shepherdstown .... *Shepherdstown, W. Va.*

Rev. Creetus A. Dowell, (1903) Rector of St. Paul's Church, Sistersville. .... *Sistersville, W. Va.*

**Rev. John Warnock,* (1903) Rector of St. Mary's, St. Albans, and in charge of St. Luke's and St. Matthew's, Kanawha County.......... *Charleston, Kanawha, W. Va.*

Rev. Edward D. Irvine, (1903) Rector of Christ Church, Wellsburg, and of St. John's, Brooke County.......... *Wellsburg, W. Va.*

**Rev. Edwin B. Snead,* (1903) in charge of Church of the Transfiguration, Buckhannon and of Spence Chapel .... *Buckhannon, W. Va.*

**Rev. Maximo F. Duty,* (1903) Assisting Rev. Jno. S. Alfriend in work of St. Philip's, Charles Town........*Charles Town, W. Va.*

Rev. Francis Van R. Moore, Deacon, (1903) in charge of St. Paul's, Elm Grove ....*Elm Grove, W. Va.*

Rev. Austin B. Mitchell, (1903) in charge of Christ Memorial Church, Williamstown; Chapel of the Good Shepherd, and Grace, Tavernersville.............*Williamstown, W. Va.*

Rev. F. A. Meade, (1902) in charge of Grace Church, Elkins...*Elkins, W. Va.*

Rev. Robt. R. Windley, (1903) in charge of St. Matthew's, Grafton..................................*Grafton, W. Va.*

***Rev. Jas. F. Plummer,* (1904) Rector of Christ Church, Clarksburg.................................*Clarksburg, W. Va.*

GEO. W. PETERKIN,
Bishop of West Virginia.

Parkersburg, May 25, 1904.

**Not entitled to seats. *Absent.

RULES OF ORDER.

Adopted by the Eighth Annual Council, June 3rd, 1885.

ORGANIZATION.

1st. The Council shall be opened each day with prayer.

2nd. After the call to order, no member shall remain standing, nor afterward stand, except to address the Chair.

ORDER OF BUSINESS.

1st. After the organization of the Council, the following order of business shall be observed:

The appointment of a committee on the Credentials of Lay Delegates.

The appointment of a Treasurer *pro tempore*, when the Treasurer is absent.

The adoption of rules of order.

The reading of the journal of the preceding day.

The reading of the pastoral address.

The appointment of committees.

Reports of standing committees.

Reports of special committees.

Unfinished business.

2nd. There shall be appointed by the President, not later than the *second* day of the Council, unless otherwise directed, the following standing committees, to consist of an equal number of each order:

A Committee on the State of the Church, to whom shall be referred the address of the Bishop on the opening of the Council.

A Committee on Parochial reports.

A Committee on the admission of new Parishes.

A Committee on the Episcopal Fund, and the Permanent Fund.

A Committee on the Brotherhood.

A Committee on Unfinished Business.

ORDER OF DEBATE.

1st. When a motion is made and seconded, it shall be stated by the President, and if in writing, be read by the Secretary before debated.

2nd. After a motion is stated by the President, or read by the Secretary, it shall be deemed in possession of the Council, but may be withdrawn by the mover at any time before amendment or decision, with the consent of his second.

3rd. Every motion shall be reduced to writing if the President or any member require it.

4th. No new motion or proposition shall be admitted under color of amendment, as a substitute for the motion or proposition under debate.

5th. When a question is under debate, no motion shall be received but to adjourn, to lay on the table, for the previous question, to postpone indefinitely, to postpone to a certain day, to commit, or to amend, which several motions shall have precedence in the order enumerated; and the first three shall be decided without debate.

6th. The previous question shall be admitted only when demanded by a majority of the members present. It shall be in this form: "Shall the main question be now put?" and until decided, all debate and amendment are precluded.

7th. A motion to adjourn shall always be in order, and shall be decided without debate.

8th. When a member desires to speak in debate, or present any matter to the Council, he shall raise from his seat, and respectfully address himself to the President, and shall confine himself to the question under debate, avoiding all personality.

9th. If any member transgress the rules of the Council, the President shall, or any member may, call him to order; in which case the member so called to order shall immediately take his seat, unless permitted to explain. If the ruling of the President be appealed from, the Council shall decide the question without debate.

10th. When two or more members rise at once, the President shall decide who is entitled to the floor.

11th. No member shall speak more than twice to the same question, without leave of the Council.

12th. The vote on all questions shall be taken by ayes and noes, whenever three members require it.

13th. Any member may call for a division of the question where the sense will admit of it, but a motion to strike out and to insert shall be deemed indivisible.

14th. Every member who may be in the house when the question is put shall give his vote, unless the Council, for special reasons, shall excuse him.

15th. No member shall vote upon a question, in the decision of which he is immediately and personally interested.

16th. Upon a division and count of the Council on any question, no member shall be counted who is not within the limits assigned as seats to the members.

17th. When a question has been decided by the Council, or postponed indefinitely, it may be reconsidered upon motion made by members voting in the majority: *provided*, such motion be made on the same or next or succeeding day of the session.

GENERAL REGULATIONS.

1st. No member shall absent himself from the meetings of the Council without leave, unless he be sick, or unable to attend.

2nd. The President shall, at his discretion, select suitable seats without the limits of those allotted to the use of the members, which shall be appropriated to the accommodation of visiting Clergymen and Candidates for Orders, who may be invited by the Rector or Wardens of the Church in which the meetings of the Council are held, under the directions of the President and Council.

3rd. No spectator shall, during the daily sessions of the Council, be admitted above or within the pews allotted to the members, and the Rector and Wardens of the Church in which the sessions of the Council are held, are directed to see that this rule is enforced.

4th. No rule of order shall be suspended except with the concurrence of two-thirds of the members present.

JOURNAL

Of the Twenty-seventh Annual Council of the Protestant Episcopal Church in the Diocese of West Virginia.

TRINITY CHURCH, MARTINSBURG, Wednesday, June 1, 1904.

The Twenty-seventh Annual Council of the Diocese of West Virginia assembled this day at 11 A. M.

The Rev. S. S. Moore, D. D. and the Rev. G. W. Easter read Morning Prayer. The Rev. Dr. Roller read the Lessons. Rt. Rev. W. L. Gravatt read the ante-communion.

The Rev. Chas. E. Shaw preached the Council sermon from the text. Acts i-8.

The Rt. Rev. G. W. Peterkin, D. D., LL. D., celebrated the Holy Communion, Bishop Gravatt assisting.

At the conclusion of the services Bishop Peterkin called the Council to order.

The roll call showed a quorum of both orders present.

The Bishop appointed the following Committee on Credentials:

Rev. Thos. J. Oliver Curran, Rev. E. H. Brosius, Mr. C. L. Thompson, Mr. George Kreglow.

On motion of Rev. J. S. Douglas, the following order was adopted by the Council: Meet at 9:30 A. M. Recess at 11 A. M. Meet at 2:30. Adjourn at 5 P. M.

The Rev. B. M. Spurr offered the following, which was adopted by a rising vote and the Secretary was instructed to wire the action of the Council to our dear brother:

Resolved, That this Council express its profound sympathy with and sorrow for our beloved brother, the Rev. Jacob Brittingham, in the sad loss of his son by drowning, and we beg to assure him of our ardent prayers, that God in his mercy will grant him the comfort and strength to endure in this, his hour of bereavement.

The Council took a recess for lunch.

WEDNESDAY, 2:30 P. M.

The Bishop called the Council to order.

The following standing committees were appointed:

STATE OF THE CHURCH.

Rev. D. W. Howard,	Mr. G. W. Parsons.
Rev. G. W. Easter,	Mr. W. E. Watson,
Rev. A. G. Grinnan,	Mr. W. G. Hubbard,

PAROCHIAL REPORTS.

Rev. A. M. Lewis,	Mr. Ben. R. Roller,
Rev. W. P. Chrisman,	Mr. George J. Rogers.

NEW PARISHES.

Rev. John S. Gibson,	Mr. Peebles Tatum,
Rev. A. J. Willis,	

EPISCOPAL AND PERMANENT FUND.

Rev. S. S. Moore, D. D.,	Dr. A. G. Aschman,
Rev. J. S. Alfriend,	Mr. B. Bryan.

UNFINISHED BUSINESS.

Rev. R. D. Roller, D. D.,	Mr. Wm. Kilmer,
Rev. R. N. Meade,	Mr. W. W. Shearer.

FINANCE.

The Rt. Rev. the Bishop of the Diocese, then read his annual address as follows:

MAY, 1904.

Wednesday, 20th: The 26th Annual Council meeting to-day in St. Matthew's Church, Wheeling, was just two weeks before the usual time, in order to be coincident with the Bishop's 25th anniversary. The services were of unusual interest, and will be found detailed in the Secretary's report. We are under special obligation to the Rev. Jno. S. Gibson, for his admirable historical sermon, and cannot soon forget the late Bishop of Kentucky, who after an interval of twenty-five years, preached on our anniversary, as he did at our consecration. The presence also of the former Rectors, the Rev. Dr. Swope and the Rev. N. S. Thomas, added great interest to the occasion. According to our custom, our services continued through Sunday, 24th, Dr. Swope preaching at the Morning service and Bishop Peterkin in the evening.

Monday, 25, Tuesday, 26: Examination of candidates for orders, in Parkersburg.

Sunday, 31: A. M., preached in St. Matthew's, S. Charleston, and Consecrated the church. P. M. St. Andrew's, Davis Creek. P. P. M. St. John's, Charleston, confirmed 5.

JUNE.

Monday, 1: In company with the Rev. Dr. Roller I visited Carbon and Wake Forest on Cabin Creek, looking to the speedy establishment of services at those points. My appointment at Pratt for the evening failed, as we were unable to secure a building.

Sunday, 1: A. M. St. John's, Willow Island, preached and confirmed 1. P. M. At the house of Mr. Norris baptized an infant. P. P. M. Church of the Messiah, Waverly, preached and confirmed 1.

Monday, 8: Theological Seminary. Examination of candidates.

uesday, 9: Board of Managers of Missions. New York.

Tuesday 16, Friday 19: In attendance on the commencement exercises of the Theological Seminary and High School, including examination of candidates, meeting of the Education Society and of the Trustees, and of the Society of the Alumni. On Thursday of this week I officiated at a wedding near Bettsville and on Friday ordained Mr. Francis Van Rensaller Moore, deacon.

Sunday 21: A. M. Christ Memorial Church, Williamstown, also visited the Sunday school. P. M. Grace Church, St. Marys.

Tuesday, 23, Wednesday, 24: Attended the commencement exercises of Kenyon, and with Bishop Gravatt and Mr. DuBois, the meeting of the Trustees.

Thursday, 25: Meeting of the Diocesan Missions Committee in Parkersburg.

Friday, 26: In Trinity Church, Parkersburg, ordained to the priesthood Rev. J. A. Hiatt, Rev. Dr. Moore presenting the candidate and Rev. W. H. K. Pendleton, of Marietta, O., preaching the sermon. There were also present and assisting, Rev. J. Brittingham and Rev. Jno. F. Woods.

On the afternoon of the same day took part in a funeral.

Saturday, 27: Met and conferred with the vestry of St. Anne's, New Martinsville.

Sunday, 28: Preached A. M. and P. M. in St. Anne's, New Martinsville, and at the morning service consecrated the church. This commodious and beautiful building having been erected on the front part of the lot in such wise as to preserve the old church for a Sunday school and lecture room, the whole property now is one of the most complete and convenient in the diocese.

JULY.

Friday, 3: In Trinity, Parkersburg, after Litany service, addressed the Woman's Auxiliary.

Sunday, 5: A. M. and P. M. Trinity Church, Parkersburg. P. P. M. St. Stephen's Church.

Friday, 10: Visited the Sheltering Arms Hospital, and in the evening preached in the Baptist Church, Pratt, and confirmed 2.

Saturday, 11: Met the ladies of Ascension, Hinton.

Sunday, 12: A. M. and P. M. Ascension, Hinton, also visited the Sunday School.

Monday 13: Preached in the M. E. Church, Beckley.

Sunday, 19: A. M. and P. M. St. Paul's Church, Sistersville. At the A. M. service confirmed 1.

Sunday 26: A. M. and P. M. Christ Church, Clarksburg.

Friday, 31: Preached in the school house, Paw Paw.

AUGUST.

Sunday, 2: A. M. and P. M. St. Mark's, Berkeley Springs. At the morning service confirmed 1.

Monday, 3: Preached in the Presbyterian church, Bayard, and made arrangements for a monthly service from Davis.

Wednesday 4: Officiated at a wedding at Harding.

Sunday, 9: In St. Thomas', White Sulphur, confirmed 1. Bishop Van Buren preaching.

P. M. Preached in Eakles school house and confirmed 2.

Tuesday 11: Preached in the Presbyterian Church, Fort Spring.

Wednesday, 12: In the Church of the Incarnation, Ronceverte, confirmed 6.

Thursday, 13: St. James' Church, Lewisburg.

Sunday, 16: A. M. Preached in the ball-room at the Old Sweet Springs, and P. M. at the Salt Sulphur.

Monday, 17: All Saints, Union.

Tuesday, 18: Preached in the school-room at Linside.

Wednesday, 19: Preached in M. E. Church, Cashmere.

Thursday, 20: Preached in the Presbyterian church, Red Sulphur Springs.

Sunday, 23: A. M. and P. M. St. Mark's, St. Albans. In the afternoon at St. John's, Scary.

Friday, 28: Preached in the Presbyterian church, Nuttall

Sunday, 30: A. M. Calvary, Montgomery. P. M. The school house, Mt. Carbon. P. P. M. St. David's Church, Powellton.

Monday, 31: Preached in the school house, Beauty.

SEPTEMBER.

sday, 1, Thursday, 3: Attended the Kanawha Association, taking part blic services and in business meetings.

Friday, 4: Preached in Baptist church, Glen Ferris.

Sunday, 6: A. M. Church of the Redeemer church, Ansted. P. M. Presbyterian church, Debree.

Sunday, 13: A. M. Trinity, Martinsburg. P. M. Christ Church, Bunker Hill. P. P. M. Mt Zion, Hedgesville, confirmed 4.

Monday, 14: New York. Commission of Bishops on Mexico.

Tuesday, 15: Board of Managers of Missions, New York.

Wednesday, 16, Thursday, 17: Attended meeting of the Eastern Convention, St. John's Ripon, taking part in public services and in business meetings. Preached at the Thursday, P. M. service.

Sunday, 20: A. M. Preached in St. John's, Brooke County, and confirmed 4. P. M. In Christ Church, Wellsburg, and confirmed 4.

Tuesday, 22: St. Stephen's Romney.

Wednesday, 23: Zion Church, North River.

Thursday, 24: Preached in the Presbyterian church, Lost City.

Friday, 25: Preached in the Presbyterian church, Petersburg.

Sunday, 27: A. M. and P. M. Emmanuel church, Moorefield, also visited the Sunday school.

Tuesday, 29: Administered the communion in Trinity Church, Parkersburg and confirmed 1, also took part in a funeral.

OCTOBER.

Thursday, 1: Visited the Sheltering Arms Hospital, also Beury, expecting to have services but was disappointed.

Friday, 2, Sunday, 4: Held services during these days in Christ Church, Boone County. On Sunday, A. M. administered the communion and in the afternoon had a special service for the children.

Sunday, 11: St. James', Richmond.

Sunday, 18: A. M. and P. M. St. Timothy's Church, Wilson, N. C. In the afternoon at Elm City.

Tuesday, 20, Friday, 23: In attendance on the Pan-American Council of Bishops, Washington, D. C.

Friday, 23: P. M. Preached in Memorial Church, Baltimore, on the occasion of the 25th anniversary of Rev. Dr. Dame, who succeeded me in 1878 as Rector of this church.

Sunday, 25: Preached in Trinity Church, St. Marys City, Md.

Tuesday, 27, Friday, 30: In attendance on the Missionary Council in Washington.

NOVEMBER.

Sunday 1: Trinity Church, Howard, County, Md., preached and administered the Communion.

Sunday, 8: A. M. and P. M. St. Paul's, Ogontz. P. P. M. Ogontz school.

Tuesday, 10: Board of Managers of Missions, New York

Wednesday, 11: At the Seminary, meeting of trustees.

Friday, 13: Preached, in the Baptist Church, White Day.

Sunday, 15: A. M. and P. M. Trinity, Morgantown. At the morning service confirmed 4.

Monday, 16: Preached in M. E. Church, Kingwood.

Tuesday 17: Preached in St. Matthias Church, Grafton.

Sunday, 22: A. M. Baptist Church, Hartford. P. M. Church of Our Savior, Mason. P. P. M. In the Chapel of Spilman, confirmed 2.

Tuesday, 24: In Baptist Church, Winfield, confirmed 2.

Thursday, 26: Thanksgiving Day. Christ Church, Point Pleasant.

Friday, 27: Preached in school house at Morgans.

Sunday, 29: A. M. Preached in Bruce Chapel and confirmed 5, also visited the Sunday school. P. M. Christ Church, Point Pleasant.

DECEMBER.

Saturday, 5: Met the vestry of St. Matthew's Church, Wheeling.

Sunday, 6: A. M. Preached in St. Paul's, Elm Grove and administered the communion. In the afternoon addressed the Sunday school, and in the evening preached in St. Andrew's, Wheeling.

Tuesday, 8: Addressed the Woman's Auxiliary, St. Matthew's, Wheeling.

Wednesday, 9: Preached in St. Matthew's, Wheeling.

Thursday, 10: Visited Reynold's Memorial Hospital, inspected the building and audited the accounts, finding them correct and sustained by proper vouchers.

Friday, 11: St. Andrew's Church, Mannington. After hard experiences, this congregation seems now in possession of a good building.

Sunday 13: A. M. and P. M. Preached in Christ Church, Fairmont, and in the morning confirmed 2.

Sunday, 20: A. M. and P. M. Trinity Church, Parkersburg.

Thursday, 24: Attended the Sunday school celebration of Trinity Church, Parkersburg.

Sunday, 27: A. M. Preached in the Chapel of the Good Shepherd, Parkersburg. P. M. Preached in Christ Church, Williamstown, confirmed 1 and baptized an infant.

JANUARY.

Sunday 3: A. M. Christ Church, Williamstown. P. M. Grace Church, Tavernersville.

Sunday, 10: A. M. and P. M. Preached in Trinity Church, Moundsville; also visited the Sunday school.

Sunday, 17: A. M. Preached in the Church of the Incarnation, and P. M. in the Church of the Holy Apostles, Philadelphia.

Sunday 24: A. M. St. John's, Ripley. P. M. Grace, Ravenswood.

Sunday, 31: A. M. M. E. Church, Cairo. P. M. M. E. Church Pennsboro.

FEBRUARY

Sunday, 7: A. M. Christ Church, Williamstown. P. M. Chapel of the Good Shepherd, Parkersburg, the minister in charge being absent at my request, filling a vacant pulpit.

Sunday, 14: A. M. Chapel of the Good Shepherd, Parkersburg. P. M. St. Luke's, Marietta, O., the minister being absent at my request, filling a vacant pulpit.

Monday, 15: Took part in a missionary service in Trinity Church, Parkersburg, and introduced the General Secretary of our Mission Board, the Rev. Dr. Lloyd.

Sunday, 21: The Rector being absent at my request, filling the vacant pulpit at Ripley, I preached A. M. and P. M. in Trinity Church, Parkersburg.

Sunday, 28: A. M. Preaching at St. Timothy's Church, Wilson, N. C. In the afternoon took part in the service and baptized an infant.

MARCH.

Sunday, 6: Preached at Eagle Point, Gloucester County, Va.

Friday, 11: Preached at the Holy Innocents Chapel, Gloucester County.

Sunday, 13: Preached in Abingdon Church, Gloucester County.

Friday, 18: Preached in St. James' Church, Richmond, Va.

Sunday, 20: A. M. Preached in St. James, Church, Richmond, and P. M. in Emmanuel, Henrico County, Va.

Sunday, 27: A. M. Preached in St. Matthew's Church, Wheeling, and confirmed 30. P. M. In St. Luke's Church, and confirmed 7.

Monday, 28: Made an address in St. Luke's Church, Wheeling.

Tuesday, 29: A. M. In St. Paul's Church, Sistersville, I preached and ordained to the priesthood the Rev. Creetus A. Dowell; the Rev. Dr. Moore presented the candidate and with the Revs. Chas. E. and Geo. C. Shaw united in the imposition of hands. P. M. I preached in St. Pauls Church and confirmed 6.

Thursday, 31: I preached in Trinity Church, Parkersburg.

APRIL.

Friday, 1: Good Friday. Preached in Trinity Church, Parkersburg.

Sunday, 3: Easter Day. A. M. Preached in Grace Church, St. Marys and confirmed 1. P. M. Preached in St. Anne's, New Martinsville and confirmed 5.

Sunday, 10: Preached morning and evening in Trinity Church, Shepherdstown. In the afternoon preached in Chapel of the God Shepard, Duffields, and confirmed 1 in private.

Tuesday, 12: Attended a meeting of the Board of Managers of the Missionary Society in New York.

Wednesday, 13: Attended the session of the N. W. Convention in Trinity Church, Morgantown, also met the vestry of the parish.

Friday, 15: Preached in the Presbyterian Church, Belington. The prospect for our building in the near future is good.

Sunday, 17: A. M. Grace Church, Elkins, confirmed 2. P. M. St. Barnabas, Davis, confirmed 6. These two churches, which were formerly united in administration, have now each a resident minister. At Elkins Rev. F. A. Meade, whom we welcome back, after his temporary sojourn in Virginia, and at Davis, Rev. Mr. Fish, who, before had charge of the whole field.

Monday, 18: Preached in the Presbyterian Church at Parsons. In this growing town we hope soon to start a building.

Sunday, 24: Preached A. M. and P. M. in St. Matthew's Church, Wheeling, the Rector being absent on a missionary tour through the Eastern Convocation.

Thursday, 28: In the Cathedral, Louisville, Ky. I took part in the memorial service for the late Bishop Dudley and preached the sermon.

MAY.

Sunday, 1: A. M. Church of the Holy Spirit, Summit Point, confirmed 1. P. M. St. Bartholomew's, Leetown, confirmed 1. P. P. M. Grace Church, Middleway.

Tuesday, 3: Grace Church, Ravenswood, confirmed 2.

Wednesday, 4: Examination of candidates in Parkersburg.

Sunday, 8: Zion Church, Charles Town, confirmed 9. P. M. St. Andrew's on the Mountains, confirmed 1. P. P. M. St. Philip's, Charles Town, confirmed 1.

Thursday, 12: Ascension Day. A. M. Christ Church, Clarksburg, confirmed 6. I was glad to welcome the new Rector, the Rev. Mr. Plummer, to the Diocese and to find that he was much encouraged at the outlook. P. M. St. Paul's, Weston.

Friday, 13: St. Paul's Chapel, Middle Run, confirmed 4.

Sunday, 15: A. M. Spruce Chapel, Spruce Run. P. M. Church of the Transfiguration, Buckhannon. After services had a meeting of the congregation. Mr. Snead, who has rendered most acceptable service at these points, has accepted a call to Southern, Ohio.

Monday, 16: St. John's, Sutton.

Tuesday, 17: Preached in the Baptist Church, Little Otter, to a large congregation.

Wednesday, 18: Preached in a school house at Centralia.

Thursday, 19: Preached in the Presbyterian Church, Richwood. We hope to be able to supply all these points during the coming year.

Sunday, 22: Preached morning and evening in All Saints, Union, and at the evening service confirmed 1.

Tuesday, 24: Attended the annual meeting of the Corporators and Directors of the Sheltering Arms Hospital.

Sunday, 29: A. M. Grace, Tavernersville and administered the communion. P. M. Chapel of the Good Shepherd, Parkersburg.

CHANGES IN THE DIOCESE.

Letters Dimissory.

Letters dimissory have been given in behalf of *Rev. W. H. Neilson, D. D.*, to the Diocese of New Jersey; the *Rev. Norman F. Marshall* to the missionary district of New Mexico; the *Rev. Thos. W. Cooke* to the Diocese of Lexington; the *Rev. Gerald Card* to the Diocese of Calgary, Canada; the *Rev. Thos. C. Darst* to the Diocese of Virginia; and to the *Rev. Jas. D. Miller* to the Diocese of Maryland.

Letters dimissory have been received in behalf of the *Rev. Edwin B. Snead* from the Diocese of Virginia; the *Rev. Maximo F. Duty* from the Diocese of Virginia; the *Rev. Austin B. Mitchell* from the Diocese of Maryland; the *Rev. F. A. Meade* from the Diocese of Virginia; the *Rev. Robt. R. Windley* from the Diocese of Pennsylvania; and the *Rev. Jas. F. Plummer* from the Diocese of Washington.

The clergy list has also been increased by the ordination to the Deaconate of *Mr. Francis VanRansellear Moore.*

The *Rev. Jno. F. Woods* has resigned the charge of St. John's Willow Island, and of Grace Church, Cresaps, and removed his residence to Philadelphia; the *Rev. Jas. L. Fish* has given up the charge of Grace Church, Elkins, and of Belington, and having removed his residence to Davis, has now charge of St. Barnaba's, Davis, and of the missions at Parsons and Bayard; the *Rev. Jacob A. Hiatt* has resigned the charge of Ravenswood Parish, with the missions attached, and has assumed charge of Ascension, Hinton, St. Peters, Glen Jean, and of the mission at Beckley; the *Rev. Paca Kennedy* has been continuing his course in Oxford, England, and on its completion this summer will return to the Diocese; the *Rev. Paris B. Stauffer* has given up the charge of Ascension, Hinton, and become Rector of Mt. Zion, Hedgesville, and in charge of St. John's, Harper's Ferry; the *Rev. Geo. C. Shaw* has given up the charge of St. Mary's, Waverly, at St. John's, Willow Island, and assumed charge of St. Andrew's, Mannington; the *Rev. Edwin B. Snead* has given up the charge of Sutton, confining his ministrations to Buckhannon and Spence; the *Rev. Maximo F. Duty* has become assistant to *Rev. Jno. S. Alfriend* in the work at St. Philip's, Charles Town; the *Rev. Francis VanR. Moore* has taken charge of St. Paul's, Elm Grove, and also of the missions at Chester and New Cumberland; the *Rev. Austin B. Mitchell* has taken charge of Christ Memorial

Church, Williamston, and of the Chapel of the Good Shepherd, Parkersburg, and Grace, Tavenersville; the *Rev. F. A. Meade* has taken charge of Grace Church, Elkins, and of the mission at Belington; the *Rev. Robt. R. Windley* has taken charge of St. Matthias, Grafton, and up to April also had charge of the missions at Cairo and Pennsboro; the *Rev. James F. Plummer* has become Rector of Christ Church, Clarksburg (including St. Thomas Chapel, North View).

Postulants.

C. Hely Molony. James Davis Gibson.

Candidates for Deacons and Priest's Orders.

W. Howard Meyers. Percy N. McDonald.
T. Getz Hill. Edmund P. Dandridge, 2nd.
Richard W. Trapnell.

For Priest's Orders.

Paca Kennedy. Francis VanR. Moore.

I have ordained during the year, *i. e.* since May 1, 1903:

Francis VanR. Moore to the order of Deacon and *Rev. Jacob A. Hiatt* and *Rev. Creetus A. Dowell* to the order of Priests.

I have also during the same time consecrated St. Matthew's Church, near Charleston, and St. Ann's, New Martinsville.

I have also, during the same, attended five meetings of the Board of Managers of the General Missionary Society in New York, the meetings of the Missionary Council and of the Pan American Conference in Washington; two meetings of the Trustees of the Seminary near Alexandria; one meeting of the Trustees of Kenyon College, at Gambier, Ohio, and have paid four official visits to the Hospitals at Paint Creek and Moundsville, attending the annual meetings of the Board of Directors.

SUMMARY.

I have confirmed 132 persons on 36 different occasions, and delivered 203 sermons and addresses. I have ordained one candidate Deacon and two Deacons Priests, and consecrated two Churches, and attended sixty-six meetings other than public services as reported, paying in all 139 visits to 101 places.

I report to the Council the following regularly organized Missions:

Mission.	P. O.	Church.
Taylor Co.	Grafton	St. Matthias
Hampshire	Romney	St. Stephens
Hampshire	Okonoko	Epiphany
Upshur	Buckhannon	Transfiguration

Elk River	Sutton	St. Johns
Morgan Co	Berkeley Springs	St. Marks
Harpers Ferry	Harpers Ferry	St. Johns
New River	Hinton	Ascension
Cresaps	Cresaps	Grace
Coal Valley	Montgomery	Calvary
Advent	Ansted	Redeemer
Princeton	Princeton	Heavenly Rest
Wayne Co	Kenova	Grace
Bluefield	Bluefield	Christ
Bramwell	Bramwell	Holy Trinity
Ripon	Ripon	St. Johns
Powelton	Powelton	St. Davids
Elm Grove	Elm Grove	St. Pauls
Wheeling	Wheeling	St. Andrews
St. Lukes	Charleston	St. Lukes
St. Matthews	Charleston	St. Matthews
Madison	Clover Lick	Grace
Norbourne	Bunker Hill	Christ
Spruce Run	Lorentz	Spruce
St. Thomas	White Sulphur	St. Thomas
Davis	Tucker	Christ
Christ Memorial	Williamston	Christ
Grace	Eckman	Grace
Elkins	Elkins	St. Barnabas
St. Marys	St. Marys	Grace
St. Andrews	Mannington	

REPORTS.

We have, now for a long time, been making efforts to secure more satisfactory reports from the various charges in the Diocese, year by year. In this we have met with some measure of success, and I believe that we now need only some slight changes in our present form to give us one that will be full and at the same time simple.

This is perhaps a more important matter than at first sight it appears to be. I know that with some persons there is a prejudice against reports as dealing too much with mere form, and with others there is a singular inaptitude for any work of this kind. Still, making all due allowance, I believe that a careless report shows a careless administration. If it were not for the consciousness that this is so, some of our reports would be positively ludicrous, as for instance where one man reports total receipts for all purposes of $430; total expenditures, $535, and yet a balance on hand of $35. He ought to give us the secret of his management; or as another reports upwards of $5,000 for current expenses, and about the same for contributions, or $10,000 in all, while the receipts from all sources, including borrowed money, amount to only one-half that sum. I think we ought to add to our Seminary curriculum a course on report making. In the meantime I hope that none of our clergy will fail to give this matter the serious attention it deserves.

I am led to make these remarks by going over the Parochial Reports that have come into my hands. I could wish that all could have that privilege. It would be quite a revelation. My attention has this year been called specially to the returns. Reports given in regard to missions, Diocesan and general, and whatever may be said of the weakness of the places represented and the strong local pressure upon them, I think many of the reports indicate but a feeble administration. I find, for instance, in 26 reports which I put aside as coming perhaps from the weakest points, that while they give as many as 635 communicants, their total contributions to missions, Diocesan and general amounted to only $225.72, and I cannot believe that this represents the real interest or ability of the people. The real explanation, I am disposed to think, is that the subject has not been frankly and wisely brought before them, and I say this al the more freely because it can be proven that if these 635 communicants had been in some way led up to give in proportion to the communicants in what is demonstrably the smallest and weakest Church in the Diocese, they would have given $1,524 instead of $225. This whole duty of Church extension is one that ought to be present continually on our hearts and consciences, so that our people would learn to regard it as fundamental and necessary. We should start out in the new year with this distinctly before us, and strive ever to impress upon all Church people, however few, or scattered that their alms as well as their prayers should go up as a memorial before God.

One word more, before I leave the subject of reports. What difficulty exists on this score is because many of the clergy will not follow the form which the Diocese has prescribed. The departure from this form is chiefly in two particulars: First, in the matter of current expenses and contributions. The form of Parochial Report which has been adopted arranges to keep these objects entirely separate, as it seems to me they ought to be in order, to give any clear idea of the administration in our several congregations. Again, the departure from the form is seen in the fact that money which is borrowed, and money secured from the outside is so often reported as if it were contributed by the congregation. Of course to do this is to give an erroneous idea as to the strength of the Parish, and indeed to make a report which is not in accordance with the facts of the case. This method of making out reports, which is not only inaccurate, but in face of the direction given on page 9 of the blank is carried to such an extent that in the report now in my hands, the contributions have been swelled to the extent of $13,498.12 beyond what they really have been, and as the result, but for the corrections I have made we would have been liable to an addition to our apportionment for General Missions to the extent of $387.93. I suppose every one is glad to see the figures in our reports swelled to the highest possible point, but that is not sufficient reason why we should report as contributions of our congregations, what we have borrowed and what has been given us from the outside. With the permission of the Council such modification will be made in certain of the headings in our present blank as to avoid the difficulties mentioned, for the future. There would have been ground for the fear that the blank itself was confusing save for the fact that out of 68 reports received only 26 departed from the prescribed form, leaving 42 correctly made out.

HOSPITALS.

Our hospitals have been doing a good work during the past year.

The Sheltering Arms Hospital at Paint Creek has cared for 389 patients, the number of nursing days being 8,444, which is 117 more than ever before. For this work there has been received from the miners and coal companies the sum of $7,520.43; from invested funds and special contributions, $1,722.39, and from the churches, i. e., chiefly, the annual offering on Thanksgiving Day, $738.36, making in all $9,981.18. The expenditures have been for salaries of doctor, nurses, matron, and the maintenance of the Training School, $3,034.49; for general expenses, $5,907.89; on account of new building, $727.25, a total of $9,669.63.

Steps have been taken to push forward the new building to completion at an early day, the hope being entertained that the 51 coal companies who in one way or another contribute to the annual expense fund, will help us towards this consummation.

The Reynolds Memorial Hospital reports through the Superintendent, the Rev. Mr. Spurr, that they have in the last year cared for 565 patients, of which number 270 were charity cases. The cost of maintaining the hospital for the year was $10,231.17 and $2,000 additional was spent on improvements.

Three nurses were graduated from the training school, to whom I delivered diplomas in December last, and there are now ten undergraduates.

THE SPECIAL FUND.

During the Councilar year the receipts for the Special Fund have been as follows:

From	Charles Town	$ 140 79
	Charleston	35 00
	Fairmont	5 00
	Grafton	5 66
	Huntington	50 00

Kenova	10 00
Parkersburg, Trinity	494 00
Parkersburg, Good Shepherd	373 30
Martinsburg	8 33
Powellton	50 00
Shepherdstown	60 00
Tavernersville	5 00
Union	1 00
Wheeling, St. Matthews	64 50
Wheeling, St. Lukes	100 00
Wilow Island	25 00
Weston	14 00
White Sulphur	100 00
Outside Sources	231 00
	$1,772 58

In the meantime the disburseemnts of this fund has been for various objects as follows:

For Sheltering Arms Hospital, 5 grants	$ 263 50
Printing, books, papers, &c	455 30
Specials to the clergy, 16 grants	647 52
American Church Missionary Society	12 50
Church buildings, 5 grants	218 76
Theological students, 2 grants	75 00
Rectories, 3 grants	100 00
	$1,772 58

The opportunities for this Fund are, as they have been, practically unlimited. I still cherish the hope that it may receive a more general support.

NECROLOGY.

I do not generally occupy the time of the Council with any extended notice of those, our friends and brethren, whom God, in his wise providence, has taken to Himself since our last meeting, but to-day I want to say a few words about two who were with us in Wheeling last May, and are now, we believe, in the Paradise of God.

The late Bishop of Kentucky was my life-long friend and has been with us more than once, on occasions of public interest and importance. He was well known, and most highly esteemed throughout the Diocese, and I am sure that many have felt a sense of personal loss in his death. His gifts were of a very high order and freely used in the public service of the

Church. In the general life of the Church there was no more prominent figure. His influence was felt everywhere. In the State which was proud of him, and in the Diocese to which he gave a prestage unknown before, in the House of Bishops, of which he was the honored chairman, in the commission for work among the colored people, of which he was the active and efficient chief, in the Board of Managers of our Missions, where he was a valuable counsellor, in the Church in Canada and the Church in England, where he was widely known and honored, and where by visits from time to time, he greatly helped to cultivate the happily prevailing fraternal feeling towards the Church in the United States. Truly one of our great leaders has passed away from us and in common with the great body of the Church, we lament his loss, and we honor his memory.

Just about the same time with the death of Bishop Dudley occurred that of Judge Rogers, of Wheeling. He was a devoted member of St. Luke's church, and Chancellor of the Diocese. Judge Rogers' interest in the Church was unfailing, and it was manifest all throughout his career by the personal service which he gave, and the substantial help he was always ready to render. In his long and active service he was more particularly identified with St. Luke's church, Wheeling. This congregation for years had the benefit of his nursing care, and in more ways than one must keenly feel his loss. Judge Rogers belonged to what we may properly call our old fashioned Virginia churchmen. Plain in his tastes, simple in his religious faith, but having devotion to the Master and His Church wrought into the very fibre of his being. He was from the first deeply interested in the Diocese, and gave it his wise counsel and his cordial support, and it was his happiness to see the blessing of God upon the labors which with like-minded men he put forth then to maintain and advance the Kingdom of God.

THE BROTHERHOOD OF ST. ANDREW.

The annual report of the Brotherhood of St. Andrew in the United States, for 1902-1903, has so brought before me the whole work for which the Brotherhood stands, that I feel I must say a few words about it.

The silence about the Brotherhood in West Virginia, is I fear, ominous. For all I see and hear to the contrary, many of its chapters must be inactive, and that notwithstanding what is called the forward movement in its present history.

I have been disposed in time past, rather to hold aloof from the active operation of the Brotherhood, not from indifference, but because it has seemed to me that it was needful to put, as far as possible, responsibility for its management upon the laymen who composed it. If it be true in any sphere of life that education consists largely in putting responsibility upon the individual, and helping him to shoulder it, and work it out, may it not be specially true in regard to the Brotherhood. It may be, in some instances that the clergy, too impatient of results, have attempted too much to direct and control the Brotherhood. My idea is to get it fairly started and then let the members work out their own salvation.

It maybe, too, that the departing—though with the best intentions—yet the departing from the simple rules of "definite prayer and personal service" have operated to check the development of the work. The Brotherhood, as I understand it, was never meant to take up all the work which laymen should do in the Church, although all departments of that work should feel the inspiration that comes from the quickened spiritual life of its members.

My advice to our chapters would be not to attempt too much, but to work strictly along the line of the Brotherhood's Rules of Prayer and Service. In my judgment, their work is rather to vitalize in the way the general work of the Church, than to attempt to do it themselves.

If they thus keep to the simplicity of their organization, they will be the better able to add to their numbers and so widen their influence. This is a vastly important point, because it is estimated that the average chapter loses ten per cent of its membership every year, and this loss must be made good if the chapter is to maintain its efficiency.

Certainly this is a matter of sufficient importance to engage the most serious attention of our clergy and laity. I say of the clergy as well as the laity, for the clergy can do a vast deal to foster and encourage such organization without attempting so to run them as to supersede the activities of the members. The great point that all can help thus to emphasize and illustrate, is that, after all, the only true Christian life is one spent in definite service in behalf of others.

TWENTY-FIFTH ANNIVERSARY.

The meeting of the 26th Annual Council of the Diocese in Wheeling, on the 20th of May last year, was to me an occasion of unmixed pleasure and gratification. To have attained to a 25th anniversary was in itself no small achievement, but to have had all these years marked by the goodness and loving kindness of the Lord as shown in the prosperity of the Diocese, and in the unbroken harmony prevailing throughout our wide bounds, was something well nigh beyond experience and expectation. But to-day, by the lapse of a whole year after those festal days, we are reminded that anniversary days are but incidents; we must come down from these mounts of observation, and take up our work and go forward as God's providence points out the way. Very much land remains yet to be possessed, and we have need to be diligent in doing what our hands find to do, the workmen change, but the work must go on, and so we, who are here to-day, having our faces steadily set to the future, rejoice in the opportunity given us to be coworkers with the

Master in hastening His kingdom. None of the clergy, save the Bishop, are forbidden to seek other fields of labor where they may be able, perhaps, to exercise their ministry for the greater glory of God, but loyalty to the great Church of which the Parish and Diocese are after all, only a small part, should prompt and oblige us to undertake with zeal and carry on with diligence that work whether it be large of small, to which in the providence of God, we have been for the time assigned. Hardly anything is more demoralizing to the man or more hurtful to the Church than to have the minister continually looking out of and beyond his charge, not only losing interest in his work in desire for some other, but so showing that loss of interest as to discourage and demoralize his people. And this will prove, after all, but a poor way to advance any interests even from a worldly standpoint. I cannot tell you how, but I am convinced that the shortest as well as the most honorable road to preferment—if we may call it by this name—is diligent, unselfish, loyal service in the charge we already have. That charge, however small and humble it may be, is, after all, the great honor of our lives, and we are to purchase to ourselves a good degree by thorough going earnestness for the Kingdom whatever our position may be. The Diocese of West Virginia is one of the smallest of the tribes of Israel, but when we do our diligence to serve here, we are approving ourselves faithful servants, who shall in no wise lose their reward.

BUSINESS METHODS.

I have taken occasion so often during the last few years to insist upon the importance of carrying business methods into the management of our congregations, that I fear the exhortation is somewhat in danger of losing its effect. It is however sufficiently important in itself, and also as rendering the churches more ready for and efficient in distinctly aggressive work, as to deserve to be insisted upon again. In visiting a congregation a few months ago I found that the rector and vestry had agreed to make an assessment for all current expenses, in place of pew rents, subscriptions, and collections on occasions of public worship, and the principle upon which they acted seems to me indisputable, although, of course, I understand that even in putting principles into exercise, we can by no means always speedily accomplish our purpose.

The rector and vestry of whom I speak, argued out the case somewhat in this wise: that a certain number of people being associated together to meet certain expenses, they had mutually agreed to incur, that the fair and honorable thing was for each one of that number to do his or her part—i. e., for all to bear their share of the common expense. It would hardly seem as if anyone could do or would be willing to be considered as doing less than so much as this. If a dozen of us associated ourselves together in any enterprise, secular or religious, in any enterprise that involves expense, undertaken by common agreement, and for our mutual satisfaction and advantage, it is hard to state on what principle any one of us should be willing to do less than our part toward the common result, as the failure of anyone must, of necessity put an additional and unfair burden on someone else. The case is so simple that its mere statement ought to be sufficient. If you call upon a congregation to contribute for missions in Africa or China, or for some work nearer home, it is after all but one of many objects, and for many reasons it does not follow that all are equally interested or obliged, but when you call upon the different members of the congregation who are associated together for a definite purpose, for the means to carry out the definite purpose of their association, whether it be to pay the rector or the sexton, or to light and heat the church, then, since these and such like things are matters of common concern, it is to say the least very unseemly for one and another to put off upon some other member of the association, any part of his or her share of the burden of making such provision, as was ordered by, and is needed for all. If you have two or three or four parties of equal means, all privy to such understanding, then the administration is very simple, the whole expense being naturally divided into two, or three, or four parts as the case may be. Of course, when the number of such associating parties is increased and their financial condition greatly varies, the difficulty of administration is increased, but the principle remains unchanged, and seems to me to be of equal obligation. I think there can hardly be any more inequitable way of meeting these common current expenses than by collections taken up in the church, because there the faithful few are again and again dunned to meet obligations incurred by all and for all—obligations which a very large proportion of the congregation practically escape, by absenting themselves, with more or less reason, from the service. And oftentimes scarcely less inequitable is the ordinary subscription when there is so little regard paid to the comparative ability of subscribers to meet the common debt. Of course there are many notable exceptions—perhaps more than enough to prove the rule—but that does not altogether relieve the general situation. In making such assessment or apportionment, call it what you will, the greatest care must, of course be taken, lest it should in some cases be considered unfair. It is believed however that if it be made by a vestry that fairly represents the people, that it will in the vast majority of cases be accepted by the people, and produce most excellent results in the working of the congregation. You will hardly find anyone who is not willing to avow that he is ready and willing to do his part, no one would like to be thought unwilling to do so much as that; if then that part be fairly assigned I believe we shall see a more hearty and efficient co-operation than is usual. Certainly the plan seems worthy of trial.

APPORTIONMENTS AND ASSESSMENTS.

The principle underlying apportionments and assessments is the same, though there seems to be a kind of tacit understanding that the failure to meet apportionments shall not be carried on in our accounts as arrears, and I very much fear that this operates at times to lessen the sense of obligation. We have had a large increase made this year in our apportionment for the General Missions of the Church, and I think it will require all our diligence to meet it. This has seemed to some to be an undue or unfair burden put upon us especially because the large increase in our contributions was due greatly to the effort we had made to increase the Permanent Fund. Still we raised the money for that fund and it stands there on the record as helping to show our ability. During the last four or five years we have increased our Permenent Fund upwards of $30,000. In addition to the help that is to us in our Diocesan administration, it shows a vitality and power we ought to be glad to utilize for the general advancement of the Kingdom. Our general contributions are in some cases twice as great as those of Dioceses of about the same size. No doubt they would be glad to take our apportionment if they could raise our contributions.

I am afraid, however, that after all the efforts made in one way or another, both by Diocesan and general agencies, that many of our clergy do by no means yet appreciate the obligations of which we are speaking. and one chief reason I have for making such statement at this time, is that I find both in the matter of general apportionment and of Diocesan assessment, that months—sometimes half the year—are suffered to pass without doing anything to meet these accumulating responsibilities. I cannot but characterize this as very poor administration. It does the congregations injustice by accumulating obligations that ought to be spread out over the year, all in a few months, and it cripples the administration of the Church when the funds that have to be regularly paid out come so irregularly in, that debts are incurred and interest has to be paid. Why should not every man, in the very beginning of the year, deliberately face all its obligations, and from the very first, begin to make provision to meet them regularly and promptly. It would be hard for anyone to tell what is gained by a delay that is demoralizing to the congregation and embarrassing to all beneficiaries.

SMALL CHURCHES.

We have been more than usually troubled during the past year in securing supply for our smaller congregations. At times the difficulties in the way seem almost insuperable, and they are not peculiar to West Virginia, or to the Episcopal Church. I find them everywhere, and they are discussed now under one aspect and now under another. The question is often proposed under the title of "The Difficulties of Our Country Churches," and that fits our case fairly well, for although we may not have many churches that we would speak of as absolutely in the country, yet often times the villages are very small, and even those that claim the more pretentious title of town, would hardly be counted as such in more populous states. Under the designation, then of country churches we may fairly place about one-half of the congregations that have regular services, perhaps 40 in number, to say nothing of double that number of places which we are trying to reach with the ministrations of our church.

These difficulties that are inherent in the situation, are being met in two ways, which seem to give reasonable promise of success.

First. We are trying more frequently so to combine various points—if you choose, many points—under the leadership of one man, that we can secure such support as will enable us to secure a man of more experience and capacity than such small places can generally obtain, being fully convinced that the services of such a man, for a part of the time, are often worth more to a church than the services of a man of less experience and ability for the whole of the time. Unfortunately many of our small congregations fail to recognize this fact, and so commit themselves to the plan of having a resident minister, that failing in this, they give but scanty support to any other plan, although it may be the only one practicable. And yet, experience shows that such congregations very much overestimate the advantages of a resident minister, and when they do from time to time secure one, they fail to make the progress predicted. The simple truth is that be our advantages what you please, yet the great mass of the people of the various communities where our services are established, are well satisfied with their church affiliations, and have no idea of leaving them to join us. Time and again our sanguine members have been encouraged by friendly expressions from outsiders, to indulge hopes which have been doomed to meet with disappointment. After the experience of these years I am the more convinced that if we can get Godly and experienced men, with the physical endurance for such work, and a sufficient sense of the proportion of things to keep them from slighting the smaller places and putting them off with the minimum of attention, that we shall find this the most effective plan for our work. There are perhaps some places that require services to be held continuously and uninterruptedly, but I believe that oftentimes the results do not justify the contention. At all events, we will have to make up our minds that unless we more freely adopt some such plan, we shall have to abandon large sections of territory in this state, and that in view of the fact that our early successes and advances were all made under this system.

Second. The second way in which these difficulties are being met is by the freer use of our women in the work of the Church. There can be no doubt but that in all lines of missionary effort, woman's work is becoming increasingly prominent and rightly so. In speaking of this some one has recently said that the modern Priscilla is not only competent to teach Appolos the things that may be lacking in his message, but also to carry the Gospel message herself to communities that are not able to avail themselves of the services of Apollos.

Boards of Missions in some states are availing themselves to good advantage of the services of Christian women in sparcely settled regions, where the churches are utterly unable to support pastors. These workers go from house to house with the Gospel message; they gather the children in Sunday schools; and hold meetings on week day evenings as well as on the Lord's day. Their house to house visitations supply a need which in such sections, the clergy seem unable to meet. May not more of our sparcely settled country, and our mining districts, yes, and our feeble missions find great help in the problems that confront them in connection with the sripitual life of the people, in the consecrated labors of Christian women, who desire to devote their time to the Master's work. We have made but a beginning in such work, yet one full of promise. On the mountain near Charles Town, in Parkersburg, at the Sheltering Arms Hospital, and at Ansted, Christian women are now doing such work with marked ability and success. These women are now reaching in Parochial schools, and boys' clubs, and sewing schools, and girls' societies of various kinds, more than 300 children, who would otherwise be practically untouched by any such uplifting and churchly influence, and in addition to that they are, by house to house visitations, and by personal ministration to the sick and to the well, reaching hundreds of individuals, who have been as sheep without a shepherd.

In these two ways we are making some little progress in what our hands find to do. We thank God and take courage.

And here I cannot but touch upon a question that I know is sometimes troublesome, especially where we have but small bands of friends and communicants in the midst of large communities who have other church associations. Some persons have a short and easy method of solving the problems of which we have been speaking, by saying that it is best for the little minority of church people in many communities, to abandon their distinctive features, and throw in their lot with some other communion which, in the providence of God, seems fully established. Of course, if a man cannot give a reason of the faith that is in him, if he be not fully persuaded in his own mind, if he be indifferent as to the various questions of doctrine, discipline and worship that distinguish the churches one from the other, if, in short, for him one church is just as good, as efficient, as scriptural as another, why, then, perhaps we had better let the matter rest as far as such an one is concerned. But I do not believe this feeling is common, and it is well it is not, for it seems to me that this spirit of indifferentism will cause a man to fail to measure up to the highest standard of excellence in character and usefulness of life. If any ecclesiastical organization in the world can claim to be on record as against division in the body of Christ, it is the Episcopal Church. She has never separated from any other organization, nor has she condemned or pronounced judgment on those who have separated from her. She stands where she has always stood, both ecclesiastically and organically, on the faith and order of the Primitive Church. There are some of her people, I grant you, who have themselves taken this matter in hand, and by their judgment and criticism have often made it appear that we stand in an arrogant attitude toward non-Episcopal churches. In the freedom they enjoy in this comprehensive church, you have an illustration of how an organization may show the defect of its merits, but meantime the Church steadily declines to criticize or pronounce judgment upon those from whom we have been unhappily separated.

The particular point, however, which I want now to insist upon is that no irenic spirit, and no recognition of the grace of God which is manifest in the abundant labors of the Christian ministers about us, can justify us in turning a deaf ear to our scattered people who are looking to us to help them to the privileges which we ourselves already enjoy. It is just along this line that plans for consolidation and co-operation often break down. We, who are in the larger centers, may, perhaps, seek to free ourselves from much responsibility and from many burdens, by advising some small band of church people appealing for help, to unite with some other body of Christians, but how would we like such advice to be given to ourselves under similar circumstances. I cannot imagine it acceptable, except in the case of those who, however, pious, have more or less that spirit of indifferentism to which I alluded.

Without entering into the discussion of church principles, or seeking to bring out distinctly what may be called the church idea, I am disposed to adopt the sentiments of a prominent divine of another church, who, contending against the idea of church indifferentism, says that the observation of twenty-five years of active pastoral work has convinced him that the usefulness of any church member is in direct proportion to the strength of his attachment to his own church, and this depends upon the intensity of his convictions as to the tenets and the distinctive features of that church. Those who have no sincere convictions, and are generally indifferent, thinking one church just as good, as efficient, as scriptural as another cannot be depended on in any good work. They will send their children to the Sunday school of other churches, and will themselves attend other churches as convenience or caprice may dictate. Some of the older ones among us may remember how, during the war between the States, we always looked askance upon a man, who, while he professed to be a soldier, yet disclaimed connection with any particular regiment or battalion. I suppose there might have been exceptions, but such a position did not commend itself to our judgment. Of course, we don't want bigots and partisans, but we do want men who have some, not only preferences, but convictions, touching the work and worth of their own churches. Loyalty to our own church, need not be synonymous with narrowness, and conscientiousness may consist with the warmest charity, but for all that the true churchman will work for Christ and the Church, all the more efficiently if he is thoroughly persuaded that his church is apostolic in its order, scriptural in its doctrine, and that its forms, hallowed by the use of so many generations, are the best for decency, comfort and edification. Every such man, however kindly his feelings toward all about him, will nevertheless feel that he has been appointed of Almighty God to stand for most important facts, and it requires such men to build up a church as it should be built, and to hasten the coming of the Redeemer's kingdom.

So we find our work goes on year after year without any great difference in method or result. While we must be hopeful, we must also avoid unreasonable expectations. After all that I have said about the importance of loyalty to our own branch of the Catholic Church, and deeply as I feel that our efficiency in advancing the Kingdom is chiefly determined by our efficiency in that organization with which in the providence of God we are identified, yet when you come to the last analysis, the great stimulating thought is that we are working for Christ and the Church, rather than simpy for our branch of the Church. We must be contented to take our place and do our part in the great work of bringing our State and country and the whole world into obedience to Christ. In certain places and at certain times that part may be very much less prominent and effective than we could desire, and as a consequence discouragement may ensue. We must, however, learn to rejoice in the progress of the Kingdom even if it be not exactly along those lines which we specialy favor. We are not the only laborers in the Lord's vineyard, the whole burden of work and responsibility for advancement does not fall upon our shoulders. Loyalty to Christ and an earnest desire to serve Him should be the great inspiration. Then we shall work along day by day, and year by year, and though we yet see not anywhere all things put upder Christ's feet, yet in all our work—whether the world calls it successful or not—we are sustained by the confident belief that Christ shall reign and that His Kingdom shall so come that every knee shall bow to him, and every tongue confess that He is Lord of all. To this work we consecrate ourselves afresh, and may the good Lord accept the imperfect offering, and make us glad and faithful in His service, even while life shall last.

The Committee on Credentials made this report:

The Committee on Credentials respectively report that the following persons are duly certified delegates and alternates to this Council.

THOS. J. OLIVER CURRAN,
E. H. BROSIUS,
C. L. THOMPSON,
GEO. T. KREGLOW.

PARISHES.

Parish.	P. O.	Church.	Delegates.
1. All Saints.... 1871.	Union	All Saints	1. John M. Rowan. 2. J. D. Logan. 3. A. S. Johnston. 1. E. S. McNeer. 2. C. A. Shanklin. 3. G. A. McCleam.
2. Bangor..	St. Albans........	St. Mark's........	....
3. Bethel	Clarksburg.......	Christ...............	1. Wm. F. Nuzum. 2. W. P. Goff.
4. Christ	Fairmont..........	Christ...............	*W. E. Watson. 1. J. E. Sands.
5. Christ	Wellsburg.........	Christ...............	....
6. Emmanuel....	Moorefield.........	Emmanuel.......	*1. Wm. H. Shearer. 2. R. D. Pollock. 3. Thomas Lakin. *1. W. W. Shearer. *2. Lester Rinker. 3 H.M.T.Gamble,M.D.
7. Greenbrier..	Lewisburg........	St. James.........	....
8. Kanawha.... 1788.	Charleston..........	St. John's.........	1. Wm. Sidney Laidley. *2. Ben R. Roller. *3. Wm. G. Hubbard. 1. J. Lynn Richardson. 2. Angus M. McDonald. 3. Alfred Phillips.
9. Norbourne... 1769.	Martinsburg	Trinity.............	*1. C. A. Miller. *2. Jacob Gassman. *3. H. L. Alexander. 1. A. M. Gilbert. 2. W. B. Colston. 3. John E. Boyd.
10. Norbourne... 1769.	Hedgesville.	Mt. Zion...........	*1. Geo. B. Kreglow. *2. P. C. Myers. 1. W. B. Lingamfetter. 2. J. H. Miller.
11. Nelson......... 1888.	Middleway........	....	1. Chas. Lucas. 2. W C. Fraser.
		Lee Town...	*3. James Grantham. 1. J. H. Strider.
		Summit	2. Geo. H. Shirley. 3. Wm. Gilbert.
12 Pt. Pleasant.	Pt. Pleasant......	Christ	1. P. C. Eastham. 2. H. E. Spilman. 3. C. K. Blackford. 1. L. S. Pomeroy. 2. M. L. Tyler. 3. C. A. Waggoner.
13. Ravenswood	Ravenswood......	Grace..............	....
14. St. Andrews.	Charles Town....	Zion..................	*1. Jos. Trapnell. *2. Richard Henderson. 3. B. C. Washington.

15.	St. Andrews.	Shepherdstown.	Trinity............	1. A. S. Dandridge.
				*2. John O. Aglionby.
				3. Dr. D. W. Border.
				1. P. P. Marshall.
				2. Dr. Hop. Gibson.
				3. F. W. Muzzey.
16.	St. John's....	Willow Island..	St. John's.........	....
17.	St. Luke's....	Wheeling..........	St. Luke's..	L. E. Sands.
				*Wylie Irwin.
				*Geo. J. Rogers.
				E. B. Bowie.
				C. H. Copp.
				W. A. Wilson.
18.	St. Matthew's	Wheeling.........	St. Matthew's....	*1. Hullihen Quarrier.
				*2. Dr. G. A. Aschman.
				*3. Prebles Tatum.
				1. J. D. DuBois.
				2. Cyrus P. Flick.
				3. Julien Hearne.
19.	St. Paul's....	Weston..............	St. Paul's.........	1. E. M. Vandervort.
				2. R. H. Harrison.
				3. E. G. Davisson.
				1. H. C. Bailey.
				2. J. S Mitchell.
				3. A. N. Kunst.
20.	Trinity........ 1846.	Parkersburg......	Trinity............	1. W. N. Chancellor.
				*2. B. D. Spillman.
				3. Simms Powell.
				1. F. Fowler.
				2. W. G. Peterkin.
				3. H. H. Moss, Jr.
21.	Trinity........	Moundsville	Trinity............	1. V. A. Weaver.
				2. Friend Cox.
				*3. H. B. Tyler.
				1. C. L. Walton.
				2. A. J. Martin.
				3. M. P. Hendrickson.
22.	Glen Allen ..	Morgantown	Trinity.............	1. L. D. Beall.
				2. Harry Zeverly.
				*3. F. W. Truscott.
23.	Trinity........	Huntington	Trinity..............	*1. C. L. Thompson.
				2. C. D. Emmons.
				3. Thos. W. Moore.
				1. Edmund Sehon.
				2. John Walton Ensign.
				3. Gustavus A Northcott
24.	Wetzel......... 1851.	New Martinsv'le	St. Anne's	1. Bruce Hall.
				2. S. R. Martin.
				3. A. L. Johnson.
				1. John F. Martin.
				2. Wm. McG. Hall.
				3. Leslie Williams.
25.	St John's.....	Cross Creek......	St. John's.........	....
26.	Tyler..........	Sistersville.......	St. Paul's.........	1. Geo. W. Stocking......
				2. George F. Durham.
				3. A. B. Hunt.
27.	Bluefield...... 1903.	Bluefield..........	Christ	....

MISSIONS.

Mission.	P. O.	Church.	Delegates.
Taylor Co	Grafton	St. Matthew's	Dr. A. H. Thayer. G. W. Lockyer, Sr. Charles W. State. Louis B. Brydon.
Hampshire	Romney	St. Stephen's	*S. W. Parsons. Wm. N. Baird.
Hampshire	Okonoko.	Epiphany	*Ned Russell. Henry M. Russell.
Upshur	Buckhannon	Transfiguration	
Elk River	Sutton	St. John's	
Morgan Co	Berkeley Spr'gs	St. Mark's	F. R. Reed.
Harper's Ferry	Harper's Ferry	St. John's	*Barnabas Bryan.
New River	Hinton	Ascension	
Cresaps	Cresaps	Grace	
Coal Valley	Montgomery	Calvary	Venable Johnson. N. R. Coles.
Advent	Ansted	Redeemer	R. C. Taylor. W. H Evans.
Princeton	Princeton	Heavenly Rest	
Wayne Co	Kenova	Grace	Frank R. Peck.
Ripan	Ripon	St. John's	
Bramwell	Bramwell	Holy Trinity	
St. David's	Powellton	St. David's	D. T. Evans. Dr. A. W. DeBell.
Elm Grove	Elm Grove	St. Paul's	
Wheeling	Wheeling	St. Andrew's	
St. Luke's	Charleston	St. Luke's	
St. Matthew's	Charleston	St. Matthew's	
Madison	Clover Lick	Grace.	
Norbourne	Bunker Hill	Christ	*John K. Cunningham. Joseph Morgan.
Spruce Run	Lorentz	Spruce	
St. Thomas	White Sulphur	St. Thomas	
Davis	Tucker	Christ	
Christ Memorial	Williamstown	Christ	J. W. Snodgrass.
Grace	Eckman	Grace	
Elkins	Elkins	Grace Church (St. Barnabas)	*C H. Scott. I. P. Gassman.
St. Mary's	St. Mary's	Grace	
St. Andrew's	Mannington	St. Andrew's	

Those marked * were present.

The Treasurer of the Diocese presented his report, which was referred to the Committee on Finance. (For report see Appendix A.)

A communication from the International Congress on Rest, was referred to the Committee on the State of the Church.

A memorial from the Diocese of California on the Revised Version of the Bible, was presented and referred to a special committee of three clergymen and one layman.

The Bishop appointed the following:

Rev. John S. Gibson.
Rev. J. S. Alfriend.
Rev. C. E. A. Marshall.
Dr. G. A. Aschman.

A request from the Diocese of Virginia was read soliciting the co-operation of this Diocese in securing the General Convention for Richmond, Va., in 1907, and the delegates to be elected were instructed to work and vote for it.

The Rt. Rev., the Bishop Coadjutor, then read his address as follows:

DIARY FROM MAY, 1903, TO JUNE, 1904.—W. L. GRAVATT.

DIARY.

May 20th, Wednesday: Sunday, 24th, Annual Diocesan Council, St. Matthew's Church, Wheeling.

The 20th: Took part in the opening services of the Council.

Sunday, 24th, A. M.: Preached in St. Luke's Church, Wheeling, and confirmed two.

Sunday, the 31st. At the request of the officials of the Presbyterian Church, Charles Town, preached A. M.

P. M. Read service and preached at St. John's Church, Ripon.

JUNE.

Sunday, the 7th: Assisted in service and preached in Zion Church, Charles Town.

Wednesday, 10th: Officiated and preached in Zion Church, Charles Town.

Tuesday, 16th: Attended meeting of the Board of Trustees of the Virginia Theological Seminary at Alexandria, Va.

Wednesday, 17th: At Mountain Lake Park, Md. Officiated at the marriage of Harvey F. Smith and Anita Collins.

Thursday, 18th: Attended a meeting of the Alumni of the Virginia Theological Seminary.

Friday,, 19th: At the Virginia Theological Seminary, ordained to the Priesthood Robert Nelson Meade, Thomas C. Darst, Edwin B. Snead; Presented by Rev. J. S. Gibson and Rev. John Moncure, D. D.

JULY.

Sunday, 1st: A. M. Read service, reached, celebrated the Holy Communion in Trinity Church, Martinsburg. 3 P. M. Read the service and preached in Grace Church, Bunker Hill.

Friday, 10th: Officiated at the funeral of Dr. Butler, Trinity Church, Shepherdstown.

Sunday, 12th: A. M. Read service and preached in Christ Church, Clarksburg. 5 P. M. Officiated at the funeral of Miss Jenny Link in Clarksburg. 8:30 P. M. Read service and preached in Christ Church, Clarksburg.

Monday, 13th: I went to Weston to confer with the Rector of the Church in Buckhannon about the work in his territory.

Tuesday, 14th: Went to Fairmont to confer with Bishop Penick about the work in Mannington.

Sunday, 19th: A. M. and P. M. Read service and preached in Christ Church, Clarksburg.

Monday, 20th: Went to Parkersburg to confer with Bishop Peterkin.

Thursday, 23rd: Visited the work on Blue Ridge Mountain.

Sunday, 26th: Preached in St. Peter's Church, Port Royal, Va.

AUGUST.

Sunday, 2nd: Preached in Zion Church, Charles Town.

Sunday, 16th: Read service and preached in Zion Church, Charles Town, A. M. P. M. Read service and preached at Harewood Mission.

Sunday, 23: Read service and preached in Zion Church, Charles Town, A. M.. 3 P. M. Read service and preached at St. Andrew's on the Mountain. 7 P. M. Officiated in Zion Church, Charles Town.

Tuesday, 25th: Preached in the Church of the Incarnation, Ronceverte, and confirmed two.

Wednesday, 26th: Preached in the Presbyterian Church, Hillsboro.

Thursday, 27th: Preached in the Presbyterian Church at Huntersville.

Friday, 28th: Preached in the Presbyterian Church, at Marlinton.

Saturday, 29th: I went, with Rev. G. H. Crook, to look over the field at Durbin.

Sunday, 31st: A. M. and P. M. Preached in Grace Church, Clover Lick.

Monday, 31st: Visited Mingo and baptized the child of Mr. Charles Bruce.

SEPTEMBER.

6th: Read service and preached in the Church of the Messiah at Alderson.

Tuesday, 8th: Visited Nuttallburg and officiated at the marriage of Miss Alice Taylor and Mr. Marion Dawson.

Sunday, 13th: Read service and preached in Christ Church, Blue Ridge Mountain, A. M. and P. M.

17th 18th and 19th: I spent in Port Royal, Va.

Tuesday, 29th: In St. Ann's Church, New Martinsville, I confirmed four and made an address.

Wednesday, 30th: A. M. In St. Ann's Church, New Martinsville, ordained to the Priesthood Rev. George Shaw. The sermon was preached by the Rev. S. S. Moore, D. D. The candidate was presented by Rev. Dr. Moore. Rev. Jacob Brittingham, Rev. C. E. Shaw, Rev. W. P. Chrisman, Rev. A G Grinnan, assisting. P. M. Made an address to the Convocation in St. Ann's Church, New Martinsville...

OCTOBER.

Thursday, 1st: Visited Reynolds Memorial Hospital and inspected the entire plant.

Friday, 2nd: Visited Grace Church, Cresaps; preached and confirmed one.

Saturday, 3rd: A. M. Visited Wheeling to confer with Rev. F. Van R. Moore about the work in Chester.

Sunday, 4th: Visited St. Paul's Chapel, Middle Run, A. M. and preached. 2:00 P. M. Consecrated the Chapel at Middle Run, and preached. 7:30 P. M. Preached in St. Paul's Church, Weston.

Monday, 5th: Preached in the Presbyterian Church, at Richwood.

Tuesday, 6th: Visited Camden-on-Gauley and preached in the Methodist Church.

Wednesday, 7th: Visited St. John's Church, Sutton; read the service and preached and had a conference about the work in that field.

Friday, 9th: Visited Fairmont.

Sunday, 11th: A. M. Consecrated the Church of The Transfiguration at Buckhannon and preached. P.M. Visited Spruce Chapel; preached and confirmed one. 7:30 P. M. Preached in the Church of the Transfiguration, Buckhannon and confirmed four.

Monday, 12th: Visited Grafton.

Sunday, 18th: Visited St. John's Church, Ripon; read the service and preached.

Sunday, 25th: Preached in St. Paul's Church, Alexandria, Va.

20th to 24th: Attended a Conference of Bishops in the Pro-Cathedral, Washington, D. C.

27th to 29th: Attended the Missionary Council held in Washington.

NOVEMBER.

Sunday, 1st: Visited Epiphany Church, Okonoko; preached morning and evening.

Tuesday, 11th: Attended a meeting of the Board of Trustees of the Virginia Theological Seminary.

Sunday, 15th: Visited St. Bartholomew's Church, Leetown; preached and confirmed one. P. M. Preached in Grace Church, Middleway.

Sunder, 22nd: Officiated in Zion Church, Charles Town.

Sunday, 20th: Vsited St. John's Church, Harpers Ferry and preached.

DECEMBER.

Sunday, 6th: Read service and preached in Christ Church, Clarksburg, morning and evening.

Monday, 7th: Was called to Piedmont to advise about the work.

Sunday, 20th: Preached in the Presbyterian Church, Charles Town, at the request of their Church officers.

Sunday, 27th: Visited Emmanuel Church, Cumberland, for the Bishop of Maryland; preached and confirmed twenty-one.

Tuesday, 22nd: Officiated at a funeral in the Presbyterian Church, Charles Town.

JANUARY.

Friday, 1st: Officiated at a funeral in Zion Church, Charles Town. A. M. Officiated in Zion Church, Charles Town.

Sunday, 3rd: Took part in the service in Zion Church, Charles Town.

Sunday, 10th: A. M. Visited St. Luke's Church, Wheeling; preached and confirmed four. P. M. Preached at St. Matthew's Church, Wheeling.

Monday, 11th: Conference with Bishop Peterkin in Wheeling.

Tuesday, 12th: Attended meeting of the Northwestern Convocation in St. Paul's Church, Sistersville and confirmed two.

Wednesday, 13th: A. M. Celebrated the Holy Communion in St. Paul's Church, Sistersville. P. M. Made an address to the Convocation.

Friday, 15th: Visited Parkersburg.

Monday, 18th: Addressed the Woman's Auxiliary, Charles Town.

Thursday, 21st: Made an address to the Brotherhood of St. Andrew in St. John's Church, Pittsburg.

FEBRUARY.

Wednesday, 3rd: Attended a meeting of the Kanawha Convocation held in the Church of the Incarnation, Ronceverte. Conducted the Quiet Hour. At the morning service celebrated the Holy Communion.

Thursday, 4th: Church of the Incarnation, Ronceverte.

Sunday, 7th: Preached in Zion Church, Charles Town.

Sunday, 14th: A. M. Visited Trinity Church, Shepherdstown, and preached. P. M. Church of the Good Shepherd, Duffields; preached.

Monday, 15th: In Zion Church, Charles Town, officiated at the marriage of Archdeacon Matthews of Ohio and Miss Collins.

Wednesday, 17th: In Christ Church, Washington, D. C., preached the sermon to the Brotherhood of St. Andrew.

Sunday, 21st: Preached in Holy Trinity Church, Richmond, morning and evening.

Sunday, 28th: Morning and evening assisted in the service in Zion Church, Charles Town.

MARCH.

Sunday, 6th: Preached, morning and evening, in Holy Trinity Church, Richmond, Va.

Wednesday, 9th: Preached in Holy Trinity Church, Richmond, Va.

Sunday, 13th: Preached morning and evening, at Trinity Church, Morgantown and at the evening service confirmed five.

Monday, 14th: Met the Vestry of Trinity Church, Morgantown.

Friday, 18th: P. M. Preached in St. Luke's Church, Wheeling.

Saturday, 19th: Visited Reynolds Memorial Hospital.

Sunday, 20th: Preached in St. Paul's Church, Elm Grove, Wheeling and confirmed seven. P. M. Preached in St. Andrew's Church, Wheeling.

Tuesday, 22nd: Visited the State Prison at Moundsville.

8 P. M. Visited Trinity Church, Moundsville; preached and confirmed one.

Wednesday, 23rd: A. M. Visited New Martinsville. P. M. Visited Spillman Chapel, Spillman, and confirmed three.

Thursday, 24th: Visited Christ Church, Point Pleasant; preached and confirmed four.

Friday, 25th: Visited Trinity Church, Huntington; preached.

Saturday, 26th: Visited Parkersburg to confer with Bishop Peterkin.

Sunday, 27th: Visited St. Matthias Church, Grafton; prached and confirmed four. 3 P. M. Made an address to the Y. M. C. A. in Grafton, 7 P. M. Visited the Boys' Reform School and preached.

APRIL.

Sunday, 3rd. Visited Trinity Church, Martinsburg; preached and confirmed thirty. P. M. Confirmed one sick person in private. P. M. Made an address to the Sunday School in Martinsburg. 7:30 P. M. Preached in Mt. Zion Church, Hedgesville.

10th. Sunday: Preached in St. John's Church, Charleston, and confirmed twelve. 3 P. M. Preached in St. Matthew's Church, Charleston, and confirmed three. 8 P. M. Preached in St. Luke's Church, Charleston, and confirmed four.

Monday, 11th: Visited St. Mark's Church, St. Albans; preached and confirmed two.

Tuesday, 12th: Confirmed in St. John's Church, Charleston, one. P. M. Preached in the Church at Mt. Carbon.

Wednesday, 13th: Visited St. David's Church, Powellton; preached and confirmed seven.

Thursday, 14th: Preached in the Church of the Redeemer, Ansted, and confirmed three.

Friday, 15th: Visited Calvary Church, Montgomery, and confirmed one.

Sunday, 17th: A. M. Preached in Trinity Church, Parkersburg, and confirmed nineteen. Made an address to the Sunday School. 7:30 P. M. Preached in the Chapel of the Good Shepherd, Parkersburg, and confirmed three.

Friday, 22nd: Met with the teachers of St. Andrew's on the Mountain.

Sunday, 24th: A. M. Preached in Zion Church, Charles Town. P. M. Visited Fairview Mission and preached. This is the first time an Episcopal service has been held at this point.

25th, 26th, 27th and 28th: I attended a meeting of the Eastern Convocation at Moorefield, and on Wednesday, the 27th, celebrated the Holy Communion.

28th, Thursday: Preached the closing sermon of the Convocation.

MAY.

Sunday, 1st: A. M. Took part in the service in Zion Church, Charles Town. P. M. With Rev. David Howard of Wheeling, visited Trinity Church, Shepherdstown.

Sunday, 8th: Visited Holy Trinity Church, Bramwell; preached and confirmed one. P. M. Preached in Christ Church, Bluefield, and confirmed two.

Monday, 9th: Visited the Church of the Heavenly Rest, Princeton and preached.

Wednesday, 11th: Visited Grace Church, Eckman; preached and confirmed one.

Thursday, 12th: Visited Welch and preached in the Presbyterian Church.

Friday, 13th: Visited Williamson and preached in the Presbyterian Church and confirmed three.

Sunday, 15th: Made an address to the Sunday School in Trinity Church, Huntington. Preached at the 11 o'clock service. 8:30 P. M. Preached in Grace Church, Kenova, and confirmed two. 8 P. M. Preached in Trinity Church, Huntington, and confirmed eleven.

Tuesday, 17th: Preached in the Presbyterian Church at Nuttall and confirmed three.

Wednesdey, 18th: Visited Dundon, Clay County; preached in the school house. This is the first time this point has been visited.

Thursday, 19th. Preached in the Baptist Church at Pratt.

Friday, 20th: Preached in the school house at Paint Creek.

Saturday, 21st. Visited Sheltering Arms Hospital.

Sunday, 22nd: A. M. Visited Wake Forrest, Cabin Creek, and preached in the school house. P. M. Visited Carbon; preached in the school house and confirmed two.

Tuesday, 23rd. Was spent in looking over the new territory along Cabin Creek and I find a splendid field for our work.

Tuesday, 24th: I attended the annual meeting of the Board of Trustees of the Sheltering Arms Hospital.

Wednesday: Officiated in Zion Church, Charles Town, at the marriage of Edward Esten Cooke and Hannah Alexander.

Sunday, 29th: Officiated in Zion Church, Charles Town, during absence of the Rector. Preached and celebrated the Holy Communion. P. M. Visited a sick person and celebrated the Holy Communion. 7 P. M. Officiatd in Zion Church, Charles Town.

SUMMARY.

Baptisms	1
Confirmations	175
Marriages	4
Burials	4
Visits made	97
Sermons	120
Addresses	57
Churches Consecrated	2
New Points Visited	7
Ordination to Priesthood	4

Moneys Received:—

Cash,from Woman's Auxiliary, Charles Town	$100.00
Check from St. John's Church, Charleston	6.00
Cash from Dundon	3.00
Cash from Pratt	1.05
Cash from Paint Creek	1.02
Cash from Wake Forrest	4.33
Cash from Carbon	11.66
Total	$127.06
St. Paul's Elm Grove	3.00
	$130.00

Amount paid out:—

Grants in Kanawha Convocation	**$ 66.00**
Three grants for education	**42.00**
One grant in Northwestern Convocation	**12.00**
Total	**$120.00**
Balance	**$ 7.06**
	3.00
	$ 10.06

On motion, the Council adjourned.

THURSDAY, JUNE 2, 1904, 9:30 A. M.

The Bishop Coadjutor called the Council to order.

Prayer by Rev. D. W. Howard.

Minutes of the previous day read and approved.

The Rev. Dr. Moore made this report and the Committee was continued.

The Special Committee on the General Clergy Relief Fund reports progress and asks to be continued.

S. SCOLLAY MOORE,
Chairman.

The Special Committee to which was referred the communication from the Diocese of California, submitted this report which was received and the appended resolution adopted:

To the 27th Annual Council of the Diocese of West Virginia:

The Special Committee to whom was referred the communication from the Diocese of California informing this Council of its having petitioned the General Convention of 1904 to permit the use of the Revised Version in the lessons in Morning and Evening Prayer, respectfully report:

Inasmuch as by authorizing the use in the lessons of Morning and Evening Prayer of "The Marginal Readings Bible" the General Convention has recognized the wisdom of giving our people who hear the word of God in the public services of the Church the light that has come to us upon the meaning of the original from the labors of the more recent devout and learned translators; and inasmuch as both by some of the English Bishops, and the action of some of our Bishops and Dioceses, the use of the Canterbury Version, in one or other of its editions, as tending to promote a fuller understanding of the revelation of God and his truth, is being urged, it is the opinion of your committee that the clergy and

people of the Protestant Episcopal Church in the United States ought to have the liberty to read such version in the public services of the Church in the parts specified, viz: the lessons of Morning and Evening Prayer. And, as the petition of the Diocese of California is that such permissive use be granted, your committee feel that it will be altogether fitting that the Diocese of West Virginia should be one of those to support the granting of such petition in General Convention in 1904.

Your committee therefore recommends the passage of the following:

Resolved, That the Deputies of this Diocese in the General Convention of 1904 be informed that the sentiment of the Church in West Virginia favors granting the permissive use of the Revised Version in reading the lessons in public worship; and that, when the matter comes to vote in General Convention, if the light then thrown upon the subject by debate and conference makes it appear wise to grant such permission, if they can support California in her petition they will be acting agreeably to the sense of their constituency.

JNO. S. GIBSON.
C. E. A. MARSHALL.
JNO. S. ALFRIEND.
G. A. ASCHMAN.

The report of the Executive Committee of the Diocesan Missions Committee submitted this report, which was made the order of the day for Friday, 10 A. M.:

The Executive Committee of the Diocesan Missionary Society submits the following report of its work for the past year:

The report of the Treasurer shows the receipts of the Society from all sources to have been $3,187.27, which is less than those of last year by nearly $150. Expenditures during the year have been $3,937.48, or $750 in excess of receipts. This large expenditure was justified by the fact that we entered the year with a considerable balance in the treasury and was due to an increase in the stipends of the men in the field, which your Committee deemed it wise, if not necessary, to make, in order that the work might be maintained and the men supported.

With this sum 27 men and one woman, working in all sections of the Diocese, have been aided—the average stipend being about $137. Five of these have now removed from the Diocese and the vacancies thus caused remain as yet unfilled. The balance in the treasury at the close of the present year is $1,127.97, which will enable us, with receipts upon the basis of the present assessment and of the experience of recent years, to meet the obligations of the coming year, but will leave us with practically no means to meet stipends falling due almost immediately after its close. We need, therefore, large increase in our receipts for the maintenance of our present work. In making our forecast we desire that the Diocese shall know exactly what the situation is—our resources and the demands of the work.

It seems impossible for us to follow rigid rules in administering this fund, but we are guided by certain general principles. We aim to give every missionary a house and $800 a year. We are still far short of this. Would need more than $3,000 additional each year to enable us to reach it. But we have made distinct advance in the past two years and have now brought the average up to about 700, subject, however, to some deduction for travelling expenses, which some of the men must pay.

For the maintenance of this standard we need $4,030 each year, which, with $1,200 from the General Board, $650 from the American Church Missionary Society and $975 from Convocational and special funds, will give us a total Missionary Fund of $6,855. This amount we propose to distribute in the manner shown in the following tables, which with the memoranda annexed, have been prepared by the Bishop for the use of the Council.

MEMORANDUM AND SCHEDULE TO ACCOMPANY REPORT OF THE DIOCESAN MISSIONS COMMITTEE TO THE COUNCIL IN MARTINSBURG, JUNE 1, 1904.

EASTERN CONVOCATION	Rectory	SALARY FUND						
		Field	Diocese	Convocation, Etc., Etc.	General Board	Amer. Ch. Miss. Society	Total Missionary	Total Salary
Romney, Moorefield, Okonoko, Paw Paw	R	$ 300	$ 250	$ 50	...	$ 200	$ 500	$ 800
Berkeley Springs	R	300	100	.....	$ 100	.....	200	500
St. Philips, Charles Town	R	100	.....	50	400	....	450	550
Middleway, Leetown, Summit Point	R	550	50	100	.....	100	250	800
Ripon, (served from Virginia)	R	100	100	.....	....	.....	100	200
Harpers Ferry, Hedgeville	R	325	300	75	.....	.....	375	700
Keyser, (served from Maryland)	....	50	50	.....	....	.....	50	100
Specials	..	.....	.....	150	....	.....	150	150
		$ 1725	$ 850	$ 425	$ 500	$ 300	$ 2075	$ 3800

NORTHWESTERN CONVOCATION	Rectory	SALARY FUND Field	Diocese	Convocation, Etc., Etc.	General Board	Amer. Ch. Miss. Society	Total Missionary	Total Salary
Wellsburg, St. John's, Brooke Co.......	R	$ 510	$ 240	.....	....	......	$ 240	$ 750
Williamstown, Good Shepherk (P.) Tavennersville........................	R	600	200	......	.....	. ....	200	800
New Martinsville..........	R	700	....	......	$ 100	......	100	800
St. Marys, Willow Island, Waverly, Ravenswood, Ripley, Mason, Leroy.	R	530	170	.. ...	.....	......	170	700
Buckhannon, Spruce...	.....	300	200	$ 100	....	......	300	600
Elm Grove, Chester, New Cumberland.	R	600	200	....	.....	.....	200	800
* Mannington	....	240	500	100	100	......	700	940
Grafton, Cairo, Pennsboro	R	450	300	......	......	.....	300	750
Davis, Bogard, Parsons.........	R	550	.....	......	200	....	200	750
Elkins, Belington..	R	300	400	... ..	... .	.. ...	400	700
Specials.............	......	.....	50	...	... ..	......	50	50
		$ 4780	$ 2260	$ 200	$ 400	......	$ 2860	$ 7640

* The sum of $240 has to be paid for rent.

KANAWHA CONVOCATION	Rectory	SALARY FUND						
		Field	Diocese	Convocation, Etc., Etc.	General Board	Amer. Ch. Miss. Society	Total Missionary	Total Salary
Bluefield, Princeton	R	$ 550	$ 150	....	$ 100	....	$ 250	$ 800
Ronceverte, Lewisburg, Fort Spring, White Sulphur, Pocahontas Co	.....	600	200	.....	.....	....	200	800
Union, Alderson	R	450	100	.....	200	.....	300	750
Point Pleasant, Spilman, Bruce Chapel	R	550	50	...	......	150	200	750
Hinton, Glen Jean, Beckley	R	600	....	......	....	200	200	800
St. Luke's, Charleston, St. Matthews, Charleston, St. Albans	R	680	120	.....	......	.....	120	800
Cabin Creek, Pratt, Clay Court House	.....	......	300	....	......	.....	300	800
Specials	....	...	......	$ 350	....	.....	350	850
		$ 3930	$ 920	$ 350	$ 300	$ 350	$ 1920	$ 5850
The Whole Mission Field	....	$10435	$ 4080	$ 975	$ 1200	$ 650	$ 6855	$ 17290

In addition to the above the women of the Diocese, by special effort, support a woman Missionary at the Sheltering Arms Hospital, who works there and at adjoining points.

It will be perceived that the above schedule leaves St. Philips, Charles Town, with $550 salary—St. Marks, Berkeley Springs, with $500 and Buckhannon and Spruce with $600, but no rectory; these are the smallest salaries. Taking into the account certain special cases indicated above, and allowing for the rent of five houses for rectories and for necessary travelling expenses, it is considered fair to estimate the average salary, in money on the above list at $675.

It will also be perceived that for the present at least, Ravenswood Parish with four churches is put with St. Mary's, etc. And it will appear later that it has seemed best also to continue Welch and its dependencies, as attached to Bramwell, to provide for these properly, and to increase the small salaries mentioned above, up to the average, would require about $1,500 additional. But as the $4,030 scheduled above as appropriated for the coming year, is $1,089 over our assessment, the Committee did not venture to make further appropriation. We expect to get through this year with the help of the balance of about $1,000 now on hand, but we earnestly ask for $4,000 for the coming year.

It must be understood that beside the 61 places mentioned above as principal points, there are about 30 that are regularly reached by our Missionaries.

So far we have been dealing only with the Missions, but to get a more complete view of the work of the Diocese, I give below a list of our self supporting charges. Eighteen in all, viz.:

Charles Town, Zion Church; Blue Ridge, St. Andrews.
Weston, Middle Run.
Wheeling, St. Lukes.
Wheeling, St. Matthews.
Moundsville.
Powellton, Ansted, Montgomery, Mt. Carbon.
Wheeling, St. Andrews.
Martinsburg, Bunker Hill.
Morgantown.
Sistersville.
Shepherdstown, Duffields.
Huntington, Kenova, Williamson.
Parkersburg, Trinity; Parkersburg, St. Stephen.
Fairmont.
Charleston, St. John.
Clarksburg, North View.
Sutton, Little Otter, Centralia, Richwood.
*Bramwell, Eckman, Welch, Elkhorn, Maybeury, etc.

Beside the 31 places mentioned in this list there are about 20 that are regularly reached by the clergy in charge. And besides the 142 places mentioned in both lists, there are about 50 which the Bishops and Clergy visit from time to time as opportunity offers.

To recapitulate, it appears that in the whole Diocese there are really 26 missionary charges or circuits, though two of them are temporarily connected with others.

Properly to care for these points we need $5,500, but in default of that we have ventured to make appropriations only to the extent of $4,030, this sum with $2,825 from other sources gives us all told a Missionary fund of $6,855 and this added to the $10,435 raised by the Missions for their own support enables us to provide Rectories, pay necessary traveling expenses, and give an average salary of about $675 in money.

These Missions have about 1,550 communicants and are expected to contribute to our Diocesna Mission work $700 a year.

Back of this work and supporting it, are the 18 self suporting charges which with 3,125 communicants are expected to contribute to our Diocesan Mission work the sum of $2,250 a year. As a help to the understanding of

---

*This is really two charges combined into one temporarily.

their financial ability it appears from the Journal that they raise a salary fund of $19,645 which after making certain deductions for house rent and traveling expenses affords an average salary of $1,040 a year.

This then is the situation as far as it can here be stated. For this work which is full of encourgement we want $4,000 for the coming year. Our last Journal reported 8,000 baptized persons in the Diocese. An average conhribution of one cent a week from all these, would give us more than the amount asked. What will you do about it?

Your Committee has but two suggestions to make, which it will put into the form of questions.

1. Are there not places in the Diocese, able and willing to assume a larger measure of obligation for this work than that imposed by the report of the Committee on Assessments? One dollar for each communicant—less than two cents a week—would seem no heavy burden to assume for work so necessary to be done. Will not each parish and mission assessed at less than this aim to bring its contribution up to this figure at least?

2. Are there not individuals in the Diocese who in response to personal appeals from their rectors can be induced to supplement the contributions from the parishes and missions by some individual gifts, either occasional or stated?

The election of Deputies to the General Convention was made the order of the day for 4 P. M. to-day.

The Rev. J. F. Plummer cordially invited the next Council to meet at Clarksburg, and on motion of the Rev Dr. Moore, the invitation was unanimously accepted.

On motion, the following Committee on Constitution and Canons was elected:

Rev. Jno S. Gibson.	Mr. Joseph Trapnell.
Rev. D. W. Howard.	Mr. W. S. Laidley.
Rev. J. S. Douglas.	

On motion, the Standing Committee was elected as follows; Tellers, Rev. A. G. Grinnan and Rev. E. H. Brosius:

Rev. G. A. Gibbons.	Mr. J. Gassman.
Rev. J. S. Douglas.	Mr. J. H. Strider.
Rev. A. J. Willis.	Judge Frank Beckwith.

The Treasurer of the Episcopal and Contingent Funds submitted his report, which was referred to the Finance Committee. (See Appendix A.)

The Rev. Dr. Moore, presented the report of the Trustees of the Permanent Fund, which was referred to the Committee on Permanent Fund.

The Rev. John S. Gibson for the Committee on Constitution and Canons, submitted the following report upon the recodification of the Constitution and Canons of the Diocese. On motion, it was made the order of the day for 2:30 P. M. Friday.

To the 27th Annual Council of the Diocese of West Virginia:

The Committee on Constitution and Canons were requested to report to this Council a recodification of the Constitution and Canons of the Diocese and to embody therein such amendments and alterations as might seem desirable. Your Committee have performed that duty to the best of their ability, acting on such suggestions and proposals of amendment as came to them from time to time, and present the result in the printed leaflet hereto attached. This leaflet was printed to contain such Canons as have been changed or added, but does not contain those which remain as they were, nor a few which need only to be rearranged or slightly modified in their language.

Your Committee recommend the adoption of the following:

Resolved, That the Constitution and Canons of the Diocese of West Virginia as presented by the Committee on Constitution and Canons be substituted for those now in force.

JNO. S. GIBSON.
JOHN S. DOUGLAS.
DAVID W. HOWARD.
JOSEPH TRAPNELL.

Council took a recess for Divine service.

THURSDAY, 2:30 P. M.

The Council was called to order by the Bishop.

Mr. W. D. Alvord was invited to address the Council upon the subject of the Anti-Saloon League of the United States, which he did in a very interesting manner.

The Rev. A. J. Willis offered the following, which was adopted:

Resolved, That the Council instructs the Committee on Assessments to assess the parishes and not the individual churches, the names of the churches being put in brackets opposite the name of the parish.

The Rev. A. M. Lewis moved that the third page of the Journal be left blank.

The motion was laid on the table.

The Rev. W. P. Chrisman presented this report from the Committee on Sunday schools.

For the first resolution appended, this substitute was adopted:

Resolved, That the Committee on Sunday Schools appoint one clergyman and one layman from each of the convocations of the Diocese to assist in the work.

The second resolution appended was laid on the table.

Your Committee on Sunday Schools beg to submit the following report:

The number of schools in the Diocese, 58; teachers, 373; scholars, 3,078; total 3,451. The Advent Offering of 31 schools was $453.47, which is the largest Advent Offering ever made by the Sunday schools. Nevertheless we would call your attention to the fact that 27 schools failed to send any offering to Diocesan Missions. Two years ago the same number were delinquent. We would therefore urge these schools to fall in line, and make an offering for Diocesan Missions, be it ever so small.

When we consider that the vast majority of scholars that attend our Sunday schools are members of Christ, the children of God, and inheritors of the Kingdom of Heaven by baptism, then we recognize that the Sunday school is part of the Church of Christ, and not an adjunct thereto. This being so it reminds us that in each congregation there are many mature Christians bound by the most solemn obligations so see that these children hear sermons that they "learn the creed, the Lord's Prayer, and the Ten Commandments, and all other things which a Christian ought to know and believe to his soul's health." This means that we cannot divorce one from the other without an injury to both. It recognizes the Sunday school as the department of instruction for the younger members of the flock, and not as a children's service that is to take the place of the regularly appointed order for morning and evening prayer. Here then your Committee would utter a warning against any system of instruction or service leaflets that leave the impression on the mind of scholars, teachers or parents that it is the children's service and therefore they are relieved from further attendance upon the regular services of the Church. Two years ago resolutions were adopted by the Council recommending the formation of teachers' training classes, more thorough Church teaching in the Sunday schools, and conferences for Sunday school workers. They were good and timely resolutions, but unless some way is devised for keeping them before the minds of those interested in the Sunday schools of the Diocese very little good will result from their adoption. The Committee on Sunday Schools as constituted at present is taken entirely from the Northwestern Convocation and this necessarily brings them in touch with a very limited number of our schools and consequently our work and report is more or less of a local nature. In order to remedy this and bring this Committee in vital touch with every school in the Diocese we would earnestly and respectfully ask the adoption of the following resolutions:

1. That the Committee on Sunday Schools be composed of one clergyman and one layman from each of the Convocations of the Diocese.

2. That it shall be the duty of such members to visit or communicate with each school within the bounds of their Convocation at least once a year, to arrange for Sunday School Institutes, to compile such data as may be necessary for an accurate and thorough report to the Council, and otherwise to lead an active and aggressive work in their respective Convocations.

W. P. CHRISMAN.
C. C. PENICK.
G. A. ASCHMAN, *M. D.*

Mr. Peebles Tatum nominated Mr. Joseph Trapnell as Chancellor of the Diocese, vice the late Judge J. P. Rogers.

Mr. Trapnell was unanimously elected.

A motion was made to take up from the table the resolution relating to the third page of the Journal. It was lost.

On motion of the Rev. Dr. Roller, the Rules of Order were ordered to be printed with the new Constitution and Canons, when printed.

On motion of Bishop Gravatt the Rules of Order were ordered to be printed in the next Journal of Council.

The Rev. D. W. Howard nominated the following Missionary Committee of the Diocese. Adopted.

Rev. S. S. Moore, D. D.
Rev. J. Brittingham.
Rev. J. S. Alfriend.
Mr. B. M. Ambler.
Mr. Simms Powell.

Mr. Joseph Trapnell offered the following, which was adopted by a vote of 34 to 16.

Resolved. That the second resolution on the third page of the cover, be expunged from the Journal.

The hour having arrived the order of the day was taken up. The Bishop appointed as tellers for the clerical vote, the Rev. R. N. Meade and Mr. F. W. Truscott and for the lay vote, the Rev. J. T. Marley and Mr. James Grantham.

The following clergymen were then nominated for deputies to the General Convention:

The Rev. Jacob Brittingham, Rev. D. W. Howard, Rev. S. S. Moore, D. D., Rev. R. D. Roller, D. D., Rev. J. S. Gibson, Rev. J. S. Douglas, Rev. C. E. Shaw and the Rev. J. S. Alfriend.

The ballot was taken.

Nominations were then made for lay deputies to the General Convention as follows:

Mr. Joseph Trapnell, Dr. G. A. Aschman, B. M. Ambler, B. D. Spilman, J. Gassman, Gen'l W. P. Craighill, W. S. Laidley, C. L. Thompson and Geo. T. Kreglow.

The ballot was taken.

Pending the count of the ballots, Mr. G. W. Parsons, of Romney, was excused from further attendance upon the Council.

The report of the Standing Committee was presented by its President, the Rev. G. A. Gibbons, from May 22, 1903, to June 2, 1904, as follows:

Standing Committee report (From May 22, 1903, to June 2, 1904).

May 28th, 1903. Rev. Geo. C. Shaw (Deacon) having served ten to fifteen years in the Methodist ministry, asked to have the time of his candidacy for Priest's Orders shortened, and being so recommended by the Bishop of the Diocese, the Standing Committee consented to shortening his time one year and a half, and then recommended him to the Bishop for ordination to the Priesthood.

At the same time the Rev. Robert Nelson Meade (Deacon) was recommended for ordination to the Priesthood.

The Rev. Edwin B. Snead (Deacon) from St. John's Church, Richmond, Va., on account of his advanced age asked for a few months of shortened candidacy, and the Bishop so recommending, the Committee consented to shorten the time, and recommended Mr. Sneed for ordination to the Priesthood.

Sept. 1st, 1903. Consent was given to the consecration of the Rev. Edwin Stevens Lines, D. D., to be Bishop of the Diocese of Newark.

Sept. 15th, 1903. Richard W. Trapnell and Edmund P. Dandridge 2nd, were recommended as candidates for Holy Orders.

At the same meeting (Sept. 15, 1903) consent was given to the consecration of the Rev. Theodore DuBose Bratton, D. D., to be Bishop of the Diocese of Mississippi. The Committee also consented to the consecration of the Rev. M. Edward Fawcett, Ph. D., to be Bishop of the Diocese of Quincy.

Jan. 6th, 1904. The Standing Committee consented to the consecration of the Rev. David Hummell Greer, D. D., to be Bishop Coadjutor of the Diocese of New York.

March 1st, 1904. The Rev. Cretus A. Dowell (Deacon) was recommended to the Bishop for ordination to the Priesthood.

May 13th, 1904. The Rev. Francis VanR. Moore (Deacon) was granted, at his own request and that of the Bishops, a few months of shortened time of candidacy for Priest's Orders, and said Mr. Moore was then recommended for ordination to the Priesthood. Also Mr. W. Howard Meyers asked for and was granted, on the Bishop's recommendation, a few months of shortened candidacy, and wes recommended to the Bishop for ordination to the Deaconate.

The Committee consented to the consecration of the Rev. Richard Henry Nelson to be Bishop Coadjutor of the Diecese of Albany.

Martinsburg, June 2, 1904. Mr. Charles Hely Molony, a Methodist minister, was recommended as a candidate for Holy Orders.

SUMMARY.

Number of meetings	7
Persons recommended as candidates for Holy Orders	3
Recommended for Diaconate	1
Recommended for the Priesthood	5
Consent given to stortening time of candidacy	3
Consented to consecration of Bishops	5

Respectfully submitted,

G. A. GIBBONS, *President.*
A. J. WILLIS.
JOHN S. DOUGLAS.
J. GASSMAN.

The tellers for the clerical vote, reported the following clerical deputies to the General Convention duly elected:

The Rev. S. S. Moore, D. D.
The Rev. R. D. Roller, D. D.
The Rev. D. W. Howard.
The Rev. J. S. Alfriend.

On motion the three persons receiving the next highest number of votes were declared to be alternates, to-wit:

The Rev. Jacob Brittingham.
The Rev. J. S. Douglas.
The Rev. J. S. Gibson.

And on motion the Rev. G. A. Gibbons was elected the fourth alternate.

The tellers for the lay vote then reported that three laymen had received a majority of all the votes cast, whereupon

Mr. Joseph Trapnell.
Mr. B. M. Ambler.
Dr. G. A. Aschman.

were declared elected lay deputies to the General Convention.

Another ballot was ordered for the remaining lay deputy.

The hour of adjournment having arrived a motion was made to continue in session. It was lost.

The Council then adjourned.

FRIDAY, June 3, 1904, 9:30 A. M.

The Council was called to order by the Bishop.

The Rev. G. W. Easter read prayers.

The minutes of yesterday were read and approved.

The tellers proceeded to take the ballot for the fourth lay deputy.

The Rev. A. M. Lewis presented the following report of the Committee on Parochial Reports. Recommendation was adopted.

REPORT OF COMMITTEE ON PAROCHIAL REPORTS.

BAPTISMS.					COMMUNICANTS.				NO. IN SUNDAY SCHOOLS	
Infants.	Adults.	Confirmations.	Marriages.	Burials.	Last Report'd	Present Nr.	Baptized Persons.	Families and Parts	Teachers.	Scholars.
94	28	90	46	61	1411	1513	2451	1086	119	1102
74	29	79	49	85	1248	1322	2383	1005	95	826
74	24	81	59	84	1518	1468	2471	1486	137	989
5	5	10	5	10	378	378	556	301	22	161
247	86	260	159	240	4550	4681	7861	3878	373	3078

DISBURSEMENTS.				GRAND TOTAL.
	CONTRIBUTIONS.			
Current Expenses	Parochial	Diocesan.	Outside the Diocese.	
$12,996 15	$ 5,455 37	$ 8,400 55	$ 2,023 64	$23,875 71
15,845 95	5,446 59	8,746 32	1,818 23	26,857 09
12,566 49	5,698 07	7,081 27	1,854 10	27,199 93
2,452 54	95 61	356 01	221 34	3,125 50
$43,861 13	$16,695 64	$14,584 15	$ 5,917 31	$81,056 23

Committee on Parochial Reports respectfully recommends that the Secretary of the Diocese, after consultation with the Bishop and Dr. Moore, be authorized to make such corections in the financial report as in his judgment will tend to the greater clearness and accuracy of the true condition of this Diocese.

ARTHUR M. LEWIS.
GEO. J. ROGERS.
BEN R. ROLLER.
W. P. CHRISMAN.

The tellers reported the election of Mr. C. L. Thompson as the fourth lay deputy to the General Convention.

Ten o'clock having arrived, the special order of the day was taken up, and the Council went into the consideration of the report of the Diocesan Missionary Committee.

The Rev. J. S. Gibson offered the following:

Resolved, That the Missions Committee, in such manner as seems wise to them, endeavor to have the Mission stations now supported in part from the Diocesan Mission funds, increase the amounts they pay to the support of their missionaries by a sum aggregating $500.00

The Council took a recess for Divine service.

FRIDAY, 2:30 P. M.

The Bishop called the Council to order.

The resolution offered by the Committee on Constitution and Canons was taken up.

The Constitution proposed as a substitute for the present Constitution, as presented by the Committee, was unanimously adopted by a vote taken by orders.

The body of Canons was then taken up. Mr. Peebles Tatum moved the adoption of the unnumbered canon relating to an ecclesiastical court.

The Rev. Dr. Moore moved to postpone the consideration of the whole body of Canons until the next Council. Adopted.

The Committee on Assessments presented their report, which was adopted. (See Appendix.)

The Rev. J. S. Gibson offered this resolution which was adopted:

Resolved, That the apportionment for General Missions be apportioned to our parishes in the same sums as those for which they are assessed for Diocesan Missions.

The Rev. A. J. Grinnan moved that the Council receive the report of the Committee on Parochial Reports. Adopted.

The Rev. G. W. Easter submitted the following report of the Committee on Education:

The resolution appended was adopted.

The Committee on Religious and Theological Education desires to call the attention of the clergy and laity of the Diocese to two matters.

1st. That by one of the Canons of the Church, it is made obligatory that at least one collection for religious and theological education shall be made in each congregation each year. It is a fact that this requirement is not complied with in many cases and in consequence the funds available for Religious and Theological Education are not commensurate with the needs and ability of the Diocese.

2nd. This Diocese has five young men preparing for the ministry at the Theological Seminary of Virginia, which is also the Seminary of this Diocese, towards whose support we contributed last year, ending April 30, 1904, $300, which is less than one-half the necessary amount. The deficiency was supplied by the Education Society of the Diocese of Virginia. We ought not to be willing thus to depend upon a sister Diocese to supply a lack which is clearly due, in large part at least, to the failure to tell our people the purpose and needs of the fund and to give them an opportunity to contribute to it. One-ninth of all the students at the Seminary are our own men and we give less than half the amount necessary for their support.

The Committee, therefore, offers the following resolution:

Resolved, That the clergy of the Diocese are hereby urged to set before all their people the purposes and needs of the fund for Religious and Theological Education and to make at least one collection for it annually as required by Canon upon some Sunday when there is likely to be a full attendance at service.

Respectfully submitted.

GEO. W. EASTER.
J. HOWARD GIBBONS.
ARTHUR M. LEWIS.
C. L. THOMPSON.
W. G. HUBBARD.

The Rev. Dr. Moore offered this resolution, seconded by the Rev. J. S. Gibson, which was adopted:

Resolved, That this Council commends to the American Church Missionary Society the importance of continuing its interest in, and support of, its domestic work, and that the Secretary be instructed to communicate to the Secretary of that Society this resolution

The Rev. Dr. Moore submitted the report of the Committee on the Permanent and Episcopal Funds.

The resolution appended was adopted.

The Committee on the Permanent and Episcopal Funds respectfully reports that we have examined with care the reports of the trustees of the Permanent Fund and of the Treasurer of the Episcopal Fund.

We find the Permanent Fund to be capitalized now at $35,919.62, which is held by the Central Banking and Security Co., of Parkersburg, Treasurer, and is represented by the following items, viz:

Bonds, pledges, notes, etc	$33,618 00
Cash to credit of trustees	1,913 56
Balance on two pledges in hands of trustees	250 00
Interest account overpaid	138 06
Total	$35,919 62

The Trustees have paid out $138.06 more than their receipts on account of interest, but this, we are informed, is an apparent, rather than an actual overpayment and will be corrected by the return of this sum to the principal during the coming year.

Comparing this report with that of last year (Journal, 1903, p. 94), it will be seen that there has been a slight increase of the fund, the capital being now about $285.00 in excess of the sum reported then.

With reference to the Episcopal Fund, the Treasurer's report shows payments on acount of the assessments amounting to $3,277.33, which is $352.69 less than the amount assessed. The bulk of this deficit comes from the failure of 29 points, upon which assessments have been laid, out of a total of 79 such points, to make any payment at all during the year These are among the weak Mission points in the Diocese, for the most part, their aggregate assessment for this Fund being only $212. There have been, however, payments from various points on account of arrearages aggregating $397.93, and small contributions amounting to $28.68 from places unassessed, which have brought contributions to the Fund to a total of $3,703.94, which, with the interest upon the invested Permanent Fund paid to the Treasurer by the Trustees, has enabled him to pay all salaries, meet all contingent expenses and close the year with a balance of $566.82 in the Treasury.

Your Committee would especially commend the care and accuracy displayed by the custodians of these two Funds in managing their trusts and presenting to the Council their reports.

We would also urge again the importance of renewed and constant efforts to increase the Permanent Fund to the sum, at least, hitherto aimed at, viz.: $50.000.

To this end we would call attention to the Canonical requirement of an annual offering from every congregation in the Diocese for this Fund and would offer the following resolution:

Resolved, That this Council commends to ministers in charge of our congregations the needs of this Fund and requests that on or about Ascension Day in each year an offering for this purpose shall be taken.

Mr. Joseph Trapnell made report for the Finance Committee.

The report and recommendations were adopted.

The undersigned Finance Committee report that they have examined and audited the accounts of the Trustees of the Permanent Fund, the Treasurer of the Diocese and the Trustee of the Episcopal and Contingent Funds.

The balance in the hands of the Treasurer of the several funds are as follows:

Permanent Fund as of May 18, 1904:

Securities	$33,018 00
Cash	1,913 56
Total	$35,531 56

Treasurer of Diocese, June 1, 1904.

Diocesan Missions	$ 1,127 97
Religious and Theological Education	14 03
Widows and Orphans	5,898 15

Episcopal and Contingent Fund.

Balance June 1, 1904	$ 566 82

The detailed statements accompany this report and should be printed as appendices to the Journal.

The disbursements charged are sustained by proper vouchers.

The Committee recommend the adoption of the following resolution:

Resolved, That the treasurer of the Contingent Fund be instructed to pay out of the funds coming to his hands the annual rent of the residence now occupied by the Bishop Coadjutor until the further order of the Council and that the said treasurer do pay to the sexton of the church of Martinsburg ten dollars for his services during this Council.

R. M. BROWNE, *Chairman*.
HULLIHEN QUARRIER.
JOSEPH TRAPNELL.
B. D. SPILMAN.
RICHARD HENDERSON.
Committee.

The Rev. J. S. Gibson offered the following resolution, which was adopted:

Resolved, That the trustees of the Permanent Fund be informed that the Council desires that contributions made annually to the Permanent Fund be invested and not treated as uninvested funds.

Mr. C. H. Scott offered this resolution:

Resolved, That this Council calls the attention of the members of this church to the action of the House of Bishops, respecting worldliness, and solemnly urges on them the duty of observing the rule of sobriety and moderation in all things; of maintaining strictly their own personal purity and integrity; and of vigorously discountenancing and wholly abstaining from participation in all forms, customs, and habits of business and pleasure that are immoral, indecent, and at variance with the spirit of Christ as revealed in His Holy Gospel.

Resolved, That the secretary of the Council be instructed to print the foregoing resolution in place of the resolution on the third page of the cover of the proceedings of the Council, prefacing it with the words: Resolution adopted at the session of the Council in Martinsburg, June 1-6, 1904.

The Rev. J. S. Gibson offered the following substitute, which was adopted:

Resolved, That the secretary of the Diocese have the Council Journal of 1904 bound in paper and printed only with the proper title and the list of places and dates of the meetings of future Councils.

The Rev. D. W. Howard submitted the report of the Committee on the State of the Church as follows:

REPORT.

Your Committee on the State of the Church begs leave to report:

The conditions of the work throughout the Diocese show a decided and steady growth. This fact we gather from several sources, and we believe, is brought about by the earnest and untiring labors of our Bishops, together with the clergy and laity working under their direction. The children of the Diocese should be commended for their zeal in the cause of Missions, both Diocesan and general, which augurs well for the future, when they shall take the place of the present generation in our parishes and missions.

This year a larger number of confirmations is reported than ever before, and from information gathered, we know of many of these candidates having been prepared and presented to the rector for the laying on of hands by our faithful body of Sunday school teachers.

During the past year, seven new points have been visited by the Bishops, and work commenced; and several mission points have been greatly strengthened, and are now, or will soon be, entirely self-supporting.

Another source of encouragement is the progress made in the woman's work throughout the Diocese. The increased interest in the Woman's Auxiliary, and the Junior Auxiliary to the Board of Missions, together with the excellent work accomplished by our deaconess and three women workers, cannot fail to bring splendid results in our Diocesan work.

With regard to the communication presented to this Council, and referred to your Committee, respecting the International Congress on Sunday Rest, we recommend that this Council express its sympathy with the object this communication has in view.

Having gathered from the statistics relative to work accomplished during the past year, the knowledge of a considerable growth in our Diocesan work, we earnestly trust that the current year may bring forth still greater fruitfulness.

Respectfully submitted,

DAVID W. HOWARD.
GEO. W. EASTER.
A. G. GRINNAN.
W. E. WATSON.
W. G. HUBBARD.

Parsons.

The Rt. Rev. Dr. Penick, the Rev. G. W. Easter, the Rev. J. T. Marley and Mr. C. L. Thompson were excused from further attendance upon the Council.

The Council adjourned.

SATURDAY, June 4, 9:30 A. M.

The Council was called to order by the Bishop. Prayers by the Rev. Thos. J. Oliver Curran.

Minutes of yesterday read and approved.

On motion a ballot was taken for alternate lay deputies to the General Convention.

The Rev. Dr. Roller, for Committee on Unfinished Business, reported that the Committees on Sunday School and Education had not been elected.

Many nominations for members of the Sunday School Committee were made. A ballot was taken which resulted in the election of the

Rev. W. P. Chrisman, Rev. C. E. Shaw, Dr. G. A. Aschman, Mr. George Rogers

The Committee on Education was elected as follows:

Rev. G. W. Easter, Rev. J. Howard Gibbons, Rev. A. M. Lewis, Mr. W. G. Hubbard, Mr. C. L. Thompson.

The Rev. John S. Douglas offered the following, which was adopted:

***Resolved*, That the secretary be requested to notify the rector of the parish in which the Council is to meet that he is expected to make arrangements with the railroad companies for special rates to Council and also to name the roads over which the delegates will travel and the number likely to come on their road, and also of any other duties he is expected to perform.**

The tellers for election of alternate lay deputies reported the following as having been elected:

Mr. Peebles Tatum, Judge Frank Beckwith, Mr. W. S. Laidley, Mr. B. D. Spilman.

The old Diocesan Committee on Foreign and Domestic Missions was elected as follows:

Rev. D. W. Howard, Rev. G. A. Gibbons, Rev. J. S. Gibson, General W. P. Craighill, Mr. C. C. Coe, Dr. G. A. Aschman.

The Secretary was requested to notify the international Committee on Sunday Rest of our sympathy with its objects as expressed in the recommendation of the Committee on the State of the Church.

The Rev. D. W. Howard addressed the Council on the importance of supporting and circulating the Church News.

The Rev. Dr. Moore offered this resolution of thanks which was unanimously adopted:

***Resolved*, That we, the members of the 27th Annual Council of the Diecese of West Virginia, assembled in Trinity Church, Martinsburg, do hereby express our thanks to the rector and vestry of this church for the admirable provision made by them for the entertainment and comfort of the Council and for the manner in which local difficulties, incident to the present session have been overcome; to the choir of this church for faith-**

ful and efficient aid rendered in the services of the Council; to the pages for the courteous and capable manner of the discharge of their duties; to the ladies of this congregation for their gracious presence and graceful hospitality, which have made our labors lighter and the hours of our stay brighter by the beauty and fragrance, which they have shed upon our proceedings; to the transportation companies for favors extended; to the pastors and official boards of other churches for courtesies shown; to the press and to the people of this community, generally, who, with full and free hospitality, have opened hand and heart and home to guests, who carry with them, as they depart, grateful memories of pleasant days.

The Rev. Dr. Moore offered this resolution which was unanimously adopted:

***Resolved,* That the thanks of the Council are hereby extended to the Committee on Constitution and Canons for the careful and admirable manner in which the work of revision committed to them has been done.**

***Resolved,* That the Committee on Constitution and Canons is hereby empowered to present to this Council at its next session a further report of revision under the terms of the original reference.**

On motion, after reading and approving the minutes of this day, and suitable devotions by the Bishop, the Council adjourned sine die.

G. W. PETERKIN,
President.

ROBT. DOUGLAS ROLLER,
Secretary.

APPENDIX A.

I. *Report of the Treasurer of the Diocese.*

II. *Report of the Trustees of the Episcopal and Contingent Fund.*

III. *Report of the Trustees of the Permanent Fund.*

TREASURER'S REPORT.

Amount of Assessment Diocesan Mis'ns.	NAME.	Paid for Diocesan Missions.	Paid Religious and Theological Education.	Widows, Orphans and Disabl'd Clergy Fund.
$ 6	Alderson	$ 4 46	$	$
20	Ansted	20 00		7 50
.....	Bayard			
5	Beury			
6	Beckley	1 45		
25	Berkeley Springs	25 82		
30	Bluefield	37 85		
30	Bramwell	45 00		21 25
5	Brooke County	7 65		
12	Bruce Chapel	15 25		
10	Buckhannon	10 00		5 00
5	Bunker Hill	1 15		
300	Charles Town, Zion	300 00	44 13	41 65
10	" St. Phillip's			
200	Charleston, St. John's	200 00	6 28	25 50
8	" St. Luke's			
8	" St. Matthews	5 72		
125	Clarksburg Church	39 25	9 25	4 26
.....	" St. Thomas			
5	Cresaps	5 00		
8	Davis	8 00		
5	Dubree	3 31		
20	Eckman	20 00		
10	Elkins	10 00	2 00	3 25
75	Fairmont	76 12		
5	Fort Spring			
10	Glen Jean			
15	Grafton	6 23		
20	Harper's Ferry	32 31	1 60	7 85
.....	Hartford	2 00		
25	Hedgesville	25 00		
30	Hinton	13 45		
75	Huntington	95 00	5 00	35 00
8	Kenova	8 13		3 20
.....	Keyser	5 50		
30	Lee Town	31 42		4 00
7	Lewisburg			
.....	Little Otter			
8	Liverpool			
5	Madison			
.....	Mannington	3 30	1 60	1 65
75	Martinsburg	120 27	7 61	33 71
.....	Mason	3 00		
15	Middleway	15 00		2 77
5	Mt. Carbon	5 00		
15	Montgomery	20 20		3 50
20	Moorefield	20 00	1 65	1 85
25	Morgantown	35 50	1 48	5 15
40	Moundsville	46 08	1 50	16 35
.....	New Cumberland			
40	New Martinsville	43 61	4 02	9 76
5	Nuttall	5 00		
10	Okonoko	12 00	2 00	2 00
350	Parkersburg, Trinity	355 00		92 60
20	" Good Shepherd	150 00	10 00	36 00
3	" St. Stephen's			
.....	Paw Paw	8 25	3 00	
50	Pt. Pleasant	106 75		
20	Powellton	23 57		4 31
6	Princeton	12 00		
10	Ravenswood	14 00	2 50	2 50
15	Ripley	20 50		
10	Ripon	11 63		
16	Romney	15 00		
8	Ronceverte	7 31		
75	Shepherdstown	43 23	10 04	14 00
5	Smithfield			
40	Sistersville	41 22	7 75	9 32

TREASURER'S REPORT.—Continued.

Amount of Assessment Diocesan Mis'ns.	NAME.	Paid for Diocesan Missions.	Paid Religious and Theological Education.	Widows, Orphans and Disabl'd Clergy Fund.
10	Spilman	15 64	$	$
4	Spruce	2 00		
15	St. Marys	15 00		
10	St. Albans	10 07	80	60
15	Summit Point	15 00		
10	Sutton	7 18		
10	Tavenersville	14 10		1 00
50	Union	100 00	10 01	17 90
10	Waverly	10 05	55	
25	Wellsburg	51 44		5 00
.....	Welch			
75	Weston	82 95		21 90
425	Wheeling, St. Matthew's	425 00	15 00	113 85
175	" St. Luke's	175 00	16 10	85 25
15	" St. Andrew's	19 85		4 00
5	" St. Paul's	14 77		4 01
10	White Sulphur			
5	Willow Island	4 02		
25	Williamstown	22 19	2 12	1 00
.....	Williamson	5 22		
.....	Winfield	7 00		
.....	Boone County	8 80		
.....	Rev. C. M. Campbell	1 00		
...	Interest and Earnings			281 00
	Total Income	3,187 27	165 99	868 94
	Balance June 1, 1903	1.878 18	148 03	5,669 21
		5,065 45	314 02	6,538 15
	Total Payments	3,937 48	300 00	680 00
	Balances June 1. 1904	1.127 97	14 02	5,898 15

PAYMENTS, DIOCESAN MISSIONS.

Rev. J. A. Hyatt	$ 225 00
Rev. Geo. C. Shaw	255 00
Rev. E. D. Irvine	240 00
Rev. J. H. Gibbons	50 00
Rev. E. B. Sneade	324 99
Rev. A. G. Grinnan	50 00
Rev. John F. Woods	233 33
Rev. John F. Woods, for Church News	25 00
Rev. G. A. Gibbons	250 00
Rev. R. U. Brooking	16 67
Rev. John Warnock	110 00
Rev. J. D. Miller	58 33
Rev. John S. Gibson	50 00
Rev. T. C. Darst	75 00
Rev. A. J. Willis	50 00
Rev. G. W. Easter	100 00

Rev. P. B. Stauffer	300 00
Rev. C. C. Pearson	100 00
Rev. G. H. Crook	250 00
Rev. E. H. Brosius	166 00
Rev. J. L. Fish	75 00
Rev. R. W. Meade	87 50
Rev. A. B. Mitchell	133 33
Rev. F. V. R. Moore	125 00
Rev. F. A. Meade	133 33
Rev. C. H. Maloney	125 00
Rev. R. R. Windley	125 00
Miss Elizabeth P. Barber	120 00
Rev. W. I. Williams	12 50
Mission Boxes	65 00
Printing	6 50
	$3,937 48

PAYMENTS, RELIGIOUS AND THEOLOGICAL EDUCATION.

February 23, 1904, P. P. Phillips, Treasurer	$ 200 00
May 24, 1904, P. P. Phillips, Treasurer	100 00
Total Payment	$ 300 00

PAYMENTS, WIDOWS, ORPHANS AND DISABLED CLERGY FUND.

Mrs. Lee	$ 150 00
Mrs. Mason	150 00
Mrs. Leavell	100 00
Rev. C. M. Campbell	150 00
Col A. Herbert	80 00
Total Payments	$630 00

RECAPITULATION.

LEDGER BALANCES.

Widows, Orphans and Disabled Clergy Fund		$5,898 15
Diocesan Missions		1,127 97
Religious and Theological Education		14 02
Total to be accounted for		$7,040 14
Bonds, Notes and Securities in hands of Treasurer	$6,747 00	
Cash in Bank	293 14	
		$7,040 14

Respectfully submitted.

LAWRENCE E. SANDS, *Treas.*

June 1, 1904.

REPORT OF TRUSTEE OF EPISCOPAL AND CONTINGENT FUNDS.

Beginning June 1st, 1903, and Ending May 31st, 1904.

NAME OF PARISH	Amount Assessed	Amount Paid	Amount Paid on Arrears	Amount Not Assessed
Alderson	$ 6 00	$ 2 83	$ 1 75	$
Berkeley Springs	30 00	17 25		
Bluefield	30 00	30 00		
Princeton	6 00			
Bramwell	30 00		30 00	
Eckman and McDowell Missions	20 00	20 00		
Brooke County, St. John's	5 00			
Buckhannon	10 00	10 00		
Bunker Hill	5 00			
Charleston, St. John's	275 00	275 00		
Charleston, St. Luke's	7 00			
Charleston, St. Matthew's	7 00			
Charles Town, Zion	425 00	425 00		
Charles Town, St. Phillip's	5 00	5 00	5 00	
St. Andrew's on the Mountain	2 00			
Clarksburg	125 00	125 00	125 00	
Cresaps	5 00			
Davis	8 00	8 00		
Elkins Mission	10 00	10 00		
Fairmont	100 00	100 00		
Grafton	15 00			
Harper's Ferry	20 00		15 25	
Hedgesville	50 00	50 00		
Hinton	20 00			
Huntington	100 00	100 00	90 00	
Kenova	7 00	5 00		
Lewisburg	10 00			
Ronceverte	8 00			
Martinsburg	100 00	100 00		
Middleway	30 00	30 00		
Summit Point	30 00	30 00		
Lee Town	30 00	37 00		
Moorefield	20 00	20 00		
Romney	16 60	16 00		
Okonoko	10 00	10 00		
Morgantown	25 00	25 00	6 00	
Moundsville	60 00	60 00		
Nuttallburg	10 00			
Parkersburg, Trinity	525 00	525 00		
Parkersburg, Good Shepherd	5 00	17 00		
Parkersburg, St. Stephen	2 00			
Tavennersville	3 00			
Point Pleasant, Christ	50 00	50 00		
Bruce Chapel	12 00	12 00		
Spillman Mission	10 00	10 00		
Powellton	20 00	20 00	29 00	
Ansted	20 00	20 00		
Ravenswood, Grace	10 00			
Ripley, St. John's	15 00			
Liverpool, Whittle	2 00			
Ripon	20 00		20 00	
Shepherdstown	75 00	68 50		
Sistersville	40 00	40 00	23 75	
New Martinsville	40 00	40 00	21 50	
Smithfield, Wetzel County	5 00			
Spruce Chapel	4 00	2 00	4 00	
St. Albans	10 00	10 00	6 68	
Montgomery	15 00	15 00	15 00	
St Mary's	15 00	5 00	5 00	
Sutton	10 00			
Union	50 00	58 75		
White Sulphur	10 00			
Fort Spring	5 00			
Waverley	5 00	5 00		
Wellsburg	25 00	25 00		
Weston	80 00	80 00		

REPORT OF TRUSTEE OF EPISCOPAL AND CONTINGENT FUNDS.—Continued.

NAME OF PARISH	Amount Assessed	Amount Paid Out	Amount Paid on Arrears	Amount Not Assessed
Wheeling, St. Matthew's	$ 600 00	$ 600 00	$	$
Wheeling, St. Luke's	175 00	150 00		
Wheeling, St. Andrew's	10 00	10 00		
Chester	4 00			
Williamson	5 00			
Wheeling, St. Paul's, Elm Grove	10 00			
Williamstown	15 00	2 50		
Willow Island	3 00			
Beckley	6 00			
Beury	5 00			
DuBree	5 00			
Glen Jean	10 00			
Immanuel, Mt. Carbon	5 00	5 00		
Winfield—Rev. J. H. Gibbons				2 00
Hartford				2 00
St. Andrews, Mannington				14 18
Little Otter				2 50
Centralia				5 00
Grace Chapel, Newport, Wood County				3 00
Totals	$3,680 00	$3,277 33	$397 93	$28 68

RECEIPTS.

Amount received on this year's assessment	$3,277 33
Amount received on arrears	397 93
Amount received from Missions not assessed	28 68
Amount received discount on Tribune bill	5 50
Amount received interest from Permanent Fund	1,985 00
Total	$5,694 44

DISBURSEMENTS.

Paid Rt. Rev. G. W. Peterkin	$2,000 00
Paid Bishop Coadputor W. L. Gravatt	2,500 00
Paid R. D. Roller, Sec'y (salary and postage)	103 50
Paid Tribune Company (printing Journal)	305 24
Paid Rev. J. S. Gibson (examining chaplain)	35 11
Paid Standing Committee (Rev. G. A. Gibbons)	22 35
Paid News Publishing Co., (Memorial Leaflets)	66 00
Paid U: S. Express Co., on Memorial Leaflets	16 24
Paid L. E. Sands (printing and postage) 6	10 00
Paid West Va. Printing Co	2 75
Paid Miss Henderson for Trustee Report (last year)	2 00
Paid rent of house for Bishop Coadjutor	300 00
Total	$5,363 19

RECAPITULATION.

Balance on hand, June 1st, 1903	$ 235 57	
Total receipts for year from every source	$5,694 44	
		$5,930 01
Bishops' salaries	$4,500 00	
Contingent expenses	863 19	
Balance on hand, June 1st, 1904	566 82	
		$5,930 01

REPORT OF THE TRUSTEES OF THE PERMANENT FUND OF THE DIOCESE OF WEST VIRGINIA FOR THE PERIOD EDNING MAY 18. 1904.

By order of Council of 1902, the Central Banking and Security Company, of Parkersburg, West Virginia, was named as Treasurer of the Permanent Fund. The accounts given below include transactions had by the Trustees direct, as well as those occurring with the Treasurer.

The accompanying statement shows in the hands of the Treasurer on May 18, 1904, the following:

1. Listed as Investments, pledges, etc.	$33,618 00
2. Cash	1,913 56
	$35,531 56
The Trustees also hold 2 pledges on Parkersburg list	250 00
	$35,781 56

The report made to the Council of 1903, published in the Journal for that year (pp. 86 to 92), closed on May 18, 1903, and showed the condition of the fund on that day to be (p. 86 of Journal):

Investments, pledges, etc.	$18,412 00
Cash	8,198 51
	$26,610 51

And on page 92 of the *Journal of 1903* is found a supplemental report, made after adjournment of Council, in order to show contributions, received from the offerings in commemoration of the 25th Anniversary of the Consecration of the first Bishop of the Diocese, Rt. Rev. Geo. W. Peterkin—Ascension Day, May 21, 1903.

That supplemental report at page 94 shows that the increase of the fund during the year, including session of Council of 1903, was $13,301.48.

To conform to the Treasurer's accounts and to official statements made to Council, we avoid confusion by now ignoring the supplemental report, and recur to the regular report of 1903, duly presented at Wheeling May 20, 1903, including May 18 of that year.

PRESENT CONDITION OF THE FUND.

Securities, bonds, pledges, notes and certificates shown by accompanying certificate	$33,618 00
Cash on hand	1,913 56

Pledges in hands of Trustees		250 00
		$35,781 56
Amount due from interest overpaid		138 06
Total resources		$35,919 62
Total reported to Council of 1903		26,610 51
Increase		9,309 11

In order to ascertain the increase of the funds since the Council of 1902, when the effort commenced to raise the Anniversary Fund—

We take the present aggregate	$35,781 56
Deduct amount reported in 1902	22,333 44
	$13,448 12
Add interest overdrawn	138 96
	$13,586 18

Detailed Statement of Receipts and Disbursements.

1903.			Interest.	
May 18	Bal. cash as per last statement			$8,198 51
May 19	Interest 6 mos. W. H. Wolfe note		150.00	
June 12	J. C. Smith Paid note $25, int. .69		69	25 00
June 12	A. T. Kreps, interest		90 00	
June 17	Subscription W. J. Robb	$ 20 00		
June 17	Subscription Mr. and Mrs. W. H. Smith	250 00		
June 17	Subscription Th. L. Broun	50 00		320 00
Aug. 4	Th. L. Broun note $100, int. $2.50		3 50	100 00
	J. H. Grimm, int. 30, Pyth Castle $15, Traders Co., $15		60 00	
Aug 17	Sub. B. M. Ambler, $250, Dr. Sharp $25			275 00
Oct. 12	St. Matthews, Mannington, paid note			300 00
Oct. 12	Interest Citizens B. A		60 00	
Oct. 30	H. H. Moss, acct. sub			62 50
Nov. 3	Int. Pyth Castle, $15		15 00	
	Subs. G. L. Watson on acct			125 00
	Trinity Church, Martinsburg			1 00
	Subs. W. N. Chancellor			250 00
	Subs. Mr. and Mrs. C. C. Martin on acct			125 00
Nov. 20	Interest Mrs. Laird		180 00	
Dec. 3	Pd. by Bp. Peterkin			5 00

Dec 9	Int. W. H. Wolfe, $150, Mrs. Tavenner, $105..	255 00	
Dec. 28	A. T. Kreps int. $90, St. Marys Ch. $27......	117 00	
	St. Marys on acct. debt....................		47 00
1904.			
Jan. 13	Int. Traders Co. $15, H. D. Perkins $75......	90 00	
Jan. 30	Int. N. A. Ogdin $60 (Feb. 1) S L. Gould $252	312 00	
Feb. 8	J. H. Grimm paid note $1,000, int. $30.......	30 00	1,000 00
Feb. 19	Interest Mrs. Laird........................	90 00	
Mar 2	Elm Grove $2.76, St. Marks, St. Albans, $1.80.		4 56
Mar. 7	H. H. Moss, bal. subs. $187.50, int. $12......	12 00	187 50
Apr. 9	Trinity Ch., Wheeling, $2.11................		2 11
Apr. 9	Interest Citizens B. A.....................	60 00	
Apr. 15	St. Marys Ch. pd. on note $60, int. $6.25.....	6 25	60 00
Apr. 20	Int. Mrs. Tavenner, $64.75, Trinity, Huntington, $2.75	64 75	2 75
May 7	Interest note Christ Church, Clarksburg,	144 00	
	Good Shepherd, $2; Shepherdstown, $1.27; Miss Gordon, $5; All Sts. Union, $7.45; Kanawha Parish, $3		18 72
	Subs. J. T. Waters, $30; St. Anns N. M., $12.10		42 10
	Christ Church, Williamstown		3 00
May 17	Int. Pyth Castle, $15; W. H. Wolfe, $150......	165 00	
		$1,905 19	$11,154 75

The following were received at Council of 1903 and shortly afterwards:

J. W. Norris	10 00	
W. T. Grier	3 00	
J. A. Davenport	5 00	
V. Johnson, Treasurer....................	7 92	
Rev. J. S. Douglas	69	
C. T. Hiteshew	5 00	
H. P. Moss	10 00	
P. E. Ch. Morgantown	136 27	
Jos. Bryan	100 00	277 80
C. Y. Ligon	10 00	
Mrs. J. J. Coyner	7 50	17 50
Elizabeth C. Breeze, Berkeley Springs....	10 00	
Mrs. McSherry, Martinsburg	12 00	
C. C. Boyer, Tr, Christ Ch. Pt. Pleasant....	32 50	
A. A. Roush, Treas. C. (C. & M. Co.) Spilman	12 00	
Rev. Guy H. Crook, Ronceverte...........	35 00	

Same	43 50		
Bishop Peterkin, Chap. Good Shepherd, Parkersburg	250 00		
St. Lukes P. E. Church, Wheeling	586 74		
St. Matthews P. E. Church	3,543 75		
St. Andrews P. E Church	67 48		
Trinity Church, Huntington	100 00		
C. C. Coe, Cashier, Kenova	21 00		
Robt. H. Browse, St. Marys	100 00		
Geo. C. Thomas, Philadelphia	500 00		
St. Pauls Church, Sistersville	31 89		
J. D. Miller, Harpers Ferry	37 00		
St. Ann's P. E. Church, New Martinsville	50 00		
Romney, W Va	446 25		
Moorefield	17 27		
Okonoko	8 25		
Paw Paw	8 14		
Cash	30		
All Saints Union	37 95		
Messiah, Alderson	1 00		
St. John's Church, Charleston	669 88		
W. D. Tyler, Treasurer, Bramwell	38 44		
L. E. Sands, Treasurer—			
Berkeley Springs	14 00		
Ravenswood	40 00		
St. Marys	10 00		
Bluefield	5 65		
Hedgeville	8 05		
Plate Collection	135 99		
Trinity Church, Moundsville	150 00		7,024 03
Mrs. Kate A. Smith	20 00		
Mrs. L. R. Via	2 00		
Mrs. S. V. Wilcox	5 00		
A member	5 00		32 00
All Saints Church Moundsville			2 41
Emmanuel Church, Moorefield			6.05
Several coupons paid			37 00
		$1,905 19	$18,551 62
			1,905 19
Total			$20,456 81

Disbursements.

1903.		
May 18	Loaned to S. L. Gould, on mortgage	$ 6,000 00
June 18	Loaned to H. H. Pennybacker, mortgage	2,000 00
June 22	Loaned to Mrs. J. A. Tavenner and Miss Tavenner	3,500 00
July 9	Loaned to H. D. Perkins	2,500 00
July 11	Paid stenographic work	5 00
July 11	Paid Parkersburg Sentinel, printing report	13 25
July 11	Loaned N. A. Ogdin	2,000 00
Aug. 16	Paid printing circulars 25th Anniversary	25 00
Aug. 16	Paid Postage and distribution	15 00
Sept. 1	Check to R. M. Browne, trustee, Bishop's salary	485 00
Dec. 16	Check to R. M. Browne, trustee, Bishop's salary	700 00
1904.		
Mar. 28	Check to R. M. Broune, trustee, Bishop's salary	800 00
Apr. 14	Loaned C. B. Gordon $4,000, out of which paid $3,500 owed by Mrs. Tavenner, as above and assumed by Mr. Gordon, check for difference	500 00
Balance of cash on hand		1,913 56
		$20,456 81

Interest Account.

Total interest received		$ 1,905 19
Paid to R. M. Browne, Treas. for Bishops' salaries, etc.	$1,985 00	
Sundry accounts	58 25	2,043 25
Overpaid		$ 138 06

Investments.

List of securities, bonds, notes, pledges and investments belonging to the Permanent Fund of the Diocese:

Bond No. 26 Traders Co., of Clarksburg	$ 500 00
Bond No. 8 Pythian Castle of Wheeling	500 00
Bal. note St. Marys Church, St. Marys	293 00
Note A. H. and A. T. Kreps, secured by mortgage	3,000 00
Note W. H. Wolfe and others	5,000 00
Note Jennie F. Laird and others, secured by mortgage	3,000 00
Certificate No. 276, Citizens B. A. Parkersburg	2,000 00
Note H. D. Perkins, secured by mortgage	2,500 00
Note C. B. Gordon, secured by mortgage	4,000 00
Note S. L. Gould, secured by mortgage	6,000 00
Note N. A. Ogdin, secured by mortgage	2,000 00

Note H. H. Pennybacker, secured by mortgage..................		2,000 00
Unpaid pledges heretofore reported.................\$	60 00	
Sundry certificates, cupons attached................	470 00	
Notes given as subscriptions..........................	2,295 00	2,825 00
		\$33,618 00
Cash on hand		1,913 56
Total assets in hands of Central Banking & S. Co...............\$		35,531 56
The Trustees hold balance unpaid on 2 pledges, made on Parkersburg list to Anniversary Fund..........................		250 00
Present aggregate of fund ....\$		35,781 56
To this should be added amount overpaid of interest account to be restored out of income		138 06
		\$35,919 62

Certificate

This is to certify that Central Banking and Security Company, of Parkersburg, West Virginia, had on hand, at close of business on May 18, 1904, bonds, notes, pledges, and items of credit belonging to the Trustees of the Permanent Fund of the Protestant Episcopal Church for the Diocese of West Virginia \$33,618 00

And cash to credit of Chairman of said Trustees to amount of 1,913 56 \$35,531 56

CENTRAL BANKING & SECURITY CO.,

By W. H. OGDIN, *Cashier*

The Trustees again request that all remittances for this fund be made to Central Banking and Security Co., Parkersburg, W. Va.

Respectfully submitted on behalf of the Trustees.

Parkersburg, May 18, 1904.

APPENDIX B.

Parochial Reports for the Year Ending April 30th, 1904, Arranged According to Alphabetical Clergy List.

PAROCHIAL REPORTS

FOR THE YEAR ENDING APRIL 30th, 1904.

PAROCHIAL REPORT.

Rev. JNO. S. ALFRIEND, address Charles Town. Zion Church, St. Andrew's Parish, Charles Town, Jefferson county. Present minister took charge March 1st, 1902.

Church Officers—Church Wardens, B. C. Washington, Frank Beckwith; other vestrymen, S. W. Washington, Geo. Eyster, Wm. Packett, Joseph Trapnell, Claiborne Green, Richard Henderson, Scott Kennedy, Richard Alexander, Jno. W. Russell, Thornton Perry; Registrar, S. W. Washington, address, Charles Town; Treasurer, S. W. Washington, address Charles Town; Superintendent of Sunday Schools, B. C. Washington, Charles Town, W. Va.; Sunday School Secretary and Treasurer, Richard Alexander; Lay Reader, Joseph Trapnell.

Official Acts—Baptisms, infants 8, adults 2, total 12; presented for confirmation since last report 9, marriages 3, burials 12, catechisings 25, public services, Sundays, 116, other days 140, total 256; holy communion, public 27, private 2, total 29.

Communicants—Number last reported 326, received by letter 2, admitted by confirmation 9, added otherwise 1, total gain 12; died 5, total loss 5; net gain 7; present number notal 333.

Congregations—Baptized persons connected with parish 450, confirmed persons connected with parish 350, families 160, number sittings in church 600, number free sittings 100, number sittings in chapel 150, number sittings in Sunday school room 150.

Rector's Salary—As pledged from this congregation $1,250.00.

Organizations—Sunday schools, officers and teachers, male 5, female 11, total 16; pupils, male 34, female 66, total 100; advent offerings $35.00, lenten offerings $40.00, other offerings $10.00, total Sunday School offerings $85.00; Brotherhood of St. Andrew, members 10; Woman's Auxiliary, members 70; Library Association, 10; Babies' Branch Auxiliary, 20; St. Andrew's Guild, 40; Mexican Guild, 10; Chancel Chapter, 5; Children of the King, 20; Rector's Aid Society, 10.

Property—Church, brick, insurance $9,000, value $13,000; rectory, brick, insurance $2,475 value $5,000; parish house, brick, insurance $1,600, value $3,000; total insurance, $13,075; total value, $21,000; indebtedness on church, $200.00.

FINANCIAL REPORT.

Receipts—For all purposes—Cash on hand, per last report, $36.32; pledges and subscriptions, $285.49; pew rent, $2,423.63; collections in church, $1,674.21; thank offerings, $343.96; Sunday School, $105.75; Woman's Auxiliary, money, $147.59; Woman's Auxiliary, boxes, value, $69.93; Guilds or other societies, $996.37; contributions from without, $88.00; income from other sources, $170.75; total receipts for all purposes, $6,342.00.

Disbursements—For Current Expenses—Salary of rector, $1,250.00; other salaries, $400.00; insurance, $112.75; ordinary repairs, $152.25; other current expenses, $234.31; total for current expenses, $2,149.31. *Contributions—For Objects in the Parish*—Communion alms, $55.00; Parish Missions, $1,156.30; maintaining Sunday Schools, $93.57; payment on debts for building, etc., $401.95; total contributions for objects in the parish, $1,706.82. *Contributions—For Objects in the Diocese*—Salary of Bishop, $425.00; Diocesan missions, $300.00; Convocation missions, $117.50; Widows and orphans, aged and disabled clergy fund, $41.65; religious and theologican education, $44.13; Sheltering Arms Hospital, $50.19; Bishop's Special Fund, $132.46; other objects, $229.99; total contributions for objects in the Diocese, $1,340.92. *Contributions—For Objects Without the Diocese*—Domestic Missions General, $107.04; Jews, $20.41; total Domestic Missions, $127.45. Foreign Missions General, $179.95; for Africa, $25.00; for Mexico, $69.00; through American Church Missionary Society, $166.50; Brazil, $273.32; total Foreign Missions, $713.77; General Clergy Relief Fund, $11.76; total contributions for objects without the Diocese, $852.98.

Financial Summary—Current expenses raised by congregation as above, $2,149.31. *Contributions*—For objects in the parish, $1,706.82; for objects in the diocese, $1,340.92; for objects without the diocese, $852.98; total of contributions, $3,900.72; all money raised by the congregation for current expenses and for contributions, $6,050.03; cash in hand, $291.97.

PAROCHIAL REPORT.

Rev. JNO. S. ALFRIEND, address Charles Town. Blue Ridge Mission, on the Mount, Jefferson county. Date of organization, 1891. Present minister took charge March 1, 1902.

Church Officers—Superintendent of Sunday Schools, Jno. Howell, Charles Town.

Official Acts—Baptisms, infants, 3; presented for confirmation since last report 1, marriages 2, burials 1, public services, Sundays, 18; Holy Communion, public, 2.

Communicants—Number last reported, 28; admitted by confirmation 1, total gain, 1; net gain, 1; present number total, 29.

Congregations—Baptized persons connected with parish, 40; confirmed persons connected with parish, 28; families, 25; number of sittings in church, 150; number free sittings, all; number sittings in chapel, 150.

Organizations—Sunday Schools, officers and teachers, male, 2; female, 5; total, 7; pupils, male, 30; female, 40; total, 70. Advent, Lenten and other offerings, $5.00; parish schools, officers and teachers, 2; scholars, 15; total, 17; mothers meetings, 10; children's society, 15.

Property—Church, wood, insurance, $600.00; value, $600; Deaconess Home, Wood, insurance, $600.00; value, $600.00; total insurance, $1,200.00; total value, $1,200.00. Money raised from outside sources, $600.00; for what objects used, building of the Deaconess House.

FINANCIAL REPORT.

Receipts—For all Purposes—Collections in church, $15.00; Sunday School, $5.00; contributions from without, $800.00; income from other sources, $475.00; total receipts for all purposes, $1,295.00.

Disbursements—For Current Expenses—Deaconess, $475.00, not raised by congregation. *Contributions—For Objects in the Parish*—Extraordinary repairs and improvements, $200.00; other objects, $5.00; building the Deaconess House, $600.00; total contributions for objects in the parish, $805.00. *Contributions—For Objects in the Diocese*—Sheltering Arms Hospital, $15.00.

Financial Summary—Contributions—For objects in the parish, $5; for objects in the diocese, $15; total of contributions, $20.

Remarks—This work so long carried on by the parish is now by consent of the bishops, rector and vestry of Zion Church to be admitted into the diocese as an independent Mission with permission of Council.

JNO. S. ALFRIEND.

PAROCHIAL REPORT.

Rev. JNO. S. ALFRIEND, address Charles Town. Harewood Mission, Harewood, Jefferson county. Present minister took charge March 1, 1902.

Church officers—Superintendent of Sunday School, A. G. Wynkoop, Charles Town, W. Va.

Official Acts—Public services, Sundays, 12.

Organizations—Sunday Schools, officers and teachers, male, 2; female, 3;

total, 5; pupils, male, 25; female, 15; total, 40. Location of schools mentioned above, Harewood, Jefferson county.

Disbursements—Sheltering Arms Hospital, $10.00.

Financial Summary—Collections in church, $10.00.

Remarks—This is a Mission point with no organization. Sunday School is held every Sunday from Easter to Christmas. I held service and preached here one Sunday afternoon in the month. Most of the children and all of teh adult congregation are connected with other denominations.

JNO. S. ALFRIEND, *Rector.*

PAROCHIAL REPORT.

Rev. JACOB BRITTINGHAM, address 66 S. Penn. Street. St. Lukes Church, The Island Parish, Wheeling, Ohio county. Date of organization, June 22, 1881. Present minister took charge, March 3, 1889.

Church Officers—Church Wardens, Lawrence E. Sands, Edward B. Bowie; other vestrymen, W. A. Wilson, Charles H. Copp; A. A. Taylor, Wylie Irwin, R. M. Wolff, Thos. Johns, Geo. J. Rogers; Registrar, W. Alfa Wilson, address care R. G. Dunn & Co.; Treasurer, Lawrence E. Sands, address Care National Exchange Bank; Superintendent of Sunday Schools, Lawrence E. Sands, Wheeling Island, W. Va.; Sunday School Secretary and Treasurer, Robt. L. Boyd; Lay Reader, A. A. Taylor.

Official Acts—Baptisms, infants, 17; adults, 2; total, 19; presented for confirmation since last report, 13; marriages, 5; burials, 17; catechisings, 6; public services, Sundays, 94; other days, 72; total, 166. Holy Communion, public, 15; private, 2; total, 17.

Communicants—Number last reported, 266; received by letter, 3; admitted by confirmation, 13; added otherwise, 2; total gain, 18; died, 4; transferred, 8; removed without letter, 11; lapsed, 2; total loss, 25; net loss, 6; present number total, 260.

Congregations—Baptized persons connected with parish, 281; confirmed persons connected with parish, 382; families, 171; individuals not thus included, 31; whole number of individuals, 413; number sittings in church, all free, 400; number of sittings in parish house, 200; number of sittings in Sunday School room, 200.

Rector's Salary—As pledged from this congregation, $1,500.

Organizations—Sunday School, officers and teachers, male, 3; female, 7; total, 10; pupils, male, 20; female, 60; total, 80; advent offerings, $15.50; lenten, $46.00; other offerings, $63.50; total Sunday School offerings, $125.00; Woman's Auxiliary, members, 18; King's Daughters, 44; Chancel Chapter, 18; Junior King's Daughters, 14.

Property—Church, frame, insurance, $6,000; value, $12,000; rectory, frame, insurance, $2,000; value, $5,000; parish house, frame, $4,500; value,

$9,000; organ, value, $2,500; total insurance, $12,500; total value, $28,500. indebtedness, about $400 in debt for current obligations, will pay it off shortly; now enlarging the rectory.

FINANCIAL REPORT.

Receipts—For all Purposes—Pledges and subscriptions, $2,213.69; collections in church, $1,221.06; money borrowed, $400.00; Sunday School, $125.00; Woman's Auxiliary, money, $70.00; Woman's Auxiliary, boxes, value, $100.80; King's Daughters, $223.20; Chancel Chapter, $227.52; total receipts for all purposes, $4,581.27.

Disbursements—For Current Expenses—Salary of rector, $1,500.00; other salaries, $673.50; insurance, $94.50; ordinary repairs, $37.69; other current expenses, $275.19; total for curent expenses, $2,580.88. *Contributions—For Objects in the Parish*—Communion alms, $26.50; payment on debts for building, &c., $1,000.00; total 'contributions for objects in the parish, $1,026.51. *Contributions—For Objects in the Diocese*—Salary of Bishops, $150.00; Diocesan Missions, $175.00; Convocation Missions, $10.00; Widows and Orphans, Aged and Disabled Clergy Fund, $35.25; Religious and Theological Education, $16.10; Sheltering Arms Hospital, $34.80; Bishop's Special Fund, $100.00; Central Fund Auxiliary, $2.00; box for Sheltering Arms, $14.00; total contributions for objects in the diocese, $537.15. *Contributions—For Objects Without the Diocese*—Domestic Missions General, $57.23; Jews, $3.10; total Domestic Missions, $60.33. Foreign Missions General, $51.01; China, $40.00 Brazil, insurance, $5.00; total Foreign Missions, $91.01; Barnesville, Ohio, $50.00; church box to Kentucky missionary, $866.80; cash, to Kentucky missionary, $25.00; total contributions for objects without the diocese, $313.14.

Financial Summary—Current expenses raised by congregation as above, $2,580.88; *Contributions*—for objects in the parish, $1,026.51; for objects in the diocese, $537.15; for objects without the diocese, $313.14; total contributions, $1,876.80; all money raised by the congregation for current expenses and for contributions, $4,457.68; overdrawn, $76.41.

PAROCHIAL REPORT.

Rev. E. H. BROSSIUS, address Bluefield, W. Va. Christ Church, Bluefield Parish, Bluefield, Mercer county. Date of Organization, May 20, 1903. Present minister took charge December 1, 1901.

Church Officers—Church Wardens, Geo. H. Hill, E. H. Smith; other vestrymen, T. H. Becker, G. H. Wade, W. H. B. Loving, R. C. Turner, R. A. Lacy, E. A. Blake, F. R. Wadleigh; Registrar, R. A. Lacy, address Bluefield; Treasurer, R. C. Turner, address, Bluefield; Superintendent of Sunday Schools, E. H. Brosius; Sunday School Secretary and Treasurer, E. H. Brosius.

Official Acts—Baptisms, infants, 5; presented for confirmation since last report, 2; marriages, 2; burials, 3; public services, Sundays, 71; other days, 15; total, 86; Holy Communion, public, 20; private, 1; total, 21.

Communicants—Number last reported, 91; admitted by confirmation, 2; added otherwise, 38; total gain, 40; died, 1; removed without letter, 24; total loss, 25; net gain, 15; present number total, 106.

Congregations—Baptized persons connected with parish, 181; confirmed persons connected with parish, 106; families, 57; individuals not thus included, 26; whole number of individuals, 205; number of scattered communicants in your section not connected with any parish, 2; number sittings in church, 200; number free sittings, 200;.

Rector's Salary—As pledged from this congregation, $466.70; from Diocesan Missions, $150.00; from General Board, $100.00; as pledged from other congregations, $83.30; total, $800.00.

Organizations—Sunday Schools, officers and teachers, male, 1; female, 3; total, 4; pupils, male, 15; female, 14; total, 29; Advent offering, $7.85; Lenten offering, $18.26; other offerings, $17.89; total Sunday School offerings, $44.00; Ladies' Guild, Chancel Chapter, Social Guild, Charity Chapter.

Property—Church, wood, insurance, $1,500; value, $2,000; rectory, wood, insurance, $800.00; value, $1,500.00; total insurance, $2,300; total value, $3,500.00; indebtedness, organ, $312.00; total indebtedness, $312.00.

FINANCIAL REPORT.

Receipts—For all Purposes—Cash on hand, per last report, $65.22; pledges and subscriptions, $767.63; collections in church, $109.98; money borrowed, $312.00; thank offering, Easter, $77.67; Sunday School, $44.00; Guilds, or other societies, $330.61; contributions from without, $179.46; total receipts for all purposes, $1,886.57.

Disbursements—For Current Expenses—Salary or rector, $466.70; other salaries, sexton, $72.00; ordinary repairs, $5.20; interest on debt, $12.82; other current expenses, $108.20; total for current expenses, $664.92. *Contributions—For Objects in the Parish*—Communion alms, $12.50; extraordinary repairs and improvements, $569.22; maintaining Sunday Schools, $44.00; payment on debts for building, &c., $140.46; other objects, organ, $312.00; total contributions for objects in the parish, $1,078.12; *Contributions—For Objects in the Diocese*—Salary of Bishops, $30.00; Permanent Fund, $5.65; Diocesan Missions, $30.00; Convocation Missions, $16.00; Sheltering Arms Hospital, $5.30; total contributions for objects in the diocese, $86.95. *Contributions— For Objects Without the Diocese—Domestic* Missions General, $16.02; Foreign Missions General, $16.02; total contributions for objects without the diocese, $32.05.

Financial Summary—Current Expenses raised by Congregation as above,

$664.92. *Contributions*—For objects in the parish, $1.078.18; for objects in the diocese, $86.95; for objects without the diocese, $32.05; total contributions, $1,862.10; all money raised by the congregation for current expenses and for contributions, $1,886.57; cash in hand, $24.47.

PAROCHIAL REPORT.

Rev. E. H. BROSIUS, address Bluefield, W. Va. Heavenly Rest Church, Heavenly Rest Mission, Princeton, Mercer county. Present minister took charge December 1, 1901.

Church Officers—Registrar, H. B. Barbor, address Princeton; Treasurer, H. B. Barbor.

Official Acts—Mariages, 2; public services, Sundays, 6; Holy Communion, public, 2.

Communicants—Number last reported, 18; added otherwise, 2; total gain, 2; removed without letter, 2; total loss, 2; present number total, 18.

Congregations—Baptized persons connected with parish, 20; confirmed persons connected with parish, 18; families, 10; number sittings in church 150.

Rector's Salary—As pledged from this congregation, $29.25; from Diocesan Missions, $150.00; from General Board, $100.00; as pledged from other congregations, $520.75; total, $800.00.

Property—Church wood. Indebtedness, due the minister, $23.25; due on diocesan assessment for Missions, $6.00; due on diocesan assessment for Bishop's Fund, $6.00; total indebtedness, $35.25.

FINANCIAL REPORT.

Receipts—For all Purposes—Pledges and subscriptions, $68.25.

Disbursements—For Current Expenses—Salary of rector, $36.00; ordinary repairs, $12.25; total for current expenses, $48.25. *Contributions for Objects in the Diocese*—Salary of Bishops, $6.00; Diocesan Missions, $6.00; Bishop's Special Fund, $8.00; total contributions for objects in the diocese, $20.00.

Financial Summary—Current expenses raised by congregations as above, $48.25; *Contributions*—For objects in the diocese, $20.00; total of contributions, $20.00; all money raised by the congregation for current expenses and for contributions. $68.25.

Remarks—No report from Athens, W. Va.

PAROCHIAL REPORT.

Rev. C. M. CAMPBELL, address Racine. Christ Church, Short Creek, Boone county. Present minister took charge April 1, 1902.

Official Acts—Burials, 2; public services, Sundays, 5; other days, 2; total, 7; Holy Communion, public, 1.

Communicants,—Number last reported, 2; present number total, 2.

Congregations—Baptized persons connected with parish, 8; confirmed persons connected with parish, 3; families, 3; individuals not thus included, 6; whole number of individuals, 14.

Property—Church, log, value, $400.

FINANCIAL REPORT.

Receipts—For all Purposes——Collection in church, $5.30.

Disbursements—Contributions—For Objects in the Diocese—Diocesan Missions, $3.80; Convocation Missions, 50 cents; total contributions for objects in the diocese, $4.30. *Contributions—For Objects Without the Diocese*—Through American Church Missionary Society, 50 cents; total Domestic Missions, 50 cents; Through American Missionary Society, 50 cents; total Foreign Missions, 50 cents; total contributions for objects without the diocese, $1.00.

Financial Summary—Contributions—For objects in the diocese, $4.30; for objects without the diocese, $1.00; total of contributions, $5.30; all money raised by the congregation for current expenses and for contributions, $5.30.

Remarks—Many more services and the Holy Communion several times, were announced, but not held, simply for lack of attendance. For six months past practically nothing has been done, but it is hoped that the Sunday School, which was closed early in November, can be reopened this summer if teachers ca nbe found. I have married one couple at Hernshaw, which is out of this county by several miles.

PAROCHIAL REPORT.

Rev. C. M. CAMPBELL, address Racine. St. Paul's Mission, Bull Creek, Boone county. Present minister took charge April 1, 1902.

Official Acts—Public services, Sundays, 2; other days, 4; total 6.

Communicants—Number last reported, 4; present number total, 4.

Congregations—Baptized persons connected with parish, 10; confirmed persons connected with parish, 4; families, 4; whole number of individuals, 10.

Remarks—No services have been held since the end of October, and there has been no Sunday School for more than a year. We have no one left at Emmanuel Mission, mouth of Robinson Creek, and I therefore send no separate report. Six (6) Sunday services, and three (3) on other days were held there however, last summer and fall; also one (1) service during the week at the Court House, Madison in the Southern Methodist Church.

PAROCHIAL REPORT.

Rev. WILSON PAGE CHRISMAN, address Moundsville, W. Va. Trinity Church, Trinity Parish, Moundsville, Marshall county. Date of organization, 1848. Present minister took charge June 1, 1902.

Church Officers—Church Wardens, V. A. Weaver, Friend Cox; other vestrymen, A. J. Martin, M. P. Hendrickson, J. T. Gallaher, C. L. Walton, J. M. Saunders, H. B. Tyler, J. D. Bruce; Registrar, J. T. Gallaher, address Moundsville, W. Va.; Treasurer, C. L. Walton, address Moundsville, W. Va.; Superintendent of Sunday Schools, W. P. Chrisman, Moundsville, W. Va.; Sunday School Secretary and Treasurer, H. B. Tyler.

Official Acts—Baptisms, infants, 3; adults, 2; total, 5; presented for confirmation since last report, 2; marriage, 3; burials, 5; public services, Sundays, 97; other days, 100; total, 197; Holy Communion, public, 24.

Communicants—Number last reported, 55; received by letter, 2; admitted by confirmation, 2; restored to communion, 1; added otherwise, 10; total gain, 15; died, 2; removed without letter, 1; lapsed, 3; total loss, 6; net gain, 9; present number total, 64.

Congregations—Baptized persons connected with parish, 153; confirmed persons connected with parish, 81; families, 50; individuals not thus included, 34; whole number of individuals, 168; number of scatered communicants in your section not connecter with any parish, 10; number sittings, in church, 200; number free sittings, 200; number sittings in chapel, 25; number sittings in Sunday School room, 225.

Rector's Salary—As pledged from this congregation, $1,250.00.

Organizations—Sunday Schools, officers and teachers, male, 4; female, 8; total, 12; pupils, male, 44; female, 65; total, 109; Advent offerings, $25.59; Lenten offerings, $42.83; other offerings, $47.09; total Sunday School offerings, $115.51; Industrial school, officers and teachers, 2; scholars, 23; total, 25; Trinity Guild, (a) Industrial Chapter, (b) Chancel Chapter.

Property—Church, frame, insurance, $4,000.00; value, $8,000.00; rectory, frame, insurance, $2,000.00; value, $5000.00; parish house brick, insurance, $5,000.00; value, $20,000.00; total insurance, $11,000.00; total value, $33,000. Indebtedness, on parish house, $3,300.00; total indebtedness, $3,300.00.

FINANCIAL REPORT.

Receipts—For all Purposes—Cash on hand, per last report, $62.81; pledges and subscriptions, $1,050.00; collections in church, $667.09; Sunday School, $115.51; guilds, or other societies, $366.09; income from other sources, $59.50; total receipts for all purposes, $2,321.00.

Disbursements—Salary of rector, $1,250.00; other salaries, $52.00; insurance, $30.00; other objects, $572.52; total for current expenses, $1,904.52. *Contributions—For Objects in the Parish*—Communion alms, $23.52; parish Missions, $3.70; parochial and industrial schools, $5.00; maintaining Sunday Schools, $4.87; other objects, $39.50; total contributions for objects in the parish, $76.59. *Contributions—For Objects in the Diocese*—Salary of Bishops, $60.00; permanent Fund, $5.15; Diocesan Missions, $44.30; Convocation Missions, $18.00; Widows and Orphans, Aged and Disabled Clergy Fund, $16.35; Religious and Theological Education, $5.00; Sheltering Arms Hospital, $11.20; Theological Seminary, $5.25; other objects, $5.00; total contributions for objects in the diocese, $170.25. *Contributions—For objects Without the Diocese*—Domestic Missions General, $16.48; colored people, $3.20; Indians, $3.95; deaf and dumb, $3.60; Jews, $3.86; Through American Church Missionary Society, $3.65; total Domestic Missions, $34.74; Foreign Missions General, $12.35; for Mexico, $2.52; Brazil, $1.00; Cuba, $1.00; total Foreign Missions, $16.87; American Church Building Fund, $3.15; General Clergy Relief Fund, $4.08; Bible and Prayer Book Society, $3.93; other objects, $57.83; total contributions for objects without the diocese, $120.60.

Financial Summary—Current expenses raised by congregation as above, $1,904.52. *Contributions*—For objects in the parish, $76.59; for objects in the diocese, $170.45; for objects without the diocese, $120.60; total contributions, $367.64; all money raised by the congregation for current expenses and for contribuions, $2, 272.16; cash in hand, $48.84.

PAROCHIAL REPORT.

Rev. THOS. J. OLIVER CURRAN, address Wheeling. St. Andrews, Wheeling, Ohio county. Present minister took charge Oct., 1900.

Church Officers—Treasurer, Wm. A. Carroll, address 3809 Jacob St.

Offical Acts—Baptism, infants 14, adults 5, total 19; marriages 12, burials 6, catechisings 44, public services, Sundays, 108, other days 75, total 183; Holy Communion, public 40, private 2, total 42.

Communicants—Number last reported 76, restored to communion 2, total gain 2; transferred 3, total loss 1, net loss 1, present number total 75.

Congregations—Baptized persons connected wth Parish 200, confirmed persons connected with Parish 75, families 15, individuals not thus included 25, whole number of individuals 315.

Rector's Salary—As pledged from this congregation $700.00, as pledged from other congregations $500.00, total $1,200.00.

Organizations—Sunday Schools, officers and teachers, male 2, female 4, total 6; pupils, male 60, female 70, total 130; advent offering $7.00, lenten offering $30.16, other offerings $239.30; total Sunday School offerings $276.46; Brotherhood of St. Andrew, members 4; St. Andrew's Guild 30 members.

Property—Church, wood, insurance $3,500.00.

FINANCIAL REPORT.

Receipts—For all purposes—Cash on hand, per last report $445.09, pledges and subscriptions $546.59, colections in Church $217.94, interest from investments $21.30, money borrowed $75.00 thank offerings 50 cts., Sunday School $276.46 Guilds or other societies $410.00, contributions from without $600.00, income from other sources $544.81, total receipts for all purposes $3,137.69.

Disbursements—For current expenses—Salary of Rector $1,269.12, other salaries $100.00, ordinary repairs $380.42, interest on debt $4.20, other current expenses $31.47, total for current expenses $1,785.21. *Contributions—For objects in the Parish*—Extraordinary repairs and improvements $125.00, maintaining Sunday Schools $172.26, flood sufferers $200.00, total contributions for objects in the Parish $497,26. *Contributions—For objects in the Diocese*—Salary of Bishops $10.00, diocesan missions $19.35, convocation missions $10.00, widows and orphans, aged and disabled clergy fund $5.00, Sheltering Arms Hospital $13.57, total contributions for objecis in the Diocese $57.92. *Contributions—For objects without the Diocese*—Domestic missions general and foreign $28.00, total contributions for objects without the Diocese $28.00.

Financial Summary—Contributions—For objects in the Parish $2,282.47, for objects in the Diocese $57.92, for objects without the Diocese $28.00, total contributions $2,368.39, all money raised by the congregation for curent expenses and for contributions $3,137.69, cash in hand $769.30.

PAROCHIAL REPORT.

Rev. JOHN S. DOUGLAS, address Martinsburg. Trinity Church, Norborne Mission, Martinsburg, Berkeley county. Date of organization 1769. Present minister took charge Oct. 1, 1899.

Church Officers—Church Wardens, Capt. W. B. Colston, C. A. Miller; other Vestrymen, Alexander Parks, John E. Boyd, Edward Rutledge, A. M. Gilbert, Dr. A. Andrews; Registrar, Capt. W. B. Colston, address Martinsburb; Treasurer, Edward Rutledge, address Martinsburg; Superintendent of Sunday Schools, Edward Rutledge, Martinsburg; Sunday School Secretary and Treasurer, C. A. Miller; lay reader, Edward Rutledge.

Official Acts—Baptism, infants, 11; total, 11; presented for confirmation since last report, 31; marriages, 2; burials, 5; catechisings, 15; public services, Sundays, 96, other days, 73; total, 169; Holy Communon, public, 18, private, 3; total, 21.

Communicants—Number last reported, 152; received by letter, 1; admitted by confirmation, 31; added otherwise, 2; total gain, 34; died, 2; removed without letter, 16; lapsed, 3; total loss, 21; net gain, 13; present number total, 165.

Congregations—Baptized persons connected with Parish, 280; confirmed persons connected with Parish, 180; families, 85; individuals not thus included, 15; whole number of individuals, 295; number sittings in Church, 350; number free sittings, 350; number sittings in Sunday School room, 250.

Rector's Salary—As pledged from this congregation, $800.00; total, $800.00.

Organizations—Sunday Schools, officers and teachers, male, 4; female, 11; total, 15; pupils, male, 40, female, 50; total, 105; advent offering, $25.00; lenten offering, $50.00; other offerings, $31.37; total Sunday School offerings, $106.37; other organizations, the Trinity Church Guild, under which have been working eight different Chapters.

Property—Church, brick, insurance $5,000, value $10,000; rectory, stone, insurance $1,500, value $7,000; Parish house, brick, insurance $2,000, value $5,000; new stable, brick, insurance $500, value $500; organ, insurance $1.800, value $1,800. *Indebtedness, on parish house, stable and approaches, $5,000. Other debts, organ, $108.64.

*$400.00 on hand to be applied on this debt, thus reducing it to $4,600.00.

FINANCIAL REPORT.

Receipts—For all purposes—Cash on hand, per last report, Tr. Guild, $304,87, Tr. Vestry, $78.33; pledges and subscriptions, $1,397.85; collections in Church, $651.84; money borrowed, $3,000.00; Sunday School, $106.37; Woman's Auxiliary, money, $140.16; Woman's Auxiliary boxes, value, $21.83; Guilds, or other societies, $563.30; contributions from without, local, 78.43; total receipts for all purposes, $6,342.92. *Disbursements—For current expenses*—Salary of rector, $800.04; other salaries, $198.67; insurance, $54.00; ordinary repairs, $32.25; interest on debt, $239.79; other current expenses, $250.24; total for current expenses, $1,574.99. *Contributions—For objects in the Parish*—Communion alms, $38.55; maintaining Sunday Schools, $29.30; other objects, $243.94; new parish house and approaches and new brick stable, $3,222.52; total contributions for objects in the Parish, $3,534.31. *Contributions—For objects in the Diocese*—Salary of Bishops, $100.00 permanent fund, $16.77; diocesan missions,

$125.47; convocation missions, $32.84; widows and orphans, aged and disabled clergy fund, $33.71; religious and theological education, $2.41; Sheltering Arms Hospital, $44.59; Bishop's special fund, $20.66; discretion of rector, $8.10; total contributions for objects in the Diocese, $384.55. *Contributions—For objects without the Diocese*—Domestic missions general, $51.16; colored people, $7.74; deaf and dumb, $8.71; through American Church Missionary Society, $30.10; total domestic missions, $97.71; foreign missions general, $137.81, Brazil, $15.06, Cuba, $15.05; total foreign missions, $167.92; American church building fund, $6.73; general clergy relief fund, $30.06; Bible and Prayer Book Society, $6.03; total contributions for objects without the Diocese, $308.45.

Financial Summary—Current expenses raised by congregation as above, $1,574.99. *Contributións*—For objects in the Parish, $534.31; for objects in the Diocese, $384.55; for objects without the Diocese, $308.45; total of contributions, $1,227 31; All money raised by the congregation for current expenses and for contributions, $2,802.30; cash in hand, $540.62.

Remarks—Note. That the cash on hand at the close of report April 30, 1903, was $78.33. To this amount we add at the beginning of this report, the balance of cash on hand held by the Treasurer of the Guild, separate and apart from the Treasurer of the Church. In like manner the balance in hands of Treasurer of the Guild is included in the amount of cash on hand at close of this report, April 30, 1904. While the money raised through the Guild has always been shown in former reports, the balances had not been carried along, and the report was, therefore, incomplete in this respect.

PAROCHIAL REPORT.

Rev. JOHN S. DOUGLAS, address Martinsburg. Christ Church, Bunker Hill Mission, Bunker Hill, Berkeley county. Date of organization, 1769. Present minister took charge Oct. 1, 1899.

Church Officers—Church Warden, Zeph S. Morgan; other Vestrymen, Joseph Morgan, J. K. Cunningham; Registrar, J. K. Cunningham, address Rest, Virginia; Treasurer, Zeph S. Morgan, address Inwood, W. Va.

Official Acts—Public services, Sundays, 18; total 18; Holy Communion, public, 2; total, 2.

Communicants—Number last reported, 7; added otherwise, 2; total gain, 2; removed without letter, 1; total loss, 1; net gain, 1; present number total, 8.

Congregations—Baptized persons connected with Parish, 15; confirmed persons connected with Parish, 7; families, 3; individuals not thus included, 1; number sittings in Church, 200; number free sittings, 200.

Property—Church, brick, value $1,500.00.

FINANCIAL REPORT.

Receipts—For all purposes—Collections in Church, $7.54; total receipts for all purposes, $7.54. *Disbursements—For current expences*—Total for current expenses, $3.97. *Contributions—For objects in the Diocese*—Diocesan missions, $1.57; convocation missions, 59 cts; total contributions for objects in the Diocese, $2.16. *Contributions—For objects without the Diocese*—Foreign missions general, 60 cts., Brazil, 84 cts.; total contributions for objects without the Diocese, $1.44.

Financial Summary—Current expenses raised by congregation as above, $3.97; for objects in the Diocese, $2.16; for objects without the Diocese, $1.44; total of contributions, $3.60; all money raised by the congregation for current expenses and for contributions, $7.57.

PAROCHIAL REPORT.

Rev. CREETUS A. DOWELL, address Sistersville, W. Va. St. Paul's Church, Tyler Parish, Sistersville, Tyler county. Present minister took charge April 266, 1903.

Church Officers—Church Wardens, George F. Durham, George B. Van Ambler; other Vestrymen, F. D. McCoy, Ed. Roome, Geo. B. Stocking, D. E. Thoenen, A. B. Hunt; Registrar, A. B. Hunt, address Sistersville; Treasurer, D. E. Thoenen, address Sistersville, Superintendent of Sunday Schools, Creetus A. Dowell, Sistersville; Sunday School Secretary and Treasurer, Mabel Choderdon.

Official Acts—Baptisms, infants, 5, adults, 8; total, 13; presented for confirmation since last report, 10; marriages, 4; burials, 3; catechisings, 25; public services, Sundays, 97, other days, 70; total 167; Holy Communion, public, 10; total, 10.

Communicants—Number last reported, 32; received by letter, 1; admitted by confirmation, 10; restored to communion, 1; added otherwise, 2; total gain, 14; died, 2; transferred, 1; removed without letter, 2; total loss, 5; net gain, 9; present number total, 41.

Congregations—Baptized persons connected with Parish, 64; confirmed persons connected with Parish, 44; families, 21; number of scattered communicants in your section not connected with any Parish, 3; number sittings in Church, 175; number free sittings, 175.

Rector's Salary—As pledged from this congregation, $800.00; total, $800.00.

Organizations—Sunday Schools, officers and teachers, male, 3; female, 8; total, 11; pupils, male, 29; female, 69; total, 98; advent offering, $7.50; lenten offering, $9.00; other offerings, $47.89; total Sunday School offerings, $64.39; Woman's Auxiliary members, 14; Young Woman's Guild, 16; Woman's Guild, 11.

Property—Church, frame, insurance $1,400, value $3,000; rectory, frame, insurance $2,000, value $3,500; total value, $6,500.

FINANCIAL REPORT.

Receipts—For all purposes—Cash on hand per last report, $78.60; pledges and subscriptions, $777.00; collections in Church, $516.89; Sunday School, $64.39; Woman's Auxiliary money, $42.05; Woman's Auxiliary boxes, value, $21.00; Guilds, or other societies, $335.00; income from other sources, $487.05; total receipts for all purposes, $2,321.98. *Disbursements—For current expenses*—Salary of rector, $800.00; salary of assistant, $222.50; ordinary repairs, $99.53; interest on debt, $20.36; other current expenses, $73.93; total for current expenses, $1,216.32. *Contributions—For objects in the Parish*—Communion alms, $21.44; extraordinary repairs and improvements, $349.28; maintaining Sunday Schools, $54.45; payment on debts for building, etc., $450.00; total contributions for objects in the Parish, $875.17. *Contributions—For objects in the Diocese*—Salary of Bishops, $44.25; permanent fund, $31.89; diocesan missions, $41,22; convocation missions, $2.50; widows and orphans, aged and disabled clergy fund, $9.32; religious and theological education, $7.75; Sheltering Arms Hospital, $11.36; other objects, $24.00; total contributions for objects in the Diocese, $172.29. *Contributions—For objects without the Diocese*—Domestic missions General, $21.30; through American Church Missionary Society, $9.49; total domestic missions, $30.79; foreign missions general, $8.45; Brazil, $9.48; Cuba, $9.48; total foreign missions, $27.41; total contributions for objects without the Diocese, $58.20.

Financial Summary—Current expenses raised by congregation as above, $1,216.32; for objects in the Parish, $875.17; for objects in the Diocese, $172.29; for objects without the Diocese, $58.20; total contributions, $1,105.66; all money raised by the congregation for current expenses and for contributions, $2,321.98.

PAROCHIAL REPORT.

Rev. MAXIMO F. DUTY, address Charles Town. St. Philip's Parish, Charles Town, Jefferson county. Date of organization, 1891. Present minister took charge June, 1903.

Church Officers—Registrar, Philip Jackson, address Charles Town; Treasurer, J. Wesley Tolbert, address Charles Town; Superintendent of Sunday School, B. C. Washington, Charles Town; Sunday School Secretary and Treasurer, B. C. Washington.

Official Acts—Baptisms, infants, 1; Adults, 1; total, 2; burials, 1; public services, Sundays, 104; other days, 64; total, 168; Holy Communion, public, 14; total, 14.

Communicants—Number last reported, 50; removed without letter, 24; lapsed, 3; total loss, 27; net loss, 27; present number, total, 23.

Congregations—Baptized persons connected with Parish, 75; confirmed persons connected with Parish, 23; families, 7; individuals not thus included, 6; whole number of individuals, 23; number free sittings, 250; number sittings in chapel, 250; number sittings in Sunday School room, 250:

Rector's Salary—As pledged from this congregation, $100.00; from general board, $400.00; as pledged from other congregations, $50.00; total, $550.00.

Organizations—Sunday Schools, officers and teachers, male, 2; female, 3; total, 5; pupils, male, 16; female, 23; total, 39; advent offering, $8.21; lenten offering, $4.75; total Sunday School offerings, $12.96.

Property—Chapel, frame, insurance $1,150.00; value $900.00; rectory, frame, value, $525.00; total value, $1,425.00. Indebtedness, due the minister, $56.50; due on diocesan assessment for Bishop's fund, $5.41; total indebtedness, $61.91.

FINANCIAL REPORT.

Receipts—For all purposes—Pledges and subscriptions, $63.36; collections in Church, $37.14; Sunday School, $12.96; Guilds, or other societies, $54.46; income from other sources, $27.36; total receipts for all purposes, $195.28. *Disbursements—For current expenses*—Salary of rector, $31.00; other salaries, $24.00; insurance, $18.00; ordinary repairs, $49.38; other objects, $42.90; total for current expenses, $165.28. *Contributions—For objects in the Parish*—Communion alms, included in "collections in church." *Contributions—For objects in the Diocese*—Salary of Bishops, $10.00; Sheltering Arms Hospital, $1.00; total contributions for objects in the Diocese, $11.00. *Contributions—For objects without the Diocese*—Domestic missions general, $10.00; total domestic missions, $10.00; foreign missions general, $10.00; total foreign missions, $10.00; general clergy relief fund, $1.70; total contributions for objects without the Diocese, $21.70.

Financial Summary—Current expenses raised by congregation as above, $165,28. Contributions for objects in the Diocese, $11.00; for objects without the Diocese, $21.70; total of contributions, $32.70; all money raised by the congregation for current expenses and for contributions, $197.98.

Remarks—The rectory, chapel and school room are very much in need of repairs. The chapel building needs bracing to render it safe. The whole propertyleaks badly.

PAROCHIAL REPORT.

Rev. GEO W. EASTER, address Union, W. Va. All Saints Church, All Saints Parish, Union, Monroe county. Present minister took charge April 18, 1892.

Church Officers—Church Wardens, Jas. W. McNeer, Chas. A. Shanklin; other Vestrymen, Jno. M. Rowan, Jos. D. Logan, A. S. Johnston, E. S. McNeer, Guy A. McClearn; Registrar, A. S. Johnston, address, Union, W. Va.; Treasurer, Chas. A. Shanklin; Superintendent of Sunday School, A. S. Johnston.

Official Acts—Baptisms, infants, 3; Total, 3; marriages, 2; burials, 1; catechisings, 50; public services, Sundays, 95; other days 74;; *total, 169; Holy Communion, public, 15; total, 15.

*Eleven of these services were held at various points in the county.

Communicants—Number last reported, 40; transferred, 1; removed without letter, 4; total loss, 5; net loss, 5; present number total, 35.

Congregations—Baptized persons connected with Parish, 78; confirmed persons connected with Parish, 40; families, 17; individuals not thus included, 6; whole number of individuals, 78; number sittings in church, 180; number free sittings, all.

Rector's Salary—As pledged from this congregation, $450.00; from diocesan missions, $100.00 from general board, $200.00; total, $750.00.

Organizations—Sunday School, officers and teachers, male, 2; female, 1; total, 3; pupils, male, 18; female, 26; total, 44; advent offerings, diocesan missions, $13.36; lenten offerings, general missions, $25.30; diocesan missions, $8.24; Mexican missions, 79 cts.; Sheltering Arms, $1.58; total Sunday School offerings, $49.27. Other organizations, Parish Aid Society.

Property—Church, wood, insurance $1,350, value $2,500; rectory, brick and wood, value $1,200; other property, $250.

FINANCIAL REPORT.

Receipts—For all purposes—Cash on hand at last report, $12.86; pledges and subscriptions, $587.44; collections in church, $275.27; Sunday School, $49.27; Guilds, or other societies, $51.23; total receipts for all purposes, $976.07.

Disbursements—For current expenses—Salary of rector, $450.00; other salaries, $62.00; ordinary repairs, $29.45; other current expenses, $16.49; total for current expenses, $557.94. *Contributions—For objects in the Parish*—Communion alms, so used, $3.30; extraordinary repairs and improvements, $75.31; maintaining Sunday Schools, $5.40; Sunday School Christmas tree, $9.43; Bibles for Sweet Springs Sunday School, $2.60; total contributions for objects in the parish, $96.04. *Contributions—For objects in the Diocese*—Salary of Bishops, $50.00; permanent fund, $9.86; diocesan missions, $100.00; widows and orphans, aged and disabled clergy fund, $17.90;

religious and theological education, $10.01; Sheltering Arms Hospital, $12.11; theological seminary, $3.88; Bishop's special fund, $1.00; other objects, expense account, $5.50; total contributions for objects in the diocese, $210.26. *Contributions—For objects without the Diocese*—Sunday School, $12.65; domestic missions general, 37.36; Indians, $1.73; deaf and dumb, $1.61; Jews, $1.96; through American Church Missionary Society, $1.93; total domestic missions, $44.59; Sunday School, $12.65; foreign missions general, $34.86; Sunday School, 79 cts; for Mexico, $1.79; Brazil, $3.19; Cuba, $3.19; total foreign missions, $43.03; American church building fund, $2.58; general clergy relief fund, $8.60; Bible and Prayer Book Society, $6.97; expense account, 31 cts; total contributions for objects without the Diocese, $106.08.

Financial Summary—Current expenses raised by congregation as above, $557.94; Contributions for objects in the Parish, $96.04; for objects in the Diocese, $210.26; for objects without the Diocese, $106.08; total of contributions, $412.38; all money raised by the congregation for current expenses and for contributions, $970.32; cash in hand, $5.75.

Remarks—This congregation has suffered greatly from deaths and removals. In the twelve years of my rectorship thirty-seven (37) communicants have been added, nine have died, twenty-five have removed and five have been dropped. As stated elsewhere eleven (11) of the 169 services reported were held at various points in the county outside of Union, viz.: Mt. Prospect, 2; Wicklines School House, 3; Sweet Springs, 2; Salt Sulphur, 1; Red Sulphur, 1; Linside, 1; Cashmere, 1.

PAROCHIAL REPORT.

Rev. GEO. W. EASTER, address Union, W. Va. Messiah Church, All Saints Parish, Alderson, Monroe county. Present minister took charge July 1, 1903.

Church Officers—Church Warden, C. W. Vandegrift; Treasurer, C. W. Vandegrift.

Official Acts—Public services, Sundays, 5; total, 5; Holy Communion, public, 1; total, 1.

Communicants—Number last reported, 5; lapsed, 1; total loss, 1; net loss, 1; present number total, 4.

Congregations—Baptized persons connected with Parish, 5; confirmed persons connected with Parish, 5; families, 3; Whole number of individuals, 9; number sittings in Church, 100; number of free sittings, all

Property—Church, wood, value $1,300; other property, $75; total value, $1,375. Indebtedness, due on diocesan assessment for missions, $1.54; due on diocesan assessment for Bishop's fund, $3.92; total indebtedness, $5.46.

FINANCIAL REPORT.

Receipts—For all purposes—Pledges and subscriptions, $12.20; collections in church, $11.03; total receipts for all purposes, $23.23.

Disbursements—For current expenses—Salary of rector, $12.20; total for current expenses, $12.20. *Contributions—For objects in the Diocese*—Salary of Bishops, $2.08; permanent fund, $1.00; diocesan missions, $4.46; total contributions for objects in the Diocese, $7.54. *Contributions—For objects without the Diocese*—Domestic missions general, $1.75; total domestic missions, $1.75; foreign missions general, $1.74; total foreign missions, $1.74; total contributions for objects without the Diocese, $3.49.

Financial Summary—Current expenses raised by congregation as above, $12.20; contributions, for objects in the Diocese, $7.54; for objects without the Diocese, $3.49; total of contributions, $11.03; all money raised by the congregation for current expenses and for contributions, $23,23.

PAROCHIAL REPORT.

Rev. JAMES LOGAN FISH, address Davis, Tucker county, W. Va. St. Barnabas Church, Davis, Tucker county. Date of organization, 1894. Present minister took charge July 9, 1899.

Church Officers—Church Wardens, A. J. McNeill, Robert Knox; other Vestrymen, Dr. W. H. Yeakley, J. M. Smith, John W. Felton, Hanson Walters, H. H. Weaver, H. N. Worden, Christopher Keller; Registrar, A. J. McNeill, address Davis, W. Va.; Treasurer, A. J. McNeill, address Davis, W. Va.; Superintendent of Sunday School, Robt. Knox; Sunday School Secretary and Treasurer, Miss A. E. Kellum.

Official Acts—Baptims, infants, 10; adults, 4; total, 14; presented for confirmation since last report, 6; marriages, 3; burials, 2; catechisings, 20; public services, Sundays, 60; other days, 12; total, 72; Holy Communion, public, 12; total, 12.

Communicants—Number last reported, 24; admitted by confirmation, 6; restored to communion, 2; added otherwise, 7; total gain, 15; removed without letter, 2; total loss, 2; net gain, 13; present number total, 37.

Congregation—Baptized Persons connected with Parish, 62; confirmed persons connected with Parish, 37; families, 19; individuals not thus included, 7; whole number of indivduals, 69; number of scattered communicants in your section not connected with any Parish, 18; number sittings in Church, 120; number free sittings, 120.

Rector's Salary—As pledged from this congregation, $400.00; from general board, $200.00; total, $600.00.

Organizations—Sunday Schools, 1; officers and teachers, male, 2; female,

2; total, 4; pupils, male, 8; female, 17; total, 25; lenten offerings, $6.60; other offerings, $13.84; total Sunday School offerings, $20.44.

Property—Church, wood, insurance, $750.00, value $1,400.00; rectory, wood, insurance $2.500.00, value $3,000.00; total value, $4,400.00. Indebtedness, or rectory, $2,000.00; total indebtedness, $2,000.00.

FINANCIAL REPORT.

Receipts—For all purposes—Pledges and subscriptions, $100.70; collections in Church, $146.00; Sunday School, $20.44; Guilds, or other societies, $161.90; contributions from without, $45.00; total receipts for all purposes, $474.04.

Disbursements—For current expenses—Salary of rector, $214.65; other salaries, $20.00; ordinary repairs, $16.00; interest on debt, $60.00; other current expenses, $65.99; total for current expenses, $376.64. *Contributions—For objects in the Parish*—Extraordinary repairs and improvements to church and rectory, $262.90; maintaining Sunday Schools, $18.00; total contributions for objects in the Parish, $280.90. *Contributions—For objects in the diocese*—Salary of Bishops, $8.00 diocesan missions, $8.00; convocation missions, $2.00; Sheltering Arms Hospital, $2.00; total contributions for objects in the Diocese, $20.00. *Contributions—For objects without the Diocese*—Domestic missions general, $5.00; total domestic missions, $5.00; foreign missions general, $5.00; total foreign missions, $5.00; total contributions for objects without the Diocese, $10.00.

Financial Summary—Contributions, for current expenses, $376.64; for objects in the Parish, $280.90; for ibjects in the Diocese, $20.00; for objects without the Diocese, $10.00; total contributions, $210.90; all money raised by the congregation for current expenses and for contributions, $739.94; cash in hand, $17.86.

Remarks—This report embraces the months from October, 1903 to April 30th, 1904. Rector moved from Elkins to Davis in October.

PAROCHIAL REPORT.

Rev. JAMES LOGAN FISH, address Davis, W. Va. Douglas Mission, Douglas, Tucker county.

Official Acts—Public services, other days, 4.

Communicants—Present number total, 5.

Congregations—Baptized persons connected fith the parish, 11; confirmed persons connected with parish, 5; families, 3.

Remarks—We hold services in school house at Douglas. There are but five communicants. Rector received $25 for all purposes.

PAROCHIAL REPORT.

Rev. JAMES L. FISH, address, Davis. Parsons Mission.

Official Acts—Sundays, 1.

Communicants—Number last reported, 6; present number total, 6.

Congregations—Baptized persons connected with parish, 6; families, 2.

PAROCHIAL REPORT.

Rev. JAMES LOGAN FISH, address Davis. Thomas Mission, Thomas, Tucker county.

Official Acts—Baptisms, infants, 1; public services, Sundays, 4.

Communicants—Present number total, 6.

Congregations—Baptized persons connected with parish, 15; confirmed persons connected with parish, 6.

Remarks—There are six communicants at Thomas; services are held in the Presbyterian church. Rector received $7.00 for past year.

PAROCHIAL REPORT.

Rev. G. A. GIBBONS, address Romney, W. Va. St. Stephens Church, Romney Mission, Hampshire county. Date of organization, 1885. Present minister took charge July 1st, 1885.

Church Officers—Church Wardens, G. W. Parsons, Wm. N. Baird; Treasurer, G. W. Parsons, (Miss Keller, Assistant), address Romney, W. Va.; Superintendent of Sunday Schools, Wm. Rusmisell, Romney, W. Va.; Sunday School Secretary and Treasurer, Mrs. G. W. Parsons.

Official Acts—Baptisms, infants, 2; marriages, 3; catechisings, 3; public services, Sundays, 24; other days, 9; total 33; Holy Communion, public, 5.

Communicants—Number last reported, 25; added otherwise, 1; total gain, 1; removed without letter, 5; total loss, 5; net loss, 4; present number, total, 21.

Congregations—Baptized persons connected with parish, 40; confirmed persons connected with parish, 21; families, 15; individuals not thus included, 5; whole number of individuals, 45; number sittings in church, 200; number of sittings in chapel, 100.

Rector's Salary—As pledged from this congregation, $100.00; from Diocesan Missions, $250.00; as pledged from other congregations, $192.00; from Convocation Missions, $50.00; from American Church Missionary Society, $200.00; total $792.00.

Organizations—Sunday Schools, officers and teachers, male, 1; female, 3;

total, 4; pupils, male, 6; female, 10; total, 16; Advent offering, $2.00; lenten offering, $11.34; total Sunday School offerings, $13.34.

Property—Church, brick, insurance, $1,200; value, $1,800; chapel, wood, insurance, $400; value, $700; rectory, wood, insurance, $1,000; value, $1,900; total insurance, $2,600; total value, $4,400.

FINANCIAL REPORT.

Receipts—For all Purposes—Pledges and subscriptions, $125.00; collections in church, $102.54; thank offerings, $22.00; guilds, $28.72; total receipts for all purposes, $278.26.

Disbursements—For Current Expenses—Salary of rector, $100.00; other salaries, $22.00; insurance, $34.50; ordinary repairs, $5.75; other current expenses, $5.95; total curent expenses, $168.20. *Contributions—For Objects in the Parish*—Communion alms, $2.00; extraordinary repairs and improvements, $22.97; other objects, rectory improvements, $22.00; total contributions for objects in the parish, $46.97. *Contributions—For Objects in the Diocese*—Salary of Bishops, $15.00; Diocesan Missions, $15.00; Convocation Missions, $5.00; Sheltering Arms Hospital, $1.75; total contributions for objects in the Diocese, $36.75. *Contributions—For Objects Without the Diocese*—Through American Church Missionary Society, $7.50; total Domestic Missions, $7.50; through American Church Missionary Society, $7.50; total Foreign Missions, $7.50; Sunday School for Domestic and Foreign Missions, $11.34; total contributions for objects without the diocese, $26.34.

Financial Summary—Current expenses raised by congregation as above, $168.20. *Contributions*—For objects in the parish, $46.97; for objects in the diocese, $36.75; for objects without the diocese, $26.34; total contributions, $110.06; all money raised by the congregation for current expenses and for contributions, $278.26.

Remarks—The chapel mentioned in this report is Zion on North River.

PAROCHIAL REPORT.

Rev. GEO. A. GIBBONS, address Romney, W. Va. Emmanuel Church, Emmanuel Parish, Moorefield, Hardy county. Date of organization, 1878. Present minister tok charge July 1, 1885.

Church Officers—Church Wardens, C. James Lobb, Thomas Lakin; other vestrymen, Wm. H. Shearer, Lisle Gamble, M. D., P. W. Inskeep; Registrar, Wm. H. Shearer, address Moorefield, W. Va.; Treasurer, Wm. H. Shearer, (Ida V. Wood, Assistant), address Moorefield, W. Va.; Superintendent of Sunday Schools, C. J. Lobb, Moorefield, W. Va.; Sunday School Secretary and Treasurer, Mrs. Annie W. Shearer.

Official Acts—Baptisms, infants, 3; catechisings, 3; public services, Sundays, 48; other days, 11; total, 62; Holy Communion, public, 6.

Communicants—Number last reported, 30; present number total, 30.

Congregations—Baptized persons connected with parish, 55; confirmed persons connected with parish, 30; families, 18; individuals not thus included, 6; number sittings in church, 200; number free sittings, 200; number sittings in Sunday School room, 125.

Rector's Salary—As pledged from this congregation, $150.00; from Diocesan Missions, $250.00; as pledged from other congregations, $142.00; from Convocation Missions, $50.00; from American Church Missionary Society, $200.00; total $792.00.

Organizations—Sunday Sschools, officers and teachers, male, 1; female, 4; total, 5; pupils, male, 9; female, 11; total, 20; Advent offering, $2.00; Lenten offering, $2.50; total Sunday School offerings, $4.50.

Property—Church, frame, insurance, $1,200; value, $3,000; rectory, frame, insurance, $1,200; value, $2,000; Sunday School room, insurance, $750; value, $1,400; total insurance, $3,150; total value, $6,400.

FINANCIAL REPORT.

Receipts—For all Purposes—Pledges and subscriptions, $150.00; collections in church, $43.82; Sunday School, $4.50; guilds or other societies, $147.00; total receipts for all purposes, $345.32.

Disbursements—For Current Expenses—Salary of rector, $150.00; other salaries, $30.00; insurance, $37.00; ordinary repairs, $60.00; total for current expenses, $237.00. *Contributions—For Objects in the Parish*—Communion alms, $3.00; extraordinary repairs and improvements, $30.00; total contributions for objects in the parish, $33.00. *Contributions—For Objects in the Diocese*—Salary of Bishops, $20.00; Permanent Fund, $1.05; Diocesan Missions, $20.00; Convocation Missions, $9.82; Widows and Orphans, Aged and Disabled Clergy Fund, $1.85; Religious and Theological Education, $1.65; Sheltering Arms Hospital, $1.00; total contributions for objects in the diocese, $55.32. *Contributions—For Objects Without the Diocese*—Through American Church Missionary Society, $10.00; total Domestic Missions, $10.00; Through American Church Missionary Society, $10.00; total Foreign Missions, $10.00; total contributions for objects without the diocese, $20.00.

Financial Summary—Current expenses raised by congregation as above, $237.00. *Contributions*—For objects in the parish, $33.00; for objects in the diocese, $55.32; for objects without the diocese, $20.00; total contribution; $108.32; all money raised by the congregation for current expenses and for contributions, $345.32; cash in hand, $5.19.

PAROCHIAL REPORT.

Rev. G. A. GIBBONS, address Romney, W. Va. Epiphany Church, Okonoko Mission, Okonoko, Hampshire county. Date of organization, 1886. Present minister took charge 1885.

Church Officers—Church Warden, Mahlon H. Russell; Registrar, E. W. McGill, address Woodrow, Morgan county, W. Va.; Treasurer, Henry M. Russell, address Okonoko, W. Va.

Official Acts—Public services, Sundays, 24; Holy Communion, public, 4.

Communicants—Number last reported, 10; present number total, 10.

Congregations—Baptized persons connected with the parish, 16; confirmed persons connected with parish, 10; families, 4; whole number of individuals, 16; number of sittings in church, 150.

Rector's Salary—As pledged from this congregation, $42.00; from Diocesan Missions, $250.00; as pledged from other congregations, $250.00; from Convocation Missions, $50.00; from American Church Missionary Society, $200.00; total, $792.00.

FINANCIAL REPORT.

Receipts—For all Purposes—Pledges and subscriptions, $42.00; collections in church, $33.50; total receipts for all purposes, $75.50.

Disbursements—For Current Expenses—Salary of rector, $42.00. *Contributions—For Objects in the Parish*—Communion alms, $2.00; total contributions for objects in the parish, $2.00. *Contributions—For Objects in the Diocese*—Salary of Bishops, $10.00; Diocesan Missions, $10.00; Widows and Orphans, Aged and Disabled Clergy Fund, $2.00; Religious and Theological Education, $2.00; Sheltering Arms Hospital, $1.50; total contributions for objects in the diocese, $25.50. *Contributions—For Objects Without the Diocese*—Through American Church Missionary Society, $3.00; total Domestic Missions, $3.00; Through American Church Missionary Society, Foreign Missions, $3.00; total Foreign Missions, $3.00; total contributions for objects without the diocese, $6.00.

Financial Summary—Current expenses raised by congregation as above, $42.00. *Contributions*—For objects in the parish, $2.00; for objects in the diocese, $25.50; for objects without the diocese, $6.00; total contributions, $33.50; all money raised by the congregation for current expenses and for contributions, $75.50; cash in hand, $2.19.

PAROCHIAL REPORT.

Rev. G. A. GIBBONS, address Romney, W. Va. Paw Paw Mission, Paw Paw, Morgan county. Present minister took charge 1893.

Church Officers—Church Warden, Thomas Korns; Treasurer, Thomas Korns, address Paw Paw, Morgan county, W. Va.

Official Acts—Public services, other days, 12; Holy Communion, public, 3.

Communicants—Number last reported, 6; added otherwise, 2; total gain, 2; removed without letter, 2; total loss, 2; present number total, 6.

Congregations—Baptized persons connected with parish, 6; confirmed persons connected with the parish, 6; families, 3; individuals not thus included, 2; whole number of individuals, 8.

FINANCIAL REPORT.

Receipts—For all Purposes—Pledges and subscriptions, $40.50; collections in church, $12.30; total receipts for all purposes, $52.80.

Disbursements—For Current Expenses—Salary of rector, $40.50. *Contributions—For Objects in the Diocese*—Permanent Fund, $1.00; Diocesan Missions, $3.00; Religious and Theological Education, $3.00; total contributions for objects in the diocese, $7.00. *Contributions—For Objects Without the Diocese*—Domestic Missions General, $1.50; Through American Church Missionary Society, $2.30; total Domestic Missions, $3.80; Foreign Missions General, $1.50; total Foreign Missions, $1.50; total contributions for objects without the diocese, $5.30.

Financial Summary—Current expenses raised by congregation as above, $40.50. *Contributions*—For objects in the diocese, $7.00; for objects without the diocese, $5.30; total contributions, $12.30; all money raised by the congregation for current expenses and for contributions, $52.80; cash in hand, $3.00.

PAROCHIAL REPORT.

Rev. J. HOWARD GIBBONS, address Point Pleasant, W. Va. Christ Church, Point Pleasant Parish, Point Pleasant, Mason county. Date of organization 1851. Present minister took charge April 1, 1901.

Church Officers—Church Wardens, Hon. P. C. Eastham, Hon. J. W. English; other vestrymen, Hon. J. S. Spencer, Hon. Rankin Wiley, Col. J. P. R. B. Smith, L. S. Pomeroy, C. C. Bowyer, J. W. C. Heslop; Registrar, Hon. J. W. English, address Point Pleasant, W. Va.; Treasurer, C. C. Bowyer, address Point Pleasant, W. Va.; Superintendent of Sunday Schools, Hon. P. C. Eastham, Point Pleasant, W. Va.; Sunday School Secretary and Treasurer, Miss K. B. Stribbling.

Official Acts—Baptisms, infants, 4; adults, 1; total, 5; presented for confirmation since last report, 4; marriages, 3; burials, 3; catechisings, 12; public services, Sundays, 61; other days, 64; total, 125; Holy Communion, public, 13.

Communicants—Number last reported, 58; admitted by confirmation, 4; added otherwise, 1; total gain, 5; died, 1; total loss, 1; net gain, 4; present number total, 62.

Congregation—Baptized persons connected with parish, 90; confirmed persons connected with parish, 62; families, 35; number of scattered communicants in your section not connected with any parish, 1; number of sittings in church (free), 250.

Rector's Salary—As pledged from this congregation, $350.00; from Diocesan missions, $50.00; as pledged from other congregations, $200.00; from American Church Missionary Society, $150.00; total, $750.00.

Organizations—Sunday Schools, officers and teachers, male, 1; female, 3; total, 4; pupils, male, 15; female, 10; total, 25; Advent offering, $5.61; Lenten offering, $8.00; other offerings, $19.84; total Sunday School offerings, $33.45; Woman's Auziliary, 16; Chancel Chapter, 9; Ladies' Guild, 29; Babies Branch Woman's Auxiliary, 13.

Property—Church, brick, insurance, $4,000; value, $6,000; rectory, frame, insurance, $1,000; value, $1,200; total insurance, $5,000; total value, $7,200.

FINANCIAL REPORT.

Receipts—For all Purposes—Pledges and subscriptions, $500.00; collections in church, $95.52; Sunday School, $33.45; Woman's Auxiliary, money, $27.30; Woman's Auxiliary, box, value, $25.00; guilds, or other societies, $360.92; total receipts for all purposes, $1,042.19.

Disbursements—For Current Expenses—Salary of rector, $350.00; other salaries, $45.95; other objects, $34.77; total for current expenses, $430.72. *Contributions—For Objects in the Parish*—Communion alms, $28.77; extraordinary repairs and improvements, $64.20; maintaining Sunday Schools, $15.59; other objects, $160.12; total contributions for objects in the parish, $268.68. *Contributions—For Objects in the Diocese*—Salary of Bishops, $50.00; Diocesan Missions, $55.61; Convocation Missions, $2.50; Sheltering Arms Hospital, $10.50; other objects, $18.99; box to Sheltering Arms Hospital, $25.00; total contributions for objects in the diocese, $162.60. *Contributions—For Objects Without the Diocese*—Domestic Missions General, $4.50; colored people, $2.50; Indians, $2.50; deaf and dumb, $2.50; Jews, $2.50; through American Church Missionary Society, $10.00; total Domestic Missions, $24.50; Foreign Missions General, $4.50; for China, $2.50; for Africa, $2.50; for Japan, $2.50; for Hayti, $2.50; for Mexico, $2.50; for Philippines, $2.50; Porto Rico, $2.50; Through American Church Missionary Society, $4.00; Brazil, $5.00; Cuba, $2.50; total Foreign Missions, $33.50; other objects, $5.00; United offering Woman's Auxiliary, $10.70; total contributions for Objects without the diocese, $73.70.

Financial Summary—Current expenses raised by congregation as above, $430.72. *Contributions*—For objects in the parish, $268.68; for objects in the diocese, $162.60; for objects without the diocese, $73.70; total of contributions, $504.98; all money raised by the congregation for current expenses and for contributions, $935.70; cash in hand, $106.49.

PAROCHIAL REPORT.

Rev. J. HOWARD GIBBONS, address Point Pleasant, W. Va. Bruce Chapel, Mason county. Present minister took charge April 1, 1901.

Church Officers—Vestrymen, J. M. H. Beale, E. L. Neale, J. Moore; Treasurer, Miss Mary Beale, address Beale, W. Va.; Superintendent of Sunday Schools, Miss Vause Beale, Beale, W. Va.; Sunday School Secretary and Treasurer, Miss Mary Beale.

Official Acts—Baptisms, infants, 1; adults, 1; total, 2; presented for confirmation since last report, 5; catechisings, 10; public services, Sundays, 25; other days, 7; total, 32; Holy Communion, public, 4.

Communicants—Number last reported, 21; admitted by confirmation, 5; total gain, 5; net gain, 5; present number total, 26.

Congregations—Baptized persons connected with parish, 60; confirmed persons connected with parish, 26; families, 15; number sittings in church, (free), 125.

Rector's Salary—As pledged from this congregation, $150.00.

Organizations—Sunday Schools, officers and teachers, female, 3; pupils, male, 14; female, 21; total 35; Advent offering, $3.25; Lenten offering, $3.00; other offering, $5.00; total Sunday School offerings, $11.25; Industrial Schools, officers and teachers, 3; scholars, 25; total, 28.

Property—chapel, brick, insurance, $1,000; value, $1,500; total insurance, $1,000; total value, $1,500.

FINANCIAL REPORT.

Receipts—For all Purposes—Pledges and subscriptions $162.00; colletions in Church, $24.05; thank offerings, $5.00; Sunday School, $15.00; total receipts for all purposes, $206.05.

Disbursements—For Current Expenses—Salary of rector, $150.00. *Contributions—For Objects in the Parish*—Extraordinary repairs and improvements, $5.00; maintaining Sunday Schools, $4.00; other objects, $3.75; total contributions for objects in the parish, $12.75. *Contributions—For Objects in the Diocese*—Salary of Bishops, $12.00; Diocesan Missions, $15.25; total contributions for objects in the diocese, $27.25. *Contributions—For Objects Without the Diocese*—Domestic Missions General, $2.00; colored people, 50 cents; Indians, 50 cents; deaf and dumb, 50 cents; Jews, 50 cents; through American Church Missionary Society, $2.00; total Domestic Missions, $6.00; Foreign Missions General, 50 cents; for China, 50 cents; for Africa, 50 cents, for Japan, 50 cents; for Hayti, 50 cents; for Mexico, 50 cents; for Philippines, 50 cents; Porto Rico, 50 cents; Through American Church Missionary Society, $1.50; Brazil, $2.00; Cuba, $1.50; total Foreign Missions, $9.00; total contributions for objects without the diocese, $15.00.

Financial Summary—Current expenses raised by congregation as above, $150.00. *Contributions*—For objects in the parish, $12.75; for objects in the diocese, $27.25; for objects without the diocese, $15.00; all money raised by the congregation for current expenses and for contributions, $205.00; cash in hand, $1.05.

Remarks—Aid is received from the D. M. S. of W. Va., and the A. C. M. S. for *all* work under my charge and is reported only under the report for Christ Church, Point Peasant.

PAROCHIAL REPORT.

Rev. J. HOWARD GIBBONS, address Point Pleasant, W. Va. Spilman Chapel, Spilman, Mason county. Present minister took charge April 1, 1901.

Church Officers—Vestrymen, H. E. Spilman; Treasurer, H. E. Spilman, address, Spilman, W. Va.; Superintendent of Sunday Schools, Miss Virginia Behan, W. Columbia, W. Va.; Sunday School Secretary and Treasurer, Mrs. M. G. Tyler.

Official Acts—Baptisms, infants, 4; adults, 1; total, 5; presented for confirmation since last report, 5; burials, 1; catechisings, 6; public services, Sundays, 13; other days, 14; total, 27; Holy Communion, public, 6.

Communicants—Number last reported, 19; admitted by confirmation, 5; total gain 5; died, 1; total loss, 1; net gain, 4; present number total, 23.

Congregations—Baptized persons connected with parish, 40; confirmed persons connected with parish, 23; families, 15; number of sittings in church, (free) 125.

Rector's Salary—As pledged from this congregation, $50.00.

Organizations—Sunday Schools, officers and teachers, female, 3; pupils, male, 12; female, 20; total, 32; Advent offering, $3.64; Lenten offering, $6.17; other offerings, $16.24; total Sunday School offerings, $26.05.

Property—Chapel, brick, insurance, $1,500; value, $1,800; total insurance, $1,500; total value, $1,800.

FINANCIAL REPORT.

Receipts—For all Purposes—Cash on hand, per last report, 53 cents; pledges and subscriptions, $50.00; collections in church, $48.33; thank offerings, $27.75; Sunday School, $26.05; total receipts for all purposes, $152.66.

Disbursements—For Current Expenses—Salary of rector, $50.00; other current expenses, $3.00; other objects, $5.25; total for current expenses, $58.25. *Contributions—For Objects in the Parish*—Extraordinary repairs and improvements, $27.75; maintaining Sunday Schools, $15.81; total contributions for objects in the parish, $43.56. *Contributions—For Objects in the Diocese*—Salary of Bishops, $10.00; Diocesan Missions, $15.64; Convocation Missions, $2.00; total contributions for objects in the diocese, $27.64. *Contributions—For Objects Without the Docese*—Domestic Missions General, $2.50; colored people, 50 cents; Indians, 50 cents; deaf and dumb, 50 cents; Jews, 50 cents; Through American Church Missionary Society, $1.50; total Domestic Missions, $5.50; Foreign Missions General, $2.00; for China, 50 cents; for Africa, 50 cents; for Japan, 50 cents; for Hayti, 50 cents; for Mexico, 50 cents; for Philippines, 50 cents; Porto Rico, 50 cents; Through American Church Missionary Society, $3.17; Brazil, $1.50; Cuba, 50 cents; total Foreign Missions, $10.67; American Church Building Fund, $3.00; total contributions for objects without the diocese, $19.17.

Financial Summary—Current Expenses raised by congregation as above, $58.25. *Contributions*—For objects in the parish, $43.56; for objects in the diocese, $27.64; for objects wthout the diocese, $19.17; total of contributions, $90.37; all money raised by the congregation for current expenses and for contributions, $148.62; cash in hand, $4.04.

Remarks—Aid is received from the D. M. S. of W. Va., and the A. C. M. S. lor *all* work under my charge, and is reported only under the report for Christ Church, Point Pleasant.

Mason City—2 Sunday services, 1 burial; offerings, $3.00 for District Missions.

Morgan's—1 week day service.

Winfield—1 week day service, 1 adult baptism, 2 persons confirmed, 3 communicants, offerings, Dis. Missions, $7.00; General Missions, $1.00; Episcopal Fund, $1.00; total, $9.00.

PAROCHIAL REPORT.

Rev. JNO. SHACKELFORD GIBSON, address Huntington. Trinity Church, Cabell Parish, Huntington, Cabell county. Date of organization 1872. Present minister took charge 1892.

Church Officers—Church Wardens, Cameron L. Thompson, Edmund Sehon; other vestrymen, F. D. Enslow, G. A. Northcott, C. D. Emmons, F. D. Fuller, E. S. Aleshire, T. L. Trimmer, F. R. Van Antwerp, John Walton Ensign, Robt. L. Archer, Harry Chambers; Registrar, C. D. Emmons, address Huntington; Treasurer, G. A. Northcott, address Huntington; Superintendent of Sunday Schools, G. A. Northcott, Huntington; Sunday School Secretary and Treasurer, Herman D. Jenkins.

Official Acts—Baptisms, infants, 5; adults, 6; total, 11; presented for confirmation since last report, 11; marriages, 4; burials, 36; catechisings, 40; public services, Sundays, 125; other days, 75; total, 200; Holy Communion, public, 25; private, 2; total, 27.

Communicants—Number last reported, 192; received by letter, 4; admitted by confirmation, 11; added otherwise, 17; total gain, 32; died, 2;

removed without letter, 12; lapsed, 10; total loss, 24; net gain, 8; present number total, 200.

Congregations—Baptized persons connected with parish, 420; confirmed persons connected with parish, 215; families, 70; individuals not thus included, 75; whole number of individuals, 450; number of sittings in church, (all free), 425; number of sittings, in chapel, 75.

Rector's Salary—As pledged from this congregation, no pledge; as pledged from other congregations, no pledge.

Organizations—Sunday Schools, officers and teachers, male, 4; female, 7; total, 11; pupils, male and femals, 80; Advent offering, $15.00; Lenten offering, $34.00; other offerings, $100.00; total Sunday School offerings, $149.00; Woman's Auxiliary, members, 11; Junior Auxiliary, members, 10; Ladies' Aid Society, members, 40; Trinity Guild of Young Ladies, members, 30; Boys' Missionary Society, members, 5.

Property—Church, brick, insurance, $8,000; value, $20,500; rectory, brick, insurance, $3,000; value, $6,000; total value, $26,500.

FINANCIAL REPORT.

Receipts—For all Purposes—Cash on hand, per last report, $75.00; pledges and subscriptions, $2,257.81; collections in church, $600.00; Sunday School, $149.00; Woman's and Junior Auxiliary, money, $107.00; Woman's Auxiliary, boxes, value, $146.00; Guilds or other societies, $663.00; total, receipts for all purposes, $3,997.81.

Disbursements—For Current Expenses—Salary of rector, $1,200.00; other salaries, $400.00; ordinary repairs, $25.00; other current expenses, $175.00; other objects, $395.00; total for current expenses, $2,195.00. *Contributions—For Objects in the Parish*—Communion alms, $65.00; extraordinary repairs and improvements, $750.00; maintaining Sunday Schools, $100.00; other objects, $30.00; total contributions for objects in the parish, $945.00. *Contributions—For Objects in the Diocese*—Salary of Bishops, $100.00; Permanent Fund, $2.75; Diocesan Missions, $75.00; Convocation Missions, $10.00; Widows and Orphans, Aged and Disabled Clergy Fund, $25.00; Religious and Theological Education, $5.00; Sheltering Arms Hospital, $132.95; Bishop's Special Fund, $50.00; Woman's Missionary, $16.00; total contributions for objects in the diocese, $416.70. *Contributions—For Objects Without the Diocese*—Domestic Missions General, $40.25; deaf and dumb, $10.56; Through American Church Missionary Society, $7.50; total Domestic Missions, $58.31; Foreign Missions General, $40.00; Brazil, $15.00; Cuba, $2.50; total Foreign Missions, $57.50; Specials, boxes, &c., $78.00; American Church Building Fund, $2.00; General Clergy Relief Fund, $2.00; total contributions for objects without the diocese, $197.81.

Financial Summary—Current Expenses raised by congregation as above, $2,195.00. *Contributions*—For objects in the parish, $945.00; for objects in the diocese, $416.70; for objects without the diocese, $197.81; total of contributions, $1,559.51; all money raised by the congregation for current expenses and for contributions, $3,754.51; cash (in hands of societies), $243.00.

Remarks—Six of the persons confirmed, four men and two women, are deaf mutes. The vestry used enough of the Easter offering to bring the payments on the rector's salary up to $1,200, the sum promised when he accepted the rectorship.

PAROCHIAL REPORT.

Rev. JNO. SHACKELFORD GIBSON, address Huntington. Grace Church, Wayne Mission, Kenova, Wayne county. Date of organization, 1890. Present minister took charge, 1892.

Church Officers—Church Warden, Charles C. Coe; other vestrymen, Frank R. Peck, R. Ney Williams; Registrar, Frank R. Peck, address Kenova; Treasurer, Charles C. Coe, address, Kenova.

Official Acts—Presented for confirmation since last report, 2; public services, Sunday, 45; other days, 8; total, 53; Holy Communion, public, 8.

Communicants—Number last reported, 8; admitted by confirmation, 2; total gain, 2; transferred, 1; not otherwise accounted for, 1; total loss, 2; present number total, 8.

Congregations—Baptized persons connected with parish, 22; confirmed persons connected with parish, 9; families, 7; individuals not thus included, 2; whole number of individuals, 23; number sittings in church, 150; number free sittings, 150.

Rector's Salary—As pledged from this congregation, no pledge.

Organizations—Advent offerings, 68 cents; Lenten offerings, $1.01; total Sunday School offerings, $1.69.

Property—Church, insurance, $1,800; value, $2,400.

FINANCIAL REPORT.

Receipts—For all Purposes—Cash on hand, per last report, $8.55; pledges and subscriptions, $157.00; collections in church, $83.13; Sunday School, $1.69; contributions from without, $43.86; total receipts for all purposes, $294.23.

Disbursements—For Current Expenses—Salary of rector, $160.00; ordinary repairs, $8.60; other current expenses, $1.60; total for current expenses, $170.20. *Contributions—For Objects in the Parish*—Extraordinary repairs and improvements, $61.64; total contributions for objects in the parish, $61.64. *Contributions—For Objects in the Diocese*—Salary of Bishops, $5.00; Diocesan Missions, $8.18; Widows and Orphans, Aged and

Disabled Clergy Fund, $3.20; Sheltering Arms Hospital, $3.00; total contributions for objects in the diocese, $19.38. *Contributions—For Objects Without the Diocese*—Foreign Missions General, $1.01; total Foreign Missions, $1.01; American Church Building Fund, $1.75; General Clergy Relief Fund, $2.00; total contributions for objects without the diocese, $4.76.

Financial Summary—Current Expenses raised by congregation as above, $294.23. *Contributions*—For objects in the parish, $231. 84; for objects in the diocese, $19.38; for objects without the diocese, $4.76; total of contributions, $255.98; cash in hand, $38.25.

Remarks—The chapel was repainted in the spring of 1904, and by town ordinance was required, in common with all property owners on Chestnut street, to lay a concrete walk in front of the property. Conditions are at present very much depressed owing to the N. & W. R. R. having in November, 1903, removed its offices and shops to Portsmouth, O., from Kenova. This financial report was prepared by Mr. C. C. Coe, Treasurer.

PAROCHIAL REPORT.

Rev. JNO. SHACKELFORD GIBSON, address Huntington. Mingo Mission, Williamson, Mingo county. Date of organization, unorganized. Present minister took charge 1902.

Church Officers—Treasurer, B. Randolph Bias, address Williamson, W. Va.; Superintendent of Sunday Schools, J. Randall Strange, Williamson, W. Va.

Official Acts—Baptisms, infants, 2; presented for confirmation since last report, 3; public services, Sundays, 2; other days, 12; total, 14; Holy Communion, public, 4.

Communicants—Number last reported, 6; received by letter, 2; admitted by confirmation, 3; added otherwise, 2; total gain, 7; transferred, 1; removed without letter, 1; total loss, 2; net gain, 5; present number total, 11.

Congregations—Baptized persons connected with parish, 28; confirmed persons connected with parish, 14; families, 7; individuals not thus included, 6; whole number of individuals, 35; number of scattered communicants in your section not connected with any parish, 3.

Rector's Salary—As pledged from this congregation, no pledge.

Organizations—Sunday Schools, officers and teachers, male, 2; female, 2; total, 4; pupils, male and female, 15; total, 19; Lenten offerings, $2,10; total Sunday School offerings, $2.10.

Property—Money raised from outside sources, $48.00; for what objects used, $10.00 put to the building fund, $2.00 to purchase books, balance in hands of Mr. Strange, to whom it was sent from St. Ann's, Annapolis, Md., his parish chapel.

FINANCIAL REPORT.

Receipts—For all Purposes—Cash on hand, per last report, $8.80; pledges and subscriptions, $103.50; collections in church, $22.64; Sunday School, $2.10; contributions from without, $48.00; total receipts for all purposes, $185.04.

Disbursements—For Current Expenses—Salary of rector, $103.50; other current expenses, $4.05; other objects, recording deed, $2.00; total for current expenses, $109.55. *Contributions—For Objects in the Diocese*—Diocesan Missions, $5.22; total contributions for objects in the diocese, $5.22. *Contributions—For Objects Without the Diocese*—Domestic Missions General, $1.36; total Domestic Missions, $1.36; Foreign Missions General, $1.35; total Foreign Missions, $1.35; Bible and Prayer Book Society, $2.00; total contributions for objects without the diocese, $4.71.

Financial Summary—Current Expenses raised by congregation as above, $109.55. *Contributions*—For objects in the diocese, $5.22; for objects without the diocese, $4.71; total contributions, $9.93; all money raised by the congregation for current expenses and for contributions, $119.48; cash in hand, $10.37.

Remarks—Services are held one a month on other days than Sunday. Presbyterian church is loaned us. Williamson has 2,000 population, is growing and we ought to have a church. $650.00 was subscribed by the people of the town to help our building, and is pledged to be paid July 1st, 1904. I have received $11.00 in cash and a pledge of $50, making about $700, or about half of such sum as will be required at present prices to erect anything of a church.

PAROCHIAL REPORT.

Rev. ANDREW GLASSELL GRINNAN, address Weston, W. Va. St. Paul's Church, St. Paul's Parish, Weston, Lewis county. Date of organization 1848. Present minister took charge 1900.

Church Officers—Church Wardens, H. C. Bailey, R. H. Harrison; other vestrymen, A. H. Kunst, E. G. Davisson, Louis Bennett, W. Ralston, J. S. Mitchell, M. B. Ralston, A. A. Warren, E. M. Vandervort; Registrar and Treasurer, E. M. Vandervort, address Weston, W. Va.

Official Acts—Baptisms, infants, 6; marriages, 1; burials, 13; public services, Sundays, 78; other days, 41; total, 119; Holy Communion, public, 15; private, 2; total, 17.

Communicants—Number last reported, 81; added otherwise, 5; died, 2; not otherwise accounted for, 9; total loss, 11; net loss, 6; present number total, 75.

Congregations—Baptized persons connected with parish, 210; confirmed

persons connected with parish, 110; families, 60; individuals not thus included, 21; whole number of individuals, 210; number of scattered communicants in your section not connected with any parish, 3; number free sittings, 300; number sittings in Sunday School room, 100.

Rector's Salary—As pledged from this congregation, $800.

Organizations—Sunday Schools, officers and teachers, female, 7; pupils, male, 26; female, 31; total, 57; Advent offering, $25.04; Lenten offering, $29.36; other offerings, $17.15; Spirit of Missions, $1.00; total Sunday School offerings, $72.55; Woman's Auxiliary, members, 18; Guild of St. Paul's, 20; Daughters of the King, 9.

Property—Church, stone, insurance, $5,000; value, $15,000; rectory, wood, insurance, $1,000; value, $2,000.

FINANCIAL REPORT.

Receipts—For all Purposes—Cash on hand, per last report, $180.93; pledges and subscriptions, $787.53; collections in church, $420.37; Sunday School, $72.55; Woman's Auxiliary, money, $40.21; Woman's Auxiliary, boxes, value, $28.26; Guilds, or other societies, $135.48; income from other sources, $64.50; total receipts for all purposes, $1,728.83.

Disbursements—For Current Expenses—Salary of rector, $800.04; other current expenses, $161.98; total for current expenses, $962.02. *Contributions—For Objects in the Parish*—Communion alms, $6.00; extraordinary repairs and improvements, $149.29; other objects, $50.11; total contributions for objects in the parish, $205.40. *Contributions—For Objects in the Diocese*—Salary of Bishops, $80.00; Permanent Fund, $6.37; Diocesan Missions, $75.00; Convocation Missions, $12.50; Widows and Orphans, Aged and Disabled Clergy Fund, $19.90; Sheltering Arms Hospital, $23.61; Bishop's Special Fund, $14.00; box for Sheltering Arms, $28.26; Woman's Missionary, $9.50; total contributions for objects in the diocese, $269.14. *Contributions—For Objects Without the Diocese*—Domestic Missions General, $32.30; total Domestic Missions, $32.30; Foreign Missions General, $32.30; Brazil, $7.00; total Foreign Missions, $39.30; other objects, $8.00; total contributions for objects without the diocese, $79.60.

Financial Summary—Current Expenses raised by congregation as above, $962.02. *Contributions*—For objects in the parish, $205.40; for objects in the diocese, $269.14; for objects without the diocese, $79.60; total of contributions, $554.14; all money raised by the congregation for current expenses and for contributions, $1,516.16; cash in hand, $212.67.

Remarks—I conducted 4 services at the Hospital for the Insane and also visited Spruce Chapel, Buckhannon, Richwood, Centralia, Camden-on-Gauley, Sutton, Burnsville and Glenville.

PAROCHIAL REPORT.

Rev. ANDREW GLASSELL GRINNAN, address Weston, W. Va. St.

Paul's Chapel, St. Paul's Mission, Lewis county. Date of organization 1903. Present minister took charge 1900.

Church Officers—Treasurer, John White Peterson, address Weston, W. Va.; Superintendent of Sunday Schools, Miss Hila McBride, Weston, W. Va.

Official Acts—Baptisms, infants, 1; adults, 2; total, 3; presented for confirmation since last report, 4; public service, Sundays, 20; other days, 10; total, 30; Holy Communion, public, 4.

Communicants—Number last reported, 9; admitted by confirmation, 4; gain, 4; present number total, 13.

Congregations—Baptized persons connected with parish, 20; confirmed persons connected with parish, 13; families, 7; whole number of individuals, 27; number sittings in church, 120; number free sittings, 120.

Rector's Salary—From Diocesan Missions, $50.00.

Organizations—Sunday Schools, officers and teachers, female, 3; total, 3; pupils, male, 15; Female, 15; total, 30; total Sunday School offerings, $3.78.

Property—Chapel, wood, insurance $750, value $1.000; one-half acre ground.

FINANCIAL REPORT.

Receipts—For all purposes—Cash on hand, per last report, $29.28; pledges and subscriptions, $56.05; collections in Church, $41.19; Sunday School, $3.78; income from other sources, $33.70; total receipts for all purposes, $164.00.

Disbursements——For current expenses—Salary of rector, $26.05; insurance, $15.00; total for current expenses, $41.05. *Contributions—For objects in the Parish*—Maintaining Sunday Schools, $3.77; payment on debts for building, etc., $86.93; total contributions for objects in the Parish, $90.73. *Contributions—For objects in the Diocese*—Widows and orphans, aged and disabled clergy fund, $2.00; Sheltering Arms Hospital, $1.70; total contributions for objects in the diocese, $3.70. *Contributions—For objects without the Diocese*—American church building fund, $3.00; total contributions for objects without the Diocese, $3.00.

Financial Summary—Current Expenses raised by congregation as above, $41.05; contributions for objects in the Parish, $90.73; for objects in the Diocese, $3.70; for objects without the Diocese, $3.00; total of contributions, $97.43; all money raised by the congregation for current expenses and for contributions, $138.48; cash in hand, $25.52.

Remarks—The chapel was consecrated Sunday, Oct. 4, by Bishop Gravatt. A stone font and solid silver mission communion service was presented to the chapel.

PAROCHIAL REPORT.

Rev. ANDREW GLASSELL GRINNAN. St. John's Church, Sutton, Braxton county.

Church Officers—Church Wardens, Amos Bright, J. S. Haymond; Registrar and Treasurer, Amos Bright, Sutton, W. Va.

Official Acts—Public services, Sundays, 4.

Communicants—Number last reported, 12; removed without letter, 1; lapsed, 1; total loss, 2; net loss, 2; present number total, 10.

Congregations—Baptized persons connected with Parish, 25; families, 5; individuals not thus included, 6; number free sittings, 125.

Property—Church, frame, insurance $1,000, value $1,500.

FINANCIAL REPORT.

Disbursements—For current expenses—Salary of rector, $20.00; other current expenses, $2.78; total for current expenses, $22.78.

Financial Summary—Current expenses raised by congregation as above, $22.78; all money raised by the congregation for current expenses and for contributions, $22.78.

Remarks—Rev. E. B. Snead was called to take charge of the mission in connection with Buckhannon. After preaching two Sundays he gave up the church at Sutton and gave all his time to Buckhannon. I find seven communicants at Richwood, W. Va.

PAROCHIAL REPORT.

Rev. JACOB A. HIATT, address Hinton. Ascension Church, Hinton Parish, Hinton, Summers county. Present minister took charge January, 1904.

Church Officers—Church Wardens, Dr. W. S. Barksdale, Hon. T. N. Read; other Vestrymen, E. P. Goodwin, C. S. Falconer, R. G. Haile, John T. Huffman, John Vromack; Registrar, Hon. T. N. Read, address Hinton; Treasurer, T. N. Read, address Hinton; Superintendent of Sunday Schools, T. N. Read, Hinton.

Official Acts—For four months, baptisms, adults, 1; total, 1; public services, Sundays, 38; other days, 30; total, 68; Holy Communion, public, 5; private, 1; total, 6.

Communicants—Number last reported, 46; received by letter, 3; total gain, 3; net gain, 3; present number total, 49.

Congregations—Baptized persons connected with Parish, 81; confirmed persons connected with Parish, 49; families, 38; individuals not thus included, 100; whole number of individuals, 150; number sittings in church, 200; number free sittings, all; number sittings in chapel, 100.

Rector's Salary—As predged from this congregation, $400.00; as pledged from other congregations, $200.00; from American Church Missionary Society, $200.00; total, $800.00.

Organizations—Sunday Schools, officers and teachers, male, 2; female, 2; total, 4; pupils, male, 10; female, 30; total, 40. Other organizations, Woman's Guild, 24.

Property—Church, frame, insurance $2,000, value $3,000; rectory, frame, insurance $1,500; value, $2,000; parish house or Sunday School room, frame; lot on which they stand, $6.000; total value, $11.000.

FINANCIAL REPORT.

Receipts—For all purposes—May 1st, 1903, May 1st, 1904, cash on hand, per last report, none; pledges and subscriptions, $356.70; collections in church, $74.87; Sunday School, $10.39; Woman's Auxiliary, money, $283.50; total receipts for all purposes, $725.46.

Disbursements—For current expenses—Salary of rector, $284.61; insurance, $15.00 ordinary repairs, $51.02; interest on debt, $39.50; other current expenses, $18.00; total for current expenses, $408.13. *Contributions—For other objects in the Parish*—Maintaining Sunday Schools, $11.50; payment on debts for building, etc., principal, $317.00; total contributions for objects in the Parish, $328.50. *Contributions—For objects in the Diocese*—Salary of Bishops, $11.00; diocesan missions, $23.45; convocation missions, $10.00; total contributions for objects in the diocese, $44.45.

Financial Summary—Current expenses raised by congregation as above, $408.13. Contributions for objects in the Parish, $328.50; for objects in the Diocese, $44.45; total of contributions, $372.95; all money raised by the congregation for current expenses and for contributions, $781.08.

PAROCHIAL REPORT.

Rev. JACOB A. HIATT, address Hinton. Glen Jean Mission, Glen Jean, Fayette county. Present minister took charge January, 1904.

Church Officers—Church Warden, W. B. Johnson; other Vestrymen, Dr. C. B. Lee, W. S. Carter; Registrar, Mrs. C. B. Lee, address Glen Jean; Treasurer, Mr. W. B. Johnson, address Red Star.

Official Acts—Public services, Sundays, 20; total, 20; Holy Communion, private, 1; total 1.

Congregations—Confirmed persons connected with Parish, 15; number of scattered communicants in your section not connected with any Parish, 70; number sittings in church, 300; number free sittings, all.

Rector's salary—As pledged from this congregation, $200; total, $200.

Property—Church, frame, insurance $1,500, value $2,500; total value, $2,500.

FINANCIAL REPORT.

Receipts—For all purposes—Pledges and subscriptions, $233.00; total, $233.00.

Disbursements—For current expenses—Salary of rector, eight months, Rev. Mr. Crook, $200.00; two months, Rev. Hiatt, $33.00; total for current expenses, $233.00.

Financial Summary—Current expenses raised by congregation as above, $233.00; all money raised by the congregation for current expenses and for contributions, $233.00.

PAROCHIAL REPORT.

Rev. J. A. HIATT. Grace Church, Ravenswood.

Church Officers—Church Warden, F. H. Green; other Vestrymen, J. V. Armstrong.

Official Acts—Public services, Sundays, 20; other days, 30; total, 50; Holy Communion, public, 2.

Communicants—Number last reported, 20; present number total, 20.

Congregations—Baptized persons connected with Parish, 40; confirmed persons connected with Parish, 20; families, 14; individuals not thus included, 25; number sittings in church, 200; number free sittings all.

Rector's Salary—As pledged from this congregation, $75; total, $75.

Property—Church, frame, insurance, $2,200, value $3,500; rectory, frame, insurance, $1.000; value, $2,000; total insurance, $3,200; total value, $5,500. Indebtedness, on church, $450; total indebtedness, $450. Money raised from outside sources, $25, for repairs.

FINANCIAL REPORT.

Receipts—For all purposes—Pledges and subscriptions, $75.

Disbursements—For current expenses—Salary of rector for nine months, $50; ordinary repairs, $35; payment on debts contracted for current expenses, $50; total for current expenses, $135. *Contributions—For objects in the Diocese*—Diocesan missions, $3.50; convocation missions, $2.00; Sheltering Arms Hospital, $14.00; total contributions for objects in the Diocese, $19.50.

Financial Summary—Contributions for objects in the Parish, $135.00; for objects in the Diocese, $19.50; total of contributions, $154.50.

PAROCHIAL REPORT.

Rev. JACOB A. HIATT, address Ravenswood. St. John's Church, Ravenswood Parish, Ripley, Jackson county. Date of organization, 1851.

Church Officers—Church Warden, W. T. Greer, Ripley, W. Va.; other Vestrymen, Mr. G. B. Crow, Dan P. Crow, W. W. Armstrong, Dr. Petty, C. W. Starcher, Sam G. Starcher.

Official Acts—Burials, 1; public services, Sundays, 16; other days, 4; total, 20; Holy Communion, public, 2.

Communicants—Number last reported, 37; died, 1; total loss, 1; net loss, 1; present number total, 36.

Congregations—Baptized persons connected with Parish, 48; families, 15; whole number of individuals, 80; number sittings in church, 200; num-free sittings, all.

Rector's salary—As pledged from this congregation, $150.

Organizations—Woman's Guild, 15.

Property—Church, frame, insurance $1,000, value $2,000. Indebtedness, due the minister, $15; total indebtedness, $15.

FINANCIAL REPORT.

Receipts—For all purposes—Pledges and subscriptions, $85.00; Guilds or other societies, $96.44; total receipts for all purposes, $181.44.

Disbursements—For current expenses—Salary of rector, for eight months, $85; other current expenses, $11.85; total for current expenses, $96.85. *Contributions—For objects in the Diocese*—Sheltering Arms Hospital, $15.00; total contributions for objects in the Diocese, $15.00.

Financial Summary—Contributions for objects in the Parish, $181.44; for objects in the Diocese, $15.00; total of contributions, $196.44; all money raised by the congregation for current expenses and for contributions, $196.44; cash in hand, Woman's Guild, $84.59.

PAROCHIAL REPORT.

Rev. DAVID W. HOWARD, address Wheeling, W. Va. Saint Matthew's church, Wheeling, Ohio county. Date of organization, May 11th, 1819. Present minister took charge Jan. 1st, 1900.

Church Officers—Church Wardens, Joseph D. DuBois, sr., Dr. G. A. Aschman; other Vestrymen, J. J. Holloway, B. Walker Peterson, W. S. Brady, Joseph C. Brady, Allen Brock, Julian Hearne, Robert M. Browne, Cyrus P. Flick, Hullihen Quarrier, Peebles Tatum; Registrar, Allen Brock, address 1413 Main street; Treasurer, Cyrus P. Flick, address 1423 Chapline street; superintendent of Sunday Schools, the Rector; Sunday School

Secretary and Treasurer, William Schwertfeger; Lay Reader, Dr. G. A. Aschman.

Official Acts—Baptisms, infants, 16; adults, 8; total 24; presented for confirmation since last report, 30; marriages, 27; burials, 16; catechisings, 12; public services, Sundays, 129; other days, 78; total, 207; Holy Communion, public, 70; private, 6; total, 76.

Communicants—Number last reported, 537; received by letter, 6; admitted by confirmation, 30; total gain, 36; died, 5; transferred, 6; removed without letter, 12; total loss, 23; net gain, 13; present number total, 550.

Congregations—Baptized persons connected with Parish, 870; confirmed persons connected with Parish, 571; families, 192; individuals not thus included, 112; whole number of individuals, 880; number sittings in church, 600; number free sittings, 170; number sittings in Sunday School room, 150.

Rector's Salary—As pledged from this congregation, $2,000.00.

Organizations—Sunday Schools, officers and teachers, male, 4; female, 9; total, 13; pupils, male, 60; female, 75; total, 135; advent offering, $60.00; lenten offering, $250.00; other offerings, $102.81; total Sunday School offerings, $412.81; Parish schools, officers and teachers, 1; scholars, 16; total, 17; Woman's Auxiliary, members, 75. Other organizations, Junior Auxiliary, 45; Swope Guild, 20; N. S. Thomas Guild, 10; Chancel Chapter, 10; King's Daughters, 25; Choir Association, 50.

Property—Church, stone, insurance, $50,000, value $65,000; rectory, stone and brick, insurance $6,000, value $12,000; total value, insurance $56,000, value $77,000. Indebtedness, vestry note at Bank of Wheeling, $2,200; total indebtedness, $2,200.

FINANCIAL REPORT.

Receipts—For all purposes—Pledges and subscriptions, $2,088.22; pew rent, $5,251.28; collections in church, $3,814.19; offerings, special, $278.00; Sunday School, $297.05; Woman's Auxiliary, money, $328.57; Guilds, or other societies, $1,130.54; total receipts for all purposes, $13,187.85.

Disbursements—For current expenses—Salary of rector, $2,000.00; salary of assistant, $500.00; other salaries, $1,871.37; ordinary repairs, $756.43; interest on debt, $262.09; payment on debts contracted for current expenses, $2,050.00; other current expenses, $1,297.32; Parish Record, $274.00; total for current expenses, $9,011.21. *Contributions—For objects in the Parish*—Communion alms, $245.83; extraordinary repairs and improvements, $150.00; parish missions, $283.60; maintaining Sunday Schools, $47.05; City Hospital, $92.00; parish house, $50.00; charities, $414.90; total contributions for objects in the Parish, $1,283.38. *Contributions—For objects in the Diocese*—Salary of Bishops, $605.75; diocesan missions, $425.00; convocation missions, $95.00; widows and orphans, aged and disabled clergy fund, $113.35; religious and theological education, $15.00;

Sheltering Arms Hospital, $419.64; Bishop's special fund, $64.00; Woman's Missionary, $100.00; Chester Mission, $33.62; total contributions for objects in the Diocese, $1,871.26. *Contributions—For objects without the Diocese* —Domestic missions general, $483.24; deaf and dumb, $5.00; Jews, $5.00; total domestic missions, $493.24; for China, $35.00; through American Church Missionary Society, $38.57; Brazil, $80.00; Cuba, $75.00; total foreign missions, $228.57; general clergy relief fund, $25.00; total contributions for objects without the Diocese, $746.81.

Financial Summary—Current expenses raised by congregation as above, $9,011.21: contributions, for objects in the Parish, $1,283.38; for objects in the Diocese, $1,871.36; for objects without the Diocese, $746.81; total of contributions, $3,901.55; all money raised by the congregation for current expenses and for contributions, $12,912.76; cash in hand, $275.09.

PAROCHIAL REPORT.

Rev. EDWARD D. IRVINE address Wellsburg. Christ Church, Wellsburg, Brooke county. Date of organization 1793. Present minister took charge January 15, 1903.

Church Officers—Church Wardens, A. C. Hall, Jos. Faussett; other vestrymen, Geo. A. Baxter, Frederick Hall, T. C. Buchanan; Registrar, Geo. A. Baxter, address Wellsburg; Treasurer, T. C. Buchanan address Wellsburg; Superintendent Sunday Schools, H. C. Hall; Sunday School Secretary and Treasurer, Rose Wheeler.

Official Acts—Baptisms, infants, 2; adults, 2; total, 4; presented for confirmation since last report, 4; marriages, 9; burials, 2; catechisings, 12; public services, Sundays, 82; other days, 75; total, 157; Holy Communion, public, 20; total, 20.

Communicants—Number last reported, 58; admitted by confirmation, 4; total gain, 4; died, 2; lapsed, 5; total loss, 7; net loss, 3; present number total, 55.

Congregations—Baptized persons connected with Parish, 75; confirmed persons connected with Parish, 60; families, 25; whole number of individuals, 125; number sittings in church, 175.

Rector's Salary—As pledged from this congregation, $450; from diocesan missions, $240; as pledged from other congregations, $60; total, $750.

Organizations—Sunday Schools, officers and teachers, male, 2; female, 3; total, 5; pupils, male, 10; female, 20; total, 30; Advent offering, $5.00; Lenten offerings, $20.16; other offerings, $40.59; total Sunday School offerings, $65.75; Parish guild, choir, chancel chapter.

Property—Church, wood, value, $3,500; rectory, wood, value $1,500; other property, value, $150; total value, $5,150.

FINANCIAL REPORT.

Receipts—For all Purposes—Cash in hand, per last report, $15.00; pledges and subscriptions, $520.39; collections in church, $101.92; Sunday School, $65.75; Parish Guild, boxes, value, $22.50; guilds or other societies, $285.08; total receipts for all purposes, $1,010.64.

Disbursements—For Current Expenses—Salary of rector, $450.00; other salaries, $30.50; other current expenses, 43.47; total for current expenses, $523.97. *Contributions—For objects in the Parish*—Communion alms, $35.98; extraordinary repairs and improvements, $236.42; maintaining Sunday Schools, $22.77; other objects, $57.18; total contributions for objects in the Parish, $352.35. *Contributions—For objects in the Diocese*—Salary of bishops, $25.00; diocesan missions, $30.16; convocation missions, $6.00; widows and orphans, aged and disabled clergy fund, $5.00; Sheltering Arms Hospital, $5.00; mission house, $7.00; box for Hospital, (Sheltering Arms) $22.50; total contributions for objects in the Diocese, $100.66. *Contributions—For objects without the Diocese*—Domestic missions general, $16.33; foreign missions general, $16.33; general missions, $32.66; specials, &c., $1.00; total contributions for objects without the Diocese, $33.66.

Financial Summary—Current expenses raised by congregation as above, $523.97. *Contributions*—for objects in the Parish, $352.35; for objects in the Diocese, $100.66; for objects without the Diocese, $33.66; total of contributions, $486.67; all money raised by the congregation for current expenses and for contributions, $1,010.64.

PAROCHIAL REPORT.

Rev. EDWARD D. IRVINE, address Wellsburg. St. John's Church, St. John's Parish, Brooke county. Date of organization 1793. Present minister took charge March 29, 1903.

Church Officers—Church Warden, Jas. Williamson; other vestrymen, Norman Pool, Jas. Allison; Registrar, Sam'l Baxter, address Route 3, Wellsburg; Treasurer, Jas. Williamson, address Route 3, Wellsburg.

Official Acts—Baptisms, infants, 8; presented for confirmation since last report, 4; burials, 1; public services, Sundays, 25; Holy Communion, public, 3.

Communicants—Number last reported, 22; admitted by confirmation, 4; total gain, 4; died, 1; total loss, 1; net gain, 3; present number total, 25.

Congregations—Baptized persons connected with Parish, 35; confirmed persons connected with Parish, 25; families, 8; whole number of individuals, 40; number sittings in church, 250; number free sittings, all.

Rector's Salary—As pledged from this congregation, $60.00; from diocesan missions, $240.00; as pledged from other congregations, $450.00; total, $750.00.

Property—Church, brick, value, $2,500; total value, $2,500. Indebtedness, due to minister, $15.00; total indebtedness, $15.00.

FINANCIAL REPORT.

Receipts—For all Purposes—Pledges and subscriptions, $411.50; collections in church, $34.62; total receipts for all purposes, $446.12.

Disbursements—For Current Expenses—Salary of rector, $45.00; other current expenses, $27.42; extensive repairs, $366.50; total for current expenses, $438.92. *Contributions—For objects in the Diocese*—Diocesan missions, $7.65; total contributions for objects in the Diocese, $7.65.

Financial Summary—Current expenses raised by congregation as above, $72.42. *Contributions*—For objects in the Parish, $366.50; for objects in the Diocese, $7.65.

Remarks—Extensive repairs have been made on the church, and the building is now in good conditions. The congregations are good, but miscellaneous, very few are church people.

PAROCHIAL REPORT.

Rev. ARTHUR M. LEWIS, address Powellton, W. Va. St. David's Church, Powellton, Fayette county. Date of organization December 5, 1886. Present minister took charge September 1, 1901.

Church Officers—Church Warden, Thomas Price; other committeemen, Godwin H. Powel, D. T. Evans, J. I. Absalom, Dr. A. W. DeBell, D. Swain; Registrar, John I. Absalom, address Powellton, W. Va.; Treasurer, D. Swain, address Powellton, W. Va.; Superintendent of Sunday Schools, D. Swain, Powellton, W. Va.; Sunday School Secretary and Treasurer, John I. Absalom; Lay reader, Godwin H. Powel.

Official Acts—Baptisms, infants, 5; adults, 5; total, 10; presented for confirmation since last report, 8; burials, 4; catechisings, 21; public services, Sundays, 42; other days, 10; total, 52; Holy Communion, public, 7.

Communicants—Number last reported, 27; admitted by confirmation, 8; added otherwise, 1; total gain, 9; removed without letter, 2; total loss, 2; net gain, 7; present number total, 34.

Congregations—Baptized persons connected with Parish, 60; confirmed persons connected with Parish, 34; families, 15; number sittings in church, 110; number free sittings, 110.

Rector's Salary—As pledged from this congregation, $402.00; as pledged from other congregations, $520.00; total, $922.00.

Organizations—Sunday Schools, officers and teachers, male, 2; female, 4; total, 6; pupils, male, 22; female, 35; total, 57; Advent offerings, $11.00; Lenten offerings, $8.26; total Sunday School offerings, $19.26; Ladies' Aid Society, 15 members.

Property—Chancel furniture, &c., value, $328.00; rectory furniture, value, $148.15; total value, $476.15. There is no indebtedness of any kind.

FINANCIAL REPORT.

Receipts—For all Purposes—Cash on hand, per last report, $174.51; pledges and subscriptions, $523.46; collections in church, $109.59; Sunday School, $49.95; Ladies' Aid Society, $206.68; income from other sources, $35.25; total receipts for all purposes, $1,099.44.

Disbursements—For Current Expenses—Salary of rector, $402.00; other current expenses, $99.34; total for current expenses, $501.34. *Disbursements —For objects in the Parish*—Communion alms, $14.68; extraordinary repairs and improvements, $28.00; maintaining Sunday Schools, $30.68; other objects, $22.34; rectory furniture, $148.15; total contributions for objects in the Parish, $243.85.*Contributions—For objects in the Diocese*—Salary of bishops, $21.00; permanent fund, $8.00; diocesan missions, $23.57; convocation missions, $2.00; widows and orphans, aged and disabled clergy fund, $4.31; Sheltering Arms Hospital, $13.42; bishop's special fund, $50.00; total contributions for objects in the diocese, $122.30. *Contributions—For objects without the Diocese*—Domestic missions general, $6.63; total domestic missions, $6.63; foreign missions general, $9.67; Brazil, $2.07; Cuba, $2.06; total foreign missions, $13.80; general clergy relief fund, $3.10; Bible and prayer book society, $5.00; society for promoting Christianity among the Jews, $2.33; total contributions for objects without the diocese, $30.86.

Financial Summary—Current expenses raised by congregation as above, $501.34. *Contributions*—For objects in the Parish, $243.85; for objects in the Diocese, $122.30; for objects without the Diocese, $30.86; total of contributions, $397.01; all money raised by the congregation for current expenses and for contributions, $898.35; cash in hand, $201.09.

Remarks—Parochial report of three mission points—St. Titus Mission at Nuttallburg—At present we have fifteen communicants here; baptized persons connected with the mission, 27; baptisms, 8; confirmations, 3; Sunday services, 1; week day services, 11; money raised, diocesan missions, $5.00; bishop's salary, $5.00; rector's salary, $49.05.

ARTHUR M. LEWIS.

Good Shepherd Mission, Ferris—Communicants, 4; Baptized persons connected with the mission, 8; baptisms, 1; week day services, 12; marriages, 2; money raised, rector's salary, $20.00; general missions, $7.18; (raised by one class in a union Sunday School.)

ARTHUR M. LEWIS.

Emmanuel Mission, Mt. Carbon—Communicants,10; baptized persons connected with the mission, 25; money raised, foreign missions general, $2.25; Sheltering Arms Hospital, $2.54; diocesan missions, $5.00; bishop's salary, $5.00; rector's salary, $50.50; sexton, $15.00; total money raised, $80.29.

ARTHUR M. LEWIS.

PAROCHIAL REPORT.

Rev. ARTHUR M. LEWIS, address Powellton, W. Va. Calvary Church, Montgomery, Fayette county. Date of organization 1878. Present minister took charge September 1, 1901.

Church Officers—Church Warden, N. R. Coles; other vestrymen, O. J. Henderson, Hubbard Smith, W. K. Bridges, Venable Josnson, L. E. Rupert; Registrar, W. K. Bridges, address Longacre, W. Va.; Treasurer Venable Johnson, address Crescent, W. Va.; Superintendent of Sunday Schools, Mrs. O. J. Henderson, Montgomery, W. Va.; Sunday School Secretary and Treasurer, Mrs. O. J. Henderson.

Official Acts—Baptisms, infants, 7; presented for confirmation since last report, 1; marriages, 1; burials, 1; catechisings, 2; public services, Sundays, 26; other days, 8; total, 34; Holy Communion, public, 4; private, 1; total, 5.

Communicants—Number last reported, 17; admitted by confirmation, 1; added otherwise, 2; total gain, 3; removed without letter, 1; total loss, 1; net gain, 2; present number total, 19.

Congregations—Baptized persons connected with Parish, 34; confirmed persons connected with Parish, 19; families, 8; number sittings in church, 200; number free sittings, 200.

Rector's Salary—As pledged from this congregation, $200.00; as pledged from other congregations, $722.00; total, $922.00.

Organizations—Sunday Schools, officers and teachers, female, 1; pupils, male, 7; female, 8; total, 15; Lenten offering, $5.10; total Sunday School offerings, $5.10; Ladies' Aid Society, 8.

Property—Church, frame, insurance, $1,200.00; value, $1,500.00; rectory fund, $1,096.47; foundation, $200.00; lot, $500.00; total value, $3,296.47; indebtedness on church, $400.00; due the minister, $100.00; total indebtedness, $500.00.

FINANCIAL REPORT.

Receipts—For all Purposes—Cash on hand, per last report, $3.85; pledges and subscriptions, $202.65; collections in church, $106.50; interest from investments, $67.72; money borrowed, (from rectory fund) $400.00; thank offerings, (donations) $11.62; Sunday School, $5.10; contingent fund, $9.00; contributions from without, $10.00; income from account repairs, &c., $82.40; total receipts for all purposes, $831.12.

Disbursements—For Current Expenses—Salary of rector, (account $200.00;) $100.00; other salaries, (sexton) $19.00; ordinary repairs, (carpet, &c.) $33.65; other curent expenses, $55.89; total for current expenses, $244.58. *Contributions—For objects in the Parish*—Extraordinary repairs and improvements, $510.32; total contributions for objects in the Parish, $510.32. *Contributions for objects in the Diocese*—Salary of bishops, $15.00; diocesan missions, $15.00; convocation missions, $1.00; widows and orphans, aged and disabled clergy fund, $2.50; Sheltering Arms Hospital, $4.10; total contributions for objects in the diocese, $37.60. *Contributions—For objects without the Diocese*—Domestic missions general, $3.15; total domestic missions, $3.15; foreign missions general, $7.30; Brazil, $1.30; Cuba, $1:30; total foreign missions, $9.90; general clergy relief fund, $3.30; total contributions for objects without the Diocese, $16.35.

Financial Summary—Current expenses raised by congregation as above, $244.58. *Contributions*—For objects in the parish, $510.32; for objects in the Diocese, $37.60; for objects without the Diocese, $16.35; total of contributions, $564.21; all money spent by the congregation for current expenses and for contributions, $808.85; cash in hand, $22.27.

PAROCHIAL REPORT.

Rev. ARTHUR M. LEWIS, address Ansted, W. Va. Church of the Redeemer, Ansted, Fayette county. Date of organization, 1879. Present minister took charge April 1, 1901.

Church Officers—Church Warden, Wm. N. Page; other vestermen, J. C. R. Taylor, Raleigh C. Taylor, W. H. Evans, Patrick Moran, John R. Brashears; Registrar, J. C. R. Taylor, address Ansted, W. Va.; Treasurer, W. H. Evans, Ansted, W. Va.; Superintendent of Sunday Schools, Wm. N. Page; Sunday School Secretary and Treasurer, J. C. R. Taylor.

Official Acts—Baptisms, infants, 5; adults, 2; total, 7; presented for confirmation since last report, 3; marriages, 1; burials, 1; catechisings, 20; public services, Sundays, 25; other days, 29; total, 54; Holy Communion, public, 6; private, 1; total, 7.

Communicants—Number last reported, 37; admitted by confirmation, 3; added otherwise, 2; total gain, 5; died, 1; removed without letter, 1; lapsed, 4; total loss, 6; net loss, 1; present number total, 36.

Congregations—Baptized persons connected with Parish, 75; confirmed persons connected with Parish, 36; families, 11; individuals not thus included, 2; number sittings in church, 200; number free sittings, 200.

Rectors Salary—As pledged from this congregation, $200.00; as pledged from other congregations, $722.00; total, $922.00.

Organizations—Sunday Schools, officers and teachers, male, 2; female, 4; total, 6; pupils, male, 20; femals, 40; total, 60; Advent offerings, $15.39; Lenten offerings, $6.00; other offerings, $36.13; total Sunday School offerings, $57.32; Parish schools, officers and teachers, 1; scholars, 40; total, 41; Ladies' Aid Society, 6.

Property—Church, frame, value, $3,000.

FINANCIAL REPORT.

Receipts—For all Purposes—Cash on hand, per last report, $75.13;

pledges and subscriptions, $200.75; collections in church, $78.01; Sunday School, $57.52; Ladies' Aid Society, $50.00; Easter offering for Parish school building, $30.00; contributions from without, $220.00; income from other sources, $253.02; total receipts for all purposes, $964.43.

Disbursements—For Current Expenses—Salary of rector, $200.00; other salaries, (janitor) $18.00; other current expenses, $8.15; other objects, $9.00; total for current expenses, $235.15. *Contributions—For objects in* added otherwise, 4; total gain, 13; removed without letter, 12; lapsed, 6; *the Parish*—Parish schools, $212.50; maintaining Sunday Schools, $56.01; other objects, $29.46; total contributions for objects in the Parish, $297.97. *Contributions—For objects in the Diocese*—Salary of bishops, $20.00; diocesan missions, $20.00; convocation missions, $27.75; widows and orphans, aged and disabled clergy fund, $4.50; Sheltering Arms Hospital, $11.00; total contributions for objects in the Diocese, $83.25. *Contributions—For objects without the Diocese*—Domestic missions general, $4.19; total domestic missions, $4.19; foreign missions, general, $9.50; total foreign missions, $9.50; general clergy relief fund, $3.00; total contributions for objects without the Diocese, $16.69.

Financial Summary—Current expenses raised by congregation as above, $235.15. *Contributions*—For objects in the Parish, $297.97; for objects in the Diocese, $83.25; for objects without the Diocese, $16.69; total of contributions, $397.91; all money raised by the congregation for current expenses and for contributions, $633.06; cash in hand, $331.37.

Remarks—Received $200.00 from Rev. B. M. Spurr on account Parish school expenses.

PAROCHIAL REPORT.

Rev. JOHN TILTON MARLEY, address Morgantown, 247 Willey street. Present minister took charge October, 1900.

Church Officers—Church Wardens, Capt. Wm. C. Marshall, Prof. S. B. Brown; other vestrymen, Col. J. C. Frazer, Bryan Gordon, L. D. Beall, Prof. Truscott, Harry Zeomly, Dr. R. H. Edmundson, Geo. Rogers, Dr. St. Geo. T. Brooke; Registrar, Mr. L. D. Beall, address Morgantown; Treasurer, Bryan Gordon, address Morgantown; Superintendent of Sunday Schools, Rector; Sunday School Secretary and Treasurer, Mr. Dean Page.

Official Acts—Baptisms, infants, 5; adults, 4; total, 9; presented for confirmation since last report, 9; marriages, 4; burials, 3; catechisings, 12; public services, Sundays, 106; other days, 60; total, 166; Holy Communion, public, 15.

Communicants—Number last reported, 91; admitted by confirmation, 9; total loss, 18; net loss, 5; present number total, 86.

Congregations—Baptized persons connected with Parish, 112; confirmed

persons connected with Parish, 86; families, 35; individuals not thus included, 15; number of scattered communicants in your section not connected with any Parish, 4; number sittings in church, 225.

Rector's Salary—As pledged by this congregation, $1,000.00.

Organizations—Sunday Schools, officers and teachers, male, 2; female, 3; total, 5; pupils, male, 18; female, 22; total, 40; Ladies' Guild; Junior Guild; Boys' Guild.

Property—Church, frame, insurance, $2,500.00; value, $3,000.00.

FINANCIAL REPORT.

Receipts—For all Purposes—Cash on hand, per last report, $175.55; pledges and subscriptions, $826.58; collections in church, $139.38; thank offering, $55.00; Sunday School, $25.43; guilds or other societies, $359.80; contributions from without, $327.78; total receipts for all purposes, $1,-904.44.

Disbursements—For Current Expenses—Salary of rector, $1,000.00; other salaries, $253.28; insurance, $50.00; ordinary repairs, $301.32; interest on debt, $18.00; other current expenses, $106.00; total for current expenses, $1,728.60. *Contributions—For objects in the Parish*—Communion alms, $32.00; Parish missions, $20.00; maintaining Sunday Schools, $5.40; total contributions for objects in the parish, $57.40. *Contributions—For objects in the Diocese*—Salary of bishops, $25.00; diocesan missions, $25.00; convocation missions, $10.00; widows and orphans, aged and disabled clergy fund, $5.15; religious and theological education, $1.48; Sheltering Arms Hospital, $20.50; total contributions for objects in the Diocese, $87.13. *Contributions—for objects without the Diocese*—Domestic missions general, $13.62; foreign missions general, $13.61; Brazil, $5.00; Cuba, $4.08; total contributions for objects without the Diocese, $36.31.

Financial Summary—Contributions—Current expenses, etc., $1,728.60; for objects in the Parish, $57.40; for objects in the Diocese, $87.13; for objects dwithout the Diocese, $36.31; total contributions, $1,909.44.

PAROCHIAL REPORT.

Rev. C. E. A. MARSHALL, address Shepherdstown. Trinity Church, St. Andrews Parish, Shepherdstown, Jefferson county. Date of organization about 1790. Present minister took charge February 1, 1903.

Church Officers—Church Wardens, A. S. Dandridge, Jno. O. Aglionby; other evstrymen, J. S. Bragonier, P. P. Marshall, Lee H. Moler, F. W. Muzzey, Dr. Hop. Gibson, Dr. D. W. Border; Registrar, J. S. Brazonier, address Shepherdstown; Treasurer, J. S. Bragonier, address Shepherdstown; Superintendent of Sunday Schools, A. S. Dandridge, Shepherdstown.

Official Acts—Baptisms, adults, 1; presented for confirmation since last report, 1; marriages, 1; burials, 6; catechisings, 15; public services, Sundays, 127; other days, 60; total, 187; Holy Communion, public, 16; private, 1; total, 17.

Communicants—Number last reported, 144; admitted by confirmation, 1; added otherwise, 8; total gain, 9; removed without letter, 3; total, loss, 3; net gain, 6; present number total, 150.

Congregations—Baptized persons connected with Parish, 272; families, 50.

Rector's Salary—As pledged from this congregation, $600.

Organizations—Sunday Schools, No. 1, officers and teachers, male, 2; female, 5; total, 7; pupils, total, 40; No. 2, officers and teachers, male, 1; No. 3, officers and teachers, female, 3; pupils, male, 8; Woman's Auxiliary, members, 8; Junior Auxiliary, 11.

Property—Church , Stone, insurance, $3,500; value, $12,300; chapel, stone, value, $3,000; rectory, brick, insurance, $3,250; value, $6.000: Chapel Good Shepherd at Duffield, frame, insurance, $1,000; value $1,500; total insurance, $7,750; total value, $22,800.

FINANCIAL REPORT.

Receipts for all Purposes—Cash on hand, per last report, $148.25; pledges and subscriptions, and pew rent, $582.63; collections in church, &c., $659.17; Woman's Auxiliary, money, $2.00; Woman's Auxiliary, boxes, value, $65.37; guilds or other societies, collections from without, income from other sources, $55.00; total receipts for all purposes, $1,512.42.

Disbursements—For Current Expenses—Salary of rector, $610.00; other salaries, (sexton) $50.00; insurance, $22.50; ordinary repairs, $68.96; other current expenses, $68.31; total for current expenses, $819.77. *Contributions—For objects in the Parish*—Communion alms, $28.60; maintaining Sunday Schools, $9.61; total contributions for objects in the Parish, $38.21. *Contributions—For objects in the Diocese*—Salary of bishops, $61.50; permanent fund, $1.27; diocesan missions, $43.23; convocation missions, $35.00; widows and orphans, aged and disabled clergy fund, $14.00; religious and theological education, $10.04; Sheltering Arms Hospital, $6.24; bishop's special fund, $60.00; total contributions for objects in the Diocese, $231,28. *Contributions—For objects without the Diocese*—Domestic missions general, $23.14; Indians, $1.38; Jews, $2.01; through American Church Missionary Society, $7.00; total domestic missions, $33.53; foreign missions general, $24.89; for Africa, $25.00; through American Church Missionary Society, $7.00; total foreign missions, $56.89; specials, boxes, &c., $65.37; American church building fund, $7.70; general clergy relief fund, $3.00; other objects, $10.00; American Bible Society, $8.47; total contributions for objects without the diocese, $185.03.

Financial Summary—Current expenses raised by congregation as above,

$819.77. *Contributions*—For objects in the Parish, $857.98; for objects in the Diocese, $231.28; for objects without the Diocese, $185.03; total of contributions, $1,274.29; cash in hand, $150.99.

PAROCHIAL REPORT.

Rev. F. A. MEADE, Elkins. Grace Church, Elkins, Randolph county. Present minister took charge December 1, 1903.

Church Officers—Church Warden, C. H. Scott; other vestrymen, I. P. Gassman, J. Lacy Dunlop, John Lingumfelter, Robert G. Read, Fred Fletcher; Registrar, Bobt. G. Read, address Elkins; Treasurer, I. P. Gassman, address Elkins; Superintendent of Sunday Schools, J. Lacy Dunlop, Elkins; Sunday School Secretary and Treasurer, Charles Stiffler.

Official Acts—Baptisms, infants, 1; adults, 1; total, 2; presented for confirmation since last report, 2; marriages, 1; burials, 3; public services, Sundays, 34; other days, 27; total, 61; Holy Communion, public, 5.

Communicants—Number last reported, 30; received by letter, 3; admitted by confirmation, 2; added otherwise, 9; total gain, 14; transferred, 3; removed without letter, 6; total loss 9; net gain, 5; present number total, 35.

Congregations—Baptized persons connected with Parish, 72; confirmed persons connected with Parish, 36; families, 16; individuals not thus included, 6; whole number of individuals, 75; number of scattered communicants in your section not connected with any Parish, 7; number sittings in church, 120; number free sittings, 120.

Rector's Salary—As pledged from this congregation, $200.00; from diocesan missions, $400.00; as pledged from other congregations, $100.00; total $700.00.

Organizations—Sunday Schools, officers and teachers, male, 1; female, 3; total, 4; pupils, male, 7; female, 13; total, 20; Lenten offering, $9.30; other offerings, $25.00; total Sunday School offerings, $34.30.

Property—Church, frame, insurance, $1,400; value, $2,900; rectory, frame, insurance, $1,000; value, $2,000; total value, $4,900. Indebtedness, on rectory, $1,750; total indebtedness, $1,750.

FINANCIAL REPORT.

Receipts—For all Purposes—Cash on hand, per last report, $2.03; pledges and subscriptions, $255.47; collections in church, $111.74; guilds or other societies, $40.00; contributions from without, $128.12; income from other sources, $5.00; total receipts for all purposes, $542.36.

Disbursements—For Current Expenses—Salary of rector, $170.43; other salaries, $11.00; insurance, $18.00; ordinary repairs, $3.40; interest on debt, $50.00; other current expenses, $23.41; other objects, $1.50; total for current expenses, $277,74. *Contributions—For objects in the Parish*—Communion alms, (not added ncluded below) $18.45; extraordinary repairs and improvements, $159.27; maintaining Sunday Schools, $13.24; total contributions for objects in the Parish, $172.51. *Contributions—For objects in the DDiocese*—Salary of bishops, $10.00; diocesan missions, $10.00; widows and orphans, aged and disabled clergy fund, $3.25; religious and theological education, $2.00; total contributions for objects in the Diocese, $25.25. *Contributions—For objects without the Diocese*—Domestic missions general, $1.25; total domestic missions, $1.25; foreign missions, general, $1.25; total foreign misions, $1.25; total contributions for objects without the Diocese, $2.50.

Financial Summary—Current expenses raised by congregation as above, $277.74. Contributions—For objects in the Parish, $172.51; for objects in the Diocese, $25.25; for objects without the Diocese, $2.50; total contributions, $200.26; all money raised by the congregation for current expenses and for contributions, $478.00; cash in hand, $105.35.

PAROCHIAL REPORT.

Rev. F. A. MEADE, address Elkins. Trinity Church, Belington, Barbour county. Present minister took charge December 1, 1903.

Communicants—Number last reported, 10; present number total, 10.

Congregations—Baptized persons connected with Parish, 25.

Remarks—Although nominally in charge since the first of December, I have not been able to hold any service on account of the impossibility of securing a suitable building. We have here a church lot and about $316.00 to meet deferred payments on lot, and to add to the fund for building a church.

F. A. MEADE.

PAROCHIAL REPORT.

Rev. ROBT. N. MEADE, address Bramwell. Grace Mission, Eckman, McDowell county. Present minister took charge April 15, 1904.

Church Officers—Church Warden, Dr. P. Killey.

Official Acts—Baptisms, infants, 1; total, 1; marriages, 2; public services, Sundays, 15; total, 15; Holy Communion, public, 3.

Communicants—Number last reported, 22; received by letter, 1; added otherwise, 2; total gain, 3; transferred, 10; lapsed, 2; total loss, 12; net loss, 9; present number total, 13.

Congregations—Baptized persons connected with Parish, 24; confirmed persons connected with Parish, 16; families, 10; whole number of individuals, 35; number free sittings, all; number sittings in chapel, 125.

Property—Church, frame, insurance $800, value $1,200.

FINANCIAL REPORT.

Receipts—For all purposes—Pledges and subscriptions, $88.00; collections in church, $76.06; total receipts for al purposes, $164.06.

Disbursements—For current expenses—Salary of rector, $67.30; salary of assistant, $9.25; total for current expenses, $76.59. *Contributions—For objects in the Parish*—Extraordinary repairs and improvements, $30.00; total contributions for objects in the Parish, $30.00. *Contributions—For objects in the Diocese*—Salary of Bishops, $10.00; permanent fund, $10.00; diocesan missions, $7.43; total contributions for objects in the Diocese, $27.43. *Contributions—For objects without the Diocese*—Domestic missions general, $8.80; foreign missions general, $8.80; total foreign missions, $17.60; American church building fund, $1.17; general clergy relief fund, $6.95; Virginia Educational Society, $4.32; total contributions for objects without the Diocese, $30.04.

Financial Summary—Current expenses raised by congregation as above, $76.59; contributions, for objects in the Parish, $30.00; for objects in the Diocese, $27.43; for objects without the Diocese, $30.04; total of contributions, $87.47; all money raised by the congregation for current expenses and for contributions, $164.06.

PAROCHIAL REPORT.

Rev. ROBT. N. MEADE, address Bramwell. St. Antipas Mission, Welch, McDowell county. Present minister took charge April 15, 1903.

Official Acts—Marriages, 1; public services, Sundays, 15; other days, 2; total, 17; Holy Communion, public, 1.

Communicants—Number last reported, 15; received by letter, 5; total gain, 5; transferred, 5; total loss, 5; present number total, 15.

Congregations—Baptized persons connected with Parish, 32; confirmed persons connected with Parish, 16; families, 10; individuals not thus included, 9; whole number of individuals, 34.

Organizations—Ladies' Guild, 15.

Property—Two lots, value, $500; building fund, (circa), $800; money raised from outside sources, $59.25, for building fund.

FINANCIAL REPORT.

Receipts—For all purposes—Cash on hand, per last report, $413.00;

pledges and subscriptions, $10.00; collections in church, $42.89; contributions from without, $59.25; income from other sources, $363.12; total receipts for all purposes, $888.26.

Disbursements—For current expenses—Salary of rector, $24.95; salary of assistant, $13.97; other current expenses, $18.00; total for current expenses, $56.92. *Contributions—For objects in the Parish*—Building fund, $802.37; total contributions for objects in the Parish, $802.37. *Contributions—For objects in the Diocese*—Salary of Bishops, $10.00; permanent fund, $5.00; diocesan missions, $11.57; total contributions for objects in the Diocese, $26.57. *Contributions—For objects without the Diocese*—General missions, $2.40; total contributions for objects without the Diocese, $2.40.

Financial Summary—Current expenses raised by congregation as above, $56.92; contributions, for objects in the Parish, $802.37; for objects in the Diocese, $26.57; for objects without the Diocese, $2.40; total of contributions, $831.34; all money raised by the congregation for current expenses and for contributions, $888,26; cash in hand, $802.37.

PAROCHIAL REPORT.

Rev. ROBT. N. MEADE, address Bramwell. Other Missions. Present minister took charge April 15, 1904.

Official Acts—Public services, Sundays, 16; total, 16.

Communicants—Number last reported, 27; received by letter, 25; total gain, 25; transferred, 14; total loss, 14; net gain, 11; present number total, 38.

Congregations—Baptized persons connected with Parish, 82; confirmed persons conected with Parish, 38; families, 21; individuals not thus included, 21; whole number of individuals, 82.

FINANCIAL REPORT.

Receipts—For all purposes—Collections in church, $40.00; total receipts for all purposes, $40.00.

Disbursements—For current expenses—Salary of rector, $6.38; salary of assistant, $32.62; total for current expenses, $39.00. *Contributions—For objects in the Diocese*—Diocesan missions, $1.00; total contributions for objects in the Diocese, $1.00.

Financial Summary—Current expenses raised by congregation as above, $39.00; contributions, for objects in the Diocese, $1.00; total contributions, $1.00; all money raised by the congregation for current expenses and for contributions, $40.00.

Remarks—This report includes Rock District, Mercer county, and Mc-

Dowell county. Services were held at Mora, 4; Elkhorn, 4; Gary, 3; Algoma, 2; Vivian, 1, and North Fork Junction, 2.

PAROCHIAL REPORT.

Rev. AUSTIN B. MITCHELL, address Williamstown, Wood county. Present minister took charge, Aug. 9, 1903.

Church Officers—Church Wardens, J. W. Snodgrass, Charles Hunter; other Vestrymen, H. C. Henderson, A. T. Henderson, R. Hammett; Registrar, H. C. Henderson, address Williamstown; Treasurer, A. T. Henderson, address Williamstown; Superintendent of Sunday School, H. C. Henderson, Williamstown; Sunday School Secretary and Treasurer, Miss F. W. Biddle; Lay Reader, H. C. Henderson.

Official Acts—Baptisms, infants, 1; total, 1; presented for confirmation since last report, 1; Catechisings, 2; public services, Sundays (this means one service each Sunday) 36; other days, 8; total, 44; Holy Communion, public, 8; total, 8.

Communicants—Number last reported, 29; received by letter, 1; admitted by confirmation, 1; total gain, 2; not otherwise accounted for, 4; net loss, 2; present number total, 27.

Congregations—Baptized persons connected with Parish, 62; confirmed persons connected with Parish, 27; families, 20; individuals not thus included, 20; whole number of individuals, 47; number sittings in church, 150; number free sittings, 150.

Rector's Salary—As pledged from this congregation, $200.00; from diocesan missions, $200.00; as pledged from other congregations, $400.00; total, $800.00.

Organizations—Sunday Schools, officers and teachers, male, 1; female, 5; total, 6; pupils, male, 12; female, 10; total, 22; advent offering, $8.56; lenten offering, $11.43; other offerings, $17.60; total Sunday School offerings, 37.59; Woman's Auxiliary, members, 14.

Property—Church, wood, insurance $1,500.00, value $2,500.00; rectory, wood, value $3,500.00. Indebtedness, on rectory, $1,500.00.

FINANCIAL REPORT.

Receipts—For all purposes—Pledges and subscriptions, $497.67; collections in church, $51.87; money borrowed, $1,500.00; Sunday School, $37,57; Woman's Auxiliary, money, $146.63; contributions from without, $242.10; total receipts for all purposes, $2,475.84.

Disbursements—For current expenses—Salary of rector, $135.80; other current expenses, $10.50; total for current expenses, $146.30. *Contributions—For objects in the Parish*—Maintaining Sunday Schools, $15.68; payment for building rectory, $2,079.20; total contributions for objects in the Parish, $2,094.88. *Contributions—For objects in the Diocese*—Salary of Bishops, $2.50; permanent fund, $3.00; diocesan missions, $28.19; convocation missions, $2.00; widows and orphans, aged and disabled clergy fund, $1.00; religious and theological education, $2.12; Sheltering Arms Hospital, $2.34; Bishop's special fund, $1.00; total contributions for objects in the Diocese, $42.15. *Contributions—For objects without the Diocese*—Foreign missions general, $18.43; Brazil, $1.00; total contributions for objects without the Diocese, $19.43.

Financial Summary—Current expenses raised by congregation as above, $146.30; contributions, for objects in the Parish, $352.78; for objects in the Diocese, $42.15; for objects without the Diocese, $19.43; total of contributions, $414.36; all money raised by the congregation for current expenses and for contributions, $560.66; cash in hand, $172.78.

Remarks—In the final summary on page 9 I have deducted from total contributions for objects within the Parish, $2,094.88, the sum of $1,742.10, balance, $352.78, which consists of funds borrowed and raised from without the Parish, leaving $352.78 the exact amount raised within the Parish and expended for objects within the Parish.

PAROCHIAL REPORT.

Rev. AUSTIN B. MITCHELL, address Williamstown. Memorial Chapel of the Good Shepherd Mission, Parkersburg, Wood county. Present minister took charge Aug. 9, 1903.

Church Officers—Registrar, W. G. Peterkin, address Parkersburg; Treasurer, W. G. Peterkin, address Parkersburg; Superintendent of Sunday School, Simms Powell, Parkersburg; Sunday School Secretary and Treasurer, W. G. Peterkin; Lay Readers, Simms Powell, W. G. Peterkin.

Official Acts—Baptisms, infants, 4; adults, 2; total, 6; presented for confirmation since last report, 3; burials, 2; catechisings, 6; public services, Sundays, 36; other days, 10; total, 46; Holy Communion, public, 3; total, 3.

Communicants—Number last reported, 9; admitted by confirmation, 3; added otherwise, 5; total gain, 8; died, 1; lapsed, 1; total loss, 2; net gain, 6; present number total, 15.

Congregations—Baptized persons connected with Parish, 25; confirmed persons, connected with Parish, 17; families, 16; individuals not thus included, 22; whole number of individuals, 39; number sittings in church, 200; number free sittings, 200; number sittings in Sunday School room, 150.

Organizations—Sunday Schools, officers and teachers, male, 3; female, 9; total, 12; pupils, male, 90; female, 95; total, 185; advent offering, $10.00;

lenten offering, $20.00; other offerings, $10.00; Ladies' Aid Society, 16; Girl Sunshine Society, 35; Sewing School, 65; Boys' Club, 15.

Property, Church, wood, value $10,000.

FINANCIAL REPORT.

Receipts—For all purposes—Cash on hand, per last report, 29 cents; pledges and subscriptions, $743.80; collections in church, $810.51; thank offerings, $373.30; Woman's Auxiliary, money, $20.00; Guilds, or other societies, $123.75; contributions from without, $50.00; income from other sources, $83.70; total receipts for all purposes, $2,205.35.

Disbursements—For current expenses—Salary of rector, $304.00; other salaries, $16.00; other current expenses, $32.23; total for current expenses, $352.23. *Contributions—For objects in the Parish*—Extraordinary repairs and improvements, $120.60; parish missions, $327.00; parochial and industrial schools, $7.74; other objects, $47.23; total contributions for objects in the Parish, $502.57. *Contributions—For objects in the Diocese*—Salary of Bishops, $17.00; permanent fund, $7.00; diocesan missions, $150.00; widows and orphans, aged and disabled clergy fund, $16.00; religious and theological education, $10.00 Sheltering Arms Hospital, $16.00; Theological Seminary, $3.00; Bishop's special fund, $373.30; total contribu_ tions for objects in the DDiocese, $592.30. *Contributions for objects without the Diocese*—Domestic missions general, $190.00; colored people, $6.00; In dians, $2.00; deaf and dumb, $10.00; Jews, $2.00; through American Church Missionary Society, $75.00; total domestic missions, $285.51; foreign missions general, $190.00; for Mexico, $2.00; Brazil, $61.00; Cuba, $61.00; total foreign missions, $314.00; American church building fund, $2.00; general clergy relief fund, $8.00; Bible and Prayer Book Society, $2.00; total contributions for objects without the Diocese, $611.51.

Financial Summary—Current expenses raised by congregation as above, $352.23; contributions, for objects in the Parish, $502.57; for objects in the Diocese, $592.30; for objects without the Diocese, $611.51; total of contributions, $1706.38; all money raised by the congregation for current expenses and for contributions, $2,058.61; cash in hand, $13.74.

PAROCHIAL REPORT.

Rev. AUSTIN B. MITCHELL, address Williamstown. Grace Chapel Mission, Newport, Wood county. Present minister took charge August.

Church Officers—Treasurer, Miss Jennie Tavenner, address Newport; Superintendent of Sunday School, Brook Thomas, Newport.

Official Acts—Catechisings, 1; public services, Sunday, 1; other days, 12; total, 13; Holy Communion, public, 1.

Communicants—Number last reported, 10; present number total, 10.

Congregations—Baptized persons connected with Parish, 20; confirmed persons connected with Parish, 10; families, 8; individuals not thus included, 20; whole number of individuals, 40; number sittings in church, 100; number free sitings, 100.

Organizations—Sunday Schools, officers and teachers, male, 1; female, 4; total 5; pupils, male, 10; female, 20; total, 30; advent offering, $2.50; lenten offering, $8.67; other offerings, $5.00; total Sunday School offerings, $16.17.

Property—Church, value $1,200.00.

FINANCIAL REPORT.

Receipts—For all purposes—Pledges and subscriptions, $65.00; collections in church, $12.32; thank offerings, $15.00; Sunday School, $16.17; total receipts for all purposes, $108.49.

Disbursements—For current expenses—Salary of rector, $50.00; other current expenses, $5.00; total for current expenses, $55.00. *Contributions—For objects in the Parish*—Parish missions, $10.00; maintaining Sunday Schools, $5.50; total contributions for objects in the Parish, $15.50. *Contributions—For objects in the Diocese*—Salary of Bishops, $3.00; diocesan missions, $8.32; convocation missions, $2.00; widows and orphans, aged and disabled clergy fund, $1.00; Bishop's special fund, $15.00; total contributions for objects in the Diocese, $29.32. *Contributions—For objects without the Diocese*—Foreign missions general, $8.67; total foreign missions, $8.67; total contributions for objects without the Diocese, $8.67.

Financial Summary—Current expenses raised by congregation as above, $55.00; contributions, for objects in the Parish, $15.50; for objects in the Diocese, $29.32; for objects without the Diocese, $8.67; total of contributions, $53.49; all money raised by the congregation for current expenses and for contributions, $108.49.

PAROCHIAL REPORT.

Rev. FRANCIS VAN R. MOORE, address Elm Grove, W. Va. St. Paul's Mission, Elm Grove, Ohio county. Present minister took charge Aug. 23. 1903.

Church Officers—Church Trustees, Mr. C. C. Woods, Mr. Samuel Patterson; other committeemen, Mr. Gilchrist, Mr. Crockard, Mr. Muhn; Registrar, Mr. Crockard, address Elm Grove, W. Va.; Treasurer, Mr. Chas. C. Woods, address Park View, W. Va.; Superintendent of Sunday School, Mr. C. C. Woods, Park View, W. Va.; Sunday School Secretary and Treasurer, Mrs. B. C. Ryan.

Official Acts—Baptisms, infants, 6; adults, 3; total, 9; presented for confirmation since last report, 7; Catechisings, Sundays; public services, Sundays, 68; other days, 24; total, 92; Holy Communion, public, 6; total, 6.

Communicants—Number last reported, 20; admitted by confirmation, 7; total gain, 7; net gain, 7; present number total, 27.

Congregations—Baptized persons connected with Parish, 30; confirmed persons connected with Parish, 27; families, 20; number sittings in church, 100; number free sittings, 100.

Rector's Salary—As pledged from this congregation, $600.00; from diocesan missions, $200.00; total, $800.00.

Organizations—Sunday Schools, officers and teachers, male, 2; female, 6; total, 8; pupils, male, 35; female, 39; total, 74; advent offering, $3.61; lenten offering, $6.10; total Sunday School offerings, $9.71; Altar Guild, Jane Pryor Society.

Property—Church, wood; other property, rectory lot, value $600. Indebtedness, on church, none; on other property, on lot for rectory, $332.00.

FINANCIAL REPORT.

Receipts—For all purposes—Pledges and subscriptions, $329.12; contributions from without, $247.49; income from other sources, $3.61; total receipts for all purposes, $580.22.

Disbursements—For current expenses—Salary of rector, 8 months, $50, $400.00; painting church, $48.00; ordinary repairs to church, $18.74; other current expenses, $8.20; Sunday School treat, $7.01; total for current expenses, $481.95. *Contributions—For objects in the Diocese*—Permanent fund, $2.76; diocesan missions, $14.77; widows and orphans, aged and disabled clergy fund, $4.01; colored work to Bishop Gravatt, $3.00; total contributions for objects in the Diocese, $24.54. *Contributions—For objects without the Diocese*—Domestic missions general, $6.24 1-2; total domestic missions, $6.24 1-2; foreign missions general, $6.24 1-2; Brazil, $1.00; Cuba, $1.00; total foreign missions, $8.24 1-2; Sunday School lenten offering, $6.10; total contributions for objects without the Diocese, $20.59.

Financial Summary—Current expenses raised by congregation as above, $230.85; contributions, for objects in the Diocese, $24.54; for objects without the Diocese, $20.59; total of contributions, $45.13; all money raised by the congregation for current expenses and for contributions, $275.98; balance on hand, $53.14.

Remarks—The church building is used for the meetings of the Sunday School.

PAROCHIAL REPORT.

Rev. S. SCOLLAY MOORE, D. D., address Parkersburg. Trinity Church;

Trinity Parish, Parkersburg, Wood county. Date of organization, 1843. Present minister took charge April 15, 1888.

Church Officers—Church wardens, Dr. W. H. Sharp, Dr. T. B. Camden; other Vestrymen, Mr. B. M. Ambler, Mr. J. N. Camden, Mr. W. N. Chancellor, Mr. C. C. Martin, Mr. H. H. Moss, Mr. Simms Powell, Mr. W. J. Robb, Mr. B. D. Spilman, Mr. W. M. Trevor, Col. W. Vrooman; Registrar, Mr. Simms Powell, address Parkersburg, W. Va.; Treasurer, Dr. W. H. Sharp, address Parkersburg, W. Va.; Superintendent of Sunday School, Mr. B. M. Ambler, Parkersburg, W. Va.; Sunday School Secretary, Mr. Cecil Fitzhugh; Sunday School Treasurer, Mr. M. Q. Shrewsbury.

Official Acts—Baptisms, infants, 16; adults, 12; total 28; presented for confirmation since last report, 20; marriages, 32; burials, 26; public services, Sundays, 101; other days, 97; total, 198; Holy Communion, public, 36.

Communicants—Number last reported, 298; received by letter, 5; admitted by confirmation, 20; added otherwise, 7; total gain, 32; died, 5; removed without letter, 17; total loss, 22; net gain, 10; present number total, 308.

Congregations—Baptized persons connected with Parish, $525; confirmed persons connected with Parish, 320; families, 200; individuals not thus included, 50; whole number of individuals, 600; number sittings in church, 550; number free sittings, 100; number sittings in Sunday School room, 200.

Rector's Salary—As pledged from this congregation, $1,800.00.

Organizations—Sunday, Schools, officers and teachers, male, 4; female, 10; total, 14; pupils, male, 42, female, 59; total 101; advent offering, $15.15; lenten offering, $22.50; other offerings, $34.33; total Sunday School offerings, $71.98; Woman's Auxiliary, members, 30; Woman's Guild, members, 60; Junior Auxiliary, members, 29; King's Daughters, members, 18.

Property—Church, stone, insurance $8,000, value $30,000; rectory, brick, insurance $3,000, value $9,000;Sunday School room brick, insurance $2,300, value $7,000; other property, insurance $3,300, value $5,500; Episcopal residence, brick, insurance $6,000, value $15,000; total value insurance $22,600, value $66,500. Indebtedness, on rectory, $550; other debts, $450; total indebtedness, $1,000.

FINANCIAL REPORT.

Receipts—For all purposes—Pledges and subscriptions, $978.56; pew rent, $2,355.75; collections in church, $1,332.09; money borrowed, $100.00; specials for permanent fund, etc, $3,555.25; Sunday School, $71.98; Woman's Auxiliary, money, $276.76; Woman's Auxiliary, boxes, value, $139.16; Guilds, or other societies, $632.30; income from other sources, $75.00; total receipts for all purposes, $9,516.85.

Disbursements—For current expenses—Salary of rector, $1,800.00; other salaries, $800.00; ordinary repairs, $339.26; interest on debt, $59.13; other current expenses, $515.21; other objects, $178.84; total for current expenses, $3,692.44. *Contributions—For objects in the Parish*—Communion alms, $34.50; Parish missions, $254.02; maintaining Sunday Schools, $49.36; payment on debts for building, etc., $72.00; total contributions for objects in the Parish, $409.88. *Contributions—For objects in the Diocese*—Salary of Bishops, $525.00; permanent fund, $3,111.25; diocesan missions, $439.00; convocation missions, $21.97; widows and orphans, aged and disabled clergy fund, $92.60; religious and theological education, $19.77; Sheltering Arms Hospital, $229.73; Bishop's special fund, $344.00; other objects, $12.00; total contributions for objects in the Diocese, $4,795.32. *Contributions—For objects without the Diocese*—Domestic missions general, $111.52; through American Church Missionary Society, $20.78; total domestic missions, $132.30; foreign missions general, $111.52; through American Church Missionary Society, $20.77; total foreign missions, $132.29; specials, boxes, etc., $202.36; woman's Auxiliary, united offering, $106.26; Woman's lenten self-denial offering, $46.00; total contributions for objects without the Diocese, $619.21.

Financial Summary—Current expenses raised by congregation as above, $3,692.44; contributions, for objects in the Parish, $409.88; for objects in the Diocese, $4,795.32; for objects without the Diocese, $619.21; total of contributions, $5,824.41; all money raised by the congregation for current expenses and for contributions, $9,516.85.

PAROCHIAL REPORT.

Rev. S. SCOLLAY MOORE, D. D., address Parkersburg, W. Va. St. Stephen's Mission (Colored), Parkersburg, Wood county. Date of organization, 1896. Present minister took charge, 1896.

Official Acts—Marriages, 2; burials, 1; public services, Sundays, 46; total, 46; Holy Communion, public, 4.

Communicants—Number last reported, 12; died, 1; removed without letter, 3; total loss, 4; net loss, 4; present number total, 8.

Congregations—Baptized persons connected with Parish, 12; confirmed persons connected with Parish, 9; families, 6; whole number of individuals, 20; number sittings in chapel, 40.

Property—Chapel, frame, insurance $600, value $900; other property, value $100; total value, insurance $600; value $1,000. Indebtedness, on chapel, $470; total indebtedness, $470.

FINANCIAL REPORT.

Receipts—For all purposes—Collections in church, $30.00; rent from investments, $50.00; Guilds or other societies, $25.10; total receipts for all purposes, $105.10.

Disbursements—For current expenses—Insurance, $4.80; ordinary repair, $13.31; interest on debt, $37.50; other current expenses, $13.47; total for current expenses, $69.08. *Contributions—For objects in the Parish*—Payment on debts for building, etc., $34.02. *Contributions—For objects in the Diocese*—Diocesan missions, $1.00; total contributions for objects in the Diocese, $1.00. *Contributions—For objects without the Diocese*—Domestic missions general, 50 cents; total domestic missions, 50 cents; foreign missions general, 50 cents; total foreign missions, 50 cents; total contributions for objects without the Diocese, $1.00.

Financial Summary—Current expenses raised by congregation as above, $69.08; contributions, for objects in the Parish, $34.02; for objects in the Diocese, $1.00; for objects without the Diocese, $1.00; total of contributions $36.02; all money raised by the congregation for current expenses and for contributions, $105.10.

PAROCHIAL REPORT.

Rev. C. C. PIERSON, address Berkeley Springs, W. Va. St. Mark's Church, Morgan county. Date of organization, 1879. Present minister took charge 1896.

Church Officers—Church Warden, J. H. Hunter; other Vestrymen, F. B. Reed, G. E. Gilpin; Registrar, G. E. Gilpin, address Berkeley Springs; Treasurer, F. B. Reed, address Berkeley Springs; Superintendent of Sunday School, the Rector.

Official Acts—Catechisings, nearly every Sunday; public services, Sundays, 50; other days, 31; total, 81; Holy Communion, public, 13.

Communicants—Number last reported, 25; admitted by confirmation, 1; total gain, 1; transferred, 3; total loss, 2; net loss, 2; present number total, 23.

Congregations—aFmilies 12; individuals not thus included, 1; whole number of individuals, 23; number sittings in church, 250; number free sittings, all free.

Rector's Salary—As pledged from this congregation, $300.00; from diocesan missions, $100.00; from generad board, $100.00; total, $500.00.

Organizations—Sunday Schools, officers and teachers, male, 1; female, 3; total, 4; pupils, male, 8; female, 9; total, 17; advent offering, $6.92. total Sunday School offerings, $6.92; Woman's Auxiliary, members, 14; St. Mark's Guild, 22.

Property—Church, wood, insurance $1,500.00; rectory, wood, insurance $1,500.00; total value, $3,000.00. Indebtedness, on diocesan assessment for Bishop's fund, $7.75; total indebtedness, $7.75. Money raised from outside sources, $41.00; for what objects used, heater in church, $9.00; insurance on church, $18.50; insurance on rectory, $13.50; total $41.00.

FINANCIAL REPORT.

Receipts—For all purposes—Pledges and subscriptions, $143.50; collections in church, $83.54; Woman's Auxiliary, money, $30.00; Woman's Auxiliary boxes, value, $50.00; Guilds, or other societies, $131.44; total receipts for all purposes, $438.48.

Disbursements—For current expenses—Salary of rector, $300.00; other salaries, $36.75; insurance, $32.00; ordinary repairs, rectory and church, $35.15; other current expenses, $20.05; total for current expenses, $423.95. *Contributions—For objects in the Parish*—Maintaining Sunday Schools, $3.07; total contributions for objects in the Parish, $3.07. *Contributions—For objects in the Diocese*—Salary of Bishops, $17.25; permanent fund, $8.00; diocesan missions, $25.82; convocation missions, $14.00; Sheltering Arms Hospital, $3.84; total contributions for objects in the Diocese, $68.91. *Contributions—For objects without the Diocese*—Domestic missions general, up to this date, $40.00; total foreign missions, $40.00; total contributions for objects without the Diocese, $40.00.

Financial Summary—Current expenses raised by congregation as above, $423.95; contributions, for objects in the Parish, $3.07; for objects in the Diocese, $68.91; for objects without the Diocese, $40.00; total, $111.98; cash in hand, to repair rectory, $20.90.

Rt. Rev. C. CLIFTON PENICK, D. D., address Fairmont, W. Va. Christ Church, Fairmont, Marion county. Present minister took charge September 15, 1899.

Church Officers—Church Wardens, J. E. Sands, J. C. Smith, other vestrymen, Geo. H. Brobst, Geo. De Bolt, Jno. Henshaw, Sam'l Holbert, Edwin Allen Russell, Wm. E. Watson; Registrar, Sam'l Holbert, address Fairmont, W. Va.; Treasurer, Geo. H. Brobst, address Fairmont, W. Va.; Superintendent of Sunday Schools, Rector; Sunday School Secretary and Treasurer, Arthur Brobst.

Official Acts—Baptisms, infants, 2; presented for confirmation since last report, 2; marriages, 1; burials, 9; catechisings, 44; public services, Sundays, 100; other days, 20; total, 120; Holy Communion, public, 14; private, 1; total, 15.

Communicants—Number last reported, 136; received by letter, 3; admitted by confirmation, 2; added otherwise, 1; total gain, 6; died, 3; transferred, 1; removed without letter, 10; not otherwise, accounted for, 4; total loss, 18; net loss, 12; present number total, 124.

Congregations—Baptized persons connected with Parish, 124; confirmed

persons connected with Parish, 124; families, 48; individuals not thus included, about 100; whole number of individuals, about 250; number of scattered communicants in your section not connected with any Parish, 6; number sittings in church, 150; number free sittings, 150; number sittings in Sunday School room, 100.

Rector's Salary—As pledged from this congregation, $1,200.00.

Organizations—Sunday Schools, officers and teachers, male, 2; female, 6; total, 8; pupils, male, 20; female, 27; total, 47; Advent offering, $8.93; Lenten offerings, $50.00; other offerings, $100.00; total Sunday School offerings, $158.93; Woman's Auxiliary, members, 26; Daughters of King, 8.

Property—Church brick, insurance, $1.500; value, $3.500; total value, $3,500; indebtedness, other debts, $625.69; total indebtedness, $625.69.

FINANCIAL REPORT.

Receipts—For all Purposes—Cash on hand, per last report, $203.23; pledges and subscriptions, $1,320.58; collections in church, $360.00; money borrowed, $625.69; Sunday School, $75.70; Woman's Auxiliary, money, $185.52; Woman's Auxiliary, boxes, value, $140.15; income from other sources, $252.72; total receipts for all purposes, $3,163.59.

Disbursements—For Current Expenses—Salary of rector, $1,200.00; salary of assistant, $200.00; other salaries, $402.92; other current expenses, $170.00; other objects, $50.00; total for current expenses, $2,022.92. *Contributions—For objects in the Parish*—Communion alms, $50.00; maintaining Sunday Schools, $10.00; total contributions for objects in the Parish, $60.00. *Contributions—For objects in the Diocese*—Salary of Bishops, $100.00; diocesan missions, $75.00; convocation missions, $50.00; religious and theological education, $100.00; Sheltering Arms Hospital, $20.00; bishop's special fund, $5.00; total contributions for objects in the Diocese, $350.00. *Contributions—For objects without the Diocese*—Domestic missions general, $50.00; deaf and dumb, $5.00; total domestic missions, $55.00; foreign missions general, $250.00; Brazil, $50.00; total foreign missions, $300.00; specials, $140.15; other objects, $235.52; total contributions for objects without the Diocese, $730.65.

Financial Summary—Contributions—For objects in the Parish, $2,082.92; for objects in the Diocese, $350.00; for objects without the Diocese, $730.67; total contributions, $3,163.59.

Remarks—The fact that the headquarters of the Consolidated Coal Company moved from Fairmont has caused many to leave here and greatly upset financial ability of this congregation. It would be wise for the Diocese not to count too largely upon Fairmont in the immediate future for fear of disappointment. Go slow and watch developments.

C. C. PENICK.

PAROCHIAL REPORT.

Rev. JAMES F. PLUMMER, address Clarksburg, W. Va. Christ Church, Clarksburg, Harrison county. Present minister took charge January 21, 1904.

Church Officers—Church Wardens, Mortimer W. Smith, J. W. Williams; other vestrymen, W. F. Nuzum, Chas. B. Alexander, Geo. L. Duncan, Percy W. Goff, M. D., E. D. Shepherd; Registrar, Chas. B. Alexander, address 670 Mulberry street; Treasurer, J. W. Williams, address 456 W. Main street; Superintendent of Sunday Schools, the Rector; Sunday School Secretary and Treasurer, Miss S. Scollay Page.

Official Acts—Baptisms, infants, 4; marriages, 1; catechisings, 2; public services, Sundays, 41; other days, 60; total, 101; Holy Communion, public, 3.

Communicants—Number last reported, 156; died, 2; removed without letter, 1; total loss, 3; net loss, 3; present number total, 106.

Congregations—Baptized persons connected with Parish, (estimated) 250; confirmed persons connected with Parish, 150; families, 67; individuals not thus included, 25; whole number individuals, 300; number free sittings, all.

Rector's Salary—As pledged from this congregation, $1,200.00.

Organizations—Sunday Schools, No. 1, officers and teachers, male, 1; female, 4; total, 5; pupils, male, 29; female, 19; total 48; No. 2, officers and teachers, male, 1; female, 3; total 4; pupils, male, 15; female, 10; total, 25; Lenten offering, $16.56; other offerings, $3.33; total Sunday School offerings, $19.89; Woman's Auxiliary, members, 15; Ladies' Aid Society, Daughters of the King. Location of schools mentioned above, No. 1, at the church; No. 2, at the chapel, Northview.

Property—Church, brick, insurance, $5,000; value, $10,000; chapel, brick, insurance, $1200; value, $2,000; rectory, frame, insurance, $2,500; value, $8,000; indebtedness, on chapel, $450; on other property, $468; other debts, $1,700; total indebtedness, $2,618.

FINANCIAL REPORT.

Receipts—For all Purposes—Cash on hand, February 1, 1904, $21.19; pledges and subscriptions, $755.55; collections in church, $1,164.36; Sunday School, $3.33; Woman's Auxiliary, money, $40.00; guilds or other societies, $170.26; total receipts for all purposes, $2,154.69.

Disbursements—For Current Expenses—Salary of rector, $500.00; other salaries, $23.75; insurance, $40.00; interest on debt, included in "payment on debts;" other current expenses, $67.86; total for current expenses, $631.61. *Contributions—For objects in the Parish*—Communion alms, $7.45; extraordinary repairs and improvements, $270.50; payment on debts for building, current expenses, etc., $567.95; relief of sick and needy by

Daughters of the King, $45.00; total contributions for objects in the Parish, $890.00. *Contributions—For objects in the Diocese*—Salary of bishops, $250.00; permanent fund, $144.00; diocesan missions, $44.25; convocation missions, $2.10; religious and theological education, $5.03; Sheltering Arms Hospital, $2.50; printing fund, Woman's Auxiliary, $2.00; total contributions for objects in the Diocese, $449.88. *Contributions—For objects without the Diocese*—Jews, $2.65; foreign missions general, $33.28; through American Church Missionary Society, $6.60; Brazil, (Woman's Auxiliary) $5.00; total foreign missions, $47.53; general clergy relief fund, $10.00; united offering, Woman's Auxiliary, $25.50; total contributions for objects without the Diocese, $83.03.

Financial Summary—Current expenses raised by congregation as above, $631.61. *Contributions*—For objects in the Parish, $8.90; for objects in the Diocese, $449.88; for objects without the Diocese, $83.03; total of contributions, $1,422.91; all money raised by the congregation for current expenses and for contributions, $2,054.52; cash in hand, $100.17.

Remarks—The present rector entered upon the rectorship of the Parish January 21 of the current year. The Parish had been vacant since the resignation of the former rector, Rev. Thos. W. Cooke, in June, 1903. The congregation of the chapel at Northview is in so unsettled a condition that no definite report from there has been found practicable. Services and Sunday School are held there Sunday afternoon, whenever sufficient number of the people appear.

PAROCHIAL REPORT.

Rev. R. D. ROLLER, D. D., address Charleston, W. Va. Assistant, C. Hely Molony. St. John's Church, Kanawha Parish, Charleston, Kanawha county. Date of organization 1788. Present minister took charge 1888.

Church Officers—Church Wardens, Jas. F. Lewis, J. Lynn Richardson; other vestrymen, S. S. Green, J. T. Waters, D. C. Gallaher, W. G. Hubbard, Alfred Phillips, C. E. Ward, O. F. Payne; Registrar, S. S. Green, address Charleston, W. Va.; Treasurer, J. T. Waters, address Charleston, W. Va.; Superintendent of Sunday Schools, the Rector; Miss E. P. Barber, Paint Creek, W. Va.; Sunday School Secretary and Treasurer, J. T. Waters.

Official Acts—Baptisms, infants, 13; adults, 3; total, 16; presented for confirmation since last report, 21; marriages, 8; burials, (hospital, 15), 34; public services, Sundays, 151; other days, 109; total, 260; Holy Communion, public, 30.

Communicants—Number last reported, 267; received by letter, 5; admitted by confirmation, 21; added otherwise, 33; total gain, 59; died, 6; transferred, 2; removed without letter, 8; total loss, 16; net gain, 43; present number total, 310.

Congregations—Baptized persons connected with Parish, 577; confirmed persons connected with Parish, 329; families and individuals not thus included, 200; whole number of individuals, 597; number free sittings, 500; number sittings in chapel and Sunday School room, 200.

Rector's Salary—As pledged from this congregation, $1,300.00; from diocesan missions, assistant, $300.00.

Organizations—Sundays Schools, No. 1, officers and teachers, male, 2; female, 11; total, 13; pupils, total, 130; No. 2, officers and teachers, 1; pupils, total 66; No. 3, officers and teachers, male, 1; pupils, total, 40; No. 4, officers and teachers, male, 2; pupils, total, 15; total officers and teachers, 17; pupils, total, 251; Advent offering, $44.81; Lenten offering, $66.83; other offerings, $103.16; total Sunday School offerings, $214.80; Woman's Auxiliary, members, 30; Ladies' Guild, 10; Ladies' Aid Society, 32; Rector's Aid, 26; vested choir, 35. Location of schools mentioned above, 1, St. John's, Charleston; 2, Crown Hill; 3, Paint Creek; 4, Carbon.

Property—Church, stone, insurance, $18,000.00; value, $48,627.00; rectory, frame insurance $2,400.00; value, $10,000.00; Parish house, brick, insurance, $4,000.00; value, $10,000.00; other property, lot, $3,000.00; Sheltering Arms Hospital, frame, insurance, $6,000.00; value, $10,000.00; total value insurance, $30,400; total value, $81,627; indebtedness, on Parish house, $5,000.00; total indebtedness, $5,000.00.

FINANCIAL REPORT.

Receipts—For all Purposes—Cash on hand, per last report, $18.00; pledges and subscriptions, $2,472.50; collections in church, $800.00; thank offerings, $109.90; Sunday Schol, $214.80; Woman's Auxiliary, money, $92.96; Woman's Auxiliary, boxes, value, $25.00; guilds or other societies, $1,143.50; income from other sources, $1,091.86; total receipts for all purposes $5,968.52; $183.50 sent direct to trustees of permanent fund.

Disbursements—For Current Expenses—Salary of rector, $1,300.00; other salaries, $812.46; insurance, $80.00; ordinary repairs, $92.82; other current expenses, $388.38; total for current expenses, $2,673.66. *Contributions—For objects in the Parish*—Extraordinary repairs and improvements, $389.15; Parish missions, $281.08; maintaining Sunday Schools, $82.29; charity, $45.30; Parish house, $1,318.50; total contributions for objects in the Parish, $2,116.32. *Contributions—For objects in the Diocese*—Salary of bishops, $275.00; permanent fund, $186.50; diocesan missions, $230.00; convocation missions, $15.00; widows and orphans, aged and disabled clergy fund, $25.50; religious and theological education, $6.28; Sheltering Arms Hospital, $109.90; bishop's special fund, $26.00; total contributions for objects in the Diocese, $693.68. *Contributions—For objects without the Diocese*—Domestic missions general, $33.35; Jews, $6.96; total domestic missions, $40.31; Brazil, $10.00; total foreign missions, $10.00; specials, boxes, &c., $44.61; American church building fund, $3.10; general clergy relief fund, $20.53; total contributions for objects without the Diocese, $118.55.

Financial Summary—Current expenses raised by congregation as above, $2,673.66. *Contributions*—For objects in the Parish, $2,116.32; for objects in the Diocese, $780.18; for objects without the Diocese, $118.55; total of contributions, $2,928.55; all money raised by the congregation for current expenses and for contributions, $5,685.71; cash in hand, $366.31.

Remarks—Twenty-one of the communicants reported under St. John's Church, are in the missions of the Parish.

PAROCHIAL REPORT.

Rev. CHAS. E. SHAW, address New Martinsville. St. Ann's Church, Wetzel Parish, New Martinsville, Wetzel county. Date of organization, 1851. Present minister took charge, April 15, 1902.

Church Officers—Church Wardens, S. R. Martin, S. Bruce Hall; other vestrymen, Jno. F. Martin, Wm. McG. Hall, Leslie Williams, Jno. H. Bridgeman, James Newman; Registrar, Wm. McG. Hall, address New Martinsville; Treasurer, S. R. Martin, address New Martinsville; Superintendents of Sunday Schools, C. E. Shaw, New Martinsville; Sunday School Secretary and Treasurer, Miss Anna Reithmiller.

Official Acts—Baptisms, infants, 5; presented for confirmation since last report, 9; marriages, 1; burials, 1; catechisings, 45; public services, Sundays, 100; other days, 66; total, 166; Holy Communion, public, 19.

Communicants—Number last reported, 36; received by letter, 2; admitted by confirmation, 9; restored to communion, 6; added otherwise, 1; total gain, 18; removed without letter, 4; total loss, 4; net gain, 14; present number total, 50.

Congregations—Baptized persons connected with Parish, 94; confirmed persons connected with Parish, 55; families, 25; individuals not thus included, 8; whole number of individuals, 101; number of scattered communicants in your section not connected with any Parish, 3; number sittings in church, 200; number free sittings, 200; number sittings in chapel, 70.

Rector's Salary—As pledged from this congregation, $700.00; from general board, $100.00; total, $800.00.

Organizations—Sunday Schools, officers and teachers, male, 1; female, 5; total, 6; pupils, male, 12; female, 12; total, 24; Advent offering, $7.00; Lenten offering, $10.16; other offerings, $4.31; total Sunday School offerings, $21.47; Rector's Aid Society, Rector's Senior Aid Society, Rector's Guild. Location of schools mentioned above, New Martinsville.

Property—Church, wood, insurance, $3,000; value, $5,000; chapel, wood, value, $1,000; rectory, wood, insurance, $1.000; value, $4,000; total insurance, $4,000; total value, $10,000; indebtedness, on church, $2,760; total indebtedness, $2,760.

FINANCIAL REPORT.

Receipts—For all Purposes—Cash on hand, per last report, $12.52; pledges and subscriptions, $1,633.64; collections in church, $548.59; money borrowed, $2,760.00; Sunday School $21.47; guilds or other societies, $191.96; total receipts for all purposes, $5,168.18.

Disbursements—For Current Expenses—Salary of rector, $700.00; insurance, $51.00; ordinary repairs, $7.50; interest on debt, $120.00; other current expenses, $48.95; Woman's guilds, $136.10; total for current expenses, $1,063.55. *Contributions—For objects in the Parish*—Communion alms, $17.54; extraordinary repairs and improvements, $1,358.00; maintaining Sunday Schools, $9.21; payments on debts for building, &c., $2,511.65; total contributions for objects in the Parish, $3,896.40. *Contributions—For objects in the Diocese*—Salary of bishops, $40.00; permanent fund, $12.10; diocesan missions, $43.61; convocation missions, $2.83; widows and orphans aged and disabled clergy fund, $9.76; religious and theological education, $4.02; Sheltering Arms Hospital, $8.34; theological seminary, $2.00; total contributions for objects in the Diocese, $122.66. *Contributions—For objects without the Diocese*—Domestic missions general, $20.59; colored people, $2.27; Indians, 69 cents; deaf and dumb, $5.82; Jews, $1.04; through American Church Missionary Society, $8.00; total domestic missions, $38.41; for Mexico, $1.50; through American Missionary Society, $3.17; total foreign missions, $4.67; general clergy relief fund, $2.91; Bible and prayer book society, $3.78; total contributions for objects without the Diocese, $19.77.

Financial Summary—Current expenses raised by congregation as above, $5,168.18. *Contributions*—For objects in the Parish, $4,959.95; for objects in the Diocese, $122.66; for objects without the Diocese, $49.77; total of contributions, $5,132.38; all money raised by the congregation for current expenses and for contributions, $5,132.38; cash in hand, $35.80.

PAROCHIAL REPORT.

Rev. GEO. C. SHAW, address St. Mary's, W. Va. Grace Church, St. Marys, Pleasants county. Date of organization, 1899. Present minister took charge June 16, 1901.

Church Officers—Church Wardens—R. L. Pemberton, R. H. Browse; other Committeemen, E. A. Sayer, J. C. Noland, George Kelsall; Registrar, J. C. Noland, address St. Marys, W. Va.; Treasurer, George Kelsall, address St. Marys, W. Va.; Superintendent of Sunday School, George Kelsall, St. Marys, W. Va.; Sunday School Secretary and Treasurer, J. C. Noland.

Official Acts—Baptisms, adults, 2; presented for confirmation since last report, 1; marriages, 1; catechisings, 6; public services, Sundays, 70; other days, 10; total, 80; Holy Communion, public, 6.

Communicants—Number last reported, 28; received by letter, 1; admitted by confirmation, 1; total gain, 2; removed without letter, 1; total loss, 1; net gain, 1; present number total, 29.

Congregations—Baptized persons connected with Parish, 30; confirmed persons connected with Parish, 29; individuals not thus included, 20; whole number of individuals, 49; number of scattered communicants in your section not connected with any Parish, 1; number sittings in church, 200; number free sittings, 200.

Rector's Salary—As pledged from this congregation, $280.00; from diocesan missions, $255.00; from general board, $100.00; total, $635.00.

Organizations—Sunday Schools, officers and teachers, male, 4; female, 3; total, 7; pupils, male, 12; female, 20; total, 32; other offerings, $24.00; total Sunday School offerings, $24.00; Grace Guild, members, 15.

Property—Church, brick, insurance $1,500.00, value $4,000.00; rectory, wood, insurance $1,200.00, value $2,200.00; total value, insurance $2,700.00, value $6,200.00. Indebtedness, on church, $280.00; on rectory, $2,000.00; total indebtedness, $2,280.00.

FINANCIAL REPORT.

Receipts—For all purposes—Pledges and subscriptions, $300.00; collections in church, $100.00; thank offerings, $71.00; Sunday School, $24.00; Guilds or other societies, $110.00; total receipts for all purposes, $605.00.

Disbursements—For current expenses—Salary of rector, $280.00; interest on debt, $144.00; other current expenses, $61.00; total for current expenses, $485.00. *Contributions—For objects in the Parish*—Maintaining Sunday Schools, $24.00; payment on debts for building, etc., $120.00; total contributions for objects in the Parish, $144.00. *Contributions—For objects in the Diocese*—Salary of Bishops, $15.00; diocesan missions, $15.00; total contributions for objects in the diocese, $30.00.

Financial Summary—Current expenses raised by congregation as above, $485.00; contributions, for objects in the Parish, $144.00; for objects in the diocese, $30.00; total of contributions, $174.00; all money raised by the congregation for current expenses and for contributions, $659.00.

PAROCHIAL REPORT.

Rev. Geo. C. SHAW, address St. Marys, W. Va. St. John's Church Parish, Willow, Pleasants county. Date of organization, 1853. Present minister took charge July 1, 1903.

Church Officers—Church Wardens, F. M. Triplett, John W. Norris; other Vestrymen, J. H. Ralston; Registrar, John W. Norris, address Willow, W. Va.; Treasurer, John W. Norris, address Willow, W. Va.

Official Acts—Presented for confirmation since last report, 1; public services, Sundays, 6; total, 6; Holy Communion, public, 1.

Communicants—Number last reported, 10; admitted by confirmation, 1; total gain, 1; net gain, 1; present number total, 11.

Congregations—Baptized persons connected with Parish, 18; families, 6; individuals not thus included, 10; whole number of individuals, 28; number sittings in church, $100; number free sittings, 100.

Rector's Salary—As pledged from this congregation, $37.50.

Property—Church, wood, value $500; total value, $500. Indebtedness, due the minister, $11.00; due on diocesan assessment for missions, $1.00; due on diocesan assessment for Bishop's fund, $5.00; total indebtedness, $17.00.

FINANCIAL REPORT.

Receipts—For all purposes—Cash on hand, per last report, $40.00; pledges and subscriptions, $26.00; collections in church, $8.00; total receipts for all purposes, $74.00.

Disbursements—For current expenses—Salary of rector, $26.00; ordinary repairs, $40.00; total for current expenses, $66.00. *Contributions—For objects in the Diocese*—Diocesan missions, $4.00; convocation missions, $1.00; Bishop's special fund, $25.00; total contributions for objects in the Diocese, $30.00. *Contributions—For objects without the Diocese*—Domestic missions general, $1.50; total domestic missions, $1.50; foreign missions general, $1.50; total foreign missions, $1.50; total contributions for objects without the Diocese, $3.00.

Financial Summary—Current expenses raised by congregation as above, $66.00; contributions, for objects in the Diocese, $30.00; for objects without the Diocese, $3.00; total of contributions, $33.00; all money raised by the congregation for current expenses and for contributions, $99.00.

PAROCHIAL REPORT.

Rev. GEO. C. SHAW, address St. Marys, W. Va. Church of the Messiah Mission, Waverly, Wood county. Present minister took charge, June 16, 1901.

Church Officers—Treasurer, Mrs. Alice Corbett, address Waverly, W. Va.; Superintendent of Sunday School, C. P. Corbett, Esq., Waverly, W. Va.; Sunday School Secretary and Treasurer, Tessie Myers.

Official Acts—Baptisms, adults, 1; presented for confirmation since last report, 1; catechisings, 10; public services, Sundays, 20; other days, 10; total, 30; Holy Communion, public, 3.

Communicants—Number last reported, 10; admitted by confirmation, 1; total gain, 1; lapsed, 1; total loss, 1; present number total, 10.

Congregations—Baptized persons connected with Parish 14; confirmed persons connected with Parish, 10; families, 5; individuals not thus included, 20; whole number of individuals, 34; number sittings in church, 100; number free sittings, 100.

Rector's Salary—As pledged from this congregation, $50.00; total, $50.00.

Organizations—Sunday Schools, officers and teachers, male, 2; female, 3; total, 5; pupils, male, 12; female, 25; total, 37; lenten offering $5.00; total Sunday School offerings $5.00.

Property—Church, wood, insurance $500.00, value $1,000.00; total value, insurance $500.00, value $1,000.00. Indebtedness, on church, $200.00; total indebtedness, $200.00.

FINANCIAL REPORT.

Receipts—For all purposes—Pledges and subscriptions, $50.00; collections in church, $45.35; Sunday School, $15.00; Guilds or other societies, $50.00; total receipts for all purposes, $160.35.

Disbursements—For current expenses—Salary of rector, $50.00; interest on debt, $15.00; other current expenses, $20.00; total for current expenses, $85.00. *Contributions—For objects in the Parish*—Communion alms, $1.10; maintaining Sunday Schools, $15.00; payment on debts for building, etc., $35.00; total contributions for objects in the Parish, $51.10. *Contributions—For objects in the Diocese*—Salary of Bishops, $5.00; permanent fund, $1.00; diocesan missions, $10.05; convocation missions, $1.50; religious and theological education, 55 cents; total contributions for objects in the Diocese, $18.10. *Contributions—For objects without the Diocese*—Domestic missions general, $1.65; total domestic missions, $1.65; foreign missions general, $4.50; total foreign missions, $4.50; total contributions for objects without the Diocese, $6.15.

Financial Summary—Current expenses raised by congregation as above, $85.00; contributions, for objects in the Parish, $51.10; for objects in the Diocese, $18.10; for objects without the Diocese, $6.15; total of contributions, $75.35; all money raised by the congregation for current expenses and for contributions, $160.35.

PAROCHIAL REPORT.

Rev. GEO. C. SHAW, address Mannington. St. Andrew's Church Mission, Mannington, Marion county. Date of organization, 1891.

Church Officers—Church Warden, Henry W. G. Bostock; other Committeemen, F. H. Armstrong, Phil. Deitz, Arnold R. Demkle, John O. Huey, James H. Bostock; Registrar, Phil. Deitz, address Mannington, W. Va.; Treasurer, John O. Huey, address Mannington, W. Va.

Official Acts—Baptisms, infants, 3; total, 3; public services, Sundays, 8; other days, 3; total, 11; Holy Communion, public 1.

Communicants—Number last reported, 21; received by letter, 3; total gain, 3; net gain, 3; present number total, 24.

Congregations—Baptized persons connected with Parish, 44; confirmed persons connected with Parish, 24; families, 16; individuals not thus included, 20; whole number of individuals, 64; number sittings in church, 150; number free sittings, 150; number sittings in Sunday School room, 100.

Organizations—St. Andrew's Guild, 20.

Property—Church, wood, insurance $2,500, value $6,000; total value, insurance, $2,500, total value $6.000. Indebtdness on church, $800; furniture, $435; total indebtedness, $1,235.

FINANCIAL REPORT.

Receipts—For all purposes—Pledges and subscriptions, $750.00; collections in church, $15.00; Guilds or other societies, $626.00; total receipts for all purposes, $1,391.00.

Disbursements—For current expenses—Insurance, $32.00; interest on debt, $30.00; other current expenses, $50.00; total for current expenses, $112.00. *Contributions—For objects in the Parish*—Communion alms, $5.00; Extraordinary repairs and improvements, $1,176.00; payment on debts for building, etc., $200.00; total contributions for objects in the Parish, $1,381.00. *Contributions—For objects in the Diocese*—Diocesan missions, $3.00; total contributions for objects in the diocese, $3.00. *Contributions—For objects without the Diocese*—Domestic missions general, $1.00. total domestic missions, $1.00; total contributions for objects without the Diocese, $1.00.

Financial Summary—Current expenses raised by congregation as above, $112.00; contributions, for objects in the Parish, $1,381.00; for objects in the Diocese, $3.00; for objects without the Diocese, $1.00; total contributions, $1,385.00; all money raised by the congregation for current expenses and for contributions, $1,497.00.

Remarks—This church has been vacant during the year and this report is as complete as data at hand will allow it to be made. The Rev. Geo. C. Shaw took charge May 1st, 1904.

PAROCHIAL REPORT.

Rev. EDWIN B. SNEAD, address Buckhannon, W. Va. Spruce Chapel Mission, Spruce, Upshur county. Present minister took charge June 21, 1903.

Church Officers—Warden, Wm. Londen, address Atlas, W. Va., Registrar, G. W. Spaulding, address Atlas, W. Va.; Treasurer, Jno. Dowell, address Atlas, W. Va.; Superintendent of Sunday School, Mrs. Olive Maple, Atlas, W. Va.

Official Acts—Baptisms, infants, 2; presented for confirmation since last report, 1; public services, Sundays, every third Sunday, 7; other days, 3; total, 10; Holy Communion, public, 1.

Communicants—Number last reported, 10; admitted by confirmation, 1; total gain, 1; net gain, 1; present number total, 11.

Congregations—Baptized persons conected with Parish, 21; confirmed persons connected with Parish, 11; families, 6; number sittings in chapel, 80.

Rector's Salary—As pledged from this congregation $50.00.

Organizations—Sunday Schools, officers and teachers, female, 3; total 3; pupils, male, 8; female, 7; total, 15.

Property—Chapel, insurance $500.00, value $800.00; rectory, value, $400; total value, insurance $500.00, value $1,200.00.

FINANCIAL REPORT.

Receipts—For all purposes—Pledges and subscriptions, $35.00; collections in church $6.00; Sunday School, $3.30; Guilds or other societies, $29.95; total receipts for all purposes, $74.25.

Disbursements—For current expenses—Salary of rector, $35.00; total for current expenses, $35.00. *Contributions—For objects in the Diocese*—Salary of Bishops, $2.00; dioceson missions, $2.00; total contributions for objects in the Diocese, $4.00. *Contributions—For objects without the Diocese*—Domestic missions general, $1.00; total domestic missions, $1.00; foreign missions general, $1.00; total foreign missions, $1.00; total contributions for objects without the Diocese, $2.00.

Financial Summary—Current expenses raised by congregation as above, $35.00; contributions for objects in the diocese, $4; for objects without the Diocese, $2; total contributions, $6; all money raised by the congregations for current expenses and for contributions, $74.25; cash in hand, $33.25.

PAROCHIAL REPORT.

Rev. EDWIN B. SNEAD, address Buckhannon, W. Va. Church of the Transfiguration, Buckhannon Mission, Upshur county. Date of organization, Aug. 1, 1903. Present minister took charge June 21, 1903.

Church Officers—Church Warden, E. C. Higginbotham; Registrar, J. J. Singleton, address, Buckhannon, W. Va.; Treasurer, C. O. Latham, address Buckhannon, W. Va.; Lay Reader, W. H. Howard.

Official Acts—Presented for confirmation since last report, 4; marriages, 1; burials, 1; public services, Sundays, 86; other days, 14; total, 100; Holy Communion, Public, 10.

Communicants—Number last reported, 19; admitted by confirmation, 4; restored to communion, 1; added otherwise, 8; total gain, 13; transferred, 1; removed without letter, 6; total loss, 7; net gain, 6; present number total, 25,

Congregations—Baptized persons connected with Parish, 28; confirmed persons connected with Parish, 25; families, 8; whole number of individuals, 28; number of scattered communicants in your section not connected with any Parish, 1; number sittings in church, 160; number free sittings, 160.

Rector's Salary—As pledged from this congregation, $450.00; from diocesan missions, $300.00; total, $750.00.

Organizations—Ladies' Guild, 7.

..*Property*—Church, insurance $1,500.00, value $3,000.00; total value, insurance $1,500.00, value $3,000.00.

FINANCIAL REPORT.

Receipts—For all purposes—Cash on hand, per last report, $5.47; pledges and subscriptions, $294.46; collections in church, $71.68; thank offerings, $54.10; Guilds or other societies, $68.50; income from other sources, $6.65; total receipts for all purposes, $500.86.

Disbursements—For current expenses—Salary of rector, $326.24; ordinary repairs, $44.59; other current expenses, $29.43; total for current expenses, $398.26. *Contributions—For objects in the Parish*—Extraordinary repairs and improvements, $19.65; total contributions for objects in the Parish, $19.65. *Contributions—For objects in the Diocese*—Salary of Bishops, $10.00; diocesan missions, $10.00; widows and orphans, aged and disabled clergy fund, $5.00; total contributions for objects in the Diocese, $25.00. *Contributions—For objects without the Diocese*—Domestic missions general, $5.00; total domestic missions general, $5.00; foreign missions general, $5.00; total foreign missions, $5.00; total contributions for objects without the Diocese, $10.00.

Financial Summary—Current expenses raised by congregation as above, $398.26; contributions, for objects in the Parish, $19.65; for objects in the Diocese, $25.00; for objects without the Diocese, $10.00; total of contributions, $54.65; all money raised by the congregation for current expenses and for contributions. $500.86; cash in hand, $47.95.

PAROCHIAL REPORT.

Rev. P. B. STAUFFER. St. John's Church, Harper's Ferry, Jefferson county. Date of organization, 1851. Present minister took charge Oct. 1, 1903.

Church Officers—Treasurer, Mr. G. H. Child; Superintendent of Sunday School, Mr. Banabas Bryan; Sunday School Secretary and Treasurer, Miss Emily Child; Lay Reader, Mr. Barnabas Bryan.

Official Acts—Burials, 1; catechisings, 6; public services, Sundays, 34; other days, 35; total, 69; Holy Communion, public, 9.

Communicants—Number last reported, 32; died, 1; total loss, 1; net loss, 1; present number total, 31.

Congregations—Baptized persons connected with Parish, 45; confirmed persons connected with Parish, 35; families, 16; number sittings in church, 150.

Rector's Salary—As pledged from this congregation, $125.00; as pledged from other congregations, $200.00; from convocation missions, $75.00.

Organizations—Sunday School, officers and teachers, male, 1; female, 5; total, 6; pupils, male, 24; female, 46; total, 70; advent offering, $17.00; lenten offering, $18.00; other offerings, $14.62; total Sunday School offerings, $49.62. This money is included in Treasurer's report.

Property—Church, wood, insurance $1,200.00, value $2,000.00; rectory, frame, insurance $800.00, value $1,000.00; total value, $3,000.00. Indebtedness, on rectory, $50.00; total indebtedness, $50.00.

Receipts—For all purposes—Cash on hand, per last report, $65.80; pledges and subscriptions, $124.25; collections in church, $174.17; Sunday School, $35.00; Guilds or other societies, $1.05; contributions from without, $17.00; income from other sources, $229.50; total receipts for all purposes, $646.77.

Disbursements—For current expenses—Salary of rector, $95.00; ordinary repairs, $17.46; interest on debt, $16.50; other current expenses, $85.23; Council expense, $6.00; total for current expenses, $220.19. *Contributions—For objects in the Parish*—Communion alms, $22.06; payment on debts for building, etc., $225.00; total contributions for objects in the Parish, $247.06. *Contributions—For objects in the Diocese*—Salary of Bishops, $15.25; permanent fund, $4.25; diocesan missions, $32.31; convocation missions, $2.25; widows and orphans, aged and disabled clergy fund, $7.85; religious and theological education, $1.60; Sheltering Arms Hospital, $5.50; Bishop's special fund, $6.01; total contributions for objects in the Diocese, $75.02. *Contributions—For objects without the Diocese*—Domestic missions general, $28.55; colored people, 2 cents; Indians, 2 cents; deaf and dumb, 45 cents; Jews, $1.36; total domestic missions, $3.76; for Mexico, 52 cents; through American Church Missionary Society, $6.72; total foreign missions, $7.24; Bible and Prayer Book Society, $1.50; total contributions for objects without the Diocese, $39.50.

Financial Summary—Current expenses raised by congregation as above, $220.19; contributions, for objects in the Parish, $22.06; for objects in the Diocese, $75.02; for objects without the Diocese, $39.50; total of contributions, $136.58; all money raised by the congregation for current expenses and for contributions, $335.27; cash in hand, $10.00.

Remarks—I have been requested to state that the financial report is in excess of the strength of the Parish. Excess due to summer visitors in the town during July, August and September. Resources, $646.77; expenditures, $581.77; balance, May 1, 1904, $65.00.

G. H. CHILD, *Treas.*

PAROCHIAL REPORT.

Rev. P. B. STAUFFER. Mt. Zion's Church, Hedgesville, Berkeley county. Date of organization, 1817. Present minister took charge Oct. 1, 1903.

Church Officers—Church Wardens, Mr. Geo. T. Kreglow, Mr. W. B. Linghamfelter; other Vestrymen, Jacob H. Miller, F. H. Robins, P. C. Myers, John H. Miller, R. B. Kilmer, Morgan Shaffer, Lee Linghamfelter; Registrar, R. B. Kilmer, address North Mountain; Treasurer, P. C. Myers, address Hedgesville, Superintendent of Sunday School, Geo. T. Kreglow.

Official Acts—Baptisms, infants, 6; catechisings, monthly; public services, Sundays, 27; other days, 2; total, 29; Holy Communion, public, 6.

Communicants—Number last reported, 65; present number total, 65.

Congregations—Baptized persons connected with Parish, 14; confirmed persons connected with Parish, 65; families, 37; number sittings in church, $200; number free sittings, 200

Rector's Salary—As pledged from this congregation, $200.00; as pledged from other congregations, $125.00; from convocation missions, $75.00.

Organizations—Sunday School, officers and teachers, male, 5; female, 5; total, 10; pupils, male, 24; female, 21; total, 45; Woman's Auxiliary, members, 15.

Property—Church, brick, value $2,000.00; rectory, frame, insurance $250.00, value $400.00; total value, $2,400.

FINANCIAL REPORT.

Receipts—For all purposes—Cash on hand, per last report, $9.46; pledges and subscriptions, $250.00; collections in church, $70.04; Sunday School, $30.39; Woman's Auxiliary, money, $64.00; Woman's Auxiliary box, value, $30.00; Guilds or other societies, $9.00; income from other sources, $36.00; total receipts for all purposes, $498.89.

Disbursements—For current expenses—Salary of rector, $168.83; other salaries, $20.00; ordinary repairs, $7.03; other current expenses, $17.30; total for current expenses, $220.19. *Contributions—For objects in the Parish*—Communion alms, $3.30; maintaining Sunday Schools, $6.76; total contributions for objects in the Parish, $10.06. *Contributions—For objects in the Diocese*—Salary of Bishops, $50.00; diocesan missions, $25.00; convocation missions, $14.50; total contributions for objects in the diocese, $89.50. *Contributions—For objects without the Diocese*—Domestic missions general, $15.20; Jews, 31 cents; total domestic missions, $15.51; foreign missions general, $9.00; Brazil, $6.00; total foreign missions, $15.00; total contributions for objects without the Diocese, $30.51.

Financial Summary—Current expenses raised by congregation as above, $220.19; contributions, for objects in the Parish, $10.06; for objects in the Diocese, $89.50; for objects without the Diocese, $30.51; total of contributions, $343.23.

Remarks—Woman's Auxiliary had an entertainment to raise money for a Sunday School library, etc., and have some $60.00 in the treasury.

PAROCHIAL REPORT.

Rev. JOHN WARNOCK, address Charleston. St. Luke's Church; St. Luke's Mission, Charleston, Kanawha county. Date of organization, 1897. Present minister took charge May 1, 1903.

Church Officers—Church Warden, J. D. Lucadoe; other Vestrymen, Geo. Grishaber, Treasurer; Elijah Steen, Registrar; Geo. M. Krauss, C. P. Payne; Superintendent of Sunday School, Thos. Liversedge, Charleston; Sunday School Secretary, Miss Williams, Charleston; Treasurer, Miss Payne, Charleston; Lay Readers, Mr. J. D. Lucadoe.

Official Acts—Baptisms, infants, 5; marriages, 4; catechisings, monthly; public services, Sundays, 45; other days, 49; total, 94; Holy Communion, public, 13; private, 1; total 14.

Communicants—Number last reported, 24; admitted by confirmation, 3; total gain, 3; net gain, 3; present number total, 27.

Congregations—Baptized persons connected with Parish, 64; confirmed persons connected with Parish, 27; families, 16; number sittings in church, 100.

Rector's Salary—As pledged from this congregation, $240.00; from diocesan missions, $50.00.

Organizations—Sunday School, officers and teachers, male, 1; female, 4; total, 5; pupils, male, 19; female, 28; total, 47; Woman's Guild, Children's Guild, Boys' Club.

Property—Chapel, frame, value $1,200.00; rectory, frame, value $1,400.00; other property, vacant lot, $300.00; total value, $2,900.00. These are the values we have been using in all former reports, but real estate values have advanced in this neighborhood recently. Indebtedness, on other property, $600.00; due on diocesan assessment for missions, $8.00; due on diocesan assessment for Bishop's fund, $7.00; estimated total indebtedness, $615.00.

FINANCIAL REPORT.

Receipts—For all purposes—Cash on hand, per last report, $3.49; pledges and subscriptions, $108.35; collections in church, $28.47; Sunday School (see Remarks); Guilds or other societies, shows $79.77; income from other sources, $4.50; total receipts for all purposes, $224.58; amount overdrawn, $50.29; total, $274.87.

Disbursements—For current expenses—Salary of rector, $227.50; ordinary repairs, $33.55; payment on debts contracted for current expenses, $1,36; other current expenses, $11.32; other objects, $2.50; total for current expenses, $274.87. *Contributions—For objects in the Parish*—Extraordinary repairs and improvements (see Remarks) $64.86; maintaining Sunday Schools, $5.90; total contributions for objects in the Parish, $70.76. *Contributions—For objects in the Diocese*—Diocesan missions, $2.00; Sheltering Arms Hospital, $2.50; total contributions for objects in the Diocese, $4.50. .

Financial Summary—Current expenses raised by congregation as above, $276.23; contributions, for objects in the Parish, $70.76; total contributions, $70.76; all money raised by the congregation for current expenses and for contributions, $346.99; amount overdrawn, $50.29. This amount is due to St. Matthews.

Remarks—Missionary stipend, $50.00 paid direct to Mr. Warnock not included in this report.

Easter offerings and other collections not handled by the Treasurer spent as follows: Rectory repairs, $40.00; Chapel repairs, $24.86, paint, fence, gas fixtures and stoves.

Sunday School Treasurer reports receipts, $17.80; Sunday School expenses, $5.90; church expenses, $1.36; total, $7.26; balance in her hands, $10.54.

PAROCHIAL REPORT.

Rev. JOHN WARNOCK, address Charleston. St. Matthew's church; St. Matthew's Mission, Charleston, Kanawha county. Date of organization April, 1897. Present minister took charge May 1st, 1903.

Church Officers—Church Wardens, J. D. Lucadoe, Comyn Lewis; other Vestryman, Geo. Grishaber; Treasurer, Comyn Lewis, address Charleston; Superintendent of Sunday School, Miss Peyton, Charleston.

Official Acts—Baptisms, infants, 5; presented for confirmation since last report, 5; marriages, 2; burials, 3; catechisings, monthly; public services, Sundays, 40; other days, 41; total, 87; Holy Communion, public, 13.

Communicants—Number last reported, 42; admitted by confirmation, 3; total gain, 3; net gain, 3; present number total, 45.

Congregations—Baptized persons connected with Parish, 136; confirmed persons connected with Parish, 45; families, 25; number free sittings, 200.

Rector's Salary—As pledged from this congregation, $240.00; from diocesan missions, $50.00.

Organizations—Sunday Schools, officers and teachers, female, 3; total, 3; pupils, male, 10; female, 20; total, 30.

Property—Church, stone, insurance, $500.00; value, $5,000.00; chapel, St. Andrews, log, insurance, $300.00; value, $650.00; total value, $5,650.00; indebtedness, due on diocesan assessment for missions, $2.28; due on diocesan assessment for bishop's fund, $7.00; total indebtedness, $9.28.

FINANCIAL REPORT.

Receipts—For all Purposes—Cash on hand, per last report, $6.62; pledges and subscriptions, $165.28; collections in church, $43.59; Sunday School, see remarks; guilds or other societies, shows, etc., $90.83; sale of cemetery lot, $10.00; income from other sources, $4.60; total receipts for all purposes, $320.92.

Disbursements—For Current Expenses—Salary of rector, $240.00; insurance, $6.00; ordinary repairs, $3.50; other current expenses, $21.13; other objects, $5.86; total for current expenses, $276.49; *Contributions—for objects in the Parish*—Maintaining Sunday Schools, $7.54; total contributions for objects in the Parish, $7.54. *Contributions—For objects in the Diocese*—Diocesan missions (also see remarks, S. S., this not yet forwarded) $1.60; convocation missions, $5.72; total contributions for objects in the Diocese, $7,32. *Contributions—For objects without the Diocese*—Foreign missions general, $1.00; for China, $7.00; for Africa, $2.00; (not yet forwarded, see remarks for amount sent by Sunday School); total foreign missions, $10.00; total contributions for objects without the Diocese, $13.00.

Financial Summary—Current expenses raised by congregation as above, $276.49. *Contributions*—For objects in the Parish, $7.54; for objects in the Diocese, $732; for objects without the Diocese, $3.00; all money raised by the congregation for current expenses and for contributions, $324.35; cash in hand, $50.29. This $50.29 has been used by St. Luke's. We expect them to pay it back.

Remarks—Missionary stipend, $50.00, paid direct to Mr. Warnock, not included in this report. Sunday School treasurer reports receipts, $28.47; Sunday School expenses, $7.54; church expenses, $5.86; diocesan missions, $5.72; foreign missions, $7.00; total, $26.12; balance in her hands, $2.35.

PAROCHIAL REPORT.

Rev. JOHN WARNOCK, address 220 Randolph Street, Charleston, W. Va. St. Mark's Church, St. Albans, Kanawha county. Present minister took charge May 1, 1903.

Church Officers—Church Warden, E. W. Chandler; other vestrymen, A. W. Howard, Luke Frazier, T. H. Mohler, W. H. Barnett; Registrar, T. H. Mohler, address St. Albans; Treasurer, T. H. Mohler, address St. Albans, W. Va.; Superintendent of Sunday Schools, E. W. Chandler, St. Albans, W. Va.; Sunday School Secretary and Treasurer, T. H. Mohler.

Official Acts—Baptisms, infants, 1; presented for confirmation since last report, 2; burials, 2; catechisings, monthly; public services, Sundays, 36; other days, 12; total 48; Holy Communion, public, 12.

Communicants—Number last reported, about 26; admitted by confirmation, 2; added otherwise, 2; total gain, 4; died, 1; removed without letter, 1; lapsed, 5; total loss, 7; net loss, 3; present total about 35.

Congregations—Confirmed persons connected with Parish, 35; families, 20; number sittings in church, 220.

Rector's Salary—As pledged from this congregations, $200.00.

Organizations—Sunday Schools, officers and teachers, male, 2; female, 3; total, 5; pupils, male, 16; female, 18; total, 34; Advent offering, $5.00; Lenten offering, $10.64; total Sunday School offerings, $15.64.

Property—Church, brick, insurance, none; value, $2,000.00; rectory, frame, insurance, $1,000; value, $2,500.00; total value, $4,500.00; indebtedness, on church none; on rectory, $161.11; due the minister, nothing; total indebtedness, $161.11.

FINANCIAL REPORT.

Receipts—For all Purposes—Cash on hand, per last report, have no record; pledges and subscriptions, $181.90; collections in church, $45.81; money borrowed, $729.08; Sunday School, $49.39; total receipts for all purposes, $1,006.18.

Disbursements—For Current Expenses—Salary of rector, $200.00; total for current expenses, $200.00. *Contributions—For objects in the Parish*—Communion alms, $4.95; extraordinary repairs and improvements, $567.97; maintaining Sunday Schools, $54.44; rector's salary, $200.00; cash on hand, $17.71; amount due on loan, $161.11; total contributions for objects in the Parish, $1,006.18. *Contributions—For objects in the Diocese*—Salary of bishops, $16.68; permananent fund, $2.15; diocesan missions, $10.07; convocation missions, 60 cents; widows and orphans, aged and disabled clergy fund, 60 cents; religious and theological education, 50 cents; Sheltering Arms Hospital, $2.55; theological seminary, 30 cents; total contributions for objects in the Diocese, $33.45. *Contributions—For objects without the Diocese*—Domestic missions general, $1.50; colored people, 20 cents; Indians, 40 cents; deaf and dumb, 35 cents; total domestic missions, $2.45; foreign missions general, 20 cents; for Mexico, 60 cents; Brazil and Cuba, 35 cents; total foreign missions, $1.15; American church building fund, 35 cents; general clergy relief fund, 20 cents; Bible and prayer book society, 30 cents; total contributions for objects without the Diocese, $4.45.

Financial Summary—Current expenses raised by congregation as above, $200.00. *Contributions*—For objects in the Parish, $59.39; for objects in the Diocese, $33.45; for objects without the Diocese, $4.45; total of contributions, $97.29; all money raised by the congregation for current expenses and for contributions, $297.29.

Remarks—Having no record for previous year, and having been treasurer for only part of this year, have not kept my books to conform with the requirements of this blank. The amounts on receipts and disbursements are in accordance with my books, and correct.

THOS. H. MOHLER, *Treasurer.*

PAROCHIAL REPORT.

Rev. A. J. WILLIS, address Middleway, W. Va. Grace Church, Nelson Parish, Middleway, Jefferson county. Date of organization, 1888. Present minister took charge November 1, 1890.

Church Officers—Church Wardens, J. J. Grantham, Wm. Gilbert; other vestrymen, James Grantham, W. E. Bates; Registrar, James Grantham, address Middleway; Treasurer, James Grantham; Superintendent of Sunday Schools, Jane Doke; Sunday School Secretary and Treasurer, Mitchell Willis.

Official Acts—Baptisms, infants, 1; marriages, 2; burials, 1; public services, Sundays, 52; other days, 15; total, 67; Holy Communion, public, 12.

Communicants—Number last reported, 47; died, 1; lapsed, 2; total loss, 3; net loss, 3; present number total, 44.

Congregations—Baptized persons connected with Parish, 47; confirmed persons connected with Parish, 47; families, 22; individuals not thus included, 200; whole number of individuals, 250; number sittings in church, 200; number free sittings, 200.

Rector's Salary—As pledged from this congregation, $150.00; from diocesan missions, $50.00; as pledged from other congregations, $400.00; from convocation missions, $100.00; from American Church Missionary Society, $100.00; total, $800.00.

Organizations—Sunday Schools, officers and teachers, male, 3; female, 4; total, 7; pupils, male, 16; female, 20; total, 43; Advent offering, $4.27; Lenten offering, $3.52; other offerings, $5.00; total Sunday School offerings, $12.79; Rector's Aid, 10; Parish Guild, embracing the three churches in the Parish.

Property—Church, brick, insurance, $1,000; value, $2,500; rectory, frame and brick, insurance, $1,500; value, $2,000; lot belonging to the Parish, $350; total value, $4,850. money raised from outside sources, $284; for what objects used, repairs and improvements to the rectory.

FINANCIAL REPORT.

Receipts—For all Purposes—Cash on hand, per last report, $10.24; pledges and subscriptions, $150.00; collections in church, $128.40; Sunday School, $12.79; guilds or other societies, $20.00; total receipts for all purposes, $321.43.

Disbursements—For Current Expenses—Salary of rector, $150.00; other salaries, $30.00; insurance, $10.00; ordinary repairs, $10.00; other current expenses, $9.21; total for current expenses, $209.21. *Contributions—For objects in the Parish*—Maintaining Sunday Schools, $20.00; total contributions for objects in the Parish, $20.00. *Contributions—For objects in the Diocese*—Salary of Bishops, $37.00; permanent fund, $3.00; diocesan missions, $15.00; convocation missions, $8.07; widows and orphans, aged and disabled clergy fund, $2.77; Sheltering Arms Hospital, $7.00; total contributions for objects in the Diocese, $72.84. *Contributions—For objects without the Diocese*—Domestic missions general, $4.00; through American church missionary society, $4.38; total domestic missions, $8.38; foreign missions, general, $7.00; through American church missionary society, $4.00; total foreign missions, $11.00; total contributions for objects without the Diocese, $19.38.

Financial Summary—Current expenses raised by congregation as above, $209.21. *Contributions*—For objects in the Parish, $20.00; for objects in the Diocese, $72.84; for objects without the Diocese, $19.38; total of contributions, $112.22; all money raised by the congregation for current expenses and for contributions, $321.43.

PAROCHIAL REPORT.

Rev. A. J. WILLIS, address Middleway. St. Bartholomew's Church, Nelson Parish, Leetown, Jefferson county. Date of organization, 1888. Present minister took charge November 1, 1890.

Church Officers—Church Wardens, L. H. Strider, Chas. Jones: other vestrymen, Dr. Chas. Lucas; Registrar, L. H. Strider, address Leetown; treasurer, L. H. Strider; Superintendent of Sunday Schools, Robt. L. Strider.

Official Acts—Baptisms, 1; presented for confirmation since last report, 2; public services, Sundays, 36; other days, 8; total, 44; Holy Communion, public, 6.

Communicants—Number last reported, 40; admitted by confirmation,

1; total gain, 1; transferred, 2; removed without letter, 4; total loss, 6; net loss, 5; present number total, 35.

Congregations—Confirmed persons connected with Parish, 60; families, 13; individuals not thus included, 100; whole number of individuals, 200; number sittings in church, 200; number free sittings, 200.

Rector's Salary—As pledged from this congregation, $175.00; from diocesan missions, $50.00; as pledged from other congregations, $375; from convocation missions, $100; from American church missionary society, $100; total, $800.

Organizations—Sunday Schools, officers and teachers, male, 1; female, 5; total, 6; pupils, male, 10; female, 15; total, 25; Advent offering, $16.42; Lenten offering, $3.30; total Sunday School offerings, $19.72; Ladies' Aid; Parish Guild, embraces all of Nelson Parish.

Property—Church frame, insurance, $1,000; value, $1,800; total value, $2,800.

FINANCIAL REPORT.

Receipts—For all Purposes—Cash on hand, per last report, $7.36; pledges and subscriptions, $175.00; collections in church, $142.92; Sunday School, $19.72; Guilds, $10.00; total receipts for all purposes, $355.00.

Disbursements—For Current Expenses—Salary of rector, $175.00; other salaries, $18.00; ordinary repairs, $10.00; other current expenses, 54 cents; total for current expenses, $203.54. *Contributions—For objects in the Parish*—Extraordinary repairs and improvements, $7.50; maintaining Sunday Schools, $10.00; total contributions for objects in the Parish, $17.50. *Contributions—For objects in the Diocese*—Salary of bishops, $20.00; permanent fund, $6.00; diocesan missions, $31.42; convocation missions, $14.20; widows and orphans, aged and disabled clergy fund, $4.00; Sheltering Arms Hospital, $7.04; total contributions for objects in the Diocese, $92.71. *Contributions—For objects without the Diocese*—Domestic missions general, $5.50; through American church missionary society, $16.25; total domestic missions, $21.75; foreign missions general, $3.30; Brazil, $16.20; total foreign missions, $19.50; total contributions for objects without the Diocese, $41.25.

Financial Summary—Current expenses raised by congregation as above, $203.54. *Contributions*—For objects in the Parish, $17.50; for objects in the Diocese, $92.71; for objects without the Diocese, $41.25; total of contributions, $151.46; all money raised by the congregation for current expenses and for contributions, $355.00.

PAROCHIAL REPORT.

Rev. A. J. WILLIS, address Middleway. Church of the Holy Spirit,

Nelson Parish, Summit Pt., Jefferson county. Date of organization, 1888. Present minister took charge, November 1, 1890.

Church Officers—Church Warden, A. P. Thomas; other vestrymen, R. O. Allen, C. C. Whiting, U. H. Willis, Registrar, G. C. Whiting, address Summit Pt.; Treasurer, R. O. Allen, address Summit Pt.; Superintendent of Sunday Schools, G. C. Whiting; Sunday School Secretary and Treasurer, Preston Biller, Summit Pt.

Official Acts—Baptisms, infants, 1; presented for confirmation since last report, 1; marriage, 2; burials, 1; public services, Sundays, 52; other days, 8; total, 60; Holy Communion, public, 12.

Communicants—Number last reported, 46; admitted by confirmation, 1; restored to communion, 1; total gain, 2; transferred, 1; total loss, 1; net gain, 1; present number total, 47.

Congregations—Baptized persons connected with Parish, 86; confirmed persons connected with Parish, 47; families, 19; individuals not thus included, 100; whole number of individuals, 242; number sittings in church, 250; number free sittings, 250.

Rector's Salary—As pledged from this congregation, $225.00; from diocesan missions, $50.00; as pledged from other congregations, $325.00; from convocation missions, $100.00; from American church missionary society, $100.00; total, $800.00.

Organizations—Sunday Schools, officers and teachers, male, 2; female, 3; total, 5; pupils, male, 5; female, 10; total, 15; Lenten offering, $2.80: total Sunday School offerings, $2.80; Parish Guild.

Property—Church, stone, insurance, $2,000; value, $4,000; total value, $4,000.

FINANCIAL REPORT.

Receipts—For all Purposes—Pledges and subscriptions, $247.71; collections in church, $38.20; Sunday School, $2.80; Guilds, $10.00; income from other sources, $32.00; total receipts for all purposes, $330.71.

Disbursements—For Current Expenses—Salary of rector, $225.00; other salaries, $24.00; total for current expenses, $249.00. *Contributions—For objects in the Parish*—Maintaining Sunday Schools, $10.00; total contributions for objects in the Parish, $10.00. *Contributions for objects in the Diocese*—Salary of bishops, $30.00; permanent fund, $2.00; diocesan missions, $15.00; convocation missions, $9.18; total contributions for objects in the Diocese, $56.18. *Contributions—For objects without the Diocese*—Domestic missions general, $2.80; through American church missionary society, $5.23; total domestic missions, $8.03; foreign missions, general, $2.50; through American church missionary society, $5.00; total foreign missions, $7.50; total contributions for objects without the Diocese, $15.53.

Financial Summary—Current expenses raised by congregation as above, $249.00. *Contributions*—For objects in the Parish, $10.00; for objects in the Diocese, $56.18; for objects without the Diocese, $15.53; total of contributions, $81.71; all money raised by the congregation for current expenses and for contributions, $330.71.

Remarks—This church was closed for three months on account of smallpox, hence contributions small.

PAROCHIAL REPORT.

Rev. ROBERT R. WINDLEY, address Grafton, W. Va. St. Mathias Parish, Grafton, Taylor county. Present minister took charge November 1, 1903.

Church Officers—Church Wardens, A. H. Thayer, M. D., Charles Steel; other vestry men, A. E. N. Means, C. W. Steel, George Lockyer, Sr., L. B. Brydon; Registrar, A. E. N. Means, address Grafton, W. Va.; Treasurer, C. W. Steel, address Grafton, W. Va.; Superintendent of Sunday Schools, Robt. R. Windley; Sunday School Secretary and Treasurer, Miss Roseline Kenedy.

Official Acts—Baptisms, infants, 6; adults, 2; total, 8; presented for confirmation since last report, 4; burials, 2; catechisings, 4; public services, Sundays, 30; other days, 14; total, 44; Holy Communion, public, 9; private, 3; total, 12.

Communicants—Number last reported, 30; admitted by confirmation, 4; total, gain, 4; died, 2; total loss, 2; net gain, 2; present number total, 32.

Congregations—Baptized persons connected with Parish, 42; individuals, not thus included, 21; number sittings in church, 125; number free sittings, 125.

Rector's Salary—As pledged from this congregation, $350.00; from diocesan missions, $300.00.

Organizations—Sunday Schools, officers and teachers, male, 2; female, 2; total, 4; pupils, male, 6; female, 18; total, 24; Advent offering, $3.72; Lenten offerings, $4.59; other offerings, $2.50; total Sunday School offerings, $10.81; Altar Guild, Ladies' Guild.

Property—Church, frame, value, $6,000; rectory, frame, value, $4,500.

FINANCIAL REPORT.

Receipts—For all Purposes—total receipts for all purposes $484 66.

Disbursements—For current expenses—Salary of rector, $177.00; other salaries, $12.00; ordinary repairs, $86.91; other current expenses, $56.35; total for current expenses, $332.26. *Contributions—For objects in the Parish*—Communion alms, $10.83; extraordinary repairs and improvements, $40.00; maintaining Sunday Schools, $29.00; other objects, $29.00; total contributions for objects in the Parish, $108.83. *Contributions—For objects in the Diocese*—Salary of bishops, $15.00; diocesan missions, $15.00; Sheltering Arms Hospital, $2.50; bishop's special fund, $5.66; total contributions for objects in the Diocese, $38.16. *Contributions—For objects without the Diocese*—Jews, 92 cents; total domestic missions, 92 cents; foreign missions general, $4.59; total foreign missions, $4.59; total contributions for objects without the Diocese, $5.51.

Financial Summary—Contributions—For objects in the Parish, $441.09; for objects in the Diocese, $38.16; for objects without the Diocese, $4.59; total of contributions, $483.84.

REPORT OF THE REV. B. M. SPURR.

My Dear Bishop:

You must forgive my tardiness in sending this report, but absence in searching for Philip Brittingham's body and bringing the same home, caused that delay and my failure to get to the Sheltering Arms.

In the past year our hospital cared for 565 patients, of which 270 were charity cases.

The cost of running the hospital for the year was $12,231.17, of which amount, $2,000 was spent for improvements. We graduated three nurses from our training school last December, who had the honor of receiving their diplomas at your hands. There are now ten under graduates in the school.

My work at the prison has been as usual, preaching, comforting, advising and preparing men for the scaffold.

I have preached in and out of the Diocese during the year, 187; baptisms, 10; burials, 9; marriages, 5; have found means for the expenses of the hospital, the building of a deaconess house and two industrial schools at Charles Town and Ansted. Provide also the means for supporting one deaconess and one teacher.

Have visited the following places in the Diocese, Mannington, (16 times) Montgomery, Paint Creek, Mount Carbon, Ansted, St. Andrews of the Mountain, (2) Charles Town, Ripley, Ravenswood, Little Otter, Sutton, Centralia, Richwood, Flatwood, Harper's Ferry.

Trusting that this report gives all the information you desire, permit me to remain,

Faithfully yours,

B. M. SPURR.

May 27. '04.

REPORT OF THE REV. OLIVER J. WHILDEN, MISSIONARY TO DEAF MUTES.

1017 W. Hopkins Avenue,
Baltimore, Md., June 10.

The Rt. Rev. G. W. Peterkin, D. D.,
Bishop of West Virginia.

My Dead Bishop:

I beg to report the following as missionary to the deaf in the Diocese of West Virginia:

I have held ten services during the year: four in Wheeling, two in Romney, one in Parkersburg, and three in Huntington. I baptized one adult deaf-mute in St. Matthew's Church, Wheeling, and four adults and one infant in Trinity Church, Huntington. I had presented for confirmation one in Wheeling and six in Huntington.

The receipts from all sources were as follows:

1903.			
Aug.	31	Mrs. G. W. Steenrod, Wheeling	$ 5 00
Sept.	4	E. M. Hoge, Wheeling	5 00
	27	Rev. D. W. Howard, Wheeling	5 00
	27	Offering at service, Wheeling	10 10
Nov.	11	Offering at service, Wheeling	7 47
	13	Offering at service, Parkersburg	50
	14	Offering at service, Huntington,	5 00
Dec.	1	Good Shepherd, Parkersburg, through Bp. P	10 00
Jan.	10	School for the deaf, Romney	10 00
Mch.	11	Rev. Mr. Howard, $5.00; offering at service, $1.87	6 87
	13	Offering at service, Huntington	4 11
May	10	School for the deaf, Romney	12 00
	13	Offering at service, Wheeling	6 00
	15	Offering at service, Huntington	1 45
			$78 50

My expenses—railroad fares, hotel bills, postage, etc., probably amounted to a little less than the above sum.

I think this is the best report of work done in any one of the other Dioceses—*ten* services, *six* baptisms, and *seven* confirmations.

The Diocese of Southern Virginia has appropriated $150 annually towards the work, Virginia gives $50, Tennessee $50 and Mississippi $50. I am waiting to hear from a few others. I hope West Virvinia may soon bein a position to allow something—the possibilities for doing good work in West Virginia are great, greater, perhaps, than in those Dioceses that allow a stipend.

I am very sorry to have to report the death of Mrs. Elizabeth Steenrod, a sainted deaf-mute woman of St. Matthew's mission, Wheeling. Mrs. Steen-

rod was very helpful and gave bountifully towards the support of the work. Her loss will be very seriously felt in the matter of support; her influence for good was so great among the half a hundred deaf-mutes I almost despair for the future. But I am hopeful that the good she did will help as a precious memory.

Very sincerely yours,

OLIVER J. WHILDEN.

General Missionary to the Deaf.

APPENDIX C.

Report of Committee on Assessments for the Year,

May 1st, 1904, to April 30th, 1905.

REPORT OF COMMITTEE ON ASSESSMENTS, AT MARTINSBURG, JUNE 3, 1904.

Name of Parish.	*Diocesan Miss.*	*Epis. & Cont. Fund.*
Alderson	$ 6 00	$ 6 00
Berkley Springs	25 00	30 00
Bluefield	30 00	30 00
Princeton	6 00	6 00
Bramwell	30 00	30 00
Eckman and McDowell Missions	20 00	20 00
Brooke County, St. John's	5 00	5 00
Buckhannon	10 00	10 00
Bunker Hill	5 00	5 00
Charleston, St. oJhn's	200 00	275 00
Charleston, St. Luke's	8 00	7 00
Charleston, St. Matthew's	8 00	7 00
Charles Town, Zion	300 00	425 00
Charles Town, St. Phillip's	10 00	5 00
St. Andrew's on the Mountain	3 00	2 00
Clarksburg	125 00	125 00
Cresaps	5 00	5 00
Davis	8 00	8 00
Elkins Mission	10 00	10 00
Fairmont	75 00	100 00
Grafton	15 00	15 00
Harper's Ferry	20 00	20 00
Hedgesville	25 00	50 00
Hinton	30 00	20 00
Huntington	80 00	100 00
Kenova	7 00	7 00
Lewisburg	7 00	10 00
Ronceverte	8 00	8 00
Martinsburg	75 00	100 00
Nelson Parish { Middleway, Lee Town, Summit Point }	75 00	90 00
Mannington	10 00	10 00

Name of Parish	*Diocesan Miss.*	*Epis. & Cont. Fund.*
Moorefield	20 00	20 00
Romney	16 00	16 00
Okonoko	10 00	10 00
Morgantown	50 00	50 00
Moundsville	40 00	60 00
Nuttallburg	5 00	10 00
Parkersburg, Trinity	350 00	525 00
Parkersburg, Good Shepherd	20 00	5 00
Parkersburg, St. Stephen	3 00	2 00
Tavennersville	10 00	3 00
Point Pleasant, Christ	50 00	50 00
Bruce Chapel	12 00	12 00
Spillman Mission	10 00	10 00
Powellton	20 00	20 00
Ansted	20 00	20 00
Ravenswood, Grace	10 00	10 00
Ripley, St. John's	15 00	15 00
Liverpool, Whittle	3 00	2 00
Ripon	10 00	20 00
Shepherdstown	75 00	75 00
Sistersville	40 00	40
New Martinsville	40 00	40
Smithfield, Wetzel County	5 00	5
Spruce Chapel	4 00	4
St. Albans	10 00	10 00
Montgomery	15 00	15 00
St. Mary's	15 00	15 00
Sutton	10 00	10 00
Union	50 00	50 00
White Sulphur	10 00	10 00
Fort Spring	5 00	5 00
Waverly	10 00	5 00
Wellsburg	25 00	25 00
Weston	75 00	80 00
Wheeling, St. Matthew's	425 00	600 00
Wheeling, St. Luke's	175 00	175 00
Wheeling, St. Andrew's	15 00	10 00
Chester	10 00	4 00
Williamson	....	5 00
Wheeling, St. Paul's, Elm Grove	5 00	10 00
Williamstown	25 00	15 00
Willow Island	5 00	5 00
Beckley	6 00	6 00

Name of Parish	*Diocesan Miss.*	*Epis. & Cont. Fund.*
Beury	5 00	5 00
Du Bree	5 00	5 00
Glen Jean	10 00	10 00
Immanuel, Mt. Carbon	5 00	5 00
Totals	$3,005 00	$3,665 00

Your committee recommends that payments on account of the assessment for the Episcopal and Contingent Fund be made to the Treasurer quarterly.

D. W. HOWARD. R. M. BROWNE.
S. S. MOORE. J. GASSMAN.
J. S. GIBSON. RICHARD HENDERSON.
J. S. DOUGLAS. L. E. SANDS.
A. G. GRINNAN. G. A. ASCHMAN.
G. W. EASTER.

APPENDIX D.

Tabulated Statement—Vital Statistics.

Tabulated Statement—Financial Statistics.

TABULATED STATEMENT—VITAL STATISTICS.

No.	ALPHABETICAL CLERGY LIST.	PARISHES, MISSIONS AND STATIONS.	Baptisms.		Confirmations.	Marriages.	Burials.	Communicants.		Baptized Persons.	Families and Parts.	Number in Sunday Schools.	
			Infants.	Adults.				Last Reported.	Present Number.			Teachers	Scholars
1	Rev. John S. Alfriend	Zion Church, Charles Town	8	2	9	8	12	326	333	450	160	16	100
		St. Andrews, Blue Ridge	8		1	2	1	28	29	40	25	7	70
		...., Harewood										5	40
2	Rev. M. F. Duty, Asst	St. Philips, Charles Town	1	1			1	50	23	75	17	5	39
3	Rev. Jacob Brittingham	St. Lukes, Wheeling	17	2	18	5	17	266	260	281	202	10	80
4	Rev. Everhard Heath Brosius	Christ Church, Bluefield	5		2	2	8	91	106	181	83	4	29
		Heavenly Rest, Princeton				2		18	18	20	10		
5	Rev. Chas. Mitchell Campbell	Christ Church, Short Creek						2	2	8	9		
		St. Paul's Mission, Bull Creek						4	4	10	4		
		Emmanuel Mission, Mouth of Robinson						4	4	7	10		
6	Rev. Wilson Page Chrisman	Trinity, Moundsville	8	2	2	3	5	55	64	158	84	12	109
7	Rev. Guy Hamilton Crook	*Incarnation, Ronceverte						21	21	38	15	2	24
		*St. James, Lewisburg						24	24	42	17		
		*Holy Comfort, Fort Spring						8	8	11	9		
		*Grace, Clover Lick						4	4	10	3		
		*Hillsboro						3	3	10	4		
		*St. Thomas, White Sulphur						41	41	75	92		96
8	Rev. Thos. J. Oliver Curran	St. Andrews, Wheeling	14	5		12	6	76	75	200	40	6	130
9	Rev. John Smallwood Douglas	Trinity, Martinsburg	11		31	2	5	152	165	280	100	15	90
		Christ Church, Bunker Hill						7	8	15	4		
10	Rev. Cretius A. Dowell	St. Pauls, Sistersville	5	8	10	4	3	32	41	64	21	11	98
11	Rev. Geo. W. Easter	All Saints, Union	8			2	1	40	35	78	23	8	44
		Messiah, Alderson						5	4	5	3		
12	Rev. Jas. Logan Fish	St. Barnabas, Davis	10	4	6	3	2	24	37	62	26	4	25
		...., Parsons						6	6	6	2		
		...., Thomas	1						6	15			

TABULATED STATEMENT—VITAL STATISTICS—Continued.

No.	ALPHABETICAL CLERGY LIST.	PARISHES, MISSIONS AND STATIONS.	Baptisms. Infants.	Baptisms. Adults.	Confirmations.	Marriages.	Burials.	Communicants. Last Reported.	Communicants. Present Number.	Baptized Persons.	Families and Parts.	Number in Sunday Schools. Teachers	Number in Sunday Schools. Scholars
	Rev. Jas. Logan Fish	............., Douglas							5	11	8		
13	Rev. Geo. A. Gibbons	St. Stephens, Romney	2			3		25	21	40	20	4	16
		Emmanuel, Moorefield	3					30	30	55	24	5	20
		Epiphany, Okonoko						10	10	16	4		
		New Creek Mission, Keyser						6	6	6	2		
		Paw Paw Mission, Paw Paw						6	6	6	5		
14	Rev. J. Howard Gibbons	Christ Church, Pt. Pleasant	4	1	4	3	3	58	62	90	35	4	25
		Bruce Chapel	1	1	5			21	26	60	15	3	35
		..............Spillman	4	1	5		1	19	23	40	15	3	32
		..............Winfield		1	2				8				
15	Rev. John Shackelford Gibson	Trinity, Huntington	5	6	11	4	36	192	200	420	145	11	30
		Grace, Kenova			2			8	8	22	9		
		Mingo Mission, Williamson	2		3			6	11	28	18	4	15
16	Rev. Andrew Glassell Grinnan	St. Paul's, Weston	6			1	13	81	75	210	81	7	57
		St. Paul's Chapel	1	2	4			9	13	20	7	3	30
17	Rev. Jacob A. Hiatt	Ascension, Hinton		1				46	49	81	138	4	40
		St. Peter's, Glen Jean						20	15				
		*............, Beckley						17	17	20	18		
		*............, Beury						2	2	2	2		
18	Rev. David W. Howard	St. Matthew's, Wheeling	16	8	30	27	16	537	550	870	304	18	135
19	Rev. Edward D. Irvine	Christ Church, Wellsburg	2	2	4	9	2	58	55	75	25	5	30
		St. John's, Brooke county	8		4		1	22	25	35	8		
20	Rev. Arthur Machen Lewis	St. David's, Powellton	5	5	8		4	27	34	60	15	6	57
		Calvary, Montgomery	7		1	1	1	17	19	34	8	1	15
		Redeemer, Ansted	5	2	3	1	1	37	33	75	13	6	60
		St. Titus', Nuttalburg	3		3				15	27			
		Good Shepherd, Ferris	1		2				4	8			
		Emmanuel, Mt. Carbon							10	25			

21	REV. JOHN TILTON MARLEY	Trinity, Morgantown	5	4	9		8	91	86	112	50	5	40
		........, Kingwood						1	1	2	1		
22	REV. C. E. A. MARSHALL	Trinity, Shepherdstown / Good Shepherd, Duffield		1	1	1	6	144	150	272	50	11	48
23	REV. FRANK A. MEADE	Grace Church, Elkins	1	1	2	1	3	30	36	72	22	4	20
		Trinity, Belington						10	10	25			
24	REV. ROBT. NELSON MEADE	Holy Trinity, Bramwell	1			2	6	37	21	54	20	5	50
		Grace, Eckman	1			2		22	13	24	10		
		St. Antipas, Welch				1		15	15	32	19		
		Algoma Mission, Mayberry " , Elkhorn " , Crane Creek "	1				2	27	38	82	42		
25	REV. A. B. MITCHELL	Good Shepherd, Parkersburg	4	2	3		2	9	15	25	38	12	185
		Grace, Tavenersville						10	10	20	28	5	30
		Christ Memorial, Williamstown	1		1			29	27	62	40	6	22
26	REV. FRANCIS VAN R. MOORE	St. Paul's, Elm Grove	6	3	7			20	27	30	20	8	74
		*New Cumberland						4	4	12	4		
		*Chester						20	20	25	10		
27	REV. S. SCOLLAY MOORE, D. D.	Trinity, Parkersburg	16	12	20	32	26	298	308	525	250	14	101
		St. Stephen's Mission, Parkersburg				2	1	12	8	12	6		
28	REV. CHARLES C. PEARSON	St. Mark's, Berkeley Springs			1	2	2	25	23	30	13	4	17
29	RT. REV. CHAS. CLIFTON PENICK, D. D.	Christ Church, Fairmont	2		2	1	9	136	124	144	148	8	47
30	REV. JAMES FITTS PLUMMER	Christ Church, Clarksburg	4			1		156	106	250	92	5	48
		St. Thomas, North View										4	25
31	REV. ROBT. DOUGLAS ROLLER, D. D.	St. John's, Charleston	13	3	21	8	34	267	310	577	200	18	130
	C. HELY MOLONEY, Assistant	........Carbon										2	15
		Pratt, Paint Creek and Crown Hill										2	106
		Dundon											
32	REV. CHARLES E. SHAW	St. Ann, New Martinsville	5		9	1	1	36	50	94	33	6	24
		........*Smithfield						7	7	7			
33	REV. GEORGE C. SHAW	Grace, St. Mary's		2	1	1		28	29	30	20	7	32
		St. John's, Willow Island			1			10	11	18	16		
		Messiah, Waverly		1	1			10	10	14	25	5	37
		St. Andrew's, Mannington	3					21	24	44	36		
34	REV. EDWIN B. SNEAD	Transfiguration, Buckhannon			4	1	1	19	25	28	8		
		St. John's, Sutton						12	10	25	11		

TABULATED STATEMENT—VITAL STATISTICS—Continued.

No.	ALPHABETICAL CLERGY LIST.	PARISHES, MISSIONS AND STATIONS.	Baptisms. Infants.	Baptisms. Adults.	Confirmations.	Marriages.	Burials.	Communicants. Last Reported.	Communicants. Present Number.	Baptized Persons.	Families and Parts.	Number in Sunday Schools. Teachers	Number in Sunday Schools. Scholars
		Spruce Church, Spruce Run	2	....	1	....	....	10	11	21	6	3	15
35	Rev. Paris Becker Stauffer	St. John's Harper's Ferry	....	....	....	....	1	32	31	45	16	6	70
		Mt. Zion, Hedgesville	6	....	....	....	....	65	65	71	37	10	45
37	Rev. Robt. Raymond Windley	St. Matthias, Grafton	6	2	4	....	2	30	32	42	21	4	24
		*Cairo	....	....	....	....	....	10	10	10	....	....	....
36	Rev. John Warnock	St. Luke's, Charleston	5	....	....	4	....	24	27	64	16	5	47
		St. Matthew's, Charleston	5	....	5	2	3	42	45	136	25	3	30
		St. Mark's, St. Albans	1	....	2	....	2	26	35	40	20	5	34
37	Rev. A. J. Willis	Grace, Middleway	1	....	....	2	1	47	44	47	222	7	43
		St. Bartholomew's, Leetown	....	1	2	....	....	40	35	60	113	6	25
		Holy Spirit, Summit Point	1	....	1	2	1	46	47	86	119	5	15
38	Rev. Orville Melville Yerger	*St. John's, Ripon	....	....	....	....	....	28	28	65	25	2	27
		*Christ Church, Blue Ridge	....	....	....	....	....	6	6	20	7	4	46
	Vacant	Grace, Ravenswood	....	....	....	....	....	20	20	40	39	....	....
		St. John's, Ripley	....	....	....	....	1	37	36	48	15	....	....
		*Whittle Chapel, Liverpool	....	....	....	....	....	9	9	30	20	....	....
		Church of Our Savior, Mason City	....	....	....	....	1	14	14	16	5	....	....
		*.............. Spencer	....	....	....	....	....	7	7	12	4	....	....
		Buffalo and Poca	....	....	....	....	....	4	4	4	2	....	....
		St. John's, Scary	....	....	....	....	....	3	3	3	2	....	....
		Pennsboro Mission	....	....	....	....	....	5	5	14	3	....	....
		*Dubrea	....	....	....	....	....	14	14	14	6	....	....
		*Keeney's Mountain	....	....	....	....	....	8	8	8	3	....	....
		*Grace, Cresaps Valley	....	....	....	....	....	9	9	18	7	....	....
	Scattered Communicants not connected with any parish		....	....	....	....	....	88	129	....	....	....	....
	Totals		251	86	263	159	242	4671	4842	8033	3817	365	3093

* Taken from last year's report.

Note.—The Bishop reports 307 from Council to Council. The discrepancy is due to the fact that the parochial reports closed Apr. 30.

TABULATED STATEMENT—FINANCIAL STATISTICS.

No.	Alphabetical Clergy List.	Parishes, Missions and Stations.	Disbursements. Current Expenses.	Contributions. Parochial.	Contributions. Diocesan.	Contributions. Outside the Diocese.	Grand Total.
1	Rev. John S. Alfriend	Zion Church, Charles Town	$ 2,149 31	$ 1,618.82	$ 1,340.92	$ 852.98	$ 5,962.03
		St. Andrew's, Blue Ridge		5.00	15.00		20.00
		Harwood			10.00		10.00
2	Rev. M. F. Duty, Asst.	St. Phillips, Charles Town	165.28		11.00	21.70	197.98
3	Rev. Jacob Brittingham	St. Luke's Wheeling	2,580.88	1,026.51	537.15	313.14	4,457.68
4	Rev. Everhard Heath Brosius	Christ Church, Bluefield	664.92	586 72	86.95	32.05	1,370.64
		Heavenly Rest, Princeton	48.25		20.00		68.25
5	Rev. Chas. Mitchell Campbell	Christ Church, Short Creek			4.30	1.00	530.00
		St. Paul's Mission, Bull Creek					
		Emmanuel Mission, Mouth of Robinson					
6	Rev. Wilson Page Chrisman	Trinity, Moundsville	1,904.52	76.59	170.45	120.60	2,272 16
7	Rev. Guy Hamilton Crook	Incarnation, Ronceverte					
		St. James, Lewisburg					
		Holy Comforter, Fort S					
		Grace, Clover Lick					
		Hillsboro					
		St. Thomas, White Sulphur					
8	Rev. Thos. J. Oliver Curran	St. Andrew's, Wheeling	582.26	480.40	57.92	28.00	1,148.58
9	Rev. John Smallwood Douglas	Trinity, Martinsburg	1,574.99	534.31	384.55	308.45	2,802.30
		Christ Church, Bunker Hill	3.97		2.16	1.44	7.57
10	Rev. Creetus A. Dowell	St. Paul's, Sistersville	1,216.32	388.12	172.29	58.20	1,834.93
11	Rev. Geo. W. Easter	All Saints, Union	557.94	96.04	210.26	106.08	970.32
		Messiah, Alderson	12 20		7.54	3.49	23.23
12	Rev. Jas. Logan Fish	St. Barnabas, Davis	376 64	235.90	20.00	10.00	642.54
		Parsons					
		Thomas	7.00				7.00

TABULATED STATEMENT—FINANCIAL STATISTICS—Continued.

No.	ALPHABETICAL CLERGY LIST.	PARISHES, MISSIONS AND STATIONS.	DISBURSEMENTS. Current Expenses.	Contributions. Parochial.	Contributions. Diocesan.	Contributions. Outside the Diocese.	Grand Total.
	Rev. Jas. Logan Fish	Douglas	25.00				25.00
13	Rev. George A. Gibbons	St. Stephens, Romney	168.20	46.97	36.75	26.34	278.26
		Emmanuel, Moorefield	237.00	33.00	55.32	20.00	345.32
		Ephiphany, Okonoko	42.00	2.00	25.50	6.00	75.50
		New Creek Mission, Keyser					
		Paw Paw Mission, Paw Paw	40.50		7.00	5.30	52.80
14	Rev. J. Howard Gibbons	Christ Church, Point Pleasant	430.72	268.68	162.60	73.70	935.70
		Bruce Chapel	150.00	12.75	27.25	15.00	205.00
		Spillman	58.25	43.56	27.64	19.17	148.62
		Winfield			8.00	1.00	9.00
15	Rev. John Shackelford Gibson	Trinity, Huntington	2,195.00	945.00	416.70	197.81	3,754.51
		Grrce, Kenova	170.20	61.64	19.38	4.76	255.98
		Mingo Mission, Williamson	109.55		5.22	4.71	119.48
16	Rev. Andrew Glassell Grinnan	St. Paul's, Weston	962.02	205.40	269.14	79.60	1,516.16
		St. Paul's Chapel	41.05	90.73	3.70	3.00	138.48
17	Rev. Jacob A. Hiatt	Ascension, Hinton	408.13	328.50	44.45		781.08
		St. Peter's, Glen Jean	233.00				233.00
		Beckley					
		Beury					
18	Rev. David W. Howard	St. Matthew's, Wheeling	9,011.21	1,283.38	1,871.36	746.81	12,912.76
19	Rev. Edward D. Irvine	Christ Church, Wellsburg	523.97	352.35	100.66	33.66	1,010.64
		St. John's, Brooke county	72.42	366.50	7.00		445.92
20	Rev. Arthur Machen Lewis	St. David's, Powellton	501.34	243.85	122.30	30.86	898.35
		Calvary, Montgomery	244.58	17.92	37.60	16.35	316.45
		Redeemer, Ansted	235.15	97.97	83.25	16.69	433.06
		St. Titus', Nuttalburg	49.05		10.00		59.05
		Good Shepherd, Ferris	20.00			7.18	27.18
		Emmanuel, Mt. Carbon	65.50		12.54	2.25	80.29

21	REV. JOHN TILTON MARLEY	Trinity, Morgantown	1,400.92	57.40	87.13	36.31	1,581.76
		........., Kingwood					
22	REV. C. E. A. MARSHALL	{ Trinity, Shepherdstown { Good Shepherd, Duffield	819.77	38.21	231.28	185.03	1,274.29
23	REV. FRANK A. MEADE	Grace Church, Elkins	277.74	172.51	25.25	2.50	478.00
		Trinity, Belington					
24	REV. ROBT. NELSON MEADE	Holy Trinity, Bramwell					
		Grace, Eckman	76.59	30.00	27.43	30.04	164.06
		St. Antipas, Welch	56.92	379.99	26.57	2.40	465.88
		Algoma Mission Mayberry " Elkhorn " Crane Creek "	39.00		1.00		40.00
25	REV. A. B. MITCHELL	Good Shepherd, Parkersburg	352.23	502.57	502.39	611.51	2,058.61
		Grace, Tavenersville	55.00	15.50	29.32	8.67	108.49
		Christ Memorial, Williamstown	146.30	352.78	42.15	19.43	560.66
26	REV. FRANCIS VAN R. MOORE	St. Paul's, Elm Grove	230.85		24.54	20.59	275.98
		New Cumberland					
		Chester					
27	REV. S. SCOLLAY MOORE, D. D.	Trinity, Parkersburg	3,692.44	409.88	4,795.32	619.21	9,516.85
		St. Stephen's Mission, Parkersburg	69.08	34.02	1.00	1.00	105.10
28	REV. CHARLES C. PEARSON	St. Marks, Berkeley Springs	423.95	3.07	68.91	40.00	535.93
29	RT. REV. CHAS. CLIFTON PENICK, D. D.	Christ Church, Fairmont	397.23	60.00	350.00	730.67	1,537.90
30	REV. JAMES FITTS PLUMMER	Christ Church, Clarksburg	631.61	890.00	449.88	83.03	2,054.52
		St. Thomas, North View					
31	REV. ROBT. DOUGLAS ROLLER, D. D. C. HELY MOLONEY, Assistant	St. John's, Charleston	2,673.66	1,024.46	693.68	118.55	4,510.35
		........., Carbon					
		Pratt, Paint Creek and Crown Hill					
		Dundon					
32	REV. CHARLES E. SHAW	St. Ann, New Martinsville	1,063.55	1,136.40	122.66	49.77	2,372.38
		........., Smithfield					
33	REV. GEORGE C. SHAW	Grace, St. Mary's	485.00	144.00	30.00		659.00
		St. John, Willow Island	66.00		30.00	3.00	99.00
		Messiah, Waverly	85.00	51.10	18.10	6.15	160.35
		St. Andrew's, Mannington	112.00	1,381.00	3.00	1.00	1,497.00
34	REV. EDWIN B. SNEAD	Transfiguration, Buckhannon	398.26	13.00	25.00	10.00	446.26
		St. John's, Sutton	22.78				22.78
		Spruce Church, Spruce Run	35.00		4.00	2.00	41.00

TABULATED STATEMENT—FINANCIAL STATISTICS—Continued.

No.	ALPHABETICAL CLERGY LIST.	PARISHES, MISSIONS AND STATIONS.	DISBURSEMENTS.				Grand Total
			Current Expenses.	Contributions.			
				Parochial.	Diocesan.	Outside the Diocese	
35	REV. PARIS BECKER STAUFFER	St. John's, Harper's Ferry	220.19	247.06	75.02	39.50	581.77
		Mt. Zion, Hedgesville	213.16	10.06	89.50	30.51	343.23
37	REV. ROBT. RAYMOND WINDLEY	St. Matthias, Grafton	332.26	108.83	38.16	5.51	484.76
		*Cairo					
36	REV. JOHN WARNOCK	St. Luke's, Charleston	276.23	70.76			346.99
		St. Matthew's Charleston	276.49	7.54	7.32	13.00	304.35
		St. Mark's, St Albans	200.00	59.39	33.45	4.45	297.29
37	REV. A. J. WILLIS	Grace, Middleway	209.21	20.00	72.84	19.38	321.43
		St. Bartholomew's, Leetown	208.54	17.50	92.71	41.25	355.00
		Holy Spirit, Summit Point	249 00	10.00	56.18	15.53	330.71
38	REV. ORVILLE MELVILLE YEAGER	St. John's, Ripon					
		Christ Church, Blue Ridge					
	VACANT	Grace, Ravenswood	185.00		19.50		154.50
		St. John's, Ripley	96.85		15.00		111.85
		Whittle Chapel, Liverpool					
		Church of Our Savior, Mason City			3.10		3.10
		*Spencer					
		Buffalo and Poca					
		St. John's, Scary					
		Pennsboro Mission					
		Dubrea					
		Keeney's Mountain					
		Grace, Cresaps Valley					
	Scattered Communicants not connected with any parish						
	TOTALS		$ 43,861.13	$ 16,695.64	$ 14,584.15	$ 5,917.31	$ 81,058.23

INDEX TO JOURNAL.

ADDRESS, THE BISHOP'S
Journal and Official Acts.................................12-21
Remarks as to Parochial Reports..........................21-23
Hospitals 23
Special Fund 23, 24
Bishop Dudley 24, 25
Judge Rogers 25
Brotherhood of St. Andrew 25, 26
Twenty-Fifth Anniversary 26, 27
Business Methods 27, 28
Apportionments and Assessments 29
Small Churches 29-33

ADDRESS, THE BISHOP COADJUTOR'S,
Journal and Official Acts 37-44

APPENDICES,
Appendix A— I. Report of Treasurer of Diocese......... 67-70
— II. Report of Trustee of Episcopal Fund.... 71-73
—III. Report of Trustees of Permanent Fund.. 74-80
Appendix B—Parochial Reports 81-170
Appendix C—Diocesan Assessments 171-175
Appendix D— I. Vital Statistics 179-182
—II. Financial Statistics 183-186

BISHOP, THE,
Journal and Address 12-33

BISHOP COADJUTOR,
Journal 37-44

CANDIDATES, For Holy Orders 20

CLERGY,
Bishop's List of 5-7
Changes Among 19, 20

COMMITTEES OF THE COUNCIL,
On Constitution and Canons 3, 4, 12
On Credentials 4
On Diocese Missions 11
On Domestic and Foreign Missions.................... 3
On Education 3
On Sunday Schools 4
On Revised Version of Bible 4

COUNCIL, Minutes of,
Wednesday, June 1st, A. M.................... 11
Wednesday, June 1st, P. M.................... 12
Thursday, June 2nd, A. M.................... 44
Thursday, June 2nd, P. M.................... 51
Friday, June 3rd, A. M.................... 56
Friday, June 3rd, P. M.................... 57
Saturday, June 4th, A. M.................... 62

DEPUTIES, to General Convocation....................

LAY DELEGATES 34-36

ORGANIZED MISSIONS 20-21

OFFICERS OF THE COUNCIL.................... 3-4

PARISHES, List of 34-35

PAROCHIAL REPORT (Appendix B)....................

REPORTS OF COMMITTEES,
Credentials 33-36
Constitution and Canons 51
Diocesan Missionary 45
Education 58
Finance 60
Parochial Report 56
Permanent Fund 59
State of the Church 61
Standing Committee 54
Sunday Schools 52
Special, on Revised Version 44

RESOLUTIONS AND MOTIONS,
Of Sympathy for Rev. J. Brittingham.................... 11

As to Hours of Meeting.............................. 11
As to Assessing Parishes.............................. 51
As to Printing Rules of Order 53
As to Mission Points, Helping Themselves.............. 57
As to American Church Missionary Society.............. 59
As to Investing the Permanent Fund 61
As to Worldliness, etc................................ 61
As to Arrangements for Annual Councils................ 63
Of Thanks for Hospitality 63
Of Thanks to Committee on Canons, etc................. 64

RULES OF ORDER 8-10

SHELTERING ARMS HOSPITAL............................... 2

SUMMARY OF STATISTICS (Appendix D)..................... 179

TABULATED STATEMENT (Appendix D) 179

TREASURER OF DIOCESE 3

TREASURER OF PERMANENT FUND 3

TREASURER OF EPISCOPAL AND CONTINGENT FUND............. 3

WOMAN'S AUXILIARY, Officers, etc....................... [illegible]

The Parochial and Fiscal Year of the Diocese begins May 1st, and ends April 30th.

Places of Meeting Determined on by the Council

CLARKSBURG, 1905.	CHARLES TOWN, 1906.
MOUNDSVILLE, 1907.	POINT PLEASANT, 1908.
WESTON, 1909.	HUNTINGTON, 1910.
SHEPHERDSTOWN, 1911.	CHARLESTON, 1912.
PARKERSBURG, 1913.	WHEELING, 1914.

MARTINSBURG, 1915.

1905.

TREASURERS OF DIOCESAN FUNDS.

SEND MONEY for Diocesan Missions, Widows, Orphans and Disabled Clergy, and Religious and Theological Education to:

L. E. SANDS, TREASURER,
WHEELING, W. VA.

For Bishops and Contingent Fund to:—
R. M. BROWNE, TRUSTEE,
WHEELING, W. VA.

For Permanent Fund:—
CENTRAL BANKING & SECURITY CO., TREASURER,
PARKERSBURG, W. VA.

For Sheltering Arms Hospital:—
H. B. LEWIS, TREASURER,
CHARLESTON-KANAWHA, W. VA.

For General Missions, Foreign and Domestic:—
GEO. C. THOMAS, TREASURER,
CHURCH MISSIONS HOUSE,
281 Fourth Ave., N. Y.

VENT

PIS

DI

MA'

JOURNAL

OF THE

TWENTY-EIGHTH ANNUAL COUNCIL

OF THE

Protestant

EPISCOPAL CHURCH,

IN THE

DIOCESE OF WEST VIRGINIA,

HELD IN

CHRIST CHURCH, CLARKSBURG,

MAY 31ST AND JUNE 1, 2 AND 3, 1905.

1905:
TRIBUNE PRINTING COMPANY PRINT,
CHARLESTON, W. VA.

DIOCESE OF WEST VIRGINIA.

OFFICERS, COMMITTEES, ETC., FOR 1905.

Bishop.

RT. REV. GEO. W. PETERKIN, D. D. LL. D., Parkersburg.

Bishop Coadjutor,

RT. REV. W. L. GRAVATT, D. D., Charles Town.

Secretary of the Council,

REV. ROBERT DOUGLAS ROLLER, D. D., Charleston.

Treasurer of Council,

L. E. SANDS, Wheeling.

Standing Committee, P. O. (Charles Town, W. Va.)

Rev. G. A. Gibbons, President.
Rev. J. S. Douglas.
Rev. A. J. Willis
Mr. J. Gassman.
Mr. Isaac H. Strider.
Judge Frank Beckwith.

Missionary Committee,

The Bishop of the Diocese, (*ex-officio*) President.
The Bishop Coadjutor, (*ex-officio*)
Rev. J. Brittingham.
Rev. J. F. Plummer.
Rev. S. S. Moore, D. D.
Mr. B. M. Ambler.
Mr. Simms Powell
Mr L. E. Sands, Treasurer.

Diocesan Committee on Foreign and Domestic Missions,

Rev. D. W. Howard.
Rev. G. A. Gibons.
Rev. J. S. Gibson.
Gen'l W. P. Craghill.
Mr. C. C. Coe.
Dr. G. A. Aschman.

Trustee of the Episcopal and Contingent Fund (Special).

Robert M. Browne, Wheeling.

Trustees of Kenyon College.

Rt. Rev. Geo. W. Peterkin, D. D., LL. D.
Rt. Rev. W. L. Gravatt, D D.
Mr. Jos D. DuBois.

Trustees of Permanent (Episcopal) Fund.

Mr. Robert M. Browne. Mr. B. M. Ambler. Mr. H. H. Moss.
Central Banking and Security Co., Parkersburg, Treasurer.

Registrar of the Diocese,

Mr. B. M. Ambler, Parkersburg.

Standing Committee on Constitution and Canons,

Rev. Jno. S. Gibson.
Rev. D. W. Howard.
Rev. J. S. Douglas.
Mr. W. S. Laidley.
Mr Joseph Trapnell.

Committee on Education,

Rev. G. W. Easter.
Rev. J. Howard Gibbons.
Rev. A. M. Lewis.
Mr. W. G. Hubbard.
Mr. C. L. Thompson.

Committee on Sunday Schools,

Rev. W. P. Chrisman.
Rev. C. E. Shaw.
Dr. G. A. Aschman.
George Rogers.

Examining Chaplains,

Rev. S. S. Moore, D. D.
Rev. J. S. Gibson.

Trustees of the Virginia Theological Seminary.

Rt. Rev. G. W. Peterkin, D. D. LL. D.
Rt. Rev. W. L. Gravatt, D. D.
Rev. S. S. Moore, D. D.
Mr. Joseph Trapnell.

Chancellor of the Diocese,

Joseph Trapnell, Charles Town.

Woman's Auxilary.

Mrs. G. A. Aschman, Wheeling, President.
Valley Convocation, Miss M. G. McSherry, Vice President.
Kanawha Convocation, Mrs. Ely Ensign, Vice-President.
North Western Convocation, Miss Gertrude Lamb, Vice-President.

Delegates to Missionary Council.

Rev. J. S. Gibson.
Rev. J. S.Douglas.
**Rev. S. S. Moore, D. D.
Gen'l B. D. Spillman.
Mr. J. T. Waters.
**Mr. H. W. Potts.

Clergy List.

DIOCESE OF WEST VIRGINIA.

MAY 24, 1905.

Rt. Rev. Geo. W. Peterkin, D. D. LL. D. Bishop (1878) *Parkersburg, W. Va*

Rt. Rev. W. Loyall Gravatt, D. D. (1893) Bishop Coadjutor (1899) ....*Charles Town, W. Va.*

Rev. Geo A. Gibons (1878) Rector of Emanuel Moorefield and in charge of Missions in Hampshire Co. ..*Romney, W. Va.*

Rev. Jno. F. Woods, (1878) ....*Philadelphia Penna.*

Rev. Robert Douglas Roller, D. D. (1879) Rector of St. Johns Ch., Charleston ....*Charleston, Kanawha, W. Va.*

Rev. Jacob Brittingham (1881) Rector of St. Luke's ch., Wheeling ....*Wheeling, W. Va.*

Rev. Chas. M. Campbell (1886) in charge of Boone Co. Mission ....*Racine, W. Va.*

Rev. S. Scollay Moore, D. D., (1888) Rector of Trinity Church,................. ....*Parkersburg, W. Va.*

Rev. Andrew J. Willis, (1890) Rector of Nelson Parish, (Grace Middleway, St. Bartholomew's Leetown and Church of the Holy Spirit, Summit Point) ....*Middleway, W. Va.*

Rev. Geo. W. Easter, (1892) Rector of All Saints Union and in charge of the Church of the Messiah Alderson........ ....*Union, W. Va.*

Rev. John S. Gibson (1892) Rector of Trinity Church Huntington, and in charge of Grace Church Kenova ....*Huntington, W. Va.*

Rev. B. M. Spurr (1894) General Misionary and Supt. Reynold's Memorial Hospital...............*Moundsville, W. Va.*

Rev. A. G. Grinnan (1895) Rector of St. Pauls Church, Weston............. ....*Weston, W. Va.*

***Rt. Rev. C. C. Penick*, D. D. (1899).................*Fairmont, W. Va.*

Rev. Jno. S. Douglas, (1899) Rector of Trinity Martinsburg, and in charge of Christ Church Bunker Hill............. ....*Martinsburg, W. Va.*

Rev. Chas. E. Shaw (1899) Rector of Mt. Zion Church, Hedgesville, and in charge of St. Mark's Church Berkeley Springs ....*Berkeley Springs, W. Va.*

Rev. David W. Howard (1899) Rector of St. Matthew's Church, Wheeling.............................. *Wheeling, W. Va.*

Rev. Jas. L. Fish (1900) in charge of St. Barnabas, Davis and Grace Church, Elkins.......................*Davis, W. Va.*

Rev. Thos. J. Oliver Curran (1900) in charge of St. Andrews, Wheeling.............................*Wheeling, W. Va.*

Rev. John Tilton Marley (1900) Rector of Trinity Morgantown and Warden of the Episcopal Hall....*Morgantown, W. Va.*

Rev. J. Howard Gibbons (1901) Rector of Point Pleasant Parish, (Christ Church and Bruce Chapel) ....*Point Pleasant, W. Va.*

Rev. J. A. Hiatt (1901) in charge of Ascension, Hinton and St. Peters, Glen Jean ....*Hinton, W. Va.*

Rev. Guy H. Crook (1901) Rector of Greenbrer Parish, (St. James, Lewisburg, Incarnation, Ronceverte, St. Thomas, White Sulphur), and in charge of the Missions in Pocohontas Co ....*Ronceverte, W. Va.*

Rev. Arthur M. Lewis (1901) in charge of St. Davids Powellton, Calvary, Montgomery, and Church of the Redeemer, Ansted ....*Powellton, W. Va.*

Rev. Everett Heath Brosius (1902) Rector of Christ Church, Bluefield, and in charge of Heavenly Rest, Princeton ....*Bluefield, W. Va.*

Rev. Jno. S. Alfriend (1902) Rector of Zion Church, Charles Town ....*Charles Town, W. Va.*

Rev. Wilson Page Chrisman (1902) Rector of Trinity Moundsville, and in charge of Grace Cresaps ......*Moundsville, W. Va.*

Rev. Paca Kennedy (1902) Rector of Ravenswood Parish, (Grace Ravenswood and St. Johns, Ripley) and of St. John's, Willow Island, and in charge of the Missions of Grace Church, St. Marys ....*St. Marys, W. Va.*

Rev. Paris B. Stauffer (1902) in charge of St. John's Church, Harpers Ferry, and St. John's Ripton,..*Harpers Ferry, W. Va.*

Rev. Geo. C. Shaw (1902) in charge of St. Andrew's, Mannington, and St. Mathias, Grafton ....*Mannington, W. Va.*

Rev. C. E. A. Marshall (1903) Rector of Trinity, Shepherdstown, ...*Shepherdstown, W. Va.*

Rev. Creetus A. Dowell, (1903) Rector of St. Paul's, Sistersville, ...*Sistersville, W. Va.*

**Rev. John Warnock* (1903) Rector of St. Mark's, St. Albans, and in charge of St. Luke's and St. Matthew's, Kanawha Co.,.................*Charleston, Kanawha, W. Va.*

Rev. Edward D. Irvine, (1903) Rector of Christ Church, Wellsburg, and of St. John's Brooke Co.,..*Wellsburg, W. Va.*

Rev. Francis Van R. Moore (1903) in charge of St. Paul's, Elm Grove ....*Elm Grove, W. Va.*

Rev. Austin B. Mitchell (1903) in charge of Christ Memorial Church, Williamstown, and of the Parkersburg Mission (Chapel of the Good Shepherd and Grace, Tavernsville,) ....*Williamstown, W. Va.*

Rev. Jas. F. Plummer (1904) Rector of Christ, Church, Clarksburg ....*Clarksburg, W. Va.*

Rev. W. Howard Meyers Deacon (1904) in charge of St. John's, Sutton, Transfiguration, Buckhannon, and Spruce Chapel, ...*Sutton, W. Va.*

Rev. C. Hely Molony, Deacon (1904) in charge of St. Ann's, New Martinsville ....*New Martinsville, W. Va.*

Rev. Jos. Livingston (1905) in charge of St. Philip's Chapel, Charles Town.........................*Charles Town, W. Va.*

Rev. Hardy H. Phelps (1905) in charge of Holy Trinity, Bramwell, and Missions at Eckman and Welch ....*Bramwell, W. Va.*

***Rev. Morton A. Barnes*, (1905) Rector of Christ Church, Fairmont ....*Fairmont, W. Va.*

GEO. W. PETERKIN,
Bishop of West Virginia.

Parkersburg, May 24, 1905.

*Absent.
**Not entitled to seats.

Ordained Deacon since meeting of Council.

Rev. P. N. McDonald.

Rev. T. G. Hill.

RULES OF ORDER.

Adopted by the Eighth Annual Council, June 3rd, 1885.

ORGANIZATION.

1st. The Council shall be opened each day with prayer.

2nd. After the call to order, no member shall remain standing, nor afterward stand, except to address the Chair.

ORDER OF BUSINESS.

1st. After the organization of the Council, the following order of business shall be observed:

The appointment of a committee on the Credentials of Lay Delegates.

The appointment of a Treasurer *pro tempore,* when the Treasurer is absent.

The adoption of rules of order.

The reading of the journal of the preceding day.

The reading of the pastoral address.

The appointment of committees.

Reports of standing committees.

Reports of special committees.

Unfinished business.

2nd. There shall be appointed by the President, not later than the *second* day of the Council, unless otherwise directed, the following standing committees, to consist of an equal number of each order.

A Committee on the State of the Church, to whom shall be referred the address of the Bishop on the opening of the Council.

A Committee on Parochial reports.

A Committee on the admission of new Parishes.

A Committee on the Episcopal Fund, and the Permanent Fund.

A Committee on the Brotherhood.

A Committee on Unfinished Business.

ORDER OF DEBATE.

1st. When a motion is made and seconded, it shall be stated by the President, and if in writing, be read by the Secretary before debated.

2nd. After a motion is stated by the President, or read by the Secretary it shall be deemed in possession of the Council, but may be withdrawn by the mover at any time before amendment or decision, with the consent of his second.

3rd. Every motion shall be reduced to writing if the President or any member require it.

4th. No new motion or proposition shall be admitted under color of amendment, as a substitute for the motion or proposition under debate.

5th. When a question is under debate, no motion shall be received but to adjourn, to lay on the table, for the previous question, to postpone indefinitely, to postpone to a certain day, to commit, or to amend, which several motions shall have precedence in the order enumerated; and the first three shall be decided without debate.

6th. The previous question shall be admitted only when demanded by a majority of the members present. It shall be in this form: "Shall the main question be now put?" and until decided, all debate and amendment are precluded.

7th. A motion to adjourn shall always be in order, and shall be decided without debate.

8th. When a member desires to speak in debate, or present any matter to the Council, he shall rise from his seat, and respectfully address himself to the President, and shall confine himself to the question under debate, avoiding all personality.

9th. If any member transgress the rules of the Council, the President shall, or any member may, call him to order; in which case the member so called to order shall immediately take his seat unless permitted to explain. If the ruling of the President be appealed from, the Council shall decide the question without debate.

10th. When two or more members rise at once, the President shall decide who is entitled to the floor.

11th. No member shall speak more than twice to the same question, without leave of the Council.

12th. The vote on all questions shall be taken by ayes and noes, whenever three members require it.

13th. Any member may call for a division of the question where the sense will admit it, but a motion to strike out and insert shall be deemed indivisible..

14th. Every member who may be in the house when the question is put shall give his vote, unless the Council, for special reasons, shall excuse him.

15th. No member shall vote upon a question, in the decision of which he is immediately and personally interested.

16th. Upon a division and count of the Council on any question, no member shall be counted who is not within the limits assigned as seats to the members.

17th. When a question has been decided by the Council, or postponed indefinitely, it may be reconsidered upon motion made by members voting in the majority: *provided*, such motion be made on the same or next or succeeding day of the session.

GENERAL REGULATIONS.

1st. No member shall absent himself from the meetings of the Council without leave, unless he be sick, or unable to attend.

2nd. The President shall, at his discretion, select suitable seats without the limits of those alloted to the use of the members, which shall be appropriated to the accommodation of visiting Clergymen and Candidates for Orders, who may be invited by the Rector or Wardens of the Church in which the meetings of the Council are held, under the directions of the President and Council.

3rd. No spectator shall, during the daily sessions of the Council, be admitted above of within the pews allotted to the members, and the Rector and Wardens of the Church in which the sessions of the Council are held, and directed to see that this rule is enforced.

4th. No rule of order shall be suspended except with the concurrence of two-thirds of the members present.

JOURNAL

OF THE

TWENTY-SEVENTH ANNUAL COUNCIL OF THE PROTESTANT EPISCOPAL CHURCH IN THE DIOCESE OF WEST VIRGINIA.

CLARKSBURG, WEST VIRGINIA,
May 31st, 1905.

Pursuant to the call of the Bishop to meet on Wednesday, May 31st instead of on the first Wednesday in June the Twenty-eighth Annual Council of the Diocese of West Virginia met in Christ Church this day at 9:45 a. m.

Morning prayer was said by Reverends Messrs. Jno. S. Douglas and Charles E. Shaw. Bishop Peterkin, assisted by Bishop Gravett, celebrated the Holy Communion, Bishop Penick reading the Epistle. The council sermon was preached by Rev. Jno. S. Alfriend, rector of Zion Church, of Charles Town, from St. Luke, xvi-31.

Immediately after divine service the Council was organized, Bishop Peterkin presiding and Rev. Jno. S. Gibson acting as Secretary for Dr. Roller, detained by having to conduct the funeral of Ex-Gov. E. W. Wilson.

The roll-call showed a quorum of both orders present.

The Bishop appointed as the Committee on Credentials of lay delegates Reverends Messrs. J. Howard Gibbons and A. B. Mitchell and Messrs. Edward Baxter and Wm. Shearer.

On motion the Rules of Order of the last Council were adopted for the government of this.

The Bishop named Mr. C. P. Flick to receive money payable to the diocesan treasurers until their arrival.

On motion of the Rector of the Parish the hours for Council

were fixed as follows: Divine service each morning at 9:30 with business session following, except on Thursday, Ascension Day, when the business session will begin at 9:30 and adjourn for service at 10:30. Afternoon sessions each day at 2 o'clock. The remainder of the order to be according to the published programme.

The Bishop read the statistical portion of his report and at 12:30 Council took a recess until 2:30 on motion of Dr. S. S. Moore.

---

2 30 P. M.

The Bishop completed the reading of his annual address as follows:

BISHOP'S ANNUAL ADDRESS.

In greeting my Brethern of the Clergy and laity—who make up this 28th annual Council, I cannot but recall the occasion of our last meeting in this Church. It was on Wednesday, July 26th, 1899, just six years ago, and in the providence of God, and under the guidance of that Spirit whose presence is the hope of the Church, you then chose to help me in the work which had grown beyond my power to compass, a Bishop Coadjutor, who has so grown into the affections and confidence of the Diocese, that today we all count his presence and faithful and efficient service to be our best endowment. I thank God for the loving and cordial and considerate cooperation which has not only lightened my personal burden but infused a more vigorous life throughout the entire Diocese. May you be as happy in long enjoying his wisdom and zeal in your service, as you were fortunate in so soon securing them.

During the past year Death has claimed one of our band of clergy, the Rev. C. C. Pearson who came to us in 1882, twenty-three years ago, entered into rest.

At our last Council in Martinsburg it was evident to his many friends that he was by no means well, but his cheerful spirit and strong will kept us from realizing how serious was the trouble under which he labored. He loved to be among his brethren as they enjoyed having him in their midst, and so in pleasant intercourse those days passed which were to be the last of our earthly association and fellowship.

Mr. Pearson at different times served various places in the Diocese, and was therefore widely known and universally admired and respected. He was counted one of our best preachers, and in his faithful presentation of the Gospel he did good service for the Master in every post which he occupied. Without personal pretence or affectation he was genial in disposition and sincere in his friendship. With a simple faith and unwavering loyalty he served his Master and helped his fellowmen, and the Church in West Virginia cherishes and honors his memory.

JUNE.

The 27th Annual Council met in Trinity Church, Martinsburg, on Wednesday, June 1st. The comfort and convenience of our sessions were much promoted by our having the use of a commodious and well arranged Parish House. It is no doubt found to be of great use in the ordinary working of the Parish.

Beside attending the usual sessions of the Council on Thursday, 2nd, I addressed a meeting of the Womans' Auxiliary.

Sunday 5. I administered the Holy Communion in Trinity Church, the Rev. Dr. Roller, a former Rector preaching. In the afternoon I visited Christ Church, Bunker Hill, the Rev. Mr. Spurr preaching; and in the evening I preached the closing sermon in Trinity Church.

Thursday 9. Made an address on the occassion of the laying the corner stone for a Y. M. C. A. building in Parkersburg.

Sunday, 12th. Visited Willow Island. Notice had failed to reach the Congregation of St. John's Church. I attended the Children's Day Services at the Baptist Church and made an address. In the evening I preached in the Church of the Messiah Waverly, having our congregation increased by the coming in of the Methodist minister with his people.

Tuesday, 14th. Friday 17th. Attended the annual exercises of the Theological Seminary of Virginia, comprising meetings of the Education Society, the Board of Trustees, the Alumni Meeting and the Commencements of the Seminary and the High School. Also on Thursday, 16th, attended a meeting for the organization of the Board of Trustees of the University College of Medicine, Richmond, Va. On Friday, 17th, I ordained to the Deaconate Mr. W. Howard Meyers, whom I assigned to have charge of the work at Sutton, Buckhanon and adjacent points, with headquarters at Sutton.

Sunday, 18th. A. M. Christ Church, Williamstown. P. M. Chapel of the Good Shepherd, Parkersburg.

Tuesday, 20th. In attendance on the meeting of the Trustees of Kenyon College, Gambier, O.

Saturday, 25th. Wednesday, 29th. In attendance on the Commencement of the University of the South, Sewanee, Tenn. During this visit I delivered an address in memory of the late Chancellor, Bishop Dudley, of Kentucky. This was my second visit to Sewanee, and I must confess the more I see of it, and the better I understand the far reaching plans of those who founded the University and of those who are now carrying it on in a like spirit, the more I am profoundly impressed with the vast possibilities for good that are bound up in that great institution.

JULY.

Sunday, 3rd. Grace Church, St. Marys, A. M., and P. M.; also visited the Sunday School.

Thursday, 7th. Visited Glen Jean, but owing to some failure in the notice, had no service. I met the congregation, however, at the house of Dr. Lee, and talked over Church matters with them.

Friday, 8th. Preached in the Methodist Church, Beckley and confirmed one, (1).

Saturday, 9th. At a very pleasant reception given at the Rectory, Hinton. I met many of the congregation.

Sunday, 10th. Preached A. M. and P. M. in the Church of the Ascension, Hinton, and in the morning confirmed five, (5). Under Mr. Hiatt's acceptable ministrations our work at Hinton, Beckley, and Glen Jean gives promise of steady growth.

Friday, 15th. Grace Church, Elkins. Here I found in charge Rev. F. A. Meade, who had before served the Diocese at other points, but who has since, I am sorry to say, been transferred to Virginia.

Sunday, 17th. Grace Church, Clover Lick.

Tuesday, 19th. At Driscol, near Huntersville. I preached in a school house.

Wednesday, 20th. Preached in the Presbyterian Church, Marlinton.

Thursday, 21st. Preached in the Presbyterian Church, Hillsboro. These last four points mentioned, in Pocohontas Co., are under the charge of Mr. Crook, of Ronceverte.

Friday, 22. Church of the Messiah, Alderson.

Sunday, 24th. Visited Lewisburg and Ronceverte, preached in both places, and in Ronceverte baptized a child in the absence of the Rector.

Sunday, 21st. Preached in St. James Church, Richmond, Va.

AUGUST.

Thursday, 4th. Sunday, 14th. In attendance on a Missionary Conference at Richfield Springs, N. Y. We had most helpful services and conferences each day during the session. I took part in many of the services made several addresses, and preached on Sunday, 14th, in St. Mary's Church, Springfield Centre.

Sunday, 21st. Trinity Church, Parkersburg, P. M., Chapel of the Good Shepherd, Parkersburg.

Sunday, 28th. A. M., and P. M., St. Luke's Church, Wheeling.

SEPTEMBER.

Friday, 9th. In St. Stephen's Church, Romney, I preached and confirmed four, (4).

Sunday, 11th. In Emanuel Church, Moorefield, preached and confirmed three, (3).

Monday, 12th. Tuesday, 13th. In attendance on the Eastern Convocation in St. John's Church, Harpers Ferry, during which time I preached twice and made an address.

Sunday, 18th. A. M., Preached in the Baptist Church, Hartford. P. M., in the Church of Our Saviour, Mason, P. P. M., in Spilman Chapel, Spilman.

Tuesday, 20th. Thursday, 22. In attendance on the Kanawha Convocation meeting in Christ's Church, Pt. Pleasant.

Friday, 23rd. Preached in the Methodist Church, Winfield.

Sunday, 25th. In Christ Church, Point Pleasant, visited the Sunday School, and preached at the morning service. P. M. preached in Bruce Chapel and confirmed one (1).

Tuesday, 27th. Wednesday, 28th. In attendance on the N. W. Convocation meeting in St. Paul's Church, Weston, and made an address at the Missionary meeting Wednesday evening.

OCTOBER.

Sunday, 2nd. Trinity, Parkersburg. P. M. Good Shepherd.

Wednesday, 5th. Tuesday, 25th. In attendance on the General Convention, Boston. During the session I took part in the Communion Service in Emanuel on Friday 21st. Preached in Christ Church, Springfield, on Sunday, 9th; St. John, Jamaica Plain and St. James', Cambridge, on Friday, 15th; and in Calvary, New York, on Sunday, 23rd.

Sunday, 30th. A. M. Preached in St. James' Church, Richmond, Va., P. M. Preached for the Church Students Missionary Association in Holy Trinity.

NOVEMBER.

Sunday, 6th. A. M. Preached in St. Paul's, Ogontz. P. M. took part in the services at St. Paul's and in the evening preached at the Ogontz school.

Sunday, 13th. A. M. Preached in Grace Church, Cresaps. P. M. in Trinity, Moundsville.

Tuesday, 15th. Addressed the Woman's Auxiliary in Parkersburg.

Thursday, 17th. Preached in the Church of the Heavenly Rest, Princeton.

Friday, 18th. Athens.

Sunday, 20th. A. M. Christ Church, Bluefield, confirmed one (1). P. M. Preached in a school house, Gary, my first visit.

Monday, 21st. Preached in Presbyterian Church, Vivvian.

Tuesday, 22. Grace Church, Eckman.

Wednesday, 23. Preached in the Baptist Church, Elkhorn.

Thursday, 24. Holy Trinity, Bramwell. In the afternoon I baptized an infant in private. P. M. Preached in Christ Church, Pocohontas, Va. Administered the Holy Communion and confirmed one (1) for Bishop Randolph.

Friday, 25th. Preached in a school house, Mora. My first visit.

Sunday, 27th. A. M. Holy Trinity, Bramwell. Administered the Holy Communion and confirmed one (1). P. M. In the Presbyterian Church, Welch. I found very much to my regret that the Rev. Robt. N. Meade, who has administered so acceptably in this extended field since Mr. Marshall's removal, had accepted a call to Pittsburg.

Monday, 28th. Preached in the Presbyterian Church, Williamson, and confirmed one (1). This mission has made decided progress under Mr. Gibson's care, and the prospect of building a chapel at any early day is good.

Tuesday, 29th. In Huntington I attended the examinations of a candidate for orders.

Wednesday, 30th. In company with Mr. Gibson I paid my first visit to Holden, near Logan Court House, going over the new railroad up Guyan River. Here, as in many other places, we have a few people who desire the services of the Church, but for whom it is as yet almost imposible to make any regular provision. I preached in a school house.

DECEMBER.

Sunday, 4th. A. M. In St. John's Church, Charleston, I preached and ordained Mr. C. Hely Malony, Deacon. Rev. Dr. Roller presented the candidate. P. M. Preached in the school house at Point Creek.

Monday, 5th. Visited the Sheltering Arms Hospital and inspected the new building, also visited Wake Forest.

Tuesday, 6th. Visited Carbon. It did not seem expedient to hold services at this place or at Wake Forest, owing to a strike prevailing.

Friday, 9th. Visited Chester and New Cumberland. It was my first visit to Chester, and I was pleased to see the eligible lot we have secured. The Rev. Mr. Moore, of Elm Grove, who now has charge of the work, was with me.

Sunday, 11th. A. M. St. John's, Brooke Co. Also visited a sick man in the neighborhood. P. M. Christ Church, Wellsburg, and confirmed one (1). I was glad to find that St. John's had been renovated and repaired, so that it is in a better condition than it has been for twenty-five years.

Tuesday, 13th. In attendance on the Board of Missions, New York.

Sunday, 18th. Spent the day in Fairmont and preached twice, also conferred with the vestry in regard to the vacancy.

Tuesday, 20th. Officiated at a wedding in St. Ann's Church, Annapolis, Md.

Sunday, 25th. A. M. Good Shepherd, Parkersburg. P. M. Christ Memorial Church, Williamstown.

Monday, 26th. Administered the Holy Communion in Trinity, Parkersburg.

Wednesday, 28th. Made an address at the Sunday School celebration of the Good Shepherd.

Friday, 30th. Made an address at the Commencement exercises of the Reynolds Memorial Hospital, Moundsville, and delivered the Diplomas to the graduating class of the training school for nurses—three in all.

1905. JANUARY.

Sunday, 1st. A. M. Preached and administered the Holy Communion in Trinity Church, Parkersburg. P. M. Preached in Chapel of the Good Shepherd.

Sunday, 8th. A. M. Preached and administered the Holy Communion in the Chapel of the Good Shepherd, Parkersburg. P. M. Went to St. Stephens to keep an appointment, but owing to some mistake, there was no service.

Tuesday, 10th. In atttendance on the Board of Misisons, New York.

Sunday, 15th. Preached twice in St. Stephen's, Culpepper, Va., my old Parish Church.

Friday, 20th. Delivered a memorial address before Camp Jenkins, Parkersburg.

Sunday, 22nd. A. M. Preached in St. Paul's, Sisterville. In the afternoon visited and addressed the Sunday School and in the evening preached in St. Ann's, New Martinsville; meeting the vestry after service to confer with them about the vacancy.

Tuesday, 24th. Thursday, 26th. In attendance on the N. W. Convocation in Trinity, Parkersburg. During the sessions, on Tuesday evening I confirmed three (3), and on Wednesday morning administered the Holy Communion, and in the evening made an address at a missionary meeting.

Sunday, 29th. A. M. Preached in the M. E. Church, Cairo. P. M. Preached in the Methodist Protestant Church, Pennsboro and confirmed one (1), after service had a meeting in a private house, of those specially interested. The Rev. Mr. Dowell has now charge of these points.

FEBRUARY.

Thursday, 2nd. Met the vestry at Moundsville to confer with them about their Parish House.

Friday, 3rd. Attended a funeral at St. Marys.

Sunday, 5th. Visited the Reform School at Pruntytown, addressed the Sunday School, and afterwards preached in the Public Hall. I was gratified at the evidence of the efficient management of this important Institution. In the afternoon I addressed the Y. M. C. A. meeting in Grafton, and in the evening preached in St. Matthias' Church.

Sunday, 12th. A. M. Preached in Christ Church, Fairmont, P. M. In St. Andrew's Church, Mannington. It gave me pleasure to worship at last in this completed Church, and to see the Rectory wisely and bravely built.

Sunday, 19th. A. M. Christ Memorial, Wiliamstown. P. M. Good Shepherd, Parkersburg.

Sunday, 26th. A. M. St. Matthew's, Wheeling. P. M. St. Andrew's.

MARCH.

Sunday, 5th. I preached twice in Trinity Church, Morgantown, and at the second service confirmed seven (7). Under a new arrangement, made since my last visit, in addition to accomodating twelve or fifteen boys, the Hall is used as a Rectory and Parish House. On Saturday evening, the 4th, I met many of the congregation at a reception.

Friday, 10th. Preached in Trinity Church, Huntington. The lecture room of this church has been recently thoroughly renovated and the Church completely lighted by electricity in very handsome style.

Sunday, 12th. A. M. In Chapel of the Good Shepherd, Parkersburg, I preached and administered the Holy Communion. P. M. Preached in St. Stephen's Chapel.

Friday, 17th. Preached in St. James' Church, Richmond, Va.

Sunday, 19th. A. M. Preached in St. James', Richmond, Va., and P. M. in Emanuel, Henrico Co., Va.

Thursday, 23rd. Preached in St. Timothy's Church, Wilson, N. C.

Friday, 24th. Preached in the same Church.

Sunday, 26th. Preached A. M. and P. M. in the same Church and in the afternoon made a public address in the Court House under the auspices of the Y. M. C. A.

APRIL.

Saturday, 1st. St. Thomas, North View, Clarksburg, and confirmed three (3).

Sunday, 2nd. Christ Church, Clarksburg A. M. and P. M., and confirmed seventeen (17). In the afternoon made an address in the Opera House under the auspices of the Y. M. C. A.

Monday, 3rd. St. Barnabas, Davis. Confirmed 7.

Tuesday, 4th. Grace, Elkins. Confirmed 6.

Rev. Mr. Fish, of Davis, in now ministering to both of these churches. Such consolidation may not be according to the ideal plan, but it is in the interest of an economy both in men and money which we are compelled to practice, and in the cases adopted, viz. Davis and Elkins, Mannington and Grafton, Sutton and Buckhanon, St. Marys and Ravenswood, it is under the wise and energetic administration of our missionaries, working admirably well.

Sunday, 9th. A. M. Trinity, Martinsburg. Confirmed 6. P. M. Mt. Zion, Hedgesville. Confirmed 1.

Monday 10th. In All Saints, Frederick, Md. I preached the last of a series of sermons in connection with the 50th anniversary of the laying of the corner stone of the Church.

Tuesday, 11th. Attended meeting of the Board of Missions in New York.

Sunday, 16th. A. M. St. Matthew's, Wheeling. Confirmed 25. P. M. St. Paul's, Elm Grove. Confirmed 3.

Monday, 17th. St. John's, Sutton. Confirmed 4.

Tuesday, 18th. In Baptist Church, Gassaway, preached to a large congregation.

Wednesday, 19th. Had an appointment at Dundon, Clay Co., but owing to some mistake about the notice it failed. In the afternoon made an address in St. John's Church, Charleston.

Thursday, 20th. A. M. Made an address in St. John's, Charleston. P. M. Preached in Methodist Church, Glen Ferris.

Friday, 21. Church of the Redeemer, Ansted. Confirmed 2.

Sunday, 23rd. Easter Day. A. M. St. David's, Powellton. P. M. Methodist Church, Mt. Carbon. P. P. M. Calvary, Montgomery. Confirmed 1.

Monday, 24th. Preached in the Presbyterian Church, Nuttall and confirmed 2.

Tuesday, 25th. In the Presbyterian Church, Dubree.

Wednesday, 26th. In the school house near Beauty. Confirmed 2.

Thursday, 27th. In St. David's, Powellton. Confirmed 8.

Sunday, 30th. In Zion Church, Charles Town, confirmed 12. Also visited and addressed the Sunday School. P. M. Visited and addressed St. Philip's Sunday School, and in the evening preached in St. Philip's Church.

MAY.

Thursday, 4th. Delivered a lecture in Wheeling before the Twilight Club.

Saturday, 6th. Met the United Guild of Nelson Parish and the vestry at the Rectory, Middleway. About 75 persons were present and I could not but think that such united meetings was a most admirable way to unify the Parish, and to excite and direct their interest. In addition to this it gave me such opportunity of meeting the people as I could not otherwise have secured.

Sunday, 7th. A. M. In the Church of the Holy Spirit, Summit Point, I preached and confirmed 1. P. M. In St. Bartholomew's, Leetown, I preached and confirmed 3, and P. P. M. Grace Church, Middleway, I preached and confirmed 1.

Tuesday, 9th. Attended the metings of the Board of Missions, in New York.

Wednesday, 10th. In St. Stephen's Church, Romney, I preached and confirmed 5.

Thursday, 11th. I preached in St. Mark's Church, Berkeley Springs. This Church in connection with Mt. Zion, Hedgesville, is now under the care of Rev. Chas. E. Shaw, while Mr. Stauffer, who was in charge at Hedgesville, has, on giving that up united St. John's, Ripon, to Harper's Ferry. This seems a more natural arrangement than that which has prevailed for some years past.

Sunday, 14th. In Trinity Church, Shepherdstown, I preached and confirmed 12. In the afternoon Mr. Marshall drove me to Duffields, where there were three to be confirmed, but the rain prevented service.

Tuesday, 16. In the afternoon I preached at Eakles school house and in the evening in the school house at Dry Creek and confirmed 7. In addition to these 7 one person was confirmed in private.

Wednesday, 17th. Attended the annual meeting of the Incorporators and Directors of the Sheltering Arms Hospital. We had a goodly number of visitors from up and down the valley. Evidence of the well sustained interest in this beneficient Institution.

Sunday, 21st. In Trinity Church, Washington, I preached before the Diocesan Convention of the Brotherhood of St. Andrew. I had the pleasure of meeting there Mr. Gardner, the President of the Brotherhood, and making arrangements with him to send some one to West Virginia that we may if possible revive our interest and activity in the Brotherhood. In the evening I preached in the Chapel at the Seminary, and had from the Professors most gratifying reports as to our four students in that Institution. I believe that most efficient and faithful work is being done at the Seminary, and that it never stood higher in the thought and consideration of the Church that it does to day. Its alumni and friends will be delighted to hear that the Bishop of New York has offered to put a new chancel to the present chapel, and this will be a very great improvement, not only to the general appearance of the building, but also as to affording additional seating capacity, now greatly needed and such enlarged space in the choir and around the chancel as will avoid the awkward crowding incident to our ordinations.

Thursday, 25th. Attended a meeting of the Diocesan Missions Committee in Parkersburg. We discussed and put forward a schedule for the next year, which the committee will lay before the Council for their information.

Sunday, 28th. A. M. Preached at the Chapel of the Good Shepherd, Parkersburg, and confirmed 4. P. M. at Christ Memorial Church, Williamstown and confirmed 1.

SUMMARY.

I have paid 123 visits to 93 places in the Diocese, and also officiated 36 times out of the Diocese, delivering 183 sermons and addresses. I have also attended 90 meetings, visited our three Convocations, and on 34 occasions I have confirmed 162 persons.

CHANGES IN THE DIOCESE.

Letters Dimissory.

Letters Dimissory have been given in behalf of *Rev. Robt. N. Meade* to the Diocese of Pittsburg, *Rev. Edwin B. Snead* to the Diocese of Southern Ohio, the *Rev. Maximo F. Duty* to the Diocese of Tennessee, the *Rev. F. A. Meade* to the Diocese of Virginia, and the *Rev. Robt. R. Windley* to the Diocese of Easton.

Letters Dimissory have been received in behalf of the *Rev. Jos. Livingston*, from the Diocese of Maryland, the *Rev. H. H. Phelps* from the Missionary District of Asheville, and from the *Rev. Morton A. Barnes* from the Diocese of Connecticut.

The clergy list has also been increased by the ordination to the Deaconate of the *Rev. W. Howard Meyer*, and the *Rev. C. Hely Molony*, The *Rt. Rev. C. C. Penick*, D. D., has resigned the Rectorship of Christ Church, Fairmont; the *Rev. Chas. E. Shaw* has resigned the Rectorship of St. Ann's, New Martinsville and become Rector of Mt. Zion, Hedgesville, and also assumed charge of St. Mark's, Berkeley Springs; the *Rev. Jas. L. Fish* retaining charge of St. Barnabas, Davis, extends his ministrations to Grace Church, Elkins; the *Rev. Wilson P. Chrisman* retaining charge of Trinity, Moundsville, has taken charge also of Grace Church, Cresaps; the *Rev. Paca Kennedy* has become Rector of Ravenswood Parish, Grace Ravenswood and St. John's Ripley, also Rector of St. John's, Willow Island, and has in addition charge of Grace Church, St. Marys and of the Church of the Messiah, Waverly; the *Rev. Paris B. Stauffer* retaining St. John's, Harpers Ferry, has given up Mt. Zion, Hedgesville, and taken charge of St. John's, Ripon; the *Rev. Geo. C. Shaw* retaining St. Andrews Mannington, has also taken charge of St. Matthias, Grafton; the *Rev. W. Howard Meyers* has been placed in charge of St. John's, Sutton, and the Transfiguration, Buckhannon; the *Rev. C. Hely Molony* has been transferred from Paint Creek and Cabin Creek, to which post he was assigned at his ordination in December last, to be in charge of St. Ann's, New Martinsville; the *Rev. Jos. Livingston*, has under the Rectorship of Rev. Mr. Alfriend, assumed charge of St. Philip's, Charles Town; the *Rev. H. Hardy Phelps* has succeeded Mr. Meade in charge of Trinity, Bramwell, and its associated missions; the *Rev. Morton A. Barnes* has become Rector of Christ Church, Fairmont.

Postulant.

James Davis Gibson.

Candidates for Deacons and Priests Orders.

T. Getz Hill. Richard W. Trapnell.
Pierce N. McDonald. Edward P. Dandridge.

Candidates for Priests Orders.

C. Hely Molony. W. Howard Meyers.

I have ordained during the year, i. e., since May, 1904:

W. Howard Meyers. C. Hely Molony.

I have also during the same time attended six meetings of the Board of Missions in New York; the Missionary Conference at Richfield, N. Y., the sessions of the General Convocation in Boston; one meeting of the Board of Trustees of the Alexandria Seminary, and one meeting of the Trustees of Kenyon College, Gambier, O. I also attended the Commencement at the University of the South, Sewanee, Tenn., and have paid four official visits to the Hospitals at Paint Creek and Glendale, attending the meetings of the Directors and the Commencement of the Training Schools.

I report to the Council the following regularly organized Missions:

LOCATION.	NAME.	CHURCH.
Ansted	Advent Mission	The Redeemer.
Buckhannon	Upshur County Mission	Transfiguration.
Bramwell	Bramwell Mission	Holy Trinity.
Bunker Hill	Norborne Mission	Christ Church.
Berkeley Springs	Morgan Co Mission	St. Marks.
Charleston	W. Charleston Mission	St. Lukes.
Charleston	S. Charleston Mission	St. Matthews
Clover Lick / Marlinton.	Madison Mission	Grace.
Davis	Tucker County Mission	St. Barnabas.
Cresaps	Cresaps Valley Mission	Grace.
Eckman	McDowell County Mission	Grace.
Elkins	Randolph County Mission	Grace.
Elm Grove	Elm Grove Mission	St. Pauls.
Grafton	Taylor County Mission	St. Matthias.
Harpers Ferry	Harpers Ferry Mission	St. Johns.
Hinton	New River Mission	Ascension.
Kenova	Wayne County Mission	Grace.
Mannington	Mannington Mission	St. Andrews.
Montgomery	Coal Valley Mission	Calvary.
Okonoko	Hampshire Mission.	
Parkersburg / Tavernersville	Parkersburg Mission	Good Shepherd. / Grace.
Powellton	Powellton Mission	St. Davids.
Princeton	Mercer CountyMission	Heavenly Rest.
Rippon	Rippon Mission	St. Johns.
Romney	Hampshire County Mission	St. Stephens.
St. Marys	Pleasants County Mission	Grace.
Sutton	Elk River Mission	St. Johns.
Spruce	Spruce Mission	Spruce.
White Sulphur / Dry Creek / Eakles	White Sulphur Mission	St. Thomas.
Williamstown	Wood County Mission	Christ Memorial.

SPECIAL FUND.

The receipts for my special fund during the year have been as follows:

Boone Co.	$ 2 00
Bramwell	10 00
Bruce Chapel	17 00

Charleston	11.00	
Charles Town	238 50	
Elm Grove	12 00	
Gary	15.00	
Glen Jean	15 00	
Grafton	11 00	
Harpers Ferry	15 25	
Hedgesville	10 00	
Huntington	45 00	
Martinsburg	38 76	
Montgomery	1 00	
New Martinsville	15 00	
Nuttall	5 00	
Parkersburg, Trinity	372 00	
Point Pleasant	5 00	
Powellton	10 00	
Rippon	1 00	
Romney	5 00	
Sheltering Arms	5 00	
Summit Point	4 00	
Shepherdstown	10 00	
Union	2 00	
Welch	8 00	
Weston	17 50	
Wheeling, St. Luke's	100 00	
Wheeling, St. Matthew's	83 00	
Williamstown	10 00	
	$ 1,094 01	
Received From Outside Sources	505 00	
Total $	1599 01	
The Expenditures have been:		
2 grants to missions		25 00
10 grants to churches		344 07
2 grants to Sheltering Arms		70 00
2 grants to miscellaneous		20 50
22 grants to clergy		690 00
Total		$ 1149 57

Leaving a balance of $449.44. As my appeal is made the first of each year this balance is to serve for the next six months.

The Managers of the Church News have made a most encouraging report to me for the year March 1904-1905. They have between 800 and 900 subscribers, have received $230.65 and expended $216.77, leaving them a balance of $13.88 with which to begin a new year. This paper which is conducted with so much spirit and efficiency by the Committee of Publication is more important than many of our people realize. Without pretending to compete with our large Church weeklies, it yet gives to us information about our own work which they cannot give. It already serves—and ought to serve still more as a means of communication between the Bishops and the Clergy and the People. We are all mutually encouraged by hearing of the welfare and activity of those who are so closely bound together as members of one Diocese.

There is no way in which we can more readily show our interest and sympathy one with another, and enlist too the aid of congregations and individuals in the common work than by using the columns of the Church News. If the paper had such a circulation as it deserves to have, we could all be sure that the word of Counsel or the appeal for sympathy and aid which appeared in its columns would reach everyone of our members and friends throughout the Diocese. This would make it still more a power for good. Shall it not be so?

HOSPITALS.

Our hospitals need no special mention at this time. They are steadily doing their beneficient work. The Reynolds Memorial cared for 525 patients during the year and the Sheltering Arms for 405. At the Sheltering Arms Hospital our plant has been greatly enlarged and improved by the erection of a new building (at a cost of about $3,000) which provides accomodation for our nurses and pupil nurses and also additional ward room. There is increasing demand for our graduate nurses. During the year the Reynolds Memorial has granted Diplomas to three.

PARISH REGISTERS.

I am gratified to be able to say that our Parochial Reports are this year in better shape than ever before. Effort has been made to make the Blank clear in its indications of requirements, and although no doubt there could yet be improvements, yet the effort has been so far successful that out of 83 reports received only 10 are not in shape. I am aware of the fact that the making up of reports is to some exceedingly distasteful, but I think all must acknowledge that the call is only for such items and facts as ought thoroughly to be known by those in charge of the work. The difficulty that seems to attach to the satisfactory performance of this duty may find an explanation in another failure that I fear is only too common, viz. in the matter of properly keeping up the Parish Register. One would think that for his own satisfaction a clergyman would make it a point of keeping an accurate record of official acts and of other things of interest and importance that ought to be recorded. But such is not always the case. Time and again I have had incoming Rectors complain to me that their predecessors did not leave the scratch of a pen to guide them; no record of families or communicants, of baptisms, marriages or burials. But recently there has come to my knowledge the fact that a certain Parish Register contained no note of the death and burial of a faithful man, who certainly during my Episcopate of 27 years—and I know not for how long before—has been in every way the main stay of his Parish. I have also information that on another Register four weddings have been noted simply by entering the names of the parties, no mention being made of parents or witnesses, and no date given—such a Register would hardly be entitled to be admitted as evidence in a Court of Law—and no doubt many similar cases of neglect could be cited. I have recently noted that the secretary of the Diocese and the Rector of St. Matthew's, Wheeling, have adopted a card system, modelled after the method which prevails in public libraries of keeping track of the books, and it must greatly simplify the problem It does not follow that one must have an expensive Register in which to keep their Records. A cheap blank book will answer every purpose, and it seems to me that every congregation however small, ought to have something of the kind so that we shall know where to find a definite record of that which has to do with the condition and progress of our Church life.

THE KALENDAR.

I do not care to make any additional statement, at this time, in regard to the value of the Kalendar which I put forth as a guide for offerings during the year, except to say that each year's experience convinces me of the great importance of the adoption, and conscientious and persistent adherance to some such scheme, in every congregation in the Diocese, be it large or small. Since I have discussed the matter so much, in time past, I shall now only call your attention to what the present parochial reports show, viz. that in the matter of offerings for the cause of Religious and Theological Education, which is called for by canonical enactment, and therefore comes to all with full canonical as well as moral obligation, and in addition to these obligations, is commended to us by our loyality to the Seminary which has supplied 26 out of our present 42 clergy, and by the need of fair dealing with the Education Society, which on an average, each year, spends in support of our West Virginia young men, about $4 for every $1 received from us. The Parochial Reports I say, show that in this matter of offerings for the cause of Religious and Theological Education, that out of our 59 organized congregations 35 representing about 2000 communicants, absolutely ignored the whole matter. To say nothing of canonical and moral obligations, I can hardly think this to be fair dealing with a Society and Seminary to whom we are so deeply indebted year by year, and to whose support we are pledged by every consideration of gratitude and duty and interest. In behalf of these 2000 communicants, I feel constrained to say that their failure is to be ascribed to the fact that the cause of which we speak was never brought to their attention. The inference is plain that if some well considered plan were adopted and faithfully followed up, then no cause that has these both canonical and moral obligation could be forgotten or ignored.

GENERAL CLERGY RELIEF FUND.

I feel I must also in this connection speak a word for the General Clergy Relief Fund, of which this Diocese is a beneficiary to the extent of $200 annually, paid to the widow of one of our former clergy. We have been and still are solicited to merge our Diocesan Fund, for which we make our offering on Christmas Day, and which paid last year to six beneficiaries about $600, but so far we have deemed it inexpedient to do this. I am not discussing the question here, but have brought it forward to remind you that while we are exercising our undoubted right to provide such a fund for ourselves and to administer it at our discretion, yet that does not justify us in ignoring the General Clergy Relief Fund, which the Church has, through the General Convocation established. This Fund has now on its list about 400 beneficiaries. It aims to give a pension or annuity to every disabled clergy whether he be young or old, and whatever his residence, and to the widows and orphans of deceased clergymen, and this it does without payment of dues or fees or premiums or age requirements or Diocesan limitations. Such a fund certainly claims our cordial cooperation and support, and especially when it comes before us endorsed by the General Convocation which recommends that a definite day of each year to be set apart for offerings for this fund. We do not need any argument to convince us of the need of providing for an old age pension which shall be available as a right, by reason of age, and years of honorable service, and yet out of our 59 organized congregations only 14 gave anything to this worthy object, which constitutes a constant and pathetic appeal for our support. The reason for this neglect has already been indicated i. e. for lack of some systematic plan cordially and persistently carried out this and other worthy objects are crowded out of our minds, and so some us may come at last to claim aid from a fund which we have, during our years of service, continually ignored.

REVIVAL IN WALES.

It is not my custom, as you know, to consume your time by the discussion of subjects that are perhaps sufficiently ventilated in the religious press of the day, but I feel that a few words about the remarkable revival in Wales may serve to direct thought in such wise as will be helpful. I suppose if the question were directly put to us, and we were pressed for an answer, we would all freely acknowledge that there was abundant room and great need for a revival of true religion throughout the length and breadth of the land. Such confession, just in proportion as it is the expression of a deep consciousness of need, lies at the foundation of every true revival or religion, and directly contributes to its progress. "They that are whole need not a physician but they that are sick." Of course you understand that we use the word revival in the sense of its permanent effect upon life in all relations, and not of its spasmodic effect artificially generated, and therefore tending to disturb and distort such relations. It is possible that we may be too conservative in our dealings with all that comes under the general head of "revivals," but certainly the whole genius of our church is rather to lead men, reverently and patiently along what we may call the permanent ways of religious life, than in anywise to seem to limit the outpouring of God's spirit to channels of our own devising, and to force men into these channels.

Some months ago, one of our papers clearly stated what it believed to be the essential difference between the revival inWales, and that which was afterward inaugurated in London; and without any reflection upon the pure zeal or Christian character of the Evangelist who under took to direct the movement in London, it seems to me that we cannot but acknowledge the truth of the statement made, that these Evangelists went to London to create a revival by organization, and by machinery upon well defined psychological principles. This may be a perfectly legitimate method of procedure, but you do not find in any such movement as that the origin of the revival in Wales. Indeed so far from it, it would puzzle anyone to tell just how it originated. You could only say "The wind bloweth where it listeth, and thou hearest the sound thereof, but cannot tell whence it cometh, or whither it goeth." Of Mr. Roberts, who more than any other person is associated in our minds with this great awakening, it is said that he seems to be working upon the principle that God is in men, and that they need but to realize and actualize His Presence among them. It is worthy of note that the revival, in which he has been prominent, seems in no way dependent upon himself, but has manifested itself where he has never been. As the result of this revival men are found fulfilling more faithfully their duty in the various relations of life. It is in the main a natural, rational, spiritual revival, so that the movement, as a whole, seems calculated not only to leave substantial impress upon the spiritual life of the people, but to make a permanent contribution to it.

Under all these conditions the lesson is very plain to us. Living as we are, under the Dispensation of the Spirit, we must be continually looking to Him, and our expectations must ever be from Him. If our need be great His power is also great and His promise is sure. He wants to be enquired of by us, then shall we know if we follow on to know the Lord. If we open our mouths wide He will fill them. For this work of advancement and revival in the Church, shall manifest itself in the purer lives of Christian men and women, and the more active gathering of the outcasts and aliens into the fold. This work shall not be by human might or power, but led by the Spirit of the Lord.

And what I have here said has a direct bearing upon an aspect of our work, which I have time and again mentioned as of importance and promise. I mean the work of Evangelization as contrasted with, or at least supplementary to the work of organization. I suppose it is perfectly natural that a minister should look for a visible tangible reward in his work, in the building up and increase of his congregation, but over and above all that, it seems to me that a great field of usefulness is opened out to us in the work of Evangelization. We can ordinarily get just as many people to come to our services, where we have no organization, and perhaps no prospect of one, as where we have organized Parish or Mission. It seems to me that this is to be taken as indicating a line of duty and of privilege. I believe that in these special services, we may have from time to time in school houses and Court Houses and it may be in the open air, we get at many persons, not otherwise accessible. Our chief responsibility, as those that have received the Gospel, is to give it to those who have not received it, and not only in the case of those who live in Heathen lands, but also to the multitudes in our own Christian land, who are scattered abroad as sheep having no shepherd. If the people will not come to us, we must, as best we can, go to them, yes out into the highways and hedges and compel them to come in. Sometimes prejudiced people will not come into one of our chuch buildings, but they will, with the crowd attend services elsewhere. I do not know to what extent tent or open air meetings are available in our towns and cities, but it really seems that these towns and cities, though not large, have already a considerable population that it is hard to reach in any other way. In speaking of all such work a representative of one of our Boards of Home Missions has wisely said that to say that we have done all that we can do to get the people into the Churches, and that they still refuse to come is to admit defeat. The people may be at fault, but you must remember that the Church was established for faulty people. The greater their fault, the greater becomes our responsibility in the matter of reaching them with the helpful ministrations of the Gospel. Even though the methods may be unusual. And it is more important to consider all this, because we canot deny the truth of an assertion recently made, that we are face to face with the tremendous and menacing fact that people are going away from the Churches by the mere growth of the population, in all our great cities. And though we, in West Virginia, may not seem to be specially exposed to the danger, yet the beginnings of it may be discovered even in our large towns and small cities. Even if there be not, in proportion, so many unattached, churchless, Godless people in small places as in large, yet, since there is a constant flow from the country and small towns and cities to the larger places, the whole subject becomes one of increasing importance.

It has been pertinently asked, in the meantime what are churches doing. Too often they are engaged in barrack-ground drill, instead of being engaged in active and effective propaganda. Cultivated parochialism is the note of too many of the churches. It is unfortunately fatally easy for a company of good and pious people to sink into this condition of cultivated parochialism We gather into our churches a community of people much alike in qualities of mind, social condition, and intellectual tastes, and the Church thus constituted is apt to become more of a social club, than a propagandist centre. We have plenty of force in our churches for the Christian conquest of our great cities, and the regeneration of our villages and towns, but we fail to mobilize these forces. The saying of Napoleon that the only way to have a conquering army is to have an army that is always fighting, applies also to the greater questions of spiritual conquest. No man can keep his own soul alive, who is not trying to save other souls, and no church that is not passionately trying to win tne world that is without, is truly alive.

GENERAL MISSIONS.

During the past winter, under the continued depression in the financial condition of our general missionary treasury, I felt constrained, after an unusually long and anxious meeting of the Board of Missions, to offer, for this Diocese, an advance of twenty per cent, on the amount that had been assigned to us as our proper apportionment for the current year. This leads the Board to expect from us $3,120 instead of $2.600. This may seem to some to have been rather a rash proceeding for a Diocese, not strong in its own resources, and essentially missionary in character, but the urgency of the situation was such as to call for special and immediate action. The enlarged scope of our general work, owing to the demands of our new dependencies, and the continued needs of many of the old fields taken in connection with the discouraging and indeed alarming failures in various parts of the church, to meet the apportionment expected of them, had brought things to such a pass, that I could not but feel that everyone who was a lover of the Church, and servant of the Master, ought to gird himself for a special effort to meet the immediate and pressing need. It seemed vain to wait for a general concerted movement to meet the emergency, for the fascinating calculation of the great results that would follow if all would lend a helping hand, and take a long pull, and a strong pull and a pull all together, have been proved by experience, to be exceedingly delusive. The question thus seemed to be, not how can we inaugurate a scheme of more general cooperation, for the Board has been and still is continually putting forth vigorous effort to do that very thing, and it would seem is leaving no stone unturned to bring about such a happy consummation. But the question seemed rather what can we ourselves do to meet the prevailing condition without waiting for others, and saying it may be with cautious reserve "what is this man or that man doing to advance the cause? It is this immediate duty as it appeared to us, we have tried to take up in making our additional pledge, and I count upon the cordial cooperation of the Diocese to make the pledge good. We gave a like amount last year, and we are not fewer in numbers, nor poorer in pocket than we were then. Even if the limit has been reached, in so far as offerings in the Church are concerned, of which their is grave doubt, yet there are many individuals among our people, who would cheerfully respond to a personal application, were it wisely and strongly made. I am convinced that in these individuals we have an undeveloped field of resources, and that also the scattered friends and members of the Church, who are not under the usual charges for the maintenance of local worship, could do a vast deal more than they do, if we of the clergy exercised a more decided leadership just along these lines. As far as the general support of the aggressive work of the Church is concerned, there are no doubt hundreds of communicants and friends of the Church, who to the question why stand ye here all the day idle, might well make answer, because no man hath hired us. Our failure to approach men directly in the great matter of personal religion, and confession of Christ, is parallelled by our failure to bring home to them patiently and judiciously the duty of personal service in and support of the Church.

THANK OFFERING FOR GENERAL CONVENTION.

In addition to the instrumentalities that are already employed it has been determined to try and unite the men of the Church, members and friends, after the example set time and again by the women in their united offerings, to unite the men I say in a thank-offering to be presented at the General Convention, to meet in Richmond, in 1907. The occasion being the 300th anniversary of our first service at Jamestown, Va., is certainly one to suggest and foster such a plan. An essential feature of the scheme is, that whatever use may be made of circular letters, yet that, at some time, a personal appeal shall be made to every man member or friend of the Church, that he will take part in this offering. In order to carry out this plan and cooperate more heartily with the Central Committee and with our Brethren all over the country, I have appointed as our Diocesan Committee, our delegation to the General Convention in Boston, in connection with Bishop Gravatt, Mr. Spurr and myself. I cannot tell yet just what form our action will take but I bespeak for this committee the cordial cooperation of the clergy and laymen throughout the Diocese. Having more than two full years in which to make this personal canvass, the task does not appear to be very onerous. If we will throw aside our timidity and false shame, and rise to the height of this great privilege and opportunity we may help kindle an enthusiasm which will in a short time do the work of many languid years.

DIOCESAN SELF SUPPORT.

And this brings me to say that in my judgment, the time has come, when for the credit of the Diocese, and the good of the common cause, we should make a still further step to show our interest in, and to render efficient aid to the general missionary work of the Church. Some of you may remember that before the formation of the Diocese in 1877, it was proposed to form the territory of the State of West Virginia into a missionary jurisdiction, and as such throw the burden of its support on the General Church. I make bold to say, that we are all now glad that this was not done. Still there were great searchings of heart at the time, as to what was really the best thing to do under all the circumstances, and naturally there were wide differences of opinion as to the wisest course An illustration of these wide differences has but recently come to my knowledge, and it may be well to speak of it just here. The truth is that with optimism on one hand and pessimism on the other, there was not only need for great caution in forming an opinion, but it was needful also to keep in mind, that in matters pertaining to the Kingdom of God, we must always remember that there are at work other factors than simply those which appear to a casual observer.

The case alluded to was simply this, that at the time of the formation of the Diocese, there were two gentlemen connected with our church than whom none, in West Virginia, were more prominent, or apparently likely to be better informed as to prevalent conditions. One of them wrote to warn the Bishop elect, though the warning never reached him, and I think I may safely say would not have been effectual if it had, and say that he ought by no means to regard the call of the Church in West Virginia, because he, knowing whereof he spoke, felt constrained in all fairness, to say that the Church people in this new Diocese had pledged themselves all together beyond their ability, and that there was no future for the movement save that of disastrous failure. I need hardly say to you, who are here today, that by the good hand of our God upon us, and by the constant and cordial cooperation of an intelligent and faithful people clerical and lay, that the Diocese has lived down that gloomy prediction.

The other one of the gentlemen took an entirely different view of the situation. Looking at the whole enterprise from a broader outlook, and with a more hopeful spirit, he pledged himself to make up such deficiency in the financial resources of the Diocese, as seemed to some so inevitable, as effectually to block the way of advance. But as he himself informed me several years ago, he has never been called upon to make good his pledge. The Diocese has promptly and fully met all its obligations, and I may add that today, although these obligations have more than doubled since my consecration, twenty-seven years ago, the Diocese still meets them promptly and fully. Might not this be taken as a good illustration of what Bishop Coleridge Patteson said, that Education consisted in teaching people to bear responsibilities, and in putting those responsibilities upon them as they could bear them.

But although West Virginia did decline to throw the burden of her general support upon the Church at large, it nevertheless seemed expedient that she should receive help in sustaining her missions. This help she has been receiving regularly during these twenty-seven years of her independent existence, and no doubt but that this help has enabled us to cultivate our widely extended field, as otherwise we could not have done. But I think that after these twenty-seven years, we may be said to have attained to our majority. During this time our fourteen Clergy have increased to forty-two, our twenty-five churches to upwards of eighty, our eleven Rectories to forty-two, our endowment from nothing to upwards of $36,000, our Fund for Disabled Clergy and the widows and orphans of deceased clergy from nothing to about $7,000, the sum total of the money we raise for all purposes from about $10,000 to upwards of $80,000, to the $175,000 worth of property we had twenty-seven years ago we have added about $750,000 more, and thus find ourselves vastly better equipped for aggressive work than the most sanguine could have expected in such time. Our little band of about 1200 communicants has grown to nearly 5,000 and we are by the labors of our faithful missionaries, extending our influence everywhere throughout the State. And beside all this, to the amazement of some of our friends, we have taken the great forward step of adding a Bishop Coadjutor to our working force, specially in the interests of aggressive work, providing for him as for the Bishop, a comfortable and commodious residence. We have also two Hospitals and Training Schools in successful operation, which during the last year cared for nearly 1,000 patients, of which number three-fourths were practically free, and all this time the General Church has been given in about $2,000 annually, in all about $50,000 to help maintain and extend our work throughout the Diocese, and inaddition to $400 year by year to enable us to carry on some work among our colored people. Under all these circumstances and conditions, it becomes a pressing question, has not the time came for us to assume more direct responsibility for the missionary work within our borders, and thanking the Board of Missions for its nursing care during all these years, now relieve that Board of further obligation, except in so far as its aid is extended for work among the colored people, and except also what we may receive from the Woman's Auxiliary united offerings, for women workers in the Diocese.

We all know enough of human nature to understand that it will perhaps never be convenient to surrender the $1,450 we now receive from the General Church. We, like other people and churches, cling to our subsidies with tenacious grasp, and always think we can show peculiar conditions prevailing which make it still expedient in our case, if not in that of others to continue former missionary appropriations. But, my Brethern, we can not always confine our activities to that which is convenient and easy to do; we must sometimes at least rise to the height of undertaking that which calls for effort and self-denial, and be ready to forego certain advantages we are enjoying, if so be that we help advance the Kingdom and honor the Master. I think that the time has now come for us whose Diocese in coterminous with this growing and prosperous state, to put forth this effort and exercise this self denial, and I ask the Diocese here in Council assembled to make this judgment their own, and lead all the people, who look to us for guidance, to make this forward movement to which we seemed to be called by all the conditions and circumstances of the case, and may we not take there conditions and circumstances as being for us the voice of the Master Himself. Yes! It is time for us to go forward in the name of the Lord, and, as far as we can, clear our skirts of any complicity in the present lagging advance of the great army.

I thus bring this matter before you, because on every account, your voice ought to be distinct and emphatic, so that it shall appear that this advance is not simply on the word of the Bishop, but in accordance with the desire and judgment of the Diocese itself. And while asking you to make this great advance, I think it but right to say that I am not acting hastily or unadvisedly, or in such a way as to imperil the support of those brave and loyal missionaries, who are holding posts that are scattered about on our thin long drawn line. I believe that the experience of the past would keep all these men from feeling that the Bishops had forgotten them in the excitement of a general advance. But for others, especially for the lay people in our small congregations, who may be disposed to think that their interests and necessities have been somewhat overlooked, I would speak this reassuring word, that an efficient plan of meeting the condition of the case has been well worked out before the proposal is now made. Let me briefly outline this plan for the information of all concerned.

The assessment for Diocesan Missions has stood at about $3,000 since 1896, nine years ago, when it was first imposed, the exact assessment that year being $2,970. Since that time the Clergy have increased from 34 to 42, and the communicants from 3,925 to about 5,000. We have also increased our Episcopal Fund from about $5,000 to upwards of $36,000 and the income from this increased fund, under the circumstances, more than provides for the support of the Bishop Coadjutor, whose constant and efficient work throughout the Diocese adds greatly to our strength. So then it would seem that we are in condition to ask our congregations voluntarily to add something, say from $250 to $500 to what they already pay to this fund. In addition to this substantial increase which seems to be altogether reasonable, it is further proposed to ask the various congregations that receive missionary assistance and they are about 50 in number to do, each one something more in self support. An average of even $5 would make up an additional sum of $250, but as the report of our

Diocesan Missions Committee will show, we expect them to do much more than that. By these means we expect to make up at least one half of the sum heretofore received from the General Church, which we now relinquish. To assure the balance and so relieve our minds of any apprehension that our work will be in any wise crippled I have appealed to three persons to join me in guaranteeing the amount, and they have readily and cordially consented, so that the way seems clear for the proposed action.

The cooperation I have secured has been sought after consultation with the Rectors of the Churches concerned, and it has been so cordially and unhesitatingly given that I am convinced that further effort along this line would have easily sceured the whole amount needed, but I felt that this could hardly be done with justice to the Churches themselves, because they ought themselves to feel and to share the increased responsibility. I present this thought however for the careful consideration of the Clergy whether others of them, besides those mentioned above, have not individuals in their congregations, who would desire to join the four persons mentioned above, as uniting with them to share proportionally the whole obligation, or as contributing some definite sum towards the amount that may be needed, and so lessening the obligation of the four who are now standing in the breach.

The Bishops naturally hesitate about making too many personal appeals to their people, but at this time, and under present conditions, we waive personal considerations and feel that you have a right to look to our leadership in a matter of such moment. In the providence of God, this advance seems now called for and we do not believe that you will be found wanting. It is our hope that the aid we now relinquish will under the careful administration of the Board prove helpful to those who may need it even more than we do.

I cannot but think that a wise decision in regard to this matter of common interest and concern will inform and inspire our people with a truer missionary spirit and if we do, what we do, with the high purpose of duty, and in a spirit of loyal devotion to the gracious Master, whose we are and whom we serve, that God, even our own God, will give us His blessing.

On motion of Rev. D. W. Howard a committee of five was appointed to consider and report upon the subject, introduced to Council by the Bishop in his address, of our relation to the Board of Missions with a view of relinquishing the aid hitherto extended by it to our missionary work.

The Committee appointed consist of:

Rev. David W. Howard.
Rev. Geo. C. Easter.
Rev. Jno. S. Alfriend.
Mr. V. A. Weaver.
Mr. Cameron L. Thompson.

The Committee on Credentials of Lay Delegates reported as follows:

The Committee on Credentials respectfully report that the following named persons are duly certified delegates and alternates to this Convention.

J. HOWARD GIBSON.
GEO. A. BAXTER,
A. B. MITCHELL,
W. W. SHEARER.

PARISHES.

Parish.	P. O.	Church.	Delegates.
1. All Saints. 1871	Union	All Saints	J. M. Rowan. H. M. Brown. M. D. A. S. Johnson. E. S. McNeer. J. D. Logan. C. A. Shanklin.
2. Bangor	St. Albans	St. Marks	
3. Bethel	Clarksburg	Christ	*I. W. Williams. M. W. Smith. W. F. Nuzum.
4. Christ	Fairmont	Christ	J. E. Sands. *Wm. E. Watson. J. O. Watson. Geo. H. Brobst. Walton Miller. E. A. Russell.
5. Christ	Wellsburg	Christ	*Geo. A. Baxter. Joseph Fausett. Fred. L. Hall. T. H. Buchanan. M. Morgan.
6. Emanuel	Moorfield	Emmanuel	Thomas W. Lakin. I. V. Seymour. W. H. Shearer. *W. W. Shearer. H. McS. Gamble. R. D. Pollock.
7. Kanawha. 1788	Charleston	St. Johns	*W. S. Laidley. C. F. Payne. Alfred Phillips. J. J. Warwick. B. R. Roller. Jos. C. Jeffords.
8. Greenbrier	Lewisburg	St. James	
9. Norbourne. 1766	Martinsburg	Trinity	*J. Gassman. *H. L. Alexander. Dr. A. Andrews. C. A. Miller. B. W. Colston. C. Wesley Small.
10. Norbourne. 1769	Hedgesville	Mt. Zion	*Geo. T. Krelow Walter B. Lingamfelter. Jacob H. Miller. Lee Lingamfelter.

	Parish.	P. O.	Church.	Delegates.
11.	Nelson 1888	Middleway	Christ	*James Grantham. Wm. C. Frazier.
		Leetown	St. Bartholemew	I. H. Strider. Wm. H. Gilbert.
		Summit	Holy Spirit	Geo. C. Whiting. J. E. Trussell.
12.	Pt. Pleasant	Pt. Pleasant	Christ.	P. C. Eastham. C. K. Blackwood. H. E. Spillman. L. S. Pomeroy. J. W. C. Heslop. M. G. Tyler.
13.	Ravenswood	Ravenswood	Grace	
14.	St. Andrews	Charles Town	Zion	Joseph Trapnell. *Richd Henderson. Geo. R. Wendling. Robt Chew. B. C. Washington. W. B. Packett.
15.	St. Andrews	Shepherdstown	Trinity	Jno. O. Aglionby. P. P. Marshall. *L. R. Lee. Dr. Hopkins Gibson. Dr. Myers.
16.	St. John	Willow Island	St. Johns	
17.	St. Lukes	Wheeling	St. Lukes	L. E. Sands. *M. R. Wolff. *Frank Zook.
18.	St. Matthews	Wheeling	St. Matthews	*J. D. DuBois. *Dr. G. A. Ashman. *C. P. Flick. H. Quarrier. J. C. Brady. Allan Brock.
19.	St. Pauls	Weston	St. Pauls	R. H. Harrison. S. C. Hess. N. C. Bailey. Louis Burnett. A. H. Kunst. E. M. Vandervort.
20.	Trinity 1846	Parkersburg	Trinity	*H. H. Moss. *Dr. W. H. Sharp. *C. C. Martin. B. M. Ambler. F. Fowler. W. G. Peterkin.
21.	Trinity	Moundsville	Trinity	*V. A. Weaver. Friend Cox. C. S. Walton. A. J. Martin. J. F. Galleger. A. B. Williams.
22.	Glen Allen	Morgantown	Trinity	*Fredk Truscott. *Bryan Gordon.
23.	Trinity	Huntington	Trinity	*Cameron L. Thompson. *G. A. Northcott. Thos. W. Moore.

Parish.	P. O.	Church.	Delegates.
			Edmund Sehon.
			C. D. Emmons.
			F. R. Van Antwerp.
24. Wetzel	New Martinsville	St. Annes	S. R. Martin.
1851			*S. Bruce Hall.
			I. F. Martin.

MISSIONS.

Missions.	P. O.	Church.	Delegates.
25. St. Johns	Cross Creek	St. Johns	
26. Tyler	Sistersville	St. Pauls	Geo. F. Durham.
27. Bluefield	Bluefield	Christ	
Tyler Co	Grafton	St. Matthias	
Hampshire	Romney	St. Stephens	Wm. R. Baird.
			Geo. W. Parsons.
Hampshire	Okonoko	Epiphany	E. W. McGill.
			Hy. M. Russell.
Spruce Run	Lorentz	Spruce Chapel	Lilburn Dowell.
			Geo. W. Spalding.
Elk River	Sutton	St. Johns	Amos Bright.
			W. E. Haymond.
Upshur	Buckhannon		C. O. Latham.
			W. H. Howard.
Morgan Co	Berkeley Springs	St. Marks	
Harpers Ferry	Harpers Ferry	St, Johns	*Barnabas Bryan.
Ripon	Ripon	St. Johns	*F. C. LaRue.
			Dr. Howard Osborn.
New River	Hinton	Ascension	
Cresaps	Cresaps	Grace	
Coal Valley	Montgomery	Calvary	
Advent	Ansted	Redeemer	
Princeton	Princeton	Heavenly Rest	
Wayne Co	Kenova	Grace	
Bramwell	Bramwell	Holy Trinity	W. D. Tyler.
			W. C. Brooke.
St. Davids	Powellton	St. Davids	
Elm Grove	Elm Grove	St. Pauls	
Wheeling	Wheeling	St. Andrews	
St. Lukes	Charleston	St. Lukes	
St. Matthews	Charleston	St. Matthews	
Madison	Clover Lick	Grace	
Norbourne	Bunker Hill	Christ	
St. Thomas	White Sulphur	St. Thomas	
Davis	Tucker	St. Barnabas	*John L. Fish.
Christ Memorial	Williamstown	Christ	
Grace	Eckman	Grace	Dr. P. H. Killy.
Elkins	Elkins	Grace	Chas. H. Scott.
			J. Lacy Dunlap.
St. Marys	St. Marys	Grace	
St. Andrews	Mannington	St. Andrews	
	Parkersburg	Good Shepherd	
	Tavennersville		

The Bishop appointed the Standing Committees of the Council as follows:

STATE OF THE CHURCH.

Rev. Jno S. Douglas.	Mr. Richard Henderson.
Rev. A. M. Lewis.	Mr. G. A. Northcott.

PAROCHIAL REPORTS.

Rev. James L. Fish.	Mr. H. L. Alexander.
Rev. F. Van R. Moore.	Mr. Byron Gordon.

NEW PARISHES.

Rev. S. S. Moore, D. D.	Mr. Joseph D. DuBois.
Rev. Chas. E. Shaw.	Mr. James Grantham.

EPISCOPAL AND PERMANENT FUND.

Rev. Andrew G. Grinnan.	Dr. W. H. Sharp.
Rev. Jno. Tilton Marley.	Mr. Geo. H. Kreglow.

FINANCE.

Dr. G. A. Aschman.	Mr. Bryan.
Mr. Bruce Hall.	Mr. Frederick Truscott.

UNFINISHED BUSINESS.

Rev. Dr. Roller.	Mr. J. Gassman.
Rev. E. D. Irvine.	Mr. Jno. L. Fish.

Bishop Gravatt read his Diary as follows:

BISHOP GRAVATT'S ADDRESS.

DIARY FROM JUNE 1904 TO JUNE 1905.

JUNE.

Wednesday, 1st. Attended the Annual Diocesan Council in Trinity Church, Martinsburg.

Friday, 3rd. Ordained to the Priesthood in Trinity Church, Martinsburg, Rev. Francis Van Rennsalaer Moore. Sermon by the Rev. J. S. Gibson, of Huntington. Assisted in the Ordination the Rev. S. S. Moore, Rev. J. S. Douglas and Rev. J. S. Gibson.

Sunday, 5th. Preached the Baccalaureate Sermon at the Shepherd Normal College, Shepherdstown, W. Va., and in the evening attended the closing services of the Annual Council in Trinity Church, Martinsburg.

Sunday, 12th. Preached the Baccalaureate Sermon at Washington & Lee University at 11 A. M. In the evening officiated at Lee Memorial Church, Lexington, Va.

Tuesday, 14th. Attended a meeting of the Trustees of the Virginia Theological Seminary.

Sunday, 19th. Preached in Holy Trinity Church, Richmond, Va.

Wednesday, 22nd. Officiated at a mariage in Zion Church, Charles Town.

Saturday, 25th. Officiated at a funeral in Martinsburg.

Sunday, 26th. A. M. Preached in St. Mark's, Berkeley Springs. Confirmed two persons. P. M. Officiated at St. Mark's Church.

Tuesday, 28th. Officiated at a funeral in Charles Town.

JULY.

Sunday, 3rd. A. M. Preached in the Church of the Holy Spirit, Summit Point, W. Va.. P. M. Preached in St. Bartholomew's Church, Leetown.

Wednesday, 6th. Officiated at an infant baptism in Zion Church, Charles Town, at the request of the Rector.

Sunday, 10th. A. M. Preached in Grace Church, Middleway, and celebrated the Holy Communion.

Wednesday, 13th. Officiated at the evening service in Zion Church, Charles Town.

Sunday, 17th. A. M. Preached in the Church of the Holy Spirit, Summit Point and celebrated the Holy Communion. P. M. Preached in St. Bartholomew's Church, Leetown.

Saturday, 30th. Officiated at a funeral at Flint Hill, Va.

AUGUST.

Sunday, 7th. Took part in the services in Zion Church, Charles Town, A. M.

Sunday, 14th. Preached in St. Thomas' Church, White Sulphur Springs, A. M. Officiated at the evening service.

Tuesday, 16th. Preached at Montague's School House, Greenbrier County.

Wednesday, 17th. Officiated at a service at the White Sulphur Springs.

Thursday, 18th. Baptized a child near Montague's School House.

Sunday, 21st. Preached in Zion Church, Charles Town.

Sunday, 28th. Ordained to the Priesthood Rev. Paca Kennedy. Sermon preached by Rev. R. W. Micou D. D. Rev. J. S. Alfriend and Rev. P. B. Stauffer assisted.

SEPTEMBER.

Sunday, 4th. Preached in Christ Church, Chapel on the mountain, baptized one child and one adult and confirmed two. P. M. Preached at St. Andrew's Church on the Mountain.

Sunday, 11th. A. M. Officiated at St. John's Church, Rippon.

Tuesday, 13th. Attended Convocation in St. John's Church, Harpers Ferry.

Sunday, 18th. Preached in St. Paul's Church, Haymarket, Va. While there received a telegram announcing the death of the Rev. C. C. Pearson and had to cancel appointment for evening service in order to reach Berkeley Springs in time for the funeral.

Monday, 19th. Officiated in St. Mark's Church, Berkeley Springs, at the funeral of the Rev. C. C. Pearson.

Tuesday, 20th. Granted Lay Reader's License to Arthur P. Gray, Jr. Officiated at a funeral in Zion Church, Charles Town.

Sunday, 25th. At St. Andrew's on the Mountain baptized three infants, preached and administered the Holy Communion.

OCTOBER.

Saturday, 1st. Laid the corner stone at the Industrial Hall on the Mountain.

Sunday, 2nd. Preached in St. Andrew's Church on the Mountain.

Wednesday, 5th to Tuesday, 25th. Attended the General Convention at Boston, Mass.

Sunday, 9th. A. M. Preached in Grace Church, Boston, Mass. P. M. Preached in St. John's Church, Lawrence, Mass.

Sunday, 23rd. Preached in St. Paul's Church, Newburyport, Mass.

Sunday, 30th. A. M. Preached in Mt. Zion, Church, Hedgesville. P. M. Preached in Trinity Church, Martinsburg.

Monday, 31st. Attended a conference in Washington, D. C.

NOVEMBER.

Wednesday, 9th. Attended a meeting of the Trustees of the Virginia Theological Seminary at Alexandria, Va.

Sunday, 20th. Preached in the School House near Middleway. In the evening preached in Grace Church, Middleway.

Thursday, 24th. Preached in St. Andrew's on the Mountain.

Sunday, 27th. Preached in St. Peter's Church, Port Royal, Va.

DECEMBER.

Sunday, 4th. A. M. Preached in St. Paul's Church, Weston and confirmed eight. P. M. Preached the opening sermon of a mission in Christ Church, Clarksburg.

Monday, 5th. to Sunday, 11th. Conducted a mission in Christ Church, Clarksburg.

Sunday, 11th. 7:30 A. M. Celebrated the Holy Communion. 10:30 A. M. Preached in Christ Church. 4 P. M. Made an address in the Opera House, Clarksburg at a Men's service. 7:30 P. M. Preached in Christ Church.

Monday, 12th. I went to Parkersburg to confer with Bishop Peterkin.

Tuesday, 13th. Visited Reynolds Memorial Hospital, to go over the books of the institution at the request of the Superintendent.

Sunday, 18th. Visited St. Andrew's on the Mountain.

Christmas Day. Assisted in the service in Zion Church, Charles Town.

Sunday, 28th. Preached in the St. Andrew's Church on the Mountain.

JANUARY 1905.

Sunday, 1st. A. M. Preached in Zion Church, Charles Town. P. M. Took part at a service in the Presbyterian Church, Charles Town.

Friday, 6th. Made an address in the Methodist Church, Charles Town.

Sunday, 8th. Assisted in a Union Service in Zion Church, Charles Town.

Monday, 9th. Made an address to the Woman's Auxiliary of Zion Church, Charles Town.

Sunday, 22nd. Made an address on Missions to the children in Zion Church, Charles Town, P. M.

Sunday, 29th. Could not keep my appointment for service in Keyser, receiving a telegram that no place could be secured in which to hold a service.

Monday, 30th. Made an adress to the Junior Auxiliary of Trinity Church, Parkersburg.

Tuesday, 31st. Attended a meeting of the Kanawha Convocation in St. Mark's Church, St. Albans.

FEBRUARY.

Wednesday, 1st. Celebrated the Holy Communion in St. Mark's Church St. Albans.

Thursday, 2nd. Made an address on Missions in St. Mark's Church, St. Albans.

Saturday 4th. I went to the Sheltering Arms Hospital to confer with Mr. Cabell about the work on Cabin Creek.

Sunday, 5th. Preached in St. John's Church, Charleston, and celebrated the Holy Communion.

Sunday, 12th. Preached in St.Philip's Church, Charles Town, and confirmed six.

Monday, 13th. Took part in a funeral in Zion Church, Charles Town.

Wednesday, 15th. Took part in a marriage in Zion Church, Charles Town.

Sunday, 19th. Preached in Trinity Church, Shepherdstown.

Sunday, 26th. Preached in St. John's Church, Harpers Ferry.

MARCH.

Sunday, 5th. Addressed the Sunday School of St. Luke's Church,

Wheeling, 11 A. M. Preached and celebrated the Holy Communion. 3:30 P. M. Made an address to men. 7:30 Preached in St. Luke's.

Monday, 6th, to Saturday, 11th. I conducted a mission in St. Luke's Chrch, Wheeling.

Saturday, 11th. I went to Parkersburg to confer with Bishop Peterkin.

Sunday, 12th. A. M. Preached in Bruce Chapel. 6 P. M. Confirmed at home a very sick person. 7:30 P. M. Preached in Christ Church, Point Pleasant.

Monday, 13th. 3 P. M. Confirmed in Grace Church, Ravenswood, one person. 7:30 P. M. Preached in Grace Church and confirmed two.

Tuesday, 14th. Preached in Whittle Chapel and confirmed one.

Wednesday, 15th. Preached in St. John's Church, Ripley.

Thursday, 16th. Preached in the Church of the Advent, Waverly.

Friday, 17th. Had to cancel appointment at Willow Island on account of the condition of the roads.

Sunday, 19th. Preached in St. Ann's Church, New Martinsville. 7:30 P. M. Preached in St. Paul's Church, Sistersville and confirmed fifteen.

Sunday, 26th. A. M. and P. M. Preached in Holy Trinity Church, Richmond, Va.

Wednesday, 29th. Preached at the Union Service in Holy Trinity Church, Richmond, Va.

APRIL.

Sunday, 2nd. A. M. and P. M. Preached in Zion Church, Charles Town.

Monday, 3rd. Visited the work at St. Andrew's on the Mountain.

Tuesday, 4th. Granted Lay Reader's license to Robert Lee Boyd, of Wheeling.

Saturday, 8th. I went to Port Royal, Va., to attend a conference.

Sunday, 9th. A. M. and P. M. Preached in Holy Trinity Church, Richmond, Va.

Wednesday, 12th. Visited the work on the Mountain at St. Andrew's.

Friday, 14th. Preached in St. Andrew's Church, Wheeling and confirmed fourteen persons.

Sunday, 16th. A. M. Preached in St. Paul's Church, Weston. P. M. Preached in the Church of the Transfiguration,Buckhannon, and confirmed two persons.

Monday, 17th. Preached in Spruce Chapel.

Tuesday, 18th. Preached at St. Paul's Chapel, Lewis County, and confirmed two persons. P. M. Preached in St. Paul's Church, Weston.

In the afternoon I officiated at a funeral at the State Hospital, Weston.

Wednesday, 19th. Preached at Christ Church, Williamstown.

Thursday, 20th. Preached at Grace Church, St. Marys.

Saturday, 22nd. Made a Lenten address in St. Luke's Church, Wheeling.

Sunday, 23rd. Easter. Preached in Trinity Church, Moundsville. Celebrated the Holy Communion and confirmed ten. P. M. Preached in St. Luke's Church, Wheeling, and confirmed twenty.

Sunday, 30th. A. M. Preached in Trinity Church, Parkersburg, and confirmed sixteen. P. M. Preached in the Church of the Good Shepherd, Parkersburg.

MAY.

Tuesday, 2nd. Preached in All Saints Church, Union.

Wednesday, 3rd. Preached in St. Peter's Church, Glen Jean.

Thursday, 4th. Preached in the Methodist Church at Beckley.

Friday, 5th. Preached in the Church of the Ascension, Hinton.

Sunday, 7th. A. M. Preached in St. John's Church, Charleston and confirmed twenty-seven. 3 P. M. Preached in St. Matthew's Church, Kanawha, and confirmed three. 8 P. M. Preached in St. Mark's Church, St. Albans, and confirmed three.

Monday, 8th. Preached in Christ Church, Boone County.

Tuesday, 9th. Preached in Methodist Church at Racine, Boone County.

Wednesday, 10th. Preached in the School House at Paint Creek and confirmed seven.

Thursday, 11th. In the Church of the Incarnation, Ronceverte, I baptized the child of the Rector and preached.

Friday, 12th. Preached in St. James' Church, Lewisburg.

Sunday, 14th. 9:30 A. M. Made an address to the Sunday School of Trinity Church, Huntington. 11 A. M. Preached in Trinity Church, 3:30 P. M. Preached in Grace Church, Kenova, and confirmed two. 8 P. M. preached in Trinity Church, Huntington, and confirmed fifteen.

Monday, 15th. Preached in St. Luke's Church, Charleston, and confirmed seven.

Tuesday, 16th. Made an address to the Auxiliary of St. John's Church, Charleston.

Wednesday, 17th. Attended a meeting of the Board of Trustees of the Sheltering Arms Hospital.

Thursday, 18th. Preached in Trinity Church, Shepherdstown, the closing sermon of the Eastern Convocation.

Sunday, 21st. A. M. Preached in St. John's Church, Rippon, P. M. St. John's Church, Harpers Ferry.

Monday, 22d. I visited St. Andrew's on the Mountain.

Sunday, 27th. Visited Fairview Schoolhouse, Jefferson County.

SUMMARY.

Lay Readers Licensed	3
Baptisms	Infant, 7; adult, 1
Confirmations	167
Marriages	2

Burials		6
Visits made		106
Sermons		133
Addresses		58
Ordination to Priesthood		2
Money Received:—		
Cash from Womans Auxiliary, Charles Town .... $	100 00	
Cash from a friend in Charles Town	3 00	
Cash from Zion Church, Sunday School, Charles Town	32 57	
Cash, "Special for Mountain"	10 00	
Check from Charles Town	50 00	
Cash, St. John's, Charleston	10 00	
Check, St. Andrew's Guild, Charles Town	30 00	
Check, Charles Town	8 00	
Cash, Charles Town	10 06	
Total	$	253 63
Money Paid Out:—		
To Six grants within bounds of the three Convocations .... $	95 00	
Three grants for education	70 00	
Paid for building of Rectory		50 00
Total	$	215 00
Balance on hand	$	38 63

Since the last Council St. Andrew's on the Mountain and Christ Church, Blue Ridge, have been placed together. Twenty acres of land have been secured for the work at St. Andrew's, costing $333.35. The Deaconess' House is being enlarged and improved at a cost of $500.00. The Chapel has had a stone foundation placed under it and the building painted at a cost of $185.00. The Industrial Hall has just been completed. It is built of stone and has cost about $2200.00. This will be a most valuable addition to the plant. The money for all this work has been secured by Rev. B. M. Spurr who has been untiring in his interest in behalf af this Mountain work.

Mr. Thornton T. Perry has given his time and thought to the construction of these buildings and without his interest in this work, it would have been impossible to have built up the "plant."

Rev. Geo. A. Gibbons presented the Annual Report of the Standing Committee as follows:

STANDING COMMITTEE REPORT.

July 2nd, 1904 to June 3rd, 1905.

July 2nd, 1904. The Standing Committee recommended the Rev. Paca Kennedy (Deacon) for Ordination to the Priesthood. The Committee at the same time consented to the Ordination and Consecration of the Rev. Robert Strange, D. D., to be Bishop Coadjutor of the Diocese of East Carolina.

Sept. 5, 1904. The Rev. C. Hely Molony, having applied to the Bishop for dispensation from the knowledge of the Latin and Greek languages, and other branches of learning not strictly ecclesiastical,—the Bishop and Examining Chaplains favoring and urging the same—the Standing Committee recommended that the application of Mr. Molony be granted.

Nov. 21st, 1904. The Bishop having laid before the Standing Committee his "urgent reasons for shortening the time of the Candidacy of the Rev. C. Hely Molony, the Committee consented and advised the Bishop in this particular case to shorten the time of his candidacy to the canonical limit. The papers of said Mr. Molony all being in due form and harmony, the Committee recommended him for Ordination to the Deaconate. At this meeting the Committee having received a communication from the Bishop concerning a proposed change in the time for the meeting of this session of the Council, and after due consideration, the Committee unanimously agreed to concur in whatever change of time for the meeting the Bishop should think best to make, and so notified him.

Jan. 2nd. 1905. The Standing Committee consented to the Ordination and Consecration of the Rev. Charles Edward Woodcock, D. D., to be Bishop of the Diocese of Kentucky.

March 7, 1905. Consent was given to the Ordination and Consecration of the Rev. James Henry Darlington, D. D., to be Bishop of the Diocese of Harrisburg.

May 9th, 1905. Mr. T. Getz Hill and Mr. Pierce N. McDonald were recommended for ordination to the Deaconate and the Rev. Walter Howard Meyers for Ordination to the Priesthood. All of which is respectfully submitted.

G. A. GIBBONS.
A. J. WILLIS.
JOHN S. DOUGLAS.
J. GASSMAN.

On motion of Rev. W. P. Chrisman Mr. McCallister, one of the traveling secretaries of the Brotherhood of St. Andrew, addressed the Council in the interest of the Brotherhood work.

The Revised Constitution having been adopted by the last Council was put upon its final passage and adopted by a two-thirds vote of both orders. There was only one dissenting vote.

The Rev. G. A. Gibbons moved to amend Art. viii of the Constitution, by adding in the second line after the word "presbyters," the word or "laymen, communicant and *ex-officio* member of the Council when elected." Referred to the Committee on Constitution and Canons.

The Rev. Mr. Irvine moved to amend the same Article, by inserting after "shall be elected," the words "each year."

Referred to Committee on Constitution and Canons.

The Committee on Constitution and Canons reintroduced the amended and revised Canons, the consideration of which was postponed to this Council by the 22nd Annual Council; and Canon 1 was amended by striking out the words "under the Canons," in the seventh line of section "a," and then adopted.

Canon 2 was adopted after striking out all of the second paragraph after the words "annual Council."

Canon 4 was amended by inserting in the fifth line of paragraph one, after the words "organized mission" these words, "each of whom shall have attained the age of 21 years," and by striking out the words "who is" before the word "each" in certificate, and inserting after the word "each" these words "of whom is," and by striking out the word "place" and inserting therefor the words "parish, congregation or missions," and by adding the word "or" after the words "minister" and "Registrar." As thus amended the Canon was adopted.

On motion the Council adjourned.

THURSDAY, JUNE 1, 1905.

Bishop Gravatt called the Council to order.

The Rev. D. W. Howard read prayers. The Rev. Mr. Gibson was requested to act as Secretary *pro tem* until the Rev. Dr. Roller arrived.

Mr. W. E. Watson was duly certified as Lay Delegate from Christ Church, Fairmont, and took his seat. The Rev. Dr. Roller at this point arrived and assumed his duties.

The Council took up the consideration of Canon 4.

The Rev. Dr. Moore moved to insert before the word Secretary in the fifth line from the bottom of the page the words, "President of the Standing Committee and," and substitute the word "who" for the words "and he" in the fourth line from the bottom.

lopted.

Whereupon Canon 4 as amended was adopted.

Canon 5 was next taken up. The Rev. Mr. Marshall moved to strike out all of the second paragraph after the word "apportionment."

The Rev. Mr. Gibson moved to make this Canon the order of the day for 2:30 p. m.

On motion the Council adjourned until 2:30 o'clock.

2:30 P. M.

The Council convened. Bishop Peterkin in the chair.

The order of the day was taken up, and Mr. Marshall's amendment was adopted on vote by orders, as follows:

Clergy—Ayes, 19; noes, 11.

Lay—Ayes, 21; noes, 6.

The Rev. J. Brittingham offered this amendment: "After the first line in the last paragraph add the following: 'The Diocesan Treasurers shall publish in the Church News each month a statement of the several assessments upon and receipts from the several Parishes and Mission Stations.'

On motion this amendment was laid on the table.

The Rev. Mr. Gibson moved the adoption of the Canon as amended. Carried.

The Secretary read Canon 6.

The Rev. Dr. Moore moved to strike out all of the second paragraph of this Canon, before the words "the income" in the second line, and also to strike out the word "therefrom" and substitute for this word, the words "from the permanent fund," which was accepted. On motion the Canon as amended was adopted.

Canon 7 was read and adopted.

Canon 8 was read and adopted.

Canon 11 was read.

The Rev. Dr. Moore moved to omit the word "baptized" in subsection "b" of paragraph three. On motion this amendment was laid on the table.

The Rev. Dr. Moore moved to strike out the words in paragraph one "preferably communicants in good standing."

On motion the Council adjourned to meet at 9:30 a. m. tomorrow.

FRIDAY, JUNE 2, 1905.

The Bishop called the Council to order.

The minutes of yesterday were read and approved.

The Secretary presented the reports of the Trustees of the Permanent Fund, of the Treasurer of the Diocese, and the Trustee of the Episcopal Fund, which were referred to the Committee on Finance.

The Rev. John S. Gibson offered the following resolution, which was adopted:

Resolved: That the Committee on Assessments is hereby requested in reporting to the 28th Annual Council, to apportion to the several parishes, congregations and missions the sum of $3,000 or thereabouts, apportioned to the Diocese by the Board of Missions, and that such apportionment be made distinct from their assessment for the maintenance of our diocesan missionary work.

The Rev. Mr. Gibson offered this, which was unanimously adopted:

Resolved: The Twenty-eighth Annual Council assembled in Christ Church, Clarksburg, expresses to its rector, Rev. James F. Plummer and to its vestry and people and to the good people of the city its grateful appreciation of the cordial hospitality extended to it and its individual members.

The Rev. J. S. Alfriend cordially invited the Council to meet in Zion Church, Charles Town, next year. The invitation was accepted.

The Rev. Dr. Moore presented the following report of the Executive Committee of the Diocesan Missionary Committee:

REPORT OF THE EXECUTIVE COMMITTEE OF THE DIOCESAN MISSIONARY SOCIETY.

We beg leave to submit the following account of our work.

We have received during the year from all sources $3735.88, as indicated by the Treasurer's report—a most gratifying increase of nearly $550 as compared with the year preceding. Our expenditures have been slightly in excess of receipts, which has resulted in a reduction of our balance to $1071.21, nearly $50 less than that of last year. Attention may again be called to the fact often noted that this seemingly large balance is necessary at this season always because we are approaching the end of a quarter, when probably all of it will be needed.

With this expenditure twenty-three men have been aided, of whom four are no longer engaged in the work in this Diocese. The places served by these men, with more or less frequency, would aggregate nearly if not quite, one hundred and would include a very large proportion of our entire list of communicants. These places have been grouped for purposes of present administration into about twenty mission fields, as more fully shown in the annexed tabulated statement.

These results have been obtained only by such combinations as merge at least seven distinct charges, into circuits with others, that are more or less convenient. The committee is fully aware of the fact that thus some of the charges are entirely too large, thus imposing upon the clergy tasks which they feel are beyond their powers, and yet there has at present seemed no way out of the difficulty.

In consequence of this consolidation, your committee has felt encouraged to take another forward step in the direction of the accomplishment of its long-cherished aim, to provide a salary of at least $800 and a rectory for each of its workers. But, in order that this may be done, it is absolutely necessary that the fields aided shall make some addition to their contributions for self support. The amount of such increase needed is not in any case large and in most fields is distributed among a number of places so as to make a very small addition to the annual contribution at each place, and it is most earnestly hoped that a faithful effort will be made everywhere to see that the scheme is carried out to its most minute detail. Your Committee would press this point with the utmost urgency and would ask that a careful study of the scheme be made and that the work, which, we believe, can in every case be done, shall be efficiently carried out. We refer for fuller information as to the details to the annexed tabulated statement which has been prepared by Bishop Peterkin with great care and labor for the guidance of the Committee and for the information of the Diocese.

In conclusion your Committee would venture to remind the Brethren that, in view of our relinquishment of the further aid of the General Board we have new fields of labor under our care and oversight and additional responsibilities to those which we have borne before. In their relation to our work these are like new possessions, not yet brought under our Master's sway, and that we may bring them, is part of the responsibility resting upon us. To meet this we need new gifts of grace. We must seek to kindle in our hearts new fires of enthusiasm for our Master and His cause, and as their warmth and glow spread out from heart to heart, from life to life, we must strive to deepen and intensify in ourselves and others that spirit of loyalty and devotion to Him, whose we are and whom we serve, which will enable us to feel every burden light, every task a joy, for the privilege of serving him.

SCHEDULE OF DIOCESE MISSIONS—DIOCESE OF WEST VIRGINIA.

NAMES.	SALARIES FROM THE FIELD.		YEAR 1904-'05 TOTALS.	Diocesan Missions.	General Boards.	Total Salary.	1905-'06 Obligations of Diocese under Old Schedule.	Expected addition from field.	Obligations of Diocese under New Schedule.	Salaries after September.	REMARKS.
Rev. E. H. Brosius....	Bluefield......	$500	$550	$150	$100	$800	$250	$ 10	$240	$800	
	Princeton..........	50									
Rev. Guy H. Crook....	Ronceverte.........	225									
	Lewisburg..........	150									
	Fort Spring	50	560	200	....	760	200	60	230	850	Extra of $50 as Rent for Rectory.
	Anthony........ ..	60									
	White Sulphur.....	75									
Rev. Geo. W. Easter ..	Union..............	450	460	100	200	760	300	....	340	800	
	Alderson...........	10									
Rev. Jas. L. Fish......	Davis..	400									
	Elkins.............										
	Belington..........		460	....	200	660	200	320	20	800	
	Parsons............										
	Bayard	50									
	Thomas............	10									
Rev. Geo. A. Gibbons.	Romney	100									
	Morefield	150									
	Okonoko	40	290	250 50 con.	200	790	450 50 con.	80	480	800	Convocation adds $50.00.
	Paw Paw										
	Keyser....										
Rev. J. H. Gibbons....	Pt. Pleasant........	350									
	Bruce Chapel	150									
	Spilman......	50	550	50	150	750	200	80	220	800	
	Winfield										
	Morgans										

Rev. J. A. Hiatt	Hinton Glen Jean Beckley Etc., Etc.	400 150 50	600	....	200	800	200	50	50	800	
Rev. E. D. Irvine	Wellsburg St. Johns, Brooke Co	450 36	486	240	....	726	240	14	300	800	
Rev. Paca Kennedy	St. Marys Waverly Willow Island Ravenswood Ripley Whittle Ch Mason City	325 50 50 110 80	615	....	....	615	....	....	85	700	Rectory not available.
Rev. C. E. A. Marshall	Shepherdstown Duffield	600	600	....	....	600	....	....	100	700	Rectory partially rented.
Rev. W. H. Meyers	Sutton Buckhannon Spruce Gassaway Etc., Etc.	400 200 10 15	625	....	....	625	....	....	75	700	No Rectory.
	Paint Creek Cabin Creek Hansford		500	300	....	800	300	....	200	700	No Rectory.
Rev. A. B. Mitchell	Williamstown Good Shepherd P'bg Grace Tavernersville.	200 400	600	200	....	800	200	50	200	850	Extra allowance of $50 as rent for Rectory.
Rev. C. Hely Molony	New Martinsville Smithfield	700	700	100	....	800	100	20	80	800	
Rev. F. Van R. Moore	Elm Grove New Cumberland Chester	600	600	200	....	800	200	200	....	800	Becomes self-supporting and so not counted in sum total.
Rev. H H. Phelps	Bramwell Eckman Elkhorn Welch, Etc., Etc.	600	600	200	....	800	200	325	....	925	Becomes self-supporting and so not counted in sum total.
Rev. Chas. E. Shaw	Berkeley Springs Hedgesville	300 250	550	50	200	800	250	20	230	800	
Rev. Geo. C. Shaw	Mannington Grafton	62 250	312	360	100	772	460	28	460	800	

SCHEDULE OF DIOCESE MISSIONS—DIOCESE OF WEST VIRGINIA.—Continued.

NAMES.	SALARIES FROM THE FIELD.		YEAR 1904–'05. TOTALS.	Diocesan Missions.	General Boards.	Total Salary.	1905–'06. Obligations of Diocese under Old Schedule.	Expected addition from field.	Obligation of Diocese under New Schedule.	Salaries after September.	REMARKS.
Rev J. B. Stauffer	Harpers Ferry	125	275	400	....	750	400	25	425	800	Convocation adds $75.00.
	Rippon	150	....	75 con.	....	....	75 con.				
Rev. John Warnock	St. Albans	200									
	St. Lukes	280	680	120	....	800	120	....	120	800	
	St. Matthews	200									
	Etc., Etc.										
Rev. A. J. Willis	Middleway	150									
	Leetown	175	550	50	100	800	150	20	130	800	Convocation adds $100.00.
	Summit Point	225	....	100 con.	....	....	100 con.				
			$11263	$ 3195	$ 1450	$15908	$ 4645	$ 1202	$ 3985	$14900	

It is to be noted that the Missionaries pay their own traveling expenses out of their salaries as given above.

Besides the 19 Mission fields mentioned above (two others listed becoming self-supporting) to be sustained by the Diocese there is a mission church for colored people to which the General Board appropriates $400 (the small congregation raising $50). There are also 16 self supporting charges which raise a salary fund of $18,747. All these the Bishop supplements by grants from his special fund to the amount of $600 So that the total salary fund and in the Diocese amounts to $34,697, of which only $400 is from the General Board.

The results tabulated above have been obtained only by such combinations as merge at least seven distinct charges, into circuits with others that are more or less convenient. The committee is fully aware of the fact that thus some of the charges are entirely too large, thus imposing upon the clergy tasks which they feel are beyond their powers, and yet there has at present seemed no way out of the difficulty.

Parkersburg, W. Va.,
May 25, 1905.

GEO. W. PETERKIN,
For the Committee.

The Rev. Dr. Moore, Diocesan Commissioner, presented this report:

DIOCESE OF WEST VIRGINIA.

Total amount contributed to the Church Building Fund by the Diocese of West Virginia from 1880 to May 1905............$	755 27
Contributions received May, 1904, to May, 1905:	
Weston (Lewis Co.)—St. Paul's Chapel....................$	3 00
Moundsville—Trinity Church	3 15
Shepherdstown—Trinity Church	2 77
Huntington—Trinity Church	2 00
Bramwell—Holy Trinity Church	6 00
Kenova—Grace Church	1 75
Spilman—Spilman Chapel	3 00
Union—All Saint's Church	2 37
Martinsburg—Trinity Church	3 56
Parkersburg—Good Shepherd Church	3 00
Huntington—Trinity Church	2 00
Weston—St. Paul's Chapel	3 00
Kenova—Grace Church	1 00
Ronceverte—Incarnation Church	3 31
Received the past year ....$	39 91
Loans have been made to churches as follows: Charleston, Huntington, Bramwell, Weston, and Hinton (all paid in full) ....$	8,250 00
Gifts have been made to Churches as follows: Kenova, Charleston, Bramwell, Boone Co., Spilman, and Weston, amounting to ....$	1,000 00

PERMANENT FUND.

Total contributions and donations received from all sources from 1880 to May 1905	$389,767 13
Total amount of gifts made since 1893 to May 1905 to build 367 Churches	$ 63,141 33
Total amount of Loans (1880 to 1905) to build 415 Churches and Rectories	$497,159 39

Copies of the Annual Report of the American Church Building Fund Commission distributed to members of the Council.

Mr. H. H. Moss appeared and took his seat.

The Council embodies in its minutes the following notice of the General Clergy Relief Fund.

GENERAL CLERGY RELIEF FUND.

GEORGE C. THOMAS, TREASURER.

Will Title: "Trustees of the Fund for the Relief of Widows and Orphans of Deceased Clergymen and of Aged, Infirm and Disabled Clergymen of the Protestant Episcopal Church in the United States of America."

The general and official society for clerical relief covering the whole Church. Canon 53, No. VI. The General Convention recommends Quinquagesima Sunday for an annual offering from every Church, and that a percentage of the Communion Alms be given to this fund.

Assistant Treasurer and Financial Agent, Rev. Alfred J. P. McClure, The Church House, Twelfth and Walnut Streets, Philadelphia.

The following Standing Committee of the Diocese was elected by ballot:

The Rev. G. A. Gibbons.
The Rev. Andrew J. Willis.
The Rev. John S. Douglas.
Mr. Isaac H. Strider.
Mr. Jacob Gassman.
Mr. Frank Beckwith.

The following Missionary Committee was elected:

The Bishops—(*Ex-Officio.*)

Rev. S. S. Moore, D. D.
Rev. Jacob Brittingham.
Rev. James F. Plummer.
Mr. B. Mason Ambler.
Mr. Simms Powell.

The Council elected the following Committee on Constitution and Canons:

Rev. John S. Gibson.
Rev. D. W. Howard.
Rev. J. S. Douglas.
Mr. W. S. Laidley.
Mr. Joseph Trapnell.

And this Committee on Education:

Rev. G. W. Easter.
Rev. J. Howard Gibbons.
Rev. A. M. Lewis.
Mr. W. G. Hubbard.
Mr. C. L. Thompson.

And this on Sunday Schools:

Rev. W. P. Chrisman.
Rev. C. E. Shaw.
Dr. G. A. Aschman.
George Rogers.

The order of the day, to-wit: Canon 11, was then taken up.

The amendment of the Rev. Dr. Moore, which was under consideration when the Council adjourned yesterday, was accepted by the Committee on Canons.

Whereupon the Rev. Dr. Roller moved to amend by inserting

the words "preferably communicants in good standing," before the words "to be," in the seventh line.

On motion the Council adjourned to 2:00 p. m.

---

2 P. M.

The Bishop called the Council to order.

On motion the vote was taken on Dr. Roller's amendment at once.

A call was made for a vote by orders, with the following result:

Clergy—Ayes, 14; noes, 2.

Lay—Ayes, 9; noes, 3.

Canon 11 as amended was then adopted.

Canon 12 was read.

Rev. Dr. Roller moved to amend by inserting "two Wardens" for the words "a Senior and a Junior Warden."

The motion was laid on the table.

The Rev. Mr. Irvine offered this amendment. Strike out the words "regular communicant," and insert "confirmed persons who have received the Holy Communion within one year."

This amendment was laid on the table.

Canon 13 was adopted.

Canon 14 was adopted.

Canon 15 was adopted.

The Rev. Mr. Gibson moved that the Council give audience to Mr. Alvord on the subject of the Anti-Saloon League, at 5 p. m. Carried.

A new Canon, to be numbered properly when printed, relating to the Disabled Clergy Fund was presented by the Committee.

The Rev. Dr. Moore moved to postpone consideration of the same, which motion was laid on the table.

The Canon was then adopted.

A Canon on Eclesiastical Court to be properly numbered was read by the Committee and adopted.

A Canon, to be numbered, relating to procedure at meetings of Council, was read and adopted.

The Committee was allowed to withdraw the Canon on Courts of Appeal.

The Rev. Mr. Smith, the Educational Secretary of the Board of Missions, was present and invited by the Bishop to address the Council, on the subject of his work.

The Committee asked permission to amend Canon 9 by inserting after the word "part" in the fourth line the words "and form a new Parish." Adopted.

And in Canon 10, to insert "Parish" for "cure" in the sixth line, and to strike out "a majority of" in the twelfth line. Adopted.

Canon 1, Title B., section 1, was amended by striking out "from any cause" in line one, and in the same section, line six, by inserting after the word "writing," these words, "to the Bishop," and in line eight the remainder of the sentence after the word "Church" was stricken out.

On motion the vote by which Canon 11 was adopted was reconsidered and an amendment was then offered, striking out the words "and organized Mission" in the third and fourth line of the first paragraph. This was adopted.

W. S. Laidley moved to strike out the words "it shall not be competent for the congregational meeting to transact any other business than the election of the vestry and." The amendment was adopted.

The Printing Committee to be appointed was authorized to transpose the sentence following the words stricken out, to the end of paragraph one.

The order of the day arrived and Mr. Alvord addressed the Council upon the subject of his work.

Consideration of Canon 1, Title B., was then resumed.

Section 3 was amended by striking out the words "when present" in line eight and by substituting the word "vestry" for "Committee" and "Vestryman" for "Committeeman" wherever they occur in the Canon.

Section 7 was amended by substituting "such" for "each" in line one.

Canon II, Section 1, was amended by substituting the word

"Presbyters" for "Ministers" in line three, and after the word Bishop in the fourth line inserting the words "Bishop Coadjutor."

Section 2, by striking out all after the word Parishes.

Section 6 was omitted and the Committee authorized to make two Canons, one on Missions, and the other on Education, from the contents of this amended Canon.

Canon III was amended by substituting "shall" for "may" in line one, striking out "at his discretion" after the word Bishop, and omitting the three last lines.

The Rev. Mr. Gibson moved that when we adjourn it be to meet at 9:30 a. m. tomorrow, and continue in session until the work of the Council is completed. Carried.

The Rev. G. W. Easter presented the following report on Education:

The Committee on Religious and Theological Education respectfully call the attention of the Clergy and Laity of the Diocese to these facts. 1st. That a yearly contribution to the fund for Religious and Theological Education is required by Canon 8 of every parish and congregation in the Diocese.

2nd. That of the 107 congregations or points in the Diocese at which services are maintained more or less frequently, only 22 have complied with the Canon and that by these only $183.04 have been contributed during the past year.

3rd. That the needs of the Diocese imperatively require larger contributions to this fund, if the Diocese would not continue to be so largely obliged to the Education Society of Virginia for two thirds or more of the money needed to assist candidates for orders in preparing for the work of the ministry.

Resolved. That the Council urges upon the Parishes and Congregations of the Diocese faithful and prompt compliance with the requirement of the Canon.

GEO. W. EASTER.
J. HOWARD GIBBONS.
ARTHUR M. LEWIS.

Mr. R. M. Browne, for the Committee on Finance, presented this report.

REPORT OF THE FINANCE COMMITTEE.

We have examined and audited the report of the Treasurer of the Diocese, the Trustee of the Episcopal and Contingent fund and the Trustees of the Permanent Fund, and find them correct, certified to, and with proper vouchers.

The Treasurers Balances May 15th are as follows:

Diocesan Missions		$ 1071 21
Widows and Orphans		7438 84
Religious and Theo. Education		72 06
Episcopal and Contingent Fund, June 1st		104 74
Permanent Fund May 15th, 1905		
Securities	$ 34,580 50	
Cash	1,450 82	
Total		$ 36,031 32

We recommend the payment of $10.00 to the Sexton of Christ Church Clarksburg, W. Va.

DR. G. A. ASCHMAN, *Chairman.*
BRUCE HALL.
BARNABAS BRYAN.
R. M. BROWNE.
W. S. LAIDLEY.

The recommendation was adopted.

The Council was invited to a trolley ride, which invitation was accepted for 3 o'clock tomorrow, if the work of the Council would permit.

On motion the Council adjourned.

SATURDAY, JUNE 3, 1905.

Bishop Gravatt called the Council to order.

Prayers were read by the Rev. J. T. Marley.

The minutes of the previous day were read and approved.

The Rev. W. P. Chrisman made this report:

REPORT OF COMMITTEE ON SUNDAY SCHOOLS.

SCHOOLS IN THE DIOCESE.

Last Reported	58	
Present Number	57	
Total loss		

TEACHERS.

Last Reported	373	
Present Number	416	
Total gain		43

SCHOLARS.

Last Reported	3078	
Present Number	3087	
Total gain		

OFFERINGS.

For Diocesan Missions last year (from 31 schools)	$ 453 47	
For Diocesan Missions this year (from 35 schools)	465 49	
Total Increase		$ 12 02
Lenten Offering last year (from 41 schools)	929 30	
Lenten Offering this year (from 45 schools)	943 38	
Total increase		14 08
Other Offerings last year	1176 88	
Other Offerings this year	1520 79	
Total increase		343 91
GRAND TOTAL OF MONEY RAISED BY THE S. S. FOR ALL PURPOSES		2887 16

W. P. CHRISMAN.
CHAS. E. SHAW.
G. A. ASCHMAN.
GEO. P. ROGERS.

The Rev. A. G. Grinnan made a verbal report as Chairman of the Committee on Episcopal and Permanent Fund, and called attention to the arrearages to this fund.

The Rev. J. F. Plummer moved that the Trustee of the Episcopal Fund be requested to make a supplemental report of monies received to the end of this Council. Carried.

The Rev. J. S. Douglas presented the following report:

The Committee on the State of the Church beg leave to report the following:

There does not seem to have been a time in the history of the Diocese when the church was in more encouraging and promising condition than she is now.

There seems to be a steady movement forward in every branch of her activity. She has been growing steadily since her organization twenty-seven years ago, and today her roots have firmer hold in the soil of parochial life, and her branches are reaching out further into the Missionary field than ever before, and a prominent feature of this growth is the healthiness of it, which is its own evidence of its being watered with the dews of divine blessing.

The financial reports will show a marked increase of money given (not only for current expenses and other parochial work—which in themselves might only signify an increased selfishness—but for aggressive work in the Diocesan Missionary field and in that yet wider field which is the world.)

There is always a difficulty in taking the spiritual measure of a Church, as of an individual but both can be known as far as man may know, by their fruits, and in these the Church has been abundant. Her hospitals are active in doing the Master's work of relieving the physical ailments of those intrusted to them, and also ministering to their moral and spiritual needs; her children in the Sunday Schools are receiving such thought and attention as they have never received before, and as ways and means are being prayerfully devised for their better instruction and more efficient usefulness, they are responding in a most encouraging way by letting their light shine in abundant measure through their good works. The laborers in the harvest are receiving more souls for their hire, as we see by the increased number of those confirmed by the Bishops during the past year. The Woman's and Junior Auxiliaries are doing invaluable service, and add to this the desire and evident determination of the Church in this Diocese to stand alone in carrying on its missionary work—that the help heretofore received from the Board might go to extend the Kingdom elsewhere, give, we think good proof of a healthy *spiritual* state of the Church.

The Committee deem it within their province to note one of the causes of these encouraging conditions. It is the wide and energetic leadership, under God, of our beloved Bishops. They are not merely sending but they are going. They are clearing the way and the Clergy are feeling—as they cannot but feel—the inspiration of such leadership, and they in their turn are trying to pass on this inspiration to the people committed to their charge.

And so we all, Bishops, Clergy and Laity as we dwell with thankfulness upon the blessings wherewith God has blessed us, and the measure of prosperity He has meted out to us, are not unmindful of the great work yet to be done for the Master and we covet a double portion of His spirit that in the years to come we may do greater works than these.

Respectfully Submitted,

JOHN S. DOUGLAS.
ARTHUR M. LEWIS.
RICHARD HENDERSON.
G. A. NORTHCOTT.

The Canons relating to Discipline were then taken up, and Canon 1 was amended as follows:

In section 2, insert "the Bishop shall immediately convene the Ecclesiastical Court" after the word "possession" in the fifth line.

Section 3 was stricken out.

In section 6, tenth line, after the word "trial," insert the words "or an appeal."

In section 10, after the word "Diocese' strike out the remainder of the paragraph.

In section 12 after the word "trial" insert these words, "excepting such as are incurred by the defendant in case he is adjudged guilty."

The Canon on Standing Committee on Constitution and Canons, was amended by striking out the words "five persons" and inserting the words "three presbyters and two laymen," and by striking out the last three lines after the word "Committee."

The Canon on Due Proclamation of Canons was amended by striking out the words "parochial" and "of their cures" and changing the word "the" to "their."

On motion the Committee on Constitution and Canons was instructed to conform the language of the Canons of the General Convention printed among the Canons of the Diocese of West Virginia, to that of the same Canons in the new Canons of the General Convention.

The following resolution was adopted:

Resolved, that the Chairman of the Committee on Constitution and Canons and the Secretary of the Diocese be and are hereby authorized to arrange in order, punctuate, re-index, and otherwise edit and print 1,000 copies of the new constitution and canons of the Diocese as amended and adopted by this Council, 750 copies to be bound in paper, and 250 copies at their discretion to be bound in cloth for the use of the Council.

Resolved, that the Rules of Order adopted by this Council be printed and bound with the Constitution and Canons.

Mr. C. P. Flick offered this resolution, which was adopted:

Resolved, that the Treasurers and Trustees of the several funds of this Diocese be, and they are hereby instructed to close their accounts on the 10th day of May of each year and include in their annual reports for the year ending with the preceding 30th day of April all sums of money received within the first ten days of May and carry over to their reports for the ensuing year all sums subsequently received within that year.

The Rev. A. G. Grinnan moved that the Secretary be requested to print the names of the treasurers of the various funds of the Diocese on the second page of the cover of the Journal. Carried.

The Rev. D. W. Howard of the Special Committee on a portion of the Bishop's address presented this report, and the recommendation was adopted:

In recognition of the importance of that portion of the Bishop's address referring to the relation of the Diocese to the General Board and the desirability of relieving that Board of the assistance now given; your Committee makes the following recommendation to this Council.

Resolved, that after the 1st day of September, 1905, the diocese of West Virginia will relieve the Board of Missions of the appropriations heretofore made, consisting of $800 from General Board and $650 from the Am. C. M. T. and that from that time the Diocese shall support its own missionary labors.

DAVID W. HOWARD.
GEO. W. EASTER.
JNO. S. ALFRIEND.
CAMERON L. THOMPSON.
V. A. WEVER.

The following resolution was adopted:

Resolved, that the President of the Standing Committee be and is hereby requested to prepare for printing in the Journal, a page to the memory of the late Rev. C. C. Pearson, so long a faithful and honored member of this Diocese.

The Rev. Mr. Curran offered this, which was adopted:

Resolved, that the Assessment Committee report to the Council each year on the second day of its assembling, the amount of assessment on the several parishes and missions.

The Rev. D. W. Howard offered this:

Resolved that all assessments for the ensuing year, shall be the same as provided for 1904-1905, except Bluefield, Huntington, Kenova, Union, and Williamstown. Adopted.

This resolution was adopted:

Resolved, that the Council desires to express its high appreciation of the services of its Secretary.

The Rev. Dr. Moore presented this report:

The Committee on the Admission of New Parishes has had no matter committed to it.

The Parochial Reports Committee made the following report:

Baptisms, Infants	304
Baptisms, Adults	103
Total	407

Confirmations		308
Marriages		180
Burials		247
Communicants last reported		4,543
Present number		5,124
Baptized Persons		7,987
Families and parts		3,553
Whole Number of Individuals		10,230
Total No. Teachers and Scholars in Sunday Schools		3,503
Total Current Expenses	$	52,645 95

CONTRIBUTIONS.

Parochial	$	29,093 42
Diocesan		12,400 52
Total Outside the Diocese		5,743 80
Cash on Hand		3,383 19
Owing to errors in tabulation the aggregate of sums contributed in the Diocese will not be correctly ascertained, but should be approximately	$	87,000 00
Public Services Sundays		3,714
Public Services other days		2,360
Sittings in Church and Chapels		15,250
Industrial or Parish School Teachers		8
Industrial or Parish Scholars		134
Brotherhoods of St. Andrew		4
Woman's Auxiliary		405
Churches and Chapels		80
Rectories		42
Parish Houses		15
Sunday School Rooms		10
Debt on Property	$	46,411 19
Due Ministers		265 70
Due Diocesan Missions		57 00
Due Bishop's Fund		118 42
	$	46,852 31
Catechizings		472
Holy Com. Public		861
Scattered Communicants not otherwise reported less Communicants of St. Andrew's on the Mountain		162

Respectfully submitted by your Committee on Parochial reports, this first day of June, 1905.

JAMES L. FISH.
FRANCIS MOORE.
H. L. ALEXANDER.
BYRAN GORDON.
Committee.

The Rev. Mr. Gibson moved that 600 copies of the Journal be printed. Carried.

On motion, after reading the minutes, and suitable devotions, conducted by the Bishop, the Council adjourned *sine die*.

GEORGE W. PETERKIN,
President.

ROBERT DOUGLAS ROLLER,
Secretary.

MEMORIAL PAGE.

By order of the Council, this page is dedicated to the memory of our lamented brother, the

REV. C. C. PEARSON,

BORN AUG. 13TH, 1827; DIED SEPT. 16TH, 1904.

He served various places in the Diocese, was widely known and universally admired and respected. He was acknowledged one of our best preachers, and in the faithful presentation of the Gospel he did good service for the Master in every post which he occupied. Without personal pretence or affectation, he was genial in disposition and sincere in his friendships.

With a simple faith and unswerving loyalty he served his Master and helped his fellow men, and the Church in West Virginia cherishes and honors his memory.

APPENDIX A.

I. *Report of the Treasurer of the Diocese.*

II. *Report of the Trustees of the Episcopal and Contingent Fund.*

III. *Report of the Trustees of the Permanent Fund.*

TREASURER'S REPORT.

Diocese of West Virginia Council at Clarksburg, May 31, 1905.

The year for Diocesan Missions runs from May 1, 1904, to April 30, 1905.
The amount paid to each fund will be credited to the Parish or Mission every month.

PARISH OR MISSION.	Assessment for Dio. Miss. Apportionment for Gen. Miss.	Paid for Dio. Miss.	Religious and Theo. Education.	Widows and Orphans and Disabl'd Clergy.
Alderson	$ 6.00	$ 4.58	$	$
Ansted	20.00	16.57		
Bayard				
Beury	5.00			
Beckley	6.00	3.00		
Berkeley Springs	25.00	85.00		5.00
Belington				
Bluefield	80.00	80.00		
Blue Ridge, Christ Church				
" " St. Andrew's				
Bramwell	30.00			
Boone Co., St. John's				
Brooke Co., St. John's	5.00	5.00		
Brookside		1.00		
Bruce Chapel	12.00			
Buckhannon	10.00	15.20		2.22
Bunker Hill	5.00	1.58		
Cairo		2.50		
Charles Town, Zion	300.00	348.94	36.79	106.94
" " St. Philip's	10.00	10.00		
" " St. Andrew's	3.00			
Charleston, St. John's	200.00	200.00		
" St. Luke's	8.00	4.89		
" St. Mathew's	8.00	5.00		
Carbon		2.05		
Centralia		5.00		
Chester	10.00		4.50	
Clarksburg, Christ Church	125.00	123.05	10.71	17.60
" St. Thomas				
Clover Lick		8.80		
Cresap's	5.00	7.81		
Davis	8.00	4.75		
Dubree	5.00	2.00		
Duffield				
Eckels				
Elkins	10.00	11.90	5.00	
Fairmont	75.00	102.63		
Fort Spring	5.00			
Glen Jean	10.00	8.00		
Grafton	15.00	16.28		
Harper's Ferry	20.00	40.00	3.00	5.00
Hartford		2.00		
Hedgesville	25.00	25.00		
Hillsboro		2.00		
Hinton	30.00	30.00		
Huntington	80.00	80.00	6.50	42.50
Kenova	7.00	2.00		
Keyser				
Lewisburg	7.00	3.30		
Little Otter		2.50		
Liverpool	3.00			
Madison	5.00			
Mannington	10.00	10.00		
Martinsburg	75.00	170.51	34.77	30.00
McDowell: Eckman	20.00	22.12		
McDowell: Welch				

PARISH OR MISSION.	Assessment for Diocesan Missions. Apportionm't for General Missions.	Paid for Diocesan Missions.	Religious and Theological Education.	Widows and Orphans and Disabled Clergy.
Mason County (Beale)	$	$ 15.00	$	$
Mt. Carbon	5.00	5.00		2.00
Montgomery	15.00	16.75		6.00
Moorefield	20.00	20.00		2.00
Morgantown	50.00	26.19		6.85
Moundsville	40.00	47.25	3.50	6.65
Nelson Parish: { Middleway, Leetown, Summit Point }	75.00	75.20	1.96	13.59
New Cumberland		6.00		
New Martinsville	40.00	40.00	4.98	
Newport, Wood Co.		8.82		
Nuttall	5.00	12.00		1.00
Okonoko	10.00	10.00		
Parsons				
Parksburg, Trinity	350.00	350.00		80.30
" Good Shepherd	20.00	117.92	8.00	20.00
" St. Stephen'	3.00			
Paw Paw		3.00	2.00	2.00
Pennsboro				
Pt. Pleasant	50.00	55.90		7.68
Powellton	20.00	20.00		4.69
Princeton	6.00			
Pratt				
Ravenswood	10.00	14.00		.67
Ripley	15.00	15.00	.52	
*Ripon	10.00	5.00		10.00
Romney, (St. Stephen's—Epiphany)	16.00	17.00	2.00	2.00
Ronceverte	8.00	13.18	3.60	2.82
Shepherdstown	75.00	75.00	4.58	2.93
Smithfield	5.00			
Sistersville	40.00	41.38	3.42	12.45
Spilman	10.00	11.00		
Spruce	4.00	1.83		
St. Mary's	15.00	15.00		
St. Albans	10.00	14.50	60.	.40
Sutton	10.00			2.18
Tavernersville	10.00	20.00		
Union	50.00	50.00	9.11	8.74
Waverly	10.00	4.00		
Wellsburg	25.00	30.65		
Weston St. Paul's	75.00	75.97	5.90	13.74
" St. Paul's Chapel		2.36		2.18
Wheeling, St. Matthew's	425.00	456.19	15.00	310.00
" St. Luke's	175.00	175.00	16.70	49.89
" St. Andrew's	15.00	15.28		5.77
" St. Paul's	5.00	15.00		
White Sulphur	10.00			
Willow Island	5.00	5.00		
Williamstown	25.00	17.95		
Williamson		2.30		
Winfield				
Miscellaneous—Holden		3.00		
Ferris ... A Friend		5.00		1,000.00
Woman's Mite ... Int. and Earnings		441.85		350.42
Total	$3000.00			
Total Income		$3,735.88	$183.04	$2,133.19
Balance last year		1,127.97	14.02	5,898.15
		$4,863.85	$197.06	$8,031.34
Total Payments		3,792.64	125.00	592.50
Balance on hand May 15, 1905		$1,071.21	$72.06	$7,438.84

*Ripon—$5.00 on last year's assessment.

Payments, Diocesan Missions.

Miss Elizabeth P. Barber	$ 120 00
Rev. E. H. Brosius	150 00
Rev. Guy H. Crook	200 00
Rev. G. W. Easter	100 00
Rev. J. L. Fish	75 00
Rev. G. A. Gibbons	250 00
Rev. J. H. Gibbons	50 00
Rev. John S. Gibson	50 00
Rev. A. G. Grinnan	50 00
Rev. E. D. Irvine	240 00
Rev. F. A. Meade	350 00
Rev. W. H. Meyers	125 00
Rev. O. B. Mitchell	200 00
Rev. C. H. Malony	450 00
Rev. F. H. Moore	200 00
Rev. C. C. Pearson	50 00
Rev. H. H. Phelps	33 33
Rev. G. C. Shaw	411 66
Rev. P. B. Stauffer	350 00
Rev. John Warnock	120 00
Rev. A. J. Willis	50 00
Rev. W. J. Williams	25 00
Rev. R. R. Windley	75 00
Rev. O. M. Yeager	25 00
Printing Treasurer's Report 1903 and 1904	7 00
Mission Boxes	35 65
Total	$ 3,792 64

Payments, Religious and Theological Education.

P. P. Phillips, Treas	$ 125 00

Payments, Widows and Orphans and Disabled Clergy Fund.

Rev. C. M. Campbell	$ 150 00
Mrs. W. T. Leavell	75 00
Mrs. Kate W. Lea	150 00
Mrs. R. H. Mason	75 00
Mrs. C. C. Pearson	62 50
Dr. C. W. Walker	80 00
Total Payment	$ 592 50

Recapitulation—Ledger Balances.

Widows, Orphans and Disabled Clergy Fund	$ 7,438 84

Diocesan Missions		1.071 21
Religious and Theological Education		72 06
Total to be accounted for		$ 8,582 11
Balance in Nat. Ex. Bank of Wheeling	$1,097 88	
Notes and Securities in hands of Treas............	2,484 23	
Bonds in hands of Treas	5,000 00—	$ 8,582 11

Respectfully Submitted,
LAWRENCE E. SANDS, Treas.

May 15, 1905.

REPORT OF TRUSTEE OF EPISCOPAL AND CONTINGENT FUNDS.

Beginning June 1st, 1904, and Ending May 31st, 1905.

NAME OF PARISH.	Amount Assessed.	Amount Received.	Amount Paid on Arrears.	Amount Received but not Assessed.
Alderson	$ 6 00	$	$	$
Berkeley Springs	30 00	20 00		
Bluefield	80 00	80 00		
Princeton	6 00			
Bramwell	30 00	30 00		
Eckman and McDowell	20 00	16 84		
Brooke County, St. John's	5 00			
Buckhannon	10 00	10 00		
Bunker Hill	5 00			
Charleston, St. John's	275 00	275 00		
Charleston, St. Luke's	7 00			
Charleston, St. Matthew's	7 00			
Charles Town, Zion	425 00	425 00		
Charles Town, St. Phillip's	5 00			
St. Andrew's on the Mountain	2 00			
Clarksburg	125 00	10 08		
Cresaps	5 00			
Davis	8 00	8 00		
Elkins Mission	10 00	10 00		
Fairmont	100 00	100 00		
Grafton	15 00	15 00	15 00	
Harpers Ferry	20 00	20 00		
Hedgesville	50 00	50 00	50 00	
Hinton	20 00			
Huntington	100 00	100 00		
Kenova	7 00	7 00		
Lewisburg	10 00	10 00		
Ronceverte	8 00	10 00		
Martinsburg	100 00	100 00		
Nelson Parish { Middleway, Lee Town, Summit Point	90 00	90 00		
Mannington	10 00	5 00		
Moorefield	20 00	20 00		
Romney	16 00	16 00		
Okonoko	10 00	10 00		
Morgantown	50 00			
Moundsville	60 00	60 00		
Nuttallburg	10 00	5 00		
Parkersburg, Trinity	525 00	500 00		
Parkersburg, Good Shepherd	5 00	20 00		
Parkersburg, St. Stephens	2 00			
Tavennersville	8 00	8 00	15 00	
Point Pleasant, Christ	50 00	50 00		
Bruce Chapel	12 00	12 00		
Spillman Mission	10 00	10 00		
Powellton	20 00	23 00		
Ansted	20 00	20 00		
Ravenswood, Grace	10 00	10 00		
Ripley, St. John's	15 00	15 00		
Liverpool, Whittle	2 00			
Ripon	20 00	20 00	20 00	
Sheperdstown	75 00	68 75	6 50	
New Martinsville	40 00	40 00		
Sistersville	40 00	40 00		
Smithfield, Wetzel County	5 00			
Spruce Chapel	4 00	4 00		
St. Albans	10 00	10 00		
Montgomery	15 00	15 00		
St. Mary's	15 00	5 00		
Sutton	10 00			
Union	50 00	46 25		
White Sulphur	10 00			
Fort Spring	5 00	5 00		
Waverly	5 00	2 50		
Wellsburg	25 00	25 00		

REPORT OF TRUSTEE OF EPISCOPAL AND CONTINGENT FUNDS.—Continued.

Beginning June 1st, 1904, and Ending May 31st, 1905.

NAME OF PARISH.	Amount Assessed.	Amount Received.	Amount Paid on Arrears.	Amount Received but not Assessed.
Weston	$ 80 00	$ 80 00	$	$
Wheeling, St. Matthew's	600 00	600 00		
Wheeling, St. Luke's	175 00	175 00		
Wheeling, St. Andrew's	10 00	10 00		
Chester	4 00			
Williamson	5 00			
Wheeling, St. Paul's, Elm Grove	10 00			
Williamstown	15 00			
Willow Island	5 00	5 00	5 00	
Beckley	6 00	3 00		
Beury	5 00			
Du Bree	5 00			
Glen Jean	10 00	8 00		
Immanuel, Mt. Carbon	5 00	5 00		
Clover Lick				20 00
Academy				2 00
Hartford				2 00
New Cumberland				6 00
Cairo				2 50
C. W. Watson, Fairmont				100 00
TOTALS	$ 3665 00	$ 3283 42	$ 111.50	$ 132.50

RECEIPTS.

Amount received on this year's assessment ....$	3,283.42
Amount received on Arrears	111.50
Amount received from Missions not assessed	32.50
Amount received from Mr. C. W. Watson, Fairmont	100.00
Amount received Interest from Permanent Fund	1,386.94
Total ....$	4,914.36

DISBURSEMENTS.

Paid Rt. Rev. G. W. Peterkin ....$	2,000.00
Paid Bishop Coadjutor W. L. Gravatt	2,500.00
Paid R. D. Roller, Secy, (Salary and postage)	109.05
Paid Tribune Company (printing journal)	284.07
Paid Standing Committee and Examining Chaplains........	37.29
Paid General Convention Capitation, $32.00 Expense $2.03...	134.03
Paid Sexton at Martinsburg	10.00
Printing report	2.00
Paid rent Episcopal residence, Charles Town	300.00
Total ....$	5,376.44

RECAPITULATION.

Balance June 1st. 1904		$ 566.82
Total receipts from every source		4,914.36
		$ 5,481.18
Bishop's Salaries, ... $	4,500.00	
Contingent Expenses	876.44	5,376.44
Balance on hand June 1st, 1905		$ 104.74

Respectfully submitted

R. M. BROWNE,

Trustee.

MONEY RECEIVED DURING COUNCIL AT CLARKSBURG.

SUPPLEMENTARY REPORT.

Trinity, Parkersburg, ...	$ 25 00
Christ Memorial, Williamstown, ...	5 00
St. Luke's, Charleston, ...	8 00
Christ Church, Clarksburg, ...	114 92
Grace, St. Marys	15 00
Union, Monroe Co.	2 61
Sutton	10 00
	$ 180 53

REPORT OF THE TRUSTEES OF THE PERMANENT FUND OF THE DIOCESE OF WEST VIRGINIA FOR THE PERIOD FROM MAY 18, 1904, TO MAY 15, 1905.

Central Banking and Security Company, Parkersburg, W. Va., Treasurer.

By order of Council, the Central Banking & Security Company of Parkersburg was named as treasurer of this Fund. The accounts below include transactions had by the trustees, as well as those occurring with the Treasurer.

The statements below show in the hands of the Treasurer on May 15, 1905, the following:

1. Listed as Investments, pledges, etc.	$ 34,580.50
2. Cash	1,450.82
	36,031.32
The Trustees hold pledges in Parkersburg list..........	187.50
	$ 36,218.82

Totals reported in 1904:

1.	Investments, pledges, etc.	$33,618.00	
2.	Cash on hand	1,913.56	
3.	Parkersburg Pledges	250.00	
4.	Due from Interest Ac	138.06	35,919.62
	Increase since May 18, 1904		$ 299.20

DETAILED STATEMENT OF RECEIPTS AND DISBURSEMENTS.

RECEIPTS.

1904.	Interest	
May 18 Bal. cash reported		$ 1,913.56
June 7 Alderson $5. Moundsville 5.15		
H. Ferry 4.25 St. Albans .35		
Sistersville 6.14 Weston 6.37		
Union 1.55 Bramwell 19.50		48.40
Interest Kreps loan	90.00	
July 25 Interest Perkins loan	75.00	
July 27 Bramwell $20 Eckman $10		
Welch 5. (Rev. R. N. Meade............		35.00
Clarksburg 1.40 St. Matthews 10...........		11.40
Int. Coupon Traders Co.	15.00	
Aug. 6 Int. Ogdin 60. Laird 90	150.00	
Aug. 29 Good Shepherd 2. Trinity 4.26		6.26
Sept. 24 Elm Grove 4.66 (Oct 14) Int. Cit. B. A. 60	60.00	4.66
Oct. 14 Int. Gordon 120. Bethel Par. 5.25	125.25	
E. Ruthledge 5. Rev. G. W. Easter 3.42.....		8.42
Nov. 23 Good Shepherd 3.00		3.00
Dec. 3 Int. Kreps $80 (Dec. 23) same $10..........	90.00	
Dec. 23 J. S. Bragonier 1.00		1.00
1905.		
Jan. 5 Payment on $ 2000 note H. H. Pennybacker .		1,000.00
Interest on same	41.83	
Jan. 21 St. Stephens Romney 1.70 Certificates $43..		44.70
Feb. 1 C. C. Martin on subscription (Parkersburg)..		62.50
Int. Perkins 75. Gould 360	435.00	
Certificates 33. Int. Ogdin 60	60.00	33.00
Feb. 10 Int. Wolfe	152.25	
Feb. 7 Certifs. 4. (13) cert. $6 (14) 7...........		
Feb. 18 Certifs. 14. (24) cert. $6		37.00
Feb. 24 Note A. H. Kreps paid $3,000.............		3,000.00
Interest $40	40.00	
Mar. 3 Certif. 5 (Mar. 20) certificate 2		7.00
Mar. 30 Legacy Miss N. W. McCandlish		150.00

Apr.	3 Int. coupons. Pyth Castle	30.00	
Apr.	5 Citizens B. A.	60.00	
Apr.	10. Certificates 15.50 Gordon int. 120	120.00	15.50
Apr.	28 St. Mary's account note		210.00
Apr.	29 Rev. G. W. Easter		4.13
May	2 Bal. St Mary's note 83. int. 18.25	18.25	83.00
May	4 St. Davids 12.83. St. Johns 5.00		17.83
May	9 Rev. A. M. Lewis 5.00 Good Shepherd 5.00		10.00
May	13 P. C. Eastham, Int. 3. Moundsville 3.70	3.00	3.70
	Sundry certificates		11.00
	Huntington, Rev. J. S. Gibson 2.00		2.00
		1,565.58	6,723.06
			1,565.58
	Total		$8,288.64

DISBURSEMENTS..

1904.		
June	7 Paid Mrs. A. B. Campbell for note $1400 and int. of H. E. Morris, et al	$ 1,421.00
July	9 Parkersburg Sentinel Report	13.50
Aug.	8 Refund and protest coupon Traders Co.	16.38
Sept.	19 R. M. Browne, Treasurer, Ac. Bps. Salaries	86.94
Sept.	22 R. M. Browne, Treasurer Ac. Bps. Salaries	500.00
Dec.	14 R. M. Browne, Treasurer, Ac. Bps. Salaries	300.00
1905.		
Feb.	14 R. M. Browne, Treasurer, Ac. Bps. Salaries	500.00
Feb.	25 Loaned W. H. Ogdin on notes	1,000.00
Mar.	23 Loaned M. A. Summers	3,000.00
		6,837.82
	Balance of cash on hand	1,450.82
		$ 8.288.64

INTEREST ACCOUNT.

Total amount credited above		$ 1,565.58
Less protested coupon Traders Co. and protest		16.38
		1,549.20
Paid Bishops Salaries	$ 1,386.94	
Paid Sentinel printing report	13.50	
Restored to Investment Account amt. advanced 1904	138.06	
Bal.	10.70	1,549.20

INVESTMENTS, ETC.

List of securities, bonds, notes pledges and contributions, and certificates given or owed to the Fund—by Items.

Notes:—

H. S. Sands, contribution	100.00	
Jos. Ruffner, contribution	100.00	
J. D. Jeffries, contribution	25.00	
Thos. Jeffries contribution	10.00	
W. G. Hubbard contribution	25.00	
Samuel R. Holbert contribution	25.00	
Lucius Hoge contribution	100.00	
Fred L. Hall contribution	50.00	
Mrs. W. H. Hogeman contribution	25.00	
C. D. Emmons contribution	50.00	
P. C. Eastham contribution	50.00	
T. J. Danner contribution	25.00	
Harriet Camp Lounsberry, contribution	10.00	
J. T. Cotten, contribution	200.00	
Christ's Church, Bethel Parish Clarksburg	800.00	
D. M. Bailey, contribution	15.00	
W. P. Wilson, contribution	100.00	
Rebecca & Edith M. Watson, contribution	25.00	
C. L. Thompson, contribution	50.00	
F. B. Enslow contribution	100.00	
Robt. L. Bland, contribution	10.00	
Fannie P. Brady, contribution	100.00	
Simms Powell, contribution	25.00	
Jos. B. Neal, contribution	100.00	
Jas. A. Wetherell, contribution	25.00	
Lawrence E. Sands, contribution	150.00	
		$2,295.00

Pledges—

L. T. Peck	$ 15.00	
L. Merrill	10.00	
R. McEldowney	15.00	
Frank Beckwith	10.00	
R. P. Chew	10.00	
		$ 60.00

Certificates—

No. 276 Citizens Building Association, Parkersburg	$ 2,000.00	
Sundry certificates with coupons attached	325.50	
		$ 2,325.50

Loans—		
W. H. Wolfe, et al	$ 5,000.00	
Jennie L. Laird, et al	3,000.00	
S. L. Gould	6,000.00	
H. H. Pennybacker	1,000.00	
Harry D. Perkins	2,500.00	
N. A. Ogdin	2,000.00	
Hortense & L. E. Morris	1,400.00	
Clifford B. Gordon	4,000.00	
W. H. Ogdin	1,000.00	
M. A. Summers	3,000.00	
		$ 28,900.00
Total amount carried forward		$ 33,580.50
Bonds—		
Bond No. 26 Traders Co., Clarksburg	$ 500.00	
Bond No. 8 Pythian Castle Asso., Wheeling	500.00	
		$ 1,000.00
Total in hands of Central Banking & Security Co.		$ 34,580.50
Balances on subscriptions Parkersburg list in hands of Trustees		
C. C. Martin $62.50 G. L. Watson $125		187.50
		$ 34,768.00

CERTIFICATE.

The Central Banking & Security Company certifies that it had on hand at the close of business on the 15th day of May, 1905, bonds, notes, pledges, and items of credit belonging to the Trustees of the Permanent Fund of the Protestant Episcopal Church for the Diocese of West Virginia ...... $ 34,580.50
and cash to credit of Chairman of Trustees 1,450.82

$ 36,031.32

(Signed) CENTRAL BANKING & SECURITY CO.,
By W. H. OGDIN, Assistant Secretary.

The Trustees again request that all remittances for this fund be made to Central Banking & Security Co., Parkersburg, W. Va.

May 15, 1905.

APPENDIX B.

Parochial Reports for the year ending April 30, 1905. Arranged according to alphabetical Clergy list.

PAROCHIAL REPORTS

For the Year Ending April 30th, 1905.

PAROCHIAL REPORT.

Rev. JNO. S. ALFRIEND, address, Charles Town. Zion Church, St. Andrew's Parish, Jefferson county; date of organization, 1819; present minister took charge March 1, 1902.

Church Officers—Church Wardens, B. C. Washington, Frank Beckwith; other Vestrymen, S. W. Washington, Geo. Eyster, Wm. Packett, Jos. Trapnell, Claiborne Green, Richd. Henderson, Scott Kennedy, Rich. Alexander, Thornton Perry, A. Byrne Hurst; Registrar, S. W. Washington, address Charles Town, Treasurer, S. W. Washington, address Charles Town; Supt. of Sunday Schools, B. C. Washington, Charles Town; Sunday School Secretary and Treasurer, Miss Mary Campbell; Lay Reader, Jos. Trapnell.

Official Acts—Baptisms, infants 9, adults 4, total 13; presented for confirmation since last report 12, marriages 8, burials 12, catechising 20, public services, Sundays 120, other days 150, total 170; Holy Communion, public, 30, private 2, total 32.

Communicants—Number last reported 333, admitted by confirmation 12, added otherwise 3, total gain 15; died 4, total loss 4; net gain 11; present number total 344.

Congregations—Baptized persons connected within Parish 500, confirmed persons connected with Parish 375, families 175, whole number of individuals 700, number of sittings in church 600, number free sittings 100, number sittings in Sunday school room, 150.

Rector's Salary—As pledged from this congregation $1,250.00; total $1,250.00.

Organizations—Sunday Schools, officers and teachers, male 4, female 10, total 14; Pupils, males 36, females 54, total 90; advent offering $34.73, Lenten offering $44.82, other offerings, $44.95, total Sunday School offering $124.50. Brotherhood of St. Andrew, members 10. Woman's Auxiliary, members 70. *Other Organizations*—Library Association 10; Babies Branch Aux. 20; St. Andrew's Guild 30; Mexican Guild 10; Chancel Chapter 10; Junior Auxiliary 10.

Property—Church, brick, insurance $9,000.00, value $13,000; rectory, brick, insurance $2,475.00, value $5,000; Parish house, brick, insurance $1,600.00; value $3,000. *Indebtedness*—On church, chapel, rectory and Parish house $800.00, total indebtedness $800.00.

FINANCIAL REPORT.

Receipts—For all purposes—Cash on hand, per last report $286.98, pew rent $2,132.67, collections in church $1,689.62; money borrowed $768.35, thank offerings $198.00, Sunday School $124.50, Woman's Auxiliary, money $172.00, Woman's Auxiliary boxes, value $78.48, Guilds, or other socities $693.09, income from other sources $210.83, total receipts for all purposes $6,354.52.

Disbursements—(1) *For current expenses*—Salary of rector $1,250.00, other salaries $420.00, ordinary repairs $136.50, interest on debts $21.93, other current expenses $245.83, other objects $5.36; total for current expenses $2,079.62. *Contributions*—(1) *For objects in the Parish*—Communion Alms $92.73; extraordinary repairs and improvements $1,160.86; Parish missions $130.95; maintaining Sunday Schools $48.81; payment on debts for building, &c. $200.00; other objects $374.40; total contributions for objects in the Parish $2,007.75. (2) *For objects in the Diocese*—Salary of Bishops $425.00; Diocesan missions $348.94; convocation missions $117.50; widows and orphans, aged and disabled clergy fund $43.29; religious and theological education $36.79; Sheltering Arms Hospital $51.98; Bishop's special fund $163.50; other objects $354.35; total contributions for objects in the Diocese $1,541.35. (3) *For objects without the Diocese*—Domestic missions general $97.16; Jews $12.72; total domestic missions $109.88; foreign missions general $161.17; for China $40.00; for Mexico $60.00; Brazil $88.00; total foreign missions $349.17; specials, boxes, &c. $78.48; general clergy relief fund $15.11; total contributions for objects without the Diocese $552.64.

Statement—Current expenses raised by congregation as above $2,079.62. *Contributions*—For objects in the Parish, $2,007.75, for objects in the Diocese $1,541.35; for objects without the Diocese $552.64; total contributions $4,101.74; all money raised by the congregation for current expenses and for contributions $6,181.36; cash in hand $54.60.

Remarks—Pew rents pay all current expenses. All Sundays in the year devoted to objects outside of current expenses. St. Andrew's Mission on the Mountain now under the Diocese with Bishop Gravatt in charge. St. Philip's Col'd. Mission is in much better shape and separate report is made by minister in charge. Harewood Mission is under charge of Rector and separate report is made by him.—JNO. S. ALFRIEND, *Rector*.

PAROCHIAL REPORT.

Rev. JNO. S. ALFRIEND, address, Charles Town. St. Andrews Mission, Mountain, Jefferson county; date of organization, 1891, present minister took charge March 1, 1902.

Church Officers—Superintendent of Sunday School, R. W. Trapnell.

Official Acts—Baptisms, infants 4, adults 1, total 5; presented for confirmation since last report 3, marriages 1, burials 1, catechisings 15, public services, Sundays, 25, other days 3, total 53; Holy Communion, public 3, total 3.

Communicants—Number last reported 28, admitted by confirmation 3, restored to communion 6, total gain 9; net gain 9; present number total 37.

Congregations—Baptized persons connected with Parish, (this includes all confirmed persons) 200, confirmed persons connected with Parish 37, families 94, whole number of individuals 375, number sittings in church 150, number free sittings 150, number sittings in Sunday School room 250.

Organizations—Sunday Schools, officers and teachers, male, 2, female 7, total 9; Pupils, male 50, female 100, total 150; Parish schools, officers and teachers 2, scholars 27, total 29. *Other Organizations*—Mothers Meetings 30; Girls Sewing Society 18; Basket Class 12.

Property—Chapel, wood, insurance $600, value $600; Parish House, stone, insurance $1,500, value $2,200; Deaconness House, wood, insurance $600, value $600. Money raised from outside sources $3,817.02. For what objects used: Land and building and salaries.

FINANCIAL REPORT.

Receipts—*For all purposes*—Collections in church $38.00, contributions from without $3,817:02, total receipts for all purposes $3,855.02.

Disbursements—(1) *For current expenses*—Other salaries $560.67; total for current expenses $560.67. *Contributions*—(1) *For objects in the Parish*—Other objects $25.00, land and industrial hall $3,083.35; total contributions for objects in the Parish $3,108.35. (2) *For objects in the Diocese*—Diocesan missions $4.00; Sheltering Arms Hospital $5.00; total contributions for objects in the Diocese $9.00. (3) *For objects without the Diocese*—Foreign missions general $4.00; total foreign missions $4.00; total contributions for objects without the Diocese $4.00.

Statement—For objects in the Parish $25.00; for objects in the Diocese $9.00; for objects without the Diocese $4.00; total contributions $38.00; all money raised by the congregation for current expenses and for contributions $38.00.

PAROCHIAL REPORT.

Rev. JNO. S. ALFRIEND, address Charles Town. Harewood Mission, Harewood, Jefferson county; present minister took charge March 1, 1902.

Official Acts—Public services, 12.

Congregations—Included in Zion Church.

Organizations—Sunday Schools, officers and teachers, male 2, female 3, total 5; Pupils, male 25, female 15, total 40; total Sunday School offerings for use in Sunday School $5.00.

Property—Public school house.

FINANCIAL REPORT.

Receipts—For all purposes—Collections in church $10; Sunday School $5.00; total receipts for all purposes $15.00.

Disbursements—(1) *For objects in the Parish*—Parish missions $5.00; total contributions for objects in the Parish $5.00. (2) *For objects in the Diocese*—Sheltering Arms Hospital $10.00; total contributions for objects in the Diocese $10.00.

Statement—For objects in the Parish $5.00; for objects in the Diocese $10.00; total of contributions $15.00; all money raised by the congregation for current expenses and for contributions $15.00.

Remarks—This is a mission point with no organization. Sunday School is held every Sunday from Easter to Christmas. The rector of Zion Church holds service and preaches every 2nd Sunday in the month. The public school house is used for Sunday School and services.—JNO. S. ALFRIEND, *Rector*.

PAROCHIAL REPORT.

Rev. MORTON A. BARNES, address Fairmont. Christ Church, Fairmont, Marion county; present minister took charge March 1, 1905.

Church Officers—Church Wardens, J. E. Sands, (senior), Wm. E. Watson, (junior); other Vestrymen J. C. Smith, George De Bolt, J. O. Watson, E. A. Russell, George H. Brobst, Walton Miller, John Henshaw; Registrar E. A. Russell, address Fairmont, W. Va.; Treasurer Geo. Brobst, address Fairmont, W. Va.; Superintendent of Sunday School Wm. H. Sands, M. D., Fairmont, W. Va.; Sunday School Secretary and Treasurer Arthur Brobst.

Official Acts—Baptisms, infants 6, adults 2, total 8; marriages 2, burials 2, public services, Sundays, about 80, other days, about 50, total 130; Holy Communion, public, about 30.

Communicants—Number last reported 124, received by letter 2, restored to communion 8, added otherwise 4, total gain 14; net gain (or loss) 14, present number total 138.

Congregations—Baptized persons connected with Parish about 200, confirmed persons connected with Parish 138, families 50, individuals not thus included about 50, whole number of individuals about 250, number sittings in church 150, number free sittings 150, number sittings in Sunday School room 75.

Rector's Salary—As pledged from this congregation $1,350.00.

Organizations—Sunday Schools, officers and teachers, male 4, female 6, total 10; Pupils, male 20, female 30, total 50; advent offering $18.00, Lenten $25.00, other offerings $50.00, total Sunday School offerings $93.00. Woman's Auxiliary, members 30. Other organizations 20.

Property—Church, brick, insurance $3,000, value $5,000; Sunday School room in church building, yes.

FINANCIAL REPORT.

Receipts—For all purposes—Pledges and subscriptions $1,886.44, collections in church $275.43, Sunday School $93.00, Woman's Auxiliary, money $250.16, Woman's Auxiliary boxes, value $75.00, Guilds, or other societies $101.00, income from other sources $373.48, total receipts for all purposes $3,054.51.

Disbursements—(1) *For current expenses*—Salary of rector $675.00; salary of assistant $60.00; other salaries $390.50; ordinary repairs $53.26; interest on debt $16.00; payment on debts contracted for current expenses $625.69; other current expenses $81.60; total for current expenses $1,902.05. *Contributions—For objects in the Parish*—Communion alms $21.07; building fund $282.65; font fund $101.00; total contributions for objects in the Parish $404.72. *For objects in the Diocese*—Salary of Bishops $100.00; Diocesan missions $25.00; Bishop's special fund $10.00; Miss Fitzhugh $25.00; support of missionary $35.00; total contributions for objects in the Diocese $195.00. (3) *For objects without the Diocese*—Boise $5.00; foreign missions general $22.22; for Japan $30.00; Brazil $5.00; total foreign missions $57.22; specials, boxes, &c., $75.00; periodicals $1.00; total contributions for objects without the Diocese $148.22.

Statement—Current expenses raised by congregation as above $1,902.05; Contributions—For objects in the Parish $404.72; for objects in the Diocese $195.00; for objects without the Diocese $148.22; total of contributions $747.94; all money raised by the congregation for current expenses and for contributions $2,649.99; cash in hand $203.28.

PAROCHIAL REPORT.

Rev. JACOB BRITTINGHAM, address, 66 So. Penn St., Wheeling, W. Va. St. Luke's Church, the Island Parish, Wheeling, Ohio county; date of organization, June 22, 1881; present minister took charge March 3, 1889.

Church Officers—Church Wardens, Lawrence E. Sands, E. B. Bowie; other Vestrymen, W. A. Wilson, C. H. Copp, A. A. Taylor, Wylie Irvin, M. R. Wolff, Thomas Johns, Geo. J. Rogers, H. S. Sands, F. E. Zook, E. E. Hodshon; Registrar, W. A. Wilson, address, The Natl. Exchange Bank Building; Treasurer, Lawrence E. Sands, address, The Natl. Exchange

Bank; Superintendent of Sunday School, Lawrence E. Sands, 43 So. Front St.; Sunday School Secretary and Treasurer, Robert Lee Boyd, Lay Readers, A. A. Taylor, Robert Lee Boyd.

Official Acts—Baptisms, infants 16, adults 3, total 19; presented for confirmation since last report 20, marriages 11, burials 11, catechisings 9, public services, Sundays 94, other days 66, total 160; Holy Communion, public 17, private 2, total 19.

Communicants—Number last reported 260, received by letter 8, admitted by confirmation 20, total gain 28; died 2, transferred 6, removed without letter 10, lapsed 1, total loss 19; net gain 9, present number total 269.

Congregations—Baptized persons connected with Parish 399, confirmed persons connected with Parish 286, families 173, individuals not thus included 27, whole number of individuals 426, number of sittings in church 400, number free sittings 400, number sittings in chapel 200, number sittings in Sunday School room 200.

Rector's Salary—As pledged from this congregation $1,500.

Organizations—Sunday Schools, officers and teachers, male 3, female 7, total 10; Pupils, male 42, female 59; total 101; advent offering $13.20, Lenten offering $40.00, other offerings $50.00, total Sunday School offerings $103.20. Brotherhood of St. Andrew, members 8. Woman's Auxiliary, members 18. *Other Organizations*—Chancel Chapter 16; King's Daughters 45; Junior King's Daughters 18; Junior Brotherhood of St. Andrew 7.

Property—Church, frame, insurance $6,000, value $12,000; rectory, frame, insurance $2,000; value $5,000; Parish house, frame, insurance $4,500, value $9,000; organ, value $2,500; total value insurance $12,500, value $28,500. *Indebtedness*—On church $2,000.

FINANCIAL REPORT.

Receipts—For all purposes—Pledges and subscriptions $1,500, communion alms $28.63, collections in church $2,930.67, thank offerings $1,500, Sunday School $90.00, Woman's Auxiliary, money $69.00, Woman's Auxiliary boxes, value $125.00, Guilds, or other societies $558.58, Bishop's special fund $100.00, total receipts for all purposes $6,901.88.

Disbursements—(1) *For current expenses*—Overdraft from last year $76.41; salary of rector $1,500.00; salary of choir $416.96; other salaries, sexton, $216.00; ordinary repairs and improvements $1,358.21; other current expenses $586.82; Sunday School expenses $50.00; total for current expenses $4,204.40. *Contributions*—(1) *For objects in the Parish*—Communion alms $28.63; extraordinary repairs and improvements $1,500; free kindergarten $164.00; day nursery $25.00; other expenses and charities $369.58; total contributions for objects in the Parish $2,087.21. (2) *For objects in the Diocese*—Salary of Bishops $150.00; Permanent Fund $5.00; Diocesan Missions $175.00; convocation missions $8.00; widows and orphans, aged and disabled clergy fund $49.89; religious and theological education $16.70; Sheltering Arms Hospital $34.82; Bishop's special fund $100.00; total contributions for objects in the Diocese $539.41. (3) *For objects without the Diocese*—Domestic missions general $54.14; Thro' American Ch. Miss. Society $28.19; total domestic missions $82.33; foreign missions general $47.79; Morrell China scholarship $45.00; Thro' American Ch. Miss. Society $28.19; total foreign missions $120.98; specials, boxes, &c., $149.00; Sunday School Lenten offering $40.00; total contributions for objects without the Diocese $392.31.

Statement—Current expenses raised by congregation as above $3,882.95. Contributions—For objects in the Parish $587.21; for objects in the Diocese $539.41; for objects without the Diocese $392.31; total of contributions $1,518.93; all money raised by the congregation for current expenses and for contributions $5,351.88; cash in hand $321.44.

Remarks—It is a pleasure to report that the Senior Brotherhood has been reorganized and is now engaged in active work, and a Junior Brotherhood has been organized.

PAROCHIAL REPORT.

Rev. E. H. BROSIUS, address, Bluefield, W. Va. Christ Church, Bluefield Parish, Bluefield, Mercer county; date of organization May 20, 1903; present minister took charge December 1, 1901.

Church Officers—Church Wardens, R. A. Lacy, W. H. B. Loving; other Vestrymen, T. H. Becker, E. A. Blake, R. C. Turner, H. A. Mitchell, Walter Perkins; Registrar, H. A. Mitchell, address, Bluefield, W. Va.; Treasurer, T. H. Becker, address, Bluefield, W. Va.; Superintendent of Sunday School E. H. Brosius; Sunday School Secretary and Treasurer E. H. Brosius.

Official Acts—Baptisms, infants 5, total 5; presented for confirmation since last report 1, marriages 1, burials 1, public services, Sundays 79, other days 17, total 96; Holy Communion, public 18, private 1, total 19.

Communicants—Number last reported 106, admitted by confirmation 1, added otherwise 30, total gain 31; died 1, removed without letter 27, total loss 28; net gain 3, present number total 109.

Congregations—Baptized persons connected with Parish 190, confirmed persons connected with Parish 109, families 56, individuals not thus included 13, whole number of individuals 200, number of sittings in church 200, number of free sittings 200.

Rector's Salary—As pledged from this congregation $500.00, from Diocesan missions $150.00, from general board $100.00, as pledged from other congregations $50.00, total $800.00.

Organizations—Sunday Schools, officers and teachers, male 1, female 3,

total 4; Pupils, male 15, female 12, total 27; advent offering $13.12, Lenten offering $23.57, other offerings $20.94, total Sunday School offerings $57.63. *Other Organizations*—Ladies Guild; Chancel Chapter; Choir.

Property—Church, wood, insurance $1,500, value $2,000; rectory, wood, insurance $800, value $1,500; dwelling, wood, insurance $1,000, value $1,500; total value $5,000. *Indebtedness*—On other property (dwelling) $3,000, total indebtedness $3,000.

FINANCIAL REPORT.

Receipts—For all purposes—Cash on hand, per last report $55.52, pledges and subscriptions $758.95, collections in church $93.76, money borrowed $3,000.00, Easter offerings $186.30, Sunday School $57.63, Communion alms $17.54, Guilds, or other societies $466.66, contributions from without $93.14, income from other sources, rent, $78.00, total receipts for all purposes $4,807.50.

Disbursements—(1) *For current expenses*—Salary of rector $536.77; other salaries $95.45; ordinary repairs $18.25; interest on debt $8.90; other current expenses $80.25; total for current expenses $739.62. *Contributions*—(1) *For objects in the Parish*—Communion alms $17.54; extraordinary repairs and improvements $370.35; maintaining Sunday Schools $44.51; payment on debts for building and organ $3,312.00; choir $110.10; Chancel Chapel $10.00; total contributions for objects in the Parish $3,864.50. (2) *For objects in the Diocese*—Salary of Bishops $30.00; Diocesan missions $30.00; convocation missions $8.00; Sheltering Arms Hospital $5.43; total contributions for objects in the Diocese $73.43. (3) *For objects without the Diocese*—Domestic missions general $15.00; total domestic missions $15.00; foreign missions general $15.00; total foreign missions $15.00; total contributions for objects without the Diocese $30.00.

Statement—Current expenses raised by congregation as above $739.62. Contributions—For objects in the Parish $864.50; for objects in the Diocese $73.43; for objects without the Diocese $30.00; total contributions $967.93; all money raised by the congregation for current expenses and for contributions $1,707.55; receipts $1,807.50; cash in hand $99.95.

PAROCHIAL REPORT.

Rev. E. H. BROSIUS, address, Bluefield, W. Va. Heavenly Rest Church, Heavenly Rest Mission, Princeton, Mercer county; present minister took charge December 1, 1901.

Church Officers—Church Warden, H. B. Barber; Registrar, H. B. Barber, Princeton, W. Va.; Treasurer, H. B. Barber.

Official Acts—Baptisms, infants 3, total 3; public services, Sundays 11, other days 1, total 12; Holy Communion, public 4, total 4.

Communicants—Number last reported 18, added otherwise 1, total gain 1, removed without letter 2, total loss 2; net loss 1, present number total 17.

Congregations—Baptized persons connected with Parish, (this includes all confirmed persons) 19, confirmed persons connected with Parish 17, families 8, number sittings in church 150.

Rector's Salary—As pledged from this congregation $25.00, from Diocesan missions $150.00, from general board $100.00, as pledged from other congregations $525.00; total $800.00.

FINANCIAL REPORT.

Receipts—For all purposes—Collections in church $34.55, total receipts for all purposes $34.55.

Disbursements—(1) *For current expenses*—Salary of rector $10.30; ordinary repairs $12.25; total for current expenses $22.55. *Contributions*—(2) *For objects in the Diocese*—Salary of Bishops $6.00; Diocesan missions $6.00; total contributions for objects in the Diocese $12.00.

Statement—Current expenses raised by congregation as above $22.55. Contributions—For objects in the Diocese $12.00; total of contributions $12.00; all money raised by the congregation for current expenses and for contributions $34.55.

PAROCHIAL REPORT.

Rev. C. M. CAMPBELL, address, Racine. Christ's Church, Short Creek, Boone county; present minister took charge April 1, 1902.

Official Acts—Marriages 1, burials 1, public services, Sundays 1, total 1.

Communicants—Number last reported 2, present number total 2.

Congregations—Baptized persons connected with Parish, (this includes all confirmed persons) 8, confirmed persons connected with Parish 4, families 3, individuals not thus included 4, whole number of individuals 12, number of sittings in church 80, number of free sittings 80.

Property—Church, log, value $400, total value $400.

FINANCIAL REPORT.

Receipts—For all purposes—Total receipts for all purposes $2.00.

Contributions—(2) *For objects in the Diocese*—Bishop's special fund $2.00; total contributions for objects in the Diocese $2.00.

Statement—For objects in the Diocese $2.00; total of contributions $2.00; all money raised by the congregation for current expenses and for contributions $2.00.

Remarks—A Sunday School was kept up with the minister and his wife as teachers from June to November with an average attendance of 22. The pupils were so irregular that the roll was soon abandoned and only the total number present each Sunday recorded. A festival was gotten up last summer, the proceeds of which, $10.00, was given to the minister. Also, the Bishop sends word to credit Boone with $2.00 for his special fund. No money has been raised by the congregation as such. On Monday and Tuesday, May 8th and 9th, just passed, we had a very pleasant visit from Bishop Gravatt. He preached in Christ's Church the first night, and the second in the Methodist Church at Racine. I have not been able to visit Bull Creek since the last report. I understand, however, there are still left 7 baptized and 3 confirmed persons in two families. Other services and the Holy Communion were announced at Christ's Church, but not held for lack of attendance.

PAROCHIAL REPORT.

Rev. WILSON PAGE CHRISMAN, address, Moundsville, W. Va. Trinity Church, Trinity Parish, Moundsville, Marshall county; date of organization 1848; present minister took charge June 1, 1902.

Church Officers—Church Wardens, V. A. Weaver, Friend Cox; other Vestrymen, A. J. Martin, J. T. Gallaher, C. L. Walton, H. B. Tyler, J. M. Sanders, W. B. Williams, J. R. Logan; Registrar, John T. Gallaher, address, Moundsville, W. Va.; Treasurer, C. L. Walton, address, Moundsville, W. Va.; Superintendent of Sunday School W. P. Chrisman, Moundsville, W. Va.; Sunday School Secretary and Treasurer H. B. Tyler, Moundsville, W. Va.

Official Acts—Baptisms, infants 12, adults 2, total 14; presented for confirmation since last report 10, marriages 4, burials 2, public services, Sundays 105, other days 106, total 211; Holy Communion, public 35, total 35.

Communicants—Number last reported 64, received by letter 1, admitted by confirmation 10, restored to communion 3, added otherwise 7, total gain 21; removed without letter 8, lapsed 3, total loss 11; net gain 10, present number total 74.

Congregations—Baptized persons connected with Parish, (this includes all confirmed persons) 166, confirmed persons connected with Parish 89, families 52, individuals not thus included 35, whole number of individuals 170, number of scattered communicants in your section not connected with any Parish 11, number sittings in church 200, number free sittings 200, number sittings in chapel 25, number sittings in Sunday School room 225.

Rector's Salary—As pledged from this congregation $1,250.00, total $1,250.00.

Organizations—Sunday Schools, officers and teachers, male 3, female 10, total 13; Pupils, male 55, female 79, total 134; advent offering $32.25; Lenten offering $51.55, other offerings $79.29, total Sunday School offerings $163.09. *Other Organizations*—Trinity Guild; (a) Industrial Chapter; (b) Chancel Chapter.

Property—Church, frame, insurance $4,000.00, value $8,000.00; rectory, frame, $2,000.00, value $5,000.00; Parish house, brick, insurance $5,000.00, value $20,000.00, total value, insurance $11,000.00, value $33,000.00. *Indebtedness*—On Parish house $3,450.00, other debts $350.00, total indebtedness $3,800.00.

FINANCIAL REPORT.

Receipts—For all purposes—Cash on hand, per last report $48.84, pledges and subscriptions $801.00, collections in church $954.93, Sunday School $163.09, Guilds, or other societies $197.96, total receipts for all purposes $2,165.82.

Disbursements—(1) *For current expenses*—Salary of rector $1,250.00; other salaries $52.00; other current expenses $521.19; total for current expenses $1,823.19. *Contributions*—(1) *For objects in the Parish*—Communion alms $20.08; total contributions for objects in the Parish $20.08. (2) *For objects in the Diocese*—Salary of Bishops $60.00; permanent fund $3.70; Diocesan missions $47.25; Convocation missions $18.00; widows and orphans, aged and disabled clergy fund $6.65; religious and theological education $1.92; Sheltering Arms Hospital $8.69; Theological Seminary $4.98; total contributions for objects in the Diocese $151.19. (3) *For objects without the Diocese*—Domestic missions general $47.77; colored people $1.85; Indians 50 cents; deaf and dumb $3.50; Jews $3.35; Thro' American Ch. Miss. Society $2.20; total domestic missions $59.17; foreign missions general $37.78; for Mexico $2.45; Brazil $1.00; Cuba $1.57; total foreign missions $42.80; American Church Building Fund $1.14; General Clergy Relief Fund $5.00; Bible and Prayer Book Society $3.85; total contributions for objects without the Diocese $111.96.

Statement—Current expenses raised by congregation as above $1,823.19. Contributions—For objects in the Parish $20.08; for objects in the Diocese $151.19; for objects without the Diocese $111.96; total of contributions $283.23; all money raised by the congregation for current expenses and for contributions $2,106.42; cash in hand $59.40.

Rev. WILSON PAGE CHRISMAN, address Moundsville, W. Va. Grace Church, Cresap's Valley Mission, Cresaps, Marshall county; date of organization, 1881; present minister took charge November 17, 1904.

Church Officers—Missionary Committee, A. Q. Whittaker, Quincy

Cresap, R. M. Gossett, Thos. Kemp; Registrar, Quincy Cresap, address Graysville, W. Va.; Treasurer, R. M. Gossett, address Graysville, W. Va.

Official Acts—Burials 1, public services 4, total 4.

• *Communicants*—(These statistics are from last report). Number last reported 9, present number total 9.

Congregations—Baptized persons connected with Parish, (this includes all confirmed persons) 18, confirmed persons connected with Parish 12, families 7, number sittings in church 75, number of free sittings 75.

Property—Church, frame, value $1,000.00.

FINANCIAL REPORT.

Receipts—For all purposes—Collections in church $10.81, total receipts for all purposes $10.81.

Disbursements—(1) *For current expenses*—Other current expenses $1.00; total for current expenses $1.00. *Contributions*—(2) *For objects in the Diocese*—Diocesan missions $7.81; convocation missions $2.00; total contributions for objects in the Diocese $9.81.

Statement—Current expenses raised by congregation as above $1.00. Contributions—For objects in the Diocese $9.81; total of contributions $9.81; all money raised by the congregation for current expenses and for contributions $10.81.

PAROCHIAL REPORT.

Rev. GUY H. CROOK, address Ronceverte. Incarnation Church, Greenbrier Parish, Ronceverte, Greenbrier county; present minister took charge June 23, 1901.

Church Officers—Church Wardens, C. N. Simms, F. A. Hauck; other Vestrymen, A. B. C. Bray, J. W. P. Eagle, Fred Buchanon; Registrar, A. B. C. Bray, address Ronceverte; Treasurer, A. B. C. Bray, address Ronceverte; Superintendent of Sunday School, Mrs. Geo. T. Brew, Ronceverte; Sunday School Secretary and Treasurer Miss May Templeton.

Official Acts—Baptisms, infants 1, total 1; presented for confirmation since last report 6, catechisings 3, public services, Sundays 32, other days 21, total 53; Holy Communion, public 6, total 6.

Communicants—Number last reported 21, admitted by confirmation 6, added otherwise 5, total gain 11; removed without letter 1, total loss 1, net gain 10, present number total 31.

Congregations—Baptized persons connected with Parish, (this includes all confirmed persons) 45, confirmed persons connected with Parish 31, families 16, whole number of individuals 45, number of sittings in church 80, number free sittings 80.

Rector's Salary—As pledged from this congregation $150, from Diocesan missions $200, as pledged from other congregations $410, total $760.

Organizations—Sunday Schools, officers and teachers, female 2, total 2; pupils, male 8, female 13, total 21; Lenten offering $17.79, other offerings, $17.00, total Sunday School offerings $34.79.

Property—Church, wood, insurance $500, value $1,050; rectory, wood, insurance $1,500, value $2,500; building lots, value $800, total value $4,350. *Indebtedness*—On rectory, $1,700, total indebtedness $1,700.

FINANCIAL REPORT.

Receipts—*For all purposes*—Pledges and subscriptions $207.13, collections in church $166.10, Guilds, or other societies $60.00, income from other sources $287.50, total receipts for all purposes $720.73.

Disbursements—(1) *For current expenses*—Salary of rector $150.00; interest on debt $90.00; other current expenses $27.00; rent $120.00; total for current expenses $387.00. *Contributions*—(1) *For objects in the Parish*—Extraordinary repairs and improvements $53.64; payment on debts for building, &c, $200.00; other objects $23.00; total contributions for objects in the Parish $246.64. (2) *For objects in the Diocese*—Salary of Bishops $10.00; Diocesan missions $13.18; widows and orphans, aged and disabled clergy fund $2.82; religious and theological education $3.60; Sheltering Arms Hospital $9.30; Theological Seminary $1.71; total contributions for objects in the Diocese $40.61. (3) *For objects without the Diocese*—Domestic missions general $3.40; colored people $2.56; Indians 80 cents; deaf and dumb $2.17; total domestic missions $8.93; foreign missions general $2.04; total foreign missions $2.04; American Church Building Fund $3.31; General Clergy Relief Fund $2.20; total contributions for objects without the Diocese $16.48.

Statement—Current expenses raised by congregation as above $387.00. Contributions—For objects in the Parish $276.64; for objects in the Diocese $40.61; for objects without the Diocese $16.48; total of contributions $333.73; all money raised by the congregation for current expenses and for contributions $720.73.

Remarks—Ronceverte is the only place which I have been able to put into operation the system recommended by the Bishop and while it does not make a perfect report owing to the limited number of services it shows its effectiveness in comparison with reports from other congregations.

PAROCHIAL REPORT.

Rev. GUY H. CROOK, address, Ronceverte. St. James Church, Greenbrier Parish, Lewisburg, Greenbrier county; present minister took charge June 23, 1901.

Church Officers—Church Wardens, D. C. T. Davis, Jr., K. M. Snyder; other Vestrymen, J. W. Harris, H. Frazier, H. L. Van Sickler; Registrar, H. L. Van Sickler, address Lewisburg; Treasurer, K. M. Snyder, address Lewisburg.

Official Acts—Baptisms, infants 1, total 1; marriages 1, burials 1, public services, Sundays 31, other days 7, total 38; Holy Communion, public 8, total 8.

Communicants—Number last reported 24, added otherwise 2, total gain 2; net gain 2; present number total 26.

Congregations—Baptized persons connected with Parish, (this includes all confirmed persons) 44, confirmed persons connected with Parish 26, families 14, indivduals not this included 1, number of scattered communicants in your section not connected with any Parish 1, number of sittings in church 200, number free sittings 200.

Rector's Salary—As pledged from this congregation $225, from Diocesan missions $200; as pledged from other congregations $335, total $760.

Organizations—Ladies Guild.

Property—Church, wood, insurance $1,200, value $2,000; rectory, wood, value $1,200, total value $3,200. *Indebtedness*—On church $42.00, due on Diocesan assessments for missions $7.00 on Diocessan assessment for Bishop's fund $10.00, total indebtedness $59.00.

FINANCIAL REPORT.

Receipts—For all purposes—Pledges and subscriptions $156.10, collections in church $34.20, income from other sources $96.00, total receipts for all purposes $286.30.

Disbursements—(1) *For current expenses*—Salary of rector $225.00; insurance $25.00; other current expenses $9.00; total for current expenses $259.00. *Contributions*—(2) *For objects in the Diocese*—Salary of Bishops $10.00; Diocesan missions $7.00; widows and orphans, aged and disabled clergy fund $2.00; Theological Seminary $2.00; total contributions for objects in the Diocese $21.00. (3) *For objects without the Diocese*—Domestic missions general $2.25; total domestic missions $2.25; foreign missions general $1.85; total foreign missions $1.85; general clergy relief fund $2.20; total contributions for objects without the Diocese $6.30.

Statement—Current expenses raised by congregation as above $259.00. Contributions—For objects in the Diocese $21.00; for objects without the Diocese $6.30; total of contributions $27.30; total $286.30.

PAROCHIAL REPORT.

Rev. GUY H. CROOK, address, Ronceverte, Pocahontas Mission, Marlinton, Pocahontas county; not organized; present minister took charge June 23, 1901.

Official Acts—Public services, Sundays 1, other days 4, total 5.

Communicants—No report. Present number total 11.

Congregations—Baptized persons connected with Parish, (this includes all confirmed persons) 16, confirmed persons connected with Parish 11, families 5, whole number of individuals 16.

Rector's Salary—Nothing. From Diocesan missions $200.00, as pledged from other congregations $560.00, total $760.00.

Property—Building fund $325, total value $325.

Remarks—No organization. It is our intention to build a church this summer.

PAROCHIAL REPORT.

Rev. GUY H. CROOK, address, Ronceverte. Grace Church, Pocahontas Co. Mission, Cloverlick, Pocahontas county; present minister took charge June 23, 1901.

Communicants—Number last reported 5, present number total 5.

Congregations—Baptized persons connected with Parish, (this includes all confirmed persons) 12, confirmed persons connected with Parish 5, families 4, individuals not thus included 1, whole number of individuals 12, number of scattered communicants in your section 7, number sittings in church 175, number free sittings 175.

Property—Church, wood, value $1,000, total value $1,000.

FINANCIAL REPORT.

Receipts—For all purposes—Collections in church $4.23, total receipts for all purposes $4.23.

Contributions—For objects in the Diocese—Diocesan missions $4.23, total contributions for objects in the Diocese $4.23.

Statement—For objects in the Diocese $4.23, all money raised by the congregation for current expenses and for contributions $4.23.

PAROCHIAL REPORT.

Rev. GUY H. CROOK, address, Ronceverte. Holy Comforter Church, Greenbrier Parish, Fort Spring, Greenbrier county; present minister took charge June 23, 1901.

Church Officers—Church Warden, D. Y. Huddlestun; Registrar, D. Y. Huddlestun, address Fort Spring; Treasurer D. Y. Huddlestun, address Fort Spring; Superintendent of Sunday School, Union S. S.

Official Acts—Public services, Sundays 9, other days 11, total 20.

Communicants—Number last reported 8, received by letter 1, total gain 1; removed without letter 1, total loss 1, present number total 8.

Congregations—Baptized persons connected with Parish, (this includes all confirmed persons) 11, confirmed persons connected with Parish 9, families 4, whole number of individuals 11.

Rector's Salary—As pledged from this congregation $50.00, from Diocesan missions $200.00; as pledged from other congregations $510.00, total $760.00.

Property—Building fund $30.00, total value $30.00. *Indebtedness*—Due on Diocesan assessments for mission $5.00, due on Diocesan assessment for Bishop's fund $5.00, total indebtedness $10.00.

FINANCIAL REPORT.

Receipts—For all purposes—Pledges and subscriptions $50.00, collections in church $16.00, total receipts for all purposes $66.00.

Disbursements—(1) *For current expenses*—Salary of rector $50.00. *Contributions*—(2) *For objects in the Diocese*—Salary of Bishops $5.00, Diocesan missions $5.00, widows and orphans, aged and disabled clergy fund $2.00, Sheltering Arms Hospital $1.00, Theological Seminary $2.00, Bishop's special fund $1.00.

Statement—Current expenses raised by congregation as above $50.00; for objects in the Diocese $16.00; total of contributions $16.00; all money raised by the congregation for current expenses and for contributions $66.00.

PAROCHIAL REPORT.

Rev. GUY H. CROOK, address, Ronceverte. Hillsboro Church, Pocahontas Mission, Academy, Pocahontas county; present minister took charge June 23, 1901.

Church Officers—No organization.

Official Acts—Public services 2, total 2.

Communicants—Number last reported 3, removed without letter 2, total loss 2, net loss 2; present number total 1.

Congregations—Baptized persons connected with Parish, (this includes all confirmed persons) 5, confirmed persons connected with Parish 1, families 1.

PAROCHIAL REPORT.

Rev. GUY H. CROOK, address, Ronceverte. Pocahontas Co. Mission, Huntersvile, Pocahontas county; no organization; present minister took charge June 23, 1901.

Official Acts—Public services, Sundays 1, total 1.

Communicants—Number last reported 4, present number total 4.

PAROCHIAL REPORT.

Rev. GUY H. CROOK, address, Ronceverte. Greenbrier Parish, Anthony, Greenbrier county; date of organization 1904; present minister took charge 1904.

Official Acts—Public services, Sundays 12, total 12.

Communicants—Present number total 1.

Congregations—Baptized persons connected with Parish, (this includes all confirmed persons) 5, confirmed persons connected with Parish 1, families 1, whole number of individuals 5.

Rector's Salary—As pledged from this congregation $60.00, from Diocesan missions $200.00, as pledged from other congregations $500.00, total $760.00.

FINANCIAL REPORT.

Receipts—For all purposes—Pledges and subscriptions $60.00, total receipts for all purposes $60.00.

Disbursements—For current expenses—Salary of rector $60.00, total for current expenses $60.00.

Statement—Current expenses raised by congregation as above $60.00; all money raised by the congregation for current expenses and for contributions $60.00.

Remarks—This place is not organized. The services are held at Hendersons lumber camp. They have organized a Sunday School during the past month but I have no statistics from it.

PAROCHIAL REPORT.

Rev. GUY H. CROOK address, Ronceverte. St. Thomas Church, Greenbrier Parish, White Sulphur, Greenbrier county; present minister took charge June 10, 1902.

Church Officers—Vestrymen, R. Cary Montague; Superintendent of Sunday Schools, R. Cary Montague, White Sulphur Springs, Mrs. T. F. Dickson, White Sulphur Springs; Sunday School Secretary and Treasurer, Miss Montague, Frank Atkinson; Lay Reader, R. Cary Montague.

Official Acts—Baptisms, infants 1, adults 3, total 4; presented for confirmation since last report 2, marriages 1, catechisings 4, public services, Sundays 18, other days 21, total 39; Holy Communion, public 4, total 4.

Communicants—Number last reported 41, admitted by confirmation 2, total gain 2; net gain 2, present number total 43.

Congregations—Baptized persons connected with Parish, (this includes all confirmed persons) 80, confirmed persons connected with Parish 44, families 21, individuals not thus included 65, whole number of individuals 145, number sittings in church 500, number free sittings 500.

Rector's Salary—As pledged from this congregation $75.00, from Diocesan missions $200.00, as pledged from other congregations $485.00, total $760.00.

Organizations—Sunday Schools, officers and teachers, male, No. 1, 2, female 3, total 5; pupils, male, 14, female 21, total 35; No. 2, officers and teachers, male 1, female 2, total 3; pupils, male 20, female 30, total 50. *Location of Schools mentioned above*—No. 1 at White Sulphur, No. 2 at Oakhurst.

Property—Church, wood, value $10,000, total value $10,000.

FINANCIAL REPORT.

Receipts—For all purposes—Pledges and subscriptions $75.00, collections in church $7.35, total receipts for all purposes $82.35. Does not include the St. Thomas Ch. in White Sulphur grounds.

Disbursements—For current expenses—Salary of rector $75.00. *Contributions*—(1) *For objects in the Diocese*—Salary of Bishops $2.10; Diocesan missions $2.15; Theological Seminary $1.05; total contributions for objects in the Diocese $5.30. *For objects without the Diocese*—(2) For Japan $2.05; total foreign missions $2.05; total contributions for objects without the Diocese $2.05.

Statement—Current expenses raised by congregation as above $75.00. Contributions—For objects in the Diocese $5.30; for objects without the Diocese $2.05; total of contributions $7.35; all money raised by the congregation for current expenses and for contributions $82.35.

Remarks—The foregoing does not reprpesent the entire work of the congregation but so far as I have been able to get reports. There is some cash in hand but I do not know how much. Report of confirmation includes those omitted last year.

PAROCHIAL REPORT.

Rev. T. J. OLIVER CURRAN address, Wheeling. St. Andrew's Church, Wheeling, Ohio county; present minister took charge October, 1909.

Church Officers—Vestrymen, Wm. A. Carroll, Wm. Weatherall, Robt. Smith; Registrar, Wm. A. Carroll, address 3809 Jacob St.; Treasurer Wm. A. Carroll; Superintendent of Sunday School Wm. A. Carroll; Sunday School Secretary and Treasurer, Wm. A. Carroll.

Official Acts—Baptisms, infants 17, adults 9, total 26; presented for confirmation since last report 14, marriages 4, burials 10, catechisings 48, public services, Sundays 115, other days 85, total 200; Holy Communion, public 45, total 45.

Communicants—Number last reported 75, admitted by confirmation 14, total gain 14; net gain 14, present number total 89.

Congregations—Baptized persons connected with Parish, (this includes all confirmed persons) 226, confirmed persons connected with Parish 89, families 36, individuals not thus included 28, whole number of individuals 379.

Rector's Salary—As pledged from this congregation $1,300; total $1,300.

Organizations—Sunday Schools, officers and teachers, male 2, female 8, total 10; pupils, male 58, female 85, total 153; Advent offering $7.50, Lenten offering $29.00, other offerings $138.26, $96.90, total Sunday School offerings $271.66; Brotherhood of St. Andrew, members 4. *Other organizations*—St. Andrew's Guild.

Property—Church, wood, insurance $3,500.

FINANCIAL REPORT.

Receipts—For all purposes—Cash on hand, per last report $769.30, pledges and subscriptions $274.05, pew rent $119.49, collections in church $22.01, Sunday School $271.66; Guilds, or other societies $543.71, contributions from without $1,455.39, total receipts for all purposes $3,455.61.

Disbursements—(1) *For current expenses*—Salary of rector $1,272.44; other salaries $104.00; ordinary repairs $113.32; other current expenses $260.59; other objects $227.27; total for current expenses $1,977.62. *Contributions—For objects in the Parish*—Maintaining Sunday Schools $165; total contributions for object in the Parish $165. (2) *For objects in the Diocese*—Salary of Bishops $10.00; Diocesan missions 15; convocation missions $5.00; widows and orphans, aged and disabled clergy fund $5.00; Sheltering Arms Hospital $20.00; total contributions for objects in the Diocese $55.00. *For objects without the Diocese*—Domestic missions general $7.50; total domestic missions $7.50; foreign missions general $7.50; total foreign missions $7.50; total contributions for objects without the Diocese $15.00.

Statement—Current expenses raised by congregation as above $1,228.47; Contributions—For objects in the Parish $1,158.47; for objects in the Diocese $55.00; for objects without the Diocese $15.00; total of contributions $1,228.47; all money raised by the congregation for current expenses and for contributions $1,228.47.

Remarks—"Statement" does not allow, nor does any part of the form allow for the showing of our saving and collecting for a specific purpose, &c. We have in the bank saved and raised by the congregation, viz. $1,242.99 for a building fund. This amount though is included in total shown on No. 1 page 6 of this form.

PAROCHIAL REPORT.

Rev. CREETUS A. DOWELL, address, Sistersville, W. Va. St. Paul's Church, Tyler Parish, Sistersville, Tyler county; present minister took charge April, 1903.

Church Officers—Church Wardens, Geo. F. Durham, Geo. B. Van Arnen; other Vestrymen, F. D. McCoy, Geo. W. Stocking, Ed. Roome, D. E. Thoenen, J. H. McCoy; Registrar D. E. Thoenen, address Sistersville; Treasurer D. E. Thoenen, address Sistersville; Superintendent of Sunday Schools, the Rector; Sunday School Secretary and Treasurer, Mabel Choderdon.

Official Acts—Baptisms, adults 5, total 5; presented for confirmation since last report 15, marriages 2, burials 7, catechisings 25, public services, Sundays 106, other days 91, total 197; Holy Communion, public 21, total 21.

Communicants—Number last reported 41, received by letter 1, admitted by confirmation 15, added otherwise 7, total gain 23; died 2, removed without letter 6, total loss 8; net gain 15, present number total 56.

Congregations—Baptized persons connected with Parish, (this includes all confirmed persons) 72, confirmed persons connected with Parish 59, families 21, individuals not thus included 14, whole number of individuals 72, number of scattered communicants in your section not connected with any Parish 4, number sittings in church 175, number free sittings 175.

Rector's Salary—As pledged from this congregation $800, as pledged from other congregations $100, total $900.

Organizations—Sunday School, officers and teachers, male 1, female 8, total 9; pupils, male 34, female 63, total 97; Advent offering $4.80, Lenten offering $11.93, other offerings $25.68, total Sunday School offerings $42.41. *Other organizations*—Woman's Auxiliary, members 14; Woman's Guild, 13; Young Woman's Guild, 15.

Property—Church, frame, insurance $1,400, value $3,500; rectory, frame, insurance $2,000, value $3,500; organ, insurance $600, value $1,000; total value $8,000. *Indebtedness*—Other debts $143, total indebtedness $143.

FINANCIAL REPORT.

Receipts—For all purposes—Pledges and subscriptions $1,313.41, collections in church $488.50, Sunday School $42.41, Woman's Auxiliary, money $11.80, Woman's Auxiliary boxes, value $30.00, Guilds, or other societies $257.72, income from other sources $461.15, total receipts for all purposes $2,584.99.

Disbursements—For current expenses—Salary of rector $800.00; other salaries $192.00; insurance $62.10; ordinary repairs $20.37; other current expenses $97.99; other objects $13.75; total for current expenses $1,185.21. *Contributions*—(1) *For objects in the Parish*—Communion alms $29.49; extraordinary repairs and improvements $1,119.45; maintaining Sunday Schools $50.68; other objects $106.55; total contributions for objects in the Parish $1,306.17. (2) *For objects in the Diocese*—Salary of Bishops $40.00; permanent fund $6.14, Diocesan missions $41.33, convocation missions $3.00; widows and orphans, aged and disabled clergy fund

$12.45; religious and theological education $3.42; Sheltering Arms Hospital $7.35; box to Sheltering Arms Hospital $30.00; total contributions for objects in the Diocese $143.69. (3) *For objects without the Diocese*—Domestic missions general $10.65; total domestic missions $10.65; foreign missions general $10.65; Brazil $9.35; Cuba $9.35; total foreign missions $29.35; united offering $6.19; total contributions for objects without the Diocese $46.19.

Statement—Current expenses raised by congregation as above $1,137.08. Contributions—For objects in the Parish $1,258.03; for objects in the Diocese $143.69; for objects without the Diocese $46.19; total of contributions $1,447.91; all money raised by the congregation for current expenses and for contributions $2,584.99; cash in hand $23.17.

Remarks—I have been conducting a monthly service on a week night at Cairo since the first of February. We have here 5 families, 16 baptized persons and 13 communicants. They have made, during this time, the following contributions: Bishop's fund $2.50; Diocesan missions $2.50; current expenses $8.25. Total $13.25.

PAROCHIAL REPORT.

Rev. CREETUS A. DOWELL, address, Sistersville. Pennsboro Mission, Pennsboro, Ritchie county; present minister took charge June, 1904.

Official Acts—Presented for confirmation since last report 1, public services, Sundays 1, other days 11, total 12.

Communicants—Number last reported 4, admitted by confirmation 1, total gain 1; net gain 1, present number total 5.

Congregations—Baptized persons connected with Parish, (this includes all confirmed persons) 15, confirmed persons connected with Parish 5, families 4, individuals not this included 2, whole number of individuals 22.

Rector's Salary—As pledged from this congregation $100.00, as pledged from other congregations $800.00, total $900.00

FINANCIAL REPORT.

Receipts—For all purposes—Pledges and subscriptions $85.00, collections in church $19.25, total receipts for all purposes $104.25.

Disbursements—(1) *For current expenses*—Salary of rector $85.00; other current expenses $19.25; total for current expenses $104.25.

Statement—Current expenses raised by congregation as above $104.25; all money raised by the congregation for current expenses and for contributions $104.25.

PAROCHIAL REPORT.

Rev. JOHN S. DOUGLAS, address, Martinsburg, W. Va. Trinity Church, Norborne Parish, Martinsburg, Berkeley county; date of organization, 1769; present minister took charge October 1, 1899.

Church Officers—Church Wardens, Capt. W. B. Colston, C. A. Miller; other Vestrymen, John E. Boyd, Alexander Parks, Arthur M. Gilbert, Dr. A. Andrews, Edward Rutledge; Registrar, Capt. W. B. Colston, address Martinsburg, W. Va.; Treasurer, Edward Rutledge, address Martinsburg, W. Va.; Superintendent of Sunday Schools, Edward Rutledge, Martinsburg, W. Va.; Sunday School Secretary and Treasurer, C. A. Miller; Lay Reader, Edward Rutledge.

Official Acts—Baptisms, infants 13, adults 1, total 14; presented for confirmation since last report 6, marriages 6, burials 11, catechisings 20, public services, Sundays 104, other days 83, total 187; Holy Communion, public 20, private 2, total 22.

Communicants—Number last reported 165, received by letter 2, admitted by confirmation 6, added otherwise 11, total gain 19; died 1, removed without letter 5, lapsed 3, total loss 9; net gain 10, present number total 175.

Congregations—Baptized persons connected with Parish 290, confirmed persons connected with Parish 188, families 90, individuals not thus included 20, whole number of individuals 310, number sittings in church 350, number free sittings 350, number sittings in Sunday School room 250.

Rector's Salary—As pledged from this congregation $900; total $900.

Organizations—Sunday School, officers and teachers, male 4, female 9, total 13; pupils, male 45, female 65, total 110; Advent offering $26.28, Lenten offering $43.83, other offerings $33.98, total Sunday School offerings $104.09; Woman's Auxiliary, members 31. *Other organizations*—Trinity Church Guild, under which are working seven different Chapters.

Property—Church, brick, insurance $5,000, value $10,000; rectory, stone, insurance $1,500, value $7,000; Parish house, new, brick, insurance $2,000, value $5,000; new stable, brick, insurance $500, value $500; organ, insurance $1,800, value $1,800. *Indebtedness*—On Parish house, stable and approaches $4,536.32. Other debts—For extraordinary repairs and improvements and for current expenses $500.00.

FINANCIAL REPORT.

Receipts—For all purposes—Cash on hand, per last report $540.62, pledges and subscriptions $1,414.93, collections in church $73.73, $1.019.67, money borrowed $500, Sunday School $104.09, Woman's Auxiliary, money $114.35, Woman's Auxiliary boxes, value $25.00, Guilds or other societies $701.29, total receipts for all purposes $4,493.68.

Disbursements—(1) *For current expenses*—Salary of rector $900; other salaries $251; ordinary repairs $67.45; interest on debt $246.73; payment on debts contracted for current expenses $316.73; other objects $21.19; total for current expenses $1,803.10. *Contributions*—(1) *For objects in the Parish*—Communion alms $45.62; extraordinary repairs and improvements $634.71; Parish missions $3.68; maintaining Sunday Schools $33.88; payment on debts for buildings, &c. $463.68; other objects $64.23; total contributions for objects in the Parish $1,245.80. (2) *For objects in the Diocese*—Salary of Bishops $100; permanent fund $5.00; Diocesan missions $255.26; convocation missions $43.62; widows and orphans, aged and disabled clergy fund $30.00; religious and theological education $34.77; Sheltering Arms Hospital $14.29; Theological Seminary $9.82; Bishop's special fund $37.82; Sunday School work in Diocese $12.85; total contributions for objects in the Diocese $543.43. (3) *For objects without the Diocese*—Domestic missions general $12.85; colored people $5.72; Indians $9.89; Jews $5.43; Thro' American Ch. Miss. Society $6.45; total domestic missions $40.34; foreign missions general 55.70, $2.00; for Mexico $2.11; Brazil $76.72; Cuba $1.51; total foreign missions $138.04; specials, boxes, &c., $25.00; American Church Building Fund $3.56; Bible and Prayer Book Society $3.44; Spirit of Missions $4.75; total contributions for objects without the Diocese $215.13.

Statement—Current expenses raised by congregation as above $1,803.10. Contributions—For objects in the Parish $1,245.80; for objects in the Diocese $543.43; for objects without the Diocese $215.13; total of contributions $2,004.36; all money raised by the congregation for current expenses and for contributions $3,807.46; cash in hand $686.22.

Remarks—Much the greater part of the cash on hand is for the purpose of curtailing the debt of the Parish.

PAROCHIAL REPORT.

Rev. JOHN S. DOUGLAS address, Martinsburg. Christ Church, Bunker Hill Mission, Bunker Hill, Berkeley county; date of organization 1769; present minister took charge October 1, 1899.

Church Officers—Church Warden, Jeph S. Morgan; other Vestrymen, J. K. Cunningham, William Seibert, Richard T. Whiting; Registrar, J. K. Cunningham, address Rest, Va.; Treasurer Zeph S. Morgan, address Inwood, W. Va.

Official Acts—Public services, Sundays 20, other days 1, total 21; Holy Communion, public 2, total 2.

Communicants—Number last reported 7, added otherwise 1, total gain 1; present number total 8.

Congregations—Baptized persons connected with Parish 16, confirmed persons connected with Parish 8, families 4, individuals not thus included 2, whole number of individuals 18, number sittings in church 200, number free sittings 200.

Property—Church, brick, value $1,500.

FINANCIAL REPORT.

Receipts—For all purposes—Collections in church $16.11; total receipts for all purposes $16.11.

Disbursements—(1) *For current expenses*—Total for current expenses $2.65. *Contributions*—(2) *For objects in the Diocese*—Diocesan missions $7.35; total contributions for objects in the Diocese $7.35. (3) *For objects without the Diocese*—Indians 55 cents; Jews 40 cents; total domestic missions 95 cents; foreign missions general $1.67; Thro' American Ch. Miss. Society $1.02; Brazil 55 cents; total foreign missions $3.24; Bible and Prayer Book Society 80 cents; total contributions for objects without the Diocese $4.99.

Statement—Current expenses raised by congregations as above $3.77. Contributions—For objects in the Diocese $7.35; for objects without the Diocese $4.99; total of contributions $12.34; all money raised by the congregation for current expenses and for contributions $16.11; cash in hand $1.12.

PAROCHIAL REPORT.

Rev. GEO. W. EASTER, address, Union, W. Va. All Saints Church, All Saints Parish, Union, Monroe county; present minister took charge April 18, 1892.

Church Officers—Church, All Saints, Union; Wardens, Chas. A. Shanklin and E. S. McNeer; other Vestrymen, Jos. D. Logan, Col. Jno. M. Rowan, A. S. Johnston, Guy A. McClearn, Richd. Mason McNeer; Registrar, A. S. Johnston, address Union, W. Va.; Treasurer, Guy A. McClearn, address Union, W. Va.; Superintendent of Sunday School, A. S. Johnston, Union, W. Va.

Official Acts—Baptisms, infants 4, total 4; marriages 8, burials 3, catechisings 40, public services, Sundays 85, other days 184, total 269; Holy Communion, public 15, total 15.

Communicants—Number last reported 35, admitted by confirmation 1, added otherwise 3, total gain 4; died 1, transferred 1, suspended 1, not otherwise accounted for 1, total loss 4; present number total 35.

Congregations—Baptized persons connected with Parish 76; confirmed persons connected with Parish 42; families 19, individuals not thus included 3, whole number of indivduals 90, number of sittings in church 180, number free sittings 180.

Rectors' Salary—As pledged from this congregation $450.00, from Diocesan missions $100.00, from general board $200.00, total $750.00.

Organizations—Sunday School, officers and teachers, male 2, female 1, total 3; pupils, male 21, female 29, total 50; Advent offering $20.35, Lenten offering $29.73, Sheltering Arms $2.20, Cuba and Brazil $4.37, total Sunday School offerings $56.65. *Other organizations*—Parish Aid Society.

Property—Church, wood, insurance $1,350, value $2,500; rectory, brick and wood, value $1,200; other property, value $250, total value $3,950. *Indebtedness*—Due the minister $101, total indebtedness $101.

FINANCIAL REPORT.

Receipts—For all purposes—Cash on hand, per last report $5.75, pledges and subscriptions $413.95, collections in church $264.33, Sunday School $56.65, Guilds, or other societies $6.67, total receipts for all purposes $747.35.

Disbursements—(1) *For current expenses*—Salary of rector $381.50; other salaries $32.00; insurance $27.00; ordinary repairs $7.50; other current expenses $5.50; total for current expenses $453.50. *Contributions* —(1) *For objects in the Parish*—Communion alms so used $5.00; maintaining Sunday Schools $17.26; other objects $6.74; total contributions for objects in the Parish $29.00. (2) *For objects in the Diocese*—Salary of Bishops $50.00; permanent fund $9.10; Diocesan missions $50.00; convocation $5.00; widows and orphans, aged and disabled clergy fund $8.74; religious and theological education $9.11; Sheltering Arms Hospital $9.10; Theological Seminary $1.10; Bishop's special fund $2.00; Childrens Home (Charleston) $1.00; expense account 10 cents; total contributions for objects in the Diocese $145.25. (3) *For objects without the Diocese*—Congregation $18.65; domestic missions general, S. S. $15.13; colored people 59 cents; Indians $3.13; deaf and dumb $3.80; Thro. American Ch. Miss. Society $10.28; total domestic missions $51.58; foreign missions general, congregation $17.92; Sunday School $15.12; For Mexico $3.83; Brazil, congregation $2.10, Sunday School $2.18; Cuba, congregation $2.10, Sunday School $2.19; total foreign missions $45.44; American Church Building Fund $2.37; General Clergy Relief Fund $2.55; Bible and Prayer Book Society $11.03; Cold. Rectory in Balto. (Bragg) $1.00; total contributions for objects without the Diocese $113.97.

Statement—Current expenses raised by congregation as above $453.50. Contributions—For objects in the Parish $29.00; for objects in the Diocese $145.25; for objects without the Diocese $113.97; total of contributions $288.22; all money raised by the congregation for current expenses and for contributions $741.72; cash in hand $5.63.

PAROCHIAL REPORT.

Rev. GEO. W. EASTER, address, Union, W. Va. Messiah Church, All Saints Parish, Alderson, Monroe county; present minister resumed charge July 1, 1903.

Church Officers—Church Warden, C. W. Vandegrift; Treasurer, C. W. Vandegrift.

Official Acts—Public services, Sundays 5, total 5; Holy Communion, public 2, total 2.

Communicants—Number last reported 4, present number total 4.

Congregations—Baptized persons connected with Parish 5, confirmed persons connected with Parish 5, families 3, whole number of individuals 9, number sittings in church 100, number free sittings 100.

Property—Church, wood, value $1,300; other property, value $75; total value $1,375. *Indebtedness*—Due on Diocesan assessment for missions 39c., due on Diocesan assessment for Bishop's fund $2.25, total indebtedness $3.84.

FINANCIAL REPORT.

Receipts—For all purposes—Pledges and subscriptions $13.00, collections in church $11.53, total receipts for all purposes $24.53.

Disbursements—(1) *For current expenses*—Salary of rector $10.00; other current expenses $1.27; total for current expenses $11.27. *Contributions*—(2) *For objects in the Diocese*—Salary of Bishops $3.75; Diocesan missions $5.61; total contributions for objects in the Diocese $9.36. (3) *For objects without the Diocese*—Domestic missions general $1.95; total domestic missions $1.95; foreign missions general $1.95; total foreign missions $1.95; total contributions for objects without the Diocese $3.90.

Statement—Current expenses raised by congregation as above $11.27. Contributions—For objects in the Diocese $9.36; for objects without the Diocese $3.90; total of contributions $13.26; all money raised by the congregation for current expenses and for contributions $24.53.

PAROCHIAL REPORT.

Rev. JAMES L. FISH, address, Davis. St. Barnabas Church, Davis Parish, Davis, Tucker county; date of organization 1894; present minister took charge 1899.

Church Officers—Church, St. Barnabas; Wardens, A. G. McNeill, R. Knox; other Vestrymen, H. H. Weaver, H. N. Warden, Dr. W. H. Holmes, John Fish, John W. Felton, H. N. Walters, J. M. Smith; Registrar, H. H. Weaver, address Davis, W. Va.; Treasurer, H. H. Weaver; Superintendent of Sunday School, John L. Fish, Davis, W. Va.; Sunday School Secretary and Treasurer, Miss M. Weimer, Davis, W. Va.

Official Acts—Baptisms, infants 2, adults 2, total 4; presented for confirmation since last report 7, marriages 2, burials 2, catechisings 12, public services, Sundays 69, other days 40, total 109; Holy Communion, public 13, total 13.

Communicants—Number last reported 37, admitted by confirmation 7, total gain 7; died 1, removed without letter 1, total loss 2; net gain 5, present number total 42.

Congregations—Baptized persons connected with Parish 66, confirmed persons connected with Parish 45, families 24, individuals not thus included 10, whole number of individuals 76, number sittings in church 120, number free sittings 120.

Rector's Salary—As pledged from this congregation $400, from general board $200; total $600.

Organizations—Sunday School, officers and teachers, male 1, female 3, total 4; pupils, male 15, female 15, total 30; other offerings $11.00, total Sunday School offerings $11.00. *Other organizations*—Ladies Guild, whose object is to raise money for the general fund of the church.

Property—Church, frame, insurance $750, value $1,400; rectory, frame, insurance $2,000, value $3,000; total insurance $2.750, value $4,400. *Indebtedness*—On rectory $2,000, due the minister 33 cents, total indebtedness $2,033.

FINANCIAL REPORT.

Receipts—For all purposes—Cash on hand, per last report $119.00; pledges and subscriptions $251.14, collections in church $121.09, Sunday School $11.00, Ladies Guild $130.81, contributions from without $45.00, total receipts for all purposes $678.04.

Disbursements—(1) *For current expenses*—Salary of rector $365.00; insurance $30.00; ordinary repairs $8.10; interest on debt $60.00; other current expenses $45.13; total for current expenses $508.23. *Contributions*—(1) *For objects in the Parish*—Extraordinary repairs and improvements $130.81; maintaining Sunday Schools $11.00; total contributions for objects in the Parish $141.81. (2) *For objects in the Diocese*—Salary of Bishops $8.00; Diocesan missions $8.00; convocation missions $2.00; Sheltering Arms Hospital $2.00; total contributions for objects in the Diocese $20.00. (3) *For objects without the Diocese*—Domestic missions general $8.00; total contributions for objects without the Diocese $8.00.

Statement—Current expenses raised by congregation as above $508.23. Contributions—For objects in the Parish $141.81; for objects in the Diocese $20.00; for objects without the Diocese $8.00; total of contributions $169.81; all money raised by the congregation for current expenses and for contributions $678.04.

PAROCHIAL REPORT.

Rev. JAMES LOGAN FISH, address, Davis. Grace Church, Elkins Parish, Elkins, Randolph county; present minister took charge February, 1905.

Church Officers—Church, Grace; Wardens, Chas. H. Scott, W. Greer; other Vestrymen, John Lingumfelter, I. P. Gassman, J. Lacy Dunlap; Registrar, John Lingumfelter, address Elkins; Treasurer, I. P. Gassman, address, Elkins; Superintendent of Sunday Schools, J. Lacy Dunlap; Sunday School Secretary and Treasurer, Charles Stiffler.

Official Acts—Baptisms, infants 3, adults 2, total 5; presented for confirmation since last report 6, marriages 1, burials 1, public services, Sundays 60, other days 43, total 103; Holy Communion, public 12, total 12.

Communicants—Number last reported 35, admitted by confirmation 6, added otherwise 2, total gain 8; died 1, transferred 2, removed without letter 6, total loss 9; net loss 1, present number total 34.

Congregations—Baptized persons connected with Parish 70, confirmed persons connected with Parish 35, families 25, individuals not thus included 8, whole number of individuals 78, number of scattered communicants in your section not connected with any Parish 6, number sittings in church 120, number free sittings 120.

Rectors Salary—As pledged from this congregation $215.70.

Organizations—Sunday School, officers and teachers, male 1, female 1, total 2; pupils, male 4, female 6, total 10. *Other organizations*—Young Ladies Guild.

Property—Church, frame, insurance $1,400, value $2,900; rectory, frame, insurance $1,000, value $2,000; one lot, value $1,100, total value, insurance $2,400, value $5,000. *Indebtedness*—On rectory $1,750, other debts, one lot $1,100, total indebtedness $2,850.

FINANCIAL REPORT.

Receipts—For all purposes—Cash on hand, per last report $105.35, pledges and subscriptions $225.50, collections in church $173.95, interest from investments $25.00, Woman's Auxiliary box, value $5.60, Guilds or other societies $66.50, income from other sources $5.00, total receipts for all purposes $606.90.

Disbursements—(1) *For current expenses*—Salary of rector $215.70; insurance $12.00; interest on debt $174.00; other current expenses $58.40; box to Sheltering Arms Hospital $5.60; total for current expenses $465.70. *Contributions*—(1) *For objects in the Parish*—Extraordinary repairs and improvements $96.40; total contributions for objects in the Parish $96.40. (2) *For objects in the Diocese*—Salary of Bishops $10.00; Diocesan Missions $10.00; religious and theological education $5.00; Sheltering Arms Hospital $9.80; total contributions for objects in the Diocese $34.80. (3)

For objects without the Diocese—Domestic missions general $10.00; total contributions for objects without the Diocese $10.00.

Statement—Current expenses raised by congregation as above $465.70. Contributions—For objects in the Parish $96.40; for objects in the Diocese $34.80; for objects without the Diocese $10.00; total of contributions $141.20; all money raised by the congregation for current expenses and for contributions $606.90.

Remarks—We have four Communicants at Huttonsville but have, as yet, not held services at this place. They are interested in the church at Elkins. We have also some Communicants at Harding, Coalton and Beverly.

PAROCHIAL REPORT.

Rev. JAMES L. FISH, address, Davis. Trinity Mission, Belington, Barbour county.

Official Acts—Public services, 12, total 12.

Communicants—Number last reported 10, removed without letter 4, total loss 4; present number total 6.

Congregations—Baptized persons connected with Parish 9, confirmed persons connected with Parish 6, families 3.

Remarks—Since Mr. Meade removed to Virginia no services have been held at Belington, but arrangements are being made to again take up services. We have completed the purchase of a lot for church, for which we paid $500. The lot is well situated. There have been several removals which have seriously affected the income.

PAROCHIAL REPORT.

Rev. JAMES L. FISH, address, Davis. Thomas Mission, Thomas, Tucker county; not organized; present minister took charge July, 1902.

Church Officers—Church, Thomas Mission; Registrar, H. Z. Blockridge, address, Thomas, W. Va.; Treasurer, H. Z. Blockridge.

Official Acts—Public services, Sundays 12, total 12.

Communicants—Number last reported 6, added otherwise 2, total gain 2; net gain 2, present number total 8.

Congregations—Baptized persons connected with Parish 15, confirmed persons connected with Parish 8, families 8, individuals not thus included 5, whole number of individuals 20.

FINANCIAL REPORT.

Receipts—For all purposes—Pledges and subscriptions $10.00; total receipts for all purposes $10.00.

Disbursements—For current expenses—Salary of rector $10.00; total for current expenses $10.00

Statement—Current expenses raised by congregation as above $10.00; all money raised by the congregation for current expenses and for contributions $10.00.

PAROCHIAL REPORT.

Rev. JAMES L. FISH, address, Davis. Parsons Mission, Parsons, Tucker county; not organized.

Communicants—Number last reported 6, added otherwise 1, total gain 1; net gain 1, present number total 7.

Congregations—Baptized persons connected with Missions 14, confirmed persons connected with Parish 7, families 7.

Remarks—The Communicants at this place are visited regularly, but it has for some time been impossible to have the use of a building for services except on week days.

PAROCHIAL REPORT.

Rev. JAMES L. FISH, address, Davis. Bayard Mission, Bayard, Grant county; not organized.

Official Acts—Baptisms, infants 2, total 2; public services, Sundays 4, total 4.

Congregations—Baptized persons connected with Parish 9, confirmed persons connected with Parish 4, families 3, individuals not thus included 2, whole number of individuals 11, number sittings in church 120, number free sittings 120.

Rector's Salary—As pledged from this congregation $50.00; total $50.00.

FINANCIAL REPORT.

Receipts—For all purposes—Pledges and subscriptions $50.00; total receipts for all purposes $50.00.

Disbursements—For current expenses—Salary of rector $50.00; total for current expenses $50.00.

Statement—Current expenses raised by congregation as above $50.00; all money raised by the congregation for current expenses and for contributions $50.00.

Remarks—Services are held in this (Emmanuel Church) or Corruna Chapel, during summer months. The services are largely attended by people in the district of all denominations. We also own a lot in the town of Bayard, which is some distance from the above named church.

PAROCHIAL REPORT.

Rev. J. HOWARD GIBBONS, address, Point Pleasant, W. Va. Christ Church, Pt. Pleasant, Mason county; present minister took charge April, 1901.

Church Officers—Church Wardens, Hon. P. C. Eastham, Hon. J. W. English; other Vestrymen, Hon. J. S. Spencer, Hon. Rankin Wiley, Col. J. P. R. B. Smith, J. W. C. Heslop, C. C. Bowyer, L. S. Pomeroy; Registrar, Hon. J. W. English, address Pt. Pleasant; Treasurer, C. C. Bowyer, address Pt. Pleasant; Supt. of Sunday School Hon. P. C. Eastham, Pt. Pleasant; Sunday School Secretary and Treasurer Miss K. B. Stribling.

Official Acts—Baptisms, infants 2, total 2; presented for confirmation since last report 1, marriages 3, burials 4, catechisings 3, public services, Sundays 55, other days 58, total 113; Holy Communion, public 11, total 11.

Communicants—Number last reported 62, admitted by confirmation 1, total gain 1; died 1, total loss 1; present number total 62.

Congregations—Baptized persons connected with Parish 167, confirmed persons connected with Parish 62, families 54, whole number of individuals 125, number sittings in church (free) 250.

Rector's Salary—As pledged from this congregation $350, from Diocesan missions $50.00, as pledged from other congregations $200, from American C'h Missionary Society $150, total $750.

Organizations—Sunday Schools, officers and teachers, male 1, female 3, total 4; pupils, male 15, female 10, total 25; Advent offering $5.90, Lenten offering $7.00, other offerings $18.34, total Sunday School offerings $31.24; Woman's Auxiliary, members 17. *Other organizations*—Ladies Guild, members 25; Babies Branch W. A., members 17; Chancel Chapter, members 9.

Property—Church, brick, insurance $4,000, value $6,000; rectory, frame, insurance $1,000, value $1,200; total value, insurance $5,000, value $7,200.

FINANCIAL REPORT.

Receipts—For all purposes—Cash on hand, per last report $106.49, pledges and subscriptions $571.45, collections in church $192.93, Sunday School $31.24, Woman's Auxiliary, money $33.50, Guilds or other societies $192.97, Babies' Branch W. A. $13.40, total receipts for all purposes $1,141.98.

Disbursements—(1) *For current expenses*—Salary of rector $350.00; other salaries $41.55; insurance $3.00; other current expenses $56.51; other objects $89.71; total for current expenses $540.77. *Contributions*—(1) *For objects in the Parish*—Communion alms $31.66; extraordinary repairs and improvements $134.27; maintaining Sunday Schools $14.30; other objects $132.93; total contributions for objects in the Parish $313.16. (2) *For objects in the Diocese*—Salary of Bishops $50.00; Diocesan missions $50.00; widows and orphans, aged and disabled clergy fund $7.66;

Sheltering Arms Hospital $9.74; Bishop's special fund $5.00; other objects $5.50; S. S. Advent off. (D. M.) $5.90; total contributions for objects in the Diocese $133.80. (3) *For objects without the Diocese*—Domestic missions general $7.50; colored people $2.50; Indians $2.50; Thro' American Ch. Miss. Society $7.50; total domestic missions $20.00; foreign missions general $10.00; for China $2.50; for Africa $2.50; for Japan $2.50; for Hayti $2.50; for Philippines $2.50; Porto Rico $2.50; Brazil $2.50; Cuba $2.50; total foreign missions $30.00; General Clergy Relief Fund $3.50; other objects $24.40; W. A. united offering for year $13.00; S. S Lenten offering (missions) $7.00; total contributions for objects without the Diocese $97.90.

Statement—Current expenses raised by congregation as above $540.77. Contributions—For objects in the Parish $313.16; for objects in the Diocese $133.80; for objects without the Diocese $97.90; total of contributions $544.86; all money raised by the congregation for current expenses and for contributions $1,085.63; cash in hand $56.35.

Rev. J. HOWARD GIBBONS, address, Point Pleasant, W. Va. Bruce Chapel, Elwell, Mason county; present minister took charge April, 1901.

Church Officers—Vestrymen, J. M. H. Beale, E. L. Neale, J. Moore; Treasurer Miss Mary Beale, address, Beale, W. Va.; Superintendent of Sunday School Miss Vause Beale, Beale, W. Va.; Sunday School Secretary and Treasurer Miss Mary Beale.

Official Acts—Baptisms, infants 3, total 3; presented for confirmation since last report 1, burials 2, catechisings 4, public services, Sundays 20, other days 3, total 23; Holy Communion, public 6, total 6.

Communicants—Number last reported 26, admitted by confirmation 1, total gain 1; net gain 1, present number total 27.

Congregations—Baptized persons connected with Parish 45, confirmed persons connected with Parish 27, families 16, whole number of individuals 60, number sittings in church (free) 125.

Rector's Salary—As pledged from this congregation $150; total $150.

Organizations—Sunday School, officers and teachers, female 4, total 4; pupils, male 14, female 21, total 35; Advent offering $3.00, Lenten offering $4.00, other offerings $5.51, total Sunday School offerings $12.51. Industrial Schools officers and teachers 2, scholars 7, total 9.

Property—Chapel, brick, insurance $1,000, value $1,500; total value, insurance $1,000, value $1,500. Money raised from outside sources $32.52 for new fence around the chapel ground.

FINANCIAL REPORT.

Receipts—For all purposes—Pledges and subscriptions $162.00, Bishop's special fund $17.00, collections in church $24.00, Sunday School $12.51; total receipts for all purposes $215.51.

Disbursements—(1) *For current expenses*—Salary of rector $150.00; total for current expenses $150.00. *Contributions*—(1) *For objects in the Parish*—Maintaining Sunday Schools $5.51; total contributions for objects in the Parish $5.51. (2) *For objects in the Diocese*—Salary of Bishops $12.00; Diocesan missions $12.00; Bishop's special fund $17.00; S. S. Advent offering (D. M.) $3.00; total contributions for objects in the Diocese $44.00. (3) *For objects without the Diocese*—Domestic missions general $1.00; colored people $1.00; Indians $1.00; Thro' American Ch. Miss. Society $1.00; total domestic missions $4.00 for China $1.00; for Africa $1.00; for Japan $1.00; for Hayti $1.00; for Philippines $1.00; Porto Rico $1.00; Brazil $1.00; Cuba $1.00; total foreign missions $8.00; S. S. Lenten offering (missions) $4.00; total contributions for objects without the Diocese $16.00.

Statement—Current expenses raised by congregation as above $150.00. Contributions—For objects in the Parish $5.51; for objects in the Diocese $44.00; for objects without the Diocese $16.00; total of contributions $65.51; all money raised by the congregation for current expenses and for contributions $215.51.

Remarks—Aid is received from the D. M. S. and the A. C. M. S. for *all* work under my care and is reported only under the report for Christ Church, Pt. Pleasant.

PAROCHIAL REPORT.

Rev. J. HOWARD GIBBONS, address, Point Pleasant, W. Va. Spilman Chapel, Spilman, Mason county; present minister took charge April, 1901.

Church Officers—Church Wardens, H. E. Spilman, M. G. Tyler; Treasurer H. E. Spilman, address Spilman, W. Va.; Superintendent of Sunday Schools Miss Virginia Behan, West Columbia, W. Va.; Sunday School Secretary and Treasurer Mrs. M. G. Tyler.

Official Acts—Baptisms, infants 1, total 1; catechisings 2, public services, Sundays 12, other days 8, total 20; Holy Communion, public 3, total 3.

Communicants—Number last reported 23, added otherwise 2, total gain 2; net gain 2, present number total 25.

Congregations—Baptized persons connected with Parish 60, families 18, whole number of individuals 70, number sittings in church (free) 125.

Rector's Salary—As pledged from this congregation $50.00; total $50.00.

Organizations—Sunday School, officers and teachers, female 3, total 3; pupils, male 10, female 14, total 24; Advent offering $1.00, Lenten offering $2.75, other offerings $20.77; total Sunday School offerings $24.52.

Property—Chapel, brick, insurance $1,500, value $1,800, total value, insurance $1,500, value $1,800.

FINANCIAL REPORT.

Receipts—For all purposes—Cash on hand, per last report $3.61, pledges and subscriptions $50.00, collections in church $43.89, Sunday School $24.52, total receipts for all purposes $122.02.

Disbursements—(1) *For current expenses*—Salary of rector $50.00; total for current expenses $50.00. *Contributions*—(1) *For objects in the Parish*—Maintaining Sunday School $20.77; other objects $13.50; total contributions for objects in the Parish $34.27. (3) *For objects in the Diocese*—Salary of Bishops $10; Diocesan missions $10; S. S. Advent off. (D. M.) $1.00; total contributions for objects in the Diocese $21.00. (3) *For objects without the Diocese*—Domestic missions general 75c.; colored people 75c.; Indians 75c.; Thro' American Ch. Miss. Society 75c.; total domestic missions $3.00; foreign missions general 75c.; for China 75c.; for Africa 75c.; for Japan 75c.; for Hayti 75c.; for Philippines 75c.; Porto Rico 75c.; Brazil $1.00; Cuba 75c.; total foreign missions $7.00; American Church Building Fund $3.00; other objects $1.00; S. E. Lenten off. (missions) $2.75; total contributions for objects without the Diocese $16.75.

Statement—Current expenses raised by congregation as above $50.00. Contributions—for objects in the Parish $34.27; for objects in the Diocese $21.00; for objects without the Diocese $16.75; total of contributions $72.02; all money raised by the congregation for current expenses and for contributions $122.02.

Remarks—Aid is received from the D. M. S. and the A. C. M. S. for *all* work under my care and is reported only under the report for Christ Church, Pt. Pleasant.

PAROCHIAL REPORT.

Rev. J. HOWARD GIBBONS, address, Point Pleasant, W. Va. For Mason City, Morning Star S. H. Morgan's S. H., Winfield; present minister took charge April, 1901.

Supt. Report—Mason City. Held 4 Sunday services.

Morning Star School House—Held 1 Sunday and 1 week day service.

Morgan's School House—Held one Sunday service; baptized 2 infants; reported under Bruce Chapel report.

Winfield—Held 1 week day service.

Remarks—Mason City is now under the care of the Rev. Paca Kennedy, Ravenswood.—J. HOWARD GIBBONS, Pt. Pleasant.

PAROCHIAL REPORT.

Rev. G. A. GIBBONS, address, Romney, W. Va. St. Stephens Church, Romney Mission, Romney, Hampshire county; date of organization, 1885; present minister took charge July 1st, 1885.

Church Officers—Church Wardens, G. W. Parsons, W. N. Baird; Treasurer, G. W. Parsons (Miss Keller, assistant), address Romney, W. Va.; Superintendent of Sunday School, Wm. Rusmisell, Romney, W. Va.; Sunday School Secretary and Treasurer, Mrs. G. W. Parsons.

Official Acts—Baptisms, infants 1, adults 3, total 4; presented for confirmation since last report 9, marriages 2, burials 1, catechisings 4, public services, Sundays 24, other days 9, total 33; Holy Communion, public 4, total 4.

Communicants—Number last reported 21, admitted by confirmation 9, total gain 9; net gain 9, present number total 30.

Congregations—Baptized persons connected with Parish 40, confirmed persons connected with Parish 30, families 16, individuals not thus included 4, whole number of individuals 44, number sittings in church 200, number sittings in chapel 100.

Rector's Salary—As pledged from this congregation $100, from Diocesan missions $250, as pledged from other congregations $190, from convocation missions $50.00, from American C'h Missionary Society $200, total $790.

Organizations—Sunday School, officers and teachers, male 1, female 3, total 4; pupils, male 6, female 12, total 18; Advent offering $6.70, Lenten offering $17.33, total Sunday School offerings $24.03.

Property—Church, brick, insurance $1,200, value $1,800; chapel, wood, insurance $400, value $700; rectory, wood, insurance $1,000, value $1,900; total value, insurance $2,600, value $4,400.

FINANCIAL REPORT.

Receipts—For all purposes—Pledges and subscriptions $122.25, collections in church $95.90, Sunday School $17.33, Guilds $31.25, total receipts for all purposes $266.73.

Disbursements—(1) *For current expenses*—Salary of rector $100.00; other salaries $22.25; other current expenses $3.00; other objects $9.18; total for current expenses $134.43. (1) *For objects in the Parish*—Communion alms $4.02; extraordinary repairs and improvements $8.50; other objects $20.00; total contributions for objects in the Parish $32.52. (2) *For objects in the Diocese*—Salary of Bishops $16.00; permanent fund $1.70; Diocesan missions $17.00; convocation missions $5.00; widows and orphans, aged and disabled clergy fund $2.00; religious and theological education $2.00; Sheltering Arms Hospital $3.75; Bishop's special fund $5.00; total contributions for objects in the Diocese $52.45. (3) *For objects without the Diocese*—Domestic missions general $10.00; total domestic missions $10.00; foreign missions general $10.00; total foreign missions $10.00; General Clergy Relief Fund $10.00; Sunday School dom. and L. miss. $17.33; total contributions for objects without the Diocese $47.33.

Statement—Current expenses raised by congregation as above $134.43. Contributions—For objects in the Parish $32.52; for objects in the Diocese $52.45; for objects without the Diocese $47.33; total of contributions $132.30; all money raised by the congregation for current expenses and for contributions $266.73.

Remarks—The Chapel in this report is Zion on North River.

PAROCHIAL REPORT.

Rev. G. A. GIBBONS, address, Romney, W. Va. Emmanuel Church, Emmanuel Parish, Moorefield, Hardy county; date of organization 1878; present minister took charge July 1, 1885.

Church Officers—Church Warden, Thomas Lakin; other Vestrymen, Wm. H. Shearer, P. W. Inskeep, Edward Rinker, F. S. Randolph; Registrar, Wm. H. Shearer, address Moorefield, W. Va.; Treasurer, Registrar and Mrs. Ida Wood, address Moorefield, W. Va.; Superintendent of Sunday School, Wm. Welton Shearer, Moorefield, W. Va.; Sunday School Secretary and Treasurer, Mrs. Wm. H. Shearer.

Official Acts—Baptisms, infants 1, adults 3, total 4; presented for confirmation since last report 3, burials 2, catechisings 5, public services, Sundays 44, other days 5, total 49; Holy Communion, public 5.

Communicants—Number last reported 30, admitted by confirmation 3, net gain 3, present number total 33.

Congregations—Baptized persons connected with Parish 60, confirmed persons connected with Parish 33, families 18, whole number of individuals 60, number sittings in church 200, number sittings in Sunday School room 125.

Rector's Salary—As pledged from this congregation $150, from Diocesan missions $250, as pledged from other congregations $140, from convocation missions $50, from American C'h Missionary Society $200, total $790.

Organizations—Sunday School, officers and teachers, male 1, female 4, total 5; pupils, male 9, female 12, total 21; Advent offering $1.60, Lenten offering $4.05, other offerings $1.50, total Sunday School offerings $7.15.

Property—Church, frame, insurance $1,200, value $3,000; rectory, frame, insurance $1,200, value $2,000; Sunday School room, frame, insurance $750, value $1,400; total value, insurance $3,150, value $6,400.

FINANCIAL REPORT.

Receipts—For all purposes—Pledges and subscriptions $170.00, collections in church $77.75, Sunday School $7.15; Guilds or other societies $10.00, total receipts for all purposes $264.90.

Disbursements—(1) *For current expenses*—Salary of rector $150.00;

other salaries $30.00; other current expenses $10.00; total for current expenses $190.00. *Contributions*—(1) *For objects in the Parish*—Communion alms $2.00; total contributions for objects in the Parish $2.00. (2) *For objects in the Diocese*—Salary of Bishops $20.00; permanent fund $1.50; Diocesan missions $20.00; widows and orphans, aged and disabled clergy fund $2.00; religious and theological education $2.50; Sheltering Arms Hospital $1.70; total contributions for objects in the Diocese $47.70. (3) *For objects without the Diocese*—Domestic missions general $10.00; total domestic missions $10.00; foreign missions general $10.00; total foreign missions $10.00; total contributions for objects without the Diocese $20.00.

Statement—Current expenses raised by congregation as above $190.00. Contributions—For objects in the Parish $2.00; for objects in the Diocese $47.70; for objects without the Diocese $20.00; total of contributions $69.70; all money raised by the congregation for current expenses and for contributions $264.90; cash in hand $5.20.

PAROCHIAL REPORT.

Rev. G. A. GIBBONS address, Romney, W. Va. Epiphany Church, Okonoko Mission, Okonoko, Hampshire county; date of organization 1886; present minister took charge 1885.

Church Officers—Church Warden, Mahlon A. Russell; Registrar, E. W. McGill, address Woodrow, Morgan Co., W. Va.; Treasurer, Henry M. Russell, address Okonoko, W. Va.

Official Acts—Public services, Sundays 19, total 19; Holy Communion, public 3, total 3.

Communicants—Number last reported 10, present number total 10.

Congregations—Baptized persons connected with Parish 16, confirmed persons connected with Parish 10, families 4, whole number of individuals 16, number sittings in church 150, number free sittings 150.

Rector's Salary—As pledged from this congregation $40, from Diocesan missions $250, as pledged from other congregations $250, from convocations missions $50, from American C'h Missionary Society $200, total $790.

Property—Church, frame, insurance $1,000, value $1,500.

FINANCIAL REPORT.

Receipts—For all purposes—Subscriptions $37.00, collections in church $10.00, thank offering $10.00, total receipts for all purposes $57.00.

Disbursements—(1) *For current expenses*—Salary of rector $37.00; total for current expenses $37.00. *Contributions*—(2) *For objects in the*

Diocese—Salary of Bishops $10.00; Diocesan missions $10.00; total contributions for objects in the Diocese $20.00.

Statement—Current expenses raised by congregations as above $37.00. Contributions—For objects in the Diocese $20.00; total of contributions $20.00; all money raised by the congregation for current expenses and for contributions $57.00.

Remarks—Long and extreme illness in the principal family in the Church here has been a great drawback to the work and contributions at this Mission.

PAROCHIAL REPORT.

Rev. G. A. GIBBONS, address, Romney, W. Va. Keyser Mission, Keyser, Mineral county.

Church Officers—Church Warden, J. M. Linthicum; Treasurer, J. M. Linthicum, address Keyser, W. Va.

Congregations—Confirmed persons connected with Parish 12, individuals not thus included 6, whole number of individuals 18.

Property—Chapel, stone, value $2,000. *Indebtedness*—On chapel $2,000.

FINANCIAL REPORT.

Receipts—For all purposes—Cash on hand, per last report $54.70, income from other sources $168.00, total receipts for all purposes $222.70.

Contributions—For objects in the Parish—Interest on debt $170.00.

Statement—Current expenses raised by congregation as above $168.00. Contributions—All money raised by the congregation for current expenses and for contributions $168.00; cash in hand $54.70.

Remarks—There have been no regular services at Keyser for a year or more, and, while not under my charge, I have at the Bishop's request, gathered the best information and data I can get and send this report.—G. A. GIBBONS, Romney, W. Va.

PAROCHIAL REPORT.

Rev. G. A. GIBBONS, address, Romney, W. Va. Paw Paw Mission, Paw Paw, Morgan county, W. Va.; present minister took charge 1893.

Church Officers—Church Warden, Thomas Korns; Treasurer, Thomas Korns, address Paw Paw, W. Va.

Official Acts—Baptisms, infants 1, total 1; public services 11, Holy Communion, public 2.

Communicants—Number last reported 6, removed without letter 1, present number total 5.

Congregations—Baptized persons connected with Parish 5, confirmed persons connected with Parish 5, families 3, individuals not thus included 2, whole number of individuals 10.

FINANCIAL REPORT.

Receipts—For all purposes—Subscriptions $28.25, collections in church $14.00, total receipts for all purposes $42.25.

Disbursements—(1) *For current expenses*—Rector expenses $28.25. *Contributions*—(2) *For objects in the Diocese*—Permanent fund $2.00; Diocesan missions $3.00; widows and orphans, aged and disabled clergy fund $2.00; religious and theological education $2.00; total contributions for objects in the Diocese $9.00. (3) *For objects without the Diocese*—Brazil $3.00; Cuba $2.00; total contributions for objects without the Diocese $5.00.

Statement—Current expenses raised by congregation as above $28.25. Contributions—For objects in the Diocese $9.00; for objects without the Diocese $5.00; total of contributions $14.00; all money raised by the congregation for current expenses and for contributions $42.25.

Remarks—We use a part of the public school for church services, and in order to do this and have it in order twelve times a year, there are no two or three individuals in the Diocese who do as much work and make as much real sacrifice by way of time and labor, as the three in the Wardens family.

PAROCHIAL REPORT.

Rev. JNO. S. GIBSON, address, Huntington. Trinity Church, Cabell Parish, Huntington, Cabell county; date of organization, 1872; present minister took charge 1892.

Church Officers—Church Wardens, Cameron L. Thompson, Edmund Sehon; other Vestrymen, Frank B. Enslow, G. A. Northcott, C. D. Emmons, F. D. Fuller, Thos. L. Trimmer, F. R. Van Antwerp, John W. Ensign, R. L. Archer, Thos. W. Moore; Registrar, C. D. Emmons, address Huntington; Treasurer, G A. Northcott, address Huntington; Superintendent of Sunday School, G. A. Northcott; Sunday School Secretary and Treasurer Herman Jenkins.

Official Acts—Baptisms, infants 5, adults 4, total 9; presented for confirmation since last report 15, marriages 5, burials 34, catechisings 40, public services, Sundays 125, other days 75, total 200; Holy Communion, public 25, total 25.

Communicants—Number last reported 200, received by letter 3, admitted by confirmation 15, added otherwise 3, total gain 21; died 1, transferred 3, removed without letter 12, total loss 16; net gain 5, present number total 205.

Congregations—Baptized persons connected with Parish 430, confirmed persons connected with Parish 220, families 72, individuals not thus included 80, whole number of individuals 460, number sittings in church, all free, 425, number sittings in chapel 75.

Rector's Salary—As pledged from this congregation $1,200; total $1,200.

Organizations—Sunday School, officers and teachers, male 3, female 8, total 11; pupils 75, total 75; Advent offering $10.76, Lenten offering $35.76, other offerings $110, total Sunday School offerings $156.52.

Property—Church, brick, insurance $8,000, value $20,500; rectory, brick, insurance $3,000, value $6,000, total value $26,500.

FINANCIAL REPORT.

Receipts—For all purposes—Cash on hand, per last report $243.00, pledges and subscriptions $1,715.00; collections in church $650.00, Sunday School $156.52, Woman's and Junior Auxiliary, money $109.73, Woman's Auxiliary boxes, value $66.75, Guilds, or other societies $900.00, total receipts for all purposes $3,598.00.

Disbursements—(1) *For current expenses*—Salary of rector $1,200; other salaries $500; insurance $45.00; ordinary repairs $75.00; other current expenses $193.00; other objects $106.00; total for current expenses $2,119. *Contributions*—(1) *For objects in the Parish*—Extraordinary repairs and improvements $618.28; Parish missions $20.00; maintaining Sunday Schools $100.00; other objects $230.00; total contributions for objects in the Parish $968.28. (2) *For objects in the Diocese*—Salary of Bishops $100.00; Permanent fund $2.00; Diocesan missions $80.00; convocation missions $10.00; widows and orphans, aged and disabled clergy fund $35.70; religious and theological education $11.50; Sheltering Arms Hospital $81.75; Bishop's special fund $45.00; other objects $35.75; total contributions for objects in the Diocese $401.70. (3) *For objects without the Diocese*—Domestic missions general $74.00, colored people $3.00, deaf and dumb $4.00; total domestic missions $81.00; foreign missions general $64.00; Brazil and Cuba $15.00; total foreign misions $79.00; special boxes, &c., $12.00; American Church Building Fund $2.00; General Clergy Relief Fund $1.60; Bible and Prayer Book Society $2.00; total contributions for objects without the Diocese $177.60.

Statement—Current expenses raised by congregation as above $2,119. Contributions—For objects in the Parish $968.28; for objects in the Diocese $401.70; for objects without the Diocese $177.60; total of contributions $1,547.58; all money raised by the congregation for current expenses and for contributions $3,666.58; cash in hands of societies $174.42.

PAROCHIAL REPORT.

Rev. JNO. S. GIBSON, address, Huntington. Grace Church, Wayne Mission, Kenova, Wayne county; date of organization, 1890; present minister took charge 1892.

Church Officers—Church Warden, Charles C. Coe; other Vestrymen F. R. Peck, R. Ney Williams; Registrar, F. R. Peck, address Kenova; Treasurer F. R. Peck, address Kenova.

Official Acts—Baptisms, adults 1, total 1; presented for confirmation since last report 2, marriages 1, public services, Sundays 48, other days 6, total 54; Holy Communion, public 9, total 9.

Communicants—Number last reported 8, received by letter 2; admitted by confirmation 2; total gain 4; removed without letter 1, total loss 1; net gain 3, present number total 11.

Congregations—Baptized persons connected with Parish 21, families 7, individuals not thus included 2, whole number of individuals 24, number sittings in church 150; number free sittings 150.

Rector's Salary—No pledge.

Property—Church and furniture, insurance $1,800, value $2,500.

FINANCIAL REPORT.

Receipts—For all purposes—Cash on hand, per last report $26.25, pledges and subscriptions $136.00, Bishop's salary $7.00; collections in church $95.14; total receipts for all purposes $264.39.

Disbursements—(1) *For current expenses*—Salary of rector $150.00; insurance $36.00; ordinary repairs $1.85; other current expenses $11.35; total for current expenses $199.20. *Contributions*—(1) *For objects in the Parish*—Extraordinary repairs and improvements $32.03; total contributions for objects in the Parish $32.03. (2) *For objects in the Diocese*—Salary of Bishops $7.00; Diocesan missions $5.00; widows and orphans, aged and disabled clergy fund $6.80; Sheltering Arms Hospital $3.65; total contributions for objects in the Diocese $22.45. (3) *For objects without the Diocese*—Domestic missions general $4.25; foreign missions general $4.25; total foreign missions $4.25; American Church Building Fund $1.00; total contributions for objects without the Diocese $9.50.

Statement—Current expenses raised by congregation as above $199.20. Contributions—For objects in the Parish $32.03; for objects in the Diocese $22.45; for objects without the Diocese $9.50; total of contributions $63.98; all money raised by the congregation for current expenses and for contributions $263.18; cash in hand $1.21.

Remarks—The recent removal of one of the families connected with and interested in this mission and the immediate removal of two others greatly depresses our work and the present outlook is not for progress, and indeed, we cannot hope to maintain our contributions to anything like their present proportions. The ministers salary has been, and will be further, reduced, and so must all assessments upon us.

PAROCHIAL REPORT.

Rev. JNO. S. GIBSON, address, Huntington. Mingo Mission, Williamson, Mingo county; unorganized; present minister took charge 1902.

Church Officers—Treasurer B. R. Bias, address Williamson.

Official Acts—Presented for confirmation since last report 1, burials 1, public services 18, total 18; Holy Communion, public, 6, total 6.

Communicants—Number last reported 11, admitted by confirmation 1, added otherwise 1, total gain 2; removed without letter 3, total loss 3; net loss 1, present number total 10.

Congregations—Baptized persons connected with Parish 30, confirmed persons connected with Parish 12, families 4, individuals not thus included 8, whole number of individuals 35, number of scattered communicants in your section not connected with any Parish 5.

FINANCIAL REPORT.

Receipts—For all purposes—Cash on hand, per last report $10.37; pledges and subscriptions $100.25, collections in church $13.55, total receipts for all purposes $124.17.

Disbursements—(1) *For current expenses*—Salary of rector $100.25; other current expenses $10.75; total for current expenses $111.00. *Contributions*—(2) *For objects in the Diocese*—Diocesan missions $2.30; total contributions for objects in the Diocese $2.30. (3) *For objects without the Diocese*—Domestic missions 50c.; total domestic missions 50c.; foreign missions general 50c.; total foreign missions 50c.; total contributions for objects without the Diocese $1.00.

Statement—Current expenses raised by congregation as above $111.00. Contributions—For objects in the Diocese $2.30; for objects without the Diocese $1.00; total of contributions $3.30; all money raised by the congregation for current expenses and for contributions $114.30; cash in hand $9.87.

Remarks—The treasurer, Mr. B. R. Bias, has in bank for the building of a church $109.00, contributed in Williamson. There is an additional $500 subscribed.

PAROCHIAL REPORT.

Rev. ANDREW G. GRINNAN, address, Weston, W. Va. St. Paul's Church, Weston Parish, Weston, Lewis county; date or oganization, 1848; present minister took charge 1900.

Church Officers—Church Wardens, Harry C. Bailey, Richard Harrison; other Vestrymen, Er. Ralston, E. G. Davisson, M. B. Ralston, Louis Bennett, A. H. Kunst, A. A. Warren, J. S. Mitchell; Registrar, Ern. Vandervort; Treasurer, Ern. Vandervort, address Weston, W. Va.

Official Acts—Baptisms, infants 6, adults 1, total 7; presented for confirmation since last report 8, marriages 9, burials 16, catechisings weekly, public services, Sundays 118, other days 79, total 197; Holy Communion, public, 40, private 1, total 41.

Communicants—Number last reported 75, admitted by confirmation 8, added otherwise 2, total gain 10; died 2, removed without letter 1, total loss 3; net gain 7; present number total 82.

Congregations—Baptized persons connected with Parish 215, confirmed persons connected with Parish 112, families 65, individuals not thus included 25, whole number of individuals 215, number free sittings 300, number sittings in Sunday school room 150,

Rector's Salary—As pledged from this congregation $800; total $800.

Organizations—Sunday school, officers and teachers, male 1, female 7, total 8; pupils, male 26, female 36, total 62; advent offering $28.22, Lenten $45.00, other offerings $36.71, total Sunday School offerings $133.41. Woman's Auxiliary, members 19. *Other Organizations*—Daughters of King 8, Guild 20.

Property—Church, stone, insurance $5,000, value $15,000; rectory, wood, insurance $1,000, value $2,000.

FINANCIAL REPORT.

Receipts—For all purposes—Cash on hand, per last report $184.74, pledges and subscriptions $855.26, collections in church $511.32, thank offerings $43.44, Sunday School $133.41, Woman's Auxiliary, money $49.00, Guilds or other societies $159.31, income from other sources $69.30, total receipts for all purposes $2,005.78.

Disbursements—(1) *For current expenses*—Salary of rector $800.04; other current expenses $218.89; total for current expenses $1,018.93. *Contributions*—(1) *For objects in the Parish*—Communion alms $22.73; maintaining Sunday Schools $48.34; other objects $113.33; total contributions for objects in the Parish $184.40. (2) *For objects in the Diocese*—Salary of Bishops $80.00; permanent fund $6.37; Diocesan missions $75.97; convocation $2.50; widows and orphans, aged and disabled clergy fund $13.74; religious and theological education $5.90; Sheltering Arms Hospital $26.54; Bishop's special fund $12.50; through Woman's Auxiliary $18.50; total contributions for objects in the Diocese $242.02. (3) *For objects without the Diocese*—Domestic missions general $61.44; total domestic missions $61.44; foreign missions general $55.94; special for China $14.58; Brazil $6.47; total foreign missions $76.99; Society of St. Philip the Apostle $43.44; total contributions for objects without the Diocese $181.87.

Statement—Current expenses raised by congregation as above $1,018.93. Contributions—For objects in the Parish $184.40; for objects in the Diocese $242.02; for objects without the Diocese $181.87; total of contributions $608.29; all money raised by the congregation for current expenses and for contributions $1,627.22; cash in hand $378.56.

Remarks—I have also conducted 4 services at Brownsville, 4 at Buckhanon, 3 at Spruce Chapel, 5 at the Hospital for the Insane, 2 at Sutton, 2 at Richwood, 1 at Centralia, 1 at Little Otter, 1 at Jacksonville.

I have begun to hold services at Brownsville (3 miles south of Weston) on the first Sunday afternoon of each month, in a school house.

PAROCHIAL REPORT.

Rev. ANDREW G. GRINNAN, address, Weston. St. Paul's Chapel, St. Paul's Parish, near Weston, Lewis county; date of organization, 1903; present minister took charge 1900.

Church Officers—Treasurer J. White Peterson, Weston, W. Va.; Superintendent of Sunday School, Miss Hila McBride, Weston, W. Va.

Official Acts—Baptisms, infants 3, adults 1, total 4; presented for confirmation since last report 2, burials 2, public services, Sundays 22, other days 8, total 30, Holy Communion, public 6, private 1, total 7.

Communicants—Number last reported 13, admitted by confirmation 2, total gain 2, died 1, removed without letter 1, total loss 2, present number total 13.

Congregations—Baptized persons connected with Parish 22, confirmed persons connected with Parish 13, families 8, number sittings in church 120.

Rector's Salary—From this congregation $28.50, from Diocesan missions $50.00, total $78.50.

Organizations—Sunday School, officers and teachers, female 3, pupils, male 16, female 18, total 34.

Property—Chapel, wood, insurance $750, value $1,000; other property, one-half acre of ground.

FINANCIAL REPORT.

Receipts—For all purposes—Cash on hand, per last report $23.69, pledges and subscriptions and collections in church $77.11, total receipts for all purposes $100.80.

Disbursements—(1) *For current expenses*—Salary of rector $28.50; other current expenses $34.58; total for current expenses $63.08. *Contributions*—(1) *For objects in the Parish*—Maintaining Sunday Schools $1.58; total contributions for objects in the Parish $1.58. (2) *For objects in the Diocese*—Diocesan missions $2.36; widows and orphans, aged and disabled clergy fund $2.18; Sheltering Arms Hospital $2.50; Bishop's special fund $2.50; total contributions for objects in the Diocese $9.54. (3) *For objects without the Diocese*—General missions $6.56; American Church Building Fund $3.00; total contributions for objects without the Diocese $9.56.

Statement—Current expenses raised by congregation as above $63.08. Contributions—For objects in the Parish $1.58; for objects in the Diocese $9.54; for objects without the Diocese $9.56; total of contributions $20.68; all money raised by the congregation for current expenses and for contributions $83.76; cash in hand $17.04.

PAROCHIAL REPORT.

Rev. JACOB A. HIATT, address, Hinton. Ascension Church, Hinton Mission, Hinton, Summers county; present minister took charge January 1904.

Church Officers—Church, "Ascension"; Wardens, T. N. Read, W. L. Barksdale; other Vestrymen, R. G. Haile, C. S. Falconer, Jno. Romick; Registrar, T. N. Read, address Hinton, W. Va.; Treasurer, T. N. Read, address Hinton, W. Va.; Superintendent of Sunday School, T. N. Read, Hinton, W. Va.

Official Acts—Baptisms, infants 5, adults 3, total 8; presented for confirmation since last report 5, marriages 2, burials 3, catechisings 15, public services, Sundays 35, other days 55, total 90; Holy Communion, public 15, private 1, total 16.

Communicants—Number last reported 49, admitted by confirmation 5, total gain 5; transferred 15, removed without letter 9, total loss 24; net loss 19, present number total 30.

Congregations—Baptized persons connected with Parish 60, confirmed persons connected with Parish 30, individuals not thus included 100, whole number of individuals 180, number sittings in church 200 (all free), number sittings in Sunday School room 100.

Rector's Salary—As pledged from this congregation $400, as pledged from other congregations $200; from American C'h Missionary Society $200, total $800.

Organizations—Sunday School, officers and teachers, male 1, female 1, total 2; pupils, male 5, female 15, total 24.

Property—Church, frame, insurance $3,500, value $4,000; rectory, frame, insurance $1,200, value $1,800; real estate, church lot, value $6,000; total value $11,800. *Indebtedness*—On church $190, on Diocesan assessment for Bishop's fund $10, total indebtedness $200.

FINANCIAL REPORT.

Receipts—For all purposes—Cash on hand May 1, 1904, $92.73, pledges and subscriptions $401.33, collections in church $66.58, thank offerings, Easter $40.29, Guilds, or other societies $210.93, total receipts for all purposes $811.86.

Disbursements—(1) *For current expenses*—Salary of rector $401.90;

other salaries, sexton, $55.80; organist $4.00; ordinary repairs $11.40; interest on debt $19.47; payment on debts contracted for current expenses $36.46; other current expenses $7.50; total for current expenses $536.53. *Contributions*—(1) *For objects in the Parish*—Payment on debts for building, &c., $271.30; total contributions for objects in the Parish $271.30. (2) *For objects in the Diocese*—Salary of Bishops $9.61; Diocesan missions $30.00; total contributions for objects in the Diocese $39.61.

Statement—Current expenses raised by congregation as above $536.53. Contributions—For objects in the Parish $271.30; for objects in the Diocese $39.61; total of contributions $310.91; all money raised by the congregation for current expenses and for contributions $847.44.

PAROCHIAL REPORT.

Rev. JACOB A. HIATT, address, Hinton. Glen Jean Mission, Glen Jean, Fayette county; present minister took charge June, 1904.

Church Officers—Vestrymen, Dr. C. B. Lee, W. B. Johnson, W. S. Carter; Treasurer, W. B. Johnson, address Red Star.

Official Acts—Baptisms, infants 1, total 1; burials 1, public services, Sundays 24, other days 6, total 30; Holy Communion, public 1, total 1.

Communicants—Number last reported 95, removed without letter 6, total loss 6; net loss 6, present number total 9.

Congregations—Baptized persons connected with Parish 25, confirmed persons connected with Parish 9, families 6, individuals not thus included 18, number sittings in church (all free) 300.

Rector's Salary—As pledged from this congregation $200; total $200.

Organizations—There is a good union Sunday School at Glen Jean.

Property—Church, frame, insurance $1,500, value $3,000; total value, insurance $1,500, value $3,000. *Indebtedness*—Due on Diocesan assessment for missions $2.00, on Diocesan assessment for Bishop's fund $2.00, total indebtedness $4.00.

FINANCIAL STATEMENT.

Receipts—For all purposes—Pledges and subscriptions $150.00, collections in Church $35.00; contributions from without $25.00; total receipts for all purposes $210.00.

Disbursements—(1) *For current expenses*—Salary of rector $200; other current expenses $25.00; total for current expenses $225.00. *Contributions*—(2) *For objects in the Diocese*—Salary of Bishops $8.00; Diocesan missions $8.00; Bishop's special fund $15.00; total contributions for objects in the Diocese $31.00. (3) *For objects without the Diocese*—Foreign missions general $5.00; total foreign missions $5.00; total contributions for objects without the Diocese $5.00.

Statement—Contributions—for objects in the Parish $225.00; for objects in the Diocese $31.00; for objects without the Diocese $5.00; total of contributions $261.00.

PAROCHIAL REPORT.

Rev. DAVID W. HOWARD, address, Wheeling, W. Va. Saint Matthew's Church Parish, Wheeling, Ohio county; date of organization May 11, 1819; present minister took charge January 1, 1900.

Church Officers—Church Wardens, Joseph D. Du Bois, Dr. G. A. Aschman; other Vestrymen, Hullihen Quarrier, W. S. Brady, J. C. Brady, James J. Holloway, Julien Hearne, B. Walker Peterson, Robert M. Browne, Cyrus P. Flick, Allen Brock, Peebles Tatum; Registrar, Allen Brock, address 1413 Main St.; Treasurer Cyrus P. Flick, address 1423 Chapline St.; Superintendent of Sunday School, Rev. David W. Howard, 1410 Chapline St., Sunday School Secretary and Treasurer, Wiliam Schwertbeger; Lay Reader, Dr. G. A. Aschman.

Official Acts—Baptisms, infants 18, adults 7, total 25; presented for confirmation since last report 25, marriages 30, burials 15, catechisings 12, public services, Sundays 130, other days 74, total 204; Holy Communion public 68, private 4, total 72.

Communicants—Number last reported 550, received by letter 5, admitted by confirmation 25, total gain 30; died 6, transferred 20, removed without letter 3, lapsed 1, total loss 30; present number total $550.

Congregations—Confirmed persons connected with Parish 561, families 187, individuals not thus included 122, whole number of individuals 871, number sittings in church 600, number free sittings 150, number sittings in Sunday School room 150.

Rector's Salary—As pledged from this congregation $2,000; total $2,000.

Organizations—Sunday School, officers and teachers, male 3, female 9, total 12; pupils, male 65, female 75, total 140; Advent offering $31.91, Lenten offering $135.00, other offerings $110.00, total Sunday School offerings $276.91. Woman's Auxiliary, members 67. *Other organizations*—Jun. Auxiliary, 45; Swope Guild, 25; N. S. Thomas Guild, 12; Chancel Chapter, 20; Choir Association, 50; Kings Daughters, 25; Seabury Club, 50.

Property—Church, stone, insurance $50,000, value $65,000; rectory, stone and brick, insurance $6,000, value $12,000; total value, insurance $56,000, value $77,000. *Indebtedness*—Vestry notes $500, total indebtedness $500.

FINANCIAL REPORT.

Receipts—For all purposes—Pledges and subscriptions $1,652.28, pew rent $5,014.67, collections in church $3,414.14, interest from investments $186.22, thank offerings $1,000, Sunday School $307.95, Woman's Auxiliary, money $853.15, Woman's Auxiliary boxes, value $178.27, Guilds, or other societies $2,772.44, total receipts for all purposes $15,379.12.

Disbursements—(1) *For current expenses*—Salary of rector $2,000; other salaries $1,934.56; insurance $48.00; ordinary repairs $1,101.45; interest on debt $142.06; payment on debts contracted for current expenses $750.00; other current expenses $1,620.35, total for current expenses $7,596.42. *Contributions*—(1) *For objects in the Parish*—Communion alms $250.63; extraordinary repairs and improvements $1,869.31; Parish missions $293.80; maintaining Sunday Schools $44.76; City Hospital $80.00; charities $507.00; total contributions for objects in the Parish $3,045.50. (2) *For objects in the Diocese*—Salary of Bishops $550.00; permanent fund $10.00; Diocesan missions $647.89; convocation missions $75.00; widows and orphans, aged and disabled clergy fund $1,310.00; religious and theological education $15.00; Sheltering Arms Hospital $141.96; Bishop's special fund $83.00; total contributions for objects in the Diocese $2,832.85. (3) *For objects without the Diocese*—Domestic missions general $514.12; deaf and dumb $10.00; total domestic missions $524.12; foreign missions general $25.00; for China $77.00; Brazil $15.00; Cuba $35.00; total foreign missions $127.00; specials, boxes, &c., $178.27; General Clergy Relief Fund $35.00; united offering of Woman's Auxiliary $536.00; total contributions for objects without the Diocese $1,400.39.

Statement—Current expenses raised by congregation as above $7,596.42. Contributions—For objects in the Parish $3,045.50; for objects in the Diocese $2,832.85; for objects without the Diocese $1,400.39; total of contributions $7,278.74; all money raised by the congregation for current expenses and for contributions $14,875.16; cash in hand $503.96; total $15,379.12.

PAROCHIAL REPORT.

Rev. EDWARD D. IRVINE, address, Wellsburg. Christ Church, Wellsburg, Brooke county; date of organization, 1793; present minister took charge January 15, 1903.

Church Officers—Christ Church; Wardens, Geo. A. Baxter, Jos. Fausset; other Vestrymen, T. A. Buchanan, F. L. Natt ——— Morgan; Registrar, Geo. A. Baxter, address Wellsburg, W. Va, Treasurer, T. A. Buchanan, address Wellsburg, Supt. of Sunday Schools, F. L. Natt, Wellsburg; Sunday School Secretary and Treasurer, Miss Rose Wheeler.

Official Acts—Baptisms, infants 6, adults 1, total 7; presented for confirmation since last report 1, marriages 6, burials 4, catechisings 12, public services, Sundays 90, other days 64, total 154; Holy Communion, public 27.

Communicants—Number last reported 55, admitted by confirmation 1, total gain 1; died 2, total loss 2; net loss 1; present number total 54.

Congregations—Baptized persons connected with parish 78, confirmed persons connected with Parish 58, families 23, whole number of individuals 125, number of sittings in church 175. All free.

Rector's Salary—As pledged from this congregation $450, from Diocesan Missions $240, as pledged from other congregations $36.22, total $712.00.

Organizations—Sunday Schools, officers and teachers, male 1, female 3, total 4; Pupils, male 10, female 20, total 30; advent offerings $6.25, Lenten affering $11.40, other offerings $36.34, total Sunday School offerings $53.99. Woman's Auxiliary, members 10. *Other Organizations*— Parish Guild 14; Choir Guild 12; Alter Chapter 5.

Property—Church, wood, value $3,500; rectory, wood, value $1,500, other property $150; toal value $5,150.00.

FINANCIAL REPORT.

Receipts—For all purposes—Pledges and subscriptions $515.84, collections in church $131.41; Sunday School $63.59, Woman's Auxiliary, money $25.66, Guilds, or other societies, $189.62, total receipts for all purposes $926.12.

Disbursements—(1) *For current expenses*—Salary of rector $450, other salaries $74.50, insurance $34.00, ordinary repairs $28.30, other current expenses $35.98, other objects, $100.39, total for current expenses $723.07. *Contributions*—(1) *For objects in the Parish*—Communion Alms $12.24; maintaining Sunday Schools $42.02; tota. contributions for objects in the Parish $54.26. (2) *For objects in the Diocese*—Salary of Bishops $25.00; Diocesan Missions $31.25; Convocation Missions $5.00; Sheltering Arms Hospital $10.00; Woman's Missionary $8.00; total contributions for objects in tne Diocese $79.25. (3) *For objects without the Diocese*—Domestic missions general $16.25; total domestic missions $16.25; foreign missions general $14.25; total foreign missions $14.25; widows and orphans $5.00; Woman's Auxiliary $14.00; total contributions for objects without the Diocese $49.50.

Statement—Current expenses raised by congregation as above $723.07. *Contributions*—For objects in the Parish $54.26, for objects in the Diocese $79.25, for objects without the Diocese $49.50, total of contributions $183.01; a.. money raised by the congregation for current expenses and for contributions $916.08.

PAROCHIAL REPORT.

Rev. EDWARD D. IRVINE, address, Wellsburg. St. John's Church, St John's Parish, Brooke county; date of organization, 1793; present minister took charge March 29, 1903.

Church Officers—St. John's Church; Wardens, Jas. Williamson; other

Vestrymen, Norman Pool, Jas. Williamson; Registrar, Samuel Baxter, address Route 3, Wellsburg, Jas. Williamson, address Route 3, Wellsburg.

Official Acts—Marriages 1, burials 2, public services, Sundays 28, other days 1, total 29; Holy Communion, public 4, total 4.

Communicants—Number last reported 25, died 1, total loss 1; present number total 24.

Congregations—Baptized persons connected with Parish 35, confirmed persons connected with Parish 24, families 8, whole number of individuals 40, number sittings in church 200. All free.

Rector's Salary—As pledged from this congregation $36.00, from Diocesan missions $240, as pledged from other congregations $4.50, total $726.

FINANCIAL REPORT.

Property—Church, brick, value $2,500.00; total value $2,500.00.

Receipts—For all purposes—Pledges and subscriptions, $36.00, collections in church $37.83, total receipts for all purposes $73.83.

Disbursements—(1) *For current expenses*—Salary of rector $36.00, other current expenses $30.38, total current expenses $66.38. *Contribuions* (2) *For objects in the Diocese*—Diocesan missions $5.00; total contributions for objects in the Diocese $5.00. (3) *For objects without the Diocese* Domestic missions general $1.23; total domestic missions $1.23; foreign missions general $1.22, total foreign missions $1.22; total contributions for objects wihout the Diocese $2.45.

Statement—Current expenses raised by congregation as above $66.38. *Contributions*—For objects in the Diocese $5.00; for objects wihout the Diocese $2.45; total of contributions $7.45; all money raised by the congregation for current expenses and for contributions $73.83.

PAROCHIAL REPORT.

Rev. PACA KENNEDY, address, St. Marys. Grace Church, St. Mary's Mission, St. Marys, Pleasant county; date of organization, 1899; present minister took charge September, 1904.

Church Officers—Church Wardens, R. L. Pemberton, R. H. Browne; other Vestrymen, E. A. Sayer, J. C. Noland, Geo. Kelsall; Registrar, J. C. Noland, address St. Marys, Treasurer, Geo. Kelsall, address St. Marys, Supt. Sunday Schools, Geo. Kelsall.

Official Acts—Marriages 3, catechisings 2, public services, Sundays 22, other days 7, total 34; Holy Communion, public, 4, total 4.

Communicants—Number last reported 29, removed without letter 1, Net loss 1; present number total 28.

Congregations—Baptized persons connected with Parish 29, confirmed persons connected with Parish 28, families 9, individuals not thus included 1, number of scattered communicants in your section not connected with any Parish 2, number sittings in church 200, number free sittings 200.

Rector's Salary—As pledged from this congregation $325, as pledged from other congregations $290, total $615.00.

Organizations—Sunday School, officers and teachers, male 5, female 1, total 6; pupils, male 9, female 20, total 29; Lenten offering $3.19, other offerings $32.59, total Sunday School offerings $35.78.

Property—Church, brick, insurance $1,500.00, value $4,000.00; rectory, wood, insurance $1,200.00, value $2,000.00. *Indebtedness*—On rectory $2,000.00, due on Diocesan assessment for Bishop's fund $15.00, other debts, Miss Appt $15.00, total indebtedness $2,030.00; money raised from outside sources $101.00; for what objects used, debt on church.

FINANCIAL REPORT.

Receipts—For all purposes—Pledges and subscriptions $136.25; collections in church $224.24; Sunday School $35.78; contributions from without $101.00; Income from other sources $56.00; total receipts for all purposes $563.27.

Disbursements—(1) *For current expenses*—Salary of rector $213.00; insurance $38.10; ordinary repairs $3.00; other current expenses $5.65; total for current expenses $259.75. *Contributions*—(1) *For objects in the Parish*—Extraordinary repairs and improvements $56.00; maintaining Sunday Schools $30.00; payments on debts for building, &c., $311.00; total contributions for objects in the Parish $397.00. (2) *For objects in the Diocese*—Diocesan missions $15.00; convocation missions $2.50; Sheltering Arms Hospital $3.65; Chester $7.25; total contribution for objects in the Diocese $28.30.

Statement—Current exenses raised by congregation as above $259.75. Contributions—For objects in the Parish $297.00; for objects in the Diocese $28.30; total contributions $325.30; all money raised by the congregation for current expenses and for contributions $585.05.

Remarks—I hope to pay our assessments at Council. The financial report is the best I can do. I imagine where a special sum is needed, i. e. insurance, the money is collected, debt paid, account kept of debt as paid but not of money as collected.

PAROCHIAL REPORT.

Rev. PACA KENNEDY, address, St. Marys. Grace Church, Ravenswood Parish, Ravenswood, Jackson county; date of organization 1855 (?); present minister took charge September, 1904.

Church Officers—Warden, F. H. Greene; other Vestrymen J. V. Armstrong.

Official Acts—Baptisms, adults 1, total 1; presented for confirmation since last report 3, public services, Sundays 11, other days 9, total 24; Holy Communion, public 1, total 1.

Communicants—Number last reported 20, admitted by confirmation 3, total gain 3; removed without letter 3, total loss 3; present number total 20.

Congregations—Baptized persons connected with Parish 30, confirmed persons connected with Parish 20, families 9, individuals not thus included 4, number sittings in church 200, number free sittings 200.

Rector's Salary—As pledged from this congregation $110, as pledged from other congregations $505, total $615.

Organizations—Sunday School, officers and teachers, male 2, female 3, total 5; pupils, male 8, female 23, total 31; Advent offerings $2.25, Lenten offerings $7.12, Children's Home $2.25, ordinary calls $18.09, total Sunday School offerings $29.71.

Property—Church, frame, insurance $2.200.00, value $3.200; rectory, frame, insurance $1,000, value $2,000. *Indebtedness*—On church $475, total indebtedness $475.

FINANCIAL REPORT.

Receipts—For all purposes—Pledges and subscriptions $48.75, collections in church $33.92, interest from investments $96.51, Sunday School $29.71, income from other sources rent of rectory $96.00, total receipts for all purposes $304.89.

Disbursements—(1) *For current expenses*—Salary of rector $82.50; other salaries $20.30; ordinary repairs $16.74; other current expenses $45.87; total for current expenses $165.41. *Contributions*—(1) *For objects in the Parish*—Maintaining Sunday Schools $17.23; payment on debt for buildings &c., $50.00; total contributions for objects in the Parish $67.23. *For objects in the Diocese*—Salary of Bishops $10.00; Diocesan missions $10.00; convocation missions assessments $2.00; widows and orphans, aged and disabled clergy fund 67c, religious and theological education 52c; Sheltering Arms Hospital $2.75;Children's Home S. S. $2.25 Advent offering $2.25; unknown $15.00; Chester collection $2.34; total contributions for objects in the Diocese $47.78. (3) *For objects without the Diocese*—Domestic missions general $5.00; foreign missions general $5.00; Lenten offering S. S. $7.12; total contributions for objects without the Diocese $17.12.

Statement—Current expenses raised by congregation as above $22.90. Contributions for objects in the Parish $17.23; for objects in the Diocese $47.78; for objects wihout the Diocese $17.12;total of contributions $82.13; all money raised by the congregation for current expenses and for contributions $105.03; cash in hand $17.82.

Remarks—The treasurer gave Mr. Spurr check for $15.00 but cannot find the check and has forgotten the object. So it is put down as "unknown." The financial report does not balance. It shows a credit of $10.47 lacking. It is the best I can do. I have had eight services at Liverpool and two school houses back in the country. Bad weather has often interfered. Good attendance. Took up $1.11 in collections, which I sent to Mr. Thomas. I also went to Mason City but found only one communicant and no congregation. I cannot get the Hartford people to have me.

PAROCHIAL REPORT.

Rev. PACA KENNEDY, address, St. Marys, W. Va. St. John's church, St. John's Parish, Willow Island, Pleasant county; date of organization 1853; present minister took charge September, 1904.

Church Officers—Church Wardens, F. M. Triplett, John W. Norris; other Vestrymen, J. H. Ralston; Registrar, J. W. Norris, Willow, W. Va.; Treasurer, J. W. Norris, Willow, W. Va.; no Sunday School.

Official Acts—Public services, Sundays 8, total 8.

Communicants—Number last reported 13, present number total 13.

Congregations—Baptized persons connected with Parish 18, confirmed persons connected with Parish 13, families 8, number sittings in church 150, number free sittings 150.

Rector's Salary—As pledged from this congregation $50.00, as pledged from other congregations $565.00, total $615.00.

FINANCIAL REPORT.

Property—Church, wood, value $500.00.

Receipts—For all purposes—Pledges and subscriptions $32.00, collections in church $34.83, thank offering $35.90, income from other sources $5.00, total receipts for all purposes $107.73.

Disbursements—(1) *For current expenses*—Salary of rector $32.00; total for current expenses $32.00. *Contributions*—(1) *For objects in the Parish*—Extraordinary repairs and improvements $55.54; total contributions for objects in the Parish $55.54. (2) *For objects in the Diocese*—Salary of Bishops $5.00; Diocesan missions $5.00; convocation missions $3.00; total contributions for objects in the Diocese $13.00. (3) *For objects without the Diocese*—Domestic missions general $3.60; foreign missions general $3.59; total foreign missions $7.19; total contributions for objects without the Diocese $7.19.

Statement—Current expenses raised by congregation as above $32.00. Contributions—For objects in the Parish $55.54; for objects in the Diocese $13.00; for objects without the Diocese $7.19; total of contributions $75.73; all money raised by the congregation for current expenses and for contributions $107.73.

Remarks—St. John's is simply holding its own.

PAROCHIAL REPORT.

Rev. PACA KENNEDY, address St. Marys. St. John's Church, Ravenswood Parish, Ripley, Jackson county; date of organization 1851; present minister took charge September, 1904.

Church Officers—Church Wardens, W. T. Green; other Vestrymen, G. B.

Crow, Dan P. Crow, W. W. Armstrong, Dr. Petty, C. W. Starcher, Sam G. Starcher; Treasurer, Miss Anna Green, address Ripley; Supt. of Sunday Schools, W. T. Greer, Ripley; Sunday School Secretary and Treasurer, Harry Armstrong.

Official Acts—Marriages 1, burials 1, public services, Sundays 11, other days 8, total 21; Holy Communion, public 1, total 1.

Communicants—Number last reported 36, died 1, removed without letter 1, total loss 2; Net loss 2; present number total 34.

Congregations—Baptized persons connected with Parish 46, confirmed persons connected with Parish 34, families 15, number sittings in church 200, number free sittings 200.

Rector's Salary—As pledged from this congregation $80, as pledged from other congregations $535, total $615.

Organizations—Sunday School officers and teachers, female 3, total 3; pupils, male 9, female 25, total 34, Lenten offering $3.15, other offerings $18.39, total Sunday School offerings $21.54. *Other organizations*—St. John's Guild, 12 members.

Property—Church, frame, insurance $1,000, value $2,000.

FINANCIAL REPORT.

Receipts—For all purposes—Pledges and subscriptions $85.00, collections in church $25.77, Woman's Auxiliary, boxes, value $14.00, Guilds, or other societies $210.51, total receipts for all purposes $335.28.

Disbursements—(1) *For current expenses*—Salary of rector $53.34; ordinary repairs $19.60; other current expenses $4.60; R. R. fare of minister $15.00; team hire $8.00; total for current expenses $100.54. *Contributions* (1) *For objects in Parish*—Extraordinary repairs and improvements $156.87; Maintaining Sunday Schools $13.25; total contributions for objects in the Parish $170.12. (2) *For objects in the Diocese*—Salary of Bishops $15.00; Diocesan missions $15.00; convocation missions assessment $2.00; Sheltering Arms Hospital $2.70; Chester coll. $3.23; box rent Sheltering Arms $14.00; total contributions for objects in the Diocese $51.93. (3) *For objects without the Diocese*—Domestic missions general $7.50; foreign missions general $7.50; total foreign missions $15.00; total contributions for objects without the Diocese $15.00.

Statement—Current expenses raised by congregation as above $100.54. Contributions—For objects in the Parish $170.12; for objects in the Diocese $51.93; for objects without the Diocese $15.00; total contributions $237.05; all money raised by the congregation for current expenses and for contributions $337.59.

PAROCHIAL REPORT.

Rev. PACA KENNEDY, address St. Marys. Messiah Mission, Waverly, Wood county; present minister took charge September, 1904.

Church Officers—Treasurer, Miss Alice Corbitt.

Official Acts—Public services, Sundays 12, Holy Communion, public 1, total 12.

Communicants—Number last reported 10, removed without letter 5, total loss 5; net loss 5; present number total 5:

Congregations—Baptized persons connected with Parish 5, confirmed persons connected with Parish 5, families 3, number sittings in church 100; number free sittings 100.

Rector's Salary—As pledged from this congregation $50.00, as pledged from other congregations $565.00. total $615.00.

Property—Church wood, insurance $800.00, value $1,300.00. *Indebtedness*—On church $175.00, due on Diocesan assessment for missions $6.00, due on Diocesan assessment for Bishop's fund $7.50, total indebtedness $188.50.

FINANCIAL REPORT.

Receipts—For all purposes—Pledges and subscriptions $40.00; collections in church $19.56, contributions from without $20.00, total receipts for all purposes $79.56.

Disbursements—(1) *For current expenses*—Salary of rector $29.00; insurance $9.00; ordinary repairs $14.00; payment on debts contracted for current expenses $4.00; total current expenses $56.00. *Contributions*—(1) *For objects in the Parish*—Payment on debts for building &c., $15.00; total contributions for objects in the Diocese $15.00. (2) *For objects in the Diocese*—Salary of Bishops $2.50; Diocesan missions $4.00; total contributions for objects in the Diocese $6.50. (3) *For objects without the Diocese*—Domestic missions general $1.03; foreign missions general $1.03; total foreign missions $2.06; total contributions for objects without the Diocese $2.06.

Statement—Current expenses raised by congregation as above $56.00. Contributions—For objects in the Parish $15.00; for objects in the Diocese $6.50; for objects without the Diocese $2.06; total of contributions $23.56; all money raised by the congregation for current expenses and for contributions $79.56.

Remarks—Waverly is very weak. The assessments are too high.

PAROCHIAL REPORT.

Rev. ARTHUR M. LEWIS, address, Powellton, W. Va. St. David's Mission, Powellton, Fayette county; date of organization December 5th, 1886; present minister took charge September 1st, 1901.

Church Officers—Church Wardens, Thomas Price; other Vestrymen, Godwin H. Powel, D. T. Evans, Dr. A. W. DeBell, J. I. Absalom, D. Swain; Registrar, Dr. A. W. DeBell, address Powellton, W. Va.; Treasurer, D. Swain, address Powellton, W. Va.; Supt. of Sunday School, D. Swain, Powellton, W. Va.; Sunday School Secretary and Treasurer J. I. Absalom; Lay Reader, Godwin H. Powel.

Official Acts—Baptism, infants 7, adults 7, total 14; presented for confirmation since last report 8, marriages 1, burials 7, catechisings 20, public services, Sundays 46, other days 8, total 54; Holy Communion, public 7, total 7.

Communicants—Number last reported 34, admitted by confirmation 8, total gain 8; died 1, total loss 1; net gain 7; present number total 41.

Congregations—Baptized persons connected with Parish 73, confirmed persons connected with Parish 41, families 19, individuals not thus included 2, number sittings in church 110, number free sittings 110.

Rector's Salary—As pledged from this congregation $402.00, as pledged from other congregations $570.00, total $972.00.

Organizations—Sunday School, officers and teachers; male 4, female 4, total 8; pupils, male 31, female 34, total 65; Advent offering $12.25, Lenten offering $17.14, other offerings $37.51, total Sunday School offerings $66.90. *Other Organizations*—Ladies' Aid Society 18 members, Rector's Guild, 8 members.

Property—Chancel Furniture, &c., value $328.00, rectory furniture, &c., $148.15, total value $476.15.

FINANCIAL REPORT.

Receipts—For all purposes—Cash on hand per last report $201.09, pledges and subscriptions $420.30, collections in church $105.59, Sunday School $37.51, Ladies' Aid Society $31.52, Guilds, or other societies, Rector's Guild $28.89, income from other sources $166.39, total receipts for all purposes $991.29.

Disbursements—(1) *For current expenses*—Salary of rector $402.00 ordinary repairs $12.00; other current expenses $113.19; total for current expenses $527.19. *Contributions*—(1) *For objects in the Parish*—Communion alms $9.09; extraordinary repairs and improvements $80.49; maintaining Sunday Schools $37.51; total contributions for objects in the Parish $127.09. (2) *For objects in the Diocese*—Salary of Bishops $23.00. permanent fund $20.83; Diocesan missions $20.00; convocation fund $2.00; widows and orphans, aged and disabled clergy fund $4.69; Sheltering Arms Hospital $116.70; Bishop's special fund $10.00; total contributions for objects in the Diocese $197.22. (3) *For objects without the Diocese*—Domestic missions general $18.98; foreign missions general $18.99; total contributions for objects without the Diocese $37.97.

Statement—Current expenses raised by congregation as above $527.19. Contributions—For objects in the Parish $127.09; for objects in the Diocese $197.22; for objects without the Diocese $37.97; total of contributions $362.28; all money raised by the congregation for current expenses and for contributions $889.47; cash in hand $101.82; total $991.29.

PAROCHIAL REPORT.

Rev. ARTHUR M. LEWIS, address, Powellton, W. Va. Redeemer Church

Ansted, Fayette county; date of organization 1879; present minister took charge September , 1901.

Church Officers—Church Wardens Wm. N. Page; other Vestrymen, Wm. N. Page, J. C. R. Taylor, J. R. Brashears, Patrick Moran, R. C. Taylor, W. H. Evans; Registrar, J. C. K. Taylor, address Ansted, W. Va.; Treasurer, W. H. Evans, address Ansted, W. Va.; Supt. of Sunday School, R. C. Taylor, Ansted, W. Va.; Sunday School Secretary and Treasurer, J. C. R. Taylor.

Official Acts—Baptisms, infants 8, total 8; presented for confirmation since last report 2, burials 1, catechisings 20, public services, Sundays, 22, other days 15, total 37; Holy Communion, public 7, total 7.

Communicants—Number last reported 36, admitted by confirmation 2, total gain 2; net gain 2; present number total 38.

Congregations—Baptized persons connected with this Parish 83, confirmed persons connected with this Parish 38, families 15, individuals not thus included 2, number sittings in church 200, number free sittings 200, number sittings in Sunday School room 50.

Rector's Salary—As pledged from this congregation $200.00, as pledged from other congregations $772.00, total $972.00.

Organizations—Sunday School, officers and teachers, male 2, female 4, total 6; pupils, male 25, female 35, total 60; Advent offering $6.57, Lenten offerings $10.00, other offerings $34.63, total Sunday School offerings $51.20, Parish schools, officers and teachers 2, scholars 50, total 52. *Other Organizations*—Ladies' Aid Society 8.

Property—Church, frame, value $3,000, Parish house, frame value $4,000, other property, value $500, total value $7,500. *Indebtedness*—On Parish House $150, money raised from outside sources $4,092.10, for new Parish building.

FINANCIAL REPORT.

Receipts—For all purposes—Cash on hand, per last report $331.37, pledges and subscriptions $122.75, collections in church $116.98, contingent fund $14.50, Sunday School $51.20, Ladies' Aid Money $50.00, Rev. B. M. Spurr $267.55, contributions from without $3,875.36, income from Parish School $158.35, total receipts for all purposes $4,988.06.

Disbursements—(1) *For current expenses*—Salary of rector $200.00; other salaries, janitor $12.00; other traveling expenses $9.00; total for current expenses $221.00. *Contributions*—(1) For objects in the Parish—Parish School $480.28; maintaining Sunday Schools $27.48; payment on debt for building, &c., $3,992.10; from Ladies' Aid Society paid on building $100.00; total contributions for objects in the Parish $4,599.86. (2) *For objects in the Diocese*—Salary of Bishops $20.00; Diocesan missions $20.00; convocation missions $2.00; Sheltering Arms Hospital $6.81; total contributions for objects in the Diocese $48.81. *For objects without the Diocese*—Domestic missions general $15.00; total domestic missions $15.00; foreign missions general $15.00; total foreign missions $15.00; total contributions for objects without the Diocese $30.00.

Statement—Contributions—For objects in the Parish $276.62; for objects in the Diocese $48.81; for objects without the Diocese $30.00; total of contributions $355.43; cash on hand $88.39.

PAROCHIAL REPORT.

Rev. ARTHUR M. LEWIS, address, Powellton. Calvary Church, Coal Valley Mission, Montgomery, Fayette county; date of organization 1878; present minister took charge September 1st, 1901.

Church Officers—Church Warden N. R. Coles; other Vestrymen, O. J. Henderson, Herbert Smith, W. K. Bridges, L. E. Rupert, W. N. Klase, Venable Johnson; Registrar, W. K. Bridges, address Smithers, W. Va.; Treasurer, Venable Johnson, address, Crescent, W. Va.; Supt. of Sunday Schools, Dr. L. E. Rupert, Montgomery, W .Va.; Sunday School Secretary and Treasurer, Miss Ora Smith.

Official Acts—Baptisms, infants 1, total 1; presented for confirmation since last report 1, marriages 1, catechisings 3; public services, Sundays, 29, other days 2, total 31; Holy Communion, public 5, total 5.

Communicants—Number last reported 19, received by letter 1, admitted by confirmation 1, aded otherwise 4, total gain 6; removed without letter 1, total loss 1; net gain 5; present number total 24.

Congregations—Baptized persons connected with Parish 37, confirmed persons connected with Parish 24, families 10, individuals not thus included 6, number sittings in church 200, number free sittings 200.

Rector's Salary—As pledged from this congregation $200.00, as pledged from other congregations $772.00, total $972.00.

Organizations—Sunday School, officers and teachers, male 1, female 2, total 3; pupils, male 13, female 7, total 20; Advent offering $2.50, Lenten offering $2.62, other offerings $12.57. *Other Organizations*—Ladies' Aid Society 17.

Property—Church, frame, insurance $1,200.00, value $1,500.00; rectory new, frame, insurance $2,500.00, value $3,500.00, lot, value $500.00; foundation $200.00, total value $5,700.00. *Indebtedness*—On church, chapel and rectory $2,500.00, due the minister $150.00, painting church $117.75, spouting rectory $40.00, total indebtedness $2,807.75.

FINANCIAL REPORT.

Receipts—For all purposes—cash on hand, per last report $22.27; pledges and subscriptions $133.60, collections in church $119.80, money borrowed $2,500.00, thank offerings, special fund $1.00, Sunday School $17.69, contingent fund $8.00, Guilds, or other societies, Ladies' Aid $167.86, income from other sources, rectory, &c., $1,263.37, total receipts for all purposes $4,233.59.

Disbursements—(1) *For current expenses*—Salary of rector $150.00; other salaries, sexton $15.00; insurance $100.84; interest on debt $37.50; other current expenses $17.35; rector's council expenses $6.00; Ladies' Aid Society $39.40; total for current expenses $366.09. *Contributions*—(1) *For objects in the Parish*—Extraordinary repairs and improvements refunding rectory fund $100.00; maintaining Sunday Schools $12.57; payment on debts for building &c., $3438.79; total contributions for objects in the Parish $3,551.36. (2) *For objects in the Diocese*—Salary of Bishops $15.00; Diocesan missions $16.75; convocation missions $1.00; widows and orphans, aged and disabled clergy fund $6.00; Sheltering Arms Hospital $5.05; Bishop's special fund $1.00; total contributions for objects in the Diocese $44.80. (3) *For objects without the Diocese*—Missions general $17.62; total contributions for objects without the Diocese $17.62.

Statement—Balance April 30, 1904, $22.27; current expenses raised by congregation as above $251.50. Contributions—For objects in the Parish $146.03; for objects in the Diocese $37.80; for objects without the Diocese $17.62; total of contributions $201.45; all money raised by the congregation for current expenses and for contributions $475.22; cash on hand $253.72.

EMMANUEL MT. CARBON.

Communicants 7, baptized non-communicants 12, Sunday services 7, week day services 24, funerals 1.

Rector's salary $29.00, Sheltering Arms Hospital $3.00, disabled clergy fund $2.00, Diocesan missions $5.00, contingent fund $5.00.

ST. TITUS, NUTTALLBURG.

Communicants 12, baptized non-communicants 8, week day services 14, communions 2, private communions 1, baptisms, infants 2, adults 3, confirmations 2.

Rector's salary $60.00, Diocesan missions $5.00, permanent fund $5.00, special fund $5.00, contingent fund $5.00.

GOOD SHEPHERD, FERRIS W. VA.

Communicants 4, baptized non-communicants 3, week day services 9.

Rector's salary $38.70, Diocesan missions $5.00.

DUBREE MISSION, DUBREE, W. VA.

Communicants 12, baptized non-communicants 25, services week day 1, Diocesan missions $2.00, hymnals for missions $1.50.

BEAUTY MISSION, BEAUTY, W. VA.

Communicants 5, baptized non-communicants 6, services week day 1.

MOUTH OF KEENEYS CREEK.

P. O. Nuttalburg, W. Va.

Comunicants 5, baptized non-communicants 4.

WYNDAL, W. VA.

Communicants 2, baptized non-communicants 6, services week day 1, infant baptisms 2, weddings 1.

PAGE, W. VA.

Communicants 6, baptized non-communicants 5, infant baptisms 2.

ARTHUR M. LEWIS.

PAROCHIAL REPORT.

Rev. JOS. W. LIVINGSTON, address Charles Town. Mission of Zion Church, St. Philips Mission, Charles Town, Jefferson county; date of organization, 1891; present minister took charge October 15, 1904.

***Church Officers*—Vestrymen, Philip Jackson, J. W. Tolbert, Eziekel Morris; Treasurer, J. W. Talbert, address Charles Town; Superintendent of Sunday School, B. C. Washington; Lay Reader, Philip Jackson.**

***Official Acts*—Baptisms, infants 1, total 1; presented for confirmation since last report 6, burials 2, catechisings 5, public services, Sundays 48, other days 24, total 72; Holy Communion, public 12, private 6, total 18.**

***Communicants*—Number last reported 23, admitted by confirmation 6, added otherwise 4, total gain 10; died 2, net gain 10, present number total 33.**

***Congregations*—Confirmed persons connected with Parish 33, families 12, whole number of individuals 75, number sittings in church 300, number free sittings 300, number sittings in chapel 300, number sittings in Sunday School room 300.**

***Rector's Salary*—As pledged from this congregation $50.00; from general board $400.00; total $450.00.**

***Organizations*—Sunday School, officers and teachers, male 5, female 3, total 8; pupils, male 20, female 20, total 40; Advent offering $1.75, Lenten offering $6.80; total Sunday School offerings $8.55.**

***Property*—Chapel, frame, insurance $1,150, value $900; rectory, frame, insurance $525; total value $1,425.**

FINANCIAL REPORT.

***Receipts—For all purposes*—Collections in church $101.99, Sunday School $8.55, Bishop Peterkin $150.00, general board $400.00, total receipts for all purposes $660.54.**

***Disbursements*—(1) *For current expenses*—Salary of rector $450.00; other salaries, sexton, $18.00; ordinary repairs $1.35; rent $12.00; total for current expenses $6.15. *Contributions*—(2) *For objects in the Diocese*—Diocesan missions $10.00. (3) *For objects without the Diocese*—Domestic missions general $10.00, total domestic missions $10.00; foreign missions general $10.00, total $20.00.**

***Statement*—Current expenses raised by congregation as above $90.54.**

Contributions—For objects in the Diocese $10.00; for objects without the Diocese $10.00; total of contributions $110.54; cash in hand $12.00.

Remarks—This report is from October 15, 1904, to May 3, 1905. There are some minor accounts not in hand at present.

PAROCHIAL REPORT.

Rev. JOHN TILTON MARLEY, address 247 Willey St. Trinity Church, Guy Allen Parish, Morgantown, Monongalia county; date of organization, 1860; present minister took charge October, 1900.

Church Officers—Church Wardens, Capt. W. C. Marshall, Prof. S. B. Brown; other Vestrymen, Col. J. C. Frazer, Mr. L. D. Beall, Mr. Bryan Gordon, Mr. Geo. Rodgers, Mr. Harry Zeverly, Dr. St. George T. Brooke, Dr. R. H. Edmundson, Prof. Fredk. Truscott; Registrar, Harry Zeverly, address North Front St.; Treasurer, Bryan Gordon, address No. 5 Cox and Boke Bld., Superintendent of Sunday School, John Tilton Marley, 247 Willey St.; Sunday School Secretary, Miss Kate Filch; Treasurer, Mr. Chas. Miller.

Official Acts—Baptisms, infants 4, adults 1, total 5; presented for confirmation since last report 7, marriages 2, burials 5, public services, Sundays 88, other days 48, total 136; Holy Communion, public 15, total 15.

Communicants—Number last reported 86.—Received by letter 2, admitted by confirmation 7, total gain 9; died 3, transferred 7, removed without letter 5, total loss 15; present number total 87.

Congregations—Baptized persons connected with Parish 113, confirmed persons connected with Parish 87, families 34, number of scattered communicants in your section not connected with any Parish 4, number sittings in church 225.

Rector's Salary—As pledged from this congregation $1,000; total $1,000.

Organizations—Sunday School, officers and teachers, male 3, female 4, total 7; pupils, male 23, female 28, total 51; Advent offering $5.10, Lenten offering $12.20, other offerings $6.20, total Sunday School offerings $23.50. *Other organizations*—Ladies Guild; Womans Home Miss. Society.

Property—Church, wood, insurance $3,500, value $9,000; other property, brick, insurance $12,000, value $18,000. *Indebtedness*—On other property $9,000, total indebtedness $9,000.

FINANCIAL REPORT.

Receipts—For all purposes—Cash on hand per last report $1,075.68, collections in church $311.24, Sunday School $18.64, Woman's Missionary Society $35.00, Ladies Guild $66.00, Guilds or other societies $50.00, income from other sources $900.00, total receipts for all purposes $2,456.56.

Disbursements—(1) *For current expenses*—Salary of rector $1,000; other salaries $188.00; insurance $37.00; ordinary repairs $10.00; interest on debt $202.50; payment on debts contracted for current expenses $362.38; other current expenses $75.63; other objects $5.00; total for current expenses $1,880.51. *Contributions*—(1) *For objects in the Parish*—Communion alms $15.00; extraordinary repairs and improvements and taxes $400.00; maintaining Sunday School $6.72; total contributions for objects in the Parish $421.72. (2) *For objects in the Diocese*—Salary of Bishops $25.00; permanent fund $25.00; Diocesan missions $5.10; convocation missions $10.00; widows and orphans, aged and disabled clergy fund $6.85; Sheltering Arms Hospital $17.00; total contributions for objects in the Diocese $88.95. (3) *For objects without the Diocese*—Domestic missions general $51.81; total domestic missions $51.81; Brazil $6.00; Cuba $6.20; total foreign missions $12.20; total contributions for objects without the Diocese $64.01.

Statement—Current expenses raised by congregation as above $2,456.56. Contributions—For objects in the Parish $421.72; for objects in the Diocese $88.95; for objects without the Diocese $64.01; total of contributions $574.68; all money raised by the congregation for current expenses and for contributions $1,880.51, $2,455.19; cash in hand $1.37.

Remarks—$900 in column of receipts for all purposes comes as rent from the hall, out of which comes interest and repairs and taxes, making the receipts and expenses in the Parish much larger than they would be otherwise. The church owes the $9,000 on the Hall property.

PAROCHIAL REPORT.

Rev. C. E. A. MARSHALL, address, Shepherdstown. Trinity Church, St. Andrews Parish, Shepherdstown, Jefferson county; present minister took charge February 1, 1903.

Church Officers—Church Wardens, A. S. Dandridge, Sr., L. H. Moler, Jr.; other Vestrymen, Jno. O. Aglionby, J. S. Bragonier, P. P. Marshall, F. W. Muzzy, Dr. D. W. Border, L. R. Lee, Dr. Hop Gibson, Dr. J. L. Meyers; Registrar, J. S. Bragonier, address Shepherdstown, W. Va.; Treasurer, J. S. Bragonier, address Shepherdstown, W. Va.; Superintendent of Sunday School, A. S. Dandridge, Shepherdstown, W. Va.

Official Acts—Baptisms, infants 7, adults 1, total 8; burials 6, catechisings 20, public services, Sundays 154, other days 84, Holy Communion, public 15, total 15.

Communicants—Number last reported 150, admitted by confirmation 12, added otherwise 2, total gain 14; died 1 transferred 2, removed without letter 5, lapsed 8, total loss 16, net gain 148, present number total 150.

Congregations—Baptized persons connected with Parish 277, families 50.

Rector's Salary—As pledged from this congregation $600 total $600.

Organizations—Sunday School, officers and teachers, male 1, female 6, total 7; total 40.

Property—Church, stone, insurance $3,500, value $12.300; rectory, brick, insurance $3,500, value $6,000; Chapel "Good Shepherd" Duffields, frame, insurance $1,000, value $1,500.

FINANCIAL REPORT.

Receipts—For all purposes—Cash on hand per last report $150.99, error $55.00, $95.99, pledges and subscriptions $697.89, collections in church $324.41, Sunday School $28.18, Woman's Auxiliary, money $2.00, Guilds, or other societies $65.40, income from other sources $63.75; total receipts for all purposes $1,277.62.

Disbursements—(1) *For current expenses*—Salary of rector $600.00; other salaries $50.00; insurance $63.28; ordinary repairs $48.20; other current expenses $128.61; other objects $25.65; total for current expenses $915.74. *Contributions.*—(1) *For objects in the Parish*—Communion alms $38.00; Parish missions $11.20; Woman's Aux. $2.00; total contributions for objects in the Parish $51.20. (2) *For objects in the Diocese*—Salary of Bishops $63.75; permanent fund $1.20; Diocesan missions $75.00; convocation missions $35.00; widows and orphans, aged and disabled clergy fund $2.93; Sheltering Arms Hospital $5.58; Theological Seminary $4.53; Bishop's special fund $10.00; total contributions for objects in the Diocese $197.99. (3) *For objects without the Diocese*—Domestic missions general $28.74; Indians $1.30; Jews $1.31; total domestic missions $31.35; foreign missions general $38.41; total foreign missions $38.41; Am. Bible Society $3.00; total contributions for objects without the Diocese $72.76.

Statement—Contributions—For objects in the Parish $51.20; for objects in the Diocese $197.99; for objects without the Diocese $72.76; total of contributions $321.95; all money raised by the congregation for current expenses and for contributions, $915.74; cash in hand $39.93; total $1,277.02.

PAROCHIAL REPORT.

Rev. WALTER HOWARD MEYERS, address, Sutton, W. Va. St. Johns Church, Sutton Mission, Sutton, Braxton county; present minister took charge July 15, 1905.

Church Officers—Church Wardens, Amos Bright, W. E. Haymond; Registrar, Amos Bright, address, Sutton, W. Va.; Treasurer, Amos Bright, address Sutton, W. Va.

Official Acts—Baptisms, adults 1, total 1; presented for confirmation since last report 4, public services, Sundays 40, other days 15, total 55; Holy Communion, public 1, total 1.

Communicants—Number last reported 10, admitted by confirmation 4, added otherwise 2, total gain 6; died 1, lapsed 5, total loss 6; present number total 10.

Congregations—Baptized persons connected with Parish 27, confirmed persons connected with Parish 16, families 10, whole number of individuals 27, number of scattered communicants in your section not connected with any Parish 15, number sittings in church 150, number free sittings 150.

Rector's Salary—As pledged from this congregation $400.00, as pledged from other congregations $425.00; total $825.00.

Organizations—Sunday School, Lenten offering $1.60, total Sunday School offerings $1.60.

Property—Church, wood, insurance $1,000, value $1,500; total value, insurance $1,000, value $1,500. *Indebtedness*—Due the minister $208, total indebtedness $208.

FINANCIAL REPORT.

Receipts—*For all purposes*—Pledges and subscriptions $482.25, collections in church $82.33, Sunday School $1.60; total receipts for all purposes $366.18.

Disbursements—(1) *For current expenses*—Salary of rector $400.00; ordinary repairs $7.00; total for current expenses $407.00. *Contributions* —(1) *For objects in the Parish*—Extraordinary repairs and improvements $100.56; other objects $2.00; total contributions for objects in the Parish $102.56. (2) *For objects in the Diocese*—Salary of Bishops $10.00; Diocesan missions $10.00; convocation missions $5.40; widows and orphans, aged and disabled clergy fund $2.18; Sheltering Arms Hospital $2.20; other objects $7.74; total contributions for objects in the Diocese $37.52. (3) *For objects without the Diocese*—Domestic missions general $9.55; total domestic missions $9.55; foreign missions general $9.55; total foreign missions $9.55; total contributions for objects without the Diocese $19.10.

Statement—Current expenses raised by congregation as above $407.00. Contributions—For objects in the Parish $102.56; for objects in the Diocese $37.52; for objects without the Diocese $19.10; total of contributions $159.18; all money raised by the congregation for current expenses and for contributions $566.18.

Remarks—Financially, the Parish is up on everything. We have over paid our apportionment $9.10, have made some contribution towards outside objects, and have made repairs to the church property. Morally, I hope things are a little improved, as we have only the increased interest in church attendance by which to judge. Perhaps the condition of our people in this respect is as good as we could expect it to be in Sutton. Those who are faithful, are so in a marked degree, but there are some that should be who are not in the least interested. The people need training in church work, etc.

PAROCHIAL REPORT.

Rev. WALTER HOWARD MEYERS, address, Sutton, W. Va. The Transfiguration Church, Upshur County Mission, Buckhannon, Upshur county; date of organization August 1, 1903; present minister took charge July 15, 1905.

Church Officers—Church Wardens, C. C. Higginbotham, W. H. Fisher; Registrar, J. J. Singleton, address Buckhannon, W. Va.; Treasurer C. O. Latham, address Buckhannon, W. Va.; Superintendent of Sunday School W. H. Meyers, Buckhannon, W. Va.; Sunday School Secretary and Treasurer, Miss Mary Higginbotham.

Official Acts—Presented for confirmation since last report 2, public services, Sundays 30, other days 18, total 48; Holy Communion, public 3, total 3.

Communicants—Number last reported 25, admitted by confirmation 2, restored to communion 1, total gain 3; removed without letter 2, net gain 3, present number total 28.

Congregations—Baptized persons connected with Parish 30, confirmed persons connected with Parish 28, families 14, indivduals not thus included 1, whole number of individuals 31, number sittings in church 250, number free sittings 250.

Rector's Salary—As pledged from this congregation $200; as pledged from other congregations $625, total $825.

Organizations—Sunday School, officers and teachers, male 1, female 1, total 2; pupils, female 8, total 8; Lenten offering $5.20, other offerings $3.75, total Sunday School offerings $8.95. *Other organizations*—Ladies Aid Society; Girls Choir Chapter.

Property—Church, wood, insurance $1,500, value $3,000; total value, insurance $1,500, value $3,000. *Indebtedness*—Due the minister $46.30, total indebtedness $46.30.

FINANCIAL REPORT.

Receipts—*For all purposes*—Cash on hand per last report $1.46, pledges and subscriptions $146.50, collections in church $42.73, thank offerings $2.80, Sunday School $8.95, Guilds or other Societies $62.32, total receipts for all purposes $264.76.

Disbursements—(1) *For current expenses*—Salary of rector $153.70; other salaries $14.00; insurance $25.50; ordinary repairs $17.25; other current expenses $7.60; other objects $5.11; total for current expenses $223.16. *Contributions*—(1) *For objects in the Parish*—Extraordinary repairs and improvements $6.30; total contributions for objects in the Parish $6.30. (2) *For objects in the Diocese*—Salary of Bishops $10.00; Diocesan missions $10.00; convocation missions $2.60; widows and orphans, aged and disabled clergy fund $2.20; Sheltering Arms Hospital $2.80; total contributions for objects in the Diocese $27.60. (3) *For objects without the*

Diocese—Domestic missions general $3.85; total domestic missions $3.85; missions general $3.85; total foreign missions $3.85; total contributions for objects without the Diocese $7.70.

Statement—Current expenses raised by congregation as above $223.16; Contributions—For objects in the Parish $6.30; for objects in the Diocese $27.60; for objects without the Diocese $7.70; total of contributions $41.60; all money raised by the congregation for current expenses and for contributions $264.76.

Remarks—The congregation has not assumed heavy responsibilities during the past year and consequently is doing very well financially. Attendance on services is very good. The people appear interested and are doing as well perhaps as could reasonably be expected. The work is small and the greatest difficulty is to keep the people from becoming discouraged. Some growth of the town seems to be reasonably assured and we are in hopes that the church may grow in proportion. The condition of the mission is perhaps in as healthy a condition as could be expected under the various adverse conditions that obtain.

PAROCHIAL REPORT.

Rev. WALTER HOWARD MEYERS, address, Sutton, W. Va. Spruce Chapel Church, Lorentz Parish, Lorentz, Upshur county; present minister took charge July 15, 1905.

Church Officers—Church Warden, William Loudin, Atlas, W. Va.; Registrar, G. W. Spaulding, address Atlas, W. Va.; Treasurer, John Dowell, address Atlas, W. Va.; Superintendent of Sunday School, Mrs. Olive Marple, Atlas, W. Va.; Sunday School Secretary and Treasurer, Miss Mary Dowell.

Official Acts—Baptisms, infants 1, total 1; public services, Sundays 10, other days 8, total 18; Holy Communion, public 4, private 1, total 5.

Communicants—Number last reported 11, removed without letter 1, total loss 1, present number total 10.

Congregations—Baptized persons connected with Parish 21, confirmed persons connected with Parish 10, families 6, whole number of individuals 21, number sittings in church 80, number free sittings 80.

Organizations—Sunday School, officers and teachers, male 1, female 3, total 4; pupils, male 10, female 12, total 22; Lenten offering $1.00, total Sunday School offerings $1.00.

Property—Church, wood, insurance $500, value $800; rectory, wood, value $400, total value, insurance $500, value $1,200.

FINANCIAL REPORT.

Receipts—For all purposes—Pledges and subscriptions $23.00, collections in church $3.40, Sunday School $4.10, total receipts for all purposes $30.50.

Disbursements—(1) *For current expenses*—Salary of rector $10.00; insurance $5.00; ordinary repairs $3.50; total for current expenses $18.50. *Contributions*—(1) *For objects in the Parish*—Maintaining Sunday School $2.10; other objects 50c.; total contributions for objects in the Parish $2.60. (2) *For objects in the Diocese*—Salary of Bishops $4.00; convocation missions 40c.; total contributions for objects in the Diocese $4.40. (3) *For objects without the Diocese*—Domestic missions general $2.50; total domestic missions $2.50; foreign missions general $2.50; total foreign missions $2.50; total contributions for objects without the Diocese $5.00.

Statement—Current expenses raised by congregations as above $18.50. Contributions—For objects in the Parish $2.60; for objects in the Diocese $4.40; for objects without the Diocese $5.00; total of contributions $12.00; al money raised by the congregation for current expenses and for contributions $30.50.

Remarks—Our people are better off here spiritually than they are financially, and they are doing as well in the latter respect perhaps as we have a right to expect. They are in earnest and attend the services well.

PAROCHIAL REPORT.

Rev. WALTER HOWARD MEYERS, address, Sutton, W. Va. Present minister took charge July 15, 1904.

Other Missions—Gassaway, Burnsville, Flatwoods, Centralia, Camden-on-Gauley, Richwood, Rupert, Webster Springs.

Official Acts—Public services 15, total 15.

Communicants—Present number total, 14.

Congregations—Baptized persons connected with Parish 34, confirmed persons connected with Parish 14, families 12, whole number of individuals 34.

Rector's Salary—As pledged from these congregations $225; total $225.

FINANCIAL REPORT.

Receipts—*For all purposes*—Pledges and subscriptions $8.00; total receipts for all purposes $8.00.

Disbursements—*For current expenses*—Salary of rector $8.00; total for current expenses $8.00.

Statement—Current expenses raised by congregation as above $8.00; all money raised by the congregation for current expenses and for contributions $8.00.

Remarks—Our people are so widely scattered at these points that it is next to an impossibility to minister to them with any degree of efficiency and thus in some instances to arouse and in others to strengthen a dying interest in a distant church. It is remarkable that they cling to the church as well as they do. Thus these scattered ones not having the spiritual interest that they might have, neither have any other kind of interest in any marked degree, excepting one or two notable exceptions.

PAROCHIAL REPORT.

Rev. AUSTIN B. MITCHELL, address, Williamstown. Christ Memorial Church, Williamstown, Wood county; present minister took charge August, 1903.

Church Officers—Church Wardens, J. W. Snodgrass, Charles Hunter; other Vestrymen, H. C. Henderson, A. T. Henderson, R. Hammatt, J. F. Snodgrass; Registrar, H. C. Henderson, address Williamstown; Treasurer, A. T. Henderson, address Williamstown; Superintendent of Sunday School, H. C. Henderson, Williamstown; Sunday School Secretary and Treasurer, Miss Fannie Biddle; Lay Reader, H. C. Henderson.

Official Acts—Baptisms, infants 1, adults 1, total 2; presented for confirmation since last report 1, marriages 1, burials 3, catechisings 4, public services, Sundays 52, other days 6, total 58; Holy Communion, public 11, total 11.

Communicants—Number last reported 27, admitted by confirmation 1, total gain 1; net gain 1, present number total 28.

Congregations—Baptized persons connected with Parish 62, confirmed persons connected with Parish 28, families 20, individuals not thus included 20, whole number of individuals 48, number sittings in church 150, number free sittings, all.

Rector's Salary—As pledged from this congregation $200, from Diocesan missions $200, as pledged from other congregations $400, total $800.

Organizations—Sunday School, officers and teachers, male 1, female 5, total 6; pupils, male 8, female 13, total 21; Advent offering $9.00, Lenten offering $10.64; other offerings $63.81; total Sunday School offerings $83.45; Woman's Auxiliary, members, 15. *Other organizations*—Juniors, 8; Sewing School, 13.

Property—Church, wood, insurance $1,500, value $2,500; rectory, wood, insurance $1,700, value $3,500. total value $6,000. *Indebtedness*—On rectory $1,500.

FINANCIAL REPORT.

Receipts—For all purposes—Pledges and subscriptions $172.90, collections in church $65.75, Sunday School $83.45, Woman's Auxiliary, money $71.07, Guilds or other societies $10.00, contributions from without $112.00, income from other sources $135.29, total receipts for all purposes $650.46.

Disbursements—(1) *For current expenses*—Salary of rector $172.90;

Insurance $39.09; interest on debt $45.00; other current expenses $9.55; total for current expenses $266.54. *Contributions*—(1) *For objects in the Parish*—Extraordinary repairs and improvements $12.65; Parish missions $14.57; maintaining Sunday Schools $17.62; rectory fund $257.01; total contributions for objects in the Parish $301.85.. (2) *For objects in the Diocese*—Salary of Bishops $5.00; Diocesan missions $12.20; convocation missions $4.50; religious and theological education $3.00; Sheltering Arms Hospital 65c; Ansted $1.00; central fund $1.00; woman's mite $5.75; total contributions for objects in the Diocese $33.10. (3) *For objects without the Diocese*—Foreign missions general $36.24; Brazil $1.00; total foreign missions $37.24; total contributions for objects without the Diocese $37.24.

Statement—Current expenses raised by congregation as above $266.54. Contributions—For objects in the Parish $301.85; for objects in the Diocese $33.10; for objects without the Diocese $37.24; total of contributions $372.19; all money raised by congregations, $638.73.

PAROCHIAL REPORT.

Rev. AUSTIN B. MITCHELL, address, Williamstown. Memorial Chapel of Good Shepherd Mission, Parkersburg, Wood county.

Church Officers—Registrar, W. G. Peterkin, address Parkersburg; Treasurer W. G. Peterkin, address, Parkersburg; Supt. of Sunday Schools, Simms Powell; Sunday School Secretary and Treasurer, W. G. Peterkin; Lay Readers, Simms Powell and W. G. Peterkin.

Official Acts—Baptisms, infants 10, adults 3, total 13; presented for confirmation since last report 4, burials 2, catechisings 5, public services, Sundays, 52, other days 6, total 58; Holy Communion, public 6, total 6.

Comunicants—Number last reported 15, admitted by confirmation 4, added otherwise 1, total gain 5, transferred 1, removed without letter 1, total loss 2; net gain 3, present number total 18.

Congregations—Baptized persons connected with Parish 35, confirmed persons connected with Parish 20, families 18, individuals not thus included 22, whole number of individuals 57, number sittings in church 200, number free sittings 200.

Rector's Salary—As pledged from this congregation $400, from Diocesan missions $200, as pledged from other congregations $200, total $800.

Organizations—Sunday School, officers and teachers, male 3, female 11, total 14; pupils, male 80, female 90, total 170. *Others organizations*—Ladies Aid, 18 members; Girls Sun Shine, 15 members; Sewing School, 70 members; Boys Club, 20 members.

Property—Church, wood, value $10,000.

FINANCIAL REPORT.

Receipts—For all purposes—Pledges and subscriptions $555.85, collections in .church $436.68, thank offerings $9.50, Sunday School $68.80, Guilds or other societies $122.89, income from other sources $59.40, total receipts for all purposes $1,254.12.

Disbursements—(1) *For current expenses*—Salary of rector $400; other salaries $59.00; insurance $82.50; other objects $23.00; total for current expenses $564.50. *Contributions*—(1) *For objects in the Parish*—Communion alms $11.00; extraordinary repairs and improvements $72.30; other objects $40.00; total contributions for objects in the Parish $123.30. (2) *For objects in the Diocese*—Salary of Bishops $20.00; permanent fund $10.00; Diocesan missions $111.48; convocation missions $9.50; widows and orphans, aged and disabled clergy fund $20.00; religious and theological education $8.00; Sheltering Arms Hospital $19.00; Theological Seminary $6.00; Bishop's special fund $50.00; other objects $7.34; total contributions for objects in the Diocese $261.32. (3) *For objects without the Diocese*—Domestic missions general $95.00; colored people $10.00; Indians $5.00; deaf and dumb $12.00; Jews $1.00; Thro' American Ch. Miss. Society $46.00; total domestic missions $169.00; foreign missions general $90.00; for Mexico $5.00; Brazil $12.50; Cuba $12.50; total foreign missions $125.00; American Church Building Fund $3.00; General Clergy Relief Fund $5.00; Bible and Prayer Book Society $3.50; total contributions for objects without the Diocese $305.50.

Statement—Current expenses raised by congregation as above $564.50. Contributions—For objects in the Parish $123.30; for objects in the Diocese $261.32; for objects without the Diocese $305.50; total of contributions $690.12; all money raised by the congregation for current expenses and for contributions $1,254.62.

PAROCHIAL REPORT.

Rev. AUSTIN B. MITCHELL, address, Williamstown. Grace Chapel Church Mission, Newport, Wood county; present minister took charge August, 1903.

Church Officers—Treasurer, Miss Jennie Tavenner, address New Port; Superintendent of Sunday School, Fred Bargeloh, R. F. D. No. 3, Parkersburg; Sunday School Secretary and Treasurer, Miss Julia Black, New Port.

Official Acts—Baptisms, infants 1, total 1; catechisings 4, public services, Sundays 7, other days 31, total 38; Holy Communion, public 4, total 4.

Communicants—Number last reported 10, present number total 10.

Congregations—Baptized persons connected with Parish 20, confirmed persons connected with Parish 10, families 8, individuals not thus included 20, whole number of individuals 40, number of sittings in church 100.

Organizations—Sunday Schools, officers and teachers, male 1, female 4,

total 5; pupils, male 10, female 15, total 25; Advent offering $5.00, Lenten offering $10.10, other offerings $5.00; total Sunday School offerings $20.10. *Other organizations*—Ladies Aid, members 14.

Property—Church, value $1,200, total value $1,200.

FINANCIAL REPORT.

Receipts—For all purposes—Pledges and subscriptions $60.00, collections in church $17.21, Sunday School $20.10; Ladies Aid Society $50.00, total receipts for all purposes $147.31.

Disbursements—(1) *For current expenses*—Salary of rector $37.00; other current expenses $5.00; total for current expenses $42.00. *Contributions*—(1) *For objects in the Parish*—Extraordinary repairs and improvements $20.00; maintaining Sunday School $9.00; total contributions for objects in the Parish $29.00. (2) *For objects in the Diocese*—Salary of Bishops $5.00; Diocesan missions $20.00; convocation missions $3.00; widows and orphans, aged and disabled clergy fund $1.00; religious and theological education $3.00; total contributions for objects in the Diocese $32.00. (3) *For objects without the Diocese*—Foreign missions general $20.10; total contributions for objects without the Diocese $20.10.

Statement—Current expenses raised by congregation as above $42.00. Contributions—For objects in the Parish $29.00; for objects in the Diocese $32.00; for objects without the Diocese $20.10; total of contributions $81.10; all money raised by the congregation for current expenses and for contributions $147.31; cash in hand $24.21.

PAROCHIAL REPORT.

Rev. C. HELY MOLONY, address, New Martinsville. St. Ann Church, Wetzel Parish, New Martinsville, Wetzel county; date of organization January 15, 1851; present minister took charge April 1, 1905.

Church Officers—Church Wardens, Saml. R. Martin, Bruce Hall; other Vestrymen, Wm. McG. Hall, John F. Martin, Leslie J. Williams, Jno. H. Bridgeman, A. B. Johnson; Registrar, John F. Martin, address New Martinsville; Treasurer, Leslie J. Williams, address New Martinsville; Superintendent of Sunday Schools John F. Martin, New Martinsville; Sunday School Secretary, A. B. Johnson; Sunday School Treasurer, S. R. Martin.

Official Acts—Marriages 6, burials 1, public services, Sundays 48, other days 15, total 63; Holy Communion, public 8, total 8.

Communicants—Number last reported 50, total loss 10, present number total 40.

Congregations—Baptized persons connected with Parish 67; confirmed persons connected with Parish 51, families 25, number sittings in church 250, number free sittings 250, number sittings in chapel 75.

Rector's Salary—As pledged from this congregation $700; from Diocesan missions $100, total $800.

Organizations—Sunday School, officers and teachers, male 3, female 5, total 8; pupils, male 9, female 16, total 25; Advent offering $4.90, Lenten offering $7.70, other offerings $13.49, total Sunday School offerings $26.09. *Other organizations*—Sr. Ladies Aid Society, 13; Jr. Ladies Aid Society, 11; Ladies Guild, 5.

Property—Church, wood, insurance $3,000, value $6,500; chapel, wood, value $800; rectory, wood, insurance $1,000, value $2,000; other property 2 lots, value $2,000; total value $11,300. *Indebtedness*—On church $2,760, total indebtedness $2,760.

FINANCIAL REPORT.

Receipts—For all purposes—Cash on hand, per last report $13.03, pledges and subscriptions $700.00, collections in church $286.08, Sunday School $39.12, Guilds or other societies $200.87, total receipts for all purposes $1,239.10.

Disbursements—(1) *For current expenses*—Salary of rector $466.88; ordinary repairs $125.91; interest on debt $165.60; other current expenses $23.95; total for current expenses $782.34. *Contributions*—(1) *For objects in the Parish*—Communion alms $7.01; maintaining Sunday Schools $11.89; total contributions for objects in the Parish $18.90. (2) *For objects in the Diocese*—Salary of Bishops $40.00; permanent fund $5.74; Diocesan missions $40.00; religious and theological education $2.70; Sheltering Arms Hospital $8.30; Theological Seminary $2.23; Bishop's special fund $15.00; total contributions for objects in the Diocese $113.97. (3) *For objects without the Diocese*—Domestic missions general $15.88; Indians 95; deaf and dumb $2.27; total domestic missions $19.10; Thro' American Ch. Miss. Society $1.40; Brazil 80c.; Cuba 76c.; total foreign missions $2.96; total contributions for objects without the Diocese $22.06.

Statement—Current expenses raised by congregation as above $782.34, for objects in the Parish $18.90; for objects in the Diocese $113.97; for objects without the Diocese $22.06; total of contributions $154.93; all money raised by the congregation for current expenses and for contributions $937.27; cash in hand $44.75.

Remarks—This report is from May 1, 1904, to December 1, 1904, Mr. Shaw, Rector, and the month of April, 1905, during which time I have been in charge, and is correct as far as my information goes. The only item doubtful that I know of is "official acts." This as reported is from the register. In comparing the report it should be borne in mind that there were four months in 1904 during which time there was no Rector, and only occasional services, consequently the regular offerings were not taken and the envelopes for the vacant days were not used by the people. —C. HELY MOLONY.

PAROCHIAL REPORT.

Rev. FRANCIS MOORE, address, Elm Grove, W. Va. St. Pauls Mission, Elm Grove, Ohio county; present minister took charge August 23, 1903.

Church Officers—Trustees, Mr. C. C. Woods, Mr. Samuel Patterson, Mr. Geo. Gilchrist; Committee, Mr. H. Mahn, Mr. E. H. Crockard, Mr. Nelson Cecil, Miss Kimmins; Registrar, E. H. Crockard, address Elm Grove, W. Va.; Treasurer, C. C. Woods, address Elm Grove, W. Va.; Superintendent of Sunday School, C. C. Woods, Elm Grove, W. Va.; Sunday School Secretary and Treasurer, Mrs. B. C. Ryan.

Official Acts—Baptisms, infants 6, adults 1, total 7; presented for confirmation since last report 3, marriages 5, burials 6, catechisings 12, public services, Sundays 80, other days 21, total 101; Holy Communion, public 16, total 16.

Communicants—Number last reported 27, admitted by confirmation 3, total gain 3, net gain 3, present number total 30.

Congregations—Baptized persons connected with Parish 50, confirmed persons connected with Parish 2, families 21, individuals not thus included 10, whole number of individuals 50, number sittings in church 80, number free sittings 80, number sittings in Sunday School room (church) 80.

Rector's Salary—As pledged from this congregation $600.00, from Diocesan missions $200.00, as pledged from other congregations $200.00, total $1,000.

Organizations—Sunday Schools, officers and teachers, male 3, female 3, total 6; pupils, male 16, female 24, total 40; Advent offering $3.66; Lenten offering $3.73; total Sunday School offerings $7.39. *Other organizations*—Chancel Chapter; Jane Pryor Society.

Property—Church, wood. insurance $1,500; rectory, wood, insurance $2,800, value $3,700. *Indebtedness*—On rectory $2,922, total indebtedness $2,922; money raised from outside sources $50, for debt on rectory.

FINANCIAL REPORT.

Receipts—For all purposes—Cash on hand per last report $53.14; pledges and subscriptions $514.90, collections in church $161.27, money borrowed $2,972, Sunday School $7.39, Guilds, or other societies $115.00, contributions from without $50.00, total receipts for all purposes $3,873.70.

Disbursements—(1) *For current expenses*—Salary of rector $600.00; insurance (for 3 years) $63.75; interest on debt $58.70; total for current expenses $722.45. *Contributions*—(1) *For objects in the Parish*—Payment on debts for building, &c. $2,972; recording deed, etc., $6.25; miscellaneous expenses $29.01; paid on rectory $50.00; total contributions for objects in the Parish $3,057.26. (2) *For objects in the Diocese*—Permanent fund $4.66; Diocesan missions $15.00; convocation missions $2.50; Sheltering Arms Hospital $6.30; Bishop's special fund $12.00; total contributions for objects in the Diocese $40.46. (3) *For objects without the*

Diocese—Domestic missions general $3.57; total domestic missions $3.57; foreign missions general $3.73; Brazil $2.16; Cuba $2.16; total foreign missions $8.05; General Clergy Relief Fund $5.37; Bible and Prayer Book Society $2.00; total contributions for objects without the Diocese $18.99.

Statement—Current expenses raised by congregation as above $722.45. Contributions—For objects in the Diocese $40.46; for objects without the Diocese $18.99; all money raised by the congregation for current expenses and for contributions $890.81; cash in hand $34.54.

PAROCHIAL REPORT.

Rev. FRANCIS MOORE, address, Elm Grove, W. Va. New Cumberland Mission, New Cumberland; date of organization October, 1904; present minister took charge November 12, 1904.

Church Officers—Church committee, Mr. S. G. Gaillard, Warden; Registrar, Mr. A. W. Brown, address New Cumberland; Treasurer, Mr. E. P. Morphy, address New Cumberland.

Official Acts—Public services, Sundays 11, total 11; Holy Communion 5, total 5.

Communicants—Present number total 10.

Congregations—Baptized persons connected with Parish 26, confirmed persons connected with Parish 10, families 10.

Rector's Salary—As pledged from this congregation $200, total $200.

FINANCIAL REPORT.

Receipts—For all purposes—Pledges and subscriptions $148.59, collections in church $10.50, total receipts for all purposes $159.09.

Disbursements—(1) *For current expenses*—Salary of rector $85.02; rent of hall $3.00; total current expenses $88.02. *Contributions*—(2) *For objects in the Diocese*—Diocesan missions $6.00; total contributions for objects in the Diocese $6.00. (3) *For objects without the Diocese*—Domestic missions general $2.00; total domestic missions $2.00; foreign missions general $2.50; total foreign missions $2.50; total contributions for objects without the Diocese $4.50.

Statement—Current expenses raised by congregation as above $88.02; Contributions—For objects in the Diocese $6.00; for objects without the Diocese $4.50; total of contributions $10.50; all money raised by the congregation for current expenses and for contributions $159.09; cash in hand $60.57.

Remarks—Service is held in the Court House at present and the congregation averages about 35 people, many coming from the various sects. I hope to have three or four persons for confirmation this Fall.

PAROCHIAL REPORT.

Rev. S. SCOLLAY MOORE, D. D., address, Parkersburg. Trinity Parish, Parkersburg, Wood county; date of organization, 1843; present minister took charge April 15, 1888.

Church Officers—Church Wardens, Dr. W. H. Sharp, Dr. T. B. Camden; other Vestrymen, Mr. B. M. Ambler, Mr. J. N. Camden, Mr. W. N. Chancellor, Mr. C. C. Martin, Mr. H. H. Moss, Mr. Simms Powell, Mr. W. J. Robb, Mr. B. D. Spilman, Mr. W. M. Trevor, Mr. W. Vrooman; Registrar, Mr. Simms Powell, address Parkersburg; Treasurer, Dr. W. H. Sharp, address Parkersburg; Superintendent of Sunday School Hon. H. H. Moss, Jr., Parkersburg; Sunday School Secretary and Treasurer, Mr. Cecil Fitzhugh.

Official Acts—Baptisms, infants 14, adults 7, total 21; presented for confirmation since last report 17, marriages 31, burials 24, public services, Sundays 103, other days 119, total 222; Holy Communion, public 34, total 34.

Communicants—Number last reported 308, received by letter 2, admitted by confirmation 17, added otherwise 7, total gain 26; died 1, removed without letter 16, total loss 17; net gain 9, present number total 317.

Congregations—Baptized persons connected with Parish 525, confirmed persons connected with Parish 325, families 200, individuals not thus included 50, whole number of individuals 600, number sittings in church 550, number free sittings 100, number sittings in Sunday School room 200.

Rector's Salary—As pledged from this congregation $1,800, total $1,800.

Organizations—Sunday School, officers and teachers, male 4, female 12, total 16; pupils, male 46, female 71, total 117; Advent offering $20.45, Lenten offering $21.86, other offerings $32.22, total Sunday School offerings $74.53; Woman's Auxiliary, members, 37. *Other Organizations*—Woman's Guild, members, 60; Junior Auxiliary, members, 34; King's Daughters, members, 18; Church Periodical Club, members, 30.

Property—Church, stone, insurance $8,000, value $30,000; rectory, brick, insurance $3,000, value $9,000; Sun. School room, brick, insurance $2,300, value $7,000; other property, insurance $3,300, value $5.500; Episcopal residence, brick, insurance $6,000, value $15,000; total value, insurance $22,600, value $66,500. *Indebtedness*—On rectory $215, other debts $850, total indebtedness $1,065.

FINANCIAL REPORT.

Receipts—For all purposes—Pledges and subscriptions $1,210.86, pew rent $2,331.61, collections in church $1,313.80, money borrowed $100, thank offerings $86.50, Sunday School $74.53, Woman's Auxiliary, money $277.00, Woman's Auxiliary Boxes, value $234.00, Guilds or other societies $538.90, total receipts for all purposes $6,167.20.

Disbursements—(1) *For current expenses*—Salary of rector $1,800; other salaries $996.25; insurance $195.00; ordinary repairs $112.55; other current expenses $359.29; total for current expenses $3,463.09. *Contri-*

butions—(1) *For objects in the Parish*—Communion alms $18.15; Parish missions $182.65; maintaining Sunday Schools $51.92; for Parochial mission $86.50; Florence Crittendon Home by King's Daughters $20.00; total contributions for objects in the Parish $359.22. (2) *For objects in the Diocese*—Salary of Bishops $500.00; permanent fund $4.26; Diocesan missions $505.50; convocation missions $78.50; widows and orphans, aged and disabled clergy fund $80.30; Sheltering Arms Hospital $68.47; Bishop's special fund $372.00; box from Woman's Auxiliary $140.00; for genl. conven. expenses $100.00; total contributions for objects in the Diocese $1,849.03. (3) *For objects without the Diocese*—Domestic missions general $61.43; total domestic missions $61.43; foreign missions general $58.43; for China $63.00; total foreign missions $121.43; specials, boxes, &c., $94.00; united offering Woman's Auxiliary $189.00; Church Periodical Club $30.00; total contributions for objects without the Diocese $495.86.

Statement—Current expenses raised by congregation as above $3,363.09. Contributions—For objects in the Parish $359.22; for objects in the Diocese $1,849.03; for objects without the Diocese $495.86; total of contributions $2,704.11; all money raised by the congregation for current expenses and for contributions $6,067.20.

PAROCHIAL REPORT.

Rev. S. SCOLLAY MOORE, D. D., adress, Parkersburg. St. Stephen's Church, Trinity Parish, Parkersburg, Wood county; date of organization 1896; present minister took charge 1896.

Official Acts—Public services, Sundays 38, total 38; Holy Communion, public 3, total 3.

Communicants—Number last reported 8, present number total 8.

Congregations—Baptized persons connected with Parish 12, confirmed persons connected with Parish 9, families 6, whole number of individuals 20, number sittings in Chapel 40.

Property—Chapel, frame, insurance $600.00, value $900.00; other property $100.00; total value, insurance $600.00; value $1,000. *Indebtedness*—On chapel $350, total indebtedness $350.

FINANCIAL REPORT.

Receipts—For all Purposes—Collections in church $21.67, interest from investments $40.00, Guilds or other societies $16.00, contributions from without $163.65, total receipts for all purposes $241.32.

Disbursements—(1) *For current expenses*—Interest on debt $19.50; other current expenses $25.15; total for current expenses $44.65. *Contributions*—(1) *For objects in the Parish*—Extraordinary repairs and improvements $45.00; payment on debts for building, &c., $150.00; total contributions for objects in the Parish $195.00. (2) *For objects in the Dio-*

cese—Diocesan missions 84c, total contributions for objects in the Diocese 84c. (3) *For objects without the Diocese*—Domestic missions general 41c, total domestic missions 41c; foreign missions general 42c, total foreign missions 42c; total contributions for objects without the Diocese 83c.

Statement—Current expenses raised by congregation as above $44.65. Contributions—For objects in the Parish $31.35; for objects in the Diocese 84c; for objects without the Diocese 83c; total of contributions $33.02; all money raised by the congregation for current expenses and for contributions $77.67.

PAROCHIAL REPORT.

Rev. H. H. PHELPS, address Bramwell, W. Va. Church of the Holy Trinity, Bramwell Mission, Bramwell, Mercer county; present minister took charge March 1st, 1905.

Church Officers—Other Vestrymen, F. L. Shaw, F. M. Archer, B. F. Keller, W. C. Brooke, A. R. Paddock, Jarius Collins, W. D. Tyler; Registrar, W. D. Tyler, address Bramwell, W. Va.; Treasurer W. D. Tyler; Supt. of Sunday School, W. D. Tyler; Sunday School Secretary and Treasurer, W. D. Tyler.

Official Acts—Baptisms, infants 4, adults 3, total 7; public services, Sundays 8, other days 20, Holy Communion, public 4.

Communicants—Present number total 23.

Congregations—Baptized persons connected with Parish 50, confirmed persons connected with Parish 25, families 13, individuals not thus included 4, whole number of individuals 50, number sittings in church 200, number free sittings all.

Rector's Salary—As pledged from this congregation $600.00, total $600.00.

Organizations—Sunday School, officers and teachers, male 2, female 5, total 7; pupils, male 16, female 23, total 39; Lenten offering $19.04, other offerings $19.74, total Sunday School offerings $38.78. *Other Organizations*—St. Margaret's Guild, Boys' Brigade.

Property—Church, frame, insurance $2,600, value $5,000; rectory, frame, insurance $3,000, value $5,000; organ, value $1,200; total value insurance $5,600, value $11,200. *Indebtedness*—On repair account $4.25, on heater account $101.73, money raised from outside sources $200; for what objects used, $100 on heater plant, and $100 on salary and general expense account.

FINANCIAL REPORT.

Receipts—For all purposes—Cash on hand, per last report $196.35, pledges and subscriptions $913.42, collections in church $200.55, Sunday School $38.78, Guilds, or other societies $696.91, contributions from without $200.00, income from other sources $454.55, total receipts for all purposes $2,700.56.

Disbursements—(1) *For current expenses*— Salary of rector $500.00; insurance $60.40; ordinary repairs $14.82; interest on debt $73.60; other current expenses, janitor, light and heat $85.75; other objects $696.91, total for current expenses $1,426.48. *Contributions*—(1) *For objects in the Parish*—Extraordinary repairs on rectory $372.50 and improvements on heater $510.00; maintaining Sunday Schools $39.15; payment on debts for building &c. $180.00; total contributions for objects inthe Parish $1,101.65 (2) *For objects in tne Diocese*—Salary of Bishops $30.00; permanent fund $19.59; Diocesan missions $30.00; Sheltering Arms Hospital $3.70; Bishop's special fund $10.00; other objects, Welch Hospital $3.70; total contributions for objects in the Diocese $96.99. (3) *For objects without the Diocese*—Colored people $3.12; total domestic missions $3.12; Lenten boxes $19.04; Bible and Prayer Book Society $2.06; total contributions for objects without the Diocese $24.22.

Statement—Current expenses raised by congregation as above $2,495.56. Contributions—For objects in the Parish $2,328.13; for objects in the Diocese $96.99; for objects without the Diocese $24.22; total of contributions $2,449.34; cash in hand $46.22.

Remarks—Having recently came into this field, my report of services, &c., is simply from the first of March.—H. H. PHELPS.

PAROCHIAL REPORT.

Rev. H. H. PHELPS, address, Bramwell, W. Va. Grace Mission, Eckman, McDowell county, present minister took charge March 1, 1905.

Church Officers—Grace Church, Warden Dr. P. H. Killey; other Vestrymen, Wm. D. Ord, W. G. Williamson.

Official Acts—Public services, Sundays 2, Holy Communion, public 1, total 1.

Communicants—Present number total, about 9.

Congregations—Families 4, whole number of individuals about 18.

FINANCIAL REPORT.

Receipts—*For all purposes*—Subscriptions $24.16, contributed $76.31, collections in church $16.84, total receipts for all purposes $117.31.

Disbursements—(1) *For Current Expenses*—Salary of rector $80.27; other current expenses $1.77; other objects $3.00; total for current expenses $85.04. *Contributions*— (2) *For objects in the Diocese*—Diocesan missions $10.96; Episcopal fund $3.24; total contributions for objects in the Diocese $14.20. (3) *For objects without the Diocese*—Domestic missions general $600; total domestic missions $6.00; foreign missions general $6.07; total foreign missions $6.07; total contributions for objects without the Diocese $12.07.

Statement—Current expenses raised by congregation as above $85.04.

Contributions—For objects in the Diocese $14.20; for objects without the Diocese $12.07; total of contributions $26.27; all money raised by the congregation for current expenses and for contributions $111.31.

Remarks—NOTE. I include in this report Eckman, Langraf and Vivian. The people—Church people—living at these points attend the services at Grace Church, Eckman. Several of the church people at these points have moved away.—H. H. PHELPS.

PAROCHIAL REPORT.

Rev. H. H. PHELPS, address, Bramwell, W. Va. Mora Mission, Crane Creek, Mercer county; present minister took charge March 1, 1905.

Official Acts—Baptisms, infants 2, total 2; public services, Sundays 1, other days 2, total 3.

Communicants—Present number total about 4.

Congregations—Families 3, individuals not thus included 3, whole number of individuals about 16.

FINANCIAL REPORT.

Receipts—For all purposes—Contributed $2.30; collections at services $6.94, total receipts for all purposes $9.24.

Disbursements—(1) *For current expenses*—Salary of rector $5.00; other current expenses $1.94, total for current expenses $6.94. *Contributions* (3) *For objects without the Diocese*—Domestic missions general $2.30; total domestic missions $2.30; total contributions for objects without the Diocese $2.30.

Statement—Current expenses raised by congregation as above $6.94. Contributions—For objects without the Diocese $2.30; total of contributions $2.30; all money raised by the congregation for current expenses and for contribtuions $9.24.

Remarks—There are two or three mining operations near Mora and we have a few church people connected with these works The people seem constantly to be on the move, so it is difficult to determine the exact number of the members of the church. At the services I have been able to hold the attendance has been quite encouraging. At my next visit to this place I hope to spend some little time in order to find out who the members of the church are and also distribute envelopes. Here we have no Sunday School nor organization of any kind.—H. H. PHELPS, minister in charge.

PAROCHIAL REPORT.

Rev. H. H. PHELPS, Bramwell, W. Va. Welch Mission, Welch, McDowell county; present minister took charge March 1, 1905.

Official Acts—Baptisms, infants 2, total 2; public services, Sundays 4, other days 2, total 6; Holy Communion, public 1, total 1.

Communicants—Present number total about 20.

Congregations—Families about 10, whole number of individuals 35.

FINANCIAL REPORT.

Receipts—For all purposes—Subscriptions $176.33; collections in church $7.46; total receipts for all purposes $183.79.

Disbursements—(1) *For current expenses*—Salary of rector $154.80; for R. N. Meade; total for current expenses $154.80. *Contributions*—(2) *For objects in the Diocese*—Diocesan missions $4.35; Sheltering Arms Hospital $1.30; Episcopal fund $11.30; total contributions for objects in the Diocese $16.95. (3) *For objects without the Diocese*—General clergy relief fund $3.33; total contributions for objects without the Diocese $3.33.

Statement—Current expenses raised by congregation as above $154.80. Contributions—For objects in the Diocese $16.95; for objects without the Diocese $3.33; total of contributions $20.28; all money raised by the congregation for current expenses and for contributions $175.08.

Remarks—At Welch. The Mission at this place has two lots upon which it hopes to build a church when funds can be raised. Altogether there is I think, in hand about $700 or $800 for building purposes. So far the attendance at the services has been quite encouraging.—H. H. PHELPS.

NOTE FURTHER—At each visit at this place I have a service on Sunday afternoon at the hospital. All seem to appreciate this service.

PAROCHIAL REPORT.

Rev. H. H. PHELPS, address Bramwell, W. Va. Elkhorn, McDowell county; present minister took charge March 1, 1905.

Official Acts—Public services, Sundays 1, total 1.

Communicants—Present number total about 8.

Congregations—Families 5, individuals not thus included 1, whole number of individuals about 18.

FINANCIAL REPORT.

Receipts—For all purposes—Contributed $3.32; collections in church $1.51; total receipts for all purposes $4.83.

Disbursements—(1) *For current expenses*—Other current expenses $1.51, other objects $2.14; total for current expenses $3.65. *Contributions*—(2) *For objects in the Diocese*—Diocesan missions $1.18; total contributions for objects in the Diocese $1.18.

Statement—Current expenses raised by congregation as above $3.65. Contributions—For objects in the Diocese $1.18; total of contributions $1.18; all money raised by the congregation for current expenses and for contributions $4.83.

Remarks—Having recently came to this section I have not yet been able to become fully acquainted with the work and the people. Having such an extensive field I have been able so far to give this place but one service. I have, however, made *four* visits, including the one at which I had service.—H. H. PHELPS..

PAROCHIAL REPORT.

Rev. H. H. PHELPS, address, Bramwell, W. Va. Gary Mission, Gary, McDowell county; present minister took charge March 1, 1905.

Official Acts—Public services, Sundays 2.

Communicants—Present number total about 3.

Congregations—Families 1, individuals not thus included 2, whole number of individuals 4.

FINANCIAL REPORT.

Receipts—For all purposes—Contributed $19.13; collections in services $7.78, total receipts for all purposes $26.91.

Disbursements—(1) *For current expenses*—Salary of rector $18.80; other current expenses $1.00; total for current expenses $19.80. *Contributions*—(1) *For objects in the Parish*—Other objects 40c; total contributions for objects in the Parish 40c. (2) *For objects in the Diocese*—Diocesan missions $6,71; total contributions for objects in the Diocese $6.71.

Statement—Current expenses raised by congregation as above $19.80. Contributions—For objects in the Parish 40c; for objects in the Diocese $6.71; total of contributions $7.11; all money raised by the congregation for current expenses and for contributions $26.91.

Remarks—Services are held here each 3rd Sunday night. The attendance has so far been encouraging, but there is no chance to build any work here.—H. H. PHELPS.

PAROCHIAL REPORT.

Rev. JAMES F. PLUMMER, address, Clarksburg. Christ Church, Clarksburg, Harrison county; present minister took charge January 24, 1904.

Church Officers—Church Wardens, M. W. Smith, J. W. Williams; other Vestrymen, W. F. Nuzum, C. B. Alexander, Geo. L. Duncan, R. S. Lowndes, Jr., Dr. W. H. Rogers, (elect); Registrar, Geo. L. Duncan, address Lowndes bldg.; Treasurer C. B. Alexander, address Horner bldg; Supt. of Sunday Schools, the rector, C. B. Alexander; Sunday School Secretary and Treasurer Miss S. Scolley Page.

Official Acts—Baptisms, infants 24, adults 7, total 31; presented for confirmation since last report 26, marriages 9, burials 10, catechisings 12, public services, Sundays 140, other days 80, total 220; Holy Communion, public, 18, private 3, total 21.

Communicants—Number last reported 106, admitted by confirmation 26, added otherwise 5, total gain 31; died 3, removed without letter 7, not otherwise accounted for 2, total loss 12; net gain (or loss) 19; present number total 125.

Congregations—Baptized persons connected with Parish 250, confirmed persons connected with Parish 150, families 75, individuals not thus included 31, number of scattered communicants in your section not connected with any Parish included in line 2, number sittings in church 220, number free sittings all, number sittings in chapel 150.

Rector's Salary—As pledged from this congregation $1,200.

Organizations—Sunday Schools, officers and teachers, male 2, female 6, total 8; pupils, male 33, female 35, total 68; No. 2: Officers and teachers, male 1, female 2, total 3; pupils, male 5, female 6, total 11; Advent offering $12.78, Lenten offering $24.44, other offerings Sheltering Arms Hospital $5.03, Children's Home Charleston $5, Cuba and Brazil $6.20, Mexico and Porto Rico $5, total Sunday School offerings $58.46, Woman's Auxiliary members 15. *Other Organizations*—Ladies' Aid Society, Christ Church Guild, Christ Church Club (for men.) Location of schools mentioned above, No. 1, Christ Church, No. 2, Northview.

Property—Same as last year. *Indebtedness*—On chapel $5.50, due on Diocesan assessment fund for Bishop's fund $73.67, note in Merchants' National Bank $1,600, note to Trustees of Permanent Fund $800, total indebtedness $3,023.67.

FINANCIAL REPORT.

Receipts—For all purposes—Cash on hand, per last report $100.17, pledges and subscriptions $1,140.35, collections in church $1,560.80, Woman's Auxiliary, money $40.00, Woman's Auxiliary boxes, value $50.00, Guilds or other societies $125.00, total receipts for all purposes $3.016.32.

Disbursements—(1) *For current expenses*—Salary of rector $1,200.00; other salaries $88.50; ordinary repairs $275.85; interest on debt $105.87; other current expenses $93.66; total for current expenses $1,763.88. *Contributions*—(1) *For objects in the Parish*—Communion alms $28.90; extraordinary repairs and improvements $100.00; Parish missions $30.00; maintaining Sunday Schools $20.00; payment on debts for building, &c., $613.89; total contributions for objects in the Parish $792.79. (2)—*For objects in the Diocese*—Salary of Bishop's $52.33; permanent fund $13.90; Diocesan missions $125.00; convocation missions $15.10; widows and orphans, aged and disabled clergy fund $17.60; religious and theological education $9.53; Sheltering Arms Hospital $12.03; Theological Seminary $10.61; total contributions for objects in the Diocese $256.10. (3) *For objects without the Diocese*—Domestic and foreign missions general $55.70; colored people $5.45; Indians $4.60; deaf and dumb 2; total domestic missions $77.75; for Mexico $6.69; through American church missionary society $5.05; Brazil and Cuba $10.20; total foreign missions $21.94;

box $50.00; general clergy relief fund $4.25; Bible and Prayer book society $13.86; special for church building at Tsingpoo, China, under care of Rev. C. F. McRae $35.75; total contributions for objects without the Diocese $203.55.

Statement—Current expenses raised by congregation as above $1,763.88. Contributions—For objects in the Parish $792.79; for objects in the Diocese $256.10; for objects without the Diocese $203.55; total of contributions $1,252.44; all money raised by the congregation for current expenses and for contributions $3,016.32.

Remarks—No organization exists at Northview beyond the Sunday School reported here as No. 2. A number of recent defections have reduced our congregation there almost to the vanishing point. The rector continues, however, to hold service there every other Sunday afternoon, alternating with the Sunday School which is faithfully kept up by its superintendent and his wife and one or two others.

PAROCHIAL REPORT.

Rev. ROBT. DOUGLAS ROLLER, D. D., address Charleston, W. Va. Asistant Rev. C. H. Molony. St. John's Church Kanawha Parish and Mission, Charleston, Kanawha county; date of organization 1788; present minister took charge April 7, 1888.

Church Officers—Church Wardens, J. Lynn Richardson, J. Talman Waters; other Vestrymen, S. S. Green, D. C. Gallaher, W. S. Laidley, W. G. Hubbard, C. E. Ward, Alfred Phillips, O. F. Payne; Registrar, S. S. Green, address Charleston; Treasurer, J. Talman Waters, address Charleston; Supt. of Sunday Schools, the rector; Sunday School Secretary and Treasurer, Ben R. Roller.

Official Acts—Baptisms, Infants 35, adults 7, total 42; presented for confirmation since last report 36, marriages 7, burials 12, public service, Sundays 113, other days 60, total 173; Holy Communion, public 24.

Communicants—Number last reported 310, received by letter 5, admitted by confirmation 36, added otherwise 15, total gain 56; died 1, transferred 1, removed without letter 18, total loss 20; net gain 36; present number total 346.

Congregations—Baptized persons connected with Parish 637, confirmed persons connected with Parish 383, families 257, number free sittings 500, number sittings in chapel 200.

Rector's Salary—As pledged by this congregation $1,300.00, from Diocesan missions, assistant $300.00.

Organizations—Sunday Schoool, officers and teachers, male 5, female 10, total 15; pupils male 48, female 63, total 111; No. 2, officers and teachers female 1, total 1; pupils, male 12, female 11, total 23; Advent offerings $29.65, Lenten offering $125.29, other offerings $105.09, total Sunday School offerings $260.03; Industrial school officers and teachers 3, scholars 38, total 41; Parish schools, officers and teachers 1, scholars 19, total 20;

Woman's Auxiliary members 39. *Other organizations*—Junior Auxiliary 19, Junior Babies Branch 20, Ladies' Guild 10, Ladies Aid 45, Rectors Aid 23, Vested Choir 36; location of schools mentioned above 1, Charleston; 2, Paint Creek; Industrial and Parish schools at Paint Creek.

Property—Church, stone, insurance $18,000.00, value $48,627.00; rectory frame, insurance $2,400, value $10,000; Parish house brick, $4,000, value $10,000;other property lot, value $3,000; Sheltering Arms Hospital, frame, insurance, $6,000, value $12,000; total value insurance $30,400, value $83,627. *Indebtedness*—On Parish House $4,000, total indebtedness $4,000.

FINANCIAL REPORT.

Receipts—For all purposes—Cash on hand, per last report $260.80, pledges and subscriptions $2,918.40, collections in church $1,448.45, thank offerings $105.89, Sunday School $260.03, Woman's Auxiliary, money $100.54, Womans Auxiliary, boxes, value $35.00, Ladies and Guilds and other societies $1,543.33, total receipts for all purposes $6,672.44.

Disbursements—For current expenses—(1) Salary of rector $1,275.00; other salaries $826.48; insurance $25.00; ordinary repairs $50.69; other current expenses $450.65; total for current expenses $2,627.82. *Contributions*—(1) *For objects in the Parish*—Extraordinary repairs and improvements $93.30; Parish missions $415.79; maintaining Sunday Schools $30.00; payment on debts for building, &c., Parish house $1,868.65; other objects $111.84; total contributions for objects in the Parish $2,519.58. (2) *For objects in the Diocese*—Salary of Bishops $275.00; permanent fund $5.00; Diocesan missions $227.00; convocation missions $5.00; widows and orphans, aged and disabled clergy fund $60.65; religious and theological education $85.89; Bishop's special fund $20.00; total contributions for objects in the Parish $678.54. *For objects without the Diocese*—Domestic missions general $108.17; colored people $1.10; Indians $1.15; deaf and dumb $8.80; Jews $5.35; total domestic missions $124.57; foreign mission general $107.58; Brazil $18.35; total foreign missions $125.93; special boxes &c. $35.00; total contributions for objects without the Diocese $285.50.

Statement—Current expenses raised by congregation as above $2,627.82; Contributions—For objects in the Parish $2,519.58; for objects in the Diocese $678.54; for objects without the Diocese $285.59; total contributions $3,483.62; all money raised by the congregation for current expenses and for contributions $6,111.44; cash in hand $561.00.

Remarks—Of the 42 baptisms reported 22 were from the Parish Mission field. Of the 36 confirmations 9 were from the same field. The new assistant is expected by July 1st, when we hope to keep a separate register for all work done in the Parish missions. Mr. Molony did a good work and he goes to his new field with our best wishes. Miss Barber beautifully fills a niche as important as any in the Diocese. Her work speaks for itself.

PAROCHIAL REPORT.

Rev. CHAS. E. SHAW, address Berkeley Springs, W. Va. St. Mark's Church, St. Mark's Mission, Berkeley Springs, Morgan county; date of organization 1879; present minister took charge December 1st, 1904.

Church Officers—Church Warden, Dr. J. H. Hunter; Registrar, Dr. G. E. Gilpin, address, Berkeley Springs; Treasurer Mr. F. B. Reed, address Berkeley Springs; Supt. of Sunday School, the Rector; Sunday School Secretary and Treasurer, Mrs. Shelly.

Official Acts—Baptisms, infants1, total 1; presented for confirmation since last report 1, burials 1, catechisings 6, public services, Sundays 40, other days 16, total 56; Holy Communion, public 12, total 12..

Communicants—Number last reported 23, admitted by confirmation 1, total gain 1; transfered 1, total loss 1; present number total 23.

Congregations—Baptized persons connected with Parish 44, confirmed persons connected with the Parish 23, families 14, individuals not thus included 2, whole nmber of individuals 44, number sittings in church 250, number free sittings 250.

Rector's Salary—As pledged from this congregation $300, from Diocesan missions $50, from general board $200, as pledged from other congregations $250, total $800.

Organizations—Sunday School, officers and teachers, male 1, female 4, total 5; pupils, male 11, female 10, total 21; Lenten offerings $6.37; other offerings $3.63, total Sunday School offerings $10.00.

Property—Church, wood, insurance $1,500, value $5,000; rectory, wood, insurance $1,500, value $3,000; total value $8,000.

FINANCIAL REPORT.

Receipts—For all Purposes—Cash on hand, per last report $14.53, pledges and subscriptions $151.30, collections in church $73.45, Sunday School $10.37, Guilds, or other societies $126.63, income from other sources $66.10, total receipts for all purposes $442.38.

Disbursements—(1) *For current expenses*—Salary of rector $224.75, other salaries $30.00, ordinary repairs 75c, other current expenses $4.64, cemetery lot $20.00, recording deed 50c., fuel $23.37, total for current expenses $304.01. *Contributions*—(1) *For objects in the Parish*—Extraordinary repairs and improvements $52.76; total contributions for objects in the Parish $52.76. (2) *For objects in the Diocese*—Salary of Bishops $20.00; Diocesan missions $25.00; widows and orphans, aged and disabled clergy fund $5.00; Sheltering Arms Hospital $2.50; total contributions for objects in the Diocese $52.50. (3) *For objects without the Diocese*—Domestic missions general $14.11; total domestic missions $14.11; foreign missions general $14.00; total foreign missions $14.00; total contributions for objects without the Diocese $28.11.

Statement—Current expenses raised by congregation as above $304.01.

Contributions—For objects in the Parish $52.76; for objects in the Diocese $52.60; for objects without the Diocese $28.11; total of contributions $133.37; all money raised by the congregation for current expenses and for contributions $437.38; cash in hand $5.00.

Remarks—Woman's Auxiliary report incomplete, will be included in this year's report.

PAROCHIAL REPORT.

Rev. CHARLES E. SHAW, address Berkeley Springs. Mount Zion Church, Norbourn Parish or Mission, Hedgesville, Berkeley county; date of organization 1817; present minister took charge December 1st, 1904.

Church Officers—Church Wardens, Geo. W. Kreglow, W. B. Lingamfelter; other Vestrymen, J. Harley Miller, Jacob H. Miller, Frank Robbins, Lee Lingamfelter, Wm. H. Kilmer, R. B. Kilmer, P. C. Myers; Registrar, R. B. Kilmer, address Hedgesville, W. Va.; Treasurer P. C. Myers, address Hedgesville, W. Va.; Supt. of Sunday School, Geo. T. Kreglow, Hedgesville, W. Va.; S. S. Supt. & Treas., Frank Robins, Hedgesville,' W. Va.

Official Acts—Baptisms, infants 5, total 5; presented for confirmation since last report 1, marriages 1, burials 1, catechisings 5, public services, Sundays 50, other days 4, total 54; Holy Communion public 12, total 12.

Communicants—Number last reported 65, admitted by confirmation 1, total gain 1; died 1, total loss 1; present number total 65.

Congregations—Baptized persons connected with Parish 72, confirmed persons connected with Parish 66, families 32, individuals not thus included 20, whole number of individuals 95, number sittings in church 200, number free sittings 200.

Rector's Salary—As pledged from this congregation $250, from Diocesan missions $50, from general board $200, as pledged from other congregations $300, total $800.

Organizations—Sunday School, officers and teachers, male 5, female 7, total 12; pupils, male 26, female 29, total 55; Advent offering $23.57, Lenten offering $16.09, total Sunday School offerings $39.66. Woman's Auxiliary, members 15.

Property—Church, brick, insurance $1,500, value $2,500; rectory, insurance $250, value $400; total value $2,900.

FINANCIAL REPORT.

Receipts—For all purposes—Cash on hand per last report $81.83, pledges and subscriptions $300.00, collections in church $66.33, thank offerings $39.63, Womans Auxiliary, money $92.28, Woman's Auxiliary, boxes, value $23.50, income from other sources $36.00, total receipts for all purposes $639.57.

Disbursements—(1) *For current expenses*—Salary of rector $250.00;

other salaries $21.73; insurance $18.80; ordinary repairs $19.00; other current expenses $27.79; total for current expenses $337.32. *Contributions*—(1) *For objects in the Parish*—Communion alms $22.65; maintaining Sunday Schools $6.74; total contributions for objects in the Parish $29.39. (2) *For objects in the Diocese*—Salary of Bishops $50.00; Diocesan missions $25.00; convocation missions $11.50; Sheltering Arms Hospital $23.50; Bishop's special fund $10.00; total contributions for objects in the Diocese $120.00. (3) *For objects without the Diocese*—Domestic missions general $13.84; total domestic missions $13.84; foreign missions general $10.00; total foreign missions $10.00; total contributions for objects without the Diocese $23.84.

Statement—Current expenses raised by congregation as above $337.32. Contributions—For objects in the Parish $29.39; for objects in the Diocese $120.00; for objects without the Diocese $23.84; total of contributions $173.23; all money raised by the congregation for current expenses and for contributions $510.55.

PAROCHIAL REPORT.

Rev. GEO. C. SHAW, address Mannington, W. Va. St. Andrew's Church Mannington Mission, Mannington, Marion county; date of organization July, 1902; present minister took charge May 1st, 1904.

Church Officers—Church Warden, H. W. G. Bostock; other Committeemen, F. H. Armstrong, Phil Deitz, A. R. Dunkle, J. A. Bostock, J. O. Huey; Registrar, Phil Deitz, address Mannington, W. Va.; Treasurer J. O. Huey, address Mannington, W. Va; Supt. of Sunday School Mrs. Annie Shaw, Mannington, W. Va.; Sunday School Secretary and Treasurer, Mrs. Ella Shaw, Mannington, W. Va.

Official Acts—Presented for confirmation since last report 1, marriages 2, burials 2, catechisings 12, public services, Sundays 73, other days 45, total 118; Holy Communion, public 12, total 12.

Communicants—Number last reported 29, admitted by confirmation 1, total gain 1; removed without letter 2, total loss 2, total loss 1; present number total 23.

Congregations—Baptized persons connected with Parish 40, confirmed persons connected with the Parish 25, families 14, individuals not thus included 20, whole number of individuals 60, number of sittings in church 150, number free sittings 150, number sittings in Sunday School room 100.

Rectors Salary—As pledged from this congregation $62.00; from Diocesan missions $360.00, from general board $100.00, as pledged from other congregations $250.00, total $772.00.

Organizations—Sunday School, officers and teachers, male 2, female 2, total 4; pupils, male 6, female 16, total 22; other offerings $15.00, total Sunday School offerings $15.00. *Other Organizations*—St. Andrews Guild, 10 members.

Property—Church, wood, insurance $2,500.00, value $6,000.00; rectory, wood, insurance $1,875.00, value $3,000.00; total value $9,000.00. *Indebtedness*—On church $700.00, on rectory $2,375.00, due on Diocesan assessment for Bishops fund $5.00, total indebtedness $3,080.00, money raised from outside sources $100.00, for what objects used, church debt and filling rectory lot.

FINANCIAL REPORT.

Receipts—For all purposes—Pledges and subscriptions $192.00, collections in church $80.00; Guilds, or other societies $407.00, contributions from without $200.00, income from other sources $100.00, total receipts for all purposes $979.00.

Disbursements—(1) *For current expenses*—Salary of Rector $62.00, in surance $27.35; ordinary repairs $50.00; interest on debt $186.00; other current expenses $60.00; total for current expenses $385.35. *Contributions*—(1) *For objects in the Parish*—Payment on debt for building, &c, $576.00; total contributions for objects in the Parish $576.00. (2) *For objects in the Diocese*—Salary of Bishops $5.00; Diocesan missions $10.00; total contributions for objects in the Diocese $15.00. (3) *For objects without the Diocese*—Domestic missions general $1.50; total domestic missions $1.50; foreign missions general $1.50; total foreign missions $1.50; total contributions for objects without the Diocese $3.00.

Statement—Current expenses raised by congregation as above $335.35. Contributions—For objects in the Parish $326.00; for objects in the Diocese $15.00; for objects without the Diocese $3.00; total of contributions $344.00; all money raised by the congregation for current expenses and for contributions $679.35.

PAROCHIAL REPORT.

Rev. GEO. C. SHAW, address Mannington, W. Va. St. Matthias Church, Grafton Mission, Grafton, Taylor county; present minister took charge July 24th, 1904.

Church Officers—Church Warden, A. H. Thayer, M. D.; other committeemen, A. E. N. Means, C. W. Steel, L. B. Brydon; Registrar, A. E. N. Means, address Grafton, W. Va.; Treasurer C. W. Steel, address Grafton, W. Va.; Supt. of Sunday Schools, Rev. Geo. C. Shaw, Mannington, W. Va.; Sunday School Secretary and Treasurer, Rosaline Kennedy, Grafton, W. Va.

Official Acts—Burials 1, catechisings 10, public services, Sundays 40, other days 6, total 46; Holy Communion, public 9, total 9.

Communicants—Number last reported 32, received by letter 1, total gain 1; died 1, removed without letter 1, total loss 2; net loss 1; present number total 31.

Congregations—Baptized persons connected with Parish 41, confirmed persons connected with Parish 31, families 21, whole number of individuals 62, number sittings in church 125, number free sittings 125.

Rector's Salary—As pledged from this congregation $250.00, total $250.00.

Organizations—Sunday Schools, officers and teachers, male 1, female 2, total 3; pupils, male 3, female 9, total 12; other offerings $5.00, total Sunday School offerings $5.00. *Other Organizations*—St. Matthias Guild, 12 members, Altar Guild 8 members.

Property—Church, wood, insurance $1,000.00, value $6,000.00; rectory, insurance $1,000.00, value $4,500.00, total value $10,500.00.

FINANCIAL REPORT.

Receipts—For all purposes—Pledges and subscriptions $279.47, collections in church $127.93, Sunday School $5.00, Guilds, or other societies $58.54, contributions from without $34.00, income from other sources $150.00, total receipts for all purposes $654.94.

Disbursements—(1) *For current expenses*—Salary of Rector $185.50; other salaries $54.52; ordinary repairs $52.71; payment on debts contracted for current expenses $50.00; other current expenses $37.00; rector s hotel expenses $37.45; total for current expenses $417.18. *Contributions*—(1) *For objects in the Parish*—Communion alms $12.80; extraordinary repairs and improvements $60.00; maintaining Sunday Schools $5.00, total contributions for objects in the Parish $77.80. (2) *For objects in the Diocese*—Salary of Bishops $15.00; Diocesan missions $15.00; convocation missions $5.50; Bishop's special fund $11.00; total contributions for objects in the Diocese $46.50. (3) *For objects without the Diocese*—Domestic missions general $3.00; total domestic missions $3.00; foreign missions general $3.23; total foreign missions $3.23; total contributions for objects without the Diocese $6.23.

Statement—Currant expenses raised by congregations as above $420.94. Contributions.—For objects in the Parish $77.80; for objects in the Diocese 46.50; for objects without the Diocese $6.23; total of contributions $130.53; all money raised by the congregation for current expenses and for contributions $551.47; cash in hand $52.76.

Remarks—The salary paid is only for nine months.

PAROCHIAL REPORT.

Rev. PARIS BECKER STAUFFER, address, Harpers Ferry, W. Va. St. John's Church, Harpers Ferry, Jefferson county; date of organization 1857; present minister took charge October 1, 1903.

Church Officers—Treasurer Mr. G. H. Child; Supt. of Sunday School Mr. Barnabas Bryan; Sunday School Secretary and Treasurer, Miss Emily Child; Lay Reader Mr. Barnabas Bryan.

Official Acts—Baptisms, infants 1, total 1; catechisings monthly, public services, Sundays 51, holy days and other days 58, total 109; Holy Communion, public 15, total 15.

Communicants—Number last reported 31, received by letter 1, total gain 1; present number total 32.

Congregations—Baptized persons connected with Parish 46, confirmed persons connected with Parish 35, families 17, individuals not thus included 10, number sittings in church 150, number free sittings all.

Rector's Salary—As pledged from this congregation $125.00; from Diocesan missions for both Harpers Ferry and Ripon $400.00, as pledged from other congregations $150.00, from convocation missions for both places $75.00, total $750.00.

Organizations—Sunday School, officers and teachers, male 1, female 7, total 8; pupils, male 31, female 57, total 88; Advent offering $20.00, Lenten offering $23.00, other offerings $23.28. *Other Organizations*—Woman's Guild.

Property—Church, frame, insurance $1,200, value $2,000; rectory, frame, insurance, $800, value $1,000; total value insurance $2,000; value $3,000.

FINANCIAL REPORT.

Receipts—For all purposes—Cash on hand, per last report $65.00, pledges and subscriptions $169.25, collections in church $152.93, Sunday School $43.00, contributions from without $20.00, income from other sources $58.75, total receipts for all purposes $443.93.

Disbursements—(1) *For current expenses*—Salary of rector $125.00; other salaries $15.00; interest on debt $3.00; other current expenses $32.79; total for current expenses $175.79. *Contributions—For objects in the Parish*—Communion alms included in offerings &c.; extraordinary repairs and improvements $26.57; payment on debt for building &c, $50.00; total contributions for objects in Parish $76.57. (2) *For objects in the Diocese*—Salary of Bishops $20.00; permanent fund $1.75; Diocesan missions $40.00; convocation missions $6.75; widows and orphans, aged and disabled clergy fund $5.00; Sheltering Arms Hospital $5.00; theological seminary $3.00; Bishop's Special Fund $15.25; total contributions for objects in the Diocese $96.75. (3) *For objects without the Diocese*—Domestic missions general $20.00; foreign missions general $21.00; for Japan $3.00; total foreign missions $44.00; general clergy relief fund $5.00; Bible and prayer book society $1.50; total contributions for objects without the Diocese $50.50.

Statement—Current expenses raised by congregation as above $170.79. Contributions.—For objects in the Parish $61.57; for objects in the Diocese $96.75; for objects without the Diocese $50.50; total of contributions $208.82; all money raised by the congregation for current expenses and for contributions $379.61; cash in hand $109.32.

Remarks—A Gift—Through the kindness of the manager of the Electric Light Co., Mr. Geo. Bready, the church is wired and is furnished with light. By the help of the Lay Reader, Mr. Bryan, the church is open every Sunday morning and evening. Summer boarders help considerable in making a fair financial showing. We have tried to eliminate such help so far as it is possible in the final statement although even here it is not absolute.

PAROCHIAL REPORT.

Rev. PARIS BECKER STAUFFER, address, Harpers Ferry. Mount Zion's church, Hedgesville, Berkeley county; date of organization 1817 A. D.; present minister took charge October 1, 1903, ceased October 31, 1904.

Official Acts—Baptisms, infants 4, total 4; marriages 1, burials 1, catechisings monthly, public services, Sundays 24, other days 2, total 25; Holy Communion, public 6, private 1, total 7.

Remarks—The offering Aug. 24, 1904, was for completion of the apportionment to general missions, which was raised and paid in full before Sept. 1. Mrs. Kreglow, widow, mother of Mr. G. T. Kreglow, died Wednesday, Oct. 12, aged 80 and more. If I mistake not, a life long member of the church. The women reorganized their branch of the Auxiliary and are doing good and aggressive work. Made gifts and had about $100.00 in the treasury. A Sunday School library was purchased at a cost of $35.00. A few necessary improvements were made to the church and grounds when my pastorate ceased Oct. 31. Others that had been arranged for had not been completed. My successor will no doubt record them. All debts, of whatever kind, were paid in full.

PAROCHIAL REPORT.

Rev. PARIS BECKER STAUFFER, address, Harpers Ferry. St. John's Parish, Ripon, Jefferson county, present minister took charge Nov. 1, 1904.

Church Officers—Church Wardens Dr. Howard Osborn, Mr. T. C. Larue; other Vestrymen, registrar, Mr. Lafayette Sommers, Mr. John Kanode, Mr. John B. Page, Mr. Lee Hulver; Registrar Mr. Lafayette Sommers, address Ripon; Treasurer, Dr. Howard Osburn, address Ripon; Supt. of Sunday Schools Dr. Howard Osburn; Sunday School Secretary and Treasurer Mrs. Kanode.

Official Acts.—Public services, Sundays 22, other days 3, total 25; Holy Communion 7.

Communicants—Number last reported 29, total gain 11; present number total 33.

Congregations—Baptized persons connected with Parish 50, confirmed persons connected with Parish 22, families 21, individuals not thus included 11, number sittings in church all.

Rector's Salary—As pledged from this congregation $150.00, from diocesan missions $400.00, as pledged from other congregations $125.00, from convocation missions $75.00, total $750.00.

Organizations—Sunday School, officers and teachers, male 3, female 4, total 7; pupils, male 10, female 18, total 28; Woman's Auxiliary members 8. *Other Organizations*—Guild members 10.

Property—Church, brick, insurance $2,000.00, value $3,000.00; total value $3,000.00.

FINANCIAL REPORT.

Receipts—For all purposes—Pledges and subscriptions $150.00, collections in church $65.75.

Disbursements—(1) Salary of rector $118.75; other salaries $11.00; insurance $12.50; other current expenses $4.45; total for current expenses $146.70. *Contributions*—(2) *For objects in the Diocese*—Salary of Bishops $20.00; Diocesan missions $10.00; convocation missions $3.00; widows and orphans, aged and disabled clergy fund $5.00; Bishop's special fund $1.00; total contributions for objects in the Diocese $39.00. (3) *For objects without the Diocese*—Domestic missions general $8.00; total domestic missions $8.00; foreign missions general $9.65; total foreign missions $9.65; total contributions for objects without the Diocese $17.65.

Statement—Current expenses raised by congregation as above $146.70. Contributions—For objects in the Diocese $39.00; for objects without the Diocese $17.65; total of contributions $56.65; all money raised by the congregation for current expenses and for contributions $203.35.

Remarks—Personal—I have found difficulty in making out report in connection with baptized and communion members, so many having gone away without letter of transfer, others living in the country, claim membership at Berryville and Wickliff, although they attend Ripon, &c., sometimes. These I have reported as belonging to Diocese.

PAROCHIAL REPORT.

Rev. JOHN WARNOCK, address Charleston, W. Va. St. Luke's Church, Charleston, Kanawha county; date of organization 1897; present minister took charge May 1st, 1903.

Church Officers—Church Warden, J. D. Lucadoe, S. W.; other Vestrymen Elijah Steen, Registrar; Geo. Grishaber, Treas., Geo. Krauss, Cobert Lucadoe, James Wilton; Registrar, Elijah Steen, address 311 Pennsylvania Ave.; Treasurer Geo. Grishaber, address Charleston P. O.; Sunday School Secretary and Treasurer Miss Williams, Miss Payne.

Official Acts—Baptisms, infants 2, total 2; marriages 3, burials 4, catechisings monthly, public services, Sundays, 40, other days 35, total 75; Holy Communion, public 12, total 12.

Communicants—Number last reported 27, added otherwise 1, total gain 1, died 1, total loss 1; net loss 1; present number total 27.

Congregations—Baptized persons connected with Parish 66, confirmed persons connected with Parish 27, families 16, number sittings in church 100.

Recetor's Salary—As pledged from this congregation $240, from Diocesan missions $50, total $290.

Organizations—Sunday School, officers and teachers, male 1, female 3, total 4; pupils, male 19, female 21, total 48; Advent offering $4.89, Lenten offering 4.00, total Sunday School offering $28.58; Ladies Guild.

Property—Church, frame, value $1,200; rectory, frame, $1,400. *Indebtedness*— Other debts $7.00, total indebtedness $7.00.

FINANCIAL REPORT.

Receipts—For all purposes—Pledges and subscriptions $137.60, collections in church $31.58, Sunday School $28.58, Woman's Auxiliary, boxes, value, $41.21, Guilds, $46.15, contributions from without $10.40, income from other sources $29.93, total receipts for all purposes $325.45.

Disbursements—(1) *For current expenses*—Salary of rector $240.00; ordinary repairs $10.40; other curent expenses $33.84; total for current expenses $284.24. *Contributions*—(1) *For objects in the Parish*—Extraordinary repairs and improvements, by Ladies Guild $24.32; total contributions for objects in the Parish $24.32. (2) *For objects in the Diocese*—Salary of Bishops $8.00; Diocesan missions $4.89; total contributions for objects in the Diocese $12.89. (3) *For objects without the Diocese*—Domestic missions general $4.00; total contributions for objects without the Diocese $4.00.

Statement—Current expenses raised by congregation as above $284.24. Contributions— For objects in the Parish $24.32; for objects in the Diocese $12.89; for objects without the Diocese $4.00; total of contributions $41.21; all money raised by the congregation for current expenses and for contributions $325.45.

PAROCHIAL REPORT.

Rev. JOHN WARNOCK, Charleston, W. Va. St. Matthew's Church, So. Charleston, Kanawha county; date of organization April 1897; present minister took charge May 1, 1903.

Church Officers—Church Wardens, J. D. Lucadoe, Comyn Lewis; other Vestrymen Geo. Grishaber; Treasurer, Comyn Lewis, address Charleston, W. Va., R. F. D., No. 1; Supt.of Sunday Schools, Comyn Lewis.

Official Acts—Baptisms, infants 10, total 10; marriages 2, burials 4, public services, Sundays 40, other days 36, total 76; Holy Communion, public 16, private 1, total 17.

Communicants—Number last reported 45, restored to communion 2, total gain 2, died 1, transferred 1, total loss 2; present number total 45.

Congregations—Baptized persons connected with Parish 136, confirmed persons connected with Parish 45, families 25, number sittings in church 200.

Rector's Salary—As pledged from this congregation $240.00, from Diocesan missions $50.00.

Property—Church, stone, insurance $500.00, value $5,000.00; Chapel, St. Andrew's, log, insurance $300.00, value $650.00; total value $5,650.00;

money raised from outside sources $85.00; for what objects used, rector's salary.

FINANCIAL REPORT.

Receipts— For all purposes—Cash on hand per last report $50.29, pledges and subscriptions, $144.52, collections in church $29.11, Sunday School (see remarks) bal 12c, sale of cemetery lot $3.00, contributions from without $25.00, income from other sources $60.00, total receipts for all purposes $261.75.

Disbursements—(1) *For current expenses*—Salary of rector $240.00; other salaries, janitor, (see remarks); insurance S. S. Pd. $2.00 more $5.50; ordinary repairs (see remarks); other current expenses, (see remarks) 54c; total for current expenses $246.04. *Contributions*—(2) *For objects in the Diocese*—Diocesan missions, S. S. Advent (see remarks) $5.00; sent to L. E. Sands $5.00. (3) *For objects without the Diocese*—Foreign missions general, sent to G. C. Thomas, S. S. Lenten $6.30.

Statement—Current expenses raised by congregation as above $173.63. Contributions.—For objects in the Parish $20.20; for objects in the Diocese $5.00; for objects without the Diocese 6.30; total of contributions $31.50; all money raised by the congregation for current expenses and for contributions $205.13; cash in hand $15.71. The $50.29 of last year's balance should be added to this balance of $15.71, but it has not yet been repaid by St. Luke's.

Remarks—Any missionary stipend has not been included in this report. Sunday School Treasurer reports receipts $28.50; church repairs paid $2.30; church expenses paid $3.10; church janitor paid $2.75; Sunday School expenses $8.93; Advent offering remitted $5.00; Lenten offering remitted $6.30, $28.38; balance 12c.

PAROCHIAL REPORT.

Rev. JOHN WARNOCK, address 220 Randolph St., Charleston, W. Va. St. Mark's Church, St. Albans, Kanawha county; present minister took charge May 1st, 1903.

Church Officers—Church Wardens, A. W. Howard, E. W. Chandler; other Vestrymen, Luke Frasher, W. H. Barnett, Thos H. Mohler; Registrar, Thos. H. Mohler, address St. Albans, W. Va.; Treasurer Thos. H. Mohler, address St. Albans, W. Va.; Supt. of Sunday Schools E. W. Chandler, St. Albans, W. Va.; Sunday School Secretary and Treasurer Thos. H. Mohler.

Official Acts—Baptisms, infants 4, total 4; burials 3, catechisings monthly, public services, Sundays 35 other days 11 total 46; Holy Communion, public, 11 total 11.

Communicants—Number last reported 35, died 3, transferred 2, total loss, 5; net loss 5; present number total 30.

Congregations—Confirmed persons connected with Parish 35, families 20, number of scattered communicants in your section not connected with any Parish 6 at Scarey, number sittings in church 220.

Rector's Salary—As pledged from this congregation $200.00, from general board (from Bp.) $120.00, total $320.00.

Organizations—Sunday Schools, officers and teachers, male 3, female 4, total 7; pupils, male 21, female 20, total 41; Advent offerings $4.38, Lenten $6.60, other offerings $41.70; total Sunday School offerings $52.68.

Property—Church, brick, value $2,000; rectory, frame, insurance, $1,000.00, value $2,500; sexton's house, frame, value, $200, total value $4,700. *Indebtedness*—On rectory $79.39, total indebtedness $79.39.

FINANCIAL REPORT.

Receipts— For all purposes—Cash on hand per last report $17.71, pledges and subscriptions $201.00, collections in church $72.20, money borrowed $211.34, Sunday School $52.68, total receipts for all purposes $554.93.

Disbursements—(1) *For current expenses*—Salary of Rector $200.00; other salaries, "collector" $9.56; payment on debts contracted for current expenses $131.95, other current expenses $19.55; due on loan $79.39; cash on hand $17.33; total for current expenses $457.78. *Contributions*—(1) *For objects in the Parish*—Maintaining Sunday Schools $46.72; total contributions for objects in the Parish $46.72. (2) *For objects in the Diocese*—Salary of Bishops $10.00; permanent fund $1.15; Diocesan missions $10.-12, convocation missions $9.21; widows and orphans, aged and disabled clergy fund 40c;religious and theological education 20c; Sheltering Arms Hospital $3.50; Theological Seminary 40c; total contributions for objects in the Diocese $34.98. (3) *For objects without the Diocese*—Domestic missions general $5.00; total domestic missions $5.00; foreign missions general $5.00, total foreign missions $5.00; specials, boxes, &c., Easter offering $4.20; general clergy relief fund $1.25; total contributions for objects without the Diocese $15.45.

Statement—Current expenses raised by congregation as above $230.00. Contributions—For objects in the Parish $200.00; for objects in the Diocese $20.00; for objects without the Diocese $10.00; total of contributions $230.00.

Remarks—You will note that I have divided the contributions to missions general equally between domestic missions general and foreign missions general. This I was advised to do by Bishop Gravatt. Therefore, do not report the amounts to each cause. I am not sure that I understand the financial statement or summary, so have just put down the amounts this Parish has agreed to give as a whole. Hope it will answer your purpose. Have spent considerable time in getting up this report and trust it is accordance with your ruling. Yours truly, THOS. H. MOHLER, Treas.

PAROCHIAL REPORT.

Rev. A. T. WILLIS, address Middleway. Grace church, Nelson Parish, Middleway, Jefferson county; date of organization 1888; present minister took charge Nov. 1, 1890.

Church Officers—Church Wardens, J. J. Granthan, Wm. H. Gilbert; other Vestrymen, James Grantham, Wm. O. Mc Caughtry; Registrar, James Grantham, address Middleway; Treasurer, James Grantham, address Middleway; Supt. Sunday School June Locke, Middleway; Sunday School Secretary and Treasurer Mitchell Willis; Lay Reader A. P. Gray, Jr.

Official Acts—Baptisms, infants 2; total 2; presented for confirmation since last report 1, burials 2, public services, Sundays 52, other days 10, total 62; Holy Communion, public, 12, total 12.

Communicants—Number last reported 44, admitted by confirmation 1, total gain 1; net gain 1, present number total 45.

Congregations—Baptized persons connected with Parish 50, confirmed persons connected with Parish 50, families 20, individuals not thus included 200, whole number of individuals 250, number sittings in church 200, number free sittings 200.

Rector's Salary—As pledged from this congregation $150, from Diocesan missions $50, as pledged from other congregations $400, from convocation missions $100, from American Church Missionary Society $100, total 800.

Organizations—Sunday School, officers and teachers, male 1, female 4, total 5; pupils, male 10, female 15, total 30; Advent offerings $3.64, Lenten offerings $3.46, other offerings $7.71, total Sunday School offerings $14.81. *Other Organizations*—Rector's Aid, 10 members, Parish Guild, embracing members of all three churches in the Parish. Location of schools mentioned above Middleway W. Va.

Property—Church, brick, insurance $1,000, value $2,500; rectory, frame and brick insurance $1,500, value $2.000; 7 acres of land, value $350; total value $4,850.

FINANCIAL REPORT.

Receipts—For all purposes—Cash on hand per last report $2.79, pledges and subscriptions $150, collections in church $142.41, Sunday School $14.81, Guilds, or other societies $20.00, income from other sources $15.00, total receipts for all purposes $345.01.

Disbursements—(1) *For current expenses*—Salary of Rector $150.00, other salaries $30.00, insurance $8.00, other current expenses $18.79, total for current expenses $206.79. *Contributions*—(1) *For objects in the Par-*

ish—Maintaining Sunday Schools $13.25; total contributions for objects in the Parish $13.25; communion alms used for missions. (2) *For objects in the Diocese*—Salary of Bishops 30.00; Diocesan misions $12.70; convocation missions $10.25; widows and orphans, aged and disabled clergy fund $7.35; religious and theological education $5.00; Sheltering Arms Hospital $7.59; total contributions for objects in the Diocese $72.89. (3) *For objects without the Diocese*—Domestic missions general $11.58; foreign missions general $3.00; Brazil $4.00; total foreign missions $18.58; work of D. Dandridge $4.25; total contributions for objects without the Diocese $22.83.

Statement—Current expenses raised by congregation as above $206.79. Contributions—For objects in the Parish $13.25; for objects in the Diocese $72.89; for objects without the Diocese $22.83; total of contributions $108.97; all money raised by the congregation for current expenses and for contributions $315.76; cash in hand $29.25.

PAROCHIAL REPORT.

Rev. A. J. WILLIS, address Middleway. St. Bartholomew's church, Nelson Parish or Mission, Lee Town, Jefferson county; date of organization 1888; present minister took charge Nov. 1st, 1890.

Church Officers—Church Wardens, I. H. Strider, Chas. L. Jones; other Vestrymen, C. C. Lucas, James Russell; Registrar, I. H. Strider, address, Lee Town; Treasurer I. H. Strider, Lee Town; Supt. of Sunday Schools, Robt. Strider, Lee Town; Sunday School Secretary and Treasurer, Robt. Strider.

Official Acts—Presented for confirmation since last report 3, public services, Sundays 36, other days 7, total 43; Holy Communion, public 6, private 1, total 7.

Communicants—Number last reported 35, admitted by confirmation 3, total gain 3; net gain 3; present number total 38.

Congregations—Confirmed persons connected with Parish 38, families 12, individuals not thus included 100, whole number of individuals 150, number sittings in church 200, number free sittings 200.

Rector's Salary—As pledged from this congregation $175, from Diocesan missions $50, as pledged from other congregations $375, from convocation missions $100, from American Church Missionary Society $100, total $800.

Organizations—Sunday School, officers and teachers, male 1, female 3, total 4; pupils, male 5, female 10, total 15; Advent offering $19.87, Lenten offering $4.53, total Sunday School offerings $24.30. *Other Organizations*—Ladies' Aid, Parish Guild, all the churches in Parish.

Property—Church, frame, insurance $1,000, value $1,800; total value $2,800.

FINANCIAL REPORT.

Receipts—*For all purposes*—Cash on hand per last report $10.30; pledges and subscriptions $175.10, collections in church $164.58, Sunday School $24.30, Guilds or other societies $5.00, total receipts for all purposes $379.18.

Disbursements—(1) *For current expenses*—Salary of rector $175.00; other salaries $18.00; insurance $10.00; other current expenses $2.15; total for current expenses $205.15. *Contributions*—(1) *For objects in the Parish*—Maintaining Sunday Schools $5.00; total contributions for objects in the Parish $5.00. Communion Alms used for missions. (2) *For objects in the Diocese*—Salary of Bishops $30.00; Diocesan missions $45.15; convocation missions $18.14; widows and orphans, aged and disabled clergy fund $3.94; Sheltering Arms Hospital $8.20; Mountain mission $2.50; total contributions for objects in the Diocese $107.93. (3) *For objects without the Diocese*—Domestic missions general $25.11; total domestic missions $25.11; foreign missions general $10.00; Brazil $9; Brazil $5; total foreign missions $24.00; to work of Durand Dandridge in Alexandria $6.83; total contributions for objects without the Diocese $55.94.

Statement—Current expenses raised by congregation as above $205.15. Contributions—For objects in the Parish $5.00; for objects in the Diocese $107.93; for objects without the Diocese $55.94; total of contributions $168.87; all money raised by the congregation for current expenses and for contributions $374.02; cash in hand $5.16.

PAROCHIAL REPORT.

Rev. A. J. WILLIS, address, Middleway, W. Va. Church of the Holy Spirit; Nelson Parish, Summit Point, Jefferson county; date of organization, 1888; present minister took charge November 1, 1890.

Church Officers—Church Wardens, A. P. Thomson; other vestrymen, R. O. Allen, Geo. C. Whiting, N. H. Willis; Registrar, N. H. Willis, address, Summit Pt.; Treasurer, R. O. Allen, address Summit Pt.; Supt. of Sunday Schools, Preston Beller, Summit Pt.; S. S. Sec. & Treas., Preston Beller.

Official Acts—Presented for confirmation since last report, 1; burials, 1; public services, Sundays 52, other days 8, total 60; Holy Communion, public, 12; total 12.

Communicants—Number last reported 47, admitted by confirmation 1, total gain 1; died 1, total loss 1; present number total 47.

Congregations—Baptized persons connected with Parish 60; confirmed persons connected with Parish 47; families 16; whole number of individuals 200; number of sittings in church 250, number free sittings 250.

Rector's Salary—As pledged from this congregation $225; from Diocesan Missions $50; as pledged from other congregations $325; from convocation missions $100; from American Church Missionary Society $100; total $800.

Organizations—Sunday School, officers and teachers, male 2, female 3, total 5; pupils male 5, female 10, total 15; Advent offering $2.00; other offerings $5.00; total Sunday School offerings $7.00.

Property—Church, material brick, insurance $2,000; value $4,000; total value $4,000.

FINANCIAL REPORT.

Receipts—For all purposes—Cash on hand, per last report $1.51; pledges and subscriptions $225; collections in church $127.20; Sunday school $7.00; total receipts for all purposes $359.20.

Disbursements—(1) *For current expenses*—Salary of Rector $225; other salaries $24; payment on debts contracted for current expenses $26; other current expenses $3.20; total for current expenses $278.20. *Contributions*—(1) *For objects in the Parish*—Communion alms (used for missions); maintaining Sunday Schools $5.00; total contributions for objects in the Parish $5.00. (2) *For objects in the Diocese*—Salary of Bishops $30.00, Diocesan missions $14.50; convocation missions $4.61; widows and orphans, aged and disabled clergy fund $2.30; Sheltering Arms Hospital $4.21; total contributions for objects in the Diocese, $55.62. (3) *For objects without the Diocese*—Domestic missions general $8.28; total domestic missions $8.28; foreign missions general $3.00; Brazil $4.08; total foreign missions $7.08; Dandridge's work in Alexandria $5.02; total contributions for objects without the Diocese $20.38.

Statement—Current expenses raised by congregation as above $278.20. Contributions—For objects in the Parish $5.00; for objects in the Diocese $55.62; for objects without the Diocese $20.38; total of contributions $81.00; all money raised by the congregation for current expenses and for contributions $359.20.

APPENDIX C.

Report of Committee on Assessment for the Year, May 1, 1904, to April 30, 1905.

REPORT OF COMMITTEE ON ASSESSMENTS, AT CLARKSBURG, JUNE 3, 1905.

Name of Parish.	*Diocesan Miss.*	*Epis. & Cont. Fund.*
Alderson	$ 6 00	$ 6 00
Berkeley Springs	25 00	30 00
Bluefield	40 00	30 00
Princeton	6 00	6 00
Bramwell	30 00	30 00
Eckman and McDowell Missions	20 00	20 00
Brooke County, St. John's	5 00	5 00
Buckhannon	10 00	10 00
Bunker Hill	5 00	5 00
Charleston, St. John's	200 00	275 00
Charleston, St. Luke's	8 00	7 00
Charleston, St. Matthew's	8 00	7 00
Charles Town, Zion	300 00	425 00
Charles Town, St. Phillip's	10 00	5 00
St. Andrew's on the Mountain	3 00	2 00
Clarksburg	125 00	125 00
Cresaps	5 00	5 00
Davis	8 00	8 00
Elkins Mission	10 00	10 00
Fairmont	75 00	100 00
Grafton	15 00	15 00
Harper's Ferry	20 00	20 00
Hedgesville	25 00	50 00
Hinton	30 00	20 00
Huntington	100 00	100 00
Kenova	5 00	7 00
Lewisburg	7 00	10 00
Ronceverte	8 00	8 00
Martinsburg	75 00	100 00
Middleway		
Nelson Parish		
Lee Town		
Summit Point		
	75 00	90 00
Mannington	10 00	10 00

Name of Parish.	*Diocesan Miss.*	*Epis. & Cont. Fund.*
Moorefield	20 00	20 00
Romney	16 00	16 00
Okonoko	10 00	10 00
Morgantown	50 00	50 00
Moundsville	40 00	60 00
Nuttallburg	5 00	10 00
Parkersburg, Trinity	350 00	525 00
Parkersburg, Good Shepherd	20 00	5 00
Parkersburg, St. Stephen	3 00	2 00
Tavennersville	10 00	3 00
Point Pleasant, Christ	50 00	50 00
Bruce Chapel	12 00	12 00
Spillman Mission	10 00	10 00
Powellton	20 00	20 00
Ansted	20 00	20 00
Ravenswood, Grace	10 00	10 00
Ripley, St. John's	15 00	15 00
Liverpool, Whittle	3 00	2 00
Ripon	10 00	20 00
Shepherdstown	75 00	75 00
Sistersville	40 00	40 00
New Martinsville	40 00	40 00
Smithfield, Wetzel County	5 00	5 00
Spruce Chapel	4 00	4 00
St. Albans	10 00	10 00
Montgomery	15 00	15 00
St. Mary's	15 00	15 00
Sutton	10 00	10 00
Union	35 00	50 00
White Sulphur	10 00	10 00
Fort Spring	5 00	5 00
Waverly	10 00	5 00
Wellsburg	25 00	25 00
Weston	75 00	80
Wheeling, St. Matthew's	425 00	600
Wheeling, St. Luke's	175 00	175
Wheeling, St. Andrew's	15 00	10
Chester	10 00	4
Williamson	....	5 00
Wheeling, St. Paul's, Elm Grove	5 00	10 00
Williamstown	15 00	15 00
Willow Island	5 00	5 00
Beckley	6 00	6 00

Name of Parish.	*Diocesan Miss.*	*Epis. & Cont. Fund..*
Beury	5 00	5 00
Du Bree	5 00	5 00
Glen Jean	10 00	10 00
Immanuel, Mt. Carbon	5 00	5 00
Totals	$3,005 00	$3,665 00

Your committee recommends that payments on account of the assessment for the Episcopal and Contingent Fund be made to the Treasurer quarterly.

D. W. HOWARD.
S. S. MOORE.
J. S. GIBSON.
J. S. DOUGLAS.
A. G. GRINNAN.
G. W. EASTER.
R. M. BROWNE.
J. GASSMAN.
RICHARD HENDEERSON.
L. E. SANDS.
G. A. ASCHMAN.

APPENDIX D.

Tabulated Statement—Vital Statistics.

Tabulated Statement—Financial Statistics.

TABULATED STATEMENT—VITAL STATISTICS.

ALPHABETICAL CLERGY LIST.	PARISHES, MISSIONS AND STATIONS.	Baptisms. Infants.	Baptisms. Adults.	Confirmations.	Marriages.	Burials.	Communicants. Last Reported.	Communicants. Present Number.	Baptized Persons.	Families and Parts.	Number in Sunday Schools. Teachers.	Number in Sunday Schools. Scholars.
REV. JOHN S. ALFRIEND	Zion Ch., Charles Town	9	4	12	8	12	333	344	500	175	14	90
	St. Andrews on the Mountain	4	1	3	1	1	18	37	200	94	9	150
	Harewood Mission										5	40
REV. MORTON A. BARNES	Christ Ch., Fairmont	6	2		2	2	124	138	200	50	10	50
REV. J. BRITTINGHAM	St. Lukes, Wheeling	16	8	20	11	11	260	269	399	200	10	101
REV. E. H. BROSIUS	Christ Ch., Bluefield	5		1	1	1	106	109	190	69	4	27
	Heavenly Rest, Princeton	3					18	17	19	8		
REV. C. M. CAMPBELL	Christ Ch., Short Creek, &c.				1	1	2	2	15	9		
REV. WILSON PAGE CHRISMAN	Trinity, Moundsville	12	2	10	4	2	64	74	166	141	18	134
	Grace, Cresaps Valley					1	9	9	18	7		
REV. GUY H. CROOK	Incarnation, Ronceverte	1		6			21	31	45	16	2	21
	St. James, Lewisburg	1			1	1	24	28	44	15		
	Marlinton							11	16	5		
	Grace Ch., Clover Lick						5	5	12	4		
	Holy Comforter, Fort Spring						8	8	11	4		
	Hillsboro						3	1	5	1		
	Huntersville						4	4	4			
	Anthony							1	5	1		
	St. Thomas, White Sulphur	1	3	2	1		41	43	80	21	8	85
REV. T. J OLIVER CURRAN	St. Andrews, Wheeling	17	9	14	4	10	75	89	226	64	10	168
REV. CREETUS A. DOWELL	St. Pauls, Sistersville		5	15	2	7	41	56	72	35	9	97
	Pennsboro			5			4	5	15	6		
	Cairo							13	16	5		
REV. JOHN S. DOUGLAS	Trinity, Martinsburg	13	1	6	6	11	165	175	290	110	18	110
	Christ Ch., Bunker Hill						7	8	16	6		
REV. GEO. W. EASTER	All Saints, Union	4			8	8	35	35	76	22	8	50
	Ch. of the Messiah, Alderson						4	4				

TABULATED STATEMENT—VITAL STATISTICS—Continued.

ALPHABETICAL CLERGY LIST.	PARISHES, MISSIONS AND STATIONS.	Baptisms. Infants.	Baptisms. Adults.	Confirmations.	Marriages.	Burials.	Communicants. Last Reported.	Communicants. Present Number.	Baptized Persons.	Families and Parts.	Number in Sunday Schools. Teachers.	Number in Sunday Schools. Scholars.
REV. JAMES L. FISH	St. Barnabas, Davis	2	2	7	2	2	37	42	66	34	4	30
	Grace Ch., Elkins	3	2	6	1	1	35	34	70	33	2	10
	Trinity Mission, Belington						10	6	9	3		
	Thomas						6	8	15	13		
	Parsons						6	7	14	7		
	Bayard	2							9	5		
REV. JAMES HOWARD GIBBONS	Christ Ch., Pt. Pleasant	2		1	3	4	62	62	167	54	4	26
	Bruce Chapel, Elwell	3		1		2	26	27	45	16	4	35
	" Spillman	1					23	25	60	18	3	24
REV. GEO. A. GIBBONS	St. Stephens, Romney	1	3	9	2	1	21	30	40	20	4	18
	Emmanuel, Moorefield	1	3	3		2	30	33	60	18	5	21
	Epiphany, Okonoko						10	10	16	4		
	Keyser							12	15	6		
	Paw Paw	1					6	5	8	5		
REV. JOHN S. GIBSON	Trinity, Huntington	5	4	15	5	34	200	205	430	152	11	75
	Grace, Kenova		1	2	1		8	11	21	9		
	Williamson			1		1	11	10	30	12		
REV. ANDREW G. GRINNAN	St. Pauls, Weston	6	1	8	9	16	75	82	215	90	8	62
	St. Pauls Chapel, near Weston	3	1	2		2	13	13	22	8	3	34
REV. DAVID W. HOWARD	St. Matthews, Wheeling	18	7	25	30	15	550	550	600	309	12	140
REV. JACOB A. HIATT	Ascension, Hinton	5	3	5	2	3	49	30	60	100	2	24
	Glen Jean	1				1	15	9	25	24		
REV. EDWARD D. IRVINE	Christ Ch., Wellsburg	6	1	1	6	4	55	54	78	28	4	30
	St. Johns, Brooke Co.				1	2	25	24	35	8		
REV. PACA KENNEDY	Grace Ch., St. Marys				3		29	28	29	10	6	29
	Grace, Ravenswood		1	3			20	20	30	18	5	31
	St. Johns, Ripley				1	1	36	34	46	15	3	34
	St. Johns, Willow Island						13	13	18	8		
	Ch. of the Messiah, Waverly						10	5	5	8		

REV. ARTHUR M. LEWIS	St. Davids, Powellton	7	7	8	1	7	34	41	73	21	8	65
	Redeemer, Ansted	8	8	2	....	1	36	38	88	17	6	60
	Calvary, Montgomery	1	....	1	1	....	19	24	87	16	3	20
REV. JOS. W. LIVINGSTON	St. Philips, Charles Town	1	....	6	....	2	23	33	40	12	8	40
REV. JOHN TILTON MARLEY	Trinity, Morgantown	4	1	7	2	5	56	87	118	34	7	51
REV. C. E. A. MARSHALL	Trinity, Shepherdstown	7	1	....	....	6	150	150	277	50	7	40
	Emmanuel, Mt. Carbon	....	....	....	....	....	....	7	19	....	....	....
	St. Titus, Nuttallburg	2	3	2	....	....	....	12	20	....	....	....
	Good Shepherd, Ferris	....	....	....	....	....	....	4	7	....	....	....
	Mission, at Dubree	....	....	....	....	....	....	12	37	....	....	....
	" " Beauty	....	....	....	....	....	....	5	11	....	....	....
	Keenys, Wyndal, Page	4	....	....	1	....	....	13	28	....	....	....
REV. WALTER HOWARD MEYERS	St. Johns, Sutton	....	1	4	....	....	10	10	27	10	....	....
	Transfiguration, Buckhannon	....	....	2	....	....	25	28	30	15	....	....
	Spruce Chapel, Lorentz	1	....	....	....	....	11	10	21	6	....	....
	Scattered places	....	....	....	....	....	....	14	30	12	....	....
REV. AUSTIN B. MITCHELL	Christ Memorial, Williamstown	1	1	1	1	3	27	28	62	40	6	21
	Good Shepherd Mission, Parkersburg	10	3	4	....	2	15	18	35	30	14	170
	Grace Chapel, Newport	1	....	....	....	....	10	10	20	28	5	25
REV. C. HELY MOLONY	St. Annes, New Martinsville	....	....	....	6	1	50	40	67	25	8	25
REV. FRANCIS MOORE	St. Pauls, Elm Grove	6	1	3	5	6	27	30	50	30	6	40
	New Cumberland Mission	....	....	....	....	....	....	10	26	10	....	....
REV. S. SCOLLAY MOORE, D. D.	Trinity, Parkersburg	14	7	17	31	25	308	317	525	250	16	117
	St. Stephens, "	....	....	....	....	....	8	8	12	6	....	....
REV. H. H. PHELPS	Holy Trinity, Bramwell	4	3	....	....	....	....	28	50	17	7	39
	Grace, Eckman	....	....	....	....	....	....	9	12	4	....	....
	Mora, Crane Creek	2	....	....	....	....	....	4	10	3	....	....
	............Welch	2	....	....	....	....	....	20	18	10	....	....
	............Elkhorn	....	....	....	....	....	....	8	10	5	....	....
	............Gary	....	....	....	....	....	....	3	5	3	....	....
REV. JAMES F. PLUMMER	Christ, Clarksburg	24	7	26	9	10	106	125	250	106	11	79
REV. ROBT. DOUGLAS ROLLER, D.D.	St. Johns, Charleston	35	7	36	7	12	310	346	687	257	16	134
REV. CHAS. E. SHAW	St. Marks, Berkeley Springs	1	....	1	....	1	23	23	44	16	5	21
	Mt. Zion, Hedgesville	5	....	1	1	1	65	65	72	52	12	55
REV. GEORGE C. SHAW	St. Andrews, Mannington	....	....	1	2	2	24	28	40	34	4	22
	St. Matthias, Grafton	....	....	....	....	1	32	31	41	21	3	12

TABULATED STATEMENT—VITAL STATISTICS.—Continued.

ALPHABETICAL CLERGY LIST.	PARISHES, MISSIONS AND STATIONS.	Baptisms.		Confirmations.	Marriages.	Births.	Communicants.		Baptized Persons.	Families and Parts.	Number in Sunday Schools.	
		Infants.	Adults.				Last Reported.	Present Number.			Teachers.	Scholars.
Rev. Paris Becker Stauffer	St. Johns, Harpers Ferry	1	......	......	......	......	31	32	46	27	8	38
	St. Johns, Ripon	4	......	......	......	......	29	33	50	31	7	28
Rev. John Warnock	St. Lukes, Charleston	2	......	......	3	4	27	27	66	16	4	48
	St. Matthews, Charleston	10	......	......	2	4	45	45	136	25	......	......
	St. Marks, St. Albans	4	......	......	......	3	35	30	40	20	7	41
Rev. A. J. Willis	Grace, Middleway	2	......	1	......	2	44	45	50	20	4	30
	St. Bartholomews, Leetown	......	......	3	......	....	35	38	40	212	4	15
	Holy Spirit, Summit Point	......	......	1	......	1	47	47	60	116	5	15
Scattered Communicants	......	......	......	......	......	......	....	157	......	......	......	......
Totals	......	315	101	305	188	252	4,414	4,991	8,205	3,695	386	2,991

TABULATED STATEMENT—FINANCIAL STATISTICS.

ALPHABETICAL CLERGY LIST.	PARISHES, MISSIONS AND STATIONS.	DISBURSEMENTS.				Grand Total.
		Current Expenses.	Contributions.			
			Parochial.	Diocesan.	Outside the Diocese.	
REV. JOHN S. ALFRIEND	Zion Ch., Charles Town	$ 2,079 62	$ 2,007 75	$ 1,541 35	$ 552 64	$ 6,181 36
	St. Andrews on the Mountain		25 00	9 00	4 00	38 00
	Harewood Mission		5 00	10 00		15 00
REV. MORTON A. BARNES	Christ Ch., Fairmont	1,902 05	404 72	195 00	148 22	2,649 99
REV. J. BRITTINGHAM	St. Lukes. Wheeling	3,882 95	2,087 21	539 41	392 31	6 901 88
REV. E. H. BROSIUS	Christ Ch., Bluefield	739 62	864 50	73 43	30 00	1,707 55
	Heavenly Rest, Princeton	22 55		12 00		34 55
REV. C. M. CAMPBELL	Christ Ch., Short Creek, &c.			2 00		2 00
REV. WILSON PAGE CHRISMAN	Trinity, Moundsville	1,823 19	20 08	151 19	111 96	2,106 42
	Grace, Cresaps Valley	1 00		9 81		10 81
REV. GUY H. CROOK	Incarnation, Ronceverte	387 00	276 64	40 61	16 48	720 73
	St. James, Lewisburg	259 00		21 00	6 30	286 30
	Marlinton					
	Grace Ch., Clover Lick			4 27		4 27
	Holy Comforter, Fort Spring	50 00		16 00		66 00
	Hillsboro					
	Huntersville					
	Anthony	60 00				60 00
	St. Thomas, White Sulphur	75 00		5 30	2 05	82 35
REV. T. J. OLIVER CURRAN	St. Andrews, Wheeling	1,228 47	165 00	55 00	15 00	1,463 47
REV. CREETUS A. DOWELL	St. Pauls, Sistersville	1,137 03	1,258 08	143 69	46 19	2,584 99
	Pennsboro	104 25				104 25
	Cairo	8 25		5 00		13 25
REV. JOHN S. DOUGLAS	Trinity, Martinsburg	1,803 10	1,245 80	543 43	215 13	3,807 46
	Christ Ch., Bunker Hill	3 77		7 35	4 99	16 11
REV. GEO. W. EASTER	All Saints, Union	453 50	29 00	145 25	113 97	741 72
	Ch. of the Messiah, Alderson	11 27		9 36	3 90	24 53

TABULATED STATEMENT—FINANCIAL STATISTICS—Continued.

ALPHABETICAL CLERGY LIST.	PARISHES, MISSIONS AND STATIONS.	DISBURSEMENTS.				Grand Total.
		Current Expenses.	Contributions.			
			Parochial.	Diocesan.	Outside the Diocese.	
Rev. James L. Fish	St. Barnabas, Davis	$ 508 28	$ 141 81	$ 20 00	$ 8 00	$ 678 04
	Grace Ch., Elkins	465 70	96 40	34 80	10 00	606 90
	Trinity Mission, Belington					
	............Thomas	10 00				10 00
	............Parsons					
	............Bayard	50 00				50 00
Rev. James Howard Gibbons	Christ Ch., Pt. Pleasant	540 77	318 16	133 80	97 90	1,065 68
	Bruce Chapel, Elwell	150 00	5 51	44 00	16 00	245 51
	" Spillman	50 00	34 27	21 00	16 75	122 02
Rev. Geo. A. Gibbons	St. Stephens, Romney	134 43	32 52	52 45	47 33	266 73
	Emmanuel, Moorefield	190 00	2 00	47 70	20 00	259 70
	Epiphany, Okonoko	37 00		20 00		57 00
	............Keyser	168 00				168 00
	............Paw Paw	28 25		9 00	5 00	42 25
Rev. John S. Gibson	Trinity, Huntington	2,119 00	968 28	401 70	177 60	3,666 58
	Grace, Kenova	199 20	32 08	22 45	9 50	263 18
	............Williamson	111 00		2 30	1 00	114 30
Rev. Andrew G. Grinnan	St. Pauls, Weston	1,018 93	184 40	242 02	181 87	1,627 22
	St. Paul's Chapel, near Weston	63 08	1 58	9 54	9 56	83 76
Rev. David W. Howard	St. Matthews, Wheeling	7,596 42	3,045 50	2,832 85	1,400 39	14,875 16
Rev. Jacob A. Hiatt	Ascension, Hinton	538 53	271 30	36 61		847 44
	............Glen Jean	225 00		31 00	5 00	261 00
Rev. Edward D. Irvine	Christ Ch., Wellsburg	723 07	54 26	79 25	49 50	906 08
	St. Johns, Brooke Co	66 38		5 00	2 45	73 83
Rev. Paca Kennedy	Grace Ch., St. Marys	259 75	297 00	28 30		585 05
	Grace, Ravenswood	165 41	67 23	47 78	17 12	297 54
	St. Johns, Ripley	100 54	170 12	51 93	15 00	337 59
	St. Johns, Willow Island	32 00	55 54	13 00	7 19	107 73
	Ch. of the Messiah, Waverly	56 00	15 00	6 50	2 06	79 56

REV. ARTHUR M. LEWIS	St. Davids, Powellton	527 19	127 09	197 22	87 97	939 47
	Redeemer, Ansted	221 00	276 62	48 81	30 00	576 43
	Calvary, Montgomery	273 77	146 08	37 80	17 62	475 27
	Emmanuel, Mt. Carbon	29 00	....	15 00	....	44 00
	St. Titus, Nuttallburg	60 00	....	20 00	....	80 00
	Good Shepherd, Ferris	38 70	....	5 00	....	43 70
	Mission, at Dubree	1 50	....	2 00	....	3 50
	" " Beauty	....	....	....	....	....
	Keenys, Wyndal, Page	....	....	....	....	....
REV. JOS. LIVINGSTON	St Phillips, Charles Town	90 54	....	10 00	10 90	110 54
REV. JOHN TILTON MARLEY	Trinity, Morgantown	1,880 51	421 72	88 95	64 01	2,455 19
REV. C. E. A. MARSHALL	Trinity Shepherdstown	915 74	51 20	197 99	72 76	1,237 69
REV. WALTER HOWARD MEYERS	St. Johns, Sutton	407 00	102 56	37 52	19 10	566 18
	Transfiguration, Buckhannon	223 16	6 30	27 60	7 70	264 76
	Spruce Chapel, Lorentz	18 50	2 60	4 40	5 00	30 50
	Scattered places	8 00	....	....	....	8 00
REV. AUSTIN B. MITCHELL	Christ Memorial, Williamstown	266 54	44 85	33 10	37 24	381 73
	Good Shepherd Mission, Parkersburg	564 50	123 30	261 32	305 50	1,254 62
	Grace Chapel, Newpor..t	42 00	29 00	32 00	20 10	123 10
REV. C. HELY MOLONY	St. Annes, New Martinsville	782 34	18 90	113 97	22 06	937 27
REV. FRANCIS MOORE	St. Pauls, Elm Grove	722 45	35 26	40 46	18 99	817 16
	New Cumberland Mission	88 02	....	6 00	4 50	98 52
REV. S. SCOLLAY MOORE, D. D.	Trinity, Parkersburg	3,463 09	359 22	1,849 03	495 86	6,167 20
	St. Stephens, "	44 65	31 35	84	83	77 67
REV. H. H. PHELPS	Holy Trinity, Bramwell	1,331 48	1,001 65	96 99	24 22	2,454 34
	Grace, Eckman	85 04	....	14 20	12 07	111 31
	Mora, Crane Creek	6 94	....	....	2 30	9 24
	.... Welch	154 80	....	16 95	3 33	175 08
	.... Elkhorn	3 65	....	1 18	....	4 83
	.... Gary	19 80	40	6 71	....	26 91
REV. JAMES F. PLUMMER	Christ, Clarksburg	1,763 88	792 79	256 10	203 55	3,016 32
REV. ROBT. DOUGLAS ROLLER, D. D.	St. Johns, Charleston	2,627 82	2,519 58	678 54	285 50	6,111 44
REV. CHAS. E. SHAW	St. Marks, Berkeley Springs	304 01	52 76	52 50	28 11	437 38
	Mt. Zion, Hedgesville	337 32	29 39	120 00	23 84	510 55
REV. GEORGE C. SHAW	St. Andrews, Mannington	335 35	326 00	15 00	3 00	679 35
	St. Matthias, Grafton	420 94	77 80	46 50	6 23	551 47

TABULATED STATEMENT—FINANCIAL STATISTICS.—Continued.

ALPHABETICAL CLERGY LIST.	PARISHES, MISSIONS AND STATIONS.	DISBURSEMENTS.				Grand Total.
		Current Expenses.	Contributions.			
			Parochial.	Diocesan.	Outside the Diocese.	
REV. PARIS BECKER STAUFFER	St. Johns, Harpers Ferry	$ 175 79	$ 61 57	$ 96 75	$ 50 50	$ 384 61
	St. Johns, Ripon	146 70	....	39 00	17 65	203 35
REV. JOHN WARNOCK	St. Lukes, Charleston	284 24	24 32	12 89	4 00	325 45
	St. Matthews, Charleston	173 63	20 20	5 00	6 30	205 13
	St. Marks, St. Albans	440 45	46 72	84 98	15 45	587 60
REV. A. J. WILLIS	Grace, Middleway	206 79	13 25	72 89	22 83	315 76
	St. Bartholomews, Leetown	205 15	5 00	107 93	55 94	374 02
	Holy Spirit, Summit Point	278 20	5 00	55 62	20 38	359 20
TOTALS		$ 50,845 01	$ 20,657 76	$ 12,423 56	$ 5,711 80	$ 89,638 13

INDEX.

ADDRESS, THE BISHOP'S.........12-34
Journal and Official Acts.........13-22
Hospitals......... 24
Special Fund.........22-23
Church News......... 23
Parish Registers.........24
The Kalendar......... 25
Genl Clergy Relief Fund......... 26
Revival in Wales.........26-29
General Missions......... 29
Thank Offering for General Convention......... 30
Diocesan Selfsupport.........31-34

ADDRESS. THE BISHOP COADJUTOR'S.
Journal and Official Acts.........38-44

AMERICAN CHURCH BUILDING FUND......... 53

APPENDICES
Appendix A— I. Report of Treasurer of Diocese......... 69
II. Report of Trustee of Episcopate Fund.... 73
III. Report of Trustees of Permanent Fund.. 75
Appendix B—Parochial Reports, according to alphabetical Clergy List......... 83
Appendix C—Diocesan Assessments......... 183
Appendix D—Tabulated Statement.
I. Vital Statistics......... 191
II. Financial Statistics......... 195

BISHOP, THE,
Journal and address.........12-34

BISHOP COADJUTOR, THE,
Journal.........38-44

CANDIDATES, For Holy Orders......... 21

CLERGY, BISHOP'S LIST OF, ... 5-7
Changes Among 21

CLERGY RELIEF FUND, GENL 54

COMMITTEES OF THE COUNCIL.
On Constitution and Canons 4
On Credentials 11
On Diocesan Missions 3
On Domestic and Foreign Missions 3
On Education 4
On Sunday Schools 4
Standing Committee 3

COUNCIL, MINUTES OF
Wednesday, May 31st, A. M 11
Wednesday, May 31st, P. M 12
Thursday, June 1st, A. M 46
Thursday, June 1st, P. M 47
Friday, June 2nd, A. M 48
Friday, June 2nd, P. M 55
Saturday, June 3rd, A. M 58

LAY DELEGATES 35-37

ORGANIZED MISSIONS 22-37

OFFICERS OF COUNCIL 3-4

PARISHES, LIST OF 35-37

PEARSON, REV. C. C., Memorial Page 65

PAROCHIAL REPORTS, (Appendix B.) 83

REPORTS OF COMMITTEES,
Credentials 35
Constitution and Canons 45
Diocesan Missionary 48
Education 57
Finance 57
Parochial Reports .... .62
State of the Church 59
Standing Committee 45
Sunday Schools 58

RESOLUTIONS AND MOTIONS,
On Bishop's Address.......... 34
As to Brotherhood Work.......... 45
As to Amount of Missionary Apportionments.......... 48
Resolution of thanks to Rector and People.......... 48
As to editing and printing new Constitution and Canons.... 61
As to date of closing Treasurer's Report.......... 61
As to printing names of various Treasurers.......... 61
As to memorial page to Rev. C. C. Pearson.......... 62
As to Report of Assessment Committee.......... 62
As to Assessments.......... 62

RULES OF ORDER.......... 8-10

SPECIAL COMMITTEE REPORT OF,
As to Diocesan Self-support.......... 62

SHELTERING ARMS HOSPITAL.......... 2

SUMMARY OF STATISTICS (Appendix D.).......... 189

TABULATED STATEMENT (Appendix D.).......... 189

TREASURERS AND THEIR ADDRESSES, 2nd page of cover.

WOMAN'S AUXILIARY, Officers.......... 7

Printed in Great Britain
by Amazon

83949210R00353